"Graham and McKay deliver a superb and comprehensive overview of the Toronto new left in the long 1960s. Like similar moments in the 1880s and the 1930s, the 1960s represented a high point of anti-capitalist struggle with innovative forms of resistance which rippled through Canadian society and culture. From the early anti-nuclear, civil rights, student, and anti-war movements to the new Trotskyist and Maoist formations, the fight for the environment, and the emergence of Black, Indigenous, women's, and gay liberation movements, the new left experience still resonates with a re-emergent socialist politics."

— Gregory S. Kealey, professor emeritus, University of New Brunswick

"*Radical Ambition*'s phenomenal evocation of the dynamic and tumultuous new left in Toronto in the last great wave of radicalization, and its assessments of the dead ends and enduring legacies of that time, provide extraordinary insight into what can be re-imagined and reworked into a politics for today."

— Varda Burstyn, writer, activist and independent scholar, author of *Water Inc.* and *The Rites of Men: Manhood, Politics and the Culture of Sport*

"What a remarkable book in terms of its depth and breadth. It captures the tenor, tone and tensions of radical Toronto politics with its local, national and international permutations; and in relation to socialism, gender, race, class, sexuality. This textured and layered study captures the radical spirit of the sixties through to the eighties, shattering the myth of Canadian innocence while making a unique contribution to global radical history, documenting a sense of hope and resistance at a time when a radical shift in the practice of politics is in dire need."

— David Austin, author of *Moving Against the System*, *Dread Poetry and Freedom*, and *Fear of a Black Nation*

"Graham and McKay bring the period's activists to life and manage to balance the numerous political differences and 'lines of demarcation' insightfully. The authors analyse not only political organizations—from the Waffle/NDP to the Maoist party formations—but also the various municipal struggles around expressways and education, the anti-war movement, and the movements around identity and sexuality. It even includes an account of the cultural left, a topic often overlooked in political histories. One of a new crop of engaging Toronto histories coming out of BTL. Local and world class. History otherwise."

— Carole Condé and Karl Beveridge, visual artists, authors, and activists

Radical Ambition

RADICAL AMBITION

The New Left in Toronto

Peter Graham
with **Ian McKay**

Between the Lines
Toronto

First published in 2019 by
Between the Lines
401 Richmond Street West
Studio 281
Toronto, Ontario M5V 3A8
Canada
1-800-718-7201
www.btlbooks.com

Library and Archives Canada Cataloguing in Publication

Graham, Peter, 1976-, author
Radical ambition : the New Left in Toronto / Peter Graham with Ian McKay.

Includes bibliographical references.
Issued in print and electronic formats.
ISBN 978-1-77113-423-1 (softcover).—ISBN 978-1-77113-424-8 (EPUB).—
ISBN 978-1-77113-425-5 (PDF)

1. New Left—Ontario—Toronto—History. 2. Toronto (Ont.)—Politics and government.
I. McKay, Ian, 1953–, author II. Title.

HN110.T6G734 2019 320.5309713'541 C2018-906074-3
C2018-906075-1

Cover and text design by Gordon Robertson
Printed in Canada

We acknowledge for their financial support of our publishing activities: the Government of Canada; the Canada Council for the Arts, which last year invested $153 million to bring the arts to Canadians throughout the country; and the Government of Ontario through the Ontario Arts Council, the Ontario Book Publishers Tax Credit program, and Ontario Creates.

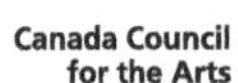

Conseil des Arts
du Canada

Canadä

Contents

Acknowledgements

Peter would like to acknowledge the many Windsor, Ont., activists who mentored him in activism and encouraged his interest in left-wing history. He would particularly like to thank Mike McLister and other movement veterans who introduced him to the inspiring social movement activity of the 1970s. He is grateful to the scholars who helped him along the way, including York University's Geoffrey Ewen and Marcel Martel, and Queen's University's Jeff Brison and Peter Campbell, as well as the activists who agreed to be interviewed for his doctoral thesis. He is indebted to his co-author and former Ph.D. supervisor Ian McKay, whose towering knowledge of left-wing history, invaluable advice, and heartening support made this book possible. He is also thankful for the enduring support of his parents, Judith and Skip, and his partner, Yen, who encouraged him to enrol in university and write about his research. Yen had to endure hearing an excessive amount of "interesting" historical anecdotes during the production of this book, which is dedicated to her.

Ian would especially like to thank his co-author Peter Graham for allowing him the opportunity to add his two cents' worth to the outstanding doctoral work that forms the basis of this study. He is also grateful to his partner, Rob, for patiently living with a preoccupied author and to the Wilson Institute for Canadian History at McMaster for offering a congenial setting for progressive scholarship.

We would both like to recognize activists like Charles Dobie, Pat Leslie, and Jearld Mordenhauer, who have helped to document the social movements we study herein. This book would also not have been possible without the help of a veritable army of archivists and librarians; we especially thank those at the Canadian Lesbian and Gay Archives, Clara Thomas Archives and Special Collections, University of Ottawa Archives and Special Collections, and William Ready Division of Archives and Research Collections. We thank the staff of Between the

Lines for their many hours of work on this book; and acknowledge the sterling editorial work of Robert Clarke, who has once again revealed why he is considered one of the Canadian left's most treasured assets.

1

Toronto: Capital of Capitalist Modernity

> To be modern is to live a life of paradox and contradiction. It is to be overpowered by the immense bureaucratic organizations that have the power to control and often to destroy all communities, values, lives; and yet to be undeterred in our determination to face these forces, to fight to change the world and make it our own. It is to be both revolutionary and conservative: alive to new possibilities for experience and adventure, frightened by the nihilistic depths to which so many modern adventures lead, longing to create and to hold on to something real even as everything melts.
>
> — Marshall Berman, *All That Is Solid Melts into Air*

WRITING for *Maclean's* magazine in 1965, Peter Gzowski saw something different about the new generation of the left. They were not the agrarian radicals of old. They did not meet in union halls. Nor were they like the Beatniks that Gzowski had rubbed shoulders with in college. "THE RADICALS of the New Left, the young men and women . . . differ from their predecessors not only in the *degree* of their protest but in its *kind*. They are a new breed."[1]

Members of the new left, women and men—this new breed of radicals—placed the ideals of self-determination and community at the core of their politics. As with all leftists, they sought to transcend capitalism. But in contrast to older formations, new leftists emphasized solidarity with national liberation movements challenging imperialism around the world. They took up organizational forms that anticipated—"prefigured," some said—in their direct, grassroots, community-based democracy, the liberated world of the future. Their ideals encouraged power relations that nurtured and respected struggles by men, women, and youth to achieve meaning and authenticity in their personal lives—a trait that encouraged them often to focus on the cultural sphere. They took their chances within movements that were actually (and not just formally) predicated on egalitarianism. They had their radical ambitions, their oft-disputed problems, their broken promises, their achievements large and small. To varying degrees in the years 1958–85 the city of Toronto was one of North America's leading centres of this new leftism.

* * *

It has always been a quiet, unassuming river. Its two branches, with headwaters far away in the picturesque Oak Ridges Moraine, converge about 7 kilometres north of Lake Ontario and the waters then flow unobtrusively south to a mouth in Toronto Harbour. Along its agreeable valley were once such pleasant retreats as Tumper's Hill, near what would become the Don Mills Road: "a gorgeous place for hiking and rambling."

Unlike more majestic rivers from Nova Scotia to California, Toronto's Don River is unlikely ever to be promoted as the "Rhine of America." When the University of Toronto historian Donald Creighton embarked on the patriotic heroization of a mighty river, he chose the St. Lawrence, Europe's gateway to the continent and the key to Montreal's acquisition of a vast western fur empire, and not the little river at his doorstep. *And Quiet Flows the Don* was the title of Mikhail Sholokhov's four-volume epic of Russian history, but the tragic flaw of the Russian river's Canadian namesake was that it flowed so slowly and, at least towards its bottom end, looked so muddy that any epic set upon its banks would be something of a snooze-fest. For much of its history Toronto's Don River quietly and unpretentiously made its long way to the harbour, with nary a *coureur de bois* or gallant Cossack in sight.

Yet on July 31, 1958, romance did finally arrive. The Don River took a starring role in an event that had Toronto spellbound. Princess Margaret, Countess of Snowdon, the younger sister of Queen Elizabeth II and second in line to the throne of England, was scheduled to make a grand visit to Toronto. Her train was to stop at a siding in Riverdale Park, just beside the Valley. According to the official plan she was to greet assembled schoolchildren from a footbridge that spanned the Don. Mayor Nathan Phillips was second to none in his Toronto-boosting zeal. Perhaps the Don location recommended itself to him because of the ease with which crowds could be accommodated in the park area, the convenience of having the Princess merely alight from her carriage, or the pleasing contrast of the rustic surroundings with the bustling city just beyond it.

Yet the designated area had one significant hitch. In the words of historian Jennifer Bonnell, by this point in its history the river was sending out a "gag-inducing stench." What to do? In preparation the city sent crews out to tidy the grounds, spruce up the river, and apply disinfectants—perhaps chloride of lime—to "sweeten the atmosphere."

The roughly two thousand Torontonians who gathered that day to greet the Princess seemed to enjoy the occasion, and the Princess, "radiant in blue," stepped slowly along the "red-carpeted footbridge across the freshly-cleaned Don river... waving and smiling at children." She apparently did not acknowledge the odour. The sensation-seeking and Liberal *Toronto Daily Star* spied an opportunity to raise a stink, so to speak: the city's efforts, it complained in an editorial under the headline "Our Perfumed Don," resembled those of "courtiers waving handkerchiefs dipped in perfume before the nostrils of the king of France as he drove through the tenements of Paris, that his majesty's nostrils might not be offended by the odor from the open drains."

From that *Star* editorial, an urban legend grew—around royal visits, the river, its stench, and the application of perfume—but, as usual, the legend contained a kind of truth. What the Don's history lacks in heart-quickening romance, it makes up for in genuine historical significance. Toronto's industrial revolution, more than a century old by 1958, had transformed the quiet river into a stinking open sewer—it was probably, Bonnell suggests, "more polluted than it had been at any other point in its history." In 1950 it had already been termed Ontario's most polluted stream, and in the twenty-first century, despite remedial efforts, it would have to be considered a top contender in any competition for Canada's most toxic. It was deadly for all but the "hardiest of fish species."[2] It had become a conduit for the wastes of industry, mechanized agriculture, and the fast-expanding suburbs. This fate, suffered in general by small rivers and streams in the vicinity of the big cities of the Great Lakes basin, was rationalized as the necessary price of progress. Sometimes being quiet and unobtrusive can be a recipe for grief.

Even beyond the royal visit, the year 1958 proved momentous for that same terrain, and in a more lasting way. That year work began on the Don Valley Parkway (DVP). From 1958 to 1966 its construction transformed the valley from "a polluted periphery of the nineteenth-century city to a vital transportation corridor in the center of a larger metropolitan region."

Torontonians had by the late 1950s fallen in love with the car—to an extent exceeded in North America only by the citizens of Detroit and Los Angeles—and planners predicted the trend would continue. The DVP was part of a master plan for a network of expressways: the Gardiner Expressway (mostly completed by 1964), and the never-to-be-completed Crosstown, Scarborough, and Spadina expressways, all linked with public transit. The entire system was designed to fulfil Toronto's aspiration to become a great modern city, moving to the driving rhythms of modernity.

The Don Valley Parkway would spur economic growth, from the city core to Don Mills—including the North York site of entrepreneur E.P. Taylor's experiment in suburban living, hailed by some as a dawn of a fully planned corporate utopia, a developer-controlled development.[3] The Parkway was popular. Because it used an existing river valley and did not require controversial mass expropriations, it could be built more cheaply than other major infrastructure projects. (The final price tag of $46.5 million *was* a bargain.) By 1966 the DVP had become the "continent's busiest artery during peak traffic periods." By 1985 traffic volumes were well in excess of the road's capacity: in the early years of this century, the DVP carried 160,000 vehicles a day on a road intended for 60,000.[4]

On a far grander scale than the attempt in 1958 to deodorize the river, the Parkway was also designed to soften the nature-threatening realities of capitalist modernity. The very name "Parkway," drawn from U.S. and Canadian examples, implied that driving along it might be construed as a wholesome experience of the natural world—offering drivers "the gentle curves, pleasing vistas, and relatively slower speeds of the suburban and regional parkways," passing through bucolic and protected landscapes. The Queen Elizabeth Way, named after the Queen Mother and connecting Toronto with Buffalo, had been intended as a grand route incorporating "majestic architecture and landscape features." Its elevated cultural ambitions are still evident in its "E/R" [Elizabeth/Regina] lamp standards. Similarly, the DVP would offer drivers an exalted and inspiring experience. As Tom Thompson, Metro Parks Commissioner, put it, "Anyone driving down to work will feel pretty close to nature."

If the concept of "nature" includes such human phenomena as road rage, Thompson was surely half-right about that: registering over a thousand accidents per year, the DVP is regularly featured on drive-home afternoon radio shows in Toronto as a source of grief and frustration. When voices speak of the "Don Valley," they do not usually mean the Valley or the River but the often maddeningly congested highway. The "nature" the drivers see is a nature transformed—with the once-picturesque Tumper's Hill flattened during construction (its dirt effectively used to supplement the highway's foundation), the lower river re-routed and its width reduced by a third, and its ecological health further undermined by more toxic chemicals, warmed by the hard surfaces of the road.[5]

The sorry story of the Don offers a suggestive parable about a city engulfed in the manifold revolutions of modernity. Toronto by 1958 was a city in which the British monarchy, the British connection, the British ideal of happy relationships between city and country folk, the rich and the poor, held deep appeal. It mattered greatly that the city appeared as an attractive place to a Royal. Yet it was also, unmistakably, an industrial capitalist city, with its little river mistreated for decades in a strictly utilitarian way as a handy conduit for the wastes of industry—with the effluent treated as so many "externalities" of production for which others (but not the capitalists or developers) could pay. The river had been transformed by industry—but it had also been transformed by the massive spread of suburbs to the north of Toronto's core, whose integration into the city as a whole was its powerful planners' major priority.

A central part of the vision of making Toronto a thrusting, progressive city was to build expressways—literally concrete manifestations of the politicians' and professional planners' sky-high aspirations. A stodgy, conservative city? Or an experimental outpost of radical modernity? Surely Toronto in 1958 was both, a contradictory process as much as a place. This was the city, then, in which, at its most creative and effective, and against considerable odds, the new left managed to establish itself as a powerful presence in a maelstrom of change.

* * *

By "modernity" we mean, first, the ways in which industrial capitalism directly transformed the lives of people (and, in the case of the Don, also non-human entities). Vast numbers of people, all trying to make a living, together generate social patterns that reshape the social and natural world around them. Just by driving to work every day, such people generate social, political, and cultural changes—which can in turn alter more than the course of a river cutting through town. "Automobility"—the "system of objects, spaces, images, and practices that surrounded private automobiles and public roads"[6]—is one important element of this experience of modernity, influencing where people live, how they perceive themselves and their worlds, the contours of civic politics—even what they eat. As part of an integrated vision of making the entire city an efficient and profitable part of a capitalist system, the state poured massive resources into highways. The majority of citizens—most of the time and in most contexts—held the values and priorities of that system to be perfectly legitimate, even if they themselves were exploited by it.

Toronto was undeniably capitalist, with most of its people dependent on wages and many of them working directly in factories; and liberal, permeated by a public political philosophy that hailed formal equality, individual liberty, and above all property; but it was also a site of modernity, with its veritable cathedrals of shopping—from the old downtown Eaton's and Simpson's department stores taking up whole city blocks (and more) to the revolutionary Eaton Centre, North America's busiest mall attracting close to fifty million visitors every year, the first million-square-feet-large portion of which was opened in 1977. Modernity also means altered relationships to space and time—and, politically, a reverence for property. "Progress" entailed the achievement of certain economic goals, which included a willingness not only to repurpose and reroute an entire river system but also to level entire city blocks, uproot tens of thousands of people, and redesign city streets. In this regard it included the wholesale uprooting and remaking of entire wards of the city to achieve a certain model of modernity, often in the name of "slum clearance." Out of a form of "creative destruction," its partisans fondly hope, will emerge ever more efficient and all-encompassing versions of profit-making. "You cannot make an omelette without breaking eggs" was a mantra of Mayor Philip Givens, who was perhaps unaware it has also been attributed to the likes of Robespierre and Lenin.

Ever since the 1950s, with the rise of a kind of commercial Keynesianism in Canada—a Keynesianism in which the vastly expanded wartime state was primarily repurposed to aid propertied individuals to make more and more money, rather than providing a promised system of social security for all—the notion of the state as a mere umpire was displaced by one that gave it a paramount position in achieving "progress"—in the specifically individualistic and capitalist meaning that word had come to acquire. The "New Brutalism" of Toronto's expressways, new subways and commuter trains, Bay Street office towers, high-rise apartment blocks, concert halls, and brand-new or vastly expanded universities was not a rival to, but supplement of, the same system that made the factories, warehouses, and shopping malls. In both form and function the "public" sphere, once clearly distinguishable from the "private," now merged with it. In the 1960s the new Toronto city hall (with its two curved towers) and the CN Tower became icons of the city, a message, in philosopher Mark Kingwell's phrase, of "thrusting modernist certainty."[7] Yet the famous city hall building and its Nathan Phillips Square essentially erased all but the faint traces of the area known as "The Ward"—a chaotic, lively zone that constituted Toronto's first immigrant neighbourhood. What seemed to some in the 1960s as the triumph of a new liberating modernity was for others a heartless eviction and displacement.

The city's 1945 "Master Plan," the overarching new Metropolitan Toronto that emerged in 1954, a city planning apparatus that sought to apply global planning precepts to local problems: all operated on the certainty that they were acting on the basis of science and rationality. These were not quasi-socialistic measures infringing on capital, but rather ways in which the state might make Toronto ever-larger, more productive, and future-focused.

Postwar consumer society "unfolded," as historian Donica Belisle puts it, "as a complex interplay among business, the state, and consumers." If the people at large—the "consumers"—were hardly the helpless or misguided dupes that critics sometimes imagined them to be, their role in this triangular relationship was certainly not one that equalled the power of the other partners. After all, it was a place and time, too, in which classically proletarian manufacturing and construction jobs remained pivotal.[8] It was in the nature of capitalism that many working people had to rely for their material survival upon their wages from jobs in which their powers were systematically sapped and the surpluses they generated appropriated. Such people, progressively alienated from the fruits of their labour time, might also become alienated from the wider culture and politics that undergirded their exclusion. They might even come to question the science of modernity that provided its proponents with their ideological certainties. They might come to see automobility, for instance, as a life-draining and even life-threatening economic and cultural system, to which whole towns, neighbourhoods, and river systems were being sacrificed. "Slum clearance" might become seen, not as an inspiring moment of human achievement, the replacement of the untidiness and messiness of old wards with rational and orderly spaces, but as cruel and irrational impositions on working people whose only crime was to be in the way of radical capitalist modernity.

Indeed, the demolition and takeover of working-class neighbourhoods did create relatively unprecedented and well-grounded movements of resistance, in which urban middle-class professionals united with endangered working-class residents. A modal moment came in 1966 in Trefann Court, an area located near Regent Park South, when leftist organizers rallied to help the cause of residents faced with eviction in a working-class neighbourhood.[9] Trefann Court had been slurred as a slum, and most Torontonians were not engaged by this uphill battle against progress. But this battle foreshadowed the full-scale wars in the 1970s over development and displacement.

The ascendency of "capitalist modernity," then, called out for something better—such as empowered "communities" of ordinary people entitled to a say in the overriding structures and conditions of their own lives. There, in a nutshell, lay much of the genesis of what came to be called the "new left," which was by no means, as often presented, just an importation into Toronto of the latest left-wing fads and fancies, but a force capable of speaking to a far wider potential audience made up of the vast population of people who came to feel alienated from the very logic of the system structuring their lives.[10]

* * *

In 1967 Canadian geographer Edward Relph arrived back in Toronto after five years in London, England. Years later he recalled his "first impressions" of the city at that time—noting that it "was not only inward-turned but stuck in the past." He saw "old-fashioned streetcars running long streets lined with wooden telephone poles festooned with wires, residential streets with tired Victorian houses, subway stations named for British patron saints, and a population with predominantly

British roots that were tangled up with romantic images of a Britain that no longer existed."[11]

He was far from alone in this response. A long-standing trope of writing about Toronto is an emphasis on its drably conformist, uniformly Anglo, stodgily anti-modern, and traditional character: "Toronto the Provincial" and "Toronto the Dull." Here was, the story goes, a place of almost overpowering Victorianism—in Relph's words: a "relatively compact, white, Anglo-Saxon, Protestant, and morally upright industrial city." Journalist Robert Fulford expressed much the same opinion, summing up the place as a "city of silence, a private city, where all the best meals were eaten at home . . . a mute, inward-turned metropolis"—and, worse, "clearly subservient to Montreal." In his 1936 novel *Jupiter Eight* the Canadian science-fiction writer Francis Pollock imaginatively described the prevailing reputation of the place as "a half-grown city, a nest of Methodists and Orangemen, of Puritans and Pharisees . . . a rube town, a hick town, an over-grown tank-town, with half a million people who confused Dada with Santa Claus."[12]

Yet was this place ever really simply "Toronto the Good" and the tedious—with the implication of a drearily provincial, ethnically homogeneous, and religiously repressive society? In truth it was always a much more complicated—and troubled—place; and the maelstrom of modernity that transformed it had its beginnings not in the 1950s and 1960s but in a much earlier era. The city's more contrary character goes back to its rampant industrialization in the third quarter of the nineteenth century, accompanied by the vigorous response of a powerful labour movement.[13] As Keith Walden, in a provocative distillation of modernity in one Toronto setting, the Industrial Exhibition ("The Ex"), points out, "The extent of change in the late Victorian Western world was staggering." It was a time when "cities grew inexorably" and "powerful new business organizations announced their presence with high-rise office towers and sprawling factories." Scientific discoveries and new technologies (not just automobiles but electric lights, telephones, motion pictures, and more) "appeared with dizzying regularity." Eaton's, with its catalogues in seemingly every home across the country, could declare itself by 1925 to be the *Largest Institution of Its Kind under the British Flag*.[14] The merchandiser had a long history of engaging in all-out labour struggles.

Toronto's ascendency to economic primacy in the country was equally venerable. In 1891 just 17 per cent of Canadian companies with branch operations were headquartered in Toronto; by 1931 Toronto's share had risen to 29 per cent, with a clear national lead in manufacturing, wholesaling, and retailing. Although skyscrapers began to proliferate especially in the 1970s and 1980s, as early as 1914 a downtown skyline had appeared, with a 1906 fifteen-storey Traders' Bank building, a twenty-storey Royal Bank building, and the gargantuan Eaton's and

Simpson's complexes.[15] By 1970 Toronto's Bay Street had overtaken Montreal's St. James Street in its financial power.

The tendency to eradicate whole working-class neighbourhoods also began early on. It can be traced as far back as the ideas of Georges-Eugène Haussmann, whose mid-nineteenth-century renovation of central Paris was motivated in part by the desire to rob working-class protesters of their best defences. The doing away of "slums" as a remedy for cancerous blots and defective people became a rallying point for urban reformers.[16] Regent Park (North) became a model of the damage that a top-down "urban renewal" scheme could inflict upon a working-class community, in this case much of the neighbourhood called Cabbagetown, long stereotyped as a slum by worried middle-class Torontonians. The Regent Park cornerstone was laid in 1948, and the following year the first family moved into the project. The *Toronto Daily Star* called it "Heaven."[17] Within two decades, a legion of people attested to their hell-like imprisonment in Regent Park.

As for the suburbanization often held to be a symptom of the postwar social order, geographer Richard Harris shows that it long antedated 1945, and cites a *Globe and Mail* editorial from 1946 complaining about Toronto's "endless dwellings of suburbia, each meticulously exact on its thirty-seven foot frontage, not an inch out of line." The early "suburbs"—such as the glorified model of Don Mills and the exclusive conclave of Forest Hill—contained their own problems; among other things they served as a prototype of a model now familiar across the famously conservative "905" zone. Writer Erna Paris would remember her life in Forest Hill as "insular and unreal," cut off from the rest of the city, whose downtown department stores were familiar, but not much else.[18] Yet not everyone who grew up in such a setting would end up a conservative or a conformist. Many a new leftist originated in such places—especially those who made the decision to leave suburbia for once and for all—with their resistance to capitalism and the liberal order sharpened by alienation and loneliness. Nor were all suburbs conservative bastions—especially in the older ones, one still found progressives and leftists. Nonetheless, over time Toronto's vastly expanded "905" has acquired a conservative atmosphere—so readily apparent whenever a federal or provincial election is called and their constituents, so reticent about their class privileges as a rule, vote decisively to reject even the mildest revision of them.

So, was it Toronto the Good, or Toronto the Troubling? C.S. Clark's *Toronto the Good* of the 1890s, although undoubtedly fiercely moralistic, was an attempt to reveal Toronto the Troubling—a city of heavy drinking, prostitution, chaos: a place of moral unruliness from below calling out for moral regulation from above. Steven Maynard's brilliant work on same-sex desire in the city, which draws on Clark, also suggests spaces for alternative modes of sexual expression well outside the official Victorian playbook.[19] Elise Chenier finds that "The Ward" accommodated sex-trade workers from the 1920s to the 1950s; they were "as much a part of the neighbourhood as the butcher, the grocer and the restaurant cook." Peter Hobbs and Cate Sandilands note that Allan Gardens—founded in 1858 by the Toronto Horticultural Society as a botanical garden, and the epitome of Victorian formality and an early site of new left cultural resistance—enjoyed a long and distinguished history as a gay cruising zone, as did David Balfour Park, one of a variety of picturesque parks branching off from the Don Valley.[20]

The descriptions of the stiflingly and uniform Anglo atmosphere of Toronto—as the site of a class-bound, blinkered authoritarianism, which, it is argued, magically dissipated with the rise of liberal "multiculturalism" sometime after 1960—are also somewhat off the mark. After the curtailment of immigration to the United States following World War One, Toronto actually became "the premier city of immigrants on the continent." Until the 1950s that influx of people was dominated by newcomers from the British Isles; to 1951 they constituted more than half the total, and in that year more than two-thirds of Torontonians "considered themselves to be of British-Canadian ethnicity." Still, those British "subjects" were hardly a homogeneous lot. Many of them, certainly, did sing the praises of the Royal Family; some were wealthy or possessed of sufficient cultural capital to render a plausible performance of aristocratic hauteur. A number of them envisaged the University of Toronto as a provincial version of Oxbridge. Yet a majority were working-class people, many of whom developed communities just beyond the city limits. "By 1907," writes Harris, "the suburbs were more clearly blue-collar than the city."[21] Many such immigrants arrived without much capital, and developed squatters' enclaves that long retained a radical reputation. Some of the immigrants came bearing the imprint of the British Independent Labour Party and developed fairly successful replicas of it in Toronto and Hamilton. Many of them later travelled into the Co-operative Commonwealth Federation (CCF). They also brought with them important ethnic and religious divisions. Although in Toronto, "The Belfast of Canada," the Orange Lodge persisted as a powerful force into the 1960s, the Irish did not speak with one Protestant voice: in a city in which Roman Catholics constituted the largest single denomination, Irish Roman Catholics were hardly without resources or influence.[22] A city nicknamed the "Belfast of Canada" was hardly going to become a byword for ethnic or religious consensus, and Toronto was not.

Nor should one overlook those who arrived who could not claim British ethnicity. Jews were the most numerous of these minorities. They confronted often ghastly conditions in sweatshops and suffered high levels of prejudice.[23] They also contributed mightily to the Social Democratic Party and then the Communist Party of Canada (CPC), sustained a lively Yiddish-language press, and colonized a large swath of downtown Toronto. That Jews were oppressed and ghettoized is not in doubt; that they were squashed by a supposedly unified Anglo hegemony can certainly be questioned, given the size and resilience of their institutions, including dynamic socialist clubs and unions. Their success in developing two provincial constituencies as "Red bases" in the 1940s and 1950s, the vitality of the United Jewish People's Order and an impressive array of other dissident institutions, the renown of their best-known MPP, the beloved J.B. Salsberg—all speak not only to their spirit and fortitude but to the deficiencies of an overdrawn portrait of "Toronto the stolidly Anglo fortress." The election of a Jewish mayor in 1955, which one newspaper proclaimed the birth of "Toronto the Tolerant," meant neither that Jews had previously been silent sufferers of oppression nor that racism or prejudice had disappeared and a gracious liberalism dawned.[24]

According to the Whig version of Toronto history, where there was once bleak stodginess, there emerged liberal enlightenment, a keen sense of tolerance, and a decent entertainment district. Yet if pre-1945 Toronto was alive with ethnic and religious tensions, post-1945 Toronto betrayed few signs of stable ethnic or racial harmony. Rather than an upwards-and-onwards liberal narrative of perpetual progress and understanding, a critical realist portrait of Toronto must attend both to the very real continuation of Anglo privilege and power—and the equally real struggles of the subaltern excluded from that realm. Toronto was never a static place—it was and is not so much an easily measured "thing" as a dynamic process. "Snowballing" immigration changed the human face of the city over the decades. There *was* something different about Toronto from the 1950s to the 1980s; but it was a radical acceleration of pre-existing trends.

* * *

That acceleration meant more than huge numbers of people in shiny vehicles pushing down heavily on the gas pedals as they negotiated the new expressways. Immigration played a huge part in the change. Post-1945 Toronto, displacing Montreal more and more as the country's economic metropolis, exerted a magnetic force over a much wider terrain. Once perhaps rightly considered a provincial industrial and commercial city whose principal hinterland lay in rural Ontario, post-1945 Toronto was plainly no longer limited to such a functional role. It now beckoned to Indigenous people across the Dominion in quest of economic survival. It called out to young people in search of adventure and their own identities, who flocked in droves to that midtown ten-year-long countercultural phenomenon called Yorkville in the mid-1960s.[25] The city was a haven (supposedly) for "Hard Luck Maritimers" and Newfoundlanders who flocked to Toronto in search of jobs—a phenomenon captured in Don Shebib's award-winning film

Goin' Down the Road. Released in 1970 to rapturous reviews—even from Pauline Kael in the *New Yorker*!—the movie featured two hapless and hopeless Maritimers trying to make it in Toronto. Although the Toronto-born Shebib shot his "Maritime" scenes in Scarborough, he did (controversially) make his way to Allan Gardens, where he depicted real live alcoholics, taken to be archetypal Maritimers.[26]

One alderman explained that such specimens were quaint hillbillies, bearers of a "rich folk culture that can be traced back to Elizabethan days." The alderman representing working-class Parkdale warned of Maritime welfare scroungers: "We don't owe these people a living. They are causing us nothing but grief." Between 1961 and 1966, as Greg Marquis observes, "The population of the Toronto Census Metropolitan Area (CMA) grew by 18 per cent," with a prevailing sentiment, stirred up by right-wing populists, that the city core could absorb no more.[27]

To such in-Canada migrants were famously added the wave upon wave of postwar immigrants—especially after the 1970s—who transformed Toronto into a city renowned for its racial and ethnic diversity. As early as the 1970s Toronto was already becoming markedly less British and more "multicultural"—to use an expression that came into vogue in that decade (with "multiculturalism" becoming official federal policy in 1971). Although it is an urban legend that the United Nations formally designated Toronto "the most multicultural city in the world," a statement "repeated in newspaper accounts, government reports, mayoral speeches and even the City's promotional literature," the city nonetheless became a remarkably diverse place, certainly one of the most heterogeneous cities in the world—even if it has also been seen, in the words of Afro-Canadian writer Austin Clarke, as a "collection of ghettoes."[28]

From 1958 to 1985 "Toronto" had two distinct meanings, depending on context. It might mean the "City of Toronto," which "had factories, offices, public transit, department stores and theatres, the wealth, the power, and most of the people." It had a population of about 670,000 in 1940 and 675,000 in 2001. On the outskirts of this core city were five other municipalities, "primarily dormitory communities of relatively low-density suburban housing surrounded by farmland."[29] These surrounding municipalities of York, East York, North York, Scarborough, and Etobicoke were brought together by the province in 1953 to form the Municipality of Metropolitan Toronto, a place of roughly two and a half million in the 1980s, which most everyone simply called "Metro." By the 1990s "Metropolitan Toronto," the core plus its periphery, had grown enormously in population: the City of North York, with more than 600,000 people, laid claim to be the sixth-largest city in Canada, within an urban area accounting for some 2,600,000 people in 2011. By the mid-2000s the Greater Toronto-Hamilton Area (GTHA)—a third meaning of "Toronto"—numbered around seven million people: the very term suggested the seemingly unstoppable expansion of the megalopolis on the shores of Lake Ontario.[30]

* * *

The decade of the 1950s was by no means the blandly conformist period that it is conventionally made out to be. It was a decade, economically, of general prosperity in North America; but also, politically, it was the time of the Cold War, McCarthyism, the Korean War, and the Suez Crisis—all amidst the ultra-dangerous arrival of the thermonuclear threat.

Onto this scene, then, came the first stirrings of what we call the new left. A standard narrative of this phenomenon posits the existence of a chasm between a decrepit old left and a youthful student-based new left—with the old left based on specific ethnic groups, weighed down by an aging generation, and lumbered with orthodox Communism. That new leftists opposed the old left's championing of conventional politics, centralized state planning, and authoritarianism is often presented as an almost self-evident truism. The old political left-wing stream was supposedly evidence of what the French-German activist Daniel Cohn-Bendit, one of the key student leaders of the French revolt of 1968, called "obsolete communism." Cohn-Bendit's widely read and cited book of that title presented a stirring denunciation of top-heavy, unspontaneous left organizations, which are counterposed against their more authentic and lively new left alternatives.[31] In Toronto, too, the words of many new leftists could be brought forward to demonstrate that an ossified "old left" served as a foil for the dynamic, revolutionary "new left" they aspired to create.

Still, although the thesis of a strict divide between old and new worked particularly well for Cohn-Bendit and France, it does not fit exactly with the Toronto evidence, which indicates a slow, ambiguous blending of one form of leftism into another. The old left was not necessarily discarded like some faded fashion that had seen its day. The new left formation undoubtedly asked new questions and proposed new solutions with respect to race, class, gender, and colonialism, taking approaches that prioritized individual emancipation, national liberation, prefigurative democracy, and grassroots community politics. But it usually did not do so in ways that presumed the dire undesirability or insufficiency of its Toronto antecedents. It was more characteristic of new leftists to sentimentalize old Reds than to denounce them. Most new leftists seemed to look with considerable sympathy at those who provided the first socialist solutions to ways of navigating the maelstrom of capitalist modernity. Some, with mixed results, even sought to emulate their successes.

Similarly, the notion of "sixties radicalism" as an entity in a certain time and place needs to be stretched out considerably—into at least the "Long Sixties," given the sense of political fervour, determination, and adaptability that lasted well into the 1970s, and beyond. The earlier years, from about 1965 to 1967, saw the emergence of a more structured movement, associated with the Student Union for Peace Action (SUPA) and other groups; and this was the modest forerunner, rather than the epitome, of the new left. In the following years some new leftists in Toronto demonstrated a fierce resistance to the educational "meat grinder" that they considered a force of repressive alienation; others (and often they were the same people) tried in many and various ways to "Bring the Revolution Home"—that is, create a movement in Toronto responsive to worldwide struggles of Third World peoples against colonialism. In these years the new left also posed a challenge to pre-existing left parties and movements, many of them shaped by Marxism-Leninism—but, even so, rather than constituting easily demarcated movements competing against each other, the left as a whole, across a broader spectrum, tended to engage in groupings that coexisted uneasily with each other and shared many ideas.

New left ideas of personal autonomy, community empowerment, and anti-imperialism and national liberation, for instance, gained surprising amounts of traction within what have been called "vanguard parties"—groups organized on the basis of a top-down or democratic centralist structure, with members who believed that a working-class revolution was the only avenue to human emancipation (and many of whom went into factories in an attempt to help achieve that goal, a scheme they called "industrializing" or "industrialization"). One key to vanguard politics was simply that revolutionaries had an obligation to *lead*—and not just to liaise, express grievances, crystallize sentiments, bear witness, or give voice. The groups included leftists who fell under the umbrella of a "new Leninist" politics—but it was a Leninism quite distinct from that of the Russian Revolution of 1917; a Leninism that in 1970 would have been unrecognizable to those sitting in the Communist Party's old Cecil Street headquarters in Toronto. As it turned out, the tense relations between new Leninists or vanguard Marxists and new leftists were often resolved on new left and not vanguardist terms. The years of the 1970s, too, saw a "turn to community," which had a lasting impact on both the new leftists themselves and the movements they sought to influence.

The new left demanded a *positive* globalization, one keenly attentive to local needs. Undoubtedly moving in response to global happenings—to the threat of thermonuclear war, the war in Vietnam, struggles against racism in the United States and around the world, and feminist and gay liberation movements challenging those specific oppressions—it was, at its best, also very local. It was equally responsive to local happenings—to the expressways threatening much more than just the Don Valley, the local liberal order's inability to provide adequate food and shelter, the Toronto-specific manifestations of racism, and the lives of drab conformity and soul-destroying ugliness that seemed the fate of so many ordinary Torontonians. The comprehensiveness of much of the new left's vision was correlated with the extraordinary scope of the processes of change transforming the city.

The new left incorporated both a *negative* critique of the capitalist modernity, of which Toronto had become a Canadian and global exemplar, and a *positive* statement of an alternative to it. It entailed, as literary critic Marshall Berman so aptly captures the tension in his brilliant diagnosis of modernity, the opportunity "to be both revolutionary and conservative . . . alive to new possibilities for experience and adventure."[32] In the twenty-seven years of its heyday in Toronto, it had many dazzlingly brilliant moments.

In Toronto the new left sought to change ways of thinking and seeing, in wide-ranging and impressive attempts to create a cultural revolution; and in turn various "leftisms" arose that were closely associated with oppressed subaltern identities—those of racialized minorities, socialist feminists, and gay liberationists in particular, all in subordinate positions to the powerful. By the 1980s neoliberalism was having its effect, to some extent sucking the oxygen out of the progressive world that the new left had helped to create—but, in the end, not entirely removing a revolutionary sensibility and a radical push for change that persists to this day.

* * *

Most Toronto new leftists lived, worked, and had their being in the city core—although the surrounding areas contained such important places for the left as York University and a good many of the factories where strikes important to many new leftists took place. Yet, as it turns out, many new leftists in Toronto were in, but not of, this community. They were, in a sense, inhabitants of a Toronto that was as much process as place.

The distinction between close identification with a community or place on the one hand, and identification with the entire planet on the other, made a huge difference to the new left—both with respect to what a good number of new leftists believed and how they were perceived. Many Toronto new leftists only sometimes thought of themselves as Torontonians. Often recent immigrants drawn from the United States and Britain, or students coming from across Ontario and the rest of Canada, they might have relatively little attachment to, or knowledge of, the history of the city in which they happened to live. They thus exemplified its radical modernity, one element of which was a marked impatience with traditional attachments and topics that might distract from the here and now. These leftists—who will appear in the pages of this book—included academics, peace activists, radical students, feminists, gay liberationists, anti-racist activists, builders of vanguard parties, and cultural workers who saw themselves as acting on stages far larger than that of Toronto. They believed themselves to be, as the University of Toronto's occasionally insightful and certainly world-famous expert on modernity would famously put it, citizens of a "Global Village"—and Marshall McLuhan's phrase, embraced with particular enthusiasm by liberals seeking to renovate the Ontario educational system, captured an important insight en route to becoming a cliché.[33]

Such leftists might spend far more time being preoccupied with the finer points of the Communist Party of the Soviet Union in the late 1920s than with the politics of contemporary Torontonians who had inherited, for instance, the traditions of the Spadina Expressway campaign and the United Jewish People's Order. For them, Toronto was merely one urban node in the much vaster entity of "Western capitalism." Its urban specificities were, at best, of limited antiquarian interest. If they were student radicals, they might see themselves as co-participants of the actions or discussions on the Berkeley and Columbia campuses, not as inheritors of radical intellectual traditions that had flourished in their own Toronto neighbourhoods in the 1930s. If they were feminists, the latest works by Simone de Beauvoir, Juliet Mitchell, Shulamith Firestone (an American feminist of Canadian descent), or Germaine Greer might count for a good deal more than the kindred explorations of Canadians Dorothy Smith, Charnie Guettel, or Margaret Bentson, not to mention a half-century of feminist struggle in Toronto. If they were gay activists working in *The Body Politic*, they might well—as historian Scott de Groot so brilliantly shows—believe themselves to be shaping a transnational discourse aiming at sexual liberation, not at something in any way rooted in or confined to Canada or Toronto.[34] Throughout such currents was a strong drive to generalize about problems on a world, not a Canadian, let alone a merely local, level. This breadth of vision could be both a source of strength and a limitation. It could be experienced as an engagement with modernity's fundamental global patterns, of which those in Canada or Toronto were merely local manifestations. It constituted an opening up to the world and to many of the most promising critical theories useful to understanding that world.

At the same time, such universalism could become seen as a limitation. Inspired strongly by the need to organize on behalf of the U.S. civil rights movement or to understand and resist the Vietnam War, many new leftists were forcibly reminded that the world remained divided up into states and superpowers. The many people who arrived as war resisters were often prompted to see the conflict as a blameworthy exercise in U.S. nationalism. Some leftists echoed, perhaps unwittingly, their ancestors of the 1920s and 1940s in posing once again the "Canada Question," and responding, in many cases, with forms of nationalism that imagined Canada as being, like Vietnam, Cuba, or Chile, poised on the brink of its own struggle against colonialism. Such new leftists might even be drawn into surprisingly sympathetic readings of such pillars of the academic establishment as Harold Innis, Donald Creighton, and George Grant, and read into them oppositional impulses with which they might not have readily identified.

New leftists were divided on the national question. Both those repelled by nationalism and those drawn by it were strongly influenced by the Toronto milieu in which they worked, which conveyed to them the increasingly insistent message that Toronto was a world-class city, really (they told themselves) the only such city in all of Canada. Equally, Toronto was the emergent cultural capital of the nation, with artists, intellectuals, publishing houses, journals, the Canadian Broadcasting Corporation (CBC), and even *Hockey Night in Canada* repeating the message that, in essence, Toronto equals Canada, or at any rate the Canada that matters. Sometimes new leftists who began at the one pole swiftly gravitated to the other. Sometimes, too, the Canada of which so many new leftists spoke bore little relation to the Canada in which many Canadians lived—there was often an abrupt disconnect between the leftists themselves and "the people" supposedly being addressed.

Sometimes, when Toronto new leftists took to generalizing about Quebec, the Maritimes, or the West, they sounded much like authorities pronouncing judgments from on high—exactly the subject-position that so many of them were desperate not to occupy. To many non-Torontonians the city's great metropolitan status seems to have not been honestly earned through any genuinely knowledgeable or sympathetic interaction with Canadians outside the metropolitan area. A sense remains that Toronto's cultural and political pretensions are misaligned with its actual world-historic significance.

Many of the new left's Toronto-centred discourses could seem of limited applicability outside the confines of the city—which hints at a scalar problem, with Toronto activists and intellectuals "scaling up" Toronto phenomena to the status of issues that should engage the attention of all revolutionaries, with which all radicals should deal, without focusing with much intensity on their determinate local co-ordinates. A Toronto that over the course of 1958–85 appeared to become the emblem of the entire country, with the CN Tower and downtown cityscape playing a nation-building symbolic role, came to be resisted precisely as the epitome of a Canadian Empire that was pretty much just as arrogant or centralist as its French, British, or American predecessors. The city, wrote a reviewer of Michael Ondaatje's novel *In the Skin of the Lion* (1987), was a "catastrophe ... ugly, formless, without character, it sits upon the banks of Lake Ontario like some diseased organ in the body, spreading pollution about it." As early as 1948, Lister Sinclair's radio play *We All Hate Toronto* set a pattern of Toronto-bashing that, from Vancouver to Halifax, and certainly not excepting Alberta, shows little sign of letting up.[35]

* * *

North America's fourth most populous city, Toronto is Ontario's capital, Canada's largest city and business metropolis, and home to the country's most prestigious university and producers of mass media, at the centre of a megalopolis stretching around the western end of Lake Ontario, whose population exceeds that of many European countries.

The city (including the people who live and work in it) exists on at least six scales: transnational (over half of the residents were born outside Canada, and a good many of those work for transnational corporations headquartered in other countries); continental (much of the industrial economy is driven in one way or the other by the North American automobile industry and the city's location on an internal sea shared with the United States); national (home to a panoply of Canada-wide banks, investment houses, and cultural and political institutions); regional (capital of a vast province and recipient of generation upon generation of in-migrants from its hinterland); local (strongly defined neighbourhoods and districts, each with its own traditions, ethnic composition, and atmosphere); and personal (as individuals and families weave together, within this maelstrom of modernity, networks that help them get through life).

A fair response to any statement about "Toronto" might be, "But that's not *my* Toronto!" Fair enough—and clearly, this sprawling metropolis is more than the sum of its parts. It has an organic unity transcending its manifold and conflicting elements—even if that unity is the conflictual, endlessly changing process of an unfolding modernity.

We keep these scales in mind when talking about Toronto's new leftists. Some of these anti-capitalists operated on a transnational level and made a significant planetary contribution to left-wing thought and practice. Many were North Americans more than they were Canadians. Energized by such issues as war resistance, a good number of them eventually left Toronto. Others operated more clearly on a regional scale, caught up, for example, in the vast bureaucracy of the Ontario government. The lives of many were lived locally—with a significant distinction between suburbanites commuting to work from outlying communities (Greater Toronto's reach now extends more than a hundred miles in all directions) and those who lived in the city's core, where most of the left-wing action took place. In such a sprawling, intimidating, fast-paced, and difficult-to-grasp context, personal friendships were indispensable—and it was characteristic of this left that they were invested with a new political significance. Stage-set, institutional nexus, or launching-pad? For the city's new leftists, Toronto was often all of these things, and more.

Toronto's new leftists—defined here as radicals committed to personal authenticity and self-determination, to solidarity with national liberation movements, to egalitarian political forms that anticipated the better world to come, and to empowered communities that might serve as the democratic antithesis of the often cold capitalist metropolis they inhabited—sometimes seemed to operate in their own universes. They often invested heavily in debates and theoretical languages that most Canadians could not understand, and were often oblivious to wider social and political contexts without which none of their dreams could be realized. But at their frequent best, their activism functioned brilliantly on all six scales. If Toronto's layered complexity often makes the city hard to grasp, it also meant that activism on one scale—say, local resistance to an expressway or gay men's fight back against a bathhouse raid—could quickly have ramifications on every scale. The heavy concentration of mass media in Toronto meant a local issue could attain national and even global dimensions with dizzying speed. All of these issues did not add up to a tightly defined agenda, which means that an evaluation of success or failure cannot simply refer to a master list of demands. New leftists did not adhere to any one party. No single organization commanded their loyalty. This diffuse history means that the new left's impact is difficult to pin down. Yet, as the evidence in this book reveals—and as subtle and intangible as the effects sometimes were—that impact endures to the present.

Critics may well dissent from this position. Any sober Canadian reckoning would have to consider the Montreal new left to be a more consequential phenomenon; with its agonistic and complicated relationship with Quebec nationalism, at one point that movement seemed on the brink of overthrowing the established political order.[36] Those people familiar with the American new left story might dismiss the Toronto activists as merely derivative, noteworthy only as a marginal addition to a U.S. movement in which it played a subordinate role as refuge, source of solidarity activism, echo chamber, and stage upon which American activists might strut their stuff. Here was a place where radicals often lip-synched to melodies written by celebrities from far away.[37] The strong presence of academics and university students meant that the movement had a tendency to invest heavily in issues unfamiliar to many of the fellow Torontonians or Canadians of the time, and many succumbed to the temptation to see themselves as cosmopolitan leftists thinking weighty thoughts beyond the understanding of the mere mortals with whom they happened to share a country or city.

Yet a countervailing tendency was also in place—to combine such international identifications with full-hearted identification with the empowerment of communities, local movements, and oppressed people sharing a stepped-upon

A Pollution Probe ad calls for a cleanup of the Don River.

Eyeopener, Oct. 3, 1969.

How would you like a glass of Don River water?

Isn't the Don River beautiful? Isn't it magnificent how it curls through the ravines of Toronto and flows beautifully into the Lake? Isn't it delightful how its banks have become the playground of children and families and other happy creatures?

It's nice to think what it could be. It's fun to think that the Don River could be pretty. That it could be useful to people. That it could be something other than a receptacle for the sewage that pours from the plants on its banks. That it could be something other than a stench that oozes into the air and makes you ashamed that it's there. And that this kind of thing could happen right here in the core of our city.

Don River water is full of everything raw and rotten you can think of. And Don River water doesn't stop in the Don River. It sort of gurgles and sludges its way with the wastes of all those progressive firms out into Lake Ontario. And the Lake goes to the St. Lawrence. And the St. Lawrence goes to the ocean. And after that, there's not much left is there?

Help us do something about things like the Don River. First write your mayor; or your Provincial Member of Parliament; or your Federal member; or even the Prime Minister. Tell them you'd like some of this stench cleaned up. If they don't believe it's there, or they give you some kind of song and dance, invite them over for a nice, cool glass of water. Don River kind.

We can use anything you'd like to contribute to help us work toward cleaning up our polluted air, water and land. If you would like to help us, we'll send you a button and a receipt for tax purposes, if you send us this coupon. Thanks.

Please Make Cheques Payable To:
UNIVERSITY OF TORONTO — POLLUTION PROBE

Name: ____________________

Address: ____________________

City: ____________________

Do it. **Pollution Probe at the University of Toronto.**

A cartoon guide to the politics of restoring the Don River.

Guerilla, Oct. 13, 1970.

racialized, gender, or sexual identity. The difficult business of operating on several scales at once was often addressed creatively—even brilliantly.

* * *

On Nov. 16, 1969, a cavalcade of about one hundred cars set out from the University of Toronto's downtown St. George campus and stopped near the Prince Edward Viaduct—a gigantic truss-arched bridge spanning the Don Valley on Bloor Street. About two hundred mourners, dressed in nineteenth-century costume and accompanied by a dirge played by two sousaphone players, descended to the riverbank.

With its elegant soaring arches supporting a busy roadway, the Prince Edward or Bloor Street Viaduct, opened in 1918, testifies to the vaunting ambition of

A wreath of mourning is placed into the Don River during a Pollution Probe demonstration; Nov. 16, 1969.

Clara Thomas Archives and Special Collections, Toronto Telegram fonds.

Toronto. Reuniting a city divided by the Don River, it accelerated the growth of the Riverdale neighbourhood, which was once home to many working-class boarding houses—dwellings now out of reach for any but the urban gentry. Starring in novels and television shows, the viaduct acquired the name of "suicide bridge" because of all the people throwing themselves off it—perhaps as many as five hundred overall by 2003, and one person every twenty-two days in the mid-1990s.[38] Modernity comes with a dark side.

On that November day in 1969, some of the participants who went down to the riverside wailed in sorrow. The crowd celebrated the life of the dear departed in moving descriptions of better days. A greedy Victorian capitalist, dressed appropriately in top hat and tailcoat, declaimed about the glories of unfettered greed, for which he was pied in the face. Then a wreath was placed on the waters, and the mourners dispersed. The death of the Don River, with its off-the-charts bacteria levels, was duly commemorated.[39]

The organizer of this event, Pollution Probe, was not a revolutionary body. Launched the previous February, it had been officially registered as a project of the Zoology Department at the University of Toronto and boasted a board of advisors chock-a-block with professors (including Marshall McLuhan). It had members who, said one participant, "couldn't be dismissed as sort of hairy radicals because they were so conformist looking. You know, tall, up-right, white Anglo Saxon." Some of them were bound for well-paid consulting jobs.[40] Pollution Probe had displaced the more "politicized" Group Action to Stop Pollution and flourished by fitting itself into the liberal-capitalist order, not fighting it.

Yet, from another perspective, in 1969 something was still happening on the banks of the Don River, something suggesting a big change in the past ten years. The capitalist abuse of the river was no longer a matter to conceal but an issue to expose—playfully and irreverently, with an eye on the media and without the air of gravity that attended many demonstrations of the day. And because it was so obviously a case of *capitalist* abuse, some of the mourners that day were bound for more radical things. Founding member Varda Burstyn, for one, went on to become one of Canada's foremost left feminist theoreticians and eco-organizers. In the 1990s Burstyn became vice-chair of Greenpeace Canada (fd.1971), whose policies of militant direct action "revolutionized the role of environmental activists."[41]

A member of Pollution Probe, taking on the persona of "Simon Greed," explains why he is responsible for polluting the Don River; Nov. 16, 1969.

Clara Thomas Archives and Special Collections, Toronto Telegram fonds.

There is, in short, another reading that claims not Pollution Probe itself but some of its members as new leftists—people who connected the dots between environmental degradation and capitalist greed and proceeded to movements dedicated to contesting the narrow concepts of property and individualism inherent in the transnational liberal order. They were, at their most creative, combining struggles on divergent scales—the local crisis of one river, a city reluctant to confront the toxic logic underlying its shimmering modernity, the myopia of the Ontario government and the hands-off stance of Ottawa, and the emerging planetary crisis—which could all be highlighted in one effective protest, reminiscent of Communist agitprop from the 1930s yet with its own youthful and irreverent spin.

In the end Toronto new leftists were historically significant people, and much of their story represents an admirable record of achievement well worth the attention of anyone who wants to advance the next left of the twenty-first century. At its frequent best, this left formation, encompassing a diversity of organizations and people, was one of the largest movements of radical resistance in Canadian

Alderwood Collegiate students participate in a "Stamp Out All Pollution" cycling tour of their neighbourhood; May 21, 1970.

Clara Thomas Archives and Special Collections, Toronto Telegram fonds.

Members of Group Action to Stop Pollution, wearing surgical masks for theatrical effect, hand out leaflets to passersby; Dec. 7, 1967.

Clara Thomas Archives and Special Collections, Toronto Telegram fonds.

history. This new left made a lasting difference to the lives of its militants and a subtle but perceptible difference in Toronto politics more generally. Without minimizing its contradictions, its fierce critics, or the reasons for its demise, we arc impressed by its achievements. In a word, we admire it.

2

A Slow, Cautious Hello: First Stirrings of a Movement, 1958–64

AROUND NOON HOUR on a summer's day hundreds of people gathered near a speaker in the park. A policeman in attendance proved to be persistent. Ignoring a cacophony of boos and jeers, he forced his way through the crowd to enforce the city's bylaw against public speaking.

As he began writing a court summons, a man at the other end of the crowd began to speak in a declamatory voice: "I still go naked where comers roam the shore." That prompted another officer to barge in to preserve order. Just then a woman shouted, "The greatest thing about Telstar is that we'll get World War III live on TV." It was a signal that the cat-and-mouse game between activists and police was not over.[1]

Others hanging around the area continued to debate philosophy and world events. As if to highlight the pro-Cuban literature displayed on a nearby ironing board, a bylaw-defying poet shouted "Fidel! Fidel!" Reporters described the "weird and wild carnival mood"—reflecting the mix of politics and the whirling cultures of what would later in the decade be called a "happening." One young participant said he had travelled as far as Vancouver in the vain hope of discovering something akin to the scene he was now experiencing. It certainly did not look like any form of the left-wing politics previously seen in the city.[2]

Throughout the summer of 1962 similar scenes played out on a weekly basis in Allan Gardens, the large park in the city's downtown east end, a space prized for its flowers and greenery. Sometimes police silently viewed the proceedings from afar; occasionally they evicted several hundred people from the park in one fell swoop. Each weekend the park's air was pungent with confrontation, culture, and politics.[3]

The impetus for these happenings had arisen the previous summer, when a handful of peace activists began regularly speaking to audiences near the park's

A crowd gathers around an anti-war speaker in front of the Robert Burns statue in Allan Gardens; Aug. 14, 1961.

Clara Thomas Archives and Special Collections, Toronto Telegram fonds.

iconic statue of the famous Scottish poet Robbie Burns. After one of the participants was arrested, members of the peace movement staged a modest demonstration in support of free speech. When a court later ruled that the activist's speech had not violated the Criminal Code but was still subject to prosecution under the city's bylaw against public speaking in parks, a new cause was born.[4]

When a group of poets joined the fray, they infused a strong countercultural component into what had been a minor political struggle. Many of the poets who came out to the park in 1962 were young, but not in university, and had taken jobs to support their passion. Some, like an eighteen-year-old railway worker, saw the battle over free speech as an opportunity to bring socially conscious poetry to the people. Although not all of the poetry delivered over those days was politically engaged, the crowds were known to regularly cheer recitations that confronted problems such as unemployment, discrimination, and the role of power and authority.[5]

The spontaneity and participatory nature of these weekly free-speech fights marked them as something new—not party-organized, perhaps not even politically coherent, but clearly defiant. The mix of culture and politics with an ever-present threat of police intervention created an enticing invitation for people who might otherwise not have gone to a more traditional meeting.

The Liberal-leaning *Toronto Star* supported the right of people to engage in these freewheeling events and dismissed the charges of subversion—pointing in one instance to the spoken words "Love, love, love" as a sign of the participants' innocent character. The more conservative *Globe and Mail* viewed the alliance of poets and anti-nuclear "zealots" as threatening and unlawful, and its reporter took care not only to cite that poet's opening lines—"I shout love . . . LOVE!"—but also his conclusion: "Listen, you money-plated bastards, when I shout love, I mean your destruction."[6]

At the end of the summer some of the free-speech protesters would have nodded as the chairman of a two-thousand-person-strong rally for peace declared, "We must make the atomic age a time for happiness, not dread." They might have listened with rapt attention as representatives from India, Nigeria, and the Soviet Union called for nuclear disarmament. They would have been especially interested in hearing from the envoy of the British Campaign for Nuclear Disarmament, an organization indirectly responsible for the city's renewed left wing.[7]

* * *

In the 1950s, left-wing activists found it difficult to win public sympathy for positions that fell outside the narrow confines of the Cold War consensus. Although the peril of a nuclear arms race was front and centre, their parties and social movements failed to benefit from the growing alarm about its dangers. The peace movement, which had once seemed a powerful presence in the country, was consigned to the margins. Its largest component, the Canadian Peace Congress, was known to have close ties to the Communist Party of Canada and had been the object of a fierce campaign orchestrated by central figures in the federal government. By mid-decade even the word "peace" might be considered a suspicious code word for a Communist project.[8]

The Cold War atmosphere inhibited a range of social movements. Some unions even expressed opposition to the concept of an independent organization of the unemployed, fearing it could be infiltrated by communists. Tenant activists had to defend themselves continuously from politicians, newspapers, and apartment owners who viewed rent control as synonymous with communism. At one moment a communist could be defined as anyone seeking to stir up hostility between classes—which included the heads of the local Labour Council and the Canadian Labour Congress. At another moment a person could become suspect just for having used the term "class." Alderman David Balfour, city hall's most vocal red-scaremonger, had an uncanny ability to find communists lurking behind any social problem that troubled him: "I wouldn't be surprised if the Communists were behind all this teen-age crime."[9]

Countless past and present communists lost jobs after RCMP visits to their employers, and the Toronto School Board banned all alleged communists from teaching. Left-of-centre writers and producers occasionally found their television shows being axed after programs made tepid criticisms of American consumerism or McCarthyism; at times they found their names deleted from show credits. When the Toronto Symphony Orchestra fired six musicians suspected of having communist sympathies, defence efforts were hindered when note-taking uniformed RCMP officers made sympathizers fear for their own jobs. Even a Progressive Conservative found himself unemployed after defending the musicians on the grounds of free speech. Some of the city's worst Red-baiters, suggested a local steelworker, were the same people who "smugly pound [their] chest and say we don't have McCarthyism here."[10]

The only substantial left-wing campus protests of the 1950s occurred precisely because some students were willing to stand up to say, "yes," McCarthyism does happen here. On Halloween night, 1953, dozens of University of Toronto students, their identities hidden by shrouds, marched down Bay and Bloor streets chanting "Burn McCarthy" and "Down with Joe." The procession swelled to a couple of hundred people before winding its way to an open space where the demonstrators mounted an effigy of the famous American senator on some scaffolding and set it on fire. Amidst lighted candles, hooded students warned that the fear of communism posed a greater danger to democracy than did communism itself. A couple of months later, protesters marched with members of Sigma Chi and other fraternities demanding that Ted Rogers, national president of the Young Progressive Conservatives and heir to a broadcasting fortune, be released from detention in the United States. Rogers was imprisoned there under the McCarthyist McCarran (or Internal Security) Act of 1950, which (among other things) required members of the Communist Party to register with the attorney general and allowed authorities to detain people suspected of subversive activities and prevent them from leaving the country. The activists must have felt vindicated. After enduring significant skepticism for arguing that McCarthyism preyed on the "innocent" as well as the "guilty," they were now listening to fraternity officials attack the McCarran Act and denounce Cold War "hysteria." An important legacy of these protests may have been that the university's student newspaper, *The Varsity*, where tense discussions about McCarthyism and its role in Canada had preceded the Halloween protest, was now more willing to support gestures against the status quo.[11]

In 1958, with an atmosphere of McCarthyism still lingering, it took a major British protest against nuclear weapons (with several thousand participants marching from London to Aldermaston over Easter weekend) to renew the peace movement in Toronto. Local activists had heard about the impending march from overseas contacts, media reports, and eventually a visiting speaker, who described the preparations being taken to organize the protest.[12]

The first organization to seize on the coming march was the Church Peace Movement (CPM), founded eight years earlier as a local branch of a U.S.-based interfaith peace network. Emphasizing the need for established churches to join the fight for peace, and seeking distance from communist-linked peace organizations, the CPM had largely confined its activity to public forums on issues such as nuclear disarmament and Third World liberation. Members took care to present themselves as "respectable" and to mark their distance from radicalism.[13]

The approaching British peace march inspired CPM to hold a public event on the same date. Designed to attract the attention of people gathered to watch the city's annual Easter parade, the demonstration had about fifty participants carrying placards calling on Christians to "raise their voices" and demanding an end to nuclear testing. Protesters distributed leaflets containing statements by respectable authorities, including scientists and the World Council of Churches, against the tests.[14]

The following month, CPM held another protest—although now with some three hundred people in attendance. Many of them, as in the earlier demonstration, appeared to hail from the Quakers (or Society of Friends), Unitarian and United churches, Holy Trinity Anglican Church, Student Christian Movement (SCM), and Women's International League for Peace and Freedom. A counter-protest by the Canadian Christian Loyalist Movement loudly accused the demonstrators of committing treason.[15]

These anti-bomb demonstrators at Toronto's 1958 Easter parade helped initiate a new social movement; April 6, 1958.

Clara Thomas Archives and Special Collections, Toronto Telegram fonds.

The CPM protests represented a departure from a politics of peace linked closely to the orthodox communist movement and from the quieter gatherings of non-communist peace organizations. Although the Canadian Peace Congress had achieved notable successes in the 1950s—a petition campaign against nuclear weapons had garnered some 300,000 signatures, and rallies in Toronto had drawn out as many as 5,000 people—the activists of this emerging peace movement proved to be more highly and increasingly visible and appeared to gain a sense of unity from their broadly humanistic and Christian language.[16]

Shortly after the Easter protest, members of the Christian social-democratic Fellowship for Reconciliation were out distributing a pamphlet attacking the "irrational futility" of the call for civil defence preparedness (that is, "duck and cover" practices and the construction of fallout shelters). Peace activists in the United Church of Canada won the national church's support for an anti-nuclear vigil, albeit after a more ambitious campaign was curtailed for fear it would "follow too closely the tactics of subversive elements." Christians of all denominations were invited to join the newly formed Toronto Committee for a Christian Use of Nuclear Energy.[17]

Although the religious basis of the new movement helped it to avoid being identified with the communist menace, its activists strove to distance themselves even further. The socialist organizer of the Student Christian Movement's peace and disarmament conference, for instance, took care to ensure that communists were not invited; and leaders made sure to tell disarmament supporters that the growth of communism was the world's biggest problem. The most secular of the movement's founding organizations, the Toronto branch of the Women's International League for Peace and Freedom, had long fought to block communist sympathizers from joining. Moving beyond such left-wing McCarthyism would later become a marker for the new left.[18]

From the start Christian socialists, then, had an enduring prominence within the city's activist community—at least until the 1960s—which clearly distinguished Toronto's left wing from radicals in other major centres of the country. From the strength of the Fellowship for Reconciliation in the 1930s to the better-known role of the Student Christian Movement, Protestant socialists in particular were central to many of the city's social movements. A number of them were leading temperance advocates. Although it is difficult to imagine someone being both a strong supporter of the Russian Revolution and head of the Ontario Temperance Federation, those positions were held in tandem by Rev. Gordon Domm, who believed in Christ's example of "serving the people."[19]

The crux of activism for a segment of these Protestant socialists was linking individual churches to social movement struggles—and placing an emphasis on "living otherwise" that was largely missing in the established left parties. In the interwar period, some of them were strongly influenced by the Japanese Christian Socialist Toyohiko Kagawa, who emphasized the practice of disciplined activists spending their lives in the service of others and the realization of a co-operative commonwealth—not as a blueprint for the future, but as a means of living and struggling in the present. While Canada's Co-operative Commonwealth Federation worked for change in the formal political sphere, these socialists sought to transform capitalism by building and supporting co-ops and communes. In that prefigurative emphasis, they captured, notwithstanding their firm Protestantism, one of the core elements of the emerging new left.[20]

A more secular footing arrived in 1959 with the establishment of the "communist-free" Toronto Committee for Disarmament (TCD). About 225 people turned out to a meeting organized by the Unitarian-affiliated Don Heights Social Action Group. Speakers included Edmonton-based Mary Van Stolk of the Canadian Committee for the Control of Radiation Hazards (CCCRH), which appeared to be composed largely of white-collar professionals, and Rabbi Abraham Feinberg. The meeting decided to form a local committee to provide "accurate information" to the public on disarmament.[21]

CCCRH envisioned a campaign that was solely educational. Believing the largest problem to be the perception that peace groups were "peculiar or pink," Van Stolk and her husband had vowed to keep "politics, Communists and cranks" outside their organization. With an emphasis on mainstreaming the movement, they opposed communists and pacifists as unpopular fringe elements.[22] Their respectability-centred approach was not just a disavowal of Peace Congress supporters, but designed to sideline the kind of boisterous in-your-face activists who had marched on Aldermaston in Britain and propelled the CPM forward. In the words of Von Stolk: "We are not pacifists. . . . We don't think there is any need for a march on Ottawa." While members of the CPM and some of its component groups had proudly identified as pacifist, the new Toronto Committee for Disarmament sought to disassociate itself from both pacifists and communists, terms that in many minds were conflated.[23]

Although it was a secular organization, TCD's leadership was dominated by religious figures who had a wealth of experience in social justice activism—people such as Rabbi Feinberg, United Church minister James Finlay, and Anglican minister John Frank. Finlay and Frank were outspoken social activists by the time they began ministering to Toronto churches in the 1930s. Feinberg had more recently established himself as a progressive activist, but he would become the city's best-known supporter of disarmament.[24]

Upon his arrival in Toronto in 1943, Feinberg had almost immediately captured the media spotlight. He became renowned for fighting against religious intolerance and racial discrimination. On several occasions he took a stand against local manifestations of McCarthyism. As rabbi at Toronto's influential Holy Blossom Temple, he was the media's go-to person for questions about Jewish-Gentile relations. While members of the press often fawned on him, he was not averse to thumbing his nose at them. His calls for the removal of religiosity from public schools, including Christmas pageants, generated considerable ire. *The Globe and Mail* lectured him that "it is just as wrong to be anti-Christian as it is to be anti-Semitic."[25]

The American son of Lithuanian immigrant parents, Feinberg had developed into a radical liberal as early as World War One, while attending seminary school. After serving as a rabbi for much of the 1920s, he became a radio and music-hall singer for several years before eventually returning to the pulpit. In the 1930s he joined the American League Against War and Fascism and passionately supported Republican Spain's fight against General Franco's fascists. He rubbed shoulders with anarchists and communists.[26]

Contrary to the account provided in his autobiography, his political record during the height of the Cold War was not consistently to the left of the political spectrum. His statements on popular culture were decidedly conservative. In one instance he compared the "comics, Coke and coddling" of Western democracies to the "chemistry, midnight oil and Communist goose step" of the Soviet Union. In 1953, when the Toronto Arts Council was being fiercely Red-baited, he publicly withdrew his support from the organization. He suggested that panels of experts should decide whether to sterilize "amoral women incapable of sufficient self-discipline." Yet, to tweak folksinger Phil Ochs's definition of a liberal, Feinberg was 10 degrees to the left of centre in good times and 10 degrees to the right of centre when things were bad.[27]

* * *

Around the time that TCD formed, four professors and a graduate student at the University of Toronto launched a campus disarmament group. It quickly accumulated an impressive list of sponsors, including around forty professors and the university's president. Committee members devoted their time to drawing up and circulating a petition demanding the end of the production, testing, and proliferation of nuclear weapons. Through the efforts of the committee, three hundred students gathered in late 1959 to hear Professor Kenneth McNaught, a significant figure in the Co-operative Commonwealth Federation and biographer of its spiritual leader J.S. Woodsworth, speak in favour of disarmament. Over two dozen attendees agreed to help obtain student signatures for the committee's petition, which contained the names of three thousand faculty and students when it was presented to Prime Minister John Diefenbaker at the end of the year.[28]

At the behest of the faculty committee, in early 1960 over a dozen students who had supported the petition drive, including organizers of a picket earlier that month against French nuclear testing, formed their own organization, the Student Union for Peace. A passage in its proposed constitution demonstrated the students' commitment to broad social change; it committed the group to "work to build a world society . . . which will suffer no individual or group to be exploited by another, and which will assure to all the means for realizing the best possibilities for life." When that formulation was criticized for sounding like the kind of communist and left-wing propaganda characteristic of past peace movements, the group replaced it with a commitment to further the principles of the United Nations' Universal Declaration of Human Rights. But when the group rebranded itself Students for Peace (SFP) the following month, it returned to a more radical-sounding goal: "remov[ing] the danger of war by attacking its economic and sociological causes, wherever they may be."[29]

In a well-publicized address to SFP in March, Rabbi Feinberg attacked the apathy of the wider student body and lambasted the university, calling it a "glorified vocational school . . . mooing at the sacred cow of conformity." Decades earlier pickets and demonstrations had occurred all over campuses, he complained, but only Elvis Presley trivia and career aspirations could be found there now: "Radicalism has become as old fashioned as the coon-skin coat and Charleston." He called on SFP members to become moral and spiritual radicals by the individual act of speaking and acting in favour of disarmament. An accumulation of such small-scale acts could, he predicted, transform classrooms from scenes of rehearsal for suburban middle age into hotbeds of revolt.[30]

As evident in Rabbi Feinberg's address, the interests of Toronto anti-nuclear activists went well beyond any single issue. In late March, when members of SFP and TCD became outraged at the mass shooting of black protesters in South Africa, popularly known as the Sharpeville Massacre, they helped organize the first sizable demonstrations of the 1960s.

In the initial event, three hundred University of Toronto students marched to Queen's Park, the site of the provincial legislature, where the demonstrators demanded an end to platitudes and the start of real action against the South African government. Protesters founded the campus-based Fellowship of Concern for South Africa to continue their campaign and promote a boycott of South African products. Off-campus activists created the Committee of Concern for South Africa, which organized a mass rally of 2,500 to condemn the apartheid system and aid the families of shooting victims.[31]

In contrast to their response to peace protests, local journalists embraced the mobilizations against South African apartheid. Sympathetic media accounts even convinced Ontario premier Leslie Frost to overrule his attorney general and

University of Toronto students protesting the Sharpeville massacre; March 25, 1960.

Clara Thomas Archives and Special Collections, Toronto Telegram fonds.

deputy provincial secretary, who had prevented the city-wide committee from incorporating because its name "indicate[d] hostility to a friendly country." But this positive reception prompted others to wonder why activists were not devoting the same energy to the deeper and less popular challenge of fighting racial discrimination at home. A letter writer to *The Toronto Star* argued, "I See No Committee Concerned with the Plight of Negroes in Commonwealth Countries Who Want to Live in Canada But Can't Because of Their Black Skin."[32]

SFP's first major protest action did not occur until after the regular school year had ended. In May around a dozen members (most of them with experience in old left organizations) drove to North Bay to protest the construction of a Bomarc missile base. (In fall 1958 the federal government had announced an agreement with the United States to have squadrons deploy this anti-aircraft missile in Canada.) Members of TCD, along with anarchist professor Roger Bray, encouraged the young activists and helped with logistics, while the faculty-led peace committee notably refused to have anything to do with the venture. Upon arriving in North Bay, the Torontonians were joined by students from Montreal and Ottawa. The Montreal contingent had formed the Combined Universities Campaign for Nuclear Disarmament (CUCND), basing it on a British organization bearing the same name.[33]

As many as a hundred activists converged at the Bomarc construction site, where they refused an order by military officials to back off. Singing "We shall not be moved," they picketed the construction site and handed out anti-nuclear leaflets to entering workers. For many participants, the opportunity to meet activists from other cities, engage in philosophical and practical discussions, and join in evening singalongs was just as valuable as the action itself.[34]

After returning to Toronto, the SFPers concentrated on educational outreach campaigns in local parks, but took note when Metro Toronto's committee for civil defence embarked on an ambitious campaign to promote the building of fallout shelters. The model bunkers provided a natural venue for anti-nuclear protest, and most activists converged on one set up at Queen's Park. SFP members used a barrage of mobilizing techniques that subtly distinguished them from older campaigners. A folk-music-themed "singing picket," led by local singers, attracted activists from the University of Toronto, Ryerson Institute of Technology, and area high schools. A more sombre twenty-four-hour protest livened up a bit when a dozen Trotskyists showed up at the twenty-third hour sporting pickets that called on people to "Organize a Labor Party," prompting annoyance and complaints about the off-message signage. The student protesters were more sympathetic when Trotskyist Ernest Tate was arrested for painting "BAN THE BOMB" onto the side of the shelter.[35]

Workers begin to paint over Ernie Tate's graffiti on the Queen's Park bomb shelter; July 11, 1960.

Clara Thomas Archives and Special Collections, Toronto Telegram fonds.

An early clash between the generations occurred at a TCD meeting held shortly after the twenty-four-hour bomb shelter protest. The meeting heard resolutions from the floor supporting removal of the Queen's Park shelter and the Bomarc missiles, as well as one calling for a public campaign to pay Tate's fine. Professor David Gauthier ruled the resolutions out of order because they had not been submitted by one of TCD's committees. Gauthier expressed his frustration as the out-of-order motions continued to be put forth during the meeting. One participant exhorted the "rash youth" to listen to older, more experienced members and submit their motions through the proper channels. In hopes of avoiding further discord, Rev. Frank offered to personally pay Tate's fine. That gesture had little appeal for the dissenters, described by a reporter as "young radicals wanting action."[36]

Friction between generations was also evident when attention shifted to a new model bomb shelter set up at the Canadian National Exhibition (CNE) in August. The activists as a whole seemed keen to protest the site, but the TCD backed off after the Ex management turned down its application for permission to petition against nuclear weapons on the CNE grounds. Anticipating a challenge to the decision, Feinberg roundly condemned those who might leaflet or petition without the CNE's permission as "extremists." A number of young activists, along with some older radicals, disregarded Feinberg's edict and surreptitiously entered the exhibition grounds to leaflet against the shelter. Although some were captured and arrested by the police, they succeeded in delivering their anti-shelter message to thousands of fairgoers. One frustrated bomb shelter salesman was caught tearing down a cartoon with the tagline "Let's hope this shelter is a waste of money." The salesman remarked, "We can't have that cartoon here. It's negative thinking."[37]

Protesters later scored an unambiguous win when picketing a fallout shelter erected by the CBC for a reality-style, televised exploration of what it would be like to live in a shelter for a week. On the seventh day, just as the featured young family was due to emerge from the shelter, protesters were booing and shouting "There's no defence" in front of the cameras. The two parents even agreed to sign the CCCRH's anti-nuclear petition, and "Mrs. Jon McCallum" told the TV audience: "I have had a lot of time to think in the last week and it is necessary to do anything we can to prevent a third world war." The federal government later announced the cancellation of its plan to construct thousands of new shelters and the discontinuance of its nuclear survival training program.[38]

* * *

In spring 1961 a dozen activists founded the Direct Action Committee (DAC), which became the first in a succession of local organizations, with overlapping

Liz Makarchuk hoists a sign during the 24-hour picket of the bomb shelter at Queen's Park; Aug. 5, 1960.

Clara Thomas Archives and Special Collections, Toronto Telegram fonds.

ideas and memberships, that would point to a new way of doing activist politics. DAC member Douglas Campbell traced the group's impetus to frustration with CUCND and its "even more" ivory-tower cousin, TCD. The DAC members expressed a willingness to go to jail for their principles, and Campbell, anticipating many a later new leftist, contrasted that militancy with the tired methods and watered-down politics of the other disarmament committees.[39]

Not unexpectedly, then, DAC's first public salvo was launched against some of its opponents on the right of the left. The CCF had recently launched the New

Party, which would soon become the New Democratic Party (NDP), and DAC organized a picket of the social-democratic party's headquarters, highlighting the need for a neutralist position between the two superpowers and urging members to retain the CCF's positions opposing the North American Aerospace Defence Command (NORAD) and North Atlantic Treaty Organization (NATO). Beyond foreign policy, DAC warned of a general move to the right that threatened to make the New Party just another liberal organization. "The Road to the Right is the Road to Oblivion," it advised New Party enthusiasts.[40]

As neutralist and pacifistic, DAC joined the fellow peace movement "bad boy," the Canadian Peace Congress, in not being invited to co-sponsor the annual Easter peace march. Yet, unlike the Congress, DAC showed up anyway. Its members were required to march with the Trotskyists because of the protest organizers' opposition to their anti-NATO signs. Despite the organizers' attempt to stay on message by banning leafleting and subjecting all signs to their approval, the major dailies both mentioned the presence of anti-NATO placards and spent a good deal of ink writing about a small group of hecklers from the University of Toronto. *The Globe and Mail*'s interview with a Communist Party organizer and copious attention to the presence of the Fair Play for Cuba and the Trotskyists' Young Socialist Alliance appeared designed to belie Feinberg's statement that the reddest thing about the protest organizers was his wife's hat.[41]

If DAC had a certain "go it alone" attitude and self-righteousness, this was most evident in Douglas Campbell, who during those years was intermittently unemployed, a student, a taxi-driver, and a café owner. Campbell himself admitted that group members complained about his image scaring people away, though he also suggested that his insistence on connecting the arms race with capitalism was a source of tension. In June most of the DAC members departed, finding Campbell too difficult to deal with, and started Canadians for Positive Non-Alignment, which held a series of small demonstrations throughout the summer.[42]

By the fall that group too had itself fallen apart, with most members dropping out because of family pressure or involvement in CUCND activities. But two of its members, University of Toronto professor Roger Bray and customs inspector Alfred Friend, along with computer analyst J.M. McNamee, decided to try again. They formed the nucleus of the Committee of 100, patterned after the well-known civil disobedience organization of that name in the United Kingdom. Their first action, in 1962, was to travel to the Soviet embassy in Ottawa to hold a sit-in protesting a nuclear test. Additional Ottawa sit-ins were co-ordinated with the Committee of 100 in Montreal, chaired by Dan Daniels, an activist who hoped to win the Quebec separatist movement over to non-violence (the two local groups formed a joint national committee). In contrast to the CUCND's

An anti-war demonstration heads down Yonge St.; Oct. 4, 1961.

Clara Thomas Archives and Special Collections, Toronto Telegram fonds.

university-based membership, some Committee of 100 protests appeared to consist mostly of high-school students, while the occupations of members arrested at an early 1962 sit-in included "printer," "housewife," and "unemployed."[43]

Was this a single-issue campaign, focused only on nuclear weapons? Some of the older members, leery of anything that smacked of the old Peace Congress, perhaps thought it to be such. But younger members were less worried about connecting various campaigns on the left. A heated discussion over whether it was within the purview of the committee to campaign against the death penalty prompted its younger members to bolt and march to the Don Jail on Human Rights Day, Dec. 10, 1962, when two men were scheduled to be executed. Joined by other groups and eventually the older members of the committee, they resisted police pressure to stay across the street with the throngs of curious bystanders. The hundred protesters picketed for four hours until the clock struck midnight—the scheduled time for the hanging—when they stopped and fell silent. Then the scene quickly descended into frenzy, as 150 protesters tried to rush past police and reach the jail, ostensibly to exercise their right to read the execution notices posted on its door.[44]

A key function of this modest demonstration—and the subsequent "riot" from which respectable organizers sought to disassociate themselves—was to create interest around a little-discussed topic, which would be a common element in many movements of the 1960s. What was most chilling about the prior year's execution was that local newspaper coverage of it appeared limited to small, business-card-sized notices. The protesters now helped make the hanging front-page news.[45]

The events at Allan Gardens in summer 1962 similarly helped to raise publicity for the issue of free speech. While the arrest of DAC's Douglas Campbell had been the initial trigger, the mainline CCCRH disarmament group, very concerned with its respectability, immediately tried to publicly disassociate itself from the free-speech fight. Committee of 100 members, on the other hand, kept returning to the park to face more police summonses and a ready-made audience for their controversial anti-NATO and anti-NORAD message. The Committee's 1962 meetings in the park were its largest. Although there would be a trickle of protests and court cases around Allan Gardens in the following year, talk of imminent change and an eventual tweaking of the bylaw led to a decline in activity.[46]

Freedom of assembly again became an issue at the tail end of 1962. About seventy activists, most of them members of Canadian Students for Nuclear Disarmament (CSND) and the New Democratic Youth (NDY), had been campaigning for a referendum on nuclear weapons amidst busy downtown streets on the last shopping day before Christmas. But their anti-nuclear chants turned to "Free speech! Free speech!" when police moved in and made twenty-one arrests. A protest march to condemn the arrests and stand up for free speech, organized by the Committee of 100, featured a "Christmas Peace Carol" that sang out their defiance. Although a judge later dismissed the unlawful assembly charges, out-of-town teacher John Glenn faced a more dire penalty. Already under suspicion for an article he had authored about a trip to Cuba and his non-literal interpretation of the Bible—some parents were disturbed by his suggestion that the story of

Jonah and the whale was a parable—members of his School Board asked for his resignation during the trial. Shortly afterwards, he was fired.[47]

* * *

In 1963 the Committee of 100 took on an ambitious venture: organizing a Canadian contingent for a protest at a military base in Rome, N.Y., in conjunction with the New England Committee for Non-Violent Action (CNVA). Committee of 100 members were impressed with CNVA's sophisticated understanding of non-violence. While several civil rights and peace organizations in the United States used non-violence merely as a tactic, members of CNVA embraced the philosophy as a way of life and even operated their own communal farm in accordance with their principles of non-violence. The Committee of 100 convinced two of its members to travel to Toronto for a seminar, from which eventually sprang an unsuccessful attempt to launch a national pacifist organization, the Movement for Non-Violent Revolution. The short-lived organization adopted CNVA's platform and anticipated later new left developments, from its references to "community" and "revolution" to its reliance on consensus decision-making and lack of an executive.[48]

The politics of groups such as DAC and the Committee of 100 extended beyond Toronto. In addition to its affiliation with the Montreal-based organization, the Committee of 100 may have seen the League for Total Disarmament (LTD) in British Columbia as a kindred organization. The LTD, founded in 1962, certainly shared a similar philosophical and tactical orientation. It embraced direct action and non-violence, and included a strain of anarchism. It sponsored protests at the Comox military base on Vancouver Island and later played an important role in establishing the Vancouver Peace Centre. In 1965 it initiated a further round of protests at the Comox base.[49]

In contrast to DAC, LTD, and the Committee of 100, CUCND was quite slow to jump on the burgeoning civil disobedience band wagon. Just before the birth of the Committee of 100, CUCND's national conference decided that "the Campaign will not endorse civil disobedience as such, but neither will it issue statements opposing such action." It was not until 1963 that three members of the CUCND's national executive (all members of the Toronto branch) proposed changing the national constitution to allow civil disobedience, which would provide the option of organizing a student sit-in if Canada acquired nuclear weapons.[50]

The libertarian socialist politics of the Committee of 100's Roger Bray, a U.S.-born botany professor and pioneering ecologist, was strongly attuned to a kind of prefigurative leftism absent in CUCND. His vision of the path to socialism, as relayed to a campus meeting in early 1961, included civil disobedience and direct action (and general strikes). The resulting society would be creative, flexible, and based on "diversity." Each workplace within it would be owned and operated directly by its workers, who would send delegates to regional councils to co-ordinate production. There would be no lawyers, police, armies, prisons, social workers, or other enforcers of the traditional family. Schooling would be transformed, and traditional forms of grading abolished.[51]

Although this line of thought may have sounded quite radical to Bray's student audience, it was more conservative than the vision of post-industrial libertarian socialism that he evoked a short time later:

> Today, the machines of destruction are nearly or altogether capable of total human annihilation and it is very probable that they will be used. It may be best, then, to abandon the whole industrial-military economy. Start with the most pernicious contrivances—rockets and jet planes, atomic weapons and reactors, electronic computers and television. Remove the works from the T.V., caulk the seams and watch fish through the picture screen. The rest will follow naturally. . . . As people move out of the cities, the land will be intensively farmed for subsistence. Even in the cities . . . gardening on rooftops, in streets and vacant lots will supply needed foodstuffs . . . motor [vehicles] filled with dirt, and sweet potatoes climbing up the auto aerial. . . . Then a withdrawal should occur, out of the state, science, and industrial society, into self-enquiry and self-subsistence, into poverty (by modern standards), into silence and joy in small things.[52]

Bray's vision was very different from that of the NDP, which wanted more government regulation, and the CPC, which was attached to the bureaucratic communism of the Soviet Union. As an early if rough statement of new leftism, it gestured towards a total refusal of capitalist life and articulated a vision of self-government beyond it. Bray was not interested in fighting for a more equal distribution of the detritus of consumer society. He wanted something entirely different.

* * *

As evident in the early peace movement's anxious attempts to distinguish itself from the Canadian Peace Congress, a big obstacle for the emerging activists to overcome was a form of left-wing McCarthyism. The response was not only frequently directed against members of the Communist Party of Canada, who were sometimes excluded from protests and public discussions out of fear that non-communist activists would be branded as "fellow travelers," but also turned up within the non-communist left through a kind of self-censorship that moderated language, demands, and tactics. As late as 1964 a speaker on a peace panel argued that a strategy centring on encouraging "responsible people" to sign petitions and write letters to newspapers was the most effective way for the peace movement to distance itself from communism.[53]

The peace group Voice of Women, founded in Toronto in 1960, largely operated within that framework during its early years. To distance themselves from potential accusations that the group was pro-communist, the group took the step of keeping the spouses of suspected former communists off their membership rolls. The organization's president decreed that any women whose husband had maintained a past association with a CPC-linked group could not hold a leadership position, and in some cases such women were also banned from general membership.[54]

Students for Peace itself had Danny Goldstick, a real, membership-holding Communist, in its ranks, and his presence became controversial. A September 1960 SFP meeting, which had intended to change the name of the group to CUCND, got bogged down with a proposal that its new constitution make membership in the Communist Party grounds for expulsion. A handful of CCFers, who were described as largely unconnected to the peace group, put forward that motion, arguing that the presence of communists would prevent the group from being non-political and result in bad publicity. Their proposal was opposed and defeated by many peace activists, including SFP president Howard Adelman.[55]

The issue of communism came up again a few months later after the group's vice-president told *The Varsity* that many students refused to associate with the Toronto CUCND branch, fearing that it was strongly influenced by communists. Although Goldstick proclaimed that he could hardly dominate the group alone, another member suggested he might be aided by closeted comrades. In response, Art Pape appealed to members of the Conservative and Liberal parties to support the group and thus remove its communist stigma. His suggestion prompted the addition of the campus Liberal president to its executive.[56]

But Goldstick's refusal to speak against Soviet nuclear testing the following year caused Adelman to put forward a resolution against the tests that appeared expressly designed to remove him. Goldstick then stated that he had changed his position and had become opposed to Soviet testing (this was after the latest round of tests had finished) and argued that the sole purpose of the motion was to expel him for being a Communist. Indeed, another member stated that if the group banned everyone who supported an organization that backed nuclear testing, it would have to expel the members of the Conservative and Liberal parties who had been wooed to counteract Goldstick's presence. Members once again rejected what amounted to an anti-communist clause. After an attempt to pass a similar motion at a subsequent meeting failed, and even after an amendment stipulating that expulsion would occur only for future offences, Adelman resigned and the branch was thrown into further disarray when five other executive members threatened to leave.[57]

Montreal CUCND leader Dimitrios I. Roussopoulos, furious about Goldstick not being kicked out, now maintained that the survival of CUCND as a national organization was at stake. Although some members cheekily dismissed Roussopoulos's Red-baiting charges, the branch executive later voted to expel Goldstick because his continued membership was detrimental to the cause of disarmament. After the executive threatened to dissolve the branch, a general membership meeting upheld the decision.[58]

A branch executive insisted, "Our executive is not controlled by Communists, but neither are we a red-baiting organization." But the line between expelling communists per se and expelling them for causing bad publicity was a fine one indeed. In the pages of *The Varsity* it was largely CUCND members opposed to Goldstick who called attention to that issue. Other items in the student newspaper criticized CUCND's fondness for demonstrations and its countercultural inclinations.[59] The era of widespread student support for left-wing protest had yet to dawn.

* * *

Amidst the overt political developments of the late 1950s and early 1960s, a small but significant portion of youth became attracted to beat or bohemian culture. They were young people who, as the press described them, often had an artistic and romantic bent, flocked to coffee shops rather than bars, and preferred jazz and folk over mainstream pop music. People identifying with this subculture had a strong yearning for authenticity and expressed antipathy towards conformity and materialism. In short, they shared some of the facets identified with the emerging new left—qualities on display during the freedom of assembly battles at Allan Gardens.[60]

The Varsity's anti-CUCND articles were at their most visceral when attacking the group for being ensconced within beatnik culture. Any protester who wore a turtleneck or beard was guilty of contributing to an image of the movement as unwashed radicals, "Castroniks" (a reference to Cuba's revolutionary leader, Fidel Castro), and, of course, beatniks. These particular articles claimed that CUCND was creating a strong link in the public mind between disarmament and beatniks, leaving the impression that only bearded radicals supported the anti-nuclear movement. Ryerson's student newspaper, which did not share *The*

Varsity's general sympathy for protesters, later emphasized the same problems of respectability and countercultural attire amongst young peace activists, as suggested particularly in its use of the word "Vietnik." Cartoons of demonstrations in *The Ryersonian* featured beatniks displaying a hipster insincerity—"To think we gave up an afternoon of espresso and Bob Dylan for this"—or obliviousness to mainstream fashion norms—"I don't understand it Marvin . . . Nobody takes us seriously!"[61]

These stereotypes carried a grain of truth. Indeed, a late 1963 article extolling the contemporary CUCND's sophisticated analysis and business-like hiereranchy pointed out that the representation of the group as "shifty-eyed bearded Trotskyists, dreamy-eyed enthusiasts, free-love, long-haired girls and troubador boys" had once been partly true. Other peace-oriented groups even appeared to double down on their association with beatnik culture. The Student Christian Movement (SCM) launched the Unmuzzled Ox, a campus-based coffee house that featured folksinging, poetry, and play readings; and in its basement the Committee of 100's Toronto Peace Centre—which had itself been previously described as "a sort of coffee house"—formally launched a coffee shop called The Shelter.[62]

Throughout the first half of the 1960s the musical interests of students attracted to the disarmament movement continued to intersect with old-left Popular Front culture, a tradition that emphasized folk music and recognized jazz as a progressive cultural form.[63] By the late 1950s folk had become an integral part of beatnik culture. It is thus no accident that the SCM sponsored an evening concert by folksinger Pete Seeger the same weekend as the first campus conference on disarmament in 1958. Or that the first local CUCND fundraiser featured the John Swann Jazz Quartet and a number of folk-music performers, including The Travellers. Subsequent CUCND social events had a similar tilt. The renewed links between young leftists and folk music were also evident at the annual Mariposa Folk Festival in 1962, which became an occasion for a ban-the-bomb rally. As folk performer Oscar Brand suggested: "People just aren't interested in hearing songs written about what happened 50 years ago. . . . Now they want to hear stuff about psychology and hydrogen weapons and other problems."[64]

Beyond beatnik stereotyping, the media occasionally derided these young protesters for wearing shorts or sneakers at a time when both were considered inappropriate everyday attire for young adults. In *The Toronto Star* journalist Larry Zolf was beside himself upon seeing the costume of one 1963 demonstrator: "When I saw a news photograph of a ban-the-bomb marcher wearing shorts and sneakers I almost collapsed on the floor. It was hilarious. A man in running shoes protesting against a nuclear bomb. What can be funnier?" *The Globe and Mail* later combined such hilarity with a symbol of beatnik culture to dismiss the seriousness of an eight-hundred-strong anti-war demonstration with the headline:

"Beards and Sneakers in Protest Parade." Such sights provided stark contrasts to the formally attired peace protesters of earlier demonstrations.[65]

* * *

A fall 1962 comment by Donald Gordon, president of Canadian National Railway, that he was unable to find French speakers qualified to hold any of the top positions in his publicly owned company, touched off an unprecedented mobilization of nationalist opinion in Quebec. In the words of historian Bryan Palmer, "All hell broke loose." In Montreal CNR's head office was besieged by demonstrators, an effigy of Gordon went up in flames, and at one particularly heated protest thousands of students fought police, smashed windows, and stripped Red Ensigns and Union Jacks from flag poles and burned them.[66]

In Toronto, mainstream opinion condemned the demonstrators and denied the existence of anti-French-Canadian discrimination. The "railway chooses its executives on the basis of ability and not language or race. To appoint a man to a top job merely because he spoke French ... would be simple discrimination," intoned a *Globe and Mail* editorial, favourably quoting Gordon. *The Toronto Star* echoed its rival, condemning Quebecers who advocated "prejudiced legislation" to rectify an inbalance in talent.[67]

At the University of Toronto, campus New Democrats saw things differently. In November-December 1962, in what was perhaps the city's first Québécois solidarity campaign, they gathered signatures on a petition protesting discrimination against French-speaking Canadians. The following September, campus NDPers declared that they would focus on publicizing the views of French Canadians. If Confederation was to be renewed, as it had to be, it was incumbent on those who lived "here, in the heart of English Canada," to push their peers to listen and act on French-Canadian concerns. To start, the club announced that it was launching a seminar series on French-Canadian nationalism, organizing an exchange with its Montreal counterpart, and planning to bring a prominent French-Canadian spokesperson to campus.[68]

Their programming proved apt as student attention turned massively to Quebec that November. The Student Administrative Council (SAC), *The Varsity*, and a host of other student organizations backed a demonstration at Queen's Park encouraging Premier John Robarts to be receptive to Quebec demands at an upcoming federal-provincial conference. As co-organizer James Laxer explained, the demonstrators would be standing in the middle, between English assimilationists on one side and French separatists on the other. If the students helped to win the acceptance of moderate French-Canadian demands, Confederation could be saved.[69]

About two thousand students responded to the well-publicized call and converged on the legislature's lawn behind a large "MARCH FOR CANADA" banner. There was a revolution going on in Quebec, SAC president Doug Ward told the marchers, that needed the understanding and support of the rest of Canada. If moderates leading that revolution were refused, they would be replaced by less compromising voices, he suggested, and the future of Canada would be imperilled: "The 20th century has witnessed that no force can stand in the road of a nation which is intent upon helping itself to find its place in the sun."[70]

Organizers had reason to be pleased with what turned out to be the largest campus-centred demonstration of the first half of the 1960s, even as they conceded that it was more of a "non-political" illustration of concern than a militant protest. Yet the reaction of student marchers was distinctly progressive in comparison to the concurrent "keep CJBT English" campaign, which fought to prevent a local radio station from converting to a French-language format. Opponents of that change apoplectically suggested that it was the thin edge of the wedge in the francization of the city and a proxy battle for the francization of the country. In contrast to campus New Democrats, local NDP MPs refused to go to bat on the issue, even suggesting that keeping CJBT English was the best means of combating anti-Quebec sentiment. This was in stark contrast to the young NDPer Laxer, who lampooned members of his party for failing to embrace the Quiet Revolution. Support for the self-determination of Quebec was on its way to becoming a "left" issue.[71]

* * *

The summer of 1963 saw two demonstrations that were simultaneously in solidarity with Black civil rights struggles in the United States and against racial discrimination in Canada. While only about a seventh of the demonstrators at the first march were Black, the composition was more mixed at the second. Black and white protesters marched arm in arm to the U.S. consulate on University Street and listened to Jack White, an NDP member and union organizer. White, who had once seen a petition circulated against him after he moved into a white Parkdale neighbourhood, called upon the gathering to help end discrimination against Black, Italian, and Jewish people in Canada. Placards at the rallies featured messages like "Yes, It Does Happen Here," "Would You Rent A Room?" and "I'm not prejudiced but . . ." The annual Emancipation Day march the following year, which in the past appeared to emphasize fealty to the British Crown, continued this emphasis on local racism as scores of Black demonstrators held up uniform placards reading, "Canada needs RACIAL EQUALITY TOO!"[72]

In the summer of 1964, the Black-led Canadian Anti-Apartheid Committee (CAAC) assembled a coalition of eighteen groups to protest a scheduled

Demanding racial equality in Canada, marchers head down Spadina Ave. on Emancipation Day; July 25, 1964.

Clara Thomas Archives and Special Collections, Toronto Telegram fonds.

appearance by Alabama's pro-segregationist governor George Wallace at the Lions Clubs International convention at Maple Leaf Gardens. Formed in 1961 to agitate for a boycott of South African products, the disinvestment of Canadian firms, and to raise money for political prisoners there, the Committee appeared to have an increasing interest in ending discrimination in Canada and the United States.[73]

Published attitudes towards the planned demonstration were mixed. A *Globe and Mail* editorial opined that a picket would violate the spirit of free speech, while a local alderman appeared to equate any discrimination that Wallace might face in Toronto to the injustice that the governor meted out in Alabama. A larger theme was anxiety that the city would sully its reputation if it did not maintain its "famous" Toronto hospitality and treat Wallace as an honoured guest. On behalf of the local Martin Luther King Fund, liberal clergymen placed an advertisement bidding Governor Wallace "Welcome," and promised the racist statesman not only free speech but the "full courtesy" of Torontonians.[74]

On the morning of the massive Lions' parade, some of the floats were found with "Racists Go Home" scrawled across them, and activists leafleted parade-goers with graphic depictions of racism in Alabama. Protesters paraded the following day, with one thousand marching from the recently liberated Allan Gardens to the site of the Lions' convention. As the *Star* told it, they were a diverse crowd, ranging from businessmen in suits and workers in overalls to young women leafleting passersby. They came from labour, church, and left-wing youth organizations to chant "We shall overcome," sing civil rights songs, and, in the case of at least one placard-holder, advance the idea that Canada needed racial equality too. A considerable number returned the next day. Inside the hall, the crowd gave Wallace's speech defending segregation a standing ovation. Demolishing the popular view that it would be a non-political speech by a man who happened to be governor of Alabama, the talk pushed *The Toronto Star* to mount a belated, but passionate, defence of the demonstrators: "There is no need to apologize for Toronto's hostile reception."[75]

* * *

There can be no doubt that incipient sparks of "new leftism"—anticipations of the later, more developed politics of national liberation, personal autonomy, cultural revolution, pre-figurative politics, and community—took place in a context heavily influenced by the CCF. Yet there were stark indications that the CCF's evolution, dramatized by its transformation into the NDP, created conditions that prompted many of its own members to seek out new inspirations from new forms of leftism.

The postwar period had been one of noticeable decline for the CCF. In an attempt to reverse its fortunes, its leadership progressively steered it closer to the political centre. The adoption of the Winnipeg Declaration in 1956 symbolized an effort to dull the party's radical edges and make peace with the capitalist economy, though it simultaneously formed part of a long-standing initiative to win the widespread support of organized labour. Some two years later the CCF and Canadian Labour Congress agreed to establish New Party clubs to help merge their memberships, attract unaffiliated liberals, and lay the groundwork for the 1961 launch of the NDP.[76]

Despite the optimism projected onto that process, in 1962 the Ontario NDP had virtually the same membership as that once claimed by the CCF. Still, the party's financial clout had substantially improved, with 90 per cent of its election spending in Toronto now coming from union contributions. This new money meant more advertising, more staff, and the means to establish a public relations committee, which worked with experts to craft the party's image and sell its program. That this committee saw itself as being "similar to a brain trust or the old Fabian group" suggests a certain triumph of marketing over ideology. During the Ontario NDP's first election campaign the party made little mention of public ownership or even planning. Regulation now seemed to be the favoured means to achieve its policy goals.[77]

Members of the University of Toronto CCF-NDP club were front-row spectators to these changes. They heard Professor Jack McLeod explain how nationalized firms were generally undesirable and that independent control commissions, like the Board of Broadcast Governors, were more efficient. They listened as Walter Pitman, the only MP elected under the New Party banner, told them that the words socialism and nationalization represented old thinking and should be avoided. If the Liberal Party should turn to the left, leaving few policy differences between the two parties, members were assured that social democrats would remain distinct by keeping their promises.[78]

The campus club debated the merits of "pragmatic" and "doctrinaire" approaches, discussed whether Keynsianism was a viable alternative to socialism, and occasionally gave speakers extolling the party's new approach a hard time. Such was the fate of Gerald Caplan, who defensively argued that the CCF's old principles had not been compromised. Sure, some of them had been modified to enhance their popularity, he confessed, but this was necessary to ensure the NDP's victory in the next election. When Caplan defended the watering down of the CCF's old anti-NATO policy and asserted, "I would rather the NDP won on a compromise NATO line than lose altogether," members responded with howls of protest. Amidst pressure to outline possible areas of nationalization, Caplan tried to defer to the nomenclature of economic planning, but eventually relented and told his audience that the question would be answered after the NDP was elected and obtained the necessary statistical information upon which to base its decisions.[79]

Members of old left organizations—above all those in the NDP—appeared to dominate CUCND's executive and general membership. Reflecting this influence, critics periodically suggested that the CUCND and NDP were too close or that a lack of political diversity might force the campus disarmament group to rename itself "C'NDP'CND." These NDP members, like others affiliated to the CPC and the Trotskyist League for Socialist Action (LSA), had a strong appreciation of the importance of working-class people and unions to the struggle for social change; and the same can be said for the many SCM activists within the disarmament group, a number of whom worked in factories as part of that organization's annual summer work project.[80]

During a 1961 strike at the Royal York Hotel, where the union had fought against a new "just in time" scheduling system, the University of Toronto NDP club, assorted campus Trotskyists, and CUCNDers all went to the hotel to express their solidarity. Influential CUCND members Ian Gentles and Art Pape, who had walked the Royal York picket line, later turned out to support striking newspaper workers in what was billed as Canada's first major strike over automation. On the Royal York picket line, James Laxer had asked: "Was a strike just Big Labour versus Big Management?" The emerging new left would have firmly responded "no." But despite the important issues, and the numbers and determination of the workers, both of these strikes were unambiguous failures and hardly the stuff to inspire a new generation of the left.[81]

CCF-NDP influence may have been responsible for CUCND being more radical than it is commonly understood to have been—in that it provided a large number of members who analyzed and acted on the connection between different issues—but also less radical, in that it was reluctant to go beyond the NDP's acceptance of NATO or engage in protests oriented towards direct action. Because the University of Toronto club was located near the centre of NDP power, in a province in which left-wing social democracy was particularly weak, and was sometimes led by the daughters and sons of such powerful NDP politicians as Andrew Brewin and David Lewis, it may have been more conservative than average.

Like their students, social-democratic professors grappled with how the NDP could thrive amidst the Cold War and the postwar compromise. The 1961 book *Social Purpose for Canada*—written as a sequel to *Social Planning for Canada*, published by the League for Social Reconstruction (LSR) in 1935—was prescient in combining ideas adopted by the emerging new left in Britain with a "third course" social democracy that sought to hoist a socialist superstructure atop a fundamentally capitalist economy. Its editor argued that the earlier book had overstated the economic virtues of nationalization and ignored problems intrinsic to any hierarchy, such as alienation and bureaucracy. Some of these problems might be remedied by promoting community and participation, as rising academic stars George Grant and John Porter argued in their chapters, but the book also called for a broader rethinking of socialist economics. Since removing the bourgeoisie from power solved neither of these problems and added new dangers, the editor argued that what the country needed was an effective middle ground between capitalism and socialism.[82]

The year after the publication of *Social Purpose*, left-wing University of Toronto professors Kenneth McNaught and Abe Rotstein founded the University League for Social Reconstruction (ULSR) as a broad-based forum for faculty to discuss current social and political issues. It too was consciously inspired by the old LSR of the 1930s, and its first meeting featured presentations by LSR alumni Frank Scott and new left–influenced philosopher Charles Taylor. Early ULSR publications reflected the efforts of local left-leaning Liberal and NDP academics to respond to the challenge posed by *Social Purpose for* Canada by suggesting how a social vision for Canada could coexist with the marketplace. By the late 1960s new ideas, and a revival of some old left thought, led the ULSR to question the very "middle ground" it had originally sought.[83]

* * *

The Communist Party of Canada was also an influence on the emergent generation of leftists. Its youthful adjunct, the Young Communist League (YCL), was incrementally transformed as the radicalism of the early 1960s grew. While its 1962 national council meeting had ended with a call to focus on the familiar slogans of unity, peace, neutrality, and independence, by the beginning of 1963 comrades were waxing enthusiastic about the new direction of young people and their growing interest in socialism. YCL discussions identified a milieu of radicalizing youth in Toronto that was culturally based and organizationally diffuse, found amongst coffee houses, the folk-music scene, and campus and high-school peace groups.[84]

YCL members decided that they had to "completely integrate and adapt ourselves to this movement." This meant slashing their endless number of bureaucratic committees and meetings, boosting the autonomy of local components, and generally ending the "old fashioned" approach to organization inherited from the 1930s and 1940s. A left-wing coffee shop and bookstore might be just the things to appeal to this new generation.[85]

This increased sensitivity to youth culture did not extend to "beatnikism." Like juvenile delinquency, "the world of the beatnik and the black leather jacket" was considered by young Communists to be a manifestation of the capitalist penetration of culture. There was perhaps some truth to this characterization, but as influential YCLer Rae Murphy pointed out, the media frequently used the term "beatnik" to refer to any young people who liked folk music, discussed serious topics, and were active in the peace movement. Yet despite this important caution, Murphy's opinion of the beatnik departed little from that of the party or "square" press, and a more positive assessment would not be reached until the label was nearing retirement.[86]

To reach collectively minded youth, the YCL was determined to reshape its public presence into something more grassroots. An important tool to reach these ends was the launch of a new magazine to reflect the militancy and élan of a radicalizing generation while including ideas from left-wing youth outside the party's immediate orbit. *Scan* became just that. Its modish graphics, extensive interviews with non-violent activists and members of New Democratic Youth, and articles by women's liberationists would set it apart from other party-affiliated publications.[87]

Through the first half of the 1960s the Communist Party was a practically uncritical supporter of the new youth political upswing. Members saw the peace movement as being fundamentally against U.S. imperialism, regardless of the intentions of its activists. They defended youth culture and even appeared to agree

Children, dressed as angels and devils, act out a post-apocalyptic scene for their entry in the "Etobicoke 2000 AD" competition. Reflecting widespread anxiety about nuclear weapons, children in the competition's winning entry dressed as insects to imply that people in Etobicoke would not survive a nuclear bomb blast; Aug. 9, 1962

Clara Thomas Archives and Special Collections, Toronto Telegram fonds.

with an article criticizing Moscow's hostility towards The Beatles. Post-1964 they presented the new left's tactics of non-violence and sit-ins as "new methods for new times" and were not at all flustered about concepts, such as "youth as class," that blatantly differed from the party's ideology. The standard image of the CPC as fossilized and resistant to the concerns of younger activists is overdrawn—especially in the Toronto context.[88]

* * *

The Trotskyist League for Socialist Action, another old left organization that regularly intersected with the emerging new left, had been known as the Socialist Education League (SEL) in the latter half of the 1950s. It argued that Stalin had betrayed the Russian Revolution and the politics of Lenin, while Leon Trotsky was the true champion of that revolutionary process. As a strategic means to increase their modest forces, SEL and its predecessors had operated within the CCF while maintaining an independent presence outside it.[89]

Like members of the two largest parties of the old left, the Trotskyists had suffered major attrition after the Second World War. Their prospects were further

Students protest against nuclear weapons in front of City Hall; Sept. 2, 1961.

Clara Thomas Archives and Special Collections, Toronto Telegram fonds.

limited by a decline in grassroots CCF activism and the expulsion of a majority of their Toronto cohort from that party. By 1955 their membership had fallen to eighteen. The slow ebbing of McCarthyism in the late 1950s, a trickle of young members, and a renewed orientation to social democracy amidst the New Party process pushed the LSA local membership to just over forty by 1963.[90]

Most recruits continued to be drawn from the working class, and their biggest influx of members was made up of Teamsters rather than university students, who tended to be considered petty-bourgeois supporters of the status quo. Following their companion U.S. organization, the Socialist Workers Party, younger members briefly established a Young Socialist Alliance branch, which had a presence at many anti-nuclear demonstrations.[91]

Members of the Young Socialist Alliance–LSA had a particularly strong role in building Canadian Students for Nuclear Disarmament, a high-school-based peace group launched in the fall of 1960. CSND claimed to have as many as two hundred members from thirty-four different Metro Toronto high schools by the following year, though its active core was probably just a dozen or two. A substantial number of its members later became involved in campus CUCND and NDP clubs. Less vibrant and increasingly influenced by the LSA at the decade's quarter mark, CSND still had the energy to launch its own newspaper, start a drive to pressure the government to pay for Grade 11–13 textbooks, and form the Committee Against School Cadets during a period in which some high schools still required military training as part of the curriculum.[92]

Reflecting LSA's attention towards high-school students, its *Young Socialist* newspaper was primarily directed to them through the first half of the 1960s. While *Young Socialist* echoed many of the themes of its parent organization, it did sound other notes that might arouse greater interest amongst its young audience, such as the "discussion, not dictation" found in Cuban schools. The newspaper appeared more openly supportive of Quebec independence than did the LSA proper, proudly reproducing a picture that boxer Reggie Chartrand had signed—"To all the young socialists of Toronto who support the struggle for Quebec's independence." Young Trotskyists were very active in the often rambunctious New Democratic Youth and in 1964 helped win Ontario NDY support for the formation of high-school student unions, replete with bargaining rights, and the immediate withdrawal of Canada from NATO.[93]

* * *

In the fall of 1961 LSA's *Workers Vanguard* enthused that the University of Toronto had seen a noticeable increase in activism, particularly via CUCND and NDP clubs. It claimed that many people familiar with the campus activist scene were now predicting how this uptick in activism signalled "a new radical generation." Though the realization of such a generation was still a while away, it was increasingly evident that the quieter atmosphere of the 1950s was coming to an end.[94]

After the election of the Liberals in 1963, with their campaign promise to continue the introduction of Bomarc missiles to Canada, CUCND became increasingly open to discussing issues beyond disarmament and exploring new techniques and philosophies that altered, but did not transcend, a social-democratic politics. It would be an exaggeration to argue that these changes represented "an analytical shift" towards understanding the connections between different social issues. Still, the civil disobedience espoused by CUCND and put into action in Quebec during the summer of 1964 at La Macaza military base—which housed nuclear weapons—did mark a shift in tactics towards the more confrontational style that would later characterize the new left.[95]

Toronto's CUCND, which since 1961 had been more reluctant to adopt an anti-NATO policy than were most other branches, resolutely upheld a resolution arguing that Canada should stay in NATO (with the goal of reforming the organization from within). But in late 1963 five of Toronto's six delegates to the

A Volkswagen Beetle disguised as a dinosaur brings artistic flair to a demonstration against nuclear weapons; March 30, 1964.

Clara Thomas Archives and Special Collections, Toronto Telegram fonds.

national CUCND conference changed their minds and voted with the majority to oppose the military alliance. In 1964 the branch contributed far more members to the La Macaza demonstrations than did any other CUCND local.[96]

In some accounts, the CUCND was the seedbed of the new left, which arose as a result of its internal contradictions. The conflation of the evolution of CUCND with the development of a new left-wing consciousness appears to have been logical enough: a bunch of youth concerned about nuclear war begin to lobby and protest; when their efforts fail they look to more radical action, begin to see a relation between peace and other social issues, and determine that democracy, economy, and government may have to be remediated before disarmament can be achieved. Yet at least in Toronto many, if not most, CUCNDers were socialists of some stripe before joining that organization. They were people who already appreciated that various other issues all had to be solved prior to winning a fight for peace.[97]

Although CUCND did evolve into the Student Union for Peace Action, often taken to be a breakthrough to new leftism, that eventuality was not necessarily a matter of changing activist mentalities. By the time of the transition, most likely few if any members saw CUCND merely as a place for supporters of disarmament who disagreed with other planks in the NDP platform, as some had previously argued.[98] When it came to adopting a more comprehensive philosophy of non-violence, CUCND was rearguard rather than avant-garde. Indeed, some of the religious groups who organized Toronto's first peace protests in 1958, as well as DAC and its successors in the early 1960s, had already embraced non-violence. The peace education program offered by the Canadian Friends Service Committee (of the Quakers) had included courses on non-violence as far back as 1962. While the CUCND's Toronto branch did provide a couple of seminars on non-violence from late 1962 through 1963, it refrained from adopting the philosophy.[99]

As a national organization, CUCND probably had several hundred active members. It was certainly larger than DAC, the Committee of 100, or groups with a similar orientation in Montreal and Vancouver. But if size were the criterion to determine the relevance of peace organizations in the early 1960s, much larger organizations like the Canadian Peace Congress and the Voice of Women would win hands down. Instead, CUCND's significance in accounts of left history of the period rests in how it comes to represent "what is new." It provides the historical origins for the "classic" new left; together with SUPA, it becomes the means of forcing events in Canada to adhere to a popular American storyline, in which SUPA in particular becomes implicitly equated with the Students for a Democratic Society (SDS).

In the first five years of the 1960s, the emerging new left had yet to attain the coherence or makeup of the political wave to be seen in following years. Yet the rejection of U.S. nuclear weapons, attention to the national struggle in Quebec, concern about civil rights, intersection with "beat" culture, exploration of non-violent philosophies, and modes of organizing all portended what was to come—as signs of an emergent paradigm of politics.

3

A Movement Emerges, 1965–67

ACTIVISTS in the fall 1964 semester at the University of Toronto were energized by the protest at La Macaza. In a newly reorganized branch of the Friends of SNCC (Student Nonviolent Coordinating Committee), women took on many of the leadership roles; as many as thirteen hundred people turned out to hear civil rights activist James Farmer, the Texan-born co-founder of the Congress of Racial Equality, speak at an Anti-Apartheid Society meeting; and a record turnout of almost a thousand students at the annual Remembrance Day peace vigil on campus was encouraging. To cap it off, at a December meeting of 150 students from eighteen different universities in Regina, a growing interest within CUCND for engagement in issues beyond disarmament led to its transformation into the Student Union for Peace Action.[1]

The new organization continued the late CUCND's commitment to non-alignment, rejecting Canada's alliance with either Moscow or Washington. To uncover the origins of, and solutions to, inequality, it undertook to study power relations within Canada. Its very nature identified students as potential leaders of social change, both on campus and in the broader society. SUPA brought together a large number of issues, ranging from the obvious (disarmament) to subtle forms of oppression in everyday life. Its preferred means of combatting injustice—through non-violent action—ensured that its methods were consistent with the egalitarian society sought by its adherents. Members increasingly attacked all the domestic underpinnings of the arms race, from economic and political elites to the media and education system. Participatory democracy rather than a hierarchically ordered democracy of delegates and leaders would, in theory, mean that SUPA itself prefigured the kind of society it was seeking. Power within the new organization would be decentralized, with internal decision-making based not on majority vote but consensus.[2] The fragments evident from 1958 to 1964 had, it seemed, finally coalesced into something more powerful, comprehensive, and transformative.

University of Toronto engineering students protest anti-war protests; Nov. 5, 1965.

Clara Thomas Archives and Special Collections, Toronto Telegram fonds.

After returning from SUPA's founding conference, Toronto members became increasingly concerned with a new issue: Vietnam. Just prior to the conference, the CUCND branch had sponsored its first demonstration against the war. It was pitched as a call for the Canadian government to work towards a truce and the removal of foreign troops. But a new Toronto bylaw requiring protesters to submit banners and picket signs to police for approval before launching a demonstration shifted attention back to the issue of freedom of expression. CUCNDers decided to openly flout the law at their anti-war demonstration. Police issued warnings but made no arrests, deciding that protests numbering less than forty people were not demonstrations. Members of the New Democratic Youth organized a subsequent protest, with the requisite numbers, in front of a downtown police station, with signs jauntily proclaiming, "This is an illegal demonstration." The police again made no arrests and issued no warnings, and shortly thereafter the bylaw was quietly rescinded. Here, then, was a significant moment: a demonstration of transnational solidarity had morphed into an opportunity to challenge a hierarchical, anti-democratic provision of local politics.[3]

The next campus-organized protest against the war, in early February, featured a more robust showing of three hundred students in front of the U.S. consulate on University Ave. Some two hundred counterdemonstrators, many of them engineers supporting the war, also turned out. Later, and reflecting the old methods of CUCND, anti-war speakers appeared in front of the Soldiers' Tower in the heart of the U of T campus and busied themselves with a petition campaign; a student delegation would present the results to the prime minister. Although a number of SUPA activists were key organizers, they notably decided to operate within a broader ad hoc committee. One activist argued that the lack of a formal structure was part of a conscious decision to maintain a sense of spontaneity: "If we get hung up on committees and subcommittees, we'll lose our supporters."[4]

* * *

While the early 1960s had witnessed significant local interest in protesting the oppression of Blacks in apartheid South Africa and the U.S. South, the events were largely organized by middle-aged activists who stuck to a routine of marches and speeches. But in March 1965, after extensive police violence disrupted a large protest march by civil rights activists from Selma, Alabama, to the state capital of Montgomery—with the actions televised for all Torontonians to see—local organizers employed a less conventional response. To a surprising extent, and less than a year after Toronto warmly welcomed Wallace, Selma provided an important moment in the history of the Toronto new left.[5]

On March 10, 1965, members of SCM, SUPA, and Friends of the SNCC blocked the entrance to the city's U.S. consulate. When police attempted to remove them, protesters used their non-violent tactical training to go limp, compelling officers to drag or throw them onto the sidewalk. But it was not just a one-time event. The action was repeated day after day, with participants maintaining their protest throughout numerous cold nights. Once the news media began to pay attention, dozens of protesters turned into hundreds. Activists collected thousands of dollars from passersby to aid civil rights efforts in the U.S. South, and the groups organized buses for a protest in Ottawa. The events proved particularly significant in enticing significant numbers of young people into political activism. Historians of the 1960s rightly emphasize the galvanizing role they had in widening the modest network of the young new left movement in Toronto.[6]

Adults were scarce amongst the sit-downers. Some said they were too old for this sort of thing, while others believed that the new activists might resent their presence. But droves of other young people joined the university students. John Gregoroff, a twenty-year-old tool-and-die-maker who labelled himself a pacifist, was a regular, as was Dan Heap, a worker-priest closer to middle age. Activist Naomi Wall, who was teaching at the New Play Drama School, was fired for having her drama students act out events at the consulate; her efforts had encouraged some of her young charges to attend the protest themselves. While Wall most likely had a university degree under her belt, none of the four sit-downers who travelled to Selma immediately after the consulate protests attended university: Allan Hood, seventeen, left his job as an office boy; George Goldie, twenty, had recently worked for a medical insurance firm; Harold McLaren, twenty, took unpaid leave from his job as dietary technician at Toronto General Hospital; and George Morgan, twenty-one, had recently quit his job making advertising signs.[7]

High-school students were a strong presence at the consulate protests, and when the cycle of protests ended, a number of them continued to be gripped by the experience. Gary Cristall was there, at age fifteen, skipping school and sitting down in front of the U.S. consulate—later citing it as the beginning of his lifetime of political activism. Among other things Cristall went on to co-found the Vancouver Folk Festival in 1978. Of the Selma demonstrations, he says, "I do remember meetings on St. George [street, in the heart of the university] and someone singing 'The Lonesome Death of Hattie Carroll,' which may be where my first consciousness of the possibility of music to change the world came from."[8] The Selma protests clearly also influenced students at Alderwood Collegiate: seven students there cut classes to attend. After the principal prevented the high school's newspaper from running an article on Selma and the Black struggle, the paper's thirteen-member editorial board resigned. When students shoved a leaflet questioning "why they could write about coloured socks but not coloured people" into every locker, the school threatened them with expulsion.[9]

When Burnley "Rocky" Jones sat down at the consulate, the action changed the trajectory of his life. Jones had grown up in the town of Truro, N.S., where he had experienced both schoolyard and institutional racism. The son of a domestic worker and stationary engineer, he had briefly joined the military before arriving in Toronto in the late 1950s. In terms of racial awareness, the big city was something of a revelation, from his initial encounters with Black activists, institutions, and professionals to his first taste of West Indian food. After working for some years as a truck driver, he had learned computer programming and got a job at the Ontario Treasury Department office, just up the street from the U.S. consulate.[10]

It was while walking to work one morning that he chanced upon the all-white crowd in front of the building. He returned at lunch hour to discuss civil rights and the aims of the protesters, went back again with his wife and child after work, and later stayed overnight. He was clearly entranced by the occasion, and felt it important that at least some Black people demonstrate their support, but he seemed most captured by the intense discussions and debates that occurred on the site. When he mentioned the protest to his co-workers, he was told that all the demonstrators were communists. His supervisor forbade him from mingling with the likes of those agitators. But he had found a new vocation as a political activist and never returned to work.[11] He would become a lifelong and effective activist in Nova Scotia.

Police officers box in student demonstrators in front of the U.S. consulate.

Clara Thomas Archives and Special Collections, Toronto Telegram fonds.

The middle-aged and a variety of other non-students were not entirely absent from the protests that week. An estimated three hundred clergy held a half-hour religious service before leading a parade of 1,700 to the consulate, and a third of the 2,000 people who marched on Queen's Park because of Selma were described as adults. Still, it was fundamentally a movement of youth and became the entry point for a number of long-term activists. Some fifty years later Judy Pocock, a member of CUCND-SUPA and an early organizer of the consulate actions, continued to be amazed by the large number of people who were first attracted to political engagement through those protests. Especially after the politicization caused by the U.S. bombing of North Vietnam that same year, the small circle of activists she had known since her days in CUCND greatly expanded.[12]

A history of SUPA, penned by activist Tony Hyde at the tail end of the group's life, labelled the Selma protests "militantly liberal," presumably because the content did not challenge the status quo in Canada or liberal opinion generally. Some activists had proposed that the consulate actions be linked to U.S. atrocities in Vietnam. The organizers agreed that the issues were related and recognized the importance of connecting them, but insisted that they simply did not have enough time to articulate the link effectively to the media and public. Going more deeply across issues might also have threatened the widespread sympathetic reaction to the protests, which at least some Friends of SNCC activists were keen to protect. Key activists Diane Burrows and Art Pape tried to discourage an

A Selma protester keeps dry, reads a book, and urges passersby to "do something"; March 13, 1965.

Clara Thomas Archives and Special Collections, Toronto Telegram fonds.

activist from handing out leaflets advertising a Black-organized fundraiser to aid the widow of Malcolm X. They presumably feared that the presence of the dead "extremist"—if only in the form of a handbill—might derail an uncomplicated message of solidarity. A picket sign observed at a demonstration a few months later—"What If MISSISSIPPI NEGROES DEMAND LAND REFORM???"—appeared designed to challenge such easy narratives.[13]

At the end of May, two rival protests were organized to greet Adlai Stevenson, the U.S. ambassador to the United Nations, who was a prominent defender of his country's invasion of Vietnam. He had been invited to the U of T campus to receive an honorary degree. A vigil organized by SUPA attracted as many as three hundred students, while the League for Socialist Action and New Democratic Youth spearheaded a protest—with seventy-five people turning out—that was more vocal and explicit in its criticisms of the ambassador. That protest attracted a large number of high-school students and smaller numbers of unaligned, off-campus activists who viewed SUPA's vigil as an intolerably weak response to the war in Vietnam. Gary Moffatt, who with other members of the Toronto Peace Centre was among the few attending both demonstrations, recalled that conversations about rival protesters were harsher than many of the remarks directed against Stevenson. Thinking of the recent Selma consulate protests, some students argued that if Friends of SNCC had organized the main campus demonstration instead of SUPA it would have been a lot more interesting than a vigil.[14]

* * *

As new activists were being won amidst this creative turmoil, SUPA was preparing an experimental series of projects that would become its signature contribution to sixties activism in Canada. These were community-organizing drives, inspired by similar efforts undertaken by the Students for a Democratic Society in the United States. Activists made plans to organize the poor in Kingston and Toronto, the Aboriginal, Métis, and Doukhobor communities in the West, and the Black population in Halifax. Individual organizers had substantial latitude in designing and executing these projects, relying on SUPA's national office in Toronto only for sponsorship, money, and advice. SUPA, said Toronto branch president Gary Teeple, was essentially just a name loosely binding together these projects.[15]

Could students activate the people? A public report back at the University of Toronto in the fall was fairly upbeat, with Burrows highlighting the unique fit of student activists in community-organizing roles:

> University students are valuable in dealing with people of a minority group or poor people. These people have a stereotyped image of the university student as someone with all the breaks on his side. When a student is working with them, it seems as if he is rejecting the society where such people don't belong. The student seems to be admitting the society isn't perfect—there's no place for me either, he seems to be saying.[16]

But behind closed doors many organizers confessed that the projects were not successful in instilling self-management in the targeted communities, and the most tangible result of these experiments may have been the disillusionment of the organizers themselves. The morale had been so bad amongst organizers in the Kootenays that the project prematurely dissolved. Other projects, hoping to marshal the presumed radicalism of poor and Indigenous peoples, found both constituencies to be more conservative than they had assumed. Some participants began to question whether the work they had been doing was radical after all: "We didn't know what made us different from ordinary social workers."[17]

Other SUPA members convincingly argued that the projects had at least helped to educate the organizers into developing a more successful praxis in the future. Linda Seese suggested that some participants had come to a better understanding of who they were and how to communicate with "regular" people. Although Jim Harding lamented, "Naive enthusiasm seems to have been replaced by cynicism for many," he also pointed out that the projects were, after all, experiments, and that the results had provided an invaluable list of questions to answer before embarking on any future project. They included: "how to reconcile local self-determination with revolutionary goals, how to avoid our organizational structures from perpetuating the mass-organizational society; whether there is a real distinction in effect between social work organizing and organizing by radical students." Harding's notion that leftists should contest the realities of a "mass-organization society" suggested that he—someone who would become renowned as one of the most intrepid of Canada's new leftists—had already absorbed key insights of the new formation.[18]

Knowledge gained from disappointment was also the salve applied to Friends of SNCC that fall after the intense enthusiasm for it ebbed. Following the Selma consulate protests, the group began to produce a newsletter and hired three paid staff members. The energy of people attending its frequent Freedom Schools was electric. That May as many as two hundred to three hundred young people attended its national conference in Toronto, where participants debated whether Friends of SNCC would remain a support group for the Black civil rights struggle in the U.S. South, with SUPA as an outlet for those who wanted to engage in local action, or if it too should take on domestic projects for social change. The crowd overwhelmingly opted for the second approach.[19]

All Friends of SNCC meetings were governed by consensus decision-making, a method that organizers believed would ensure participation by all—in order that people would not feel railroaded, that strong personalities would be less dominant, and that factions would be prevented from forming. Not everyone was convinced. Liora Proctor reported that every meeting she attended featured a debate on whether or not to use this form of decision-making. Trotskyists tended to argue that the need for consensus impeded not just decision-making but clear discussion. Those criticisms might be dismissed as a symptom of old left thinking and an attachment to *Robert's Rules of Order*, but some new leftists, arguing their case in the pages of the archetypically named Toronto Friends of SNCC publication *Freedom Now*, also shared this critique.[20]

In a late August *SUPA Newsletter* Barry O'Neil complained that the need for consensus had stalled the work of the organization: "All matters large and small were discussed. Meetings sometimes ran to four hours and tasks were left undone. Members became dissatisfied with the consensus method. Finally the method was abandoned and an executive was elected." Referring to these frustrating meetings, Heather Dean commented: "I have been to one Friends of SNCC meeting. . . . I have great respect for the courage of anyone who has attended two." Broaching other issues, Harvey Shepherd reported that attendance at meetings had plummeted from around fifty to almost nothing. Most money collected was now going to local office operations, instead of being sent south to SNCC. Although everyone had agreed to the group's reorientation to local action, Shepherd complained that most concrete proposals received little enthusiasm. The group found it impossible to recapture the enthusiasm of the Selma protests in a meeting room.[21]

Less than half a year after its buoyant consulate protests, Friends of SNCC was on life support, and some SUPA members interpreted this outcome as illustrating the inadvisability of mounting spectacular actions. An objection to SUPA planning an anti-war demonstration in Ottawa was later tied to a critique of what was dubbed the "Selma cycle." The name denoted the belief that even if a dramatic protest proved successful, any gains made would peter out, leaving the movement in a state similar to where it had been before the exemplary action in question. The proposed demonstration might prove to be nothing more than a distraction from the serious work of movement building. John Seeley disagreed with this analysis, arguing that action cycles were intellectually productive and that the back end or ebb of such cycles, though dispiriting to some, was responsible for advances in individual and collective thinking.[22]

SUPA's leadership may have already had its hands full, but the "Great SUPA Debate" had begun. That was author Margaret Daly's term for the late 1965–early 1966 discussions in SUPA about a new government program, the Company of Young Canadians (CYC). Members were torn over this government-backed program aimed at facilitating youth volunteering by providing them with guidance, projects, and a paid stipend. Would it help or hinder their efforts for social change? A number of Toronto SUPA members—above all, leader Art Pape—had already become committed to working with CYC and convinced that SUPA would be able to take advantage of CYC's resources. Others worried that the opposite would occur—that the CYC would drain energy and resources from SUPA.[23]

In November, in the pages of *The Varsity*, two Toronto SUPA members announced their resignations from the organization. Both expressed differences over SUPA's abstentionist electoral position, which meant that it would not be supporting the New Democratic Party, and condemned the branch for its anti-democratic elitism. Marvin Ross alleged that there had been no outreach, no public recruitment, and no decision-making by an elected leadership. It was a travesty, he argued, that an organization committed to grassroots participatory democracy was top-down, manipulative, and operated by a "small ruling elite." In rebuttal, Harvey Shepherd pointed out that what appeared to be a lack of democracy reflected an imbalance of commitment and experience, which, combined with decentralized decision-making, may have contributed to the appearance of authoritarianism. But, he argued, SUPA's democracy was actually more substantive than the NDP's version, in which everyone had a vote no matter how little they were concerned with a problem, and people who made decisions were generally not those who carried them out.[24]

Yet charges of elitism and undemocratic functioning did not go away. Around the same time the complaints surfaced, Gary Teeple, who had recently resigned his presidency of the Toronto branch, made similar comments in the *SUPA Newsletter*. Teeple alleged that SUPA was undemocratic and run by an informal elite whose social ties had been cemented during their CUCND years. This elite declared that decisions had been made by consensus when in fact they had never been discussed, and they decided who got organizational plums, like meetings with George Grant or appearances on CBC. Teeple announced his suspicion that many who had left SUPA had done so for this reason and that he was now joining them.[25]

Similar allegations of undemocratic functioning plagued the organizing of SUPA's anti-war action in Ottawa. Christopher Powell, in his history of anti-war activism in Canada, notes the discord that the event's planning caused within the group and finds SUPA's participatory democracy to have been largely a chimera in this instance. The action itself, a sit-in at Parliament Hill, took place in March 1966, just weeks shy of the first anniversary of the Selma consulate protests. Like those protests, civil disobedience was to be its signature, distinguishing it from "boring and bureaucratic" marches. Its advocates understandably thought it had the potential to create a larger movement. In contrast to the Selma protests, the Ottawa action had entailed months of planning and a clear domestic angle, and it took place in the country's seat of political power, which led to larger initial numbers. The protest resulted in sixty-one arrests, but received little media attention and failed to inspire a new cohort of activists. It was, as Powell's history concludes, largely a failure.[26]

Yet Powell too quickly dismisses the idea of civil disobedience, emphasizing its elitist undertones while favouring the importance of mass demonstrations. Although that critique has its strengths, there was nonetheless something to be said for the exuberance of the new action and the electricity of defiance. Civil disobedience was attuned to a media-saturated and increasingly self-reflective age, one in quest of authenticity and individualism. In Toronto, such a pattern had already been evident at Allan Gardens and the U.S. consulate. Not everyone at those locations participated in civil disobedience themselves, yet it was a tactic that moved observers, converts, and organizers. It was a mark of the beginning of the new left movement, where new ideas coupled with new tactics—on the part of DAC, the Committee of 100, and finally CUCND—galvanized activists and pushed them in new directions. Civil disobedience, although not really new, frequently possessed the *image* of something new and had the potential to inspire people in ways that orderly marches seldom could.[27]

Civil disobedience was also not just a device for peace demonstrators in 1966. Others who employed it tended not to name it or fit it within a wider philosophical rubric such as non-violence, but it was civil disobedience nonetheless. More than a quarter of all strikes in Ontario that year were illegal as thousands of workers in Toronto expressed their discontent with the limits of the postwar labour/capital compromise by moving beyond the respectable boundaries of legalism in their workplaces. Farmers also employed illegal means, slowing traffic around Toronto with their highway protests, defying threats of arrest and the seizure of their tractors. During a day of "Bedlam at Queen's Park," long-haired youth from Yorkville looked on as hundreds of farmers split from a larger demonstration and invaded the legislature, banging on office doors and forcing their way into committee rooms in search of the premier.[28]

SUPA displayed an energy and creativity that lasted long after the organization's demise. Its core concepts—justice-seeking neutralism in foreign policy, self-determination, participatory democracy, and a critique of the market economy—continued to be expounded well beyond its borders.[29]

* * *

At first SUPA refused to take part in the city's anti-war coalitions. Although one of its leaders noted that the organization was "not opposed to 'united front' concepts per se," potential allies were expected to concur with its philosophy and appreciation of non-violent tactics. SUPA's position was "that 'unity' must be based on common humanitarian and political principles, and the implementation of those principles in specified programs of action and policy." But community-based efforts against the war continued to advance and attract larger numbers of youth.[30]

Despite SUPA's absence, the new left was hardly missing in action. In an anti-war protest in April 1965 some six hundred people took to the streets amidst spring showers, and heard speeches delivered not only by long-time disarmament activists Rabbi Abraham Feinberg and Rev. John Morgan, but also Diane Burrows of Friends of SNCC. In a notable departure from the past, the organizing committee's slogan—"Negotiation Not Escalation"—was complemented by a plethora of competing slogans, marking an end to the enforcement of uniform placard signage. In the fall two demonstrations took place on the same day, with three hundred marching under the banner of the Toronto International Vietnam Day Committee (TIVDC) and twice that number attending a protest sponsored by SUPA, Voters for Peace, and other groups.[31]

In what was perhaps the most audacious speech that day, a middle-aged man, David Middleton, declared: "We should dissociate ourselves from all the institutions that support U.S. policy in Vietnam: we should leave the churches, the universities, the schools, and establish institutions of our own, on our own standards of morality." He called on Canadians to sabotage factories producing weapons for the U.S. war effort in Vietnam. Referring to the recent arrest of a man who had blown up a handful of U.S. fighter jets near Edmonton, he proclaimed: "This is a Canadian hero; he should be honored, not hung." A protest organizer emphasized that the anti-war committee did not share these views.[32]

In early 1966 SUPA came under fire for refusing to sponsor a co-ordinating structure being launched by local anti-war groups. Some of the five hundred participants at an organizing meeting were clearly upset that SUPA members were attending, selling literature and seeking support for their upcoming action in Ottawa, but refusing to endorse the efforts of other groups. In the meeting, SUPA's Tony Hyde denounced the proposed coalition's structure as unintentionally comic in its top-down bureaucracy. Such an approach would only lead to "more talk and more ineffective protests." Later, possibly chastened by the ineffectiveness of their own Ottawa action, members of SUPA's federal council wondered if their refusal to sponsor that meeting had been a mistake. The local branch reversed course and joined the Toronto Co-ordinating Committee to End the War in Vietnam (TCC), the group that resulted from the organizing meeting.[33]

The Labour Committee to End the War in Vietnam, formed at TCC's initial meeting, actively encouraged the participation of union members in the anti-war movement. The year before, a number of unions (disproportionately those historically associated with the CPC) began to back efforts against the war, and the president of the Canadian Labour Congress called for a ceasefire. The Labour Committee reached out to additional unions, inviting them to join the Toronto and District Labour Council and Ontario Federation of Labour in opposing the war, and worked to build the demonstration that TCC was helping to organize in Ottawa on March 26. They met with some success.[34] Judy Pocock, one of eight hundred to a thousand Torontonians to attend the protest in Ottawa, remembers her surprise upon boarding the train reserved by TCC:

> We went up in the train and I remember there were all these union guys! I didn't know working-class people; my parents weren't working-class. The movement that I was a part of was not working-class, and here were all these working guys. . . . I remember that and I'm sure there were many others, but I was oblivious at that point in time to the trade union movement.[35]

Morale and a sense of unity were high following the Ottawa demonstration. Hundreds of Torontonians descended upon Niagara Falls, where they picketed border crossings and, in nearby Welland, the Cyanamid chemical factory, which produced products used by the U.S. military in Vietnam. When six hundred people marched from Queen's Park to city hall, they witnessed something unthinkable just a short time before: Rabbi Feinberg of the TCC and James Endicott of the Peace Congress speaking on the same platform.[36]

That Feinberg was willing to speak in conjunction with Endicott indicates both a new confidence and the ebbing of McCarthyist fears within the left. Toronto activist William Spira, interviewed by a reporter from the CPC's *Canadian Tribune* while demonstrating at the TCC-backed Ottawa protest, said the very fact that he was willing to be interviewed by a communist paper demonstrated how perceptions were quickly changing. Even a year earlier he would have been too afraid to talk to such a reporter, for fear of being smeared as a communist himself. Peace, once presented as a moral issue, was increasingly couched in political terms. As Brewster Kneen, the thirty-three-year-old national secretary of the Christian-based Fellowship for Reconciliation in Canada (and also a member of the Latin America Working Group), now put it, "You can't talk about loving your neighbor without being left-wing."[37]

There was even a rejuvenation of left-wing sectarian conflict, signalled by the expulsion of four LSA-linked organizations from TCC. Communists, liberals, new leftists, and social democrats all joined together against a new common enemy in what LSA dubbed a "CP-liberal-pacifist bloc." The alleged LSA front organizations were readmitted into TCC at the end of the year, probably because the strong work ethic of Trotskyist organizers had been recognized in the breach.[38]

Efforts against the war continued to build steadily through 1967 and, with four thousand in attendance, the annual fall protest was the largest to date.[39] The following month saw the most significant campus anti-war mobilization of this period, a protest against Dow Chemical, the U.S. company that produced the napalm used in Vietnam. Other cities had seen protests against Dow recruiting students, and locally the Voice of Women and Save Lives in Vietnam Committee had promoted a boycott of the company's products. Activists at the University of Toronto now announced that Dow was not welcome on their campus.[40]

The campus demonstration lasted from 9 a.m. to nightfall, as protesters marched and then sat down in front of the old building housing the campus's placement service. As many as seventy-five students and three professors, ringed by fifty supporters, sat down to obstruct potential recruits, passing a bullhorn between them to amplify their calls against the war and for student power. Many were stepped on, as engineering students and university officials attempted to enter the building, but the action was largely successful as the Dow recruiter was virtually imprisoned in the building, with protesters sitting and lying across its porch, front yard, and sidewalk. Although the sit-in had its detractors, the Student Administrative Council passed a motion opposing recruitment by companies materially supporting the U.S. war effort. The motion's passage prompted a recall petition against SAC president Tom Faulkner, who resigned, ran against a pro-recruitment candidate, and handily won re-election. Dow, Vietnam, and Canadian complicity in the war had been thrust into the spotlight.[41]

The response from some quarters to the Dow sit-in anticipated later forms of discourse about new left movements as violent and authoritarian. In criticizing the protest, a *Globe and Mail* editorial referred to the sit-in as a "violent expression," and the members of St. Michael College's council made clear that they "abhor[red] violence." Labelling the protesters "censors," economics professor Arthur Kruger called the sit-in a threat to "academic freedom" and "freedom of speech." Even history professor Natalie Zemon Davis, who attended the demonstration and remained supportive of its aims, criticized those who tried to humiliate the recruiter upon his departure as "cowardly and warlike."[42]

New leftists did not necessarily accept the liberal doctrine that individuals should be free to do as they wished provided they did no harm to others. In solidarity with national liberation, and in the context of the human rights disaster in Vietnam, new leftists believed in their moral right to compel individuals to adhere to a political and ethical standard. A protest organizer, responding to the liberal rejection of new left tactics, argued that freedom of speech in the classroom and the freedom to manufacture chemical weapons were distinct issues and that students had a moral duty to stop human suffering.[43]

* * *

As activists at the University of Toronto joined a global pattern of revolutionary solidarity with Vietnam, the nascent left at other local post-secondary institutions struggled into being. A small coterie of activists at York University complained of having to endure all sorts of ridicule, even for just wearing a protest button. While students at other universities were gaining institutional influence, those at York had to put up with a council president who fought with his peers at Ryerson and U of T against the idea of free tuition. They had to suffer campus newspaper editorials decrying their lack of objectivity about the war in Vietnam and denouncing the "poor taste and undignified behaviour" of Selma protesters. One activist, close to his breaking point, fumed: "The way things look right now, York is one of the most conservative and backward campuses anywhere. York is intellectually dead, politically reactionary, and entirely alienated from the major issues of our age."[44]

A man wades through a crowd of activists to reach Dow's recruitment officer.

This Magazine Is About Schools, Summer 1968.

At York through the first half of the 1960s, Trotskyists, first via an NDP club and then the York Socialist Forum, appeared to sponsor most left-wing events. Efforts to organize against the Vietnam War via an ad hoc coalition in 1965 represented an important first step in mustering larger forces. By autumn small chapters of SCM and SUPA were functioning and working closely with the York Social Action Committee, a group fostered by York's student government.[45] That fall the first large mobilization of York students took place in a march to Queen's Park demanding universal accessibility to education. Despite U of T's relatively massive student population and a greater history of movements of "social concern," more than half the six hundred marchers came from Ryerson and York, reflecting the more modest economic backgrounds of students from those schools. The following year's demonstrations, demanding better accessibility for post-secondary education, were significantly larger and focused on the issue of student grants and loans. About 2,400 students from the University of Toronto alone protested at Queen's Park.[46]

A march of nine hundred Ryerson students to Queen's Park was more impressive given that school's smaller student body. In this protest, noticeably unruly, students began marching on their own initiative, leaving their student union president running to catch up. Photos show scenes outside the standard template for demonstrations, with cheerleaders whipping up the protest and young men crowd-surfing. Union executives repeatedly pleaded with demonstrators to tone it down. When a union official announced that the march was over and told everyone to return to campus, more than half of them, refusing to comply, engaged in a sit-in.[47]

These demonstrations were part of a larger social movement against tuition fees, which peaked in 1965–66 and died off soon after, largely because students had successfully pressured the government to increase loans and freeze fees. The temporary resolution of that battle encouraged members of the U of T student council to attack their university's "paternalism," fighting for autonomy against limits placed on the powers of student governments. When these demands were largely won, the council began to seek student power within the university as a whole.[48]

At mid-decade, the evolution of the Canadian University Press, an association of English-language campus newspapers, reflected wider changes within campus activist milieus: from a 1963 push to have newspapers adopt an outlook of "social concern" to a 1965 change in its charter that made advocating for "social change" a major focus. Through the second half of the 1960s many campus journalists would no longer see themselves as mere purveyors of information. Instead they took on the identity of transformative agents, rejecting the idea that news media could, or should, be objective and unbiased. While the content of the revolution that the association was seeking remained largely undefined, there was a sense "that the membership was working towards a socialist, even Marxist, idea of social change."[49]

* * *

"They Sit for 'The Queen,'" proclaimed the headline, pointing to the recent public presence of Canadian nationalism in the city. Refusing to stand for "God Save the Queen" was just the latest tactic by members of the Native Sons of Canada to release the city's "brow-beaten colonials" from the grip of Empire. The decades-old group had experienced a very public re-emergence in 1958 after local aldermen expressed outrage that "O Canada" and not "God Save the Queen" had been played following a toast to Queen Elizabeth. Was the switch in anthems subversive? The public did not appear to think so. The general lack of indignation, and even support for the idea of a made-in-Canada anthem and flag, suggested a growing impatience with Toronto's ruling-class fascination with monarchy, Empire, and deference.[50]

The Toronto left was not interested in the conservative Liberal nationalism of the Native Sons of Canada. But during the late 1950s it was developing its own vision of what a truly independent country might look like. Canadian nationalism, after all, had an impeccable old left pedigree. Since the 1940s the CPC had emphasized how much communists loved Canada. But in contrast to the Native Sons, who campaigned against symbols of British rule, old leftists who embraced Canadian nationalism emphasized the structural issue of U.S. economic domination. In 1958 Progress Books, the CPC's locally based publishing company, issued *The Power and the Money* by Frank Park, which advanced the case for a made-in-Canada economy. Quoting from C. Wright Mills's *The Power Elite*—the book most often cited as a first flowering of new left sociology—and utilizing new research by Canadian sociologist John Porter, Park minimized Marxist language, avoided references to the CPC, and called for an alliance of unions, farmers, professionals, and business people to take back the country from the national elites and Americans who controlled it.[51]

Economic nationalism entered the mainstream in the early 1960s with Walter Gordon's crusade against the dangers of foreign investment. Gordon's nationalist statements were regularly circulated in *The Toronto Star*, which also published comments by James Coyne, governor of the Bank of Canada, warning that U.S. investment threatened Canada's economy. Riding this nationalist wave, Progress Books published Frank and Libby Park's *Anatomy of Big Business*, which argued that the nationalization of large U.S. corporations was the only solution to U.S. dominance.[52]

Unlike the CPC, the CCF did not view the "national question" as central to its politics. Its Winnipeg Declaration made no explicit or implicit references to Canadian independence, although a failed motion to add a position against U.S. capital demonstrates at least some party members' awareness of the issue. By the end of the 1950s leading CCFers were calling for a national investment board to reduce U.S. domination of Canadian industry. By 1964 the NDP had adopted a more strident tone. When Prime Minister Lester B. Pearson moved to adopt a new flag that year, the NDP's federal leader, Tommy Douglas, suggested: "A symbol of national independence will have little meaning if, in the meantime, Canada has become an economic satellite of the United States." The social-democratic-leaning University League for Social Reconstruction was more tepid, but held a long series of meetings at the University of Toronto devoted to Canadian nationalism during 1964 and 1965.[53]

Canadian nationalism also popped up in the late 1950s–early 1960s peace movement. The first petition campaign at the University of Toronto to support disarmament was explicitly couched in those terms: "As we find ourselves bound ever more closely to American policies, we shall less and less be able to effectively present an independent viewpoint, to seek to prevent the spread of nuclear weapons."[54] James F. Minifie's *Peacemaker or Powder-Monkey*, which became a best-seller upon its release in 1960 and enticed some people to join the peace movement, was in many respects more a call to enhance Canadian independence than it was an argument for opposition to nuclear weapons. Although TCD, like other peace groups, largely refrained from extolling Canadian nationalism, it did occasionally evoke calls for national independence and the "Canadian values" of compromise and toleration.[55]

With the acceptance of U.S. nuclear weapons on Canadian soil, CUCND's eventual support for Canada's withdrawal from NATO, attentiveness to national liberation struggles from Quebec to Vietnam, a new commitment to multi-issue organizing, and the growth of nationalist sentiment in Canadian society, SUPA began to take up the cudgels of Canadian nationalism. Don Roebuck's "U.S. Ownership and Control of Canadian Industry," a working paper for SUPA's founding conference at the end of 1964, may have been the first concrete manifestation of this trend. Roebuck's document outlined the growing U.S. ownership of Canadian business assets, concluding that national independence was an illusion because "economics is fundamental to everything else."[56]

By the time SUPA was setting its sights on organizing a protest in Ottawa against the war in Vietnam, two of its leading figures, Toronto's Art Pape and Montreal's Dimitrios Roussopoulos, were revealing an interest in Canadian nationalism. Pape wondered how activists in Canada ("notably the most important and most servile U.S. colony") could find sufficient support amongst a populace resenting the bigness and bullying of the United States, on the one hand, and keen on the economic benefits they received from this relationship on the other. Roussopoulos's conception of SUPA strategy had begun to focus on Canadian nationalism. He wanted SUPA to send a delegation to the NDP announcing SUPA's intent to build a movement for self-determination and to win allies for the group's direct action. The group would later tell the public that Washington, not Ottawa, was the real seat of power and that domestic protests were largely useless because of this colonial relationship. Roussopoulos expressed a hope that SUPA's embrace of nationalism would attract union locals unhappy with Canadian dependence and open up new areas of community organizing, providing the basis of a mass movement. In his mind at least, national liberation and community organizing were closely linked.[57]

Reflecting this vision, organizers of the Ottawa protest embraced the Canadian nationalist theme as a means of understanding both Canadian complicity with the U.S. war in Vietnam and the logic of coalition-building. Many hoped that student radicals, Red Tory nationalists, community people in their project areas, parts of the B.C. labour movement, Prairie farmers, members of co-op movements, and radical academics would all join the action under a left-nationalist rubric. A half-page advertisement for the Ottawa action showcased the names of supporters from some of those sectors. Headlined "Reverse the Lament," it began with a quote from George Grant—author of *Lament for a Nation*—asserting that Canada was no longer a nation.[58]

A SUPA regional conference a couple of months later again highlighted the issue: "At times the workshops were intense as the participants came to grips with the implications of the speeches and attempted to integrate this new concept of

Canadian nationalism into the thinking of SUPA and its predecessor, CUCND." Debates about how to inject positive content into this anti-American form of nationalism included participants maintaining that Canadian nationalism could be used as an umbrella theme to unify SUPA concepts such as positive neutralism, self-determination, participatory democracy, and a critique of the market economy.[59]

The use of Canadian nationalism to transmit new left politics to new audiences and forge a broader coalition for change persevered, even as the rhetoric employed to this end turned closer to old left expressions in 1967. As Toronto new leftist Philip Resnick warned:

> In assessing our own attitude towards Canadian nationalism, we can have one, and only one criterion. Does nationalism promise to be a progressive force in Canadian society, shifting the focus of political power in this country from the present corporate elite with its technocratic allies to strata which are currently powerless? Does a critique of American control of our economy link up with a demand for reorientation of a Canadian-controlled economy in the direction of popular control and direct participation? ... To utter long live a socialist Canada! Vive le Québec socialiste! These are the slogans pointing in the right direction, though it is our duty as radicals to give new and concrete meaning to these terms.[60]

There is a tendency to attribute the new left's Canadian nationalism to the influence of *Lament for a Nation*, published in 1965. Although the Red Tory Grant, in the words of one activist, "greatly influenced the minds of many SUPAmen," the old left's interest in the issue was no less influential. James Laxer was notably enthusiastic about *Lament for a Nation*—a factor used to suggest that Grant's book was responsible for the new left's interest in Canadian nationalism and ultimately the creation of the Waffle movement as an offshoot of the NDP. That line of thought ignores Laxer's close relationship with his old left father, the Canadian nationalist Robert Laxer, and the pre-*Lament* writing on the subject.[61]

What is more likely is that SUPA members decided to attribute their Canadian nationalism to an eminent academic philosopher for public relations purposes. Comments made in the group's internal bulletin by Roussopoulos indicate that Grant's chief importance rested in how "for once someone other th[a]n the old left has maintained that Canada is part of a massive technological Empire, the US empire." Grant's conservative, yet distinctly consensus-rattling viewpoint, was more acceptable to liberals and could be more effectively integrated into SUPA's strategic vision than anything that savoured of the old CPC. "Again the importance of his position," Roussopoulos wrote, "is that he gives this critique a new legitimacy."[62]

* * *

Moreover, the new Canadian nationalism was also directly influenced by the new left politics of revolutionary solidarity—as with struggles in Latin America, which from the early 1960s had a hold on the hearts of Toronto's leftists. Liz Makarchuk, one of the few women to attend the May 1961 anti-Bomarc demonstration in North Bay, had been so inspired by the Cuban Revolution that she temporarily moved to Havana later that same month. Inspired by the writings and pro-Cuban statements of sociologist C. Wright Mills and activist philosophers Bertrand Russell and Jean-Paul Sartre, she helped the young government by assisting with translating, editing, and broadcasting; she also hosted a midnight jazz program with political commentary. Given that both CUCND and SCM organized educational meetings on Cuba, Makarchuk was clearly not alone in her interest in the Cuban Revolution.[63]

Still, Cuban solidarity efforts were largely co-ordinated by old left organizations. The most prominent group, Fair Play for Cuba (FPFC), was established in February 1961 before a packed meeting of four hundred people. Members of LSA played a key role in setting up and operating the committee, following the lead of its U.S. ally, the Socialist Workers Party, which had initiated the first FPFC committees. The Toronto-based Canadian incarnation of FPFC quickly won support from members of the CCF-NDP, unions, academics, and churches.[64]

But just months after its founding meeting, FPFC was hit by damaging allegations from the *Toronto Telegram*, and rumblings from assorted social democrats, that the committee was overrun with communists. Following a statement by the RCMP that the group was under observation, U of T professors Leslie Dewart and McNaught proposed that the committee rename itself, adopt an anti-communist clause, and remove at least one person from its executive. When most of the FPFC members rejected this proposal, Dewart and McNaught resigned. Anxiety over the Red-tinged committee resurfaced when the John F. Kennedy assassin Lee Harvey Oswald was tied to the U.S. FPFC; a member of the Toronto group tore up his membership card in front of witnesses. Despite such temporary setbacks, FPFC persevered, and its 1964 student tour of Cuba left an indelible mark on many of its emerging new left participants.[65]

The first new left organization devoted to solidarity with Latin America was the Latin American Working Group (LAWG), established in 1966. At first the group was almost akin to an international arm of SUPA, in that its members planned to travel to developing countries and undertake experiments in participatory democracy and radical social action there. Although LAWG's membership included many SUPA activists, in notable contrast to that organization, women in this group played leading roles in organizing, speaking, and writing.[66]

At first LAWG focused much of its overseas activity on the Dominican Republic, with members in particular taking part in a community project in a poor area of Santo Domingo. But from its beginning, educating Canadians about and researching topics related to Latin America were at least as important as physically travelling to the region. To that end the group hosted a range of research projects and seminars, sometimes featuring Latin Americans as resource people.[67]

By summer 1967, before the first round of projects was even completed, LAWG participants were questioning their usefulness. Their unease was a result of an increasingly common conclusion amongst new leftists about the necessity of some form of revolution. They saw genuine solidarity as requiring something broader and more reciprocal than just helping people "over there." Activists were wondering about "how to make the revolutionary changes needed in both North and South American societies."[68]

One aspect of this new understanding caused a debate around the focus of LAWG's outreach. Linda Seese advocated that the group concentrate on recruiting radicals, a constituency she identified as springing from SUPA, NDY, and Kairos (a Christian coalition), former members of SUPA, and possibly hippies and members of peace groups. She argued that many of the people in these groups had become disillusioned with community organizing, anti-war activism, and the left in general. They were cynical about the possibility of making real change in Canada, and many of them had begun to engage in serious study, trying to find a way out of the impasse. Latin America could be used as a focus for refining a left-wing analysis.[69]

Supporting Seese, another member emphasized that the main purpose of the group should be to provide an international perspective to movement activists in Canada. Instead of being a small pressure group of Latin Americanists, LAWG should communicate the ideas and experiences of Latin American revolutionaries to radical Canadians—including everything from theories about developing consciousness to the methodology of guerrilla warfare. LAWG members could continue to give presentations to churches, high schools, and other appropriate groups, but that activity would be secondary.[70]

Brewster Kneen, in contrast, argued in favour of LAWG continuing to engage all constituencies, especially high-school students. Reaching out to liberals, rather than radicals, was paramount. Members of liberal church groups could readily be converted into radicals, he contended, and might prove superior to the "alienated" activists of the new and old lefts. A weekly seminar series, combining areas studies with readings from the works of theorists like Frantz Fanon and Régis Debray, could utilize "Latin America as a front for the '*conscientizacao*' [consciousness-raising] of Canadians."[71]

Despite this minor disagreement, LAWG members appeared to be united in deciding to end their overseas projects, which a later document derided as "educated tourism," to focus on education at home. Participants in any future projects would be Canadians who were already working for fundamental social change. Many of them, they argued, already had a keen interest in the global south:

> Young adults in Canada, talking about a new society based on 'participatory democracy,' trying experiments in 'radical' social action, on Indian reservations, in coffee houses, and in the slums, looked admiringly upon the revolutionaries in the Third World as brothers in a common struggle against the 'system.'[72]

LAWG members also shared the early new left's embrace of Canadian nationalism. In the months prior to its establishment, solidarity activism had already convinced some of them that Canada itself was an underdeveloped country with limited self-determination. By the summer of 1967 Kneen appeared to be speaking for the group in suggesting that an understanding of the causes of oppression and suffering in Latin America would necessarily lead to considering "how Canada functions in ways similar to the U.S. on the one hand, and how Canada is a victim of the U.S. in a way analogous to Latin America on the other." This nationalist analysis became stronger in subsequent years. By 1969 LAWG saw itself as "an integral part of what might be called a movement to liberate Canada as well as Latin America"—a movement that was "visible in academic, labor and political circles and in such documents as 'For an Independent Socialist Canada.'"[73]

Canadian nationalism, as the new left reinterpreted it, had more to do with the politics of transnational solidarity than it did with George Grant's conservative vision of Canada.

* * *

Feminist issues had been starkly absent from SUPA. There was nothing in the group's publications comparable to the occasional articles in old left publications such as CPC's *Marxist Quarterly*, which termed women as "super-exploited" and emphasized themes extolled by the later women's liberation movement. In the NDP's equally staid publication *The Commonwealth*, Aileen Hall, criticizing women's subordination, made mention of an early British suffrage leader: "Mrs. Pankhurst would surely feel she had fought in vain if she could see the position women are now content to occupy."[74]

An early left feminist tract in Toronto was activist Heather Dean's "On Passing Two Whores and a Nun," which appeared in October 1966 as the cover story of the premier issue of the U of T's slickly hip *Random* magazine. The introduction establishes the nun, at first depicted as an oppressed and somewhat derisive character, as someone who had escaped everyday societal expectations of women: "She wasn't in the game. She was liberated from the game." Dean did not, of course, advocate that women don habits and join a church, but she predicted that, like the nun, women would have to pay a price for their liberation. She believed that much of that price would be extracted by white, male liberals, who would claim—as they had for unions and Black power activists—that women were going "too far."[75]

The heart of Dean's essay emphasized the similarity between the Black American struggle for freedom and a future movement for the liberation of women: "Read 'woman' for 'black man.' Read 'real woman' for 'good nigra.' Read 'male chauvinist' for 'Southerner.'" Like some Black leaders, Betty Friedan and her book *The Feminine Mystique* (1963) were weak on solutions, Dean argued. Instead of just getting jobs, as Friedan had suggested, women must share a process of self-discovery and independent decision-making. Then, consciously following the schema for Black power, they could unite with men in a common struggle for a revolutionary restructuring of society to liberate them both.[76]

A month after Dean's article appeared, a group of women from the university's Whitney Hall residence began to agitate for the right of women to enter Hart House, a largely male-only preserve. The women asked to be allowed to participate in debates and attend concerts without escorts, and to be granted greater access to its art gallery. Some argued that there would have been an uproar on campus had any other minority been treated in the way they had been. In early December 1966, forty-five women lined up, seeking entry to a Hart House debate on the motion of "This House Would Rather March on Ottawa Than Stand for Parliament." The women were turned away (and the motion defeated).[77]

The following month, three women—Laurel Limpus, Jennifer Penney, and Laurel Sefton—sat down in the Hart House cafeteria. Persistently asked to leave, they remained, as several men shouted "out, out" and threw a torrent of crumpled paper bags and empty milk cartons at them. Student council president Tom Faulkner, considered something of a progressive, publicly denounced the women, telling them he agreed with the objective of integrating Hart House, but their sit-in tactic was counterproductive and had turned the men against them. The women needed a go-slow approach, which he likened to the push for integration in the American South: "You can't legislate it. You have to change the men's attitudes."[78]

All these women had some experience on the left. A year earlier, Penney had been elected to SAC. Alongside ex-SUPA members Marvin Ross and Gary

Teeple, she had campaigned under the banner of the left-wing Student Democratic Union, which promised to combat housing discrimination, make birth control information readily available, and pursue student power. Limpus was a member of SDS in the United States before relocating to Canada and had recently penned articles promoting student power and decrying sexual puritanism, replete with several references tying sexual repression to U.S. war-making in Vietnam.[79]

At a time when discussions about birth control and gender inequality were increasingly reaching the public sphere, SUPA remained silent. These new left women were clearly taking action and speaking up, yet their proto-feminist organizing did not appear to substantively extend beyond the small Hart House occupations, and Dean's call for an extensive process of female decision-making would have to wait a little longer. Sefton, at the time, expressed her distaste for "groups of somewhat hysterical and certainly unattractive, out-and-out feminists, who are usually anti-men (in itself unfeminine) and who make the thought of 'twentieth century female equality' terrifying to the male sex." Despite those reservations, a new left-wing voice had clearly arrived in Toronto by 1966.[80]

* * *

In early 1965, SUPA and the NDP remained fairly close—an activist song sheet even featured an "SCM, NDP, SUPA, SNCC Song"—but cracks were becoming discernible. Just prior to SUPA's founding, Pape and Laxer had sparred on the issue of electoral politics at a seminar on student syndicalism organized by the Ontario University New Democrats. Pape, clearly soured on electoralism, told the gathering that organized party politics was largely irrelevant to the real issues of society. Laxer, maintaining that real change continued to be possible through the NDP, charged Pape with failing to appreciate the history of democratic socialism. By the end of 1965, many people involved in SUPA had swung to Pape's position, and anti-parliamentarism became the de facto position of the group. A late 1965 article by SUPA's Dean aptly sums up this new stance. In it, she portrays the "Free Enterprise Electoral System" as completely akin to a consumer economy—as something in which "political entrepreneurs" create "products" for voters to "shop" for and seek to maintain "brand loyalty" and "profit margins." A system designed to sell products to passive consumers could never be used to alleviate alienation or to attain significant political power, she argued. The consumption of commodities did not equal active self-determination. She concluded, "Don't vote."[81]

Dean singled out the NDP for being entrenched in this system—and must have had that party in mind when she issued a warning against a vote for the "lesser evil." She pointed to a recent NDP campaign directive indicating that the most effective political arguments had a maximum length of three seconds.

There were "socialists" and "purists" within the party who did seem to want an alternative to such dumbing-down. But in its place they merely sought a more "sophisticated consumption of political products." As she put it, "Thus, the NDP, the only party that pretends to address itself to the question of power, fails even to define the question."[82]

Dean refused to provide any alternatives to the electoral system, believing that any top-down advice would be akin to the very manipulation she was critiquing. In an interview after the article appeared, SUPA and Friends of SNCC member Pocock said that people had to make up their own minds concerning both domestic and foreign policies and that her fellow activists were against the idea of adopting a particular doctrine or ideology. "The communists use the philosophy that the ends justify the means. We at SNCC believe that the means justify the ends."[83]

This vague-sounding process was much clearer in evoking what was "new" than what was "left." But new left language was inching towards greater specificity. A letter from a student active in the Selma protests listed many of the soft apolitical words regularly used by the movement throughout the first half of the 1960s: concern, involvement, responsibility, commitment, relevancy. But as the year progressed, these keywords were retired in favour of the more robust phrase: "social change." By the end of the year some SUPA speakers were even talking about "revolution."[84]

While both of those concepts still hinged on the philosophy of non-violence, there were hints of a challenge to that approach as well. Some two months after the Selma protests, Jewish groups mobilized against John Beattie, the leader of the Canadian Nazi Party, who was scheduled to speak at Allan Gardens. Young leftists plugged into the Jewish community recognized the risk of violence in this event, and in response, SUPA, Friends of SNCC, and a handful of Jewish youth organizations decided to host a "live-in." Their rally would centre on singing and folk dancing, which they hoped would alleviate tensions in the crowd and channel feelings of hatred into a spirit of humanitarian uplift. But on the day of the demonstration, about three thousand Jews and supporters showed up to challenge Beattie and his compatriots, who numbered less than a dozen. A section of the crowd attacked the neo-Nazis, and police prevented the young activists from continuing their "live-in" as the protests turned into a full-fledged riot.[85]

Afterwards SUPA member Donna Rosenthal argued that it was difficult to evaluate the "live-in" because of its forced dispersal. Yet the Allan Gardens riot appeared to show the limits of the strategy of non-violence. The "live-in" had, after all, failed in its goal of preventing violence and did not seem to pose a constructive alternative to combatting anti-Semitism or racism. Rosenthal's stance—that paying attention to the small band of Nazis had been a mistake, and that the riot was wrong—largely mirrored the views of the establishment and local media. Non-violence, which had proven so successful at the U.S. consulate, appeared to be a philosophical and tactical failure just two months later.[86]

Non-violence continued to be considered crucially important for a time. A SUPA activist who attended SDS's Economic Research and Action Project (ERAP) training institute saw non-violence as a key difference between American and Canadian activists. While ERAP members considered it merely a tactic to be used when circumstances warranted, for SUPA members it tended to be central to both their philosophy and strategy.[87]

Yet even before the establishment of SUPA questions had been raised within CUCND about the feasibility of non-violence. As early as 1964 Pape was taking note of a decline in support for non-violence amongst Black activists in the United States. Pape's contacts were telling him that Southern activists of all ages had grown impatient with the strategy's "slow success." Another CUCND branch executive wrote that the Cuban Revolution, which had been victorious in large measure because of armed struggle, had caused her to question her past advocacy of non-violence.[88]

In late 1965 Toronto author Austin Clarke, a proponent of Black power, debated non-violence with SUPA members at U of T and York. Clarke maintained that pacifism was "immoral"—an argument rejected by the SUPA participants, who continued to support non-violence as a revolutionary strategy. Yet others in SUPA disagreed. One member repeated a question from SNCC: "Why bother to integrate non-violently into a violent society?" The Vietnam War and SNCC's move away from non-violence were probably important factors leading to SUPA's shift of emphasis away from non-violence as a universal solution. Earlier Pape had vehemently criticized American pacifists who favoured a peace settlement in Vietnam at any price; he believed that such a deal would violate Vietnam's right to national self-determination.[89] His position suggested a new left politics that went well beyond a push for the sensible adjudication of conflicts; the old approach would at best produce a harmonious, but unjust, outcome.

In essence, the new left emerging during these years, seemingly well-removed from the hippies and the counterculture, had absorbed some of the unrelenting opposition of that lifestyle to bourgeois compromise and daily life—the "rat race." In the mid-1960s Toronto's counterculture was evolving from a beat-informed vision to a hippie-centred alternative that would become most evident in the late 1960s and early 1970s. SUPA publications carried a few hints of this later subculture, but the countercultural thrust of new leftism was much more apparent in *Sanity*, which had started as a CUCND publication. In 1966–67 the newly independent newspaper devolved from a standard professional layout to an eclectic style anticipating later underground newspapers. By fall 1965 *Sanity* had begun to distinguish itself from other left-wing papers by highlighting ecological concerns; by spring 1966 it was clearly moving in a "neo-primitive" direction. The poisoning of the environment and oppression of Indigenous peoples were not merely "issues" or "problems" to be solved through social change, but vital to the creation of a "new man" and a new society. "Natural," pre-capitalist economics was upheld and "overdeveloped" economies disparaged.[90]

Industrial society, whether capitalist or socialist, was a dead end. The Russian Revolution had tried to inaugurate a new way of living within industrial society and failed. Although it had created greater income equality than seen in Western nations, the Union of Soviet Socialist Republics (USSR) was a state capitalist society with fundamentally the same values and puritanical work ethic. Developments in Communist China were more encouraging, but the newspaper was ultimately pessimistic: "With the Chinese revolution the Marxist concept that man will change when the economic structure changes has received another lease on life." Yes, capitalism had to be abolished, but the creation of new ways of living was not automatic or inevitable.[91]

Recalling the early new left's interest in existentialism, *Sanity* proposed that individuals had a responsibility to establish a new creative culture and find a new purpose and meaning to life. Members of the newspaper collective suggested that they were embarking on the discovery of this new culture by embracing spontaneity and a move "back to the land." By opening a rural peace centre, which would advocate social change as play, they would go beyond the rituals of both the establishment and those protesting against it:

> To the extent that a play spirit is beginning to take its place alongside purposive, planned thought and action in the peace movement, the movement is in a better position to understand the social forces it wishes to control, it is in a better position to break free of the existing order, and most importantly, it is in a better position to live now the full life it is confident man is able to lead.[92]

New leftists were at least implicitly challenging the political and cultural conventions of their society. By early 1966, some of them were forming commitments to "living otherwise" that would stand them in good stead for the remainder of the twentieth century.

* * *

As early as the fall of 1965 SUPA began its decline as a major local and national activist organization. The following year was considered "pretty discouraging in that there has seemed to be little significant activity going on across the country.

It has also been terribly obvious that our numbers have been dropping." In a late 1966 eulogy Peter Gzowski, a supporter who tended to identify SUPA as *the* new left, dubiously claimed that potential recruits had decided to become marijuana smokers instead.[93] When SUPA was formally dissolved in 1967, an obituary in *The Varsity* suggested that its longevity and importance had both been overblown:

> Of course, SUPA's decline comes as no surprise because it has not been much more than an office staff, a newspaper and an idea for over a year now. Even before that, though, SUPA was a victim of its own myths.... Never more than a loose collection of radicals, it was trumpeted by others as the vanguard leading a major youth revolution. It was never that ... but historians researching years from now just might get that impression from the articles, radio and TV shows of two years ago.[94]

That final comment was starkly accurate. Nevertheless, the discussions and debates within SUPA during 1966–67 are immensely revealing, both about its own "myth"—which has tended to set the standard by which historians have judged subsequent new left organizations—and in encapsulating many of the challenges to the new left ideology of the mid-1960s, which would shape the movement for years to come.

In fall 1966, for example, SUPA debated whether it should be moving in a different direction. Allan Marks, of Montreal, arguing that branches outside Ontario wanted the next SUPA conference to be more tightly organized, called for a discussion of ideological differences within the group. For him, SUPA's democracy was a "myth," and its loose structure meant that charismatic leaders continued to control the organization. He posited that Toronto members, fighting to maintain the status quo, were responsible for SUPA's continued decline.[95]

In Toronto Heather Dean insisted on maintaining the current organization. She saw a large gap between the consciousness of young people and the awareness needed to become a political activist, arguing that a loosely structured environment was most conductive to bridging it:

> We think in terms of creating politicals out of what we have, which is <u>not</u> a pool of radicals hungering for expression, but at best a bunch of confused middle class kids in a degenerating social system who need to be led gently out of their confusion, and a potential constituency who are already afraid of the degree of ideology we have.[96]

Toronto members understood, better than those in other provinces, that politicization had to be subtle and informal until political conditions improved: "You will never make a SUPA member into a materialist by sitting him in front of a Marxist intellectual for an hour. . . . You can do this more effectively in a bar—not more pleasantly, more effectively." Denying that SUPA's decision-making was undemocratic, Dean told Marks she would "be happy to discuss this with you over beer, as it is a prime example of something that requires intensive and immediate interaction."[97]

While activists agreed on the surface about the long-term need for a more structured and ideological organization, for the present competing outlooks remained irreconcilable. They could not even agree about the make-up of SUPA's membership. For Toronto's Tony Hyde, the people he saw in the group lived outside of conventional society, did not consciously engage in social change, and were preoccupied with personal relationships. While it might have seemed as though he was referring to a constituency of potential members in the hippie haven of Yorkville, he clearly indicated that the "kids" he was referring to were a majority of SUPA members.[98] Montreal's Jim Best disagreed with that assessment, but insisted that even the type of member Hyde referred to was "still able to participate" in a planned conference. "They may be alienated but they are not stupid. They are capable of understanding social problems and what needs to be done about them. Around here SUPA has earned contempt not only from the old leftists but also from some of the alienated kids you talk about."[99]

The stark differences between leaders and the led upheld and reinforced by Dean and Hyde evoke caricatures of Marxist-Leninist structures more than they reflect the essence of a new left participatory democracy. Despite the importance that SUPA placed on the democratic ideal, its execution was tremendously flawed, with decision-making often restricted to activists at the top of the organization in its Toronto-based national office. Discussion, while more democratic in some respects than that of the old left—as suggested by public criticisms of its leadership—could also be more constrained. In contrast to old left groups such as the CPC and LSA, only a select minority of SUPA members received its de facto internal discussion bulletin.

Although SUPA never did have anyone with the power and esteem of the Communist Party's Tim Buck or NDP's Tommy Douglas, both Art Pape and Dimitrios Roussopoulos projected an outsized influence. Their roles generated significant speculation about the negative influence of such emphatic personalities on the organization's participatory democracy. Don McKelvey, an SDS member who had moved to Toronto to assist SUPA, summed up how he thought each "camp" saw the other:

> Art is seen as a righteous, moralistic, consciously manipulative political operator who thrives on "unstructured situations" in which he can bring his

> considerable charisma to bear—his manipulation being that much worse for being so subtle and for a good cause. Dimitri is seen as a cold-hearted type of political operator who "wheels and deals" behind the scenes, influencing people and events through manipulation, outright lies (or at least distortions), and building a political machine in miniature, complete with semi-puppets. It is interesting that each of these individuals is known by the "other camp"—only half-jokingly—as "The Prince of Darkness."[100]

The criticism was a telling indication of the negative side of what might be called the "new left style," which entailed a personalized politics that placed a heavy onus on the charismatic male individual. McKelvey attributed the dominance of these personalities, and the divergence of their "camps," to a host of factors, including Toronto's dominant control over SUPA's central office and national decision-making, but above all the organization's lack of activity.

As impatience grew in some quarters for a new kind of model that would be more democratic, tightly structured, and ideologically coherent—moving to study, debate, and eventually adapt some kind of socialist ideology—a national SUPA conference finally took place in Goderich, Ont., during the summer of 1967.[101] By that time SUPA had virtually ceased operating in Toronto, despite having its national office there. Those who continued to consider themselves members held private biweekly study sessions, exploring issues such as the transition of the CCF to the NDP, but made only scant efforts directed at growth or outreach. Even so, two-thirds of the thirty-five-odd SUPA members attending the Goderich conference lived in Toronto. Aside from two Albertans, three Quebeckers, and a handful of Americans, everyone else hailed from Ontario. SUPA, as a national organization, was in effect already dead.[102]

The gathering at Goderich included few of the alienated young "lifestylists" that Hyde had mentioned, and many of the organization's "heavies," including Pape and Roussopoulos, were conspicuously absent. For those who persevered, conversation turned to two subjects that had never been explored in depth at a national SUPA conference: Marxism and women's liberation.

Although SUPA's newsletters contained the odd reference to Marxism, the political tendency had been relegated to the margins of the organization, though at least some members were studying and discussing the political philosophy behind the scenes. Marxism had been examined in several courses held by Toronto SUPA's School for Social Theory in 1965, and a report back from one class noted the challenge of synthesizing Marxism with psychoanalysis. The strong presence of Marxism and class issues in an early 1967 draft SUPA manifesto indicates that this interest had most likely been percolating below the surface for some time.[103]

At Goderich a paper penned by Montreal member Stan Gray advocated a turn to Marxism, offering a kind of analysis to which many attendees, worn out by SUPA's lack of coherence, structure, and success, were now receptive. But everyone did not embrace it. When one member ventured that the working class had sold out in exchange for two cars, a washer, and a dryer, Gray replied, "So what?" Another member, recalling her years of working in a factory, suggested that those material possessions did not mean that the working class had "sold out" or that it could not be an agent for revolutionary social change.[104]

While the emergence of Marxism as a major topic of discussion at Goderich was hardly sudden, the appearance of a women's liberation manifesto was probably somewhat surprising. Indeed, the subject had been completely off SUPA's radar until women at a meeting in the spring announced that they were going to meet separately in a caucus. There, they discussed SUPA's inequitable division of labour—for instance, how men did all the writing while women readied their words for publication. Some women complained that their own status in the group was in direct proportion to the influence of the men they were dating.[105]

A handful of men took umbrage at the very idea of women meeting separately. Former activist and SUPA historian Cyril Levitt viewed such gender-specific meetings as undemocratic and exclusionary. He quoted extensively from a "prominent Canadian student leader" who claimed that allegations of discrimination and the formation of women's caucuses were just excuses to "split the movement."[106] Harvey Shepherd, a key local activist in both CUCND and SUPA, suggested that the women were expressing a sense of self-loathing because they had become estranged from their gendered essence:

> The thrust of women's liberation is all too often towards homogeneity: the abandonment of women's roles by women (eschewing cosmetics, for instance), the assumption of men's roles by women (strong language, for instance) and the attempt to eliminate from human experience specifically men's roles (the resentment of male organizations, for instance).[107]

Peggy Morton, the only manifesto author to have grown up in Toronto, came from a middle-class family that had encouraged her intellectual inquiry. She had become interested in disarmament in high school and when she was only seventeen moved to Kingston to attend Queen's University, where she was active in the peace movement. In her first year she became head of her CUCND branch; in her second year she helped organize the La Macaza protests and attended SUPA's inaugural conference in Regina. She was instrumental in setting up SUPA's Kingston Community Project, and after working on that moved to Toronto to work in SUPA's national office. Morton recalls attending a SUPA meeting and how her thoughts drifted. She would think to herself, "Gee I said that an hour ago and nobody listened. Now some guy said it and everybody's talking about it." After that, she said, "I started noticing that's what happens every time a woman speaks."[108]

Myrna Wood was older than the other manifesto co-authors and arguably had more life experience. She had worked at an aircraft factory in Los Angeles and at a bunch of jobs across the Southern United States, including in a bookstore where she watched the Ku Klux Klan parading outside. She had been married and divorced and felt pained that knowledge about birth control had been denied her. In contrast to many of her activist peers, she did not have a university education and spent most of the first half of the 1960s working in the special collections department at the University of Toronto.[109]

When Wood heard about the new branch of Friends of SNCC on campus she joined it, which was just before the Selma consulate protests. She returned to the U.S. South that summer to lend a hand to the civil rights struggle. Beyond having to deal with bigoted whites, she found that working there exposed a host of troubling gender and racial dynamics internal to SNCC. She admired how some Black female activists had dealt with this situation. Upon her return, Wood quickly decamped to work on the Kingston Community Project and later moved again to Toronto, where she worked in SUPA's national office for a time. Like Morton, Wood was sitting in a SUPA meeting when she had a "click moment" about the status of women in the group.[110]

Linda Seese hailed from a middle-class family in the United States and like Wood had experienced civil rights organizing in the American South. She lived in Mississippi for a year, where she registered Black voters and worked on other civil rights ventures. It was tough. A school she taught at burned down, and a house she stayed in was attacked with Molotov cocktails. Upon leaving she raised funds for an ongoing cotton workers strike and joined a project helping Indigenous people organize in Northern Ontario. She became active in SUPA towards the end of that organization's first year. Although two or three SUPA colleagues knew she was a lesbian, she was mostly closeted while living in Toronto. Her partner was the only other lesbian she knew of in the city's burgeoning women's movement.[111]

Judy Bernstein came from an old left family that fell somewhere between the working and middle classes. She had been active in the peace movement and other causes and saw SDS's community-organizing projects as an opportunity to escape the isolation of her campus, where her activism had tended to support movements elsewhere. She became active in a couple of projects, including one in Chicago in which she worked mostly with poor women on issues such as daycare and welfare. Because of this community-organizing experience, Bernstein was recruited by the Company of Young Canadians and moved to Toronto, where she worked primarily with immigrants, especially those from Italy.[112]

Bernstein, who had attended only a handful of SUPA meetings, became part of the group writing the manifesto partly because of her friendship with Wood. She had been distressed upon hearing about the position of women in SUPA—it brought to mind problems she had experienced as a community organizer in the United States. While she had seen women suffer oppression and was frustrated by the lack of women in leadership positions, she did not have an analysis that would encompass her individual complaints. Recalling her earlier fieldwork in Chicago, Bernstein remembered: "We saw abuse, we saw beatings of women by the men . . . and we never went to that next step of seeing that as something that needed collective response."[113]

The essay penned collectively by these four women, "Sisters. Brothers, Lovers . . . Listen," marked a distinct stage in new left thinking. It is a remarkable document of its time, exploring for the first time most of the themes later developed within socialist feminism—revealing its "socialism" clearly if implicitly in its opening critique of liberalism. In the postwar consumerist miracle, it argued, a "bigger piece of the pie for women" was decidedly beside the point if the pie itself was rotten. The manifesto contained the standard new left threads—authenticity, egalitarianism, individuality, spontaneity, participatory democracy—but articulated them together in a way that radically transformed their meanings.[114]

The authors turned the rhetoric of participatory democracy against the gender politics of the new left itself, exposing the elitism and discrimination hidden behind its rhetoric. Women had cleaned, cooked, and undertaken boring jobs to sustain the creative and political work of their male activist partners. They patiently laboured to organize poor and minority communities while "a few stars" decided the agenda for their "many followers." Women, who had tacitly been promised equality and self-management, realized they had neither.[115] As Morton later recalled:

> We were people who just assumed we were in this movement that was about freedom and liberation and justice and rights, and that we were going to be treated with freedom and justice and rights. Then we found out that we weren't, that we were expected to do all the grunt work in the organization. All the leaders with big egos would do their thing, and we would make sure that everything got done and they would take all the glory. I don't think we were looking for glory, but we just wanted some recognition.[116]

Like Dean before them, the authors drew parallels with the status of Blacks and the civil rights movement in the United States to analyze the status of women and the emerging women's liberation movement. To explore how production, reproduction, sexuality, and child socialization had contributed to the oppression of women, they leaned heavily on the Marxist-feminist analysis of Juliet Mitchell, whose article "Women: The Longest Revolution" had recently been published in Britain's *New Left Review*. In new left style, the authors would not wait until after the revolution to seek their liberation. Twisting a Biblical phrase popular with Canadian and Québécois nationalists, they announced their decolonization in the manifesto's conclusion: "We are going to be the typers of letters and distributors of leaflets (hewers of wood and drawers of water) NO LONGER."[117]

The co-authors certainly knew their subject matter. SUPA's proposed 1967 manifesto, which had attempted to create a cohesive framework for the group, was probably typed by a woman, but the collective effort of writing it was a male-only affair. An earlier, hand-written, list of potential writers for that manifesto included no women amongst the many names suggested. As women cooked and cleaned communal SUPA–Kingston Community Project houses, men claimed that they were prefiguring future social relations in those very same houses. While male leaders dominated internal discussions, women saw their contributions to debates ignored. The organization had no mechanisms to deal with sexual harassment or philandering leaders.[118]

While those SUPA leaders had their laureates, and other young men obtained something of a rebel cachet, with stories drawing attention to their beards and longish hair, such flair was seldom ascribed to young women. Peter Gzowski's glowing article about SUPA, which appeared in *Maclean's* and was subsequently reprinted and distributed by the group, concluded: "Most of the girls are chubby. I have no idea why this should be so, but it is. Some of them are pretty—pretty but chubby—with firm chubby knees."[119]

Activists at the Goderich conference, aware of both their organization's bare existence and the urgency of the new ideas percolating within it, voted to disband their organization and erect a new one, the New Left Committee (NLC). Representatives of this committee, elected at Goderich, subsequently wrote a biting indictment of their predecessor. SUPA, they argued, had never gone beyond liberal protest and had never been a radical organization. A coherent analysis, they stated, was key to transcending the problems that SUPA had experienced. This ideology (socialism or Marxism) would lay bare the structural roots of issues (capitalism) so that members could finally develop a relevant and successful practice.[120]

NLC was "not" putting itself forward as some kind of vanguard, they emphasized. It would be but one organization amongst many in the Canadian left's broad "regroupment." (They were adapting a French term from the Québécois movement.) NLCers indicated that their priority would be organizing working-class youth, but they would also pursue other issues such as student power. With the committee's limited mandate, much of their work would be analytical, investigating the cultural, economic, political, and social facets of "monopoly capitalism," which, they hastened to add, included sex roles and the family.[121]

NLC—which tellingly referred to itself as a Toronto organization—never did call the national conference it was mandated to organize. Some members had envisioned a meeting of young independent socialists based on carefully chosen activists they already knew and people affiliated to a handful of groups they felt close to. But the new group quickly became almost irrelevant to those elected to guide it. An early 1968 article in the group's *New Left Committee Bulletin* announced that the members would henceforth devote their time to local projects.[122]

* * *

Clearly, by 1967—even, as Gzowski affirmed, as early as 1965—something new was happening among leftists in Toronto. What moved many of them were global issues: the struggles for peace, racial equality, the individual's search for meaning in a materialistic capitalist world. They were not as moved, yet, by local, provincial, or (for the most part) Canada-wide concerns. They were "new leftists" in an obvious sense—they were not easily pigeonholed in the positions or the parties of the 1930s to 1950s, and they responded to ideas and movements that were not in any clear sense tied to a particular party or tendency. Yet in many respects this was still an inchoate and diffuse set of dissenters. They had yet to construct a movement of movements unified and animated by common ideals.

In the international literature, 1968 looms large as the climactic "year of years" of the new left, the epitome of its politics of personal authenticity, self-determination, solidarity with national liberation movements, prefigurative politics, and community empowerment. In Toronto, though, 1968 is better seen as a year in which a new left, for which SUPA was but a first draft, started, often within well-established left movements and parties that a new cohort sought to change. For SUPA was unquestionably the first national attempt to apply the multiple ideals of the new left to the English-Canadian context. Although ultimately unsuccessful in uniting theory and practice, the SUPA experience left an indelible mark on the later praxis of the Canadian new left. Yet at this early stage new left thinking was certainly not the exclusive purview of SUPA members, as the prevailing tendencies of the time—the anti-war movement, the rise of student power and left-wing Canadian nationalism, and early moves towards a women's liberationist perspective—make clear. SUPA was also an organization that contained more "old left thinking" than its leaders were prepared to publicly admit.

In the end its inability to become a viable, lasting organization, even in Toronto, suggests the folly of identifying SUPA as *the* new left in Toronto, let alone Canada.[123] SUPA was a Toronto-based and Toronto-centric organization;

and its weakness in the city calls into question its oversized role in new left historiography. It is troubling that an organization that peaked in 1965 has served in large measure to represent the new left, a movement that substantively expanded in subsequent years. This tendency seriously distorts the appreciation of this activist decade. SUPA was at best, much like its CUCND predecessor, a prelude to a more substantial period of activism.

An anti-war demonstration heads down Yonge St.; May 29, 1970.

Clara Thomas Archives and Special Collections, Toronto Telegram fonds.

4

Out of the Meat Grinder: Confronting the Educational Leviathan, 1968–71

"THERE'S NOTHING to see here," said Principal Sydney Watson. "Reports of unrest are not only misleading and exaggerated but also damaging to the college and its graduates," said one of his supporters. It was the spring of 1968 and Minister of Education William Davis had just turned down a plea from students for his intervention in a dispute at the Ontario College of Art. Some of the students were no doubt recalling a remark that Watson had made in the past: "The student can't rebel or he isn't going to graduate."[1]

Yet residents curious enough to drop by the student-occupied campus cafeteria found a very different scene than the one depicted by the principal. The place was packed with students boycotting classes. Some were playing guitar, or cards, and others were debating the meaning of student power. Cheers went up when representatives from the George Brown College, Ryerson Polytechnic, U of T, and York student councils came along to promise their support—and when one of the college's professional models announced that she and others were going out on a sympathy strike. More cheers burst out when an instructor said she was joining nine of her peers in supporting the students.[2]

Even the most conservative of the city's newspapers admitted that a majority of the one thousand students at the college were boycotting classes. Students wanted a reduction in mandatory courses and, in general, more say in decision-making—a cause behind sit-ins the previous year—but emphasized a demand for the return of two fired instructors. Both of the teachers had been let go for disrespecting the principal amidst an alleged secret reorganization of the Fine Arts Department. The incident threw a spotlight on the lack of democracy at the college and

Although Humber College activists could boast of having a women's centre before any of the local universities, they lamented their relatively quiet campus.

Coven, March 24, 1972.

Humber College students are just entering 1958 when it comes to demanding their rights.

created an immediate rallying point. On day nine of the strike, the education minister reversed course and intervened to rehire the instructors. When Davis unexpectedly showed up at the victory party in the cafeteria, the crowd of 1,200 put their music and dancing on hold to give him a standing ovation.[3]

After the party, students hashed out new plans to democratize their classes. Their strike had won them unprecedented representation on the college's new governing board, and the administration promised to drastically reduce the number of mandatory classes. For a time it looked like they, along with the faculty, might share half of the board's seats. Although students ended up with only 15 to 20 per cent of the seats, their spring strike was an unambiguous victory, considering their relatively modest opening demands. Their triumph also extended outward. The principal of George Brown College blamed the strike for inspiring unrest at high schools and colleges across Metro Toronto, including a minor rebellion at his own institution. University officials expressed fear that the Wright report, commissioned by the provincial government as part of the strike settlement, would force all post-secondary institutions to hand over 50 per cent of their decision-making power to students and faculty.[4]

Reverberations from the victory also extended forward, as instructors became emboldened to fight for "faculty power" and the art college briefly adopted a radical free-school structure: classes were transformed into "probes" and instructors into "co-ordinators," individual departments were abolished, and the college's traditional course calendar was replaced by a deck of tarot cards. The revolution had truly arrived, or so it seemed.

* * *

The University of Toronto, English Canada's largest university, was in the throes of its own institutional upheaval, and its campus activists immediately began analyzing the Ontario College of Art insurgency. It was, after all, a classic example of how student power could develop. At first a core group of fifteen had done most of the organizing and speaking, focusing on three demands. After a few days, students began discussing wider issues, such as the role of education, and a broader circle of new and old activists took on speaking and organizing roles. That the protest had been started by "average" students, who formed their own committee and refused to heed objections from their student council, was believed to have been key to this radicalization. If U of T activists wanted to go from discussion to action, they too would have to work outside existing structures.[5]

Jerry Farber's pamphlet was a touchstone for white student activists of the 1960s.

Jerry Farber, *The Student as Nigger* (Madison: Connections, Undated).

That strategy was embraced by the campus's Toronto Student Movement (TSM), which formed later in 1968. TSM argued that if the radical minority on student council were to succeed, it would need an extra-electoral movement capable of providing a greater sense of continuity and pursuing a more ambitious radical agenda. TSM reflected the "new" new left thinking that emerged from SUPA's 1967 Goderich conference. It aimed to provide a venue for the construction of a socialist strategy that would avoid the pitfalls of both vanguardism and social democracy.[6]

Tactically, TSM tended towards theatrical confrontations, and a key coterie of its activists was fascinated with the "student as nigger" concept as advanced by American Jerry Farber to illustrate the subservient position of students. A short time before the formation of TSM, campus activist Ken Stone had told students, whilst tearing up his university diploma at convocation, "Fellow niggers, look what Mr. Charlie's done to your minds." That was the focused message that TSM activists deployed during the 1968–69 school year. New left activists greeted arriving students by doling out slices of watermelon alongside copies of Farber's article whilst a radical student council executive imitated the speech of Southern Blacks to emphasize the "student as nigger" argument. York University activists,

who also handed out slices of watermelon, teamed up with their U of T peers to distribute the tract at local high schools, two of which had amongst the largest population of Black students in the city. Today, gazing at a press photo showing student radicals with their massive "Welcome Back Niggers" banner in front of one of those schools, we would find it hard not to consider the approach insensitive, white-centric, or racist.[7]

An October episode of the CBC's *Public Eye*, taped at U of T, was devoted to debating the general applicability of the "Student as Nigger" theme with Farber himself, alongside campus activist Peter Warrian, defending the thesis. To Warrian, there was not an exact parallel between the conditions of Blacks and students, but the rubric remained a useful tool to highlight power relations within universities and society at large. U of T political science professor James Eayrs adamantly opposed the tract, evoking the spectre of George Orwell's *Animal Farm* to describe what the university would be like if students were to achieve the power they sought. In dismissing the activism of the era, Eayrs argued, "All the major battles have been won. The fundamental things have been conceded. We are living in the post-revolutionary era."[8]

As its warm reception of Farber suggested, TSM was committed to in-your-face confrontations with the educational authorities, a strategy that garnered considerable publicity. An early 1969 campus visit by Clark Kerr, who had been president of the University of California during the famous Berkeley free-speech

York University activists arrive at Bathurst Heights Collegiate, where their "Welcome back niggers" banner becomes a flashpoint for debate; Sept. 3, 1968.

Clara Thomas Archives and Special Collections, Toronto Telegram fonds.

fight of 1964, was occasion for a stormy TSM protest. In the middle of this formal lecture at the Royal Ontario Museum, around a hundred radicals surged towards the stage. Several TSM members hopped up, wrested the microphone from Kerr, and started chanting for Kerr to go back to the United States. That, more or less, was it. Nobody, including Kerr, was injured.[9]

Nonetheless, many media outlets implied that barbarians from restive American colleges had finally breached the gates of the Canadian academy. TSM hastened to explain its tactics. Kerr had played a key part in the evolution of the modern university. He exemplified a U.S. manager seeking to extend his influence to the Canadian campus. While the TSM members understood that some students were upset at the violence of their "gestures," they argued that their actions paled in comparison to the violent economic system represented by Kerr.[10]

TSM was the first activist group that Ulli Diemer had ever joined, and for a recent high-school graduate, it was quite an experience. Diemer's background was roughly typical of many university new leftists of the late 1960s. His mother was a secretary and his father a photographer. Some leftists may have considered them middle class, but they did not enjoy the kind of privilege often implied by that term in books about the activist 1960s. Intellectually, Diemer had decided in Grade 8 that he was an atheist. He probably read more than average in high school, where he dabbled in political philosophy and encountered his first new left periodicals. He was concerned about capital punishment, civil rights, and the

Students taking part in a demonstration against the American invasion of Vietnam; May 29, 1970.

Clara Thomas Archives and Special Collections, Toronto Telegram fonds.

Vietnam War. He was involved in student power fights, chiefly over censorship of the student paper, but did not have contact with activists beyond his high school. He was certainly a leftist in a general sense, but did not have a label or a strong sense of the left's ideological spectrum.[11]

The TSM meetings that Diemer attended every week or two were quite large, with fifty to sixty people. At first he mainly sat there without saying anything, trying to figure out exactly what was going on around him. Graduate students, along with fourth-year undergrads, tended to do most of the talking. The meetings clearly had their tensions, and he knew that groups of TSMers sometimes met separately in caucuses, but it took a while for him to figure out the political dimensions of what was going on. Amidst all of this, TSM planned actions around Vietnam and the university's new disciplinary policy. It also organized frequent study groups on topics ranging from health care to Marxism—with sessions held at the newly founded Rochdale College, an experimental high-rise "free university" and residence on the edge of the U of T campus. There were also discussions about women's liberation, which Diemer remembers as fascinating and "part of what was new."[12]

Over the summer of 1969 TSM split into two new groups, the New Left Caucus (NLC) and the Worker-Student Alliance (WSA). The new organizations were more noticeably ideological, but not sharply defined. While WSA was Leninist—inspired by such ideals as a vanguard party and the formation of disciplined, well-trained leaders—NLC was neither Leninist nor anti-Leninist. Strategically, the differences were clearer. NLCers were more interested in organizing students and youth and WSA was more focused on the traditional working class. NLC's structure was loose, and WSA's much tighter. NLCers tended to have long hair and identify with the counterculture, while WSAers tended to have short hair and to frown on drugs. Diemer remembers one WSA activist in particular who turned up at first with an almost classic hippie appearance; when he returned after the summer break he had short hair and dressed "straight." This was in accordance with WSA's belief that if you were going to organize workers, you had to look like one—or at least your stereotype of one.[13]

Diemer went to both NLC and WSA meetings for a while. He liked that NLC was anti-authoritarian and had a certain dynamism. He liked that WSA prioritized the working class (but not that they seemed to define that class as largely one of industrial workers). By fall 1969 Diemer had concluded that Marxism and Leninism were not compatible. Reading Daniel Cohn-Bendit's 1968 book *Obsolete Communism: The Left-Wing Alternative* had crystallized that for him. The book strongly influenced a lot of NLC members.[14]

York University, the epitome of university expansion in the era of Premier John Robarts, was also shaken by new left protests. The initiation of a mandatory social science class with an enrolment of 1,800 in the 1968–69 school year prompted a massive revolt, seemingly spontaneous, that entailed classroom disruptions, the advent of counter-courses, and ultimately the elimination of the offending course altogether. Other struggles were organized by the York Student Movement, which appeared similar to TSM in orientation. It made links between the top-down, elite-run, and supposedly objective education process at York and capitalist society. Members of the group maintained that the purpose of their interventions was to break down the one-way, passive learning experiences that had students listening to professors or outside experts.[15] They launched similar critiques of courses provided by leftists on the faculty. One professor who taught a course on alienation received a blistering attack for refusing to believe that alienation existed in his classroom. Although much of the professor's analysis was "right on," he allegedly rejected the idea that his class's coursework was work and considered complainers ungrateful. As one student remarked:

> So what I found out was that many radicals, or people who call themselves radicals, can't be judged radicals until you see what they do with their own lives, unless you see what they do when they have real power. Are they willing to relinquish their power? If they're not, then they're no different than anybody else.[16]

Judy Darcy, an activist in a York Women's Liberation group, had taken that same class and came to a similar conclusion about the role of young, "hip" left-leaning

Even left-wing history professors could find themselves under attack from radical students.

Eyeopener, "Day Before Valentine's Day," 1970.

professors: "Although the packaging is different (they wear the same bell-bottoms and beards that we do) the authority of the professor remains unchallenged."[17]

Although 350 students and several professors launched a protest over preferential faculty parking in late 1968, York's later radical proclivities were not yet much in evidence. A referendum vote took place that fall over whether companies supporting the U.S. war effort in Vietnam should be allowed to recruit on campus. It revealed that activists had a long way to go, as students voted overwhelmingly—1,126 to 295—to allow this recruitment to continue. York Students to End the War in Vietnam complained about the referendum's wording, and the distracting issue of free speech it had engendered, but the lopsided result appears to have been a rebuke of their efforts.[18]

Ryerson, a polytechnic college linked closely to the demands of industry, presented new leftists with a very different, less "academic" and "middle-class" venue. Aside from tuition and loan protests, Ryerson had been remarkably quiet in the mid-1960s, but that began to change in 1967 with the advent of student power. Campus activists regularly defended radical resolutions from the Canadian Union of Students and the Ontario Union of Students—motions that critics deemed too revolutionary—and raised the issue of the streaming of working-class students in high schools.[19]

In autumn 1968 radical student president David Maxwell launched a referendum in which students could vote in favour of a plan to democratize their campus. The scheme involved the elimination of bureaucracy, the replacement of both the board of governors and student council with direct-democracy mass meetings, and a free-school style of education. When the proposal was overwhelmingly defeated, Maxwell resigned. Yet the struggle had achieved something, as Ryerson joined the Ontario College of Art as one of the few post-secondary institutions in Canada to have student spots on its board of governors. Although self-proclaimed moderates bested new leftists in the first election for these positions, they were in turn replaced, in a following election, by new leftists, who saw in the administration's attempt to "turn the tide of student rebellion" a good illustration of the pitfalls of tokenism.[20]

While *The Ryersonian* as a student publication tended to be exceptionally parochial and conventional, complete with a cheesecake photo of a female student adorning each of its issues, activists mobilized to create their own publication, *The Eyeopener*, imbued by the atmosphere of the underground press. It was sufficiently feisty to irritate lecturer David Crombie (who would become mayor of Toronto in 1972). Crombie variously threatened to press the newspaper's advertisers to cancel their ads and/or to seize control of the paper. The newspaper published a large cartoon likening such authorities to classic British colonial administrators arrogantly declaring their subjects unfit for self-government.[21] The new left trope of national liberation had once again found a rather unlikely venue. It was a sign of growing radicalism at Ryerson, where in early 1970 the firing of five English professors prompted a massive outcry on the campus. Close to a thousand students attended a series of protest meetings that were broadcast live throughout the campus. Members of Students for Social Change, the Free Ryerson Movement, and the *Eyeopener* staff all entered the fray. After one meeting, 150 students embarked on a sit-in outside the president's office.[22]

All three of the largest post-secondary institutions in Toronto were, then, to varying degrees influenced by new left activists, whose protests were markedly more militant and confrontational than were those of previous years. Most participants had a holistic approach to social change, but the most visible forms of activism on campuses were struggles for student power.

* * *

The new left was sufficiently powerful that some contemporaries identified it as a fount of violence and disorder. In wake of the Ontario College of Art victory, the chair of the institution's governing board charged that "communist" and "fascist" strike organizers had used violent intimidation to force student involvement: "I've never seen such a scared bunch of kids in my life." Referring to a "rising tide of student violence" at York, lecturer John Ridpath called for the expulsion of misbehaving students from his campus before it was too late. "It is certainly disheartening, if not chilling," he argued, "to contemplate that force and violence, so typical of the pre-civilized barbarian, are re-appearing in the very institution that man looks to for reasoned guidance."[23]

Such baseless charges of violence proliferated because of a very liberal definition of the term. Claude Bissell, the president of U of T and a prime target of much new left critique, defined violence as negotiation "by threat and not by persuasion," a capacious description that encompassed many of the period's radical protests. Other authorities appeared to take Bissell's definition as their own, making it possible for sit-ins to be variously described as "inevitably" leading to violence, a form of "implied violence," or even intrinsically violent. Bissell was himself accused of supporting violence by refusing to call in the police to end campus sit-ins.[24]

Academic opponents of the new left were echoing a growing chorus on the far right. The Edmund Burke Society, a local neo-fascist organization, began emphasizing the theme of student activist violence in 1967 after its members failed to block an anti-war march but succeeded in provoking some scuffles. Linked to assaults on members of the American Nazi Party at a U.S. anti-war demonstration, the incident was used to depict anti-war activism as monolithically menacing. The *Toronto Telegram* rejoiced in publicizing such incidents as an exposure of the peace movement's violent nature. An editorial cartoon typical of that genre depicts a protester returning home, her clothing and picket sign torn and arm broken, as her father asks, "Another peace march?" Alarmist statements, like those of renowned McGill University professor John Humphrey—who claimed that student activists were threatening the very existence of Canada—were reliably seized on and amplified by such right-wing pundits. That single comment of

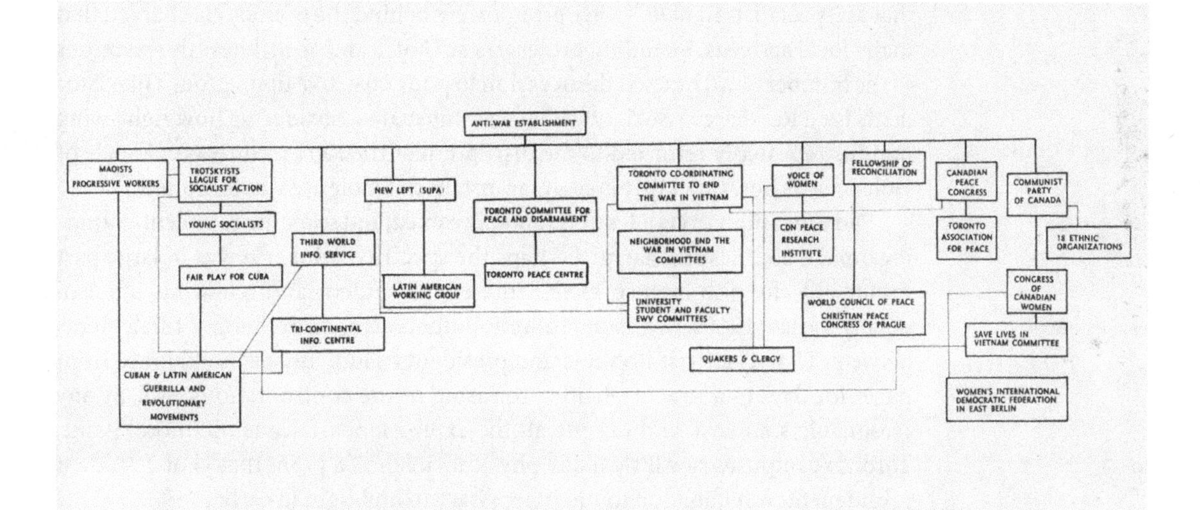

Peter Worthington worked hard to "expose" the connections between local anti-war groups; circa January 1968.

Peter Worthington fonds, Library and Archives Canada.

Humphrey's was used by *Telegram* columnists, editors, and even a cartoonist—who depicted students throwing bricks and bottles—as fodder for their campaign for a crackdown on allegedly violent student activists.[25]

Toronto's only substantive instance of activist violence in this period occurred on Sept. 24, 1968, when the homes of thirteen executives of Hawker Siddeley, a military manufacturer, were bombed within a few hours of each other. Attached to acid-based timing devices, which jettisoned their payloads through living-room windows, the bombs generally resulted in minor fire damage. Leaflets mailed to each executive's home read: "You have been judged guilty of active complicity in America's war against the Vietnamese people. Until you desist, it is our avowed program to carry the war back to you."[26]

In the aftermath police called up their reserves for what was said to be the largest investigation in the force's history. The Toronto force announced to the press that it was scrutinizing pictures taken at anti-war meetings and visiting the homes of anti-war activists. Although a police inspector claimed to know which anti-war groups had been responsible for the bombing, no one was ever charged. The city's major peace groups, for their part, went on record in opposition to the bombings and released a statement of condemnation to the press: "The acts of individual terrorism obscure the peaceful ends of our movements and achieve nothing."[27]

While no existing evidence linked campus radicals to the bombing campaign, it had become obvious that establishing such a link promised ample political payoffs—and that the new left's opponents were finding it important to make the connection. The *Telegram*'s Peter Worthington quickly entered the fray, writing that as "specialists in hate," peace groups were behind the bombs. He charged that many local activists, including professors at U of T and York, knew the identities of the bombers, and he used the occasion to pour invective upon groups like "Students for a Red Fascist Society." What was unusual—considering how right-wing pundits repeatedly returned to the disruption of the Kerr lecture as evidence of violence—is how quickly this singular instance of violence was forgotten.[28]

Did the campus new left's undoubtedly robust, and sometimes violent-sounding, image do it lasting harm? Perhaps the spectre of violence was in large part responsible for the intense media interest in student and left-wing activism during the late 1960s. Even something as innocuous as an exchange of statements between U of T activist Bob Rae and president Claude Bissell could grace front pages for days in a row, implicitly promising future confrontations. Still, by any reasonable standard, and despite all the expressions of academic moral panic, Toronto campuses saw little if any physical violence, a point that U of T student president Steven Langdon found it necessary to highlight in early 1969.

Certainly, Toronto schools saw nothing close to the February 1969 "Sir George Williams Affair" in Montreal, where a peaceful computer lab sit-in—around issues of racism in the teaching faculty—erupted into a full-scale "riot," or so it was called. The event was notable for computers and punch cards being tossed out of the high-rise university building onto the street, a fire breaking out, and the destruction of school records. The protest was peaceful until the police arrived, "dressed in riot gear," and broke into the centre. It was, David Austin writes, "not just the largest student occupation in Canadian history, but internationally the most destructive (to property) act of civil disobedience on a university campus." Although Toronto's experiences proved less volatile, there is no evidence that the mass of students, shocked by violence at other Canadian institutions, promptly lost their interest in protest. Following the Sir George Williams event, which generally serves as the primary evidence of campus violence, Toronto had an anti-war demonstration of 10,000, roughly double the attendance of past marches.[29]

Linked to the spurious critique of the campus new left as violent was the suggestion that it was inherently authoritarian. Denunciations of the new left along such lines by NDP-affiliated *Telegram* columnists Harry Crowe and Douglas Fisher became increasingly hysterical as the 1968–69 school year went on. In the fall they argued that the new left was a new barbarism rather than a new form of radicalism, and pleaded with university administrations to avoid playing into the new left's "game" with heavy-handed tactics. By springtime the student radicals had become fascists and universities were being urged to avoid "appeasement" and to immediately call in the police to deal with campus disruptions. Although not utilizing the term "liberal death wish," which had become increasingly popular amongst people on the political right, Crowe and Fisher adopted the essence of the phrase when decrying capitulation to new leftists. They attacked influential NDPer David Lewis for having blessed direct action "of the most outrageous kind" and denounced U of T professors who criticized corporate interests on university boards as "intimidated" and "stupid."[30]

Crowe and Fisher had never been on "the left" of either the CCF or NDP, but alarm at new left tactics was in evidence there as well. An apt example of conservative backlash from those quarters came from historian Kenneth McNaught. The son of rich and intellectually minded parents, McNaught had joined the CCF in the 1930s while attending Upper Canada College and later became president of the party's club at the University of Toronto. As many of his CCF and former LSR colleagues retreated towards liberalism with the advent of the Cold War, he held steadfast to his social-democratic beliefs. Within academia, McNaught was willing to take risks—he resigned from his first teaching position to protest the unjust firing of historian Harry Crowe—and did not shirk from being identified with the CCF, as his 1959 book, *A Prophet in Politics: A Biography of J. S. Woodsworth*, attests. Objectivity, he believed, was an illusory device used by historians defending the status quo.[31]

The early 1960s found him closely tied to U.S. publications *Labor History* and *Studies on the Left*, serving on the advisory board of the Student Christian Movement, and briefly joining Fair Play for Cuba. As the CCF was in the midst of transforming itself into the NDP, McNaught passionately fought for it to renounce NATO and NORAD and retain the old party's emphasis on public ownership, arguing that its socialist principles were being abandoned in favour of a "domesticated J.K. Galbraith progressivism." At mid-decade, McNaught was involved in a flurry of anti-war activities that included helping draft dodgers, taking part in demonstrations, and participating in the Faculty Committee on Vietnam. Coming from a rare exponent of left-wing history, his lectures became very popular.[32]

But as the student movement expanded and set its sights on winning "student power," McNaught became increasingly uneasy. By early 1967 he was calling proposals for student participation in university governance "dangerous," a term he would later attach to the new left itself. Its disdain for structures, rules, and leadership, as well as its "American" ideology, could only create violence and irresponsibility, and in turn lead to anarchy or authoritarianism. To oppose the new left was to acknowledge "the danger of losing liberal-constitutional values in one grand, amorphous assault upon 'the establishment.'"[33]

While labour activist Ed Finn had condemned intemperate attacks on new leftists only the year before, he viewed the Sir George Williams "riot," and the failure of student activists to condemn it, as a crossing of the Rubicon. Unionists, he stated, no longer saw any difference between the "old right" and the anarchic and nihilist new left, whose "combination of political extremism, long hair, unconventional attire, sexual promiscuity and drug addiction disgusts even the most broad minded." Even the term new left was a misnomer, he now argued, because its "far right" tactics could only create a society along the lines of Hitler's Germany or Mussolini's Italy.[34]

In the wake of the Sir George events, the left-wing magazine *Canadian Dimension*—to which Finn was a regular contributor—struck a similar chord by printing a series of articles written by academics defending the university administration and attacking the new left. One professor argued that the new left had proven itself to be unreasonable, pseudo-fascist, racist, and authoritarian, and that it now had to be defeated at any cost. Its proclaimed anti-elitism was only a thinly veiled philistinism, he said, a symptom of the increasing number of university students coming from uncultured homes. Another professor informed readers that he was similarly re-evaluating his past support for new left actions. He used the presence of Black foreign students and their allegedly American or American-educated supporters to testify to the "non-Canadian character" of the "riot." Philip Resnick countered that such hostility was reflective of many Marxists who were employed at universities. These professors maintained a certain theoretical socialism, but had given up applying their Marxist politics for the promise of employment. With the rising strength of the new left, these professors aligned with liberals to protect their personal interests, and thus their campuses, from demands for radical change.[35]

* * *

New leftists' critique of an alienating educational system designed to meet the needs of a dehumanized and mechanized society obviously struck a chord with thousands of university students. Yet the most surprising evidence of an unheralded success in Toronto from 1968 to 1971 appeared lower down the educational echelon: in the public-school system.

The beginning of the 1968–69 semester marked an increase in collective action by local high-school students, frequently around the lifestyle-related axis of hair, dress, and smoking. Notable demonstrations included a protest by 250 Scarborough students who left classes to demand a smoking lounge, and a three-day walkout by Castle Frank technical school students protesting hair and dress regulations. An escalating series of demonstrations struck Danforth Collegiate and Technical School, where a dozen students were suspended for the length of their hair and skirts. A hundred students were later suspended for leaving class to protest that decision, prompting yet another walkout. Students opposed to the protesters shouted "dirty hippies" and "cut your hair" from the windows.[36]

Systemic critiques of education percolated within many lifestyle protests of the late summer and early fall. November valedictorian speeches carried echoes of the more far-reaching sentiments of university activists. In her speech at Downsview Secondary School, Judy Feldman attacked not only the injustices of discipline, but also the status quo in general. Mimico High School's Harold Coldwell refused to give any address at all when told to jettison the one he had planned in favour of a talk lauding happy memories. His banned speech traced the links between education and mass production and urged students to join the minority of people striving for social change.[37]

High-school students protest a plan to lengthen the school year; Dec. 18, 1968.

Clara Thomas Archives and Special Collections, Toronto Telegram fonds.

In early fall the general secretary of the Ontario Secondary School Teachers' Federation (OSSTF) announced that his union had "become alarmed with respect to student power and outside influences affecting our students." A conservative board trustee more specifically placed the blame for unrest on the organizers of the Ontario Union of Students; he threatened to charge them with inciting juvenile delinquency. There was some truth to these allegations. The student union had initiated the High School Union of Students earlier that year, and one of its organizers had been spotted during the disturbances at Castle Frank. The High School Union of Students demanded student power and attacked the regimentation of high-school life, including everything from the now long-standing issues of hair and dress to students having to walk silently in single file between classes.[38]

An OSSTF ad paralleled the moral panic gripping conservative academics. Purporting to represent principal and union opinion, it called for discipline and lashed out at wayward students, trustees, parents, and "outside pressure groups." Fearing the prospect of boards caving in to student demands, principals underscored their role as the sole guardians of discipline and the only hope for returning the schools to normalcy. Although some trustees had called for more democracy in schools and less concern for hair and dress, a meeting of the Toronto board readily backed the principals, prompting students in attendance to denounce it as a farce. Scarborough principals played a similar restraining role, successfully pressuring their board to reverse a plan to abolish the strap from kindergarten to Grade 6. Yet even as the ad helped principals marshal short-term support, it made them a target for the burgeoning education reform movement. North York trustee Val Scott flatly said principals had no business regulating hair and skirt

The controversial issue of Forest Hill's radical student paper.

This Magazine Is About Schools, Autumn 1969.

length. At a meeting to discuss the OSSTF ad, a majority of rank-and-file teachers expressed their disagreement with both principals and their union. Desmond Dixon, a teacher who became a union employee after being fired for supporting student activists, suggested that the position of principal be abolished and replaced by a three-person administrative committee elected by teachers.[39]

A December announcement—that the provincial government was considering extending the school year—predictably fanned the flames of unrest. It led to scattered walkouts, most notably by 1,000 students at George Harvey Secondary School. Some 1,500 students, many from Etobicoke, descended on Queen's Park and city hall, where they threw peanuts and apples while shouting at Mayor William Dennison. That some of the protest organizers had ties to organized labour and groups such as High School Students Against the War in Vietnam and the New Democratic Youth is hardly surprising. Yet the wide organic appeal of such protests suggests that they were not simply the work of a handful of experienced activists. Within a couple of months, during a province-wide boycott of classes in opposition to the school-year extension, some of the largest mobilizations—like the majority of Owen Sound students who left class or the 95 per cent of Brantford Secondary students who walked out—were in cities largely untouched by contemporary social movement activity.[40]

The most notorious high-school protest of the period took place in one of the wealthiest neighbourhoods of the city, at Forest Hill Collegiate. At that school in late spring 1969 the administration handed out a series of suspensions to three members of a Maoist-influenced club called the Student Guard. All three students had previously tussled with school authorities over a series of issues, from the undemocratic nature of the education system to the revocation of their club's official status. The immediate trigger for the suspensions was a mimeographed newsletter published by the club. It depicted the school's principal as a "paper tiger" (a Maoist-associated reference to opponents who appear strong but can be readily toppled). Instead of staying at home, the students began organizing sit-ins in the school's lobby and picket lines out front. Students from other schools flocked to Forest Hill to show their support—along with some union members who had met up with the Student Guard on factory picket lines. A who's who list of radical post-secondary groups endorsed a set of demands: for the club to exist without a staff sponsor, the right to organize and publish, and an amnesty for past actions.[41]

For the *Toronto Telegram*, the small rebellion at Forest Hill Collegiate was proof that student activism was out of control. Articles emphasized that the school was far too liberal, a place that allowed boys to grow their hair long and girls to wear jeans during winter months. U.S. exchange students at the school told the paper that the schools they came from were like jails in comparison. The newspaper delved into the family background of one Guard member to suggest that only a communist-tainted student could have a problem with such a school.[42]

In the end, it was the vaunted liberalism of the school that denied the Guard a building block for a possible "workers' and students' state." In stark contrast to the clumsy authoritarianism of most high-school administrations, the school authorities tasked a student-staff committee with finding a solution to the dispute, which would then be voted on by a general assembly of staff and students. The joint committee adopted most of the Students Guard's demands, with the proviso that freedom of expression could be curtailed by a vote of the student body. The "bill of rights," adopted by a general assembly, included sweeping provisions for freedom of expression and gave assemblies the power to suspend students and teachers (although the rule in effect could apply only to students). The suspensions of Student Guard members would be lifted if they agreed to abide by the school's new regulations. Eventually, they agreed.[43]

The circumstances of the Forest Hill protests were atypical: the school was in a high-income area; only a tiny percentage of students at the school participated; the activists all had strong ties to left-wing campus groups; the participants favoured the theatrical far-left style popular at U of T over the lower level of politics typical of other collective high-school actions; and media coverage greatly exceeded that accorded any other high-school protest of the 1960s and 1970s. The principal's use of student opinion to curtail the teenage rebels was also unique. That the technique of using student assemblies for this purpose was repeated elsewhere suggests that the school's head was a particularly wily "paper tiger."

The following month, the principal of Sir John A. Macdonald Collegiate Insitute called an assembly to rebuke the school's student president, who had criticized dress codes and called his school a "hole." Students stood up and disagreed with their president's statements, successfully pressuring him to resign. As the student president himself said, questions like "Is there a better collegiate in all Ontario than Sir John A?" received the answers expected by the principal. But here, as with other schools, there were some supportive teachers, two of whom publicly disagreed with the principal's tactics. They called the assembly "a heavily manipulated move" and a "hysterical orgy."[44]

That summer, thirty Ontario high-school leaders were sent to a leadership seminar at Queen's University to learn how to counter student unrest, and a meeting of principals announced that they would refuse to cave in to further student demands. Their resolve would be tested during the 1969–70 school year, as students began campaigning for school boards to curtail "principal power." Initial efforts to force principals to allow school assemblies to discuss the Vietnam War were stymied by board intransigence. The North York board ignored written requests, adjourned their meetings when students tried to address them, and called in the police. But student persistence paid off when the board finally agreed to urge principals to allow assemblies about the war and to incorporate gatherings to discuss and debate current issues, such as pollution and the Middle East, into the regular school program. Although these changes appeared to be a huge gain for those wanting to inject political issues into their schools, activists considered them meaningless because the calling of assemblies remained the prerogative of principals.[45]

One of those activists was Barry Greenwood, a member of the League for Student Democracy (LSD). Formed by a handful of Sir Sandford Fleming Academy students in fall 1969, it now claimed 270 local members. LSD president Barry Weisleder explained the group's basis of unity: "We want out of the meatgrinder of marks and grades. . . . We feel the educational process should be unstructured so that individual needs can be met." LSD's newspaper, *Third Eye*, was printed at Rochdale College with help from U of T's student council and financial assistance from the New Democratic Youth. It was one of many high-school underground newspapers circulating in the city. Radicals gravitated to those newspapers because principals and staff advisers were known to censor "aboveground" student newspapers—in violation, some leftist students believed, of their basic human rights. Even jibes at hippies and dissent were going a step too far for the principal of Lawrence Park Collegiate, causing newspaper club member Shirley Hong to lament: "So bring back the pictures of cheerleaders and football players, they don't threaten the system." But principals were prickly about criticism, and the long arm of high-school administrators sometimes reached the underground newspapers. The president and vice-president of the Royal York Collegiate student council were permanently banned from their school after their newspaper *Underwear* criticized and graded teachers. But discipline across the system was arbitrary. The producers of the North Toronto Collegiate Institute's *Montgomery Tavern Revival* newspaper, which reviewed the quality and prices of drugs, seemingly persisted without persecution.[46]

During the 1970–71 school year the prevailing struggles were against budget cuts. In light of a possible teachers' strike, several student councils voted to call for a student strike against recently imposed budget ceilings and to pressure the

These students from Monarch Park Collegiate, protesting cafeteria prices, are likely heading to another high school to drum up more support; May 7, 1971.

Clara Thomas Archives and Special Collections, Toronto Telegram fonds.

school boards, government, and teachers to resolve their issues. When teachers and the government appeared to reach a settlement, the councils decided to focus their protests on a new 50 per cent hike in cafeteria prices. Earlier cafeteria protests had been local struggles—such as the one at Birchmount Park Collegiate, where the entire student body had boycotted the cafeteria and won concessions on service and food quality—but those in May 1971 were often jointly co-ordinated by activists from different schools. When students protested with their wallets, the board responded by laying off fifty-seven cafeteria workers and shuttering some facilities entirely.[47]

When these high-school students marched, the journey was truly no less important than the destination. They tended to travel school-to-school trying to augment their numbers, leading to a host of confrontations. During the May marches, a number of schools locked their doors to keep students from leaving; fire alarms went off at some schools, and were deactivated in others; activists shouted "walk out, walk out!"; traffic was stopped; windows were broken. The ad hoc Toronto Secondary School Strike Committee, composed of representatives from five schools, decided to escalate matters by calling a general walkout for May 18. No fewer than two thousand protesters from a dozen schools, half of them vocational, converged on Queen's Park. They chanted "We want Davis!"—referring to the high-profile education minister and now premier, Bill Davis. Complaining about budget ceilings, but above all about the 50 per cent hike in cafeteria lunch prices, some students entered the legislature, where they created

These high-school students climbed a lamppost at Queen's Park to get a better view of their demonstration against cutbacks.

Clara Thomas Archives and Special Collections, Toronto Telegram fonds.

a disturbance before being chased out by police.[48]

Far from being a middle-class movement mounted by privileged university students whose activism was confined to their own "corporatist" demands, new left student radicalism had by 1971 expanded far beyond its initial confines to encompass a much more diverse population. Indeed, a significant characteristic of this wave of high-school unrest was that it involved at least as many working-class as middle-class schools. Although the wave was nearing its crest, the most explosive year of high-school activism still lay ahead.

* * *

"Where O where is Hall-Dennis?" asked LSD's *Third Eye* in early 1970. Students should be dancing in the streets, singing "Ontari-ari-ario." They should be celebrating their liberation and praising the "great white gods" of liberal educational reform. But instead, they were writing exams. Where was Hall-Dennis? Certainly, truant from the classroom.[49]

Lloyd Dennis and Emmett Hall were the authors of *Living and Learning: The Report of the Provincial Committee on Aims and Objectives of Education in the Schools of Ontario*, which had been commissioned by Education Minister Davis and published in 1968. Its abundant photos and graphic style, including pop art and psychedelia, immediately distinguished it from other government reports. But it was the report's substance that was really far out. Like many student activists, it recommended getting rid of authoritarian principals, anachronistic structures, rote memorization, and traditional exams. On the surface, it looked like the report was a victory for new left parents, students, and teachers who had been fighting to change the education system from the outside.[50]

In the mid-1960s a small, but important, circle of activists had begun experimenting with what a truly free and social-justice-oriented education might look like. They were strongly influenced by A.S. Neill, who in the 1920s had opened the Summerhill school in England. Summerhill had tried to free children not only from the structures of compulsory education, but also from traditional family hierarchies, sexual Puritanism, and sexism. Neill was from a prior generation of the left, but, like his close friend, the Austrian psychoanalyst and Marxist theorist Wilhelm Reich, was atypically interested in the psychological and cultural sources of oppression.[51]

The activists' first free-school experiment, Everdale Place, was founded in 1966. Although the school was located on a former farm about 80 kilometres outside the city, most of its students and teachers were from Toronto. Everdale had no grades or exams, unless a student requested them for university applications, and its curriculum encouraged intellectual inquiry, play, and relationship building. After the initial financial planning, admission of students, and hiring of teachers was complete, decision-making devolved to everyone. While Everdale catered to the children of well-off professionals, Point Blank School, which opened in Toronto's low-income Cabbagetown neighbourhood in 1967, offered a free-school environment to teenage dropouts. Much of the new left impetus for these schools could be found in *This Magazine Is About Schools*, a seminal source of alternative approaches to education from its first issue in 1966.[52]

But there were high barriers to a free-school education. As small islands of freedom, they offered only very few students the opportunity to enrol. Point Blank relied on volunteer labour, and later small grants, while Everdale depended on a poorly paid workforce and tuition fees beyond the means of low- and middle-income families. High-school activists would have been envious had they known of Everdale's field trip to the United States, where students attended demonstrations and a trial of anti-war activists. But they may have had trouble identifying with the oppression that some students complained of when their request to extend the week-long trip was undemocratically denied. Would Hall-Dennis turn a small island of privilege into a sea of freedom?[53]

The short answer is no. The sweeping reform vision of the Hall-Dennis report was never implemented, which was something high-school activists began complaining about within a year of the report's release. One activist conceded that around 100 of the 240 recommendations may have been adopted, but plausibly claimed no more than a handful were in effect at a given school.[54] Hall-Dennis expert Josh Cole observes that a major function of the radical-sounding report was to re-assert the legitimacy of a beleaguered educational establishment:

> Hall-Dennis almost outdid *This Magazine Is About Schools* in denouncing the hierarchies, rigidities and even cruelties of Ontario schools—all the while concluding that the system was progressing and its leadership in good hands. To pre-empt the radicals, Hall-Dennis to a considerable degree began to speak their language and even toy with certain of their ideas.... Yet throughout Hall-Dennis there was no serious intention of turning the Ontario system into a network of free schools, suffused with a democratic spirit.[55]

Still, the report may have helped to legitimize the demands of free-schoolers, and local school boards showed a new willingness to endorse part-time or after-hours free schools. Just before the report's release, a group of parents and education activists created the board-sanctioned Summer of Experience, Exploration and Discovery. The parents were anxious for their children to stay out of trouble during the summer. Young people enrolling in the program demanded courses to satisfy a wide array of interests, from watch-making to "Economics as It Affects the Social Order." After the program closed at the end of summer, students kept in touch and organized a "First Inter-Galactic Synergy" conference. A baffled trustee complained that they "look like acid people, like they are way out on Cloud 9." Another trustee was baffled at their lack of hierarchy. There was no president or secretary, he fumed, just a young woman who signed letters "Peace, Diana Smith."[56]

"Won't wait for Hall-Dennis," was an apt tagline for the many free schools that continued to be founded in 1968–69. Superschool, where parents, students, and teachers had to reach consensus before anything was taught, was probably the largest. It grew from a single old house in September 1969 to encompass four buildings two years later. Like Everdale, it charged tuition, yet still had far more applicants than it could handle. Another effort, Laneway School, was not a free school. Its founders, a group of low-income working-class mothers, were concerned that their children were not doing well in mainstream schools and thought ungraded schools had the potential to make things worse. Having failed to get support from the School Board—and knowing that its class-based system of streaming would limit their children's potential for upward mobility—the mothers founded their own school in a local community centre.[57]

* * *

In March 1969 the firing of school teacher Fiona Nelson proved a cause célèbre for educational reform. Nelson had been fired for the crime of criticizing the Toronto School Board. This was a rare course of action for the board to take, and the evidence against her being three years old added to the mystery. A trustee tried to further muddy the waters by hinting that Nelson was the perpetrator of unspeakable moral crimes. No evidence was offered for that. Students from her elementary school organized a protest, members of OSSTF's Toronto council voted unanimously to back her, and she received support from other quarters as well. Facing what was most likely unprecedented pressure, the board retreated and apologized. Nelson nonetheless quit her position. She would soon return—as head of the School Board.[58]

Unhappiness with "authoritarianism" in Toronto schools led to the formation of the Citizens' Committee for Change in Schools in late 1969. The committee adopted an ambitious thirteen-point program: ungraded open schools, promotion by subject, elimination of Grade 13, parent-teacher dialogue, citizen-school committees, participation of staff and students in forming school policy, participation by students in shaping curriculum, free student council elections, uncensored school newspapers, unlimited right to form political and social clubs and invite outside speakers, right of teachers to design their own courses, more free periods for lesson preparation, and a leave of absence for teachers to run for any political office.[59]

Despite its bold demands, the program was not an idle wish list. It was the basis for an electoral campaign to transform public education in Toronto. The Citizens' Committee interviewed just over sixty potential trustee candidates, settling on eighteen names. But the new slate was not necessarily radical. Candidates did not have to agree with the entire program to receive the committee's backing, and some of those endorsed by the Committee ran under labels connected to the Liberal Party. Some eleven of the Committee's candidates, all under the age of forty, won election that year, leaving only eight, much older, incumbents. Some of the new trustees, such as Gordon Cressy—who reported that two hundred young people had helped out with his campaign—credited youth supporters for their success. The election was clearly a loss for the principals, who had made themselves lightning rods for both students and teachers seeking reform. The new board quickly moved to prevent principals from interfering in hair styles, a significant cause of high-school unrest that semester. A journalist summed up the new board's positions: "Among the Good are student power, citizen participation, change, open meetings, and activism; the Bad includes parking lots, school principals, authority, and politicians."[60]

The new trustees ordered a battery of experimental programs and a number of studies. One report substantiated the charges of the working-class Trefann Court mothers and left-wing trustees that a link existed between poverty and academic performance. Trustee David Sanoff wanted an investigative report on the feasibility of busing students between rich and poor areas, but could not garner enough support. Such ideas did not enamour conservative trustee Mahlon Beach, who insisted that sex education was a communist plot and saw the termination of regular prayers at board meetings as "an additional step to the takeover of our country by communism."[61]

If the new trustees included some people interested in soothing the conflicts that had simmered in Toronto high schools, others were made of sterner stuff. Ernest Barr and Val Scott were two trustees not satisfied with anything short of the dismantling of the school system. Both were pre-boomers who embraced the radical politics and counterculture of the time. They were particularly influenced by the current of ideas sweeping up many who thought deeply about education in a mass society. They dreamt, not of a society served by more efficient schools, but of one that had been "de-schooled."

Barr was a one-term trustee with the Toronto board and the only Committee-endorsed candidate to be excluded from entering the reform caucus struck shortly after the election. Once a member of the Liberal Party, Barr had come to reject all parties and sought "a classless society, composed of freely-cooperating non-alienated people." Inspired most by radical psychologist Erich Fromm, Barr saw personal change as a prerequisite for societal transformation. He urged others to follow the path he had taken, which included self-psychoanalysis, free association exercises, and communal living. As a board member, he argued strenuously for steps leading to de-institutionalization and de-professionalization. His was an abstract new leftism transposed into the practical politics of a working school board.[62]

He was soon embittered by the refusal of other trustees to support his plans, particularly one to have Toronto teachers trained by disciples of Fromm. To Barr, both the permissive and authoritarian models of schooling advocated by other trustees were equally alienating. People were "not being asked whether or not they want a big, expensive, compulsory, bureaucratic, monopolistic school system. They are being asked what kind of big, expensive, compulsory, bureaucratic, monopolistic school system they want." This non-choice ensured that schools would continue to "hollow-out" people and fill the emptiness with alien feelings, beliefs, and values.[63]

Like Barr, Val Scott acknowledged that a new consciousness was a prerequisite for change, but he did not share his colleague's emphasis on transforming individual consciousness. He brought with him a panoply of new left influences—Paul Goodman, *This Magazine Is About Schools*, *Guerilla*, *Third Eye*, and *Community Schools*—all of which were central to the radical left's reading of education. Scott found schooling and the "Educational Establishment" to be fundamentally unreformable. Yet, until 1973 an ardent and powerful member of the New Democratic Party, he was still concerned with combating class and anti-immigrant bias in the prevailing system and highlighted the role of the "hidden curriculum" in normalizing these and other prejudices. Such were familiar benchmarks and attitudes of a host of new leftists interested in education in the late 1960s and early 1970s. Not many of them were, like Scott, occupiers of important positions in the educational power structure—in his case, vice-chair of the North York Board of Education.[64]

* * *

The election of the new trustees had clearly boosted free-school supporters. The Summer of Experience, Exploration and Discovery group, which had riled some trustees on the previous board, worked with the new trustees to form a publicly funded free school called SEED in 1970. The Toronto board created a Sub-Committee on Alternatives in Education as an ongoing body to facilitate the creation of other new schools. One reporter quipped that all it took to start a public school in the early 1970s was "a duplicating machine, several people who know what they want, and a delegation to a board subcommittee." The city's second public free school, known as ALPHA (short for A Lot of People Hoping for an Alternative) was approved the following year.[65]

But by 1971 education radicals, both on and off the board, had grown distinctly less enthusiastic for free schools. A minor reason for this reassessment was that the conservative Parent Action League and the Committee Against Moral Pollution in the Schools had petitioned for a school of their own based on Christian values. Although the board turned them down, a free-school activist recalled:

> They presented a proposal for a parent-run, extremely right-wing program, under the same logic of course that we were going for, that parents had a right to define the educational possibilities for their children. There was some pause about what we were doing and what that potentially was opening up.[66]

A larger reason was increasing skepticism over the usefulness of free schools. As George Martell, *This Magazine*'s co-editor and for half a century a stalwart of educational new leftism in Toronto, saw it, "Free schools taught us that they don't work." Or, as another activist put it, "Free schools end up complementing the schools rather than undercutting them." Free schools, or even alternative schools generally, were increasingly seen as "safety valves." New leftists were wasting their energy on these islands of freedom while the educational leviathan sailed on without them. Activists who wanted to confront the "psycho-social underpinnings of oppression" needed a broader strategy.[67]

But the main reason, which surfaced prior to locally published critiques of free schools, was an embrace of the community-school concept. *This Magazine Is About Schools* revealed an early indication of this change in the form of a new analytic line that increasingly looked to a revolutionary overhaul of the existing school system. While it had formerly doted on free schools, from the end of the 1960s to the mid-1970s it focused more on community schools and on developing both a local and national analysis. The new locally produced magazine *Community Schools* took up similar positions.

Rather than opting out with free schools, these education activists urged people to stay within the public-school system and work there for broader change. They wanted community schools to be jointly controlled by teachers, students, parents, and local residents. While some education activists may have seen this as an isolated struggle, virtually all of the voices presented in the magazine did not. "As educational radicals," declared Martell, "if we are not practicing socialists, we shall be failures." He considered the NDP too capitalist and the Marxist and new left groups too campus-focused, tiny, fragmented, and arrogant. He called on the new left to "go into cities and towns where most of us come from and organize block by block, neighbourhood by neighbourhood, ward by ward, riding by riding. In the process we must build a political party, but unlike the socialist parties of the past it must develop a very high degree of local control." In 1971 the editors of *This Magazine* expressed hope that they would be able to link their publication with the wider community-control movement.[68]

The new left's opponents were certainly cognizant of the new community emphasis. The executive secretary of the Ontario Teachers' Federation warned of unnamed civic groups circulating claims that inner-city children received inferior education, believing that "ethnic parents" were particularly vulnerable to such falsehoods. The past president of the Toronto Teachers' Federation was a little more specific, warning that some of the new trustees were out to wreck the school system. Ronald Jones, the board's director, spoke of unnamed left-wingers who wanted to destroy not only the education bureaucracy, but the board itself. Jones had some reason to be hostile, as he had only been hired after the first choice of the radical trustees—an American experienced in running a community school who had been dubbed "an opponent of establishments"—was ruled ineligible for the position.[69]

That all the trustees, except for Ernest Barr, had voted for Jones after the reform candidate had been eliminated was a cause of consternation for many new left educationalists: "Why do they have to be so bloody gutless?" A crowd of 150 activists had been regularly attending the board meetings focused on the selection of a new director, and they were already upset that the board had voted eighteen to four against an alternative selection process proposed by Citizens' Committee for Change in Schools. While the Citizens' Committee had been strategizing and organizing to defeat Jones, reform trustees lamely claimed that they had been hoodwinked by conservatives because they were not politicians. A belated effort to remove the new director, supported by none other than Marshall McLuhan along with the president of the Ontario Federation of Labour and other notables, failed.[70]

Loren Lind, the education reporter for *The Globe and Mail* and regular contributor to *This Magazine*, was clearly exasperated with the limited progress of the left-wing trustees. He credited them with giving parents a veto over strapping, with refusing to support a motion that would have condemned the prospect of marijuana legalization, and with establishing SEED, but thought the negative side of the balance sheet loomed larger: strapping itself had not been abolished and community councils, crucial to the new left's educational program, remained unrealized. Activists, smarting from the board's many inadequacies, were already planning how they could mobilize for the next election. In subsequent years, as radical alumni from the *Community Schools* and *This Magazine* collectives began winning seats, substantive change at the board became possible.[71]

* * *

Students and board trustees were not the only ones caught up in the fierce storms of ideas and protests sweeping through Toronto high schools. Teacher Brian Clow's 1971 conviction for the possession of marijuana brought the issues of community schools, unionization, and changing social mores into widespread contestation. In similar cases in the past, teachers charged with the possession of marijuana had seen their teaching certificates revoked and quietly moved on to other jobs. It was a sign of the times that Clow, a teacher at Don Mills Collegiate Institute, fought his case so vigorously—and received so much support. The school had once been something of a laboratory for a community-oriented approach to schooling that involved many parents as volunteers, curriculum planners, and even lecturers.[72]

Given the Don Mills tendency to experiment, itself a reflection of new left ideas, any decision involving a teacher like Clow was highly likely to be influenced by the decisions made by the community as a whole. The Don Mills Community School Association held a mass assembly on Clow's pending removal and voted 402 to 47 to keep him at the school. Although any decision to retain or fire him remained in the hands of more senior administrators, in the climate of the early 1970s any top-down exercise of power would have carried the opprobrium of imposing a diktat upon the power of the people. It seemed that the democratic assembly spoke for the community. The news media were unusually supportive of this exercise in new left political theory. Together, *The Globe and Mail* and *Toronto Star* printed six supportive editorials on the case. Clow had suffered enough; an excellent teacher should not be barred for such an offence. One editorial maintained that had a group of parents decided on a similar case five years ago, Clow would have been thrown to the wolves, but the assembly had demonstrated that social values had changed.[73]

Despite such favourable coverage, the case prompted a backlash. After the assembly, sixty parents formed a dissident group, raising the key conflict of who spoke for the community. The new group maintained that it was the large assembly that was illegitimate because it only represented an eighth of the two thousand parents who had children at the school. Dissident parents also critiqued the community-school concept itself, which they defined as a mix of poor administration and lax discipline. They complained about the consumption of alcohol at dances, and about theft, truancy, and sexual permissiveness. To these parents, a weakening of academic standards had resulted in courses such as "Women in Literature," which they saw as propaganda for the women's liberation movement. The most vocal of the dissident parents suggested that the school's teachers were at the root of the problem: "We feel the kids are becoming far too socialistic and it's not coming from the parents." Despite their moral panic, the dissidents may have had a point. In court Clow had argued that he had grown the marijuana plants on the advice of friends and fellow teachers—and students—in order to experience the drug and thus better understand the students' viewpoint. In a sense, he was walking the walk of de-professionalization and de-schooling.[74]

A report by an employee of the community council and YMCA added fuel to the flames. The man, hired to bring students, teachers, and parents together, delivered a report that not only included a selection of four-letter words but also, and most objectionably, recommended Mao's *Little Red Book*, then circulating widely in left political circles, as "a first reading in community school." He suggested: "Mao's methods may not be entirely applicable to the Canadian scene, but his ideas, philosophy, leadership, and faith in human beings and community certainly are." That statement, and the project's grant from the federal Local Initiatives Project (LIP), signalled to some dissident parents that the problem went well beyond Don Mills: "We are alarmed with the intent of [a] mass student movement across Metro to eliminate administrations, school boards and even a formal school program."[75]

Having received overwhelming support from the school's assembly, Clow found that his next hurdle was the disciplinary committee of the Ontario Teachers' Federation (OTF). The committee proposed Clow's immediate reinstatement. But OTF's executive, strongly wedded to the union's traditional ideal of professionalism, overturned that decision and recommended that Clow's teaching certificate be suspended until the following year. Any further action was left up to the education minister, who was on record as stating that his ruling would be strongly influenced by the union's decision.[76]

The union's stance particularly interested writers for the local magazine *Community Schools*, whose focus was increasingly moving beyond alternative models of education to an interest in reforming "regular" public schools and teachers' unions. In its pages Mark Golden attacked the union's ruling, explaining that even teachers who were ruled incompetent did not face the severe sanctions meted out to Clow for marijuana possession. To Golden, the Clow case solidified the impression that OTF was "worse than a sweetheart union." The union had no rank-and-file teachers on its executive and was concerned with little beyond salaries and status. Harkening back to the 1930s–40s, Golden presented an alternative vision of teachers identifying with other workers and bluntly attacking the economic system. In his mind, the phenomenon of professionalism had led both to the victimization of Clow and teachers' estrangement from the rest of organized labour.[77]

The outlook for Clow was bleak after the education minister passed the final decision over to the North York School Board. Numerous trustees said their constituents were calling them to oppose reinstating Clow. One trustee was the founder of the Committee Against the Legalization of Marijuana, and the board's president expressed dismay that the education minister had not removed Clow's licence. A disciplinary meeting was scheduled to be held behind closed doors, but leaflets titled "Justice Is an Open Meeting" circulated at Don Mills urging parents and students to attend. When a crowd of students, parents, and teachers showed up, the trustees relented and opened the doors, allowing 350 people into the board room and having loudspeakers transmit the proceedings to the overflow crowd outside. The vote was eleven to two to place Clow in a job in which he would not have contact with students; only two trustees held out for him to teach.[78]

On the surface Clow lost. He gave up hope of ever returning to the classroom and in 1973 resigned from his staff job to work as a bookstore clerk. But the decision was still a victory in that his teaching certificate was not suspended or cancelled and that the board did offer him continued employment. Clow himself said that if it were not for the publicity the assembly had given him, he would have been quietly fired. He had officially contended that not all parents would want to see the back of him, and in that too he was right. Even the dissident parents, seemingly victorious, conceded the ambiguity of the outcome.[79]

* * *

For youth outside of school, hitchhiking was growing increasingly popular. Each summer, tens of thousands of young people hit the roads, stuck out their thumbs, and embarked on a thrifty adventure, occasionally leaving moral panic in their wake. In spring 1971 Torontonians were told that their city was on the brink of a massive youth invasion. The local news media were hyping a government statement predicting that 400,000 youth would be travelling across the country that summer, with 150,000 of them passing through Toronto and needing places to stay. The government had to intervene immediately if the city hoped to avoid a "messy and possibly violent summer."[80]

It was the city's good fortune that a group of young activists already had a plan to avoid such a calamity. Back in 1970 a group called "Project 71" had envisaged the creation of a tent city. Now, with the city facing a crisis and the federal government opening its purse strings, representatives from a variety of local progressive projects came together to realize the concept. The new committee, named Grass Roots to reflective its democratic sensibilities, decided the tent city could be hosted in a local park, which would be called Wacheea, from the Cree word meaning a place where everyone is welcome.[81]

Although providing a housing service was the reason that Grass Roots was promised $40,000 in funding, that was not the most important rationale for its members. A *Toronto Star* reporter remarked that the organization contained three distinct groups. One, not especially interested in politics, was focused on creating a new youth culture. A second, the majority, wanted to build a co-operative, self-sufficient youth community set apart from the present political system. The third group was a revolutionary formation, Red Morning (RM), which had an agenda of its own. Amongst all of this, the question arose: where to locate this temporary alternative community of wandering young people?[82]

No clear answer was forthcoming from the authorities. City council passed a motion to oppose the volatile "freak show" and asked the Toronto Board of Education, which despite its lawyer's opposition had voted to sponsor Grass Roots' application, to withdraw its support. Some of the discussion on Wacheea became a debate on the nature of contemporary youth, with dissenters, including some Labour Council delegates, highlighting concerns about morality and poor behaviour.[83]

After their requests for space had been turned down, Grass Roots members realized that their tent city would not be able to go ahead. But organizer Judy Rebick expressed hope that "The spirit of what Wacheea is . . . the whole community thing . . . will be kept alive." A *Toronto Star* reporter who met with a half-dozen Grass Roots members noted that they used the word "community" a lot. Although the precise connotation of the term remained elusive, these activists certainly had a countercultural idea of community in mind. For Grass Roots, the "community" was made up of "freaks, with waist-length hair or electric Afros, blue jeans, sandals, burlap purses or army rucksacks, faded workshirts and army jackets with peace symbols sewn on where stripes should be, living in communal houses and eating organic food and not 'working' as we know it." At Wacheea they would enjoy a completely participatory environment. It would not be, as a spokesperson put it, "just like the Salvation Army only made up of freaks."[84]

Yet it was a condition of government funding that "the community" (that is, those already living in the neighbourhood of the prospective temporary village) be in agreement with the establishment of the encampment, wherever it was to be. Residents of High Park proved unenthusiastic. The University of Toronto also signalled its displeasure. As the summer approached, organizers decided to risk both jail and their government grant by setting up on university-owned property. Once more new leftists were calling upon U of T to change its spots—to become, not the aloof bastion of elite culture and gatekeeper to the bourgeoisie, but the centre of a dynamic and free-floating movement of young people.[85]

Around two hundred people pitched tents and slept on the university campus on the first night, July 11, after tucking into a communally prepared dinner of brown rice, cabbage salad, and bread. The new community was abuzz the next day when there were now six hundred people crowding onto the site. Toronto newspapers ran with the "Grass Roots" idea. Reporters from the sympathetic *Canadian Tribune* emphasized that it was a community with a purpose and hinted that one of its components was the melding of the political with the counterculture, as witnessed by an on-site screening of a movie about guerrilla struggles in Venezuela being followed by Walt Disney's *Alice in Wonderland*. Educational sessions and workshops proliferated. Some of the meetings addressed general issues; many others were of a practical nature, discussing what to do about stealing, drugs, or possible police raids. When the subject of the police came up, fierce arguments ensued about the advisability of non-violent resistance. A security committee was formed to keep the peace and evict undercover police officers. It was all a bit reminiscent of Woodstock, 1969, albeit with a federal grant in hand and taking place on the campus of a prestigious university.[86]

From the outset the university's president maintained that the occupation was illegal and unacceptable. The federal government agreed: Grass Roots must either leave the campus or lose its funding. The organizers were offered the use of an abandoned lot in Parkdale as an alternative location, but the occupiers voted to stay at the university and ignored a noon deadline to leave. At an emergency general meeting, some pushed for the encampment to move to Queen's Park, but a majority decided to ignore the court injunction against them and to guard the camp, which they did until a downpour forced them into their tents at 3 a.m.[87]

At 7:30 the next morning, July 18, 180 police officers and members of campus security ringed the campsite and announced an 8:00 deadline to vacate. The campers reluctantly left, but what police interpreted as an attempt to return to the site was met with violence. A chaotic scene followed as police intermittently punched and kicked their way into the demonstration. Some Grass Roots occupiers ran into backyards and alleys to escape. Members of the new left Red Morning were out in force, apparently having taken on the job of security. Many press accounts focused on the statements or actions of the RM members, with some reports blaming the group's supporters for throwing stones at the police after the Wacheea site had been evacuated. Although some activists denied that version of events, organizer Wally Seccombe was less generous and condemned Red Morning for actions that he said had confused and alienated people: "If it doesn't build the left, it isn't part of the left I want to be a part of." Red Morning agreed with that sentiment and, after failing to win support in Grass Roots for a demonstration, formally left the organization. Its members believed that Grass Roots was holding back the militant majority and credited themselves for the few hundred people who demonstrated at Queen's Park following the eviction.[88]

After twenty-one occupiers were arrested, a column marching from the Wacheea site reached The Hall, a left-tinged social centre run by American exiles, which was quickly surrounded by hundreds of police. As the protesters planned strategy, the police slowly melted away and a demonstration there the next day passed without incident. For the U of T radicals, the president's decision to call in the police constituted a shameful betrayal of the university's promise to avoid an extreme response.[89]

Instead of continuing the campaign for the university site, the occupiers elected, with the blessing of the university and the Ontario government, to move to the site in Parkdale, which quickly became a hive of activity. The youth set up about thirty or forty tents in a semi-circle around a hub that contained a first-aid tent, a kitchen, and a space for seminars on subjects including birth control and sexuality. Each day the inhabitants sat in a wide circle to make decisions about their camp by consensus, considering everything from how to collect garbage to the hours that journalists would be allowed to enter the camp. When a reporter complained about a lack of identified leaders, a resident explained: "We prefer to just be known as spokesmen—everyone here speaks for the community, we're all together on this." But not all residents were equally committed to what must have been a hectic meeting schedule, and the daily meeting to plan food was typically attended by only half a dozen people. While some residents built wash-basin stands and set up washrooms, a greater number, according to reports, could be found playing Frisbee or soccer or sitting around a guitar player at night.[90]

Some residents of this south Parkdale neighbourhood were clearly opposed to what was happening in their neighbourhood, and the conflict of the hip community versus the established community became the theme of much of the media coverage. Petitions against the site were immediately organized, and a group calling itself Stop Tent City formed. One unwilling neighbour complained of public urination, sex, and violence, while another, who styled himself as something of an expert on hippies—he apparently had a nephew who once lived nearby some of them—said he had personally witnessed acts of kissing and hugging. A prominant beef was that the executive of the local ratepayer group had approved the tent city without calling a public meeting.[91]

Stop Tent City, like the dissident parent group at Don Mills Collegiate, was led by the president of a local Liberal Party association. The ad hoc group organized a well-publicized meeting to have local residents vote on the issue, but despite talk of an angry community and predictions of a crowd of nearly 1,000, only 145

Parkdale residents showed up. Both the local Member of Parliament and alderman in attendance were stridently opposed to the encampment—the tent city, said the alderman, was a "horizontal Rochdale." The president of the ward's property owners association delared that the occupiers did not meet the moral standards of the neighbourhood and centred his comments on young Americans as being particularly culpable. But the big show was the mostly verbal clash between Tent City supporters and members of the far-right Edmund Burke Society, who demanded that the occupiers be kicked out and threatened a violent eviction of Wacheea if the assembled residents refused to act. In the end, only a narrow majority of participants at the meeting voted against Tent City, with the votes of Burke Society members claiming to live in the area probably contributing greatly to the outcome. Although a subsequent meeting decided to take a wait-and-see approach to Wacheea, city council voted to evict the campers. A court appeal by the organizers and the support of a committee of Parkdale residents forstalled eviction.[92]

A poster showing the location of Wacheea's second campsite.

Revolutionary Marxist Group fonds, William Ready Division of Archives and Research Collections.

Wacheea organizers liked the idea of linking their community with working-class Parkdale. A poster advertising the site even concluded: "Part of defending our site means building links with the working people around our community. Some of them think that we're a bunch of 'rich kids' who are more privileged than they are—but we feel that this 'system' gives us both a lot of hassle." But any kind of systematic approach to building such a relationship was most likely beyond the resources of the organizers. As many as five thousand leaflets were distributed door to door in an attempt to woo long-term residents to the site, but only a tiny portion of residents paid a visit. Organizers were able to stem fallout from anti-hippie sentiments, but unable to change a narrative that focused on youthful vs. traditional social mores. A Wacheea spokesman admitted that it was hard to explain to an assembly-line worker or library clerk why it did not matter to him if fifteen-year-olds slept together. The student-worker alliance of which many U of T radicals dreamt was not to be easily consummated.[93]

Towards the end of the University of Toronto occupation, the campers had taken over control from the original Grass Roots organizers, an act that Rebick maintained was the plan all along. Shortly after the encampment moved to Parkdale, a number of the organizers took a week-long leave in order to hand over their power to a coterie of activists who had only recently become involved. In mid-August a hundred Wacheea residents voted to have Grass Roots turn over any remaining grant money to them and expressed dissatisfaction with food and facilities. Grass Roots organizers dismissed the charges, largely on the grounds that those complaining had not bothered to participate in the allocation of funds. But the vote revealed that relations at Wacheea were not all egalitarian and suggested tensions with, and a certain power inherent in, the initiating organization. Most of the government money had been spent on the salaries of the project's forty-five full-time and part-time staff.[94]

Toronto's main countercultural newspaper, *Guerilla*, blamed the controversy on the fantastic turnover rate of the campers and the resulting lack of knowledge about Wacheea's internal politics. This fluid membership was also the basis of *Guerilla*'s conclusion that the key lesson of the experiment was that a population as transient as Wacheea's could never be organized as a community. The occupiers, though they did not all agree with each other, were more upbeat. Organizers stated that the main lessons of Wacheea were that direct action was more effective than working with the establishment; that it was only when they set up the tents illegally that Wacheea became a reality; and that each confrontation created a radicalizing experience. Other radical occupiers stressed Wacheea's prefigurative vision and the experience of living in an alternative community as its main success. Seccombe explained that by constructing an alternative, people became more aware of the status quo and better equipped to change it: "You create an opposition, a resistance to those predominant institutions and to the extreme specializations of roles and statuses." In short, Wacheea was a place to politicize people.[95]

As Wacheea went through its planned shutdown in early September, a group of the occupiers rented an abandoned factory so they could continue living communally into the winter. But the occupation's most tangible impact may have come when classes resumed at the University of Toronto. The cover of the annual undergraduate *Handbook* released that month featured police marching onto campus to surround Wacheea. Its editorial, "The Year of the Siege," linked the university's use of police at the encampment to other grievances. Student council was in an uproar about the police being called to campus and the lies they believed the university's president had told to make that happen. Not only students felt this way: the issue of police on campus was cited in the formation of the Faculty Reform Caucus, set up by fourteen professors as a liberal and left-wing coalition to campaign for the democratization of the university, a reassessment of the nature of teaching and learning, and an increased social involvement of the university in society. Caucus members complained that past disorganization had left progressives in a minority on a faculty association that they faulted for at least a couple of reasons: opposing parity with students on the councils of the university and having a narrow view of faculty interests. They viewed with displeasure the evidence that the head of the faculty association had approved of the police action.[96]

The question of policing also haunted Rochdale College, with its career that unfolded from 1968 to 1975 in an eighteen-storey "new brutalist" building on Bloor Street.[97] The University of Toronto was interested in the structure as a solution to meet the housing needs of students who were arriving in numbers that seemed destined to overwhelm the long-established Campus Co-operative Residence organization. The new fortress-like high-rise college, Toronto's most famous experiment in countercultural communal living, could be seen as just one more component of its student accommodation system. For visionaries such as Howard Adelman and Dennis Lee, Rochdale might not only fulfil long-cherished hopes of transcending capitalist competitiveness—its very name appealed to the British co-operative tradition—but also offer an alternative to the meaningless seminars and lectures of the mainstream university, which they had both critiqued in a 1968 book, *The University Game*: "The overcrowded classes, the superficiality of assignments, 'the piecemeal life of the mind' were supplanting 'classical university ideals.'"[98]

Rochdale could be seen as a gradualist response to a crisis of liberal order that, throughout the educational system, was reducing the vaunted individuals at the core of the theory to mere raw materials for a vast machine—the pedagogical meat grinder. As would repeatedly be the case with such left liberalism, a chasm developed between the altruistic ideal and the grimly capitalist world that such liberals generally left unexamined. In the case of Rochdale, the building attracted many vulnerable young émigrés from the fast-vanishing Yorkville counterculture, who were in turn preyed upon by thuggish drug dealers. In Michael Valpy's expression, Rochdale was "Yorkville gone high-rise."[99] Operating on new left political precepts, the Rochdale Governing Council sought to regulate the drug problem by discriminating between life-threatening and merely recreational drugs. It succeeded in evicting dealers in methamphetamines and supported the establishment of the Rochdale Clinic to respond to addictions.

Like so many experiments in finding richer forms of democracy in the 1960s and 1970s, this experiment in community control and self-government had its problems. At times, writes historian Stuart Henderson, the "highly fractious" and "mutable" Governing Council was "able to get things accomplished, but it was prone to crippling debate and indecisiveness." Repeated police raids were resisted by bombardments of objects ranging from bricks to stoves; street battles occurred in August and early September 1970. The Toronto media sensationalized Rochdale and dwelt with particular avidity upon suicides related to it—even though far more suicides took place in the subway and on the Prince Edward Viaduct (and many of the so-called Rochdale cases did not actually involve Rochdale residents). In 1975, citing financial irregularities, U of T shut the college down.[100]

One lesson of Rochdale, driven home by the mainstream Toronto press and underlined by John George Diefenbaker when he addressed the Empire Club in 1972, was that it showed the great dangers of attempts at building an alternative to bourgeois liberalism. Many new leftists could draw a different lesson. Pat Shafter of Rochdale Women responded to the threat of macho violence and a pervasive culture of sexism with arguments for a practice of consciousness-raising that would highlight such issues as economic dependence on men, sexual objectification, and the drug culture's pervasive machismo. For other groups, Rochdale also exemplified the political consequences of structurelessness and undisciplined personal behaviour. New leftists could see in Rochdale the perils of investing themselves too heavily in a mainstream institution that followed the propertied precepts of mainstream liberalism to the letter—one devoted not to encouraging their programs of political and social transformation, but merely to containing them.

* * *

On the face of things, the new left's tangible achievements in revolutionizing the vast leviathan of the Ontario educational system were meagre. Most post-secondary institutions had been engulfed in sometimes serious struggles, especially efforts sparked by the new left's support of national liberation struggles and its demand for the educational equivalents of self-management in the design of programs and curriculum and in the overall governance of the academy. Yet such projects had not led to forms of advanced education that were strikingly different than any that had gone before. Links between universities and industries were strengthened, not severed. In high schools, even with the percolation of new left ideas and *The Student as Nigger* as a popular manifesto, the trend was not towards ever-greater democracy but a more thorough penetration of education by the corporate sector.[101] There is ample room, in considering the institutional legacy of the new left's educational career, for skepticism.

Yet a broader perspective on educational change leaves room for an entirely different conclusion. Professorial privilege remained, but the professor as an unquestioned classroom authority and the textbook as an unchallengeable source of wisdom were fast-fading. Women's activism and peace activism forced changes in the curriculum; the wider currents of Marxist and socialist thought were taught with a freedom on Canadian campuses such as had never been seen before. When academics spoke out against poverty, they no longer needed to fear the ends of their careers. Attempts to smear new leftists as violent terrorists bore little fruit. New leftists started to influence, and in some instances *become*, school trustees. If Clow's case suggests the survival of age-old patterns of privilege and oppression, it also points to how such patterns had become newly contested. In the short term, new left victories in education looked modest from 1968 to 1971. Yet the longer term would tell a different story: of how the planting of seeds of resistance and the emergence of inspirational leaders would enduringly change the experiences of Toronto's students.

The educational struggles of new leftists in Toronto from 1968 to 1971 were nothing if not local—protests against the victimization of pot-smoking teachers, having to take a mandatory social science class, and even preferential faculty parking—but they also were important on other scales. They challenged a vast provincial bureaucracy and stimulated it to change, albeit in ways that ultimately proved to be principal-empowering. They were also suffused with transnational educational ideas that took old notions of progressive education and turned them towards radical and even revolutionary ends. Although published in Toronto, *This Magazine Is About Schools* was read around the world because it resonated powerfully with a generation determined to transform alienating processes of schooling into a transformative *praxis* of education—one that would answer to the new left's core demand for a new form of life in which personal authenticity and self-determination, and not the brutal anonymity of the meat grinder of industrial capitalist education, would become the animating principles of a revolutionary way to be human. This story of student resistance in Toronto, then, spoke to the experiences of students around the world—and in doing that provided an enduring legacy.

5

Bringing the Revolution Home: Black Power, Feminism, and Turning the Local into the Global, 1968–71

In late 1967 Ted Watkins of the Hamilton Tiger-Cats appeared on CBC-TV's *The Public Eye*. His team had just won the Grey Cup. He had scored the game's second touchdown goal, and was now a star.

But Watkins wanted to speak about something more important than his big win. He wanted the public to know what it meant to be Black in 1960s Canada. Since moving to Canada from the United States to play in the Canadian Football League (CFL), he had been the object of numerous racial taunts and acts of discrimination. There were times, Watkins told the CBC audience, that he felt he was in Mississippi.[1]

With highly publicized statements like this one, the politics of race in Canada entered the mainstream, soon to be followed by the Black power movement as an element, however uneasy, of the new left.

In November 1967 three authors of SUPA's women's manifesto initiated something completely new. They invited female activists to enter U of T's Hart House, "that bastion of male supremacy," where they had surreptitiously organized a meeting. The women who attended were introduced to the Women's Liberation Group and embarked on drafting a radical brief to the government on abortion law reform. Believing that women should have full say about their own bodies, they voted to support a women-only national referendum on abortion. Organizers emphasized that their goal was not to create a perfect position paper, but to use the issue of abortion as an organizing tool to spur discussion about the role of women in society.[2] That meeting was a harbinger of a debate that would shape new left feminist politics from 1968 to 1971.

As it happened, the advent of a Black power cohort and an emerging feminist movement became crucial aspects of an expanding late 1960s new left. By the close of the decade the Toronto new left was developing new energy and gaining new constituencies. Contrary to narratives of decline, which posit 1970 as a critical year for the end of the sixties, the new politics largely represented fissures of growth rather than pockets of fragmentation. While the conventional narrative of the 1960s activists has generally focused wholly on the participants as white, middle-class students, scholars more recently have recognized that much more was happening and that, as U.S. historian Van Gosse puts it, "The white-student New Left coexisted alongside all the other radical causes."[3] Oddly enough, too, while Black power and left feminism had a lot of differences, they shared many common features of new leftism.

* * *

After the CBC's Watkins telecast, newspaper reporters and columnists sprang into action to call into question, not their own city's race relations, but Watkins's credibility. *The Toronto Star* followed up with Watkins's football coach, asking him whether Watkins would be fired for his statements and if he thought Watkins had any plans to kill white people.[4]

The issue of whether professional athletes had a right to speak about social and political issues also came up. Both Watkins's former coach and the sports journalist Richard "Dick" Beddoes argued that Black athletes did not have such a right, and that Watkins should have stayed quiet. Their criticisms recalled a fracas of the prior year, when it had been announced that legendary boxer Muhammad Ali was coming to Maple Leaf Gardens. Beddoes had stated that some of Ali's anti-war statements were too dangerous to be defended on the grounds of freedom of speech, and repeatedly pushed for the boxing match to be cancelled. Although the event went ahead, Conn Smythe, the former majority owner of the Toronto Maple Leafs, resigned his Gardens directorship in a pique of indignation over Ali's appearance, and a hyperbolic critic suggested that the stadium should henceforth be called "Black Muslim Gardens." Beddoes was similarly vexed when Tommie Smith and John Carlos later gave Black power salutes during their medal ceremony at the 1968 Olympics in Mexico. Beddoes decried "the same old tattered generalization about all U.S. whites being prejudiced" and insisted that the two athletes had given "fascist" salutes.[5]

Oddly enough, writers for the conservative *Telegram* took Watkins's accusations more seriously than their competitors did. They noted that the CBC's phones had been besieged by racist callers following the on-air interview and expressed disappointment that reactions to his comments had "ranged from the offensive to the absurd." Watkins had encouraged other Black athletes to share their stories of racism, which the paper saw as an understandable, if not positive, development: "Yesterday it was Ottawa and Ted Watkins. . . . Tomorrow it could be a Negro athlete anywhere in Canada who can no longer be silent about racial discrimination in this country." Player George Reed of the Saskatchewan Roughriders was emboldened to complain that "Regina is like living in the heart of Alabama as far as I'm concerned." Winnipeg Blue Bomber Dave Raimey, in itemizing the discrimination he faced in that city, lamented, "Whenever I mention it, people around here say I have a chip on my shoulder."[6]

Watkins, taking advantage of his recent notoriety, continued to speak up. "Watkins Calls Canada 'Lesser of Two Evils'" blared a subsequent *Globe and Mail* headline. In that story Watkins carefully rebutted suggestions that he was anti-white. Yes, Black people had the right to respond with force to those violently repressing them, but no, he did not hate white people. He just loved Black people more. After Watkins made other provocative comments—the footballer said that he would have joined the rioting in Detroit had he lived there—the *Star* printed a story with yet another inflammatory headline: "The Dapper Young Negro—Who Hates Whites." It placed this eye-catching headline above an article in which Watkins nowhere expressed an explicit, or even implicit, hostility towards white people.[7]

Following the negative caricatures in the press, rumours spread about how Watkins was the aggressive, bitter, and ill-educated product of a tough childhood in a Chicago slum. Watkins may have been born in such circumstances, but by the time he was three his family was following a nomadic life, moving through a series of cities and towns as his father chased construction work. When Watkins was eleven they finally settled down in Modesto, Cal., where they had a house and regularly attended church. In Modesto Watkins became consumed by a love of sport, including running and basketball. He became a star high-school athlete and won election as student president in a popularity-driven campaign. Attending a nearby college on a football scholarship, Watkins married his high-school sweetheart and had the first of his four daughters. But he began to lose interest in his classes and became tired of the drudgery of a janitorial job. When an Ottawa Rough Riders recruiter made him an offer in 1963, he jumped at the chance to escape.

The Canada that Watkins encountered was no oasis from racism. As teammates recalled, when Watkins was called "nigger," he responded with his fists. Around mid-decade he became more racially conscious. He had encountered some bigots over the years, but his friends said he had never looked at racism in any analytical kind of way. A close friend and former teammate insisted that the reason for Watkins's transformation was personal: "Ted couldn't bear the idea that his little girls would be hurt because of their color. He used to say it was alright for him, he could look after himself, but nobody was going to push his little girls around." Yet growing Black ferment in the United States must have been a factor, and friends acknowledged that his growing sense of identity was sharpened by the racism he experienced while playing for Ottawa.

By 1966 Watkins was finding less physical ways of responding to racism. He had decided to resume his college studies part-time and was jolted when an instructor dismissed the achievements of Black Americans. When he protested, the instructor said he could leave if he did not like the class. "I'll leave the whole damn school!" he responded, and he did. He also threw himself into the study of Black American history and culture with the kind of passion he had formerly reserved for sports. He decided he would be a propagandist for the Black struggle once his football career was over. But patience was not his strong suit. Shortly after being transferred to the Tiger-Cats in Hamilton, he started the publication *Al Kitab Sudan*, which was sympathetic to the Nation of Islam. He also founded a publishing house (with the same name) that brought out a series of pamphlets, one of which—*The Confessed Bewilderment of Martin Luther King and the Idea of Non-Violence as a Political Tactic*—was authored by writer Austin Clarke, who had opposed adherence to non-violence during debates with SUPA members in 1965.[8]

By 1968 Watkins had decided it was time to move from publishing to more overt acts of political activism. Early that year he became a founder of the Afro-American Progressive Association (AAPA), Toronto's first Black power organization. With his speaking skills, knowledge, and relative celebrity, he immediately became a leader. But his prominence made his family the target of threatening racist phone calls. Fearful for his family's safety, he quickly relocated them to California. A few months later, when Watkins went there to visit them, a liquor-store owner shot and killed him and injured his brother, who survived a bullet wound to his neck. An angry Black crowd outside the store said that police had stood by while Watkins bled to death. The police, alleging that the brothers had tried to rob the store, circulated a story about Watkins's mother being on welfare to suggest a possible financial motive. But Watkins's brother was later acquitted of robbery charges. The store had a reputation as an unfriendly place for Black customers, and perhaps Watkins had been simply demanding more respectful customer service.[9]

In Toronto the AAPA firmly rejected the police version of events. Members said Watkins's involvement in such a robbery was inconceivable, and demanded an inquiry. A rally of six hundred people was organized to support Watkins's brother and the Black Panthers' Huey Newton, both of whom languished in jail. They also organized a memorial service. Everyone attending was handed a mimeographed poem written as a tribute to the activist football player. Its opening words could very well have been a rebuke to Watkins's popular depiction: "He didn't Hate; He Loved . . . the Hell out of Black People."[10]

* * *

The media's response to Watkins's critical reflections on race in Canada suggests how sensitive the topic of racism was in the late 1960s. The federal government and the mainstream media had long been telling Canadians that their country was a non-racist oasis, free of the prejudice and riots south of its border. The notion that Canada was itself founded upon the creation of a racialized Indigenous minority or that it had flourished as part of an empire nourished by the chattel slavery of Africans was distant from most Canadians' understanding of the past. Toronto's dramatically changing demographic and social makeup had, by 1967, not generated mainstream awareness of how racialized minorities were caught up in systemic relations that oppressed them. Racism was understood to function on the individual level, a result of poor education or social backwardness—and not as a structural phenomenon imbricated in the realities of the city's social and cultural life.

Watkins had strenuously emphasized that structural fact: when speaking about racially segregated accommodation and the prohibition of white wives and girlfriends, while playing for the Rough Riders; or when talking about a Ti-Cat teammate who had been subjected to a racist petition after buying a home outside Hamilton. He linked the incidents to a wider system of racial oppression, but the media and his detractors wanted to make everything be about the individual—or specifically about Watkins as a flawed individual.

Responses from CFL officials to his *Public Eye* interview typify a rhetorical strategy widely used in subsequent years. Commissioner Allan McEachern explained that Black players fell into two categories, the "intelligent, well-adjusted man" and "the man with a chip on his shoulder." As to whether there was racism in the CFL, McEachern chose to deflect the footballer's criticism: "Discrimination works both ways. You can say the Negroes discriminate against the whites because they tend to stick so closely together." The general manager of Watkins's former team, the Ottawa Rough Riders, used the same playbook: "Watkins had chips piled on both shoulders." Too many Blacks on a team cause anti-white discrimination, he suggested. The only discordant note came from Watkins's Ti-Cat coach, who said he had worked with "other colored boys with a chip on their shoulder," but Watkins was not one of them.[11]

The "chip on his shoulder" argument had a long pedigree in Toronto. Prior to the Second World War it had frequently been used to explain away Jewish accusations of anti-Semitism. It implied that charges of discrimination reflected a flawed individual psychology rather than the problem of an Anglo-dominated society. It also suggested that the accuser, rather than the accused, was prejudiced. The phrase became increasingly popular in the late 1960s and early 1970s, both to describe the minority of local Black activists who had been born in the United States and as an explanation for the rise in complaints about racism. Used in this way, it implied that both the "chips" and allegations of racism were American problems imported to Toronto.

The alleged racism of Black players, pointed to by football officials, and the *Star*'s conclusion that Watkins was guilty of "reverse racism," were unsurprising considering the reception that American advocates of Black power received in the local press. A *Globe and Mail* story on Stokely Carmichael prominently accused the former chairman of the Student Nonviolent Coordinating Committee of reverse racism and compared his speaking style to Hitler. A *Star* editorial, "Fuelling the Fires of Race Hate," summarized Carmichael's ideas on Black self-defence and revolution as "get guns and prepare to kill white people." Even a rare sympathetic interview, with noted African-American writer and radical LeRoi Jones (later known as Amiri Baraka), was prefaced with a biographical note describing him as "a militant racist." It was not a label used for white Torontonians who refused to provide jobs, accommodation, or service to people from other races.[12]

The prevailing rhetorical style had partly been borrowed from the U.S. press, but also reflected an attitude ingrained in the city's white conservative Protestant majority. Since the 19th century, Toronto's economic and political order had been dominated by an anti-Catholic organization called the Orange Order. Members of the Order insisted they were fighting for equal rights and against prejudice, as they systematically worked to exclude Catholics from coveted jobs and political decision-making. Public employees received paid time off for the organization's parades and conventions, while the Order condemned Catholics for demanding "special privileges." After the Second World War, the Orange Order's strongest supporters on city council claimed that discrimination either did not exist, or that it was only practised by non-British immigrants. The Black and Jewish communities, who were foremost in demanding anti-discriminatory bylaws, were characterized as the most prejudiced elements of society. Reflecting the Order's strong identification with the British Empire, *The Globe and Mail* routinely used racist tropes to support British colonization around the world, while simultaneously decrying the anti-white prejudices of colonized peoples. Restive Africans were sometimes cited as proof that racial prejudice "cuts two ways."[13]

In Toronto, postwar opposition to racist practices focused on a local-provincial-national axis. Civil rights activists, usually tied to left-wing parties, relied on moderate rhetoric to change minds and agitate for legal reforms in those jurisdictions. Efforts against the racism of the British colonial project were scarce. Reflecting the city's Cold War atmosphere, rare meetings on that topic tended to take place in progressive churches under the safe sponsorship of organizations such as the Universal Nations Association. Yet one group of activists focused on combining these seemingly disparate local and international issues. They were members of the United Negro Improvement Association (UNIA), an international organization of the African diaspora founded in 1914 by Jamaican-American Marcus Garvey, which promoted racial pride and the idea that African-descended peoples should return to Africa. In its heyday the largely working-class, Caribbean-émigré-based Toronto branch of UNIA had regularly attracted hundreds of people, but by the early 1950s it barely had a dozen members.[14]

Still, that small group remained extremely active, sometimes working with white-dominated civil liberties organizations or initiating Black-led campaigns. They would occasionally transcend the standard language of civil liberties activists by evoking anti-colonial struggles or using intemperate rhetoric. When UNIA member Don Moore pointedly "reminded" the minister of immigration in 1954 that "yellow and black races are arising," he was foreshadowing the late 1960s technique of using provocative language to draw out an enemy. It certainly drew out the *Globe* editor, who simultaneously denied that racism was a problem, accused Moore of spreading racial hatred, and, in atypically frank terms, upheld the idea of a white Canada.[15] That UNIA activists anticipated Black power is obvious from Rocky Jones's recollection of meeting some of them in the early mid-1960s:

> It is strange now that I think about it, but we weren't talking about the civil rights movement in the United States. These guys were talking about Africa, and our need to organize and do things like that. They were really focused. They would have functions, dances, parades, you know all kinds of things way before the [1965 Selma] sit-in on University Avenue, and yet none of these people were involved in that sit-in. Not one of those organizations was involved and yet they were political organizations, they were cultural and political. Their politics were Canada and the Diaspora.[16]

Watkins's 1967 observation that Canada was not unlike Mississippi came at a moment when the "race question" in Toronto was about to attain a new salience. Canadians looked over the border and, from 1968 to 1971, saw burning cities and racialized killings. They also saw significant moments of resistance, some of which had drawn them in directly. They focused especially on the Black Panther Party, with some of its members fleeing north to evade an increasingly violent campaign to stamp it out; many of the writings of its key proponents were enjoying a considerable vogue. The patent decline of the British Empire created space for many Torontonians to see their city, not as a node of Empire, but as a plausible venue for movements of solidarity with a decolonizing world. Older currents traceable back to the 1920s—Pan-Africanism, gradual liberal meliorism, socialist anti-racism—were reactivated in this highly charged climate, as the "race question" suddenly seemed to be an issue that no serious progressive could fail to ponder.

* * *

It was no accident that AAPA was founded on Malcolm X's birthday. Members were calling out for a new form of activism, one with a more combative and transnational perspective. Some argued that the "tame Negroes" recognized as spokespersons for the Black community had lost the ability to communicate with the younger generation. All of the members saw Canada not as an oasis in a racist world but as part of a transnational system of oppression and exclusion that they sought to overthrow. Reflecting this new politics, AAPA invited the militant Black Panthers to talk to local audiences. But its Canadian speakers alone were challenging, especially for any white new leftist hoping for an easy multiracial coalition. At one AAPA rally, Rocky Jones stopped a speech about Canada's structural racism to reprimand his largely white audience, which was applauding him furiously: "You're damn fools to applaud me when I call you racists." The applause ceased. "You're a symbol of what has happened to me. Every cop I ever came across, every teacher I ever knew, was white."[17]

AAPA had been formed by members of the American, Canadian, and West Indian Black communities. Its most visible spokespeople—Watkins, Jan Carew (a novelist and playwright), and José Garcia (an electrical worker)—were all recent immigrants from the United States or West Indies. These militants coexisted, sometimes uneasily, with longer-established Afro-Canadian activists. One of those was Toronto-born Leonard Johnson. Leonard was linked to the Communist Party and talked into involvement in AAPA by his daughter. He thought the organization was plagued with "rabble rousers" and criticized the Black power advocates for their brashness and lack of sensitivity to the Toronto context. He was particularly worried, not without reason, by the state intelligence agents whom he suspected were working within the movement, perhaps as provocateurs urging its members to participate in rash and dangerous actions. Johnson's penchant for tactical caution also led him to argue against AAPA forming ties with groups south of the border. He feared they would ensnare the organization in "U.S. problems." That Johnson was sometimes dubbed "the Black conservative" for his cautious approach suggests that Communist Party members, formerly portrayed as a dangerously radical bunch, were increasingly being viewed as insufficiently revolutionary by a new generation of activists.[18]

If *The Toronto Star* is to be believed, Johnson had reason to be concerned. After 150 people attended an AAPA meeting to mourn Martin Luther King Jr.'s assassination and raise money for imprisoned American activist Rap Brown, the crowd marched to the U.S. consulate, where they shouted, "Burn, kill, shoot the white savages." AAPA member Don Blackman reportedly called for violence, burning, shooting, and killing, "in a tirade against all whites." Watkins, the only member authorized to give statements to the media, refused to do so and warned his audience: "If things get hot down there . . . then things will get pretty warm up here."[19]

The local mainstream media focused relentlessly on Black power's supposed violence, and predictably missed the far-more-nuanced aspects of the movement's consciousness-raising. The AAPA was much more concerned with fostering Black empowerment. The literature that AAPA promoted—dismissed by a *Globe and Mail* reporter as "Honky-this, Whitey-that"—included works of history and academic sociology alongside books and speeches by two key voices: Frantz Fanon, a Martinican anti-colonial activist and Marxist intellectual; and Malcolm X, the key figure challenging the established U.S. civil rights movement. The organization referred to all Black people in the Western hemisphere as Afro-American, rejected Martin Luther King Jr.'s non-violence strategy, and was deeply attuned to Black ferment south of the border. The cultural impact of American Black power was evident from its lauding of brightly coloured African clothing and natural hairstyles and the adoption of "We're a Winner," a 1968 song recorded by American soul sensations The Impressions, as the AAPA's official anthem. In a slogan that countered claims of Canadian exceptionalism, members defined Canada as "Cold, Anti-Negro and Definitely American."[20]

If the AAPA was emphatically new left in style and content—its very name testifying to its members' sense that they were part of a transnational community of resistance—it was also new left in experiencing complicated relationships with the activists who preceded it. They shared an anti-racist mission, after all, with the Universal Negro Improvement Association, which had been a fixture of the Black community through much of the century. The UNIA had a hall, a few aging members, and a reputation, and AAPA successfully agitated for it to open its membership to young people. AAPA also became involved, to a degree, in the Home Service Association, another historic (albeit more liberal) Black institution, encouraging the city to back off on its plans to take over the municipally owned building occupied by that organization. Despite the drawing of generational lines, the movements—much like new leftists and old leftists in other contexts—also had shared interests, as evident when Toronto's Black new left developed an interest in figures such as UNIA founder Marcus Garvey.[21]

As 1968 came to a close, the AAPA was drawing as many as one hundred militants to its meetings. After only a few earlier signs that the organization was heading in a Marxist direction, many of its speakers now began to tie racial oppression to capitalism and advance a Marxist analysis of society. When asked if the association was like a Black Panther chapter, AAPA secretary José Garcia said: "We're part of the same political line, which is a Marxist-Leninist line."[22]

The Black Panther model and the growing influence of Marxism inspired some members to form a new organization in early 1969. Most leading AAPA members joined the new group, called the Black Liberation Front (BLF) and also headed by Garcia, but Johnson and a few others elected to stay with the much-weakened older organization. BLF's ultimate objective was social revolution—"We will not rock the boat of discrimination—we will sink it"—but most of its struggles revolved around fighting the day-by-day racism experienced by Blacks in Toronto. Pointing to an increase in police brutality and harassment, BLF tried to mobilize both the Black and left communities in demanding an elected civilian review board with guaranteed minority representation for the city's police.[23]

In 1969 it was not fanciful to imagine a Toronto poised on the edge of a general race crisis. In downtown Alexandra Park, a neighbourhood near Dundas St. W. and Bathurst St., Portuguese and Black Canadians were involved in a public dispute, apparently provoked by an altercation in the Portuguese-owned Algarve Billiards room. The dust-up was soon blown up, at least in some minds, into a "Black Power Riot." It started when police showed up at 1:30 a.m. and tried to make an arrest. Bottles flew towards the police, store and car windows were smashed, and a crowd estimated at four-hundred-strong taunted police with Black power slogans. Some chanted "Toronto's going to burn." Following an hour and a half of sporadic fighting, the police left after making a few arrests. The BLF's Frank Cleare said the dynamic of the so-called riot was that every time more police showed up, more Blacks would come outside to watch, which caused more police to be called, until there were forty police cruisers on the scene.[24]

John Crawford, whose right cheek was swollen from a police club, said problems between Blacks and Portuguese occurred "once in a blue moon," and that police had tried to exploit the situation. "If there's any race problem it's with them." Other "rioters" vouched that it was police rather than Portuguese who would call them "nigger." Pointing to police overreaction and racism, the BLF used the Alexandra Park incident to launch a campaign for a civilian review board, which would investigate cases of beatings and intimidation and curtail police powers.[25]

In BLF's *Black Liberation News*, discussions of local organizing campaigns appeared alongside extensive coverage of events in Africa, the Caribbean, and the United States. Toronto appeared to be but a single node in a global struggle for Black liberation. Even a local story itemizing racism at an auto factory became instantly transnational with the insertion of a graphic showing the Third World origins of the metals, rubber, and petroleum products in the assembled vehicles, challenging colonial relationships and the very idea of a "North American–made" car. Much of the paper's political line seemed congruent with the analysis of the Black Panthers' Huey Newton, for whom socialism was a precondition of Black liberation, and divergent from the AAPA's emphasis on cultural struggle. From a BLF perspective, cultural nationalism was empty if unaccompanied by a more comprehensive social revolution. Black businesses, far from being important signs of a community attaining respect, showed how a minority could grow rich by using the language and images of cultural nationalism.[26]

Foregoing Black-only public events, the BLF emphasized that the situation called for unity with other "progressive forces" and that it would prioritize racially mixed coalitions. The group held many events with multiracial audiences, including seminars organized in Rochdale College. Other radicals, such as Rocky Jones, whose speech at the end of 1968 seemed to preclude such alliances, appeared to rethink their previous positions. Jones now spoke of a looming confrontation with the privileged and conservatives on one side and the have-nots and revolutionaries on the other. Blacks would ultimately join with the working class to transform society.[27]

Toronto's Black liberationists also foresaw an alliance with Indigenous activists. While the AAPA had once considered opening its Black-only meetings to Native peoples—seeing them as part of the oppressed Third World—the BLF argued that it had formed a "coalition" with Native activists. Garcia projected a long-term relationship "with our Indian Brothers and eventually with other minority groups similarly oppressed by the white power structure." Red power activist Fred Kelly, who travelled from Kenora to discuss this coalition proposal, spoke favourably of exploring common grievances and goals with Black power activists and likened Native reserves—"rural ghettos"—to Black ghettos.[28]

White activists occasionally voiced their desire for a similar alliance, but Black activists were more persistent. The goal of supporting and understanding Indigenous struggles was not just an exercise in solidarity, nor was it wholly the idea that different peoples experiencing racism would be stronger working together. Black power activists considered the Indigenous experience foundational to both an understanding of Canada and their own place within it. As Jan Carew explained:

> In analyzing race relations in this country it is impossible to deal with the Black minority without reference to the Indian one. The two are indivisible since racism springs from the same tap root in this society—a history

of exploitation and greed where profits were more important than human rights. The Blacks and Indians were dispossessed for the same reasons.[29]

The aftermath of the Sir George Williams affair, frequently cited as a trigger for declining student activism, prompted many Black students to become politically active. Some, like thirty students from York University who demonstrated under the banner of the Black People's Movement, became active in fighting to support the defendants and called for an official inquiry. For many others, the Sir George affair marked a more general rise in racial consciousness and politicization.[30]

New Black organizations appeared that appealed especially to the young. The Black Youth Organization (BYO), which had started as a youth-based adjunct of AAPA, attracted some of these new activists. It also mobilized AAPA members who, unlike those setting the tone for the BLF, were deeply interested in mobilizing Afro-specific memories and energies. Like the Black Liberation Front, the Black Youth Organization prioritized goals—better education and housing, full employment, community centres, and opposition to police brutality—that could conceivably be achieved without a revolution. Yet unlike BLF, BYO—rather more attuned to new left notions of self-management and local autonomy—emphasized a vision of a "co-operative, communal" post-revolutionary society and had a markedly less state-centric discourse.[31]

The different conceptions of Black revolution held by the two groups were fully apparent in their duelling appreciations of pan-Africanist Marcus Garvey. BLF central committee member Peter Robinson set himself the difficult challenge of claiming Garvey for Marxism. He insisted that by liberating his own country Fidel Castro was doing exactly what Garvey had fought to achieve. Black liberationists were enjoined to make a political revolution—not a cultural one. By contrast, BYO's Horace Campbell focused on how Garvey had transcended national boundaries to organize Black people and made vital contributions to Black culture. Both speakers exemplified left transnationalism, but in radically contrasting ways.[32]

As 1960s activists, BYO militants prioritized cultural change in general and educational change specifically. In 1969, after the Portuguese-Black disturbances of that year, they established the Black Educational Project (BEP) to serve as a cultural school and organize against racism. They found volunteers to teach aspects of Black history and culture, including practical courses in African sewing and dance—although when they learned that most of their pupils were having difficulty reading and writing, they shifted the courses to teaching basic skills.[33]

In 1970–71 the advent of Black student unions changed BEP's horizons. The first Black Student Union (BSU) was formed at Toronto's Centennial College in 1970 after a representative of the college's student government, a member of the

Black activists, in front of the federal government building on St. Clair Ave. East, supporting arrested Sir George Williams students; Nov. 2, 1969.

Clara Thomas Archives and Special Collections, Toronto Telegram fonds.

far-right Edmund Burke Society, advertised his racist views in the student newspaper. When dozens of Black students got together to respond, they shared complaints about racial discrimination at the college and decided to form a Black campus-based organization. The idea spread like wildfire. At least a dozen BSUs were established at high schools and post-secondary institutions throughout the decade. They held weekly meetings, formed study groups, and planned political actions. Dozens of BSU militants lent BEP their assistance.[34]

Demonstrating the utility of the new group to existing Black activist organizations, U of T's BSU was able to wrest $5,000 from the student council. It contributed the funds to BEP and other community-organizing initiatives, including a planned breakfast program for poor children inspired by a similar project run by the Black Panthers. Right-wing student representatives strenuously complained about the circumstances under which the grant had been given. They argued that it was unjust that the money had gone to a racially based organization—a criticism that also heard from the more liberal wing of Toronto's establishment, who saw nothing wrong with the city's white-dominated religious-based charities and service organizations but viewed similar Black organizations as harmful and unnecessary. The *Star*'s editorial page, consistent with a newspaper that had emphasized Watkins's supposed anti-white bias, lambasted the student council funding and questioned why it was not providing money to poor whites. It concluded that the funding was "conscience money for the sins of whites in other times and other places."[35]

The BSU was hardly to the *Star's* taste—nor was the newspaper's easygoing liberalism any more agreeable to the BSU. In general, members of the BSU, as good new leftists, wanted Revolution Now—not Revolution Someday. They had a marked impatience for the go-slow approach of many Black civil rights activists. Speaking to a Queen's Park demonstration against the Human Rights Commission, the BSU's Deborah Clarke declared: "We don't want a bunch of old, tired Jews and blacks, who sold their souls 20 years ago, telling us what to do." Yet while Clarke was skewering the immediate postwar cohort of activists, this was not a purely generational divide. Stanley Grizzle, one of the outstanding figures in that same cohort, joined her at the same rally in lambasting the commission for being both passive and toothless.[36]

Though not averse to highlighting political divisions, a major goal of all Black new leftists was to unify the Black community by overcoming historical divisions among its American, Canadian, and Caribbean-born members. By upholding Africa as the centrepiece of Black identity and concern, Africanists in BYO and other groups hoped cultural, political, and island differences could be subsumed under a common struggle. Some radicals hoped that negative aspects of the community's constituent parts—a tendency of those born in Canada to underplay racism in Canadian society and for those born in the Caribbean to view their stay in Canada as temporary—could be countered by uniting in struggle. Thus all the groups argued that it was essential for Blacks to join organizations and struggles based on Blackness rather than on identities predicated on countries of origin, and they regularly evoked the Black community as their base and constituency. Although activists argued that local Blacks had a long-standing sense of community, which they were only endeavouring to serve and unite further, they themselves also played a substantial role in bolstering and defining that community. One reporter, questioning whether local Blacks "in any way" formed a community, astutely observed, "Militants have a vested interest in solidarity."[37]

Where, then, was Black power in Toronto? Some activists referred to the geographic centre of the city's Black community—sometimes placed within the boundaries of Queen St. West, Ossington Ave., Bloor St. West, and Huron St.—as the "black belt." J. Ashton Brathwaite's consciousness-raising novel *Niggers, This Is Canada* depicts this belt as the vibrant heart of the city's Black community, a place teeming with businesses, people, and politics. The lively scene he depicts in front of the Bathurst subway station, where copies of the city's leading Black newspaper, *Contrast*, and BYO's *Black Voice* were being distributed, would be familiar to anyone who frequented the area in the early 1970s. But a distinct part of the radical fostering of community was not readily apparent by walking the streets. Black new leftists nurtured a historical view of community, forged by class, nation, and race. The movement-produced film *Born Black* (1972) was emblematic of this popular line of analysis. It placed contemporary manifestations of Black activism—from *Contrast* newspaper and the Harriet Tubman Centre to Gwen and Leonard Johnston's Third World Bookstore and Crafts—squarely within a historical continuum of struggle stretching from pre-Confederation slave resistance to 20th-century battles by Black trade unionists.[38]

Black militants, keen to expand the historical horizons of their struggle, laboured to make it speak to people far beyond Toronto itself. On Oct. 6, 1969, dozens of Black organizations and many more individuals convened in Toronto to form the National Black Coalition of Canada (NBCC) as a country-wide co-ordinating body. The initial backers of NBCC defined Canadian society as WASP and not multiracial or multicultural. The country's predominant social makeup, they believed, led to Black alienation, which would only be overcome by the Black community defining a role for itself and then seeking to influence the policies of governments and institutions. The NBCC's first chair, Howard McCurdy, said Black power in Canada, in contrast to the United States, must be predicated on unity rather than numbers. This comment was directed at least partly to the many young militants who attended NBCC's founding meeting. Some were expressing their dissatisfaction that a request to discuss the Sir George Williams affair had been ignored and that government money had helped to finance the conference. McCurdy himself came under fire for characterizing young radical activists as transients who had little understanding of Black people in Canada beyond their immediate concerns and ideologies. He was later forced to apologize for expressing his grievances in the white press.[39]

In light of NBCC's first conference, a number of Black power activists thought the new organization was bound to be a replica of the National Association for the Advancement of Coloured People, which U.S. proponents of Black power saw as a fundamentally conservative organization. The BLF condemned McCurdy for his refusal to debate the Sir George Williams affair and was highly critical of NBCC's servility-inducing dependence on state funding. As the Black new left became more engaged with Marxism, others accused the NBCC of representing the interests of the "petty-bourgeois class." Activist Rosie Douglas, who had come to national prominence following the Sir George Williams events and would later become prime minister of Dominica, believed the NBCC's state funding was an attempt by the government to develop a black bourgeoisie, that is, "to control black people through other black people." Another activist called NBCC a neo-colonialist agent.[40]

That critique provided only a partial picture of the NBCC. Many Black new left activists saw the NBCC as a kind of united front organization, a place where they could engage with the mainstream of the politically active Black community and benefit from some of its personal and material resources. The Black new left and the large-circulation Black weekly *Contrast* had a similar relationship. The paper at its most tepid welcomed Liberal Party stalwarts and middle-of-the-road journalists; yet in its editorials and news reporting it regularly supported Black nationalism and Pan-Africanism. Members of the Black power new left were frequent contributors to the publication, which in turn consistently advertised and reported on the movement's activities.

After McCurdy left the chair of NBCC, the influence of radicals on the coalition became increasingly evident. His 1972 successor declared her support for Black nationalism and Pan-Africanism; and her successor supported Amiri Baraka (formerly known as LeRoi Jones and lionized by many BYO and BSU members) as a featured speaker for the coalition's annual conference and approved bail money to students jailed in the Sir George Williams affair. Later in the decade a chairman fighting impeachment appeared to pander to Black power activists, demanding more fundraising for Black liberation movements and calling for NBCC to prioritize Black nationalism and Pan-Africanism. At one point the immigration minister withdrew a grant to NBCC's Ontario region because intelligence reports indicated that leftists would control the money.[41]

Although the movement was split on whether to work within NBCC, members showed virtual unanimity in the early 1970s against working in coalition with whites. Horace Campbell presented his decision as an easy one: "I naively thought I would work with progressive white groups—living in a integrated environment for a while until I found out that racism pervaded the white society at every level—whether left or right." Rosie Douglas, in explaining his refusal to work with white leftists, accused the white new left of being ultra-left and unable to revolutionize the white proletariat. White workers were themselves dismissed for identifying with capitalism and viewing Black workers as a threat to their jobs. Douglas believed that the revolutionary overthrow of capitalism would abolish institutional racism, but individual racism would continue (the distinction between personal and structural racism was fairly new). Rocky Jones, concurring with Douglas, suggested that Blacks would have to organize a second revolution.[42]

The focus of Black new left activists was squarely on the Black community, but they did reach out to white radicals on occasion. The Committee to Aid the Sir George Williams Students, though established by Black radicals, included a number of white-based left-wing groups. At a 1971 rally, the committee's chairman challenged the left to fight racism by taking up the cause of the convicted former students. Rosie Douglas, who served a prison sentence for his involvement in the Sir George events, linked the judicial proceedings to larger issues of capitalism and imperialism, but showed sympathy for Quebec independence struggles. He noted that the only non-racist whites he had encountered in prison were Québécois militants. Mel Watkins of the NDP's Waffle wing, which was one of the committee's co-sponsors, expanded on part of Douglas's statement by focusing his remarks on the role of Canadian imperialism in the Caribbean.[43]

Black new left activists' day-to-day efforts were rooted in their local community, but the pan-Africanist underpinnings of their ideology situated Toronto within a transnational community that encompassed Blacks in Africa, the Caribbean, North America, and elsewhere. But of all these transnational links, those binding Toronto with the United States were the most practically significant; and at first relationships with the Black Panther Party were foremost. Over time, adulation of the Panthers gave way to more critical characterizations. Douglas argued that the Panthers had discredited themselves by working with groups such as the Communist Party that had "a history of selling out." A speaker at a BYO event accused the Panthers of being "counter-revolutionaries."[44]

Some local activists may have thought the Panthers "sold out" by only gingerly criticizing Canada. In one instance, while addressing a Toronto rally of 1,500, members of the Panthers emphasized that "Canada was a colony of the states," while declaring the country to be progressive when compared to the United States. Most white new leftists believed that Canada was a U.S. colony, but local Black power advocates had declined to support Canadian nationalism and would have seen statements about a relatively progressive Canada as anathema to their campaign to expose domestic racial discrimination. Moreover, the Panther statement was hardly an anomaly. A number of prominent Black American activists, including Martin Luther King Jr., had made similar comments. Even Malcolm X had declared, "As far as I am concerned, Mississippi is anywhere south of the Canadian border."[45]

In the early 1970s ties between local groups and the Detroit-based League of Revolutionary Black Workers supplanted former allegiances to the Panthers—accompanied, as time passed, by a rising interest in Marxism-Leninism as a way of explaining and transforming Black Torontonians' lives. Discontent with Afro-centric nationalism increased. Especially within the BYO, Garvey-like enthusiasms for Africa waned as activists increasingly oriented themselves to Marxist formulations of their struggle. A November 1970 *Black Voice* article lashed out at the "dashiki wearin" crowd expected at a Black People's Conference to be held that month, reflecting a new assessment that downgraded the importance of Africanist symbols.[46] A passage in that same issue, by a member commemorating the life of Malcolm X, suggests that BYO was evolving towards a position closer to that of its old BLF rival:

> Before Malcolm's murder he stressed close identification with Africa. This, however, has come to mean identifying with anything African instead of with revolutionary forces waging a war of liberation in the Mother country.

> I am not coming down on Afro[s] and dashikis, but I would like to stress that power does not come out of the sleeve of a dashiki, but out of a united people armed with a correct political ideology. A good example being the People's Republic of China.[47]

By 1971 significant numbers of Black activists were turning to new forms of transnational radicalism that would be less culturally specific and more Marxist-Leninist in orientation.[48]

* * *

The emergence of identity politics in the form of Black power did not undermine a once-unified new left. No new left group could boast of having even a handful of Black members prior to the emergence of Black power. But racially based organizing did provoke flashpoints. Recalling earlier opposition to women meeting separately, articles in *Guerilla* expressed disbelief that whites were barred from some Black-led meetings. Much of the newspaper's coverage of the Black People's Conference reflected a dismay at whites being excluded, causing one female reporter to state, rather oddly, that she felt like the "Invisible Man." Conference organizer Sister Akousa explained that the Black-only spaces were necessary to foster an atmosphere of togetherness. Confrontations between Black and white attendees had sidetracked the agendas of past meetings.[49]

The type of confrontation Akousa referred to resurfaced almost immediately following that conference, when a young white woman was reprimanded for referring to Rocky Jones as brother. "You haven't got the right to call us brother," thundered visiting speaker David Murphy, as the two-hundred-strong mostly Black audience shouted "right on" and stamped their feet. As Murphy mused on what derogatory depiction best fitted white people, almost two-thirds of the white audience got up from their seats and walked out. Jan Carew congratulated Murphy for his forthright and angry response and called after the retreating whites: "Walking out of the room isn't going to bring you any comfort. The voices of our anger will reach you wherever you go."[50]

But if excluding whites from meetings proved uncontroversial, the issue of white females in the bedrooms of Black activists—the "white woman question"—proved a thorny one. The BLF's Garcia and other activists faced criticism, emanating from the new left's "the personal-is-political" logic, for having white wives. When speaking in Toronto, Amiri Baraka made numerous references to this situation, at one point declaring that the first revolution was in your head, while the second was in your bed: "You've got people trying to organize the community and have got the enemy right there with them, telling them how to do it." The

A press conference held during a 1971 Black power gathering; Feb. 20, 1971.

Clara Thomas Archives and Special Collections, Toronto Telegram fonds.

feminists of the era were not the only ones to theorize that the politics of the bedroom and the politics of civil society writ large were linked. A cheap shot from a *Contrast* columnist later suggested that some Black nationalists were turning Marxist purely to justify having relationships with white women. Bedroom politics later periodically surfaced amongst Asian new leftists, who were concerned about white male–Asian female relationships, and amongst at least a handful of Latin American new left women, who similarly worried about Latin American men getting together with Anglo-American women.[51]

In the end, not one of the dozens of local Black activists drawn into this movement during 1968–69 came to it because of a "split" from SUPA—or were, indeed, ever members of SUPA or other organizations identified as *the* new left, which is a sobering indication of the narrowness and parochialism of our existing historical understandings of this complicated formation. In the case of Black power new leftists, they sought the transnational liberation of people of colour, their communities' autonomous right to meet and identify its own objectives, and to manage its cultural and political destinies without the oversight of a society increasingly defined as racist. In so doing they also defied, quite fundamentally, the self-conception of many other Canadians. As Gosse remarks, "The centuries-old presumption that the normative [North] American was a white, heterosexual man of undefined class status, neither rich nor poor, was overturned, suddenly and decisively."[52]

* * *

Some new left activists embraced "children's liberation."

Transformation, Summer 1972.

Women's liberation, like Black power, worked within, against, and beyond classic new leftism—also standing as a towering refutation of any attempt to limit the creative subversive energies of "the Sixties" to the 1960s. While a mid-1960s new leftist may never have thought about women's oppression, by the close of the decade women's liberation had become part of the new left "package." Identifying as a new leftist, or even as part of the left, would eventually require a comprehensive political and personal commitment far beyond the scope of traditional "women's issues."

After the late 1967 meeting at Hart House and the issuing of a brief on abortion reform, feminist activists took up the debate. Should the struggle to decriminalize abortion be seen as the primary issue around which women should unite, or did it constitute just one of a host of issues—everything from sexuality, men's power in the home as interwoven with their power more generally, and social responsibility for the care of infants to equal pay for equal work—each of which was, in its own way, as significant as reproductive rights?

The women's liberationists spent much of the following year holding educational meetings. They now referred to themselves as the Toronto Women's Liberation Movement (TWLM). By January 1969 selected members had begun participating in beauty pageants, using their time on stage (sometimes aided by seizing the MC's microphone) to denounce the contests as an obscene insult to women. It was vintage new leftism—a subversive strategy that made serious fun of a social institution.[53]

By then members of TWLM had created a labour-force subgroup, the first of over a dozen internal collectives to be established, which initiated an intensive support campaign for striking Hanes textile workers in the district of Rexdale, northwest of the city core. Members trekked to the picket line on a daily basis to help out and discuss personal and political matters with the strikers, most of whom were women. The strike was viewed as a particularly potent symbol of gender wage inequality, and the activists hoped that a successful outcome would inspire non-unionized women to organize. They argued that male supremacy—they were not yet using the term "patriarchy"—helped bosses and not male workers. Later, deciding that strike support activities were a poor means of organizing working women, some members suggested that activists had to enter factories

Occupiers celebrate after winning a struggle over daycare at the University of Toronto.

This Magazine Is About Schools, Spring 1970.

to do this; others pointed out that women workers could not be organized in the same way as men. A women-centred approach had to contend with their role in the family and reproduction.[54]

What today's generation would call "intersectionality" was born, not from the brains of academic theorists, but from those of activists struggling to understand the real world around them. In the midst of the Hanes strike members of the subgroup began discussing problems that working mothers faced in finding day-care and the related issue of how young children were socialized. Inspired by students at Simon Fraser University, who had started their own daycare, they began a survey in the summer of 1969 to establish the need for daycare services on the U of T campus. After securing a low-rent space from the university, these left feminists inaugurated the Campus Cooperative Daycare Centre in the fall.[55]

The co-operative was not like most other daycares in the city. Its originators preferred to view it as a community where parents, children, and volunteers were brought "into a social and communal experience with each other." TWLM day-care activists criticized the professionalism of existing daycares and wanted to challenge the idea that children were best raised in a traditional family structure. Together with other new left daycare activists, they critiqued the corporate model

A hand-drawn sign advertising a rally for the Campus daycare.

This Magazine Is About Schools, Spring 1970.

of child care, explored the different needs of poor and working-class women, and debated concepts of "tribal parenting." They arrived at their decisions about the daycare by consensus, rather than voting, they shared responsibility for chairing meetings, and parents were obliged to contribute their labour to help run the centre.[56]

When the daycare failed to gain a licence and was threatened with closure if it could not raise enough money to conform to fire regulations, TWLM and its supporters held a demonstration and occupied the building housing the university president's office. Having won their demands and secured the future of the daycare, they subsequently occupied another building that they used as a second daycare site. Activists stayed there twenty-four hours a day for ten months until they won control of the facility. The energy unleashed in that second occupation led to a strong push for government-funded, co-operative daycares for everyone.[57]

This new emphasis paralleled the shift in education, where calls for freer structures were supplemented with demands focused on ensuring universal and accessible services. It was, after all, difficult for working-class parents to spend the volunteer hours required to run a fully parent-controlled daycare. These women's liberationists were obliged to be aware of such class realities. True, there was an inherent contradiction for some new leftists in a demand for free, state-supplied child care—did one really want to apply the pedagogical authoritarianism so evident in public and high schools to young children? Nonetheless, it seemed obvious that government-run daycare was infinitely superior to no daycare at all.[58]

This car's message provoked extensive debate amongst Abortion Caravan participants.

Nancy Nicol, *Struggle for Choice – Part 1: Abortion Caravan* (1986).Courtesy of Vtape.

In spring 1970 the other great issue stirring the feminist new leftists of Toronto was the Abortion Caravan. The last leg of the Vancouver-initiated Caravan was reaching Toronto, as were militants in the Vancouver Women's Caucus. Like TWLM, members of the Vancouver group wanted both radical abortion law reform and the mobilization of women on a host of other issues. Some of them had even painted "Smash Capitalism" on one of the Caravan's vehicles; others wanted to debate the seemingly ancillary issue of whether militants could smoke marijuana while caravanning. In Toronto, they found a more heated conflict, between local Caravan organizer TWLM and other left-wing feminists who had been prevented from taking part. The out-of-town activists were perplexed by the split, which seemed "too heavy, too ideologically intense."[59]

In Ottawa some Caravan participants famously chained themselves to seats in the Parliament's viewing gallery and interrupted proceedings before heading to 24 Sussex Drive. There, at the prime minister's residence, they informed the police, who were inquiring about the movement's leaders, that "There are no leaders here." (There, one might say, spoke the new left.) After reviewing the day's events, at least one member of TWLM was unhappy. She believed the caravanners in the House of Commons should have been shouting "Victory to the NLF" (the National Liberation Front in Vietnam). Criticisms along those lines would soon bedevil TWLM itself.[60]

This attempt to combine anti-imperialism in Vietnam with feminism in Canada would resurface at an April 1971 Indochinese Conference in Toronto, organized in part by TWLM. This conference was the catalyst, if not the cause, of a vast number of ideological divisions among the left feminists of Toronto. The Toronto conference, and a similar one in Vancouver, had been initiated by Americans, who would not have been allowed to bring pro-NLF speakers from Cambodia, Laos, and Vietnam to U.S. cities. Thus Vancouver and Toronto were "stand-ins" for American locales, not places with their own identities and politics. The allegedly domineering role of the U.S. activists may have been a factor

A protest organized to coincide with the Abortion Caravan's arrival in Toronto; May 7, 1970.

Clara Thomas Archives and Special Collections, Toronto Telegram fonds.

pushing some Canadian feminists to become more enthusiastic about Canadian nationalism.

Some members now suggested that TWLM had been complicit in not challenging members who brought U.S. new left politics into the group, including the idea that the anti-imperialist struggles in Canada and the United States were simply one and the same. TWLM had been implicitly anti-national, they alleged, with fears of bourgeois nationalism having prevented an appreciation of very real differences between the two countries. A major divergence was that Canadians were themselves victims of U.S. imperialism. Nationalist grievances convinced members of TWLM's "Discussion Collective No. 6" to publish a book, *Women Unite! An Anthology of the Canadian Women's Movement*, by and about Canadians, as a corrective to a left that they found all too frequently adopting the American left's analyses and solutions.[61] The remark about "hewers of wood and drawers of water" contained in the 1967 women's liberation manifesto returned to an earlier nationalist spirit in describing the oppression of *Canadian* women: "Major decisions about the conferences were made by the American women, while the Canadians carried out the menial tasks and basic organization. Disagreement within the Canadian movement was intensified by the anger sparked in many women by the American chauvinism and internal factionalism."[62]

A second major issue was lesbianism. As a former member of TWLM recalled, some women had tried to discuss the subject with the South East Asian delegation, but the interpreter had refused, stating that no Vietnamese word existed for the concept. This refusal was followed by a dramatic moment, when one woman stood up from the crowd and asked every lesbian to stand up with her. Several did. More women stood up in solidarity. But others became agitated, upset with what they believed was an inappropriate gesture. The regular use of rival labels—"anti-imperialistic women," "feminists," "radical lesbians"—seeded the conference's divisive atmosphere.[63]

Post-conference, it was evident that the issue of same-sex relations had been crystallized for a number of TWLM members. Many would have heard something about U.S. debates on the subject at a lesbian-focused meeting the previous year, and there had once been a TWLM lesbian collective. But the exchange in the conference's auditorium had caused a number of straight TWLM members to seriously think about the issue for the first time. They were encouraged to do so by lesbian members, whose very presence complicated conventional categories concerning motherhood, womanhood, and sexuality.[64]

Exemplifying new left decentralization, TWLM contained at least a dozen collectives, along with semi-autonomous discussion and study groups.[65] Some of these groupings were vested in struggles familiar to old leftists, such as the Working Women's Collective's strike support and internal debates about who did, and who did not, belong to the working class. By 1971 the Working Women's Collective had shifted its energies at least partly to the Well Baby Clinic, jointly staffed and operated by the Women's Liberation Health Collective and People's Health Organization. Beyond working at the clinic, members made home and hospital visits to follow up with patients, initiated a support group for mothers, and, after the clinic closed for the day, jointly discussed their cases and otherwise engaged in "political struggle."[66]

For another left feminist collective, the core issue was Quebec. The Quebec Collective undertook independent initiatives, such as publishing a "Quebec Fact Sheet," but largely worked within the mixed-gender Committee for a Free Quebec on public events. Collective members ensured that the committee featured women from Quebec in their forums and that women's workshops were included at larger events. They also sought out information about women's liberation struggles in Quebec and debated the relationship between the Québécois struggle and the oppression of women. With their male peers in the Committee, they jointly discussed issues that most new left activists faced, including ways of attracting working-class people, the nature of solidarity work, and how their activism related to building socialism in English Canada.[67]

Towards the end of TWLM's active life, many of the collectives were already anticipating the post-1971 direction of women's liberation in Toronto. One collective, which did not appear to have official status, centred on developing a women's culture, to foster "writing, singing, dancing, loving and struggling with our sisters in new ways." This subgroup designed guerrilla theatre actions to accompany demonstrations and organized an all-women's picnic, but nurtured much more ambitious hopes of founding permanent women's theatres and musical bands, of producing their own graphics and publications, and of establishing a women's centre. Members of the Marriage Breakup Collective, who found that many of the women they tried to help had nowhere to stay after leaving their husbands (the city's shelters were, remarkably, men-only), developed a blueprint for starting a "Women's House." All of these ideas would be realized within a year or two.[68]

But TWLM, plagued by the kind of splitting and fissuring typical of the revolutionary left, would not be around to oversee these exciting advances. In fall 1971 seven women announced that they were leaving. TWLM's co-ordinating committee had fallen apart, they said, and had been replaced by unrepresentative and unaccountable meetings that did not even bother to record their decisions. Evoking critiques of SUPA's functioning, the activists alleged that TWLM's increasingly decentralized structure had given rise to "personalism," with decisions often made on the basis of friendship. The lack of a defined structure added in turn to another big problem: the group's inward-looking focus. Members looked down on mass, public work, they claimed, in favour of sponsoring consciousness-raising groups, service projects, and sporadic educational efforts, which was no substitute for the public outreach and union-geared activism needed if the group was to grow.[69]

In early 1969 TWLM had already faced a split from women who disagreed with its broad political focus and Marxist politics and wanted to establish a straightforwardly feminist group. As one of the leading dissenters explained, "The sexual oppression underlies all others, so we feel, and therefore we think it obscures the primary issue to approach it with, say, a Marxist analysis." Yet a small group of women who were also members of the Trotskyist League for Socialist Action and Young Socialists were part of this new opposition. To them, TWLM was too disorganized, too countercultural, too multi-issue, too inactive, and too Marxist. It was nothing but a new left–dominated "talk shop."[70]

Laurel Limpus, one of the most intellectually astute of Toronto's left feminists, recalled a series of "terrible fights" over a period of two months before the dissidents left and founded the New Feminists (NF) in March 1969. By the following month NF had expanded beyond its half-dozen co-founders and boasted of having a membership of twenty-five who met twice a week. The new organization's liberal-reform tendencies were quite pronounced during its first year, though it would later be recognized as a radical-feminist group. In contrast to the TWLM, the New Feminists attracted women who tended to be slightly older and more apt to be married with children, white-collar professionals, or those living in upper-middle-class households. But like WLMN, NF remained as decentralized as possible. It avoided having a president, or even a steering committee. To enhance its democratic ethos, internal committees with rotating memberships carried out its organizing activities.[71]

Within that collective form of leadership, thirty-two-year-old Bonnie Kreps was the organization's de facto spokesperson. Older than many of her feminist peers, Kreps had been active in feminist and new left circles in California. Her sister had authored a well-known tract exposing "The Myth of the Vaginal Orgasm" shortly after Kreps moved to Toronto in 1967. From the outset, NF received significant media publicity, aided by contacts that Kreps had made as a researcher for Toronto's CTV. Television shows that she and a fellow NFer produced were used to publicize the group and educate new members.[72] The philosophy of NF, as Kreps summarized it, defined the organization's politics for most of the following four years:

> Radical feminism is called "radical" because it is struggling to bring about really fundamental changes in our society. We, in this segment of the movement, do not believe that the oppression of women will be ended by giving them a bigger piece of the pie, as Betty Friedan would have it. We believe that the pie itself is rotten. We do not believe that women should be integrated into the male world so that they can be "just as good as men."[73]

In a pattern stretching back to Heather Dean's important 1966 feminist essay, NF was inspired by Black political organizing. Members held up Malcolm X as an author who had influenced them the most, and Kreps argued that the position of the feminist movement was analogous to that occupied by Black power five years before.[74]

NF become more radical and less liberal after 1969 as its members continued to develop as feminists. In contrast to the professional and upper-class women recruited during NF's much-publicized first year, the newer members tended to be more economically marginal, with some struggling to make ends meet on welfare or in lower-income white-collar jobs. These members attended organizational meetings and consciousness-raising sessions at NF's office. But the real engine of the group became a series of "cells," composed of about eight members each, which centred on consciousness-raising analysis and discussion.[75] As an NF document stated:

> Our chief task at present is to develop female class consciousness through sharing experience and publicly exposing the sexist foundations of all our institutions. Consciousness-raising is not "therapy," which implies the existence of

This generation had new dialectics to grapple with.

Other Woman 2-4, 1974.

> individual solutions and falsely assumes that the male-female relationship is purely personal, but the only method by which we can ensure that our program for liberation is based on the concrete realities of our lives.[76]

The very expression "female class consciousness" suggested some of the febrile debates that were engaging the left feminist world over the question of class vs. gender.

NF at first carried out protests similar to those conducted under TWLM's banner. Its members picketed *Maclean's* magazine because of its cover story on "The Natural Inferiority of Women." They demonstrated for equal pay and protested beauty pageants. In the early 1970s NF took part in three sit-ins at the Royal York Hotel's male-only dining room; one member was arrested for spray-painting over the hotel's "Men Only" sign. Members may have been responsible for a disproportionate amount of graffiti and "This Ad Insults Women" stickers that began appearing over sexist advertising. This campaign suceeeded in torpedoing at least one advertising drive when the targeted company's replacement costs spiralled out of control. It was vintage new leftism in its spontaneity, disrespect for authority, and media savvy.[77]

Despite NF's radical-feminist philosophy, the group was not necessarily receptive to lesbians. Some former NFers said Kreps worried about the presence of lesbians in the group and had even denied that any lesbians were members. After several disgruntled lesbians challenged this "bourgeois, anti-lesbian attitude," they were kicked out. Kreps may have been broadly referring to this situation when she complained of having been accused of being a liberal by members who said they were more radical than her because they hated men more. Kreps later maintained that she resigned from the group after pleading with members to avoid rage, anger, and overcommitment to the cause. It seemed as though her movement was radicalizing all around her.[78]

Most likely a general disdain of lesbianism, on one side, and a desire for a radical lesbian strategy, on the other, played a large role in NF's demise. A major part of the divergence probably came down to political differences between married and sexually conservative members such as Krep and those who did not want to relate to men at all. The definition of a lesbian provided by one NF member suggests that a more stringent definition of the "women's community" would inevitably have demanded new ways of practising radical-feminist politics: "A Lesbian is a female who moves independently of men. Lesbianism is not sex. Lesbianism is moving independently of men in every sphere of your life. . . . You do not live with a man, you do not associate with men, you do not go to parties where men are around."[79]

By 1972 many former members had switched their allegiances to new projects that embraced lesbianism. Some joined small women's separatist groups, whose "guerrilla feminism" included physical confrontations with sexist men. They believed that general feminist organizations were insufficient. Lesbian activists needed a lesbian movement.[80]

If abortion rights constituted one of the great campaigns of early 1970s feminism, and lesbianism was emerging as a significant if polarizing issue, one of the most contentious of all feminist issues in the period was raised by the "entryist" tactics of Leninist parties, particularly the Trotskyists. In late spring 1970 a small group of women, some of them members of the LSA-YS, decided to break from the NF and establish their own feminist organization. For them, NF had become too inward-looking. In its place they established the Toronto Women's Caucus (TWC), which was to be a broad, action-oriented group that would be able to recruit more women. It quickly launched a series of modest protests in which members picketed beauty pageants and held rallies against other manifestations of sexism. After starting with five women, in a matter of months TWC boasted an activist core of twenty-five to thirty. It opened an office, organized a "housewives group," and began publishing *Velvet Fist*, which was far more professional-looking than the NF or TWML periodicals and most likely had a greater readership.[81]

Reflecting the terms of its split from NF, TWC critiqued consciousness-raising—stale and pacifying, it said—and suggested that the task of the women's movement was to combine talk, action, and activism. These activities had at least a marginal benefit to the Trotskyist LSA, which recruited eight members of the TWC during the feminist group's first year and a half.[82] Still, an open letter written by TWC members Corileen North and Yvonne Trower highlighted the difficulties of a single socialist group animating a much broader social movement. They announced their resignation from the organization, alleging that it was controlled by LSA members and it was impossible to have a broad-based group with Trotskyist leadership. They complained that LSA/YS women caucused before every TWC meeting and that their members always constituted at least 60 per cent of women in attendance, allowing them to control the agenda. TWC depended on the LSA for both financial and human resources, they pointed out, which meant that the caucus had become a front group in a "classic sense." Along with distorting the TWC's internal functioning, the Trotskyist intervention also served to isolate the group from broader social movements.[83]

The open letter came only a year after the TWC tasked North to rebut a *Guerilla* article claiming that the caucus reflected "the politics of the YS almost to a T." North, a psychologist and Ph.D. student at York, had emphasized the caucus's superdemocratic structure and the plurality of its membership—with women from the Vietnam Mobilization Committee, Pollution Probe, Zero Population Growth, and the Conservative and Liberal parties. Trotskyists were a minority incapable of dominating the group. North upheld the "non-political" nature of the caucus, contrasting it favourably with "other" women's liberation groups that were prone to expel non-conforming members.[84] Her new, more critical position claimed the credibility of an insider's perspective.

The YS and the women's commission of the LSA responded that the open letter's allegations could only be taken seriously if a reader assumed that socialism and women's liberation were incompatible, that the women of LSA/YS were not really women, and that other women were "sub-intelligent dupes." They concluded that the letter was a form of Red-baiting and hinted that North, Trower, and the *Toronto Telegram* (which had featured the letter on its front page) had been motivated by a desire to divide the women's liberation movement. It appears that the open letter itself did not have a serious impact on the TWC, most likely because, as the LSA women recognized, they had been forthright about their politics and open about their ties to organized Trotskyism. The points they raised would periodically resurface and in a sense were responsible for the demise of the organization a year later.[85]

Although their newspaper *Velvet Fist* was only a year and a half old, Liz Angus (the sole staff member of TWC and a member of LSA) argued that its general feminist approach had become obsolete. Angus wanted the group to transform its paper into the organ of the abortion repeal coalition, arguing that TWC women were influential in establishing the coalition and already formed its "core staff." The coalition would create the mass movement of the future that everyone had been working towards.[86]

Many of the non-LSA women in the group were unreceptive to that proposal. They liked the paper as it was and could not imagine many women subscribing to a paper centred on abortion issues. More substantively, they disagreed with abortion being the ideal vehicle to draw women into the feminist movement. They questioned the coalition's narrow middle-class base and asserted that many women involved in the coalition were not feminists. They argued that new women who came to TWC meetings were already wondering if abortion was the only issue that the group was involved in. Using a historical analogy long favoured by new left women liberationists, they raised the issue of the dissolution of the women's suffrage movement after winning the vote as proof of the danger of adopting such a single-issue orientation.[87]

Angus countered that the reactionary social climate that the suffragists had inhabited was responsible for their dissolution and that focusing on winning the vote had probably extended that movement's lifespan. Besides, abortion was not necessarily a single issue; it raised all sorts of arguments about the status of women. Even if many of the women in the coalition were not conscious feminists, they were feminists by virtue of their activism. Moreover, a repeal victory would spur further struggles. The same focus on action and numbers that LSA had used to justify earlier splits from TWLM and NF resurfaced. Members wanting to maintain the paper were excessively concerned with generating consciousness rather than action and seemed content with a readership of 1,500 at best. Even this modest number was due to abortion repeal groups taking bundles of papers. While general feminist groups were declining in activity, "floods of women" were joining the repeal campaign.[88]

For many in the LSA, including Angus, abortion had become the "dividing line" in the women's liberation movement between supporters of mass action and the inward-looking and passive currents of the new left and reformism. Members of TWC who had previously been open to Trotskyist politics and "accepted our leadership" had come to prefer "individual solutions" over mass action and now sat on "the other side of the fence." Although these members claimed to want to get involved with issues other than abortion, they were less and less willing to do anything but talk. Their inactivity turned off new people who considered joining.[89]

In internal League bulletins long-time LSA activist Pat Schulz strongly disagreed with this negative representation of the TWC. She believed that the caucus had been flourishing and recalled going to a meeting of forty women and seeing new faces amongst them. The decline of the group had not been caused by a lack of interest or an alleged preponderance of "armchair" activists. Rather, it had come about because of the LSA's singular focus on abortion and its subsequent withdrawal from the caucus.[90] It was LSA members who were turning inward, Schulz opined, as abortion subsumed all other areas of women's oppression. YS members were being instructed to launch abortion action committees instead of general feminist groups. In recent years around three-quarters of the coverage of women's issues in LSA's *Labour Challenge* had centred on abortion. LSA was essentially saying "Forget about women's liberation" instead of using the abortion issue to build further interest in both socialism and women's liberation: "We have not taken women concerned with a single issue and broadened their view. We have reversed this process."[91]

Schulz argued that many working women viewed workplace discrimination and daycare as being more pressing concerns than abortion. Among high-school women, birth control appeared to be a more urgent issue. Women activists at U of T had gravitated to daycare, while more women had been drawn into the struggle by the union movement than any single-issue campaign. Despite LSA's best efforts, non-members were not being convinced that abortion should be the primary focus.[92] Instead of an emphasis on abortion, Schulz wanted the group to orient itself to the existing struggles and organizations in which women were already active. She conceded that the single-issue action coalition, largely created by LSA, could facilitate the organization's "intervention," allowing comrades to choose the issue, program, organizational form, and level of activity, but it came with the burden of carrying all the work. It limited the group's ability to be involved in other issues or to influence those already active in the feminist movement. With two LSA full-timers assigned to abortion work and a short-lived *Spokeswoman* newspaper largely produced by LSA staffers, the abortion struggle had become more their own movement than it was the mass movement they portrayed it to be.[93]

In the immediate aftermath of TWC's dissolution, unaffiliated members of the caucus may not have blamed the Trotskyists for the decline of their group and might even have defended them against women trying, as some LSA women said, to "Red-bait" them for their actions.[94] Yet some of these independents had at least a change of heart—and politics—shortly thereafter and came to fault the LSA for TWC's demise. Linking their experiences to those of women in Edmonton and Vancouver, they concluded that LSA/YS did not really believe in autonomous women's movements and that Trotskyist women were de facto controlled by the men in their organization.[95]

Such feminists disagreed with the LSA's prioritizing of class over sex, objecting that the class struggle was "only one aspect of feminism," and stressed that sexism could exist in a non-capitalist society. "A revolutionary women's move-

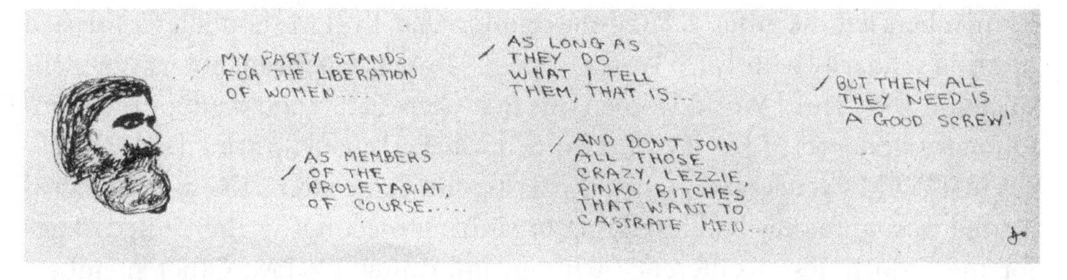

Some former members of TWC were not reluctant to show their disdain for male-dominated Marxist politics.

Other Woman 2, 4, 1974.

ment must understand the integral nature of all these struggles [class, race, and sexuality] and combine them into a single fight," they argued, anticipating late-twentieth-century social theory. Projecting grassroots organizing around "radical demands" as the only way forward, they criticized the LSA for its parliamentarism, its distinction between leaders and masses, and above all its emphasis on single-issue "liberal" campaigns. They argued that the LSA "intentions are not to stop the women's movement but to divert its direction away from smashing male supremacism and all the attending evils of racism, classism, etc., and towards getting more reforms and basic civil liberties."[96]

If the LSA had gained a much larger membership, it could easily have left a minority of its female activists to engage TWC and other locales of feminist organizing. That they did not speaks to the larger issue of how Leninist groups in English Canada, with dozens or hundreds of members, could emulate the Bolsheviks in Russia, whose ranks were often counted in the tens of thousands. One method to cope with Canadian conditions was to prioritize a small number of issues and campaigns so that the party or group could play a role out of proportion to its size. But this strategy had a number of downsides. In this instance it meant viewing "their" sector of the women's movement as being more important than the women's movement writ large. It meant severing ties with non-party women's liberationists, and increasingly isolating members from competing left-wing and feminist analyses. This approach was especially problematic for an organization claiming to be the vanguard of both left-wing social movements and the working class. The LSA/YS intervention in feminism had aroused feminist new left fears of being subtly controlled by male-dominated groups whose internal workings and motivations were opaque to them. The resulting splits, which came about after much anguish and left enduring scars, influenced how Marxists and feminists, and feminist Marxists, would interact in the following years.

No less painful, in their way, were the splits occasioned by Third Worldism. In the fall of 1970 a crisis developed within TWLM with an internal group called the Leila Khalid Collective (LKC), consisting of fifteen women who held membership in the radical anti-imperialist May 4th Movement (also called Rising Up Angry and Red Morning). The women were developing political perspectives at odds with the political beliefs of most adherents of TWLM. LKC's statement on why its members left the group offered the opinion that TWLM should have focused more on solidarity with Third World women—by which it meant not just an identification with Third World women but that Canadians should adopt the revolutionary strategies of Third World women who had taken up armed struggle.[97]

In TWLM's version of events, the flashpoint came after LKC members had started raising money and attending organizing meetings in the United States for the Indochinese Conference without informing TWLM. Other members of TWLM found this conduct unacceptable. When members of LKC were confronted, they argued that their actions exemplified a new type of leadership. They had initiated work on the Indochinese Conference to make TWLM more political. TWLM's co-ordinating committee issued an ultimatum:

> Everytime we try to talk to LKC about their practise you manipulate the discussion to talk about politics, which you incorrectly distinguish from your practise. We will not talk about your paper until you self-criticize your practise and agree to be under the discipline of WLM as a whole. If you don't want to meet these conditions you should no longer consider yourselves part of Women's Liberation.[98]

LKC representatives said they were not interested in discussing their practice or debating and preferred to separate from TWLM.[99]

The LKC collective's distinct political viewpoints made cohabiting with TWLM untenable—as two essays by LKC's Peggy Morton and the group's statement on leaving TWLM make clear. LKC criticized TWLM's views on "consumerism," targeting the past campaigns against beauty pageants. The gist of LKC's position was that a serious politics of revolutionary solidarity meant setting to one side such trivial issues, which were of interest only to middle-class Western women. Even organizing working women in the workplace was a waste of time, and so too was the reformist struggle for more daycare spaces.[100]

Some women within the Toronto feminist movement did respond to Morton's appraisal. Workers at the York University Day Care Centre took up LKC's critique of daycare. They now repudiated their past practice for being reformist and adopted the same strategy for daycare that Morton had outlined. Although the York University Day Care Centre had hardly been apolitical—parents were warned that the nuclear family was repressive; they were encouraged to raise their children communally; and instructed on how authoritarian child-rearing practices served the capitalist system—it had not lived up to LKC's ideal: "The students and faculty at York have already chosen to be liberal professionals rather than fight a repressive economic system. They are bourgeois privileged people and daycare on campus for them only enhances their privileges."[101]

Following the split some members of TWLM accused LKC of being Third World vanguardists, who at best ignored the working class and at worst identified them as part of the system. LKC could never understand the oppression of women, they argued, because that oppression was rooted in the capitalist division of labour. LKC understood exploitation only in terms of morality and global anti-imperialism. TWLM members lambasted LKC for downplaying fights for abortion, daycare, and equal pay, and for counterposing such "reformist" struggles to their own "anti-imperialist politics."[102]

At the end of 1971 left feminism in Toronto was still mired in the messy process of being born. Feminists had written manifestos, launched newspapers, published the first book-length expositions of their position, challenged mainstream leftists, and wrestled with profoundly unsettling issues. If some of this might be dismissed as so many tempests in a Toronto teapot—and that was the response of at least some sympathetic outsiders as they received the latest word from Canada's metropolis—much of it was far more significant. Such debates would play out in the far larger and more powerful left feminism that gained traction in Toronto from 1972 to 1978—again, a periodization of left feminism that, in itself, places a large question mark over any attempt to confine Toronto's "sixties" to the 1960s.

* * *

The histories of feminism and Black struggle in North America generally pay no attention to Canada or Toronto—even though the Black power and feminist movements in Toronto, in their earliest phases, were quite busily re-enacting transnational debates sweeping the Western world. From 1968 to 1971 the "balance of trade" in ideas, inspirations, and defining struggles was not running in Canada's favour. Many of the manifestations of left politics were unfolding on a world scale, and Toronto leftists were adding their voices to them, rallying, for instance, to the U.S. civil rights movement or deriving inspiration from, and offering shelter to, the Black Panthers.

In both forms of identity leftism, nothing was more typical than the visiting left celebrity performing on a Toronto stage as one appearance amongst many. Yet such re-enactments were not without lasting local effects. Lip-synching gradually turned into homegrown creativity. Abstractly conceived ideals of racial and gender liberation came to be rooted in local organizations and struggles. Over time the transnational call for liberation came to be heard and lived on the local level.

From 1968 to 1971 activists in both camps—feminist and Black power—had to respond to worried commentators who feared their politics was based on hateful exclusion. Watkins was falsely depicted as a Black man who hated whites;

feminists were routinely quizzed on whether they really hated men. In both cases, reporters sometimes found evidence of what they considered a "reverse discrimination"—from some of the more honky-hating and male-deriding proclamations of their targets—and happily broadcast the results. The framing of such issues served to sideline the complaints that both groups made about a sexist and racist society. The dominant opinion attributed charges against male and white supremacy to flawed, hateful individuals with "chips on their shoulders."[103] New left men would rarely if ever deny the structural basis of racism or sexism in the late 1960s, but they were not exempt from the tendency of male reporters to trivialize both women's issues and women's liberation activists. Just as some white new leftists objected to Black activists meeting without them, some men expressed discomfort with meetings that were attended by women only.[104]

Echoes of these positions were to be heard much later on amongst those who lamented the "identity politics" that undermined a supposedly once-cohesive movement. But the new left was never particularly unified—not in its earliest days before 1965, and not from 1968 to 1971. The new left operated without an authoritative central committee and was inherently disinclined to unity. Yet it was also inherently disinclined to self-satisfaction and stagnation.

Much of what we now take for granted about the politics of racial equality was first elaborated in the 1960s by much-maligned Black power advocates, who pointed out the obvious durability of racism in Canadian society and strove to overcome it. Much of what we now take for granted about the politics of gender equality was first elaborated by equally maligned left feminists, who argued, with themselves as much as with the rest of society, about what genuine equality between men and women might look like. That their debates were messy and often painful is obvious. That they were of enduring value is no less so. Thanks to the debates of this early period, those entering the Toronto new left after 1971 would find that anti-racism and anti-sexism were no longer strenuously debated by most serious new leftists. For many, such struggles had simply become part of the new left package.

6

Obsolete Communism and Conflicting Visions? Wafflers, Liberals, and New Leninists, 1968–71

"Revolution!"

"Kill the pigs!"

"They can't stop you . . . Over the gate!"

The Canadian National Exhibition was engulfed in chaos. Hundreds, even thousands, of people had crashed through the Exhibition gates or climbed over its fences. Applause rang out each time someone breached the perimeter. A young man waving a toy machine gun yelled for others to come on in.

Police chased after the fence climbers. They tried to disperse the 2,500 protesters who remained outside by driving horses and motorcycles into the crowd. Some protesters shouted, "Don't throw rocks!" Others yelled, "______ pigs" and threw firecrackers and black pepper at the horses. Speaking to reporters, the police chief predicted: "This is only the beginning. . . . It's an indication of the growing militancy of youth. . . . They don't want to go along with anything that smacks of the establishment."[1]

All of this took place in June 1970, at what was supposed to have been the largest pop festival in Canadian history. Its bill was packed with popular American acts. Janice Joplin, the Grateful Dead, the Flying Burrito Brothers, and The Band were all there. But songs were few and far between. It was not because of some sort of spontaneous chaos. This disorder had been very well organized. An astute headline later declared, "Music Takes Back Seat to Politics at Festival." The politics of a new organization called the May 4th Movement (M4M) was in the driver's seat.[2]

The countercultural sensibilities of M4M members had been offended by the festival's announcement. They also saw a strategic opportunity. The Walker-Eaton Festival, popularly known as the Festival Express, had been organized by Ken Walker along with George and Thor Eaton. The idea was to take a number of popular bands on a "portable" tour, by train, which would also go to Winnipeg and Calgary. The organizers, sons of rich and prominent Toronto families, were practically poster boys for what had been derisively labelled "hip capitalism." The festival's indirect connection to Eaton's—"a place that's anti-union, anti-woman, and anti-young people" and pro–Spadina Expressway—made it even more loathsome. At $16 a ticket, it promised to be the city's most expensive concert ever.[3]

In a poster proclaiming, "EATON-WALKER (RIP-OFF) FESTIVAL IS FREE FREE FREE (yeah) IF WE TAKE IT TAKE IT TAKE IT (dig it)," M4M encouraged people to crash the two-day event en masse. Youth, it said, had invented their own music, dress, politics, and lifestyle only to have it stolen by the capitalist "pig" system. By forcefully entering the festival and refusing to pay, this authentic and liberating culture could be restored. "Peace, Love and $16" was the group's pithy slogan satirizing the bourgeois appropriation of the counterculture. A member of M4M had approached the festival's producers with a host of demands. He instructed them to drop their admission fee entirely or put 20 per cent of the take into a fund for daycare, bail money, and the development of "people's parks." The producers showed little interest in those options. Walker later boasted of taking the activist by the neck and throwing him down a flight of stairs. It proved to be a tactically flawed decision.[4]

When it later became evident that the festival was paralyzed and might have to be completely shut down, the producers panicked. The police had already approached them, suggesting that order might be restored if ticket prices were reduced. One performer walked away from the stage mid-act, having failed to win the crowd's attention. In the end the organizers gave in to, or at least compromised with, the protesters. The Grateful Dead and other acts would now be performing for free in a neighbouring park. Some six thousand people turned out to the first free concert, which lasted until four a.m., and a couple of thousand turned out to a subsequent event. There were lots of drugs, some nude dancing, and the music was excellent. Food and underground newspapers became communal property, and M4M members raised money for some of the young people in police custody.[5]

Word quickly spread about what had happened, and the festival's producers were dogged by restive audiences and demands for free concerts at subsequent stops on the tour. Calgary's mayor even got into the act, demanding that the festival be free in his city. The large communications company that had quietly partnered with the producers subsequently declared the festival a $200,000 loss. Preventing the exploitation and appropriation of the counterculture was probably an impossible task, but M4M had at least made some companies think twice about the matter. More importantly, it had shown thousands of young people that collective action could be successful, inspiring a series of largely spontaneous gate crashes later that summer. In one instance, well over a thousand people forced their way into the Mariposa Folk Festival, despite M4M's agreement to leave the non-profit event alone. In analyzing this new trend, a reporter dramatically predicted that large, admission-based concerts would become a thing of the past in Toronto.[6]

Most of the M4M members involved in successfully organizing against the festival looked like hippies. They had a countercultural bent, but their politics included a retro ideology. The activists adhered in practice and theory to a "new Leninism," quite set apart from new leftism (although many of them were indeed former new leftists).

New Leninists were distinguished from their Leninist forebears in a number of ways. The adherents, instead of being organically anchored in factories, were a more diffuse lot, encompassing larger numbers of students and white-collar workers as a proportion of their total membership. Indeed, both their memberships and leaderships were largely university-educated. During a time when office and service-sector employment was on the increase and union organizing campaigns were signing up public-sector workers in record numbers, new Leninists were largely focused on recruiting factory workers, a section of the workforce on the verge of a steep decline in the city centre. Post-secondary students and white-collar workers often took factory jobs as part of their party-building projects.

While an earlier generation of Leninists had played a part in shaping the terrain of left-wing Canadian politics as a whole, new Leninists were less successful on that front. They had less philosophic unity and influence. Their forces were divided amongst several competing organizations, each claiming to be the vanguard of the Canadian proletariat. Reflecting their times, most of the devotees were inspired by Third World revolutions, and they emphasized the importance of "the national question." They were more suspicious of the middle class, petty bourgeoisie, and intellectuals. To varying degrees they were both attracted to, and repulsed by, new left ideas.

Many new Leninists were Maoists, inspired by the direction of the Communist Party of China. Some were Trotskyists, aligned to small groups of co-thinkers around the world. Others did not identify with any major Leninist tradition. Most of their organizations debated, romanticized, and sought to emulate aspects of the pre–Second World War Communist Party. They largely favoured the "go-it-alone" approach of the Communist Party's Third Period (1928–35) over the collaboration of the Popular Front (1935–39). Leninists today tend to draw from the same well of history, ignoring the contribution of their fellow new Leninists.

Marxist-Leninists, as part of this stream, emerged as a significant force in the Toronto left after 1968. Although plainly intent on stealing the new left's thunder, capturing its base, and opposing it philosophically and strategically, they came to articulate political ideas and organize political forms that were just as plainly influenced by the very new leftism they so vociferously opposed. Far from being a "flash-in-the-pan," easily subsumed by other organizations on the left, new leftism's enduring influence continued even amongst those who had sworn to replace it.

* * *

As they pushed their agenda from 1968 to 1971, new leftists challenged the pre-existing institutions of Toronto's progressive politics—the CCF-NDP, the Communist Party, even the Liberals. Especially after 1968, the social democrats, communists, and left liberals had to contend with an upstart formation calling their left-wing credentials into question. All three camps displayed a complicated pattern of selective appropriation and dissemination of new left ideas.

Some old leftists had reacted negatively to the new modes of thinking and organizing, and were pushed to the right. Others dove in and embraced those changes. Rabbi Feinberg, formerly a vocal foe of communism, became a big fan of Vietnamese Communist leader Ho Chi Minh. He stopped criticizing activists for being hooked on popular culture and recorded a song with pop-cult icon John Lennon. His later sympathy for America's urban guerrillas suggests that he no longer considered activists who handed out leaflets without a property owner's permission as being beyond the pale. Other local old leftists began to latch onto new left ideas, or were at least more apt to describe their politics in new left terms. University of Toronto math professor Chandler Davis (a long-time leftist and key faculty activist), for example, now emphasized that the main task of radicals was to create a new relationship between people and power—not after the revolution, but as soon as possible. Suggestions arose that the revolutionary Che Guevara—whose pictures adorned many activist homes and offices—had borrowed his statements on love and revolution from the new left.[7]

The New Democratic Party, in small steps, tried to orient itself to new left concerns. Ontario party leader Donald MacDonald spoke of developing participatory structures within both the NDP and society to attract new leftists alienated from his party. The federal NDP's president, Toronto-based MPP James Renwick, admitted that he would have joined the new left had he been younger. The head of the Ontario NDP's policy review committee insisted that a series of party discussion papers had included "a considerable amount of New Left influence." The papers raised calls for participatory democracy, community organization, and an end to government control over personal behaviour and preferences: "If our proposals for ending the cruelty and selfishness of society only produce new bureaucracies, we shall, in great part, have failed our ideals. The bridge between enlightened legislation and an enlightened society is community participation."[8]

A far more significant new left push came from within the local grassroots of the party. In 1968 activists began calling on the party to adopt a politics of Canadian national liberation and working-class self-management. Edward Broadbent was among those suggesting the transformation. As a doctoral student under the renowned C.B. Macpherson at the University of Toronto, and then as a York University lecturer, Broadbent was clearly considered a middle-class radical. At the same time he was keenly interested in worker self-management—touting the Yugoslavian example of it as a model for Canadian leftists—and would eventually arrive in Parliament as the MP for working-class Oshawa.

To the question "Do we wish to remain with the welfare state or do we want to go beyond it?" Broadbent had enthusiastically argued for moving forward. The welfare state, he explained, was a liberal brand of democracy in which power was concentrated in the hands of a few and capitalism reigned supreme. The task of democratic socialists in the 1960s necessitated not only "going beyond" capitalism, working for the elimination of inequality and the extension of democracy to the workplace, but also advancing towards a new kind of socialism that would transcend even the old radicalism of the CCF: "And socialism, we must show as Czechs, French workers and students and North American students have demonstrated, does not mean the concentration of more and more power in the central government, but rather the decentralization of power."[9]

In spring 1969 Broadbent and ten other members of the NDP began meeting in Toronto to discuss how a new left–influenced version of socialism could be brought into the mainstream of the party. Together they produced a proposal called the "Manifesto for an Independent Socialist Canada."[10] In urging NDP members to take their party in a nationalist direction, the manifesto did not try to define what it meant to be a Canadian, or anything like that. Its demand for independence rested wholly on extricating Canada from its economic and military entanglement with the American Empire. In calling for a "truly socialist party" rooted in factories, offices, farms, and campuses, the manifesto carefully positioned the NDP as the parliamentary arm of a larger mass movement. Like many old left manifestos, it suggested that unions were the most important component of that movement. But the manifesto also evoked a distinctly new left kind of socialism—a socialism promising to liberate people from their spiritual oppression and to foster decentralized, participatory decision-making:

> A socialist transformation of society will return to man his sense of humanity, to replace his sense of being a commodity. But a socialist democracy implies

> man's control of his immediate environment as well, and in any strategy for building socialism, community democracy is as vital as the struggle for electoral success. To that end, socialists must strive for democracy at those levels that most directly affect us all—in our neighborhoods, our schools, and our places of work.[11]

As historian Robert Hackett observes, this version of socialism was quite different than the one presented in the CCF's technocratic *Regina Manifesto* (1933), which had envisioned a large centralized state strongly influenced by experts.[12]

The manifesto circulated privately during the summer—with many new supporters adding their signatures, although Broadbent himself ultimately refrained from doing so. In September the group of NDPers publicly released the manifesto at a conference. The news media were largely critical—some reactions were described as "hysterical"—but the manifesto garnered substantial publicity and won support from surprising figures: even Tommy Douglas, the NDP's leader, was sympathetic. Senior NDPers agreed to have the manifesto debated at the party's federal convention, scheduled to take place the following month.[13]

The manifesto signers continued to organize supporters, eventually forming a caucus within the party called the Waffle—an irregular name based on one participant's comment that he would rather "waffle to the left" than "waffle to the right." James Laxer and Mel Watkins soon became the Waffle's most visible leaders. Laxer had a strong socialist, nationalist, and activist pedigree stretching back to his Communist childhood. Watkins was a University of Toronto political economics professor who had recently chaired a government taskforce on foreign investment. The taskforce's recommendation for greater Canadian economic independence, contained in what was popularly dubbed "The Watkins Report," received significant attention. Prior to the founding meetings of the caucus, Watkins had written: "To implement the Watkins Report is decidedly second-best; the first-best solution is socialism, and a radical socialism at that."[14]

Before the debate at the NDP's convention, the party's national council tried to dilute support for the manifesto by advertising a new interest in "extra parliamentary activity." Members also commissioned a manifesto of their own. Penned by deputy party leader David Lewis and Montreal-based philosopher Charles Taylor (who had signed the Waffle manifesto but then changed his mind), their "For a United and Independent Canada" called for regulations to curtail U.S. capital and included public ownership as a potential tool for democratic socialists. Recognizing that it was designed to circumvent the manifesto's influence, its detractors quickly dubbed it the "Marshmallow Resolution," a pointed reference to one of the new left's favourite terms for wishy-washy liberals.[15]

At the convention, after intense debate the Waffle's manifesto was voted down 499 to 268. But eight supporters were elected to the party's federal council, and Watkins became one of the NDP's vice-presidents. Wafflers were also able to pass a number of motions, including one calling for Canada to withdraw from all U.S.-Canadian military agreements. Their proposal to add party council seats exclusively for women, which was narrowly defeated, suggests that feminists were beginning to make themselves heard within the caucus. Despite the manifesto's defeat, the Waffle continued to attract considerable attention and new recruits.[16]

A poster for a Toronto Waffle women's conference.

Author's collection.

Toronto members became intensely involved with efforts to save the Dunlop Canada rubber products plant, which had been a fixture on Queen Street East since 1919. After the British-based multinational announced the immediate layoff of all of the factory's workers (numbering about six hundred), the militants organized demonstrations and a 30,000-signature petition demanding government intervention to halt the closure. But when their solidarity efforts extended to critiquing the union and NDP for insufficient responses, leaders of both organizations made it clear that the Waffle had overstepped its bounds. Pushback from union and party officials increased when the Ontario Waffle released its own manifesto, "For a Socialist Ontario in an Independent Socialist Canada," which placed a greater emphasis on the importance of unions and workers than the federal manifesto had done, especially in critiquing the role of U.S.-led unions and calling for their replacement by new autonomous organizations.[17]

Despite blowback from the party establishment and organized labour, the Waffle demonstrated its strength at the Ontario NDP's convention in October 1970. Delegates approved parts of their resolutions on housing and women's liberation and fully backed a Waffle motion on nationalizing Canada's energy industry. The defeat of the Ontario manifesto was surprisingly narrow, at 744 to 628, revealing a substantial base within a major Ontario party for a politics that was unmistakably new leftist in many of its key demands. Reflecting that radicalism, motions guaranteeing collective bargaining rights for tenants and an impressive environmental package, which allowed the "forfeiture of ownership" for persistent pollution offenders and supports for workers harmed by environment-related layoffs, both passed. Several other resolutions had an unmistakable new left hue. These included calls for a provincial department of co-operative living, the creation of powerful community councils, the wide-scale establishment of co-operative daycares controlled by parents, and a full-time NDP organizer to assist social movement organizations.[18]

The highlight of the federal NDP's 1971 convention was Laxer's campaign for party leadership. He placed second on each of the four ballots, but David Lewis ultimately beat him by a two-to-one margin. This time the Waffle was much less successful on the policy front, with most of its resolutions resoundingly defeated. Nonetheless, the Wafflers continued to shape discussions—and to update their agenda: most notably, their manifesto had not referenced two of the issues that they now heavily promoted at the convention (a guarantee of a percentage of federal council seats for women and support for Quebec self-determination). The Waffle thus showed itself capable of expressing a diversity of new left positions. Although the issue of workers' control did not make it to the convention floor, it too was a sign of the Waffle's new left inclinations. Some Wafflers viewed workers' control as an immediate goal that could increase a general political consciousness and go beyond wages, benefits, and other common collective-bargaining demands. Workers were increasingly attracted to this concept, they argued, pointing to the CLC's recent convention, where the issue had been frequently raised under the cautious term of industrial democracy.[19]

By judging the Waffle in a harsh Cold War light, David Lewis and other top party officials aligned themselves with one way of seeing the offshoot—as a political tendency shaped by Communist antecedents (and even echoing, in its call for "self-determination," some older Communist formulations). Other comments stressed the Waffle's deep roots in social democracy itself—as suggested by the Wafflers' penchant for championing the legacy of the CCF's J.S. Woodsworth—or, more simply, as yet another new left movement. But in his study, Robert Hackett is undoubtedly right to call the Waffle a "heterogeneous coalition" that reflected all three of these tendencies. Watkins himself hinted of such a coalition when he suggested that the Waffle's new left strategy for social change allowed different styles and approaches to politics to coexist in way that did not occur in university-based new left groups: "In some sense, the students think they're too radical for us."[20]

Waffle enthusiasts themselves were sometimes divided over matters of new left politics and mores. One member, Jackie Larkin, recalled that while most Wafflers joined together to chant "power to the people" on the NDP's convention floor in 1971, some were clearly "uptight" about identifying the faction with the slogan. (It did not help that, for Canadian nationalists, the SDS slogan had an unmistakably American provenance.) Laxer, for one, disliked that slogan, and often used the phrases new left and "new middle-class left" interchangeably. Yet he was not completely beyond appealing to such sentiments. In one instance he pitched a proposal that he favoured for organizing the industrial hinterland of the province as an opportunity for the new leftists to finally integrate their sentiments about community control and community organizing with a "complete strategy for socialism."[21]

In another instance, a group of Wafflers engaged in mental gymastics to avoid using the term "community organizing" because many of their fellow members viewed the concept as reformist, American, and "new left." They instead fastened upon "social animation" as a means of shaking the Waffle out of its "rather static, meeting-oriented view of building socialism." In contrast to the earlier term, *animation sociale* had Québécois, and perhaps more revolutionary, overtones. Their reluctance to idenfity too closely with U.S. new left concepts made European new left philosophers all the more attractive. André Gorz, the French theorist who argued for a fundamental reconsideration of Marxist thinking about the working class and emphasized the demand for workers' control, wielded considerable influence.[22]

* * *

In 1972 the leadership of the Ontario NDP gave members of the Waffle an ultimatum: disband or leave. Those who left founded the Movement for an Independent Socialist Canada, but most activists continued to call the group the Waffle. It is telling that, while the old leftists running the NDP (and the Communist Party) targeted the Wafflers for criticism, new leftists did not join in the attack—and that is probably because many of them, convinced they had completely avoided the "social-democratic stage" in their process of radicalization, supported the faction. A 1972 guide to U of T leftist groups, written by *Varsity* new leftists, lambasted all of the campus new Leninist groups but pointedly avoided making critical comments about the politics of either the Waffle or another radical grouping, the Old Mole (OM).[23]

The Old Mole had begun as an informal venue for campus activists to discuss theory and strategy. Members bonded through a shared new left understanding of issues and their criticisms of rival social-democratic and new Leninist perspectives. At a time when activists showed a tendency to abandon the campus as the central focus of struggle, the Old Mole continued to advance student power, sometimes resorting to tactics that recalled the in-your-face activism of the Toronto Student Movement. Notably, most OM members were also affiliated to the Waffle. They saw most Wafflers as allies in the struggle for revolutionary change, but criticized some caucus members for being "social democrats in their approach to politics." A broadly similar orientation—both supportive and critical—could be

New leftists hoped that workers' self-management (evoked here during the 1978–79 Bell Canada strike) would become a sign of the times.

Strike! November-December 1981.

found among activists attached to the Montreal-based publishing collective Our Generation, which for a time had a Toronto contingent in place. The new left–anarchist-oriented group supported Toronto members who wanted to join the Waffle during the period when it was being forced out of the NDP.[24]

Communists and Trotskyists were, on many occasions, much less keen on the Waffle, which had emerged so quickly and powerfully as their competitor. Both strains were especially suspicious of the Waffle activists who pursued politics with a new leftist tilt. The League for Socialist Action condemned caucus members for betraying their lack of class analysis by using "utopian concepts" such as participatory democracy. The LSA unfairly attacked a document written by Winnipeg socialist and *Canadian Dimension* editor Cy Gonick as being representative of the Waffle's non-revolutionary orientation and typical of its middle-class and petty-bourgeois leadership.[25] While the paper had been discussed inside the Waffle, Gonick was clearly struggling to find a way of combining a new left vision of a transformed world, in which participatory democracy prevailed, with the challenges of organizing in actually existing Western societies. In Gonick's vision, the socialist movement would be active in a constellation of organizations—farm unions, tenant unions, student unions, associations of teachers, social workers, community and neighbourhood clubs, peace movements, environmental groups—within which they would help people become politically conscious by formulating demands for community and worker control and student power:

> In short, it must do what socialists like G.D.H. Cole and Erich Fromm and Antonio Gramsci have advocated—and that is to develop socialist man within the old society, to begin thinking and living in a new way, through continuous and persistent struggle to win majorities throughout the civil orders of society.[26]

LSA members essentially criticized the Waffle for not sharing their own conception of politics. They wanted the Waffle to centre on work within the NDP and slammed the group for focusing too much on industrial workplaces. They complained that the Waffle's strong involvement in a strike at the Texpack textile factory in Brantford, Ont., had diverted energy that could have been used for the

NDP's election campaign. Outside the NDP, they advised Wafflers to focus on the anti-war and abortion campaigns. These areas—not unions or the general feminist movement—were where most people were radicalizing.[27]

But it was the Communists who could be the most prickly. To be sure, they professed to be encouraged by the heightened presence of leftists within their NDP rival. On the other hand, the party seemed threatened by the Wafflers' commitment to ideals of Canadian nationalism and socialism—which, in its own eyes, it owned. The Communist Party members were quite cognizant that the Waffle, within which old Communist names like "Laxer" were prominent, had the potential to cause problems within its own ranks.

CPC leader William Kashtan waxed harshly critical of "those forces in the Waffle movement, however well-intentioned, who insist on coupling the questions of Canadian independence, the fight against monopoly and the question of a socialist 'Ontario.'" Such a strategy played "objectively . . . into the hands of the Tories and monopoly, and also the most right-wing element of their own party." Canada would need a higher level of struggle before socialist demands could be made, he said, while simultaneously arguing that the Waffle's demands were not really socialist at all. He invited Wafflers and other "genuine" leftists to join his Communists in fighting for the public ownership of resources via a broad anti-monopoly coalition "headed by the working class and its Marxist-Leninist Party, as a transition to the building of a socialist Canada."[28]

Targeting one of the new left–influenced aspects of the Waffle's program, articles in CPC's press denounced the caucus's demands for industrial democracy and workers' control as petty-bourgeois and reformist, while linking the concepts to the influence of German-American philosopher and political theorist Herbert Marcuse. As the author of the severely critical *Soviet Marxism: A Critical Analysis* (1958), Marcuse was a perennial Communist target. The demands were appropriate in a post-revolutionary situation, Kashtan allowed, but it was counter-revolutionary to raise them prior to the abolition of private property. In this spirit, CPC writers generally refused to distinguish between new left calls for workers' control and Western European co-management schemes:

> What is this, but anarchist gobbledegook and syndicalist phrase-mongering that negates ideological and political struggle and capitulates before the class enemy [?] Simply another form of capitalist-fostered co-determination, or workers' control in the form of class collaboration.[29]

These views reflected the party's rising hostility towards the new left, which was first publicly aired in a late 1968 *Canadian Tribune* article that criticized all facets of student lifestyle and protest. This theme quickly became the de facto party line after a missive criticized some party members for their "opportunistic" acceptance of new left ideology. Urgent action was now needed, the document stated, because petty-bourgeois radicals were exerting dangerous pressure on both the party and the working class. The new policy did encounter internal dissent from within the CPC. Stanley Ryerson emphasized that the progressive thrust of the new left overshadowed any class and ideology deficiencies its adherents might have and warned that by treating them as enemies the party would lose any chance of influencing them. But effectively speaking for the majority opinion, Communist veteran Sam Walsh countered that such deficiencies did in fact define the young leftists. Tailing after them—to use the parlance of vanguard party enthusiasts—would repudiate the privileged role of the party.[30]

Support or hostility to the new left was closely tied to assessments of the Soviet invasion of Czechoslovakia in 1968. Russian tanks figured inadvertently as vivid counterpoints to the joyous, spontaneous energies of Paris 1968. The CPC was split on the 1968 invasion, and such division was particularly marked in Toronto, where a substantial "Eurocommunist" tendency had emerged centred on U of T and identifying closely with Ryerson. For a time there was a real possibility that the existing party leadership would be overturned and the reformers come to power. Toronto Communists opposed to the invasion tended to see sectarianism as the main danger to the party and had a more positive view of the new left. Those supporting the Soviet action, and hostile to the new left, saw revisionism as the main danger—and that position came to the fore amidst the inward and orthodox turn that the party made in rallying around the Soviet flag in the invasion's aftermath.

The official history of the CPC refers to these events under a section entitled "In Defense of Communist Principles." Its main argument is that an "opportunist" tendency had taken root in the party but was only revealed after the central committee supported the "revisionist" changes taking place in Czechoslovakia and expressed disagreement with the Soviet invasion. A fight was on, and in October support for the invasion was affirmed and a house cleaning began that removed the supposed opportunists from important party roles and closed down the party-affiliated publications *Scan* and *Horizons*.[31]

* * *

If many of the established left-wing organizations in Toronto reacted to the rise of the new left with a mix of appreciation of its new energy and suspicion of its hegemonic ambitions, more surprising was the extent to which new leftism penetrated the consciousness of some Toronto Liberals. Their federal party, after all, had been governing Canada since 1963. As the official opposition in Ontario, the

Liberals had often spoken on behalf of rural Ontarians far removed from the hotbed political realms of downtown Toronto and the urban universities. Nonetheless, new left energies were at work within the Liberal Party, in which members sometimes outdid social democrats and communists in swearing allegiance to an entirely refurbished and participatory society. Some of them were influenced by Pierre Trudeau's somewhat ambiguous ideal of the "Just Society," and others could also remember the prime minister's warm words of endorsation for "Participatory Democracy." It was also under federal funding from the Liberals that the Company of Young Canadians began to speak out with a voice of youthful idealism and Opportunities for Youth (OFY) grants financed a legion of left initiatives.

The youth wing of the Liberal Party took on a new left atmosphere from 1968 to 1971. A York University member of the party even wrote at this time of the "Student Liberal as Nigger," evoking the notorious student-power manifesto of the day. He likened his party's version of participatory democracy to controlled elections in Russia and asked why student, community, and anti-war activists were outperforming his own party in political relevance.[32] Ryerson's fabled student president, Janet Weir—with her ambiguous support for Communism—was also active in the Liberal Party. Her tenure in office received positive reviews from leftist activists and at one point created a storm of controversy after she had been quoted as saying she was a communist. The context for that comment, she later explained, was an argument over the idea of a classless society: "If they want to call the classless society Communist, then I'm for it."[33]

Institutionally, this trend became more noticeable after 1968. Debate at a federal Liberal youth convention in 1969 centred on whether to get involved with the "global student power movement." The Liberal Party's youth director told the delegates: "Radical liberalism is the key and often the solution to many problems affecting the students. . . . We cannot survive unless we become relevant." Closer to home, the Ontario Young Liberal Association voted to disband in an attempt to increase its leverage with the "adult" party, and local young Liberals dragged out a Toronto and District Liberal Association meeting to seven hours in their quest for additional youth delegates.[34]

Meanwhile, the Ontario Student Liberals threatened to quit the party if it did not start responding to the needs of the "politically disenfranchised." In 1969 provincial convention delegates approved a "manifesto of revolt" by a 35 to 22 vote. It stated: "Without a new definition and commitment to the building of a humanistic society, we believe that we can no longer support the Liberal party." The new definition included party alignment with the protest movements of tenants, the poor, students, Indigenous peoples, and other minorities. The student Liberals emphasized that their work with the oppressed would be neither charitable nor top-down. Rather, they would form a community with them and not try to impose their own middle-class values.[35]

David Cole, the re-elected Toronto-based president of the Ontario Student Liberals, told the gathering that the Liberal parties were controlled by large economic interests, and that agents of insurance companies within the party were responsible for the downfall of the nationalist minister of finance, Walter Gordon. Although Ontario Liberal leader Robert Nixon, who was no radical, urged delegates to be less critical and questioned the manifesto's use of the phrase "perverted Liberalism," he also told the students: "You've served notice you want to be part of the party on the street and on the Indian reserve and in that spirit I welcome it."[36]

The young Liberals had some older Liberals as allies. MPP Tim Reid had, with his wife Julyan, edited the anthology *Student Power and the Canadian Campus*. He chaired the social change committee that created the Ontario Student Liberals' controversial manifesto. Colin Vaughan, who later became a well-known Toronto councillor, lectured the Young Liberals on the importance of devolving political power to make it more locally responsive and on the need to reorient urban planning to focus on people instead of "coldblooded developers." Young Liberals were encouraged to study a plan he favoured for eliminating provinces and replacing them with largely autonomous city states.[37]

Young Liberals were most likely heartened by Stephen Clarkson's Liberal 1969 mayoral campaign. Clarkson pledged to strengthen the rights and the associations of tenants, humanize welfare, hold monthly citizen forums in each ward, promote continual community participation in the planning process, and investigate how the city could implement free public transportation. He used stronger rhetoric than what might have been expected from a Liberal, describing tenants as living in a state of "legal serfdom." Anticipating the explosion about to erupt over the Spadina Expressway, he asked voters to choose between an "automobile city" and a "people city."[38] In short, Clarkson genuinely appeared to take the advent of sixties activism to heart. He insisted that welfare recipients, students, and other unprivileged Torontonians needed to control the policies that had an impact on their lives, and that the Liberal Party had to change to accommodate this new era of activism: "At a time when Poor Power and Red Power are joining Student Power and Labor Power with direct demands on government, it is essential for the successful adaptation of our political system that the parties be capable of integrating and transmitting into action the general demand of People Power."[39]

Young Liberals maintained their move to the left in 1970. John Varley, the English vice-president of the Canadian Student Liberals and a student at York, published a manifesto that damned the party as the "voice of the Establishment" and depicted Trudeau as a Mackenzie King–style conservative whose participatory democracy rhetoric was just that. Varley's kindest words implied that the other parties were no better. He called for government subsidies to replace large corporate donations and urged the party to "get to the people" and join them in demonstrations. When an elder Liberal put a damper on the prospect of the party getting involved in such action, a young Liberal suggested that similar pragmatism had led to Auschwitz.[40]

That July the executive of the Canadian Student Liberals, now headed by Varley, unanimously adopted a paper that called for the legalization of soft drugs for youth as young as fourteen. The paper explained: "The use of psychedelic and hallucinogenic drugs, particularly cannabis, is an integral part of a developing culture whose system of values differ from the prevailing culture and norms of the majority population." The students were supported on this radical proposition, to a degree, by the Toronto and District Liberal Association, whose policy conference voted 105 to 30 in favour of pot being sold in the same way as liquor.[41]

That policy convention also signalled that Toronto Liberals were moving close to many of the Waffle's positions. They voted for tough anti-pollution laws, that abortion be left up to women, for strong controls on U.S. ownership and influence, and that all unions should be autonomously Canadian. Some of the resolutions passed had a new left air: public housing was to be managed at the community level, with tenants having a voice; welfare recipients were to be involved with the planning and administration of welfare programs; in prisons, now to be smaller and community-oriented, inmates were to be allowed to make decisions over policies affecting them. At the federal party's convention, Toronto and student Liberals joined together to try to have these resolutions passed.[42]

Like the local NDP, Toronto Liberals also distinguished themselves by their strong nationalism—participating, at least to a degree, in the discourse of national liberation. According to one account, at a parliamentary committee meeting on foreign ownership in Ottawa, the Toronto and District Liberal Association's policy committee was said to have harsher criticism of the government than did many of the speakers from opposition parties. James Conrad, speaking for the Toronto and District Liberal Association, blamed an anti-Toronto and rural bias for the Ontario party's uninspired platform and promised that the Association's two hundred delegates would lobby just as intensely as the Waffle had done at the Ontario NDP convention.[43]

Social democrats, communists, and liberals all indicated an awareness of something new, and important, being afoot in Toronto politics—the rise of a new left that challenged their traditional ways of thinking and doing things. Significantly, none of these quarters showed any indication of the dissipation of radical energies by 1971. Rather, in all three camps, new leftism aroused both enthusiasm and concern—and a wide array of strategies for containing and channelling its energies in ways that would allow political leaders to continue to function without looking over their shoulders at an insurgent cohort of ardent radicals.

* * *

A quite different logic prevailed on Toronto's far left—which, from 1968 to 1971, saw the rise and consolidation of a considerable diversity of groups aspiring to revive Marxism-Leninism and lead the revolution. Although the new Leninists' tactics and the containment strategies of the more established parties had their similarities, they also had this profound difference: a good number of the new Leninists, as former new leftists, brought into organizations many of their previously established ideas about left politics. What they sought in new Leninism was a way of safeguarding and developing the revolution that they had glimpsed as new leftists and that they feared was being placed at risk by habits of spontaneity and leaderlessness.

One of the first of these new Leninist groups arose at the time of the April 27, 1968, demonstration against the war in Vietnam. This demonstration began as many of its predecessors had, with around 1,500 protesters milling around Nathan Phillips Square. Among the crowd was a contingent of some 150 to 200 protesters who had clustered together beneath Vietnamese National Liberation Front flags. The protest later moved over to the U.S. consulate, where another group, the Spring Mobilization Committee, led by the League for Socialist Action, had organized another demonstration. At the consulate the police, as usual, forced the protesters to congregate across the street because of the presence, in front of the building, of pro-war Edmund Burke Society demonstrators. Later, claiming that pre-emptive action was needed to prevent violence between the rival camps, police moved to disperse the anti-war crowd entirely. The familiar routine exasperated many demonstrators, and some flat out refused to move. Even a clergyman was amongst the refuseniks: "First of all you [police] tell me to get on the median, now you tell me to get off. I'm not moving." When the police began making arrests the crowd relented and headed north to Queen's Park, where an anti-war rally and teach-in organized by a coalition of CPCers, liberals, and independent radicals was taking place.[44]

As the numbers at Queen's Park swelled to 3,500, a man asked to use the microphone to make an appeal for money to bail out the activists who had just been arrested at the consulate. He had been amongst the contingent holding the NLF flags at city hall before joining the march to the consulate. After this solicitation was denied, the group with the NLF flags started their own rally, which quickly attracted six hundred people. Chanting "Victory to the NLF," they lined up behind the flags and returned south, first gathering outside the nearby police station on Dundas Street W., where the arrestees had been sent, and later returning to the consulate. Both the contingent and rally had been organized by a new organization called Canadians for the NLF (CNLF).[45]

An editorial in CNLF's bulletin later declared that the April 27 demonstration marked the transformation of an anti-war movement into an anti-imperialist movement. The six hundred who had marched from Queen's Park to the police station represented a heightened radicalism, newly attentive to Canadian reality and struggles, that had decided to discard American-style strategy and slogans and cease being a "Yankee import." The very tone suggests an important element of much of the early Maoism that arose in Toronto—the centrality of Canada's "national question."[46]

Members of CNLF slammed the insufficient politics of the CPCers, liberals, and independent radicals who had organized the Queen's Park rally and teach-in. They condemned the CPC in particular for selling out the Vietnamese people by pursuing peace at any price. But they directed most of their ire towards the Spring Mobilization Committee, condemning the LSA marshals at the consulate for telling people to leave there for Queen's Park, thus allowing police to make arrests and retake ground held by demonstrators. They also critiqued the Trotskyists for discouraging people from marching on the police station and pilloried them for allegedly downplaying the existence of U.S. imperialism. The LSA, they alleged, even opposed Canadian independence, and thus exemplified "the colonized mind"—referring here to a concept developed by Frantz Fanon in probing the psycho-dynamics of racism in Algeria.[47]

The CNLF had its origins in the Toronto-based Canadian Party of Labour (CPL), which had its start three years prior as a branch of the Progressive Workers' Movement (PWM)—which in turn had been established by former members of the Communist Party of Canada in British Columbia; they were activists who had sided with China during the Sino-Soviet split and thus left the CPC. The originators of PWM had unsuccessfully tried to gain adherents in Toronto and other parts of the country before founding their Vancouver-based group in 1964. Hoping to grow into a pan-Canadian party, PWM sent members Joe Hendsbee and Roger Perkins to Toronto in 1965 to form a local branch of its movement.[48]

The Toronto PWM branch immediately began issuing its own publication, *Left Leaf*, which pointed to the 1965 anti-Nazi demonstration at Allan Gardens to differentiate the group from its old Leninist competitors. It was not up to the left, the publication said, to defend the free speech of Nazis, as the LSA had supposedly done, or to create illusions about the government by demanding the Nazis' suppression, which was allegedly the CPC's position. Instead it was up to working people to decide how to respond, regardless of any law—a formula that appeared to back the violent attacks on Nazis in Allan Gardens.[49]

MAY DAY AND THE 8 HOUR MOVEMENT P 2

Progressive Worker

Workers of All Countries, Unite!

Volume 1, Number 8 10¢ MAY 1965

USA

HIS MASTER'S VOICE

STORY PAGE 8

ALSO in this issue THE A. F. L. -C. I. O. 'S FOREIGN POLICY Page 14

N. D. P. CONVENTION Page 10 TEAMSTER'S STRIKE Page 3

The Progressive Workers' Movement promoted a socialist road to Canadian independence. This cover featured a satirical image of Prime Minister Lester Pearson kowtowing to the U.S. government.

Progressive Worker, May 1965.

Like the PWM's mentor Jack Scott, *Left Leaf* was distinctly nationalist. It sported a red maple leaf and the slogan "Dedicated to an Independent and Socialist Canada" affixed to its masthead (the same slogan used just a few years later by the Waffle). The publication blamed the appearance of local Nazis on "Yankee" influences. It supported a made-in-Canada car, lauded the nineteenth-century Métis rebel Gabriel Dumont ("Riel should be understood, Dumont imitated"), and ran a cover illustration of Canada being menaced by the giant hand of U.S. imperialism. When members of LSA tried to disperse a demonstration that was

American imperialism in Canada as seen by *Left Leaf*.

Left Leaf, Winter 1966.

about to burn a U.S. flag—explaining that the American flag represented U.S. workers and that burning it was childish—*Left Leaf* concluded that the action simply exposed the pro-imperialist and counter-revolutionary politics of its Trotskyist rival.[50]

In his autobiography, a chagrined Jack Scott said that PWM would have been better off having not sent anyone to Toronto. Hendsbee and Perkins were "terrible." Yet the two men succeeded in getting a branch off the ground that over time attracted a significant number of young radicals. In an early action foreshadowing later worker-student alliances, they brought a number of Friends of SNCC members together to march with striking Teamsters in 1965. The following year they began encouraging their members to take jobs in construction-related unions, a strategy that would become popular amongst new Leninists in the 1970s. Bill Lewis, who at the behest of the branch started working as a member of the ironworkers union in 1966, may have been the earliest local new Leninist to "industrialize," that is, to take up factory work with the encouragement of his organization.[51]

The industrialization strategy led to serious, and revealing, problems when a young PWM member intervened in a Teamster local. When he found himself in disagreement with the union's opposition caucus (which was supported by members of the CPC and LSA), he began to collude with his local's conservative leadership. The PWM suspended him until his "genuine repudiation" of his error restored his organization's discredited image. According to an internal report, the comrade renounced his actions at every opportunity. He declared himself to be no longer overconfident in his own abilities and condemned his secret aspiration to win a place within the union bureaucracy. He had become a new man. The Toronto branch had thus already grasped the "criticism and self-criticism" model that Chinese Communists had made central to party functioning.[52]

It was in midst of learning the ropes of industrial organizing that the PWM branch established CNLF in fall 1967. The new anti-war coalition included veterans from Canadian Students for Nuclear Disarmament and SUPA, students who had participated in the Hart House occupation and a sit-in at a Dow chemical plant, workplace militants who had never attended university, and novice activists. CNLF quickly adopted a monthly dues structure and an ambitious schedule of meetings and film screenings. Many of its members seemed to be looking for something more concrete and organized than the grassroots spontaneity of the classic new left.[53] Many of them believed that Canadian nationalism and socialism were integral to the fight against the war and that fighting U.S. imperialism in Canada was the best way to support the Vietnamese.[54]

The question of Canadian nationalism was seldom far from the early manifestations of new Leninism in Toronto. During the summer of 1968 discussions in CNLF's bulletin became increasingly dynamic and pushed well beyond the issue of the war movement. It was a way of moving beyond the single-issue, "lowest-common denominator" approach of bodies led by the established Leninists of the CPC and LSA. A working paper stated: "We must recognize that Canada is Vietnam. That tomorrow, Canada could be like Vietnam in the military sense." They were attempting to apply in Canada an inspiring model of decolonization they had first glimpsed in Indochina.[55]

CNLF began holding seminars exploring Canada's national question. Many speakers argued that the fight for national liberation in Canada was part of the class struggle. Some of these voices would become important figures in the later debate over the national queston in the 1970s. At this time Daniel Drache held that Canada was half a colony and half a neo-imperialist power, while Steve Moore, later a strong critic of the Canadian nationalist position, decried the "continentalist view" that the Canadian left might have to wait for initiatives taken by the U.S. left. An American revolution would never free Canada from "Yankee Imperialism."[56]

By the end of the summer of 1968, CNLF had launched what it called a movement for an independent Canada. Some of the initial attempts to liken Canada to Vietnam were sidelined; Canada's status was compared, rather, to that of Scotland or Ireland. The organization envisioned a public education campaign, taking place over several months, which would culminate in a call for a constituent assembly. Separate committees were struck for students, student-labour, culture, and "captive unionists" (most likely referring to those in U.S.-headquartered unions). Although the CNLF's size is difficult to estimate, and so too is the proportionate weight of its Leninist and new left elements, after the collapse of SUPA and before the rise of the Toronto Student Movement, it was plainly a significant area of activity for some new leftists.[57]

Yet tensions between the CNLF and the larger Canadian Party of Labour, between nationalism and a burgeoning anti-nationalism, and between new Leninists and new leftists would all work to destroy the fledgling movement during the fall and winter of 1968. The first attack against the developing Canadian nationalist line in the *CNLF Bulletin* came in September, when Chandler Davis penned an article attacking the Canada-Vietnam comparison. The response to his missive was unsympathetic. One reply hammered Chandler over his contention that white Canadian workers, enjoying the same living standards as those in the United States, were in effect a labour aristocracy. It condemned him for downplaying the plight of Canadian workers and argued that their gains had been won in struggle rather than being gifts awarded by imperialism. Canada might not be Vietnam, but it certainly was not the United States.[58]

Although the leaders of the CPL appear to have become increasingly skeptical of Canadian nationalism, they largely avoided openly contesting the nationalist position in favour of arguing that the offshoot CNLF and its Canadian independence movement had constituted a distraction from the main task: party-building. A key CPL position paper argued that too much time had been spent in building CNLF and that the amount of energy necessary to sustain it had prevented work on other priorities. The immense work put into CNLF had won recruits to CPL, but the position paper questioned the ideology of some of these newcomers. Had they been won to the CPL line and Leninism or to the Vietnamese line and national liberation? It concluded that the "front organization" had compromised the integrity of the "vanguard party" and needed to be shut down.[59]

The position paper also argued that setting up a Canadian independence movement was at best premature and certainly a repeat of the "substitutionalist" mistakes made with CNLF: "We are not 'anti-imperialists,' 'nationalists,' or 'Joe Workers.' We are communists." The temptation to keep "communism" out of propaganda was strong, and revisionism was already taking root in the party, the paper claimed, so it was best to have the party itself push for national liberation instead of creating an independence movement. It accused those wanting such a movement of romantic nationalism.[60]

As to the suitability of Canadian nationalism, the authors of the paper undogmatically confessed that the whole question was "tricky." As an oppressed nation, Canada was also the site of a class struggle, but uncertainty existed over what constituted socialist nationalism (good) and petty-bourgeois nationalism (bad). Perhaps an independence movement could be a way of winning recruits to the party and of helping it avoid isolation, but that remained to be seen. The paper suggested that a nationalist movement might never become strong enough because of the country's proximity to, and integration with, the United States: "Canada is not Vietnam. Canada is Bulgaria."[61]

In October the CNLF reprised its rivalry with the LSA by announcing a demonstration that would coincide with a similar gathering (and march) planned by the Trotskyist-influenced Vietnam Mobilization Committee. The resulting scene at Queen's Park indicated the visible costs of competitive inter-Leninist feuding. The proponents of both events made their pitches from duelling loudspeakers. In the end, CNLF marched to the U.S. consulate with about five hundred followers, twenty-four of them later being arrested. At least three times that number stuck with the Vietnam Mobilization Committee, which for the first time engaged in direct action, trying to make good on a promise by organizer Joe Young that they would try to march on the city's busy main thoroughfare—Yonge Street—even though the city had denied permission for them to do so. Demonstrators were prevented from marching on Yonge and suffered nine arrests amidst what *The Toronto Star* called a massive police presence. Taking credit for the Mobilization Committee's new approach, CNLF suggested that its rival had only planned the "usual demonstration with the usual political line and the usual tactics," but changed its mind after hearing of the growing support for CNLF's protest march.[62]

The CNLF's last hurrah was its participation in organizing a rally in support of the NLF and spearheaded by the CPC and related groups such as the Canadian Peace Congress—which the militants derided as the "Canadian Peace-At-Any-Price Congress." CNLF spokespersons expressed the view that the event was being organized as a response to the attractiveness of their own policies. Despite being outnumbered by the other planning groups, the CNLF members were not inclined to be conciliatory. They did not want union leaders to speak at the rally, arguing that the unionists worked full-time for U.S. imperialism. They tried to get a "strikebreaker" delisted as a supporter—an attack on the dedicated local left activist Dan Heap—and pushed for the main banner to read "Death to the U.S. imperialists—Our common enemy" (they decried the "old CP women of either sex" who had instead voted for "Welcome NLF"). Their reportage of the rally itself dripped with disdain towards the more liberal activists involved. Even on the brink of dissolution, CNLF was preoccupied with distinguishing itself from other elements of the left.[63]

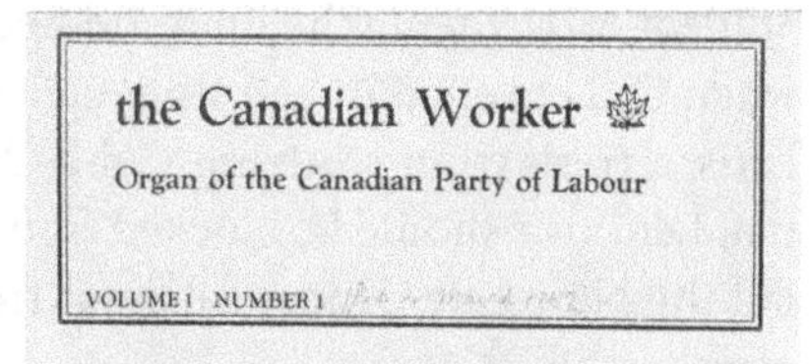
the Canadian Worker

Organ of the Canadian Party of Labour

VOLUME 1 NUMBER 1

The inaugural issue of *The Canadian Worker*.

William Ready Division of Archives and Research Collections.

Once freed of its CNLF entanglements, the Canadian Party of Labour launched a new monthly publication, *The Canadian Worker*, in early 1969. Its inaugural front page was devoted to continuing the attack on Dan Heap, who was eviscerated as a scab and a purveyor of "bosses' ideas" inside the workers' movement. The immediate cause for this vitriol was that Heap was a member of one of the U.S. "company unions" at the Continental Can factory, where CPL was supporting a new Canadian union. Heap also had a long history of working with both rival old left tendencies and new leftists, making him an attractive target for a group wanting to demarcate its politics from the rest of Toronto's left-wing movement. *The Canadian Worker* spent much time and energy denouncing those on the "phoney left," including the "Marcusians" of the League for Socialist Action and Young Socialists—a choice of epithet suggesting a keen interest in associating its rivals with the evidently outdated philosophies and practices of the new left.[64]

On the U of T campus the lines between the CPL and its new left opponents were not always as starkly drawn. An early CPL document saw the classroom as the main arena of struggle on campus and argued against the efficacy of large events or meetings. It urged members to intervene in social science classes with comments, leaflets, and even guerrilla theatre critiquing (or satirizing) course texts and professors, an approach highly reminiscent of the tactics of the Toronto

Student Movement. The lines did become deeper during the summer of 1969, when CPLers encouraged student-worker alliances on picket lines, while new leftists, fresh from studying Cohn-Bendit's *Obsolete Communism*, concluded that Leninists should be blocked from participating in the TSM altogether. That fall the New Left Caucus offshoot from the TSM barred CPL members from membership.[65]

The CNLF's bulletin in fall 1968 had attacked the new leftists for their "student as nigger" discourse and other trends adopted from the U.S. student movement; and now the CPL was itself caught in a somewhat contradictory position in encouraging a worker-student alliance in which its own ideology was put at risk of disappearing. Yet for a time at least CPL displayed surprisingly little bitterness for the new left. The party's internal report from its 1969 summer project at the Wiener Electric factory, for instance, notably avoided any criticism of new left ideology. Its *Combat Bourgeois Ideology* pamphlet series, produced around this time, featured writings reproduced from the U.K. publication *New Left Review* by authors such as Perry Anderson, Robin Blackburn, and André Gunder Frank—just the kind of intellectuals that a later CPL would condemn for *transmitting* bourgeois ideology.[66]

In its early years, the CPL was often remarkably undogmatic, awake to other currents in the political and intellectual world that its members were anxious to inhabit. It was quite open to arguments made by early women's liberationists. One of its student-worker alliance reports notes the superexploitation of female factory workers and even remarks on the problems that some of those women had experienced with their husbands. The report predictably accused feminism, along with nationalism and male chauvinism, of ignoring class and being divisive, but it unexpectedly credited women's liberationists for providing an antidote to "anti-male" ideology. CPL itself announced that it would combat male chauvinism by eliminating the gender division of labour within its own ranks and encouraging women to become leaders. Added to the list of bourgeois courses to which it committed its disruptive energies was economics, which tended to justify the exploitation of women, and history, which often did not mention women at all.[67]

CPL was understandably upset by the disintegration of TSM and being shut out of the New Left Caucus. It criticized Caucus members for prioritizing the student movement and for emphasizing women's liberation more than the working class. It also ridiculed claims that the Caucus was Marxist. Its rivals, failing to understand the theory, had only adopted Marxism to maintain a facade of credibility to counter the growing popularity of CPL. After the split, CPL continued to centre its campus efforts on aligning students with blue-collar workers. It defined both anti-war work and campus worker struggles as part of the same fight against imperialism and looked to the student movement to represent the working class on the educational front.[68]

The relationship between new leftism and new Leninism—with all its tensions—was packed with subtleties and ambivalences. The CPL was prepared to admit that the new left had done some good, chiefly in encouraging increasing numbers of students to grasp the need of comprehensively analyzing capitalist society. Thus it was only logical that the new left was moving towards a Marxist position and an increasing realization of the importance of class. Some of the CPL's more cogent critiques of the new left included its emphasis on superstructure, personal experience (which led to spontaneous politics and "action freaks"), and decentralization. CPL argued that decentralization could only begin after both the revolution and the destruction of all counter-revolutionaries. Wed to the belief that a single, strong Leninist organization was a necessity, members lampooned the new left notion that a number of groups could coexist and then "magically" come together in a pre-revolutionary situation.[69]

New left writings tended to be critical of popular culture, but entertainment reviews in *The Canadian Worker* were much more heated and conspiratorial. The magazine reserved most of its ire for movies that some activists might have found relatively progressive. The films *Easy Rider* (1969) and *Joe* (1970), for example, were presented as co-ordinated attempts to inspire anti-worker prejudice and undermine worker-student alliances. Robert Altman's *M*A*S*H* (1970) served up ample helpings of sex and gore to undermine the self-confidence of the working class. CPL reviewers insisted on the primordial significance of class and the marginal significance of most everything else, even when most people would have interpreted such cultural phenomena quite differently. The Canadian film *Goin' Down the Road* (1970) was uniquely credited for revealing some of the drawbacks of working-class life, but ultimately dismissed for not endorsing socialism.[70]

In the early 1970s CPL devoted less and less time to organizing on campus but still maintained a presence. Its rationale for involvement in U of T's daycare struggle was quite forthright. It saw the united front as an opportunity to expose "misleaders"—by which members most likely meant the Communists and Trotskyists involved in the struggle—and win recruits to CPL and its Worker-Student Alliance. The CPL argued that its left-wing opponents were agents for the bosses and used quotation marks to surround the words communist, left, or socialist when citing the titles of rival organizations. The CPL did make compelling points about the lack of democratic functioning of the daycare occupation, but its main line was to attack its erstwhile allies, including Professor Natalie Zemon Davis. It exposed her class privilege through a reference to the installation of an extra home phone for the use of her children. In new Leninist hands, the "personal is the political" could take on a venomous tone.[71]

CPL's involvement in a campus referendum for parity in university governance in 1971 had a similarly sectarian character. It spent most of its time attacking parity activists for wasting everyone's time on such an unimportant issue. Yet, when it became apparent that the parity referendum was becoming one of largest mobilizations in campus history, CPL quickly changed course and criticized its own past line as sectarian. But instead of supporting the referendum (a yes vote would have obliged students to strike for parity), group members continued to set themselves apart from everyone else by urging students to boycott the referendum and engage in an immediate strike.[72]

In the meantime, for all its earlier Canadian nationalism, by the early 1970s the CPL was remoulding itself in the image of the U.S. Progressive Labor Party. It was now defining Canada as an imperialist country and no longer describing Quebec as a colony or even a nation: the Québécois were merely a collection of people who suffered from racism. It even dismissed Indigenous and Inuit nationalisms as harmful schemes to prevent working people from turning to socialism. CPL argued that everyone in Canada was a foreigner and that Aboriginal peoples had just been here longer. This new analysis dovetailed with the party's prior suggestion that Black power and immigrant-based organizations were guilty of dividing workers and obscuring their class interest. It was now incumbent upon revolutionaries to destroy these backward "ethnic" cultural forms and replace them with a new culture of everyday struggle and worker internationalism.[73]

As part of its perspective of uniting the working class, CPL began offering English- and French-language classes and started an Italian-language CPL newspaper. Yet members used their commendable efforts to communicate with immigrants in their first languages as a means to attack the unilingual leaflets of their opponents as racist. They made similar charges against Waffle members, in part because CPL now believed anti-Americanism could be a form of racism. CPL referred to the Waffle's politics as "national socialist," linked its calls for nationalizations to similar schemes in fascist Germany and Italy, labelled the promotion of industrial democracy "Hitlerite," and claimed that the Waffle planned to deport all immigrants from Canada. Yet when the Waffle was faced with expulsion from the NDP, members of CPL joined the caucus, hoping to create a schism between the Waffle's leadership and its rank and file. In a 360-degree turn, *The Canadian Worker* lauded Wafflers for their revolutionary consciousness and assured them that the ideas that had made their caucus popular were also at the core of the CPL's own thinking. A short time thereafter, when the Waffle purged the CPLers, *The Canadian Worker* immediately returned to its previous form, leaving new readers to ponder why CPL would have had anything to do with such a frankly racist organization in the first place.[74]

* * *

Another new Leninist organization to arise out of PWM's Toronto Branch was the curiously named Canadian Workers Project Century: 2 (CWPC2). It did not have the influence, members, or profile of the CPL, but proved to be remarkably prescient about the strengths and limits of revolutionary politics in Toronto. Although its philosophy and praxis ultimately marked out a path not taken, its brief history does suggest that an alternative vision of Marxism-Leninism need not have waited until the early 1980s.

CWPC2 was founded in the mid-1960s by a small group of Toronto PWM members, including branch co-founder Joe Hendsbee, who were significantly older than their peers. Core members of the group had quit CPC during the mid- to late 1950s and had only joined PWM after a few years' sojourn in the League for Socialist Action. Members identified themselves as Marxist-Leninists filling a vacuum created by the discredited old left. Rather more than CPL, whose relationship with new leftism was ambiguous, CWPC2 expressed warm sympathy with aspects of 1960s youth culture. They lauded youth for being more aware and realistic than any previous generation and defended their music from Marxist-Leninists who heard only indoctrination and bourgeois decadence in it. They did not have any problems with pot and LSD per se. Upholding conventional ideas about drugs was necessary only because doing otherwise raised the risk of alienating workers. CWPC2 did condemn new leftism as a form of militant liberalism, but it also advocated a long-term patient approach to new leftists. It strongly denounced those Marxist-Leninists who dismissed the new left, arguing that the critics had relied on an approach combining arrogance, Puritanism, and sectarianism.[75]

As to its chief differences with PWM, CWPC2 largely centred on practices that it termed sectarian, such as PWM's alleged characterization of social democracy as fascist. In contrast to other Maoist-identified new Leninists, CWPC2 emphasized that social democracy could be both progressive and reactionary, depending on country, period, and other factors. CWPC2 also panned PWM for relying too much on China for its ideology. Canadian communists, it complained, tended to adopt the programs of other national parties holus bolus, while the Cuban and Vietnamese revolutions had proven that national struggles and aspirations had to be integrated into the life of the organization to achieve not only national, but also international objectives. Flowing from this, CWPC2 argued that Maoist tactics needed a rethink in non-revolutionary situations such as Canada's, where parliament was not irrelevant, "even if we wish it to be."[76]

Although members of CWPC2 must have known the prospect of working with revolutionaries of all varieties would not go down well with their fellow Marxist-Leninists, they nevertheless argued for the necessity of this co-operation in Canada. CWPC2 believed that all revolutionaries were in motion. Their positions of today would not be their positions of tomorrow. Denouncing the kind of overblown, invective lines of attack that became increasingly popular at the end of the decade, it argued, "We have never met any person (police agents excepted) who has joined a political tendency on the left for the purpose of counter-revolutionary or anti-working class activities."[77]

By the end of the 1960s, supporters of CWPC2 became convinced that the deification of Mao and the adoption of revolutionary Chinese practices had hurt attempts to build a strong movement in Canada. While allowing that the application of criticism and self-criticism held some promise, they complained that it was only being applied to personal shortcomings and errors in practice and method—instead of being used to question the principles and methods of a person's own ideological tendency. In this spirit they denounced Maoist calls for a "return" to Marxist-Leninism. Revolutions like those in China and Russia had instead been all about "going beyond," which meant discarding rather than adopting old methods and practices.[78]

By 1970 CWPC2 had begun to consider the Leninist model valuable but outdated. It contrasted such unreflexive Leninism to an undogmatic "creative Marxism." In a rare, if not unique, argument in Toronto at this time, CWPC2's publication *The Nationalist* spent many pages outlining the thinking of Rosa Luxemburg as an antidote to popular Leninist conceptions. In further contrast to other Maoist-inspired groups, CWPC2 strongly embraced the rise of women's liberation and recent changes to sexual mores (*The Nationalist* urged its readers to "discover yourself . . . Read Wilhelm Reich's 'sexual revolution'"). For a time every issue of *The Nationalist* had prominently repeated the formula: "For an independent Canada; Support self-determination for native peoples; Support self-determination for Quebec." The editors now added, "Accept the demand for women's liberation." For members of CWPC2, it was possible to consciously carry aspects of new leftism into a new Leninist organization.[79]

* * *

The May 4th Movement, picking up CNLF's banner of direct action, was established on May 5, 1970, just a day after a mass shooting by National Guardsmen killed four students at Kent State University in Ohio. It was an appropriate birthdate for an organization that later tried to replicate the praxis of the U.S. urban guerrillas known as the Weather Underground Organization, or Weathermen. After its founding, members immediately began organizing a demonstration at the U.S. consulate to oppose both the war and the college shooting: "We announce the death of the silent majority. You are cordially invited to the funeral wake with us. Riots, macings, clubbings, fights, killings and a splendid time is guaranteed for all." With tongue firmly in cheek, leaflets encouraged attendees "NOT" to bring eggs, paint, rocks, or other projectiles to the protest because "THESE THINGS HAVE PROVEN TO BE EFFECTIVE IN THE PAST." The lesson of the Kent State shooting was that you had to fight if you wanted to survive.[80]

The May demonstration of five thousand appeared unremarkable at first, but when the inevitable scuffles with Edmund Burke Society members broke out and police moved to disperse the crowd, officers were met by a hail of bottles, eggs, and other makeshift missiles. An initial melee saw some of the consulate's windows broken, a police officer injured, and a number of demonstrators arrested. After that about two thousand protesters yelling "The streets are ours" surged off towards Yonge Street. The sound of smashing glass added to the panopoly of noise as several large Eaton's department store windows were shattered. Seizing Yonge Street, protesters headed north to College Street, where they attacked a second Eaton's location. By the end of the day the police had made ninety-one arrests, and the deputy chief reported that the city had not seen a day of unrest like this since the unemployed demonstrations at Queen's Park during the 1930s.[81]

Members of M4M, who complained of indiscriminate police violence, announced that Toronto's reputation for peaceful protest was now over and the fight for survival had begun. Reflecting aspects of both new leftism and new Leninism in its philosophy, style, and political priorities, M4M introduced itself as "a tightly disciplined, centrally-organized collection of anarchists, freaks, students and even communists. It is a movement of youth that after it has dealt with the Amerikan Consulate will disperse and attack rising unemployment, pollution, the Spadina Expressway, and other issues that make this city unliveable." The statement seemingly implied that new leftism might be able to survive in a new organizational form.[82]

During the summer, M4M held regular discussion groups in Rochdale College, trained its members in self-defence, gave away cheap or free food as part of its "serve the people" campaign, and organized the Festival Express protest in 1970. It went through organizational changes and became Rising Up Angry before settling on the name Red Morning. Members complained of having grown tired of the endless discussions and ineffective actions of the new left. While many of those activists were adopting the kind of militant rhetoric popularized in the United States, RM activists were committed to putting action behind those heretofore empty phrases.[83]

In analyzing the prospects for revolution, Red Morning argued that street people, those living on welfare, young workers, and students were the folks who most frequently rose up against their oppression. They later called upon a more Marxist terminology in defining their constituency as working-class youth, especially those who could be considered "lumpen," shorthand for lumpen-proletariat, Karl Marx's term for a permanent underclass that included criminals and the chronically unemployed. For RM, lumpens were the subalterns most conscious of their class oppression and would be the quickest to embrace revolution. The young had the least stake in "the system" and were yet to have had their spirits ground down; and the number of lumpen youth—"freaks and grease alike"—was growing. With this perspective, believing "All busts of youth in this city are political," RM offered security against police raids. They believed that "gangs" could provide a revolutionary means for people to survive and defend themselves and their communities, and invited gang members to come along and "rap" with them.[84]

This analysis of lumpen youth was tied to Red Morning's strong integration with the counterculture. RM's political platform—unique amongst the new Leninist organizations in Toronto—included the demand for the legalization of all psychedelic drugs and good clean dope. But while the group believed that drugs such as acid could beneficially bring people closer together, it considered harder drugs such as speed as "the man's way of keeping us down." At a time when many new Leninists were running away from countercultural mores, RMers were fiercely encouraging their growth. "Spray-painting the walls of Toronto with what kind of beautiful, strong people we are and what we're about, is an important way of communicating among ourselves," declared an RM article alongside a graphic of a weapon-wielding Zig Zag rolling paper man.[85]

RM's militant, direct action focus did not endear it to groups trying to gear their messages to middle- and working-class constituencies. These other groups would not have been happy to see RM, with its banner featuring a blue machine gun superimposed over a red star, appear at their demonstrations. RM blamed marshals at such protests for preventing "the people" from fighting for their survival and acting on their anger: "It doesn't matter where the people are at or what they want to do," their paper stated. "Marshals will try to hold the people back from fighting." Leadership was necessary at demonstrations, RM conceded, but its goal should be to maximize political and material damage (that is, breaking windows) while minimizing arrests.[86]

After initially adopting a horizontal leadership structure, members decided RM should be less pluralist and more vanguardist. They developed a tripartite vertical structure with central staff at the top, cadre in the middle, and street workers at the bottom. An article in *Red Morning* couched this move as a means to expand the democracy of their organization: "In the past, what we've had was <u>implicit leadership</u>, that is, formally there was no leadership, but actually a few people functioning as leaders. When that's going on, you can't criticize or change leadership because supposedly it doesn't exist." While there was undoubted merit to that argument, RM quickly accumulated a centralist surplus and a democratic deficit.[87]

Central staff appeared to make all of the decisions, while street workers—a category of members tasked with making everyday links with the young "lumpens" the organization hoped to attract—were expected to obediently follow the dictates of their leaders. In contrast to the group's leadership, most of these street workers had never attended university—a relative lack of schooling that leaders saw as beneficial in communicating to their target audience. Yet the streaming of RM's working-class members into the lowest echelon of this democratic centralist organization appeared to mirror the class-based streaming of schools and workplaces that leftists generally opposed. The street workers, too, were supposedly serving as the ears and eyes of RM in the community—which would have best situated the group as a whole to "learn from the people." Yet when it came to decision-making the leadership generally ignored their input.[88]

Cover: Peggy Morton's pamphlet published by Hogtown Press.

Pamphlet Collection, William Ready Division of Archives and Research Collections.

Although RM did have a distinct women's liberationist current, most visible in the actions of its Leila Khaled group, collective member Peggy Morton remarked how the organization upheld both "street fighting" men and women as a model. As the first page of her pamphlet *They Are Burning, They Are Burning Effigies* declares:

> We also need to kill another pig—our own socialization—that forever oinks to us that we'll never take leadership of the white revolutionary left in North Amerika, because we're still somehow mystically chained to the image of what everyone always told us we were. But with the advent of Panther women with shotguns and the Vietnamese sisters with AK-47's, both pigs, imperialism and our white socialization are dying sure deaths.[89]

Conditions, she argued, had forced activists to go beyond the existentialism popular in the early 1960s, when the commitment to be a revolutionary was an abstract, moral choice. Now, at the turn of the decade, fighting back and becoming a revolutionary was the only way to become human. (The echoes of Fanon's theme of personal transformation through violent struggle were audible.) A key reason why the Abortion Caravan protest in Ottawa had inspired so many women was that the caravanners had shown themselves to be bold, strong, and tough. Giving women the confidence to "destroy the monster that is sucking our blood" had marked that protest as being far from the realm of the standard liberal and reformist approaches.[90]

American militants had clearly influenced the language in Morton's essay and were a strong factor in shaping RM's conception of itself. RM's newspaper regularly carried items about armed struggle groups, including the Black Panthers and Weather Underground, as well as the Front de libération du Québec (FLQ) in Quebec. Beyond adopting the strategy and rhetoric of such groups—above all the Weathermen—RM members helped to hide some of their American cousins in Toronto, including members of the Black Panthers.[91]

In fall 1971 RM used the anniversary of the declaration of the War Measures Act (October 1970) as an occasion for the kind of exemplary action that Morton had hoped for. About one hundred members and supporters turned out for a downtown march, where they were closely followed by a detachment of fifty police officers. As the crowd neared the Eaton's department store on Yonge Street, at a signal from leaders the protesters hurled a barrage of placard handles, flag-holders, and rocks at the store's display windows, breaking fifteen in all. Police officers rapidly descended upon the crowd and made about a dozen arrests. All of those detained were charged with mischief to private property and conspiracy, and some faced charges such as assault and possession of a deadly weapon.[92]

In the aftermath, RM lauded the relatively minimal arrests as a victory. They had shattered not only windows but also to some degree the police force's "aura of invincibility." Clearly, the police would have a rough time preventing similar actions in the future. Yet their Eaton's "riot"—so reminiscent of the "Days of Rage" perpetrated by the Students for a Democratic Society in Chicago a few years earlier—proved to be the last of RM's spectacular activities. The arrests, modest in relation to the number of the demonstrators, meant that a good number of RMers faced time-consuming legal struggles and ultimately jail time. In contrast to some of the group's earlier feats, this one inspired neither imitators nor joiners.[93]

A former member was not impressed. Suggesting that RM had not understood the level of struggle in Toronto, he saw the borrowing of Weatherman ideology and tactics as the root of his organization's troubles. For him, RM's strategy of building a "fighting force" was petty-bourgeois and anarchist. RM had tried to guilt people into action by evoking their privilege and had called people refusing to fight chauvinists and racists. All of that rhetoric about getting rid of the pig in your head, he concluded, was "mindfucking . . . bullshit." Like a number of his peers, he would look towards Marxist-Leninist strategies centred on the working class as a new way forward.[94]

* * *

The most lasting, and one of the most audacious, of the new Leninist groups emerging from 1968 to 1971 was the Communist Party of Canada (Marxist-Leninist) (CPC-ML). In a vivid contrast to Red Morning, it steered clear of all things countercultural and tried to replicate a highly orthodox version of Depression-era communism.

The CPC-ML had its origins in a University of British Columbia–based group called the Internationalists, founded in 1963. Hardial Bains, a postgraduate student who had emigrated from India in 1959, was a leading figure of that group. In his autobiography Bains, whose father was a Communist, recalled joining the student wing of the party in India while in elementary school. In Canada he found himself being disappointed at the CPC's revisionist policies and the NDP's anti-communism. He saw the early Internationalists as being somewhere between a left-leaning discussion group and a scheme to turn youth towards Marxism-Leninism.[95]

A year and a half after his group's founding, in December 1964, Bains and other members of the Internationalists attended SUPA's inaugural conference in Regina. His refusal to hide his Marxist politics, he said, helped to arouse a significant interest amongst delegates to meet members of his group: "It was well known that only at UBC and around Vancouver was serious work taking place, and that the name of Hardial Bains was connected to it." Bains was thoroughly unimpressed with the amateurish conference and its deficient Ontario-based leadership. He became convinced that he alone could do the political work necessary to advance the movement.[96]

Within a year Bains had begun establishing groups of co-thinkers in the British Isles, starting with the Irish Internationalists, founded while he was working at Dublin's Trinity College. Beginning with an internal "struggle against bourgeois hang-ups" campaign in 1966, followers there and in Canada began to adopt increasingly more disciplined organizational structures. In 1967 they began moving towards what some Marxist-Leninists would refer to as a "pre-party formation."[97]

Bains's *Necessity for Change*, published in 1967, became the Internationalists' seminal document. Its key proposition was that Anglo-American society was infected with "anti-consciousness," a set of beliefs imprinted with capitalist values instilled through everything from culture and education to parents and history. This anti-consciousness reinforced itself by filtering out experiences and information that questioned those values. People needed to liberate themselves and overturn this truncated, consumer-oriented definition of humanity.[98]

The problem was, most so-called Marxists were imprisoned within consumerism. They believed that "whenever there is a lack of objects there will be a revolt in favour of restoring the availability of these objects." Social movements fell into a similar consumerist trap. Unions were focused on ensuring a more equitable distribution of consumer goods. Attempts to win freedom and equality for women had resulted in the transformation of women themselves into commodities. In sharp contrast to the old left's sociological approach to social change, *Necessity for Change* suggested that the beginning of capitalism's end might instead be psychological: "What is going to happen is that the entire capitalist, imperialist and colonialist psychology is going to crumble and the consumer-based society will be exposed." It is surprising, but not far-fetched, to find parallels in Bains's arguments here and reflections commonly associated with Herbert Marcuse, the Frankfurt School, and other new left icons.[99]

It was up to individuals to overturn the consumer society. The document sought to reclaim the terrain of the individual from capitalist values rooted in private property. Bains attacked the way in which "anti-consciousness" linked the self-realization of the individual to the progression of capitalism and identified socialism as the antithesis of individuality. Under capitalism, "The more obediently you get yourself processed, the more rewards you will get in terms of consumer goods.... Everybody is in the process of homogenising themselves." To break away from anti-consciousness, individuals had to actively struggle to find the truth. They needed to serve the people by fighting for working people and others who were oppressed.[100]

Much later, on the 30th anniversary of *Necessity for Change*'s publication, Bains suggested that the document had transformed the Internationalists and paved the way for the formation of the CPC-ML: "Activists of the Internationalists, the cadre and the sympathizers, all of a sudden, rose out of their anti-consciousness, took their place in the society as revolutionists and created the subjective conditions for the development of the workers' and communist movement." Anyone who took up this analysis became a new human being. The creation of a new society depended upon everyone striving to reform themselves in such a way.[101]

Necessity for Change betrayed an obvious debt to existentialism, new leftism, and radical humanism. Some of these themes may have sat uncomfortably with the CPC-MLers who were more attracted by the party's aura of discipline and science. A view expressed in the party's press in 1971 downplayed the document's importance. It had served but a temporary, utilitarian purpose:

> The basic feature of the slogan (Necessity For Change) was to change the cadres who have come forward in struggle from petty bourgeois individuals interested in revolutionary ideas and action in a detached and isolated manner and hostile to revolutionary discipline, into revolutionary cadres who

> consciously participate in revolutionary struggles and enthusiastically and on a voluntary basis come under revolutionary discipline.[102]

In 1968, though, the document was clearly important to the Internationalists. That year they founded many organizations, including the Necessity for Change Institute of Ideological Studies, which was designed to provide an alternative to imperialist universities and petty-bourgeois free schools. Reflecting the Internationalists' unusually strong interest in culture, the Institute published a journal, *Literature and Ideology*, devoted to applying Marxist-Leninist analysis to literature and art with articles such as "Two Lines in the Teaching of Macbeth."[103]

A graphic produced by the "Committee to Oppose U.S. Imperialist 'youth culture,'" depicting a clean-cut proletarian kicking an American hippie holding drugs, pornography, and rock 'n' roll records, nicely summarizes the general stance of the Internationalists and CPC-ML towards sixties youth culture. Attacks on rival leftists could sound very much like those of sixties conservatives decrying "permissiveness"—"a marijuana smoking, drug-taking, sexual degenerate"—or even evoke the social conservatism of an earlier era: "a slime, at one time a 'communist' another time a 'jazz fan', a 'play boy' etc."[104] Testifying to the socially conservative leanings of its members in Toronto, a reporter noted:

> The organized Maoist is the antithesis of the 'hippie' and his passive, drug-centred philosophy. Most Maoists are neatly dressed, clean and devastatingly articulate. Some use alcohol in moderation; all abhor the use of drugs, deride the emphasis on sex in this 'decadent' culture. They fight birth control and firmly support the family unit.[105]

The Internationalists in Canada, largely situated in Montreal through 1967–68, established a base of operations in Toronto in the fall of 1968 when members began holding meetings on the University of Toronto campus under the guise of the Canadian Student Movement and the Canadian Internationalists (Marxist-Leninist). They made an impression strong enough that student Andy Wernick, in his guide to the U of T campus left, considered them the most objectionable of all the new Leninist groups. He accused them of reducing Marxism to "magical incantations" and dismissed their "interminable front groups." "The entire left, from NDP to CPL," he announced, "regards them as utterly lunatic."[106]

The Internationalists had appeared at a smattering of local demonstrations in 1969 but became much more visible after the founding of CPC-ML in early 1970. Their unofficial debut was marked by an anti-war protest in Ottawa at Parliament Hill, where they marched with red flags and pictures of Mao and tried to seize the speaker's platform and drown out speeches whilst engaging in clashes with police.

One report noted that a police officer who seized a CPC-MLer there had been immediately set upon by members who fought "with no holds barred" to free their comrade. Even a "pretty girl flung herself into the melee, scratching, biting, kicking."[107]

After the disruption of the Ottawa rally, a spike of local reports followed about confrontations involving members of the group. The Toronto press began dubbing them "The Maoists," no doubt to the chagrin of others who identified with Mao. Reporters gravitated to the oversized rhetoric of the group's leading Toronto member, Bob Cruise, who publicized his intention for the group to acquire weapons in preparation for a coming "armed people's war":

> Very shortly there will be a vast acceleration of revolutionary activity. Poor old Toronto will never be the same again. We are prepared and we're pushing deep into the masses at the place of work. Eventually, something will trigger fighting in the streets, and we will lead the way into a full-scale revolution.[108]

But the success of the party's organizing in workplaces was questionable at best. A "mass democracy" staged in a factory cafeteria, by one worker and some outside supporters, was not atypical of the party's theatrical interventions. For such a strongly collective organization the symbolism employed frequently appeared to be highly individualistic. For instance, Ann Briggs, a dishwasher at the Hospital for Sick Children, was probably fired for supporting a union drive. In protest, she held her own twenty-one-day sit-in and hunger strike. She decorated the hospital's lobby and emergency ward with pictures of Mao. She literally spat in the faces of hospital administrators. Although the union hoped to use her labour board hearing to press for the protection of its supporters, she forced its cancellation because she did not want to have anything to do with capitalist institutions. After a series of physical evictions from the hospital, Briggs was forced to go to court, where she told the judge, "I don't plead to servants." It is doubtful that any workers were won to the party during her campaign.[109]

An episode a few months later encapsulates much of CPC-ML's direction in the early 1970s. In August Cruise and another party militant travelled to Hamilton after the party's bookstore there had been repeatedly vandalized. They took with them "a shotgun in order to shoot down anyone who dared to violate the bookstore again." When both men were arrested for charges relating to an alleged threat to a police officer with that gun, they used their trial as a political opportunity to speak the truth and expose the fascist press, police, and court.[110] This situation was not anomalous. Just before leaving for Hamilton, Cruise told a Toronto reporter that there had been four hundred arrests of CPC-MLers and that he himself had been arrested twice in the past four months. Augmenting the severity of these arrests was the tendency for members to use their appearances in court to denounce the judiciary as illegitimate and fascist, frequently garnering contempt of court charges. In many cases the original charges were dropped—which was especially so for the party's newspaper sellers, who were regularly arrested for disturbing the peace in public places such as subway entrances—but contempt charges led to stays in jail for thirty to ninety days.[111]

At his court appearance Cruise declared, "The unarmed struggle of the Canadian people is bound to develop into armed struggle and there is nothing the fascist courts and police can do to prevent it!" According to his party, that statement would prove strikingly prophetic. While Cruise's subsequent incarceration was designed to dampen the revolutionary struggle, its practical effect, the party said, was the opposite. The jailing exposed the fascist court system, and Cruise's "bold, pathfinding" act of armed self-defence captured the imagination of the people: "This was a heroic act, an act which has brought a new factor into Canadian politics. THIS IS DEFINITELY THE WAVE OF THE FUTURE!"[112]

As the struggle to liberate Comrade Cruise continued, CPC-ML's inflated rhetoric grew apace. The party claimed that the "broad masses" were rallying to his defence. Their only criticism of Cruise's conduct was that he should have taken out his shotgun sooner. Within days the city was experiencing a "developing revolutionary situation," and in the following month *The People's Canada Daily News* announced that a full-fledged revolution was underway. In the midst of its panic, the ruling class had turned Hamilton into an armed camp to prevent demonstrations in support of Cruise. But local repression could not disguise how the politics of the nation had undergone a tectonic shift: "The struggle now is at the stage of ARMED SELF-DEFENSE and ARMED MAO TSETUNG THOUGHT PROPAGANDA TEAMS."[113]

The party's newspaper lionized Cruise as a "living model" who never doubted the party, did not own private property, and had "always hated his parents." For him, "Mao Tsetung Thought, The Party and revolution is everything and 'personal interest' is nothing." When he was eventually released after undergoing a fifty-six-day hunger strike (which had landed him in hospital), party members and hospital workers flocked to his bedside to celebrate. In a scene reminiscent of a revolutionary Chinese opera, they congratulated him for his heroism and sang revolutionary songs to mark the occasion. Hospital workers purchased party literature, and some expressed their desire to become communists. "No wonder the ruling class is running scared," one of them exclaimed.[114]

That moment undoubtedly made sense within a Marxist-Leninist epistemology and ontology unshared by most Torontonians, but it was also immersed in the new left atmosphere of the times. The extreme fervour of CPC-ML members, their depiction of the working class as being in sync with their party, and their position that a revolution was breaking out recall a John Lennon–Yoko

Onoesque "Capitalism is over if you want it." CPCer Danny Goldstick suggested that the CPC-MLers were attracted to the "mind over matter" zeal of the Chinese Red Guards, who could seemingly create their own objective conditions by the depth of their conviction.[115] Revolutionary idealism was of a piece with the emphasis of *Necessity for Change* on the transformative power that individuals could wield if they only attained the requisite consciousness.

Goldstick contended that under some circumstances Maoism could "present itself as a quasi-religious conversion experience, complete with moralistic personal 'rebirth,' as in Christianity, and the mindless spewing of violent slogans representing the symbolical antithesis of the individual convert's own 'petty-bourgeois' background and past." Membership testimonies of conversion portray life before joining the Internationalists or CPC-ML as empty and phony, enmeshed in bourgeois culture and mired by anti-consciousness. Despite the apolitical tenor in which their prior lives were depicted, members also confessed to having been reactionaries or on the precipice of becoming servants of imperialism.[116] Although allegories linking Leninist groups with religious movements are often substantially overdrawn, CPC-ML may be an exception. Lots of activists, new leftists and new Leninists alike, sacrificed safety, security, and leisure in pursuit of a post-capitalist society. But a synthesis of *Necessity for Change*, the party's increasingly confrontationist line, and the more militant style of protest seen in the late 1960s and early 1970s appears to have conjured up a new type of activist: a militant who "feared neither hardship nor death" and was willing to sacrifice her or himself again and again, with seemingly little consideration for the immense costs and dubious benefits of such actions. The party would later state that its members had been arrested over 1,600 times between 1968 and 1973 and that twenty-two immigrant members had been deported.[117]

The number of deportations points to the significant involvement of immigrants. Although some of them were American, many were immigrants from India, whose involvement in CPC-ML made it the country's only new Leninist group whose membership was not overwhelmingly white (until the later advent of Black new Leninist organizations). The integration of local Marxist-Leninists with their cousins in India, who were waging a rural-based guerrilla war, may have contributed to the Canadian party's unusual interest in armed struggle and active resistance against the police. The party would later claim that the Canadian proletariat was "deeply aware that the success of the Indian revolution is crucial to the success of its own revolution."[118] CPC-ML's significant South Asian following was facilitated by Bains, who headed an organization called the Hindustani Ghadar Party (Marxist-Leninist Organization of Patriotic Indians Overseas) (HGP), which followed in the tradition of a party established in North America in 1913 aiming to seek independence for India and combat racism in the West.[119]

The term "Maoism," although it was the one that stuck, was not favoured by these new Leninists. They preferred to call themselves "Marxist-Leninists," or "MLs" for short, a name implying that other tendencies associated with conventional communism or Trotskyism were by contrast not really Leninist at all.[120] What drew so many new leftists to Maoism? Many contemporaries, not just leftists, saw the Cultural Revolution in China as a remarkably democratic experiment. The barefoot doctors brought medical care to remote villagers; students were given permission to criticize their instructors; ordinary citizens could "bombard the headquarters" with their opinions. As it was represented in much of North America, the Cultural Revolution could be made to look like new leftism, with the additional attraction of being part of a world-reshaping and disciplined movement that organically responded to such grassroots initiatives. Looking upon the Chinese Cultural Revolution, new leftists could not have failed to see some similarities with what they were trying to do in Canada. The advent of "mass democracies," the overthrowing of "experts" and smashing of bureaucracies, and the idea of learning from and serving the people were attractive ideals. In Vancouver, PWM activists, notably Scott, conducted on-the-ground investigations in China that culminated in their disillusioned appraisal of vanguard Leninism. But in Toronto, neither new leftists nor Maoists ever seem to have attempted any kind of in-depth or even schematic analysis of Mao or China. Maoist slogans would pop up in all sorts of places, from the *Guerilla* and *Harbinger* underground newspapers to the *New Left Committee Bulletin*. This was, to be sure, a "soft" kind of Maoism, with activists indicating that they liked a particular slogan or policy, without necessarily offering blanket support for Chinese-style communism.[121] Yet it was suggestive of the extent to which new leftists might be predisposed to respond sympathetically to what they thought was the Maoist program. Maoism can be represented not so much as new leftism's termination as its continuation—albeit in a very different framework that sometimes seemed intent on reviving the most top-down features of Depression-era Communism.

Given that new leftism was never monopolized by one party or tendency, it often seems to have been everywhere and nowhere. The histories of the CCF-NDP, Communist Party, Liberals, and Maoists suggest the extent to which new and established parties all had to engage with a large population of articulate Toronto radicals pushing for a different kind of politics. For these people the old political world (and not just Cohn-Bendit's "Communism") was indeed obsolete. For some of them, history's most pressing challenge was to transform old parties into carriers of new left ideals. For others, it was to create new parties to bear witness to individuals' existential choice to heroically challenge the status quo. Over time and probably for the majority of activists, new leftism transcended any and all parties. It values would be best fought for in a host of new social movements, those predicated upon oppressed identities foremost among them.

From "Kill the Pigs" to "Victory to the NLF" to "Destroy the Monster that is Sucking Our Blood" to "Armed People's War": many of the slogans that echoed through this period suggest a left indifferent to its social and cultural context, essentially treating "Toronto" as one small venue for a planetary drama about world revolution or one relatively minor city in an undifferentiated North America. This Toronto was not so much a place as one more stage upon which to re-enact a replay of the revolutions in Russia or China that had, in essence, no Toronto or Canadian precursors worth noticing.

At the same time, other slogans, such as "For an Independent Socialist Canada," "Riel Should Be Understood, Dumont Imitated," and "Self-determination for Quebec" suggested a contemporaneous "Toronto left" that imagined itself to be operating, in essence, as the brains trust of a Canada-wide left (a status that many in the outlying regions were reluctant to concede to them). For some militants, any integration of these scales of analysis was tantamount to a dilution of revolutionary purity. But for others, there was plainly a hunger for a left politics that would be simultaneously local and personal, national and provincial, transnational and global.

7

"We Must *All* Be Politicians": Urban Resistance and the Turn to Community, 1971–78

> Community organization of the late 1960s was more radical, more pervasive and longer lasting, and had far greater impact on the socio-political structure of Toronto than anything that had preceded it. . . . After 1970, a significant degree of power shifted from City Hall to the neighbourhoods, even if it was only for a short period.
>
> —Kevin Brushett, "Blots on the Face of the City: The Politics of Slum Housing and Urban Renewal in Toronto, 1940–1970"

IN JUNE 1971 Ontario premier Bill Davis shocked Toronto, and the province, by announcing the reversal of a decision of the Ontario Municipal Board that had approved a loan for construction of the William R. Allen (Spadina) Expressway. The expressway had been promoted by planners and politicians since even before the consolidation of Metro Toronto in 1953. From 1961 to 1971, and especially after 1969, the city had been rocked by an intensive debate about the proposal. The expressway would have extended south from the northern cross-city Highway 401 into the heart of the city's Spadina garment district. For its proponents it was the epitome of liberal modernity. Individuals decided to buy cars, and individuals drove them to work, which thanks to millions invested by

This issue of *Guerilla* highlighted its opposition to the Spadina Expressway.

Guerilla, June 1970. Illustration by Mike Constable.

the government, they would now be able to do on an "aesthetically pleasing" motorway. For Sam Cass, who would become the Metro Commissioner of Roads and Traffic later in the 1970s, Los Angeles provided the model for a Toronto wrestling with the implications of an increasingly suburbanized city.[1]

For its opponents, Spadina epitomized the selfish short-sightedness and greed of capitalist development. By 1970 the Stop Spadina Save Our City Co-ordinating Committee—whose awkward name echoed both U.S. civil rights struggles and the communitarian notion that "our city" was a living entity that could be saved—had drawn as many as fifteen hundred active members into a body whose activist core consisted of white-collar professionals. The huge interest in stopping the expressway reflected a growing interest in participation, technology, and the environment. It also pointed to a new populist moment in which many were questioning the role of elected politicians, and especially whether they were acting in the best interests "of the people."[2]

Opponents of Spadina could draw inspiration from the successful struggle, unfolding at the same time, to block the redevelopment of the working-class neighbourhood of Trefann Court. Yet the victory over the expressway in 1971 constituted an even more noteworthy achievement, shifting as it did the spatial pattern of downtown Toronto and stopping an infrastructure project upon which the state had already lavished much money. It seemed that community organizing had achieved the impossible. It revealed that a "minority group of radicals" (to cite one critical evaluation of Stop Spadina) could prevail over the combined forces of business, state, and the suburban middle class.[3]

Was it a new left victory? The anti-expressway coalition included *The Globe and Mail*, prominent CBC-TV journalist and writer Adrienne Clarkson, Rosedale ratepayers, elite lawyer J.J. Robinette, and the top brass of the University of Toronto; they were hardly devotees of new leftism. Nor was Conservative premier Davis, even though he borrowed a (highly edited) slogan from Students for a Democratic Society and other radical groups when he proclaimed, "The streets belong to the people." As in the case of the Hall-Dennis Report, Davis was selectively appropriating and neutralizing elements of a world view he opposed, and there is little evidence to suggest that Toronto over the next decade ever became committed to progressive, non-automotive, and collective forms of transportation.[4]

Yet it would also be a mistake to write off the Spadina struggle as a minor concession to bourgeois highway haters. It propelled a cadre of reformers, including future mayor John Sewell, into the spotlight; it encouraged people to express, in often unconditional terms, their opposition to rampant capitalist modernity; it popularized the hitherto uncommon ideas that "progress" might be deadly and that alternative models of urban living were well worth considering; and it suggested to those anti-expressway activists who *were* hard-core socialists and Marxists that they could win victories if they operated within broader alliances and articulated their ideas in an accessible language. The very people whom one Liberal MPP dismissed as "hairy, snaggle-toothed academics" and others termed a "very small, but vocal minority" had prevailed.[5]

Certainly the RCMP believed something was seriously amiss with the coalition that blocked Spadina. In late 1968 Stephen Clarkson and Abraham Rotstein, both professors at the University of Toronto, launched a research institute bearing the Marxist-sounding name "Praxis." If the initial prospectus of the institute announced its anodyne intention "to encourage research and long-range imaginative thinking on the various aspects of the future development of our society," on which basis it won support from the federally funded National Council of Welfare, the RCMP suspected that it was part of a broader conspiracy. The RCMP saw Howard Buchbinder, formerly a community organizer and radical social work professor in St. Louis, and an activist in the U.S. War on Poverty, as being intent on subverting the Metro Toronto Social Planning Council. One police analyst thought that Praxis constituted the "central nervous system" of a new left extraparliamentary opposition.[6]

On December 18, 1970, persons unknown, but plausibly linked to the Edmund Burke Society, broke into offices at 373 Huron Street and seized records belonging to Praxis, the Just Society (which sought to mobilize welfare recipients), Metro Tenants, and the Stop Spadina group. Some of the Praxis documents ended up in the hands of right-wing *Toronto Telegram* columnist Peter Worthington, who then turned them over to the RCMP; others made their way directly to the RCMP's security service. Under pressure because of misdeeds in Quebec, the police evidently destroyed them, apparently to protect the identity of a police informant inside the Burke Society. The force was thus complicit not only in the receipt of stolen goods but also in arson because the burglars had also burned down the Huron Street house. Similar arson attacks severely damaged or destroyed the offices of a Black newspaper, a left-wing theatre, the Communist Party's headquarters, and the Arab Community Centre, from which files were also stolen.[7]

In addition to illustrating the extent to which activists were under aggressive surveillance, the Praxis affair tells us something about the new alignment of forces in Toronto in the early 1970s. Praxis may have started off asking the most innocent of questions about how to enhance citizen participation, and some partisans of Stop Spadina may have been interested in maintaining placid professional lives in downtown Toronto—but both cases indicate the radical potential of such openings for the new left. As the RCMP analysts were well aware, the subversive elements of a resurgent left could, if the groups played their cards well, find receptive audiences and raise popular consciousness around down-to-earth concerns, such as a looming highway. The notion of neighbourhoods uniting to resist capitalist development, and then building larger alliances with other neighbourhood groups and city-wide interests, was no left-wing chimera.

Yet, in the eyes of at least some leftists, community control over various aspects of daily life might not even *be* leftist. Writers in the long-standing social-democratic publication *Canadian Forum* were alarmed at the decentralist ethos of the "hardline" reformers. Michael S. Cross wrote that the central demand of local control was "necessarily a conservative doctrine," part of a "new anarchism" whose adherents ranged from prominent right-wing commentator William F. Buckley to maverick writer Norman Mailer. Alan Powell, who had served as chairman of Stop Spadina, discerned two poles in such reformism: "class-conscious-centralist-socialist-ideology inspired by Marx" and "consensus-decentralist-populist pragmatism inspired by Jane Jacobs." Many community organizers clearly straddled both categories.[8]

* * *

The first significant local new left community organizing project was initiated in 1966 to help working-class residents of the Trefann Court neighbourhood who were faced with eviction. Activists rallied to help them obtain better compensation, and eventually to save their homes. Sarah Spinks, of SUPA, Marjaleena Repo, of *This Magazine Is About Schools*, and novice organizer John Sewell were all involved. That same year, James Lorimer, a recent graduate student (and later a prominent city activist and book publisher), began his "participant observation" study of neighbouring Don Vale, which marked his entry into community activism. Lorimer's research was eventually published in *Working People: Life in a Downtown City Neighbourhood* (shades of the Praxis affair, documents stolen during a break-in at the book's publisher resurfaced in the offices of the right-wing *Toronto Sun*).[9]

In striving to organize their communities, residents of both neighbourhoods engaged in door-to-door organizing and picketed the homes of politicians. In solidarity with Don Mount residents, who lived further to the east, activists from both neighbourhoods protesting evictions occupied city council chambers, where they sang civil rights songs such as "We Shall Not Be Moved" and "We Shall Overcome." While other community struggles at that point lacked such tell-tale signs of leftist involvement, the sheer size of some mobilizations—like the nearly one thousand tenants who protested rent increases in East York—suggests that the foundations for a social movement were already being laid. Community organizations would soon win concessions "of which," writes researcher Kevin Brushett, "their predecessors only dreamt."[10]

This far-ranging and largely forgotten atmosphere of activism and opposition, which extended well beyond the organized left, was also present in the Spadina struggle. But police may have had more trouble with middle-aged pro-Spadina Expressway supporters than with the more youthful anti-Spadina campaigners. Residents north of Eglinton Avenue, the major east-west thoroughfare where the expressway construction came to a halt, were furious with the project's cancellation. The city had already bulldozed through their neighbourhoods, and the route remained unpaved and in limbo for years (as debate around its future continued). It was still no easier for people in that area to get downtown, and, worse, the project's termination at Eglinton left a lot of new traffic going through local streets in search of a convenient route south. To press their case, the neighbourhoods organized delegations, symbolically burned the money wasted on the project, and even blockaded rush-hour traffic. Their aura of militancy was so striking that a mislabelled picture of a pro-Spadina rally was later used to illustrate the anger of downtown anti-expressway activists.[11]

Another expressway story, this one suggesting that activists established bases of support in working-class communities, has similarly been erased. The Scarborough Expressway would have been a major, city-altering project. It was to have headed north from the Gardiner Expressway, up Leslie Street, and then eastward, above Gerrard Street. About 1,200 working-class houses were scheduled for demolition. Community activists had been agitating against the plan since the late 1960s and gained new confidence with the cancellation of the Spadina route. Feeling the pressure, officials offered a modified plan in 1973 whereby only half the number of houses would be torn down; they contemplated giving evicted tenants compensation.[12]

But protests only escalated. Many saw the expressway as a class issue, arguing that the city was discriminating against low-income and working-class residents of the city's east end. In contrast to the many well-known opponents of the Spadina Expressway, people speaking out against the Scarborough Expressway tended to be working-class residents and activists embedded in east-end groups like the new left–tinged, but largely social-democratic, Forward 9 and the new left-leaning Greater Riverdale Organization.[13] A *Globe and Mail* reporter made a slightly exaggerated comparison between the two anti-expressway efforts:

> Unlike the Spadina Expressway protesters, the people opposed to the Scarborough Expressway are not a small intellectual group fighting for a concept. Rather, they are a large and voracious body of residents.... The people who will be most affected by the expressway and noise are largely blue-collar workers, many of ethnic origin, who have struggled to buy a house of their own.[14]

Residents held several large meetings and rallies in the second half of 1973. A small protest at the home of Metro chairman Paul Godfrey provoked an angry response about the mixing of politics and private lives. But a rally of seven hundred residents lauded that action. A man in the multilingual crowd, drawing loud applause, asked, "Didn't you tell him that his politics on the expressway are ruining the lives of hundreds of people whose homes are being destroyed?" After a key expressway supporter reversed course in front of a community meeting of five hundred in the late summer of 1973, advocates for the Scarborough Expressway became scarce. Its last diehard supporters, Godfrey and *The Toronto Star*, eventually capitulated.[15]

The *Star*'s strong editorial support for the expressway, its dubious use of statistics to back it, and its scant reporting of opposition activities (until the tide had clearly turned)[16] pointed to a long-recognized problem: the interests of the mainstream media and activists and leftists often ran counter to each other. New left activists found it difficult to compete with the substantial circulation of the mainstream press. But in the early 1970s over a dozen new community newspapers worked to close that gap. While the major local dailies supported the Conservative or Liberal parties, these newspapers—with a collective circulation of around 100,000—leaned strongly towards the NDP at the provincial and federal levels and favoured independent left candidates and coalitions municipally.

With the *Star*'s blockade of anti-expressway views, residents of the city's east end relied on *Ward 9 Community News* to read about the latest developments and to discover impending meetings and protests. Like other ward-wide newspapers, it was delivered door to door. The exceptionally long-lived *Seven News* (1970–85) served Ward 7, a hot spot for anti-development activism. Its regular readers were introduced to a host of social movement activities and debates. *Ward 8 News* incorporated regular Greek- and Chinese-language pages and occasionally subverted the often-staid community newspaper format, most memorably in a left-wing send-up of *The Toronto Sun*. Even a boiler-plate community article might be supplemented with a more critical analysis. A piece covering an Indo-Canadian film premiere at the local Naaz Theatre, for instance, came with a review by budding sociologist and writer Himani Bannerji decrying the class, race, and gender biases of the film.[17] Virtually all of the community newspapers were free, with varying publication schedules (often bi-weekly or monthly).

A host of neighbourhood-based newspapers ranged from the left-of-centre *Community* (North Jarvis) to the eclectic *Riverdale Review* and atypically conservative *Parkdale Citizen*. The influence of the *Parkdale Citizen* was partly counteracted by the left-wing *Parkdale Tenant*. Other community media operated on a severely local level. The circulation of the *Sunday Brunswick* might have been limited to few city blocks, but a political fissure over parking was significant enough to give it a car-skeptic competitor, *The Original Brunswick Guardian*.

Neighbourhood activists would have found much of interest in the *City Hall* newsletter, the *Toronto Citizen* newspaper, and the locally produced *City Magazine*, which was a forum for analyzing municipal politics and social movements across the country. The independent *Toronto Clarion*, in which new left ideas found a most emphatic expression, could be found in convenience stores, subway stations, and newspaper boxes throughout the Metro area. Journalist Tom Walkom shrewdly profiled its journalistic stance by noting two models it might follow: Leninist, espousing a specific political line (even if not necessarily Leninism); and populist, which did not preclude reporting stories that might raise eyebrows among conventional leftists. The *Clarion* was, he thought, a paper for the "downtown lumpen intelligentsia," aiming to attract white-collar workers as readers but more often winning over "people like us," meaning radicals, hippies, and others who wanted something of a different perspective.[18]

Anyone interested in following local political issues could, in short, gather information from subtly or explicitly left-wing media. Even though, as Walkom suggested, the *Clarion* wore its politics lightly, it sometimes used explicitly anti-capitalist language. One editorial opined that the development of co-ops and "other democratic organizations" served as useful models for a future socialist society, while allowing more affordable food and housing in the present. Another urged readers to vote NDP but to remember that real change would stem only from their own grassroots organizing.[19] Through the alternative media, new left ideals with respect to affordable housing, co-operative daycare, and locally raised organic food became common-sense matters for a large number of Torontonians.

A paradox for many of these small newspapers—and of much "community activism" in Toronto in the early 1970s—was their direct or indirect funding from the federal state. From 1971 to 1977 (when government financial support for community organizing dried up) dozens of projects, many of them new left in atmosphere and personnel, flourished in Toronto, funded in part by government money. Grants from the Local Initiatives Program fed a galaxy of left projects in Toronto. Significant bounties also appeared courtesy of Opportunities for Youth, which provided even Red Morning with money for a drop-in centre. Lesser sources of funding included grants under the Secretary of State's multicultural program and Canada Works. Many of Toronto's LIP and OFY grant recipients were assiduously tied to new left and countercultural activists in a right-wing "exposé" called *The Big Rip-Off* (1972).[20]

New left activists intent on challenging the state could often go from LIP grant to OFY grant to LIP grant to avoid completely starving themselves for the revolution. The state frequently intervened to edit out bothersome applicants—*Guerilla* was excluded in 1972, as was CHAT, a gay liberation group. To resist arbitrary measures, and press for the renewal of their grants, 110 recipient organizations formed the Toronto Metro Working Group, which engaged in demonstrations at and occupations of Liberal Party offices. If, as often contended, the Liberals were using grants to absorb their radical critics, they did not always succeed in doing so. After 1977 a general tightening up occurred in all such forms of largesse. Budget cuts undermined programs that left conspirators had created and forced some activists to compete with others for money. An article in *City Magazine* that year maintained that community organizing was in a state of severe decline because the state had terminated or absorbed so many promising autonomous agencies. But for much of the decade the state was in effect financing many people who longed for its overthrow.[21]

* * *

A slogan of many new left activists in the 1970s was "community control," an expression that captured the drive for decentralized political power and neighbourhood councils. The term could encompass such traditional left objectives as public ownership of land, housing, and businesses. People should exert a maximum amount of democracy in small local units—participating in the decisions that had an impact on their daily lives. For activists like Paul Weinberg, the local level was the place to start constructing "a world untouched by the polluting ravages of Industrial capitalism." Community control was seen as an antidote both to ruling capitalists and the old left, who were said to have accepted the ideology of liberalism, a philosophy that, according to Weinberg, permeated "virtually all Canadian political groups from the Liberal Party to the Young Socialists, endorsing growth, efficiency and technocracy to the detriment of the individual and the community."[22]

Some new leftists were ardent nationalists, and many more were ardent internationalists, focused on struggles in Cuba, Chile, and, later, Nicaragua. But many new leftists were convinced that the key to social transformation lay in local struggles. In discussing upcoming Toronto elections, Weinberg wrote:

> For radicals, the place of action lies on the local level. There the contradictions between the quality of life and the growth ethic of our profit-making economic system are clearest. These will cause a high level of conflict across Canada in the urban centres where the majority lives. The issue of power from below rather than from above, comes through very strongly in the fight by neighbourhoods for the right to control their own design, education, planning and for that matter destiny.[23]

Education activist George Martell agreed. He advocated a trench-by-trench strategy for community control, utilizing support bases won in local campaigns for broader assaults on the system:

> In the process we must build a political party, but unlike the Socialist parties of the past it must be committed to developing a very high degree of local control at the same time as it develops the power to challenge the Corporations. Indeed, its commitment to community control of the major institutions of the society will come only through the party being born out of the struggle of local people for self-determination, with its structure reflecting the vastly increased power of the neighbourhood.[24]

Here was a theorization of the very strategy that had worried the RCMP when it encountered the anti-Spadina movement: an ever-expanding circle of resistance that, established on the basis of local struggles for control, could culminate in a system-challenging movement. It was a movement that seemed capable of eliciting unlikely responses from unlikely allies, as in the case of professors William Kilbourn and Jack Granatstein, who pitched themselves into a whole-hearted battle, including moments of direct action, against a large development project that would have transformed midtown Marlborough Avenue.[25]

Some of this outlook is preserved in a book manuscript, "The Politics of Change," prepared by Howard Buchbinder and Gerry Hunnius, who went on to become a major writer on workers' control (a concept that applied new left ideals of participatory democracy to the industrial workplace). Their first chapter looked at liberal democracy as a means of elite control—as an indirect and compartmentalized democracy in which citizens had some freedom of speech on the street corner but none in the workplace or school. They argued that Leninism and social democracy were but variations of elite control. The way to move beyond those dead ends was through extraparliamentary social movements directed towards transforming power rather than taking it (via social ownership of the means of production coupled with self-governing community and workplace collectives). "The new socialist man and woman" would be created during this struggle, rather than after an election or revolution.[26]

They examined around 150 books, articles, and unpublished manuscripts—from scholarly books to Ontario government publications—on the theme of participatory democracy. Virtually all of them advocated a politics of liberalism, they concluded, whereby isolated participatory techniques would be grafted onto an otherwise status-quo society. They predicted that this kind of participation would become popular with managers, under the guises of "creativity" and "teamwork." But Buchbinder and Hunnius also worried about statements made by members of local social movements and radical organizations, which also threatened to keep things as they were. Many of these activists were directing their demands to governments, implicitly recognizing the state as the key venue for social change. This could only feed into the continued expansion of the welfare state, the authors warned, which ultimately served the interests of corporations. New leftists should have been aware of this danger, but in practice they were repeating the history of the old left, whose pursuit of reforms had led to the welfare state in the first place. Underlining this argument, the authors emphasized that the labour movement, once radical and grassroots, had been corrupted by the state-focused postwar compromise: "Trade unionism has ceased to be a social movement and has become a business."[27]

Harkening back to the student movement of the late 1960s, their final chapter acknowledged that the movement for control—for real participation—had been sown in schools, workplaces, and families. The authors spoke favourably of the delegitimizing function of alternative institutions and of the new women's movement, but refrained from directly prescribing a way forward: "There was no blueprint for them and there is no blueprint for you."[28] Buchbinder also developed these themes in the *Our Generation* journal. A 1972 editorial, written by the Toronto Our Generation collective, called for joint struggles for worker and community control, a combination seen as the very essence of participatory democracy.[29]

The ideas distilled in Buchbinder and Hunnius's manuscript could be found in countless new left quarters in 1970s Toronto. For some thinkers, such as Sarah Rothschild writing in *The Varsity*, calls for community control distracted leftists from more global patterns of power and tended to overlook the class and other divisions within any given community. Others noted how "participation" and even "participatory democracy" could be liberal ruses, persuading people that what they really wanted was something small and easily acquired. It was necessary, said Lorimer, to begin "smoking out the liberals." Wayne Roberts, a veteran of the Spadina Expressway campaign, pointed to the limitations of urban reformers, who tended to create *unions sacrées* of homeowners, small businessmen, and "good capitalists." Warren Magnusson, writing in a more academic vein, agreed: urban reform would only be genuinely radical if it involved the rejection of centralizing measures and the re-creation of "small, directly democratic institutions." Encapsulating some of these criticisms, *Seven News* printed a "pyramid of participation," breaking the elements down into eight parts, with "manipulation" at the bottom and "citizen control" at the top. Many local examples (falling under "placation" and "consultation") were situated in the middle.[30]

In 1974 Eric Blair, writing in the left-wing *Last Post* (a Montreal-based magazine founded partly by Toronto émigrés), found it encouraging that activists' ill-defined notions of a "common front" uniting the "poor, working-class and middle-class residents" of a given neighbourhood had yielded to more rigorous forms of analysis: "The very fuzziness of the coalition made it easy for them to think in fuzzy populist terms about 'the people' and 'citizen participation' without being plagued by hard questions about class interests." Now those hard questions had come to the surface, which reflected Toronto's transition to a city in which 50 per cent of the population consisted of renters.[31]

If "community development" and "neighbourhood control" could have conservative connotations, in their implication that "the community" and "the neighbourhood" had one homogeneous identity and interest, new leftism generally broke with such comfortable consensual assumptions. In the University of Toronto's School of Social Work, students were introduced to models of community control that emphasized confrontation, the redistribution of power, and the social genesis of problems manifested on the individual level.[32] Although often accused of romanticizing "community," new leftists tended instead to see community as an important level of struggle. As debates erupting in 1975 at the Cowan Avenue Firehall (a Parkdale community centre) suggested, the achievements of the left, such as a co-operative daycare, the Parkdale Single Parents Association, a food co-op, a community law office, and the Parkdale Tenants' Association, were all being assailed from the right, fuelled by stories in a new right-wing tabloid, *The Toronto Sun*. The leftists prevailed in the discussion at that centre, leading one alderman to condemn the "Commie hangout."[33] The radicals knew, and perhaps he also knew, that in such a location, geared as it was to local and personal struggles, links could be formed that might sharpen, not soften, the contradictions of a capitalist society. New leftists did not embrace the local in the pursuit of quieter lives. They embraced it in search of a revolution.

* * *

Housing had never been considered a central pillar of the Canadian welfare state. By design, the free market was left to make the most fundamental decisions. But as the city's population mushroomed, so too did the cost of accommodation. A great number of people did not own their own homes and were looking for affordable and collective ways to live. New leftists responded to this issue by organizing tenants, pushing for legal reforms, and establishing co-operative housing.

The late 1960s and early 1970s saw a dramatic increase in different kinds of alternative housing spaces. These ranged from places where people lived fairly conventional middle-class lives under one roof to experiments in which private rooms were abolished, clothing was equally shared, and everyone slept with everyone else.[34] Sociologist Meg Luxton, after examining eleven local experiments in communal living in a 1973 study, concluded that all the participants had been influenced to some degree or other by left-wing ideas. Although differing in their exact analysis, her subjects agreed on a number of points: middle-class society demanded change; the nuclear family was oppressive; new patterns of interpersonal relationships were needed; communal living arrangements were part of a broader move towards radically changing society; and this was all a part of building "the movement."[35]

Houses sharing all financial and other resources tended to be called "communes," while houses sharing resources to a lesser degree were called "co-ops." In everyday talk, people living together in common would speak of their "house" (as in, "My house is going to a demonstration tomorrow"), but in the often hostile eyes of the mainstream media, all such experiments were "communes." Some leftists saw an important distinction lurking in the "co-op/commune" combination. Despite being featured in an article headlined "Commune on McCaul St.," the residents saw their house as a co-op rather than a commune. As one of them explained: "I think that communes are just an idealistic dream in the confines of a capitalistic society. They just don't work." Politically oriented leftists tended to agree with that assessment. When asked why she referred to her past communal living arrangements as co-ops, Maureen Hynes said, "We never called it a commune—that was a hippie thing. But looking back . . . maybe." Norm Rogers similarly viewed "commune" as a "hippie term" associated with vegetarianism, free love, and incessant dope-smoking. Certainly some of that existed at the co-op he lived in, he allowed, but its focus was on politics.[36]

Those who identified more closely with the counterculture than with left-wing politics per se were indeed more apt to use the term "commune." Alex, a freelance writer who lived with two students, a welfare worker, and an unemployed woman, insisted that the house they lived in "is a commune, not a co-operative. We do everything communally, including eating. There are two reasons. It is cheaper and it brings us closer together." It was this tightness that most distinguished a commune from a co-op; and just as important were the social and political goals related to the living environment. According to Alex, many communes in the city had the goal of eventually moving out to the countryside to further their experiment. Tanis, a musician who tie-dyed clothing to pay her bills and shared Alex's outlook, emphasized that the community-building aspect of communal living was paramount.[37]

Contrary to stereotype, the typical residents of these co-ops and communes were not students or drop-outs. While twenty-nine of the people Luxton studied were full-time students, forty-three were workers, either part-time or full-time. A number connected their work, like their living arrangements, to a broader political outlook. Some chose manual-labour occupations to further long-term radical goals, while others taught in free schools, laboured in worker co-operatives, or had jobs as paid community organizers. Some were employed in "people's institutions," providing daycare, or legal or medical services, places that hoped to radicalize people in the process of helping them.[38]

The largest concentration of these co-ops was in a block bordering Beverley, Sullivan, and Huron streets, which many activists simply referred to as the "red belt." Like many areas of the downtown, the block had been targeted for development and in the interim a company was renting out houses it had purchased. Over time, the twenty to thirty political and counterculture houses on the block formed a community, with significant intermingling between its left-wing and hippie residents. Together they built a coalition that thwarted the developer's plans to demolish their houses. Norm Rogers, whose "red belt" co-op progressively became more politically active as it shifted from a student to a worker demographic, estimated that a total of seventy to eighty people lived at his house during his ten-year stay there. This Beverley Street house provided its residents with cheap rent, a base for launching activist projects, and a vibrant forum for political discussion ranging from weighty philosophical debates to whether residents should purchase butter or margarine.[39]

Some of the centrality assumed by the "politics of housework" in early-1970s feminism stemmed from women's perceptions that they were stuck in these houses doing all the cleaning and cooking, even in communes that were supposedly challenging the status quo. For them—and for many new leftists—a "house" was not just a place to live, but a space to prefigure the social relations of a better world. Activists such as Sylvia Hauge of the Toronto Women's Liberation Movement explicitly embraced the ideal that such patterns of housing should challenge both the traditional family and the wider social system. A few groups took this idea further by founding communes and integrating them into their organizational structures. The group Alternative to Alienation—in which radical school trustee Ernest Barr was active—established their own commune to pioneer a new way of living and take up Reich's challenge to "restructure man."[40]

Red Morning set up a handful of communes so that members could take care of basic things like rent, cooking, and cleaning in a collective fashion. Everyone in these houses gave their income to the group, which in turn paid expenses and doled out individual allowances. Yet their vision for collective living went far beyond such practical benefits. Communes, they said, could eliminate "patterns and games that we've learned from pig society" and "build the new man, new woman, new world." Gerald Dunn, who moved from Rochdale College into a Red Morning house, explained that for him communal living was part of being a communist. It was inconceivable that genuine radicals would not live in accordance with their wider principles.[41]

* * *

In addition to solving housing problems for themselves through communes and co-ops, leftists turned en masse to organizing tenants' struggles. They saw housing as a public utility, with most of it community-controlled, a sector in which profit-making should not occur. They envisaged a Toronto that would be largely tenant-run, with public ownership of land and community services controlled by users. A growing tenant movement proved an ideal opportunity to test many of these ideas.[42]

By the late 1960s, Toronto tenants were visibly disgruntled with rising rents and arbitrary landlords. In early spring 1970 two back-to-back tenant revolts broke out, illustrating the breadth of such complaints. Leading one was eighty-five-year-old Lillias Scott. After her apartment building was hit with a 40 per cent rent increase, she handed her rent money over to the Bloordale Tenants' Association. Dozens of other tenants, many on fixed incomes, followed her lead. They demanded a rent reduction and called on their landlord to repair their dilapidated apartments, get rid of the cockroaches, and turn up the heat. They picketed in front of their building with homemade signs: "Slum Landlord," "Rent Strike On," "Strikebreakers Keep Out!" Meanwhile, in a more prosperous part of town, Dick Lightbown was demanding justice. Tenants in his apartment complex had been promised swimming pools, squash and tennis courts, saunas, and other such facilities, but his landlord had failed to come through on all of these luxury amenities. In response, a hundred irate tenants pledged not to pay their rent. Picket lines, organized by the Graydon Hall Tenants' Association, ratcheted up the pressure by turning prospective tenants away.[43]

The largest and most sustained rent strike that year took place in an apartment, managed by the Ontario Housing Corporation, for married U of T students. In August tenants in three hundred units began deducting $50 from their rent to protest high rents and a lack of say in running their building. In November

125 of them began withholding all their rent. They organized demonstrations, mass meetings, and even street theatre performances to highlight their demands. In one sketch, black-hooded figures representing housing corporation officials herded tenants towards a guillotine until "Supertenant" saved the day. The real-life tenants, however, had no such luck and conceded defeat in March 1971 after a court upheld their eviction notices.[44]

Nothing was easy when it came to mobilizing tenants. Steven Langdon, a renowned U of T activist, reported on one fraught attempt to establish a tenants' union in a North York apartment building. He described a meeting that was "heated" and "out of control, marked by frenzied attacks by tenant on tenant."

> Every so often, someone would shout louder than the rest and he would become chairman for a while, letting one or perhaps two speakers talk to the crowded room before interruptions back and forth returned things to general disorder and formless argument. It was people trying to work out participatory democracy.[45]

The barriers to tenant organizing were even higher when initiated from the "outside." Activists in the Ward 4 Community Association, dedicated to increasing the number of tenant associations in their ward, eventually acquired the necessary expertise. A former member who organized a large three-building complex at Bloor and Dovercourt recalled a painstaking process of going door-to-door to find people willing to set up an association. They experienced cat-and-mouse games with the superintendent and suspected intimidation from the landlord (slashed tires), but the end result was success.[46]

To increase their collective power, tenant associations as diverse as those at Bloordale and Graydon Hall worked together in the Metro Tenants' Association (MTA), created in 1969. Its activists included new leftists, old leftists, and plenty of the "regular people" that both camps hoped to recruit. Hitting on the radical themes of community power, tenant control, and unionization, new left and Waffle stalwarts were featured speakers at MTA's first annual meeting in 1970.[47]

The Ontario Tenants' Association (OTA), spearheaded by Kingston activists to support collective bargaining for tenants across the province, was another key coalition. U of T professor Lee Patterson, who had earlier led seventy-five Eastmount Avenue families in a rent strike that one judge characterized as a "revolution," became its chairman.[48] Shortly after its 1969 founding, OTA sponsored a Toronto demonstration calling for rent control and an end to discrimination and security deposits. The NDP MPP James Renwick pleased the crowd by echoing OTA's view that tenant groups be given a similar status under the law as unions. But the minister of trade and development proved less obliging, arguing that rent controls were unrealistic. The housing minister, for his part, said the protest was populated by all sorts of unsavoury radicals and had been secretly organized by the NDP. He publicly scolded tenants for allowing children to carry picket signs with "the filthiest four-letter words that anyone could write." Sympathizing with his outrage, the city's Board of Control referred one psychedelic sign to the police to see if the tenant holding it could be prosecuted—it contained cutouts portraying nude men and women under the heading "Tenant Joy."[49]

In 1971 the Ontario Tenants' Association was hit by a wave of resignations amidst complaints that the MTA dominated the group, did not care about associations outside of Toronto, and was too left-wing. OTA's resigning treasurer grumbled, "I believe tenants' organizations should be radical and militant, but I don't believe the solution to problems lies in overthrowing the system. I'm a militant—not a revolutionary." MTA's president admitted that his organization's large size—it had 1,500 more members than OTA's second-largest affiliate—made equitable relations difficult, but rejected being characterized as a wild-eyed revolutionary: "We get accusations of being too conservative all the time.... We're not generally regarded as being radical."[50]

A third tenant coalition, the Ontario Housing Tenants' Association, was formed in 1970. Despite its name, it was initially limited to activists from nineteen Metro Toronto public housing projects. Given that public housing tenants had engaged in successful direct-action protests that year (in one instance delivering bags of garbage to their public-sector landlords), this development was hardly surprising. In addition to demanding recreation facilities for their children, repairs, pest control, and a role in decision-making, these tenant association members faced a bunch of issues seldom experienced by other housing activists. To prevent drug dealers and "hoodlums" from coming near their buildings, a few joined baseball-bat-wielding vigilante squads. Others organized against conservative homeowners who were demanding that fences be put up to segregate public housing projects from their surrounding neighbourhoods.[51] Many were fed up with visits from tenant relations officers: "They sent this nice university girl with middle class ideas in to tell me that my floor was not as clean as it should be. She knows from beans what it is like to live in poverty."[52]

While government leaders had first mocked the very idea of tenants serving on public housing boards, the growing militancy of the tenant movement began to convince bureaucrats and politicians that some form of token representation was necessary. *The Telegram*, ever eager to bolster "moderate" demands to curtail the power of "extremists," began demanding the inclusion of tenants on all public housing boards. In later years city hall explored more ambitious participation schemes in municipally owned housing, and the Canadian Mortgage and Housing Corporation (CMHC) launched an experimental tenant co-management project.[53]

Rent control, implemented by the provincial government in 1975, was a more tangible gain from this widespread tenant unrest. In addition to their own campaigns, tenant organizations joined with a broad range of left-wing allies to push for the introduction of controls. A particularly influential joint body was a city hall committee (composed of five tenant representatives, two labour and community delegates, and two left-wing councillors). Although the committee came under fire for its ideological and structural biases, council nevertheless passed its recommendation for the city to implement its own rent controls, creating additional pressure on the provincial government to act. Ontario's new rent controls were not as progressive as those demanded by tenants' groups (or the City of Toronto), but their benefit to a majority of Torontonians represented a substantial victory for the tenant movement.[54]

Despite this win, organizing continued apace, with hundreds of angry tenants besieging new rent review board hearings. The MTA (relaunched as the Federation of Metro Tenants Associations in 1974) continued to fight for collective bargaining rights and other issues dear to the movement. Control by tenants remained a prominent demand, and its tenant bill of rights included the "right to self-management." A popular slogan was "People or property?" By the following decade, one list enumerated over six hundred building-based tenants' associations active in the city.[55]

* * *

New leftists also strove to change the overall framework of housing in Toronto. In 1972 an article from the Toronto Community Press Service (an organization formed to create content specifically for Toronto's community newspapers) complained that co-operative housing remained little more than an idea. With housing costs skyrocketing, the article demanded that governments give more subsidies to increase the viability of community-based non-profit housing. This "third force" housing was considered a vital alternative to both government and private sector–operated rental units. Some five years later the situation had changed dramatically. With changes to the regulations governing the Canadian Mortgage and Housing Corporation in 1973, co-ops sponsored by community groups became eligible for the same loan arrangements enjoyed by government housing projects. In the mid-1970s, more units were being provided by Toronto's third sector than by the government.[56]

The struggle to obtain CMHC funding for co-ops only came to fruition via legislation from the federal Liberal minority government backed by the NDP. Senior CMHC officials had seen co-ops as "unhealthy and unCanadian." One official proclaimed that he could not "imagine anything more likely to jeopardize

[the] stability of family life than becoming involved in a venture of co-operative housing." Even after the change, a CMHC brochure juxtaposed co-ops to "more socially acceptable" forms of housing.[57]

The city's co-op housing sector took off immediately after the new regulations were in place. Several ward-based community organizations set up non-profit corporations to build their own housing. Forward 9, which had prominently organized against the Scarborough Expressway, saw co-ops as a good projection of what it was *for*. Its Ward 9 Co-op quickly accumulated over a half-dozen properties. In conjunction with the Labour Council, Forward 9 formed the Main-Gerrard Community Development Co-operative, which owned several apartment complexes. During the mid- to late 1970s and early 1980s, similar neighbourhood groups and community-labour partnerships created thousands of co-op units.[58]

Among all of the co-op housing built, two developments were particularly controversial. One of them, the Don Area Co-operative Homes Inc., had been set up by the Federation of Don Area Residents' Associations. More than 450 people turned up at a meeting to discuss and vote on whether to take over a block of rental properties assembled by a private developer and turn it into co-op housing. The meeting supported the co-op proposal by a vote of 198 to 158, thereby launching a running battle: on one side were new "white-painting" homeowners, who sought a more gentrified area and worked with right-wing Progressive Conservative Party activists; on the other were longer-term tenants supported by the left.[59]

Tory MPP Margaret Scrivener saw the co-op as part of an alarming growth of "hastily-organized ratepayers' groups, environmental groups, peaceniks, ban-the-bomb types, marches and demonstrations." She hired a party member to work alongside party activists in opposition to the project. Angry homeowners joined the crusade, insisting that the vote in support of the co-op be thrown out. They believed that tenants should not have been allowed to vote on the issue and argued that the middle class (like the French, the poor, and the rich) should be able to live amongst their own kind. The real estate broker selling to the co-op said he had experienced dozens of people telephoning him in the middle of the night calling him a "commie bastard." When the mayor began to be swayed by the opposition, reform members of city council successfully rallied to obtain city endorsement and the plans went forward.[60]

The second of the controversial co-op projects, Bain Avenue Apartments, involved a fight in which both sides were left-wing. The early and mid-1970s had witnessed intense battles between the Bain Avenue Tenants' Association and Toronto Housing and the landlord. During a fight over repairs, the site's general manager called the employers of tenant activists to complain about their conduct. When tenants were served notice that their apartments would be converted into condominiums, they decided to strike up a co-op and resist the efforts to evict them. They picketed the model suites set up to attract buyers and, with the assistance of the city government, agreed to buy the apartments as a whole. The plan involved a two-year trial period, starting in 1974, in which the city would own the complex but allow full tenant participation in its management.[61]

Trouble began in 1977 when the co-op management announced an 18 per cent rent increase, the third substantial increase in two years (co-ops were not covered by rent controls). A group of tenants, including members of Bain Avenue Tenants' Action (an OFY project) and Wages for Housework (a feminist group), announced that they would refuse to pay the increase. Supporters of the rent freeze said they had the backing of one hundred tenants, but the residents' council voted against the freeze. Disagreements escalated, with debate increasingly focusing on the desirability of co-ops. Freeze opponents spoke of community control and cheaper housing in the long term, and warned that a rent freeze would threaten the future of the co-op. Freeze supporters challenged the whole concept of co-op ownership, characterizing it as "a way of exploiting yourself for the government's purpose." They wanted the complex to be run as municipally owned housing. A referendum confirmed that a majority of residents favoured the co-op concept. While that vote largely settled the matter, freeze supporters voted to fight on.[62]

* * *

Whether campaigning against anti-commune bylaws, agitating for rent controls, or struggling to build a housing co-op, urban activists found reliable allies amongst a coterie of city counsellors. From 1971 to 1978 a fairly steady polarization occurred in Toronto electoral politics. Over the years the left-urbanist *City Magazine* distinguished between two groups of progressives: "soft-line" (liberal) and "hardline" (radical). Alderman Michael Goldrick, conventionally considered a radical, nonetheless saw the binary's limitations. "Hardline" politicians wanted to redistribute wealth and power and ensure the people's actual, not token, participation in politics. Yet, he argued, they had failed to rally around a coherent and unifying philosophy. The "soft-line" contingent had done rather better, he thought, because they shared a "liberal framework" and sought measures that would adapt the city to "fundamental changes in the accumulation of capital."[63]

The news media preferred to use the term "reformer" to describe the aldermanic candidates seeking to overthrow the conservative establishment at city hall. It initially referred to candidates who had self-identified with the label during the 1969 municipal elections, such as the independent John Sewell, Liberal

William Kilbourn, and NDPer Karl Jaffary. The term became more current during the 1972 election, which saw candidates identified as reformers running in every ward. Although a large minority of them were seated in city hall that year, they had little common ground other than their opposition to the incumbents they ran against and their hostility to the large-scale redevelopment of the downtown. The election as mayor of David Crombie, recognized as a reformer in the media, created the impression that reformers, or even the left, had control of city hall.[64]

Writing for *Last Post*, Rae Murphy expressed a skepticism shared by much of the left, both new and old, to pronouncements about Toronto's new reform council. Murphy noted that the only difference between the new "reform" city council and the previous one was the appearance of change. Much of the left concurred. James Lorimer, for one, believed that the only option was to "destroy the status quo" with a "radical alliance of citizens' groups, tenant organizations and labour." For Lorimer, the reformers were middle-class liberals who believed, or pretended to believe, that they were not beholden to ideology.[65]

Although they showed little awareness of it, the "hardline" members of council were part of a long-running left tradition; and one of the richer paradoxes of Toronto municipal politics in the 1960s and early 1970s was provided by William Dennison, a member of the CCF/NDP since the 1930s and Toronto's mayor from 1967 to 1972. Some party members hoped he might build on the legacy of Jimmy Simpson, who had served as Toronto's first socialist mayor in 1935. The two men, both ardent teetotallers and Orangemen, had been allies. But Dennison's successful 1966 mayoral campaign had focused on economic constraint and low taxes. By the late 1960s he seemed, in one journalist's words, to be "one of the more reactionary figures at City Hall." Even *The Telegram*, which had once warned its readers that Dennison and his CCF colleagues had to be "snuffed out now before they get the power to snuff you out," endorsed him.[66]

On the eve of Dennison's 1969 re-election campaign, there was an attempt to line the party up behind somebody else, but the mayor's supporters prevailed. The chair of the Labour Council's political education committee proclaimed him a "good socialist, a good friend of the labor movement and all trade unionists." But if Dennison's first term as mayor had been ambiguous, his second was unreservedly conservative. Headlines like "We Need Cash for Expressways, Not Subway: Mayor" and "Dennison Scorns 'Bike-City' Idea" illustrate his firm rejection of the "new urbanist" ideas floating around amongst young leftists and liberals. He dismissed ideas of participatory democracy—an impossible notion, he argued—and social movements espousing popular participation. His staunch support for developers and advocacy for the Spadina Expressway only heightened his reactionary reputation. On the political right, even the formerly xenophobic *Telegram* objected to some of the mayor's anti-immigration statements. As one columnist lamented, Dennison appeared to be a figure from another time, a throwback to the narrow cultural conservatism of the old Anglo city in defiance of a fast-changing Toronto.[67]

The Riverdale Community Organization was a favourite target—Dennison regularly accused it of espousing one brand of radical communism or another. Their meetings were calls to violence, their protests were "Red Guard" actions, and their use of the phrase "free and open society" was proof of anarchist intrigue. He aimed similarly vitriolic dismissals at his major opponent, Sewell, describing him as "either a left-wing Communist or an anarchist." He regularly attacked the counterculture in Yorkville and served as honorary chair of the Citizens Committee for the Closing of Rochdale. It would be difficult to imagine a more archetypal anti–new leftist.[68]

With a lack of unanimity at city hall, civic activists and council hardliners hoped that the establishment of community councils would be the key driver of systemic change. At council meetings, residents could exert control over their representatives in city government and have direct oversight over the policies that shaped their urban lives. Yet, as the mixed record of the council meetings of wards 6 and 7 suggests, the approach was to place a huge burden on the shoulders of average Torontonians, whose after-work agenda might call more for the necessary fulfillment of tasks at home or enjoyment of recreation time than it did for non-stop civic politicking. Some community council meetings started with ample crowds, but over time stabilized with average attendances of one to three dozen. Both aldermen and activists considered this as being too unrepresentative to provide an effective unit in a people's democracy. Gradually leftists shifted their focus from the highly decentralized strategy of empowering ward councils to the creation of quasi-parties on the ward and municipal levels.[69]

The Confederation of Resident and Ratepayer Associations (CORRA), established in 1969, was in many respects the predecessor of these later quasi-parties. Future mayor John Sewell had been a founding member, as was Jane Jacobs, the emergent philosopher of new urbanism. To its core associations, generally drawn from prosperous middle- and upper-class areas of the city, were added others from less privileged areas. By 1970 thirty-five community organizations had affiliated to it. CORRA exemplified the radical-liberal crossovers characteristic of its day. It could claim some of the credit for blocking the Spadina Expressway, and it brought together advocates of participatory democracy and ward councils. It could be associated with such democratizing demands as more frequent election cycles and the doubling of the number of the city's wards. At the same time it left cold many new leftists, such as some writers on *The Varsity*. Here was a group, they complained, made up of "bourgeois community groups" different in tone but not in substance from the property-holders who already ruled Toronto. A more sympathetic mainstream reporter approvingly noted that CORRA was liberal and middle class and that it refrained from using labels such as "people power"—all of which helped it to legitimize new ideas while blunting any of the radicalism normally associated with them.[70]

In CORRA, "hip" urbanists drawn from middle-class parts of the city did predominate, but at least some of their rhetoric and program could be aligned with a new left outlook. Architect Colin Vaughan, a member of the Liberal Party who hailed from the Wychwood Park Ratepayers Association and served as CORRA's chair during its fight against the expressway, adopted a variety of new left positions without taking them to their anti-capitalist conclusions. When Dennison, in a long analogy, compared community groups to "swamp rabbits," CORRA members defended extraparliamentary activity and in rebuke sported buttons bearing an image of a rabbit. The group did back striking garbage workers and supported students protesting the closed stacks of the Robarts Library. Under the leadership of U of T professor James Lemon, elected in 1973, the umbrella group demanded the immediate establishment of ward councils that would prepare their own budgets and assume many of the tasks carried out by city hall's departments. Members of these councils would be elected during the regular municipal election cycle.[71]

In the last half of the 1970s, the Movement for Municipal Reform, better known as ReforMetro, became the main civic left-wing coalition in the Metro Toronto area. Envisioned as a means to institutionalize linkages among community organizers, left-wing alderman, and their constituents, it was established in 1975 after a public callout for a federation or political party to fill this role. Activists at its inaugural meeting voted to form a federation after a two-hour debate, though some of its organizers continued to see it as a local version of Montreal's Citizen Movement, a new left–inspired political party. All the elected hardline reformers joined it, with the exception of Sewell, who worried about being under the control of an unrepresentative body. In contrast to CORRA, ReforMetro was based on individual membership and working-class wards and strongly tended towards new left philosophy. Vaughan dismissed it as "a remnant of the late 1960's children's crusade."[72]

ReforMetro's politics certainly shared the ambitiousness of late 1960s demands, but its approach was far more comprehensive and reflected the growth of radical community organizations in the 1970s. It viewed housing as a public utility in which profit-making should not occur. Allying with the tenant movement, it envisioned the collective control of tenant housing and the eventual public ownership of all land. It strongly supported existing community-controlled services and wanted local government to help them expand. With a decentralized system and the opening of more community-controlled clinics, neighbourhood residents would be able to gain control of health care. ReforMetro opposed urban sprawl, supported bike lanes and a host of environmental measures, and saw cars and cities as incompatible. Although it often supported the grassroots activity of community organizations, ReforMetro occasionally initiated its own activist campaigns. When transit fare increases were announced, its transportation committee collected 15,000 signatures and organized a 400-strong protest. After racist and homophobic remarks by police were publicized, city hall's council chambers became packed with hundreds of protesters calling for the officers to be disciplined.[73]

The candidates that ReforMetro endorsed ranged from left-liberal to Communist, and it encountered recurring friction with the NDP. In the late 1970s, Diana Fancher, ReforMetro candidate for "alderman" (as the position was still called) and frequent contributor to the *Toronto Clarion*, wrote that disagreements between ReforMetro and the NDP were a replay of the earlier debates that had pitted the Waffle against the mainstream party. According to Fancher, ReforMetro was far more influenced by community activists than was the NDP. The role of labour in the conflict between the two left bodies also harkened back to the earlier conflict between the NDP and the Waffle. An anonymous Labour Council staffer said that the NDP re-emerged on the municipal scene in the late 1970s because the Council saw ReforMetro as a middle-class group not concerned with the real interests of labour, a charge disputed by ReforMetro. In 1978 a ReforMetro convention pointedly voted to change a reference in its platform from working closely with the NDP to working closely with "progressive political associations."[74]

In 1978 Sewell was elected mayor of Toronto. Thanks to conservative candidates dividing the anti-reform base, he gained the mayoralty with less than 50 per cent of the vote. His election seemingly portended a left-wing Toronto in which the dreams of a generation of new leftists would be realized. Yet the intricacies of combining new left idealism with the pragmatics of civic governance proved challenging, confounding many of these dreams even before Sewell's defeat and Toronto's return to political normalcy in 1980. A year earlier Sewell himself had wondered, "Where have all the people gone!" With respect to his home ward, he found *Seven News* disinclined to focus on local politics and ward residents little energized by struggles over increased transit fares. Some ward organizations were struggling to maintain quorums at their meetings. Complaining about this lack of popular participation, a cynical Riverdale activist wrote that change was now coming "to the people and for the people," not *by* the people. "And remember, 'Power to the People' is just a bed-time story told by communists, anyhow." A new left model demanding round-the-clock mobilization of highly energized citizens had apparently run into substantial obstacles, well before Sewell's election as mayor.[75]

* * *

On May 9, 1970, an estimated 23,000 people attended "The City Is For People" festival. There was abundant food and entertainment. Several activist groups set up booths. Some political speeches were made. The festival was hardly "capital-P" politics, even according to the new left's expanded definition of the term, yet its implied populism and vague community-building aspects were important. American war resisters had recognized this the year before with their first annual Baldwin Street Festival. During subsequent summers, hundreds and sometimes thousands attended events like the Blake Tenants Union Festival or the Ontario Anti-Poverty Festival (where attendees drew on the "people's art wall" and enjoyed an outdoor screening of the U.S. Mine, Mill–produced film *Salt of the Earth* [1954]). The vast majority of neighbourhood festivals—which skyrocketed in number during the 1970s—were not outwardly political at all. But they reflected a new interest in geographic communities that complemented civic activist campaigns.[76]

In Sewell's Ward 7, resident left-wing activists seemed to relish their ward's burgeoning political reputation and boasted of having their own community-based anti-racist and grape boycott groups. But Ward 7 did not have the historical cachet of Cabbagetown or evoke a sense of community in the way exhibited, for instance, by residents of Riverdale, just across the Don Valley. It was an administrative label reflecting civic political boundaries. Yet municipal activists, most notably the citizen journalists of *Seven News*, worked to make this clearly "imagined community" more meaningful. By the mid-1970s residents were increasing adopting the label as a community identifier and even had a Ward Seven Community Orchestra.[77]

In addition to well-known efforts against "block busting" (when developers would buy several houses, fill them with tenants, and let the properties deteriorate, to encourage remaining homeowners to sell), the widespread urban activism of the era extended to protecting community spaces and residents. Although providing an adequate supply of crossing guards might not seem the most radical of issues, picketing mothers forced the appointment of a crossing guard in one particular intersection near a housing development. It was the culmination of a struggle that had seen the erection of barricades, hundreds of women and children demonstrating on the street, and defiant mothers challenging police officers who were threatening them with arrest. Police were usually reluctant to arrest the mothers, but a few of the women were apprehended for blocking traffic during the St. Clair Avenue crossing-guard struggle. "Mother power" successfully forced the return of twenty crossing guards to Avenue Road.[78]

Refecting the semi-spontaneous nature of basic community struggles, militants—many of them described as grandmothers—successfully blocked a work crew believed to be preparing to build a road through their neighbourhood park.[79] Adults affiliated with the Avenue-Bay-Cottingham Residents' Association, along with their children, also actively tried to thwart construction crews tearing up their neighbourhood playing field. When residents concluded that Ramsden Park was under threat from an adjacent high-rise development, a whopping two thousand people attended a rally to oppose its construction. Residents of an Ontario Housing Corporation project won a new park after seventy-five of them staged a sit-in at the corporation's downtown office.[80]

New leftists also pushed hard for the expansion and protection of existing parks. There were even a few blatantly leftist attempts to establish "people's parks," reminiscent of a similar campaign in Berkeley, California. In 1970 as many as five hundred people attended a "plant-in" on vacant land owned by the University of Toronto. After having cut down part of a fence and sown grass, members of the May 4 Movement inaugurated the new park with a rock concert, and on subsequent days people watched skits and danced to the music of the People's Revolutionary Concert Band. The following year—after a series of broken promises from the city and developers for a park in St. James Town—young people went ahead and tried to build their own park on privately owned vacant land. Organizers denounced statements by the owners, Meridan Co., that characterized them as trespassers and denied rumours that they were controlled by militant tenant unions (they allowed that some of them might have had overlapping memberships). Co-organizer Leslie McFarlane crowed: "They're scared to let the people get together. They're afraid of the power they might have." The eighteen-year-old William Bucci agreed that the real issue for both company and activists transcended the issue of green space: "It goes beyond the park. . . . It would bring people together and when people are together, that might be a threat to Meridan and some of the things they are proposing for this neighbourhood."[81]

The neighbourhood food co-op, that most ubiquous of 1970s counterinstitutions, could also be tied into broader political and organizational prespectives. New left-leaning books that attacked the capitalist food industry anticipated that co-ops would be part of a post-capitalist food economy. Don Mitchell's *The Politics of Food* (1975) envisioned a socialist food system whose components ranged from state-owned property and co-ops to workers' control of food manufacturing plants. *The Land of Milk and Money* (1980), the report of the People's Food Commission, focused more on the utility of co-ops in the present. Launched in 1977, the People's Food Commission had visited seventy-four cities and towns across the country and collected testimony. The authors of the resulting book found individualism and support for capitalism to be the largest barriers to a socialist food system. Some presentations before the committee had presciently emphasized organic, local, and individually produced food, and the authors suggested that the collective nature of co-ops could be used to expand political consciousness. A comic book devoted to food co-ops published by a Toronto collective—inspired in its form and content by experiments conducted during Salvador Allende's presidency in Chile—concluded that the stores were beneficial in any economic system.[82]

Some co-op advocates, like one member of the Community Service Grocery Store, were more conservative, emphasizing the emotional draw of co-ops and evoking the image of a strong community anchored by "old corner grocery stores." A member of a Don Vale food co-op sympathized with emotive motivations—"big is bad because of impersonality and treating people as numbers rather than fellow humans"—but also tied co-ops to a broader fight for social justice in which "controlled people" worked towards redistributing wealth and power. Yet many new leftists viewed the co-ops as too local, too incremental, and too focused on consumption. From a pragmatic perspective, the editor of *Seven News* argued that the lower prices of supplies in food co-ops were largely a myth because of limited selection and store hours. The need for bulk purchases and membership fees made them exclusive sites of consumption. He mocked their participatory model as "the in thing" and, as to their more intimate atmosphere, declared he did not "experience the feeling." Where he discerned trendiness, others saw social utility: as *The Toronto* Star explained in 1973, the burgeoning food co-op movement offered a choice of "co-operation as opposed to corporations, people versus companies."[83]

The most successful food co-op was probably Karma (I), which survives today in the city's Annex neighbourhood. Like many of its peers, Karma avoided buying from multinationals whenever possible, preferring to purchase from small independent businesses, communal farms, and local co-ops such as Jubilation Bakery. The politics of solidarity was particularly prominent when deciding where *not* to buy from, with Karma boycotting numerous companies and countries in support of striking workers and against human rights abuses. Although the politicization of Karma's supply chain was widely supported, some members hesitated to extend that analysis further. A debate over whether Karma would implement policies to attract lower-income members—its membership was largely made up of professionals and students—exposed some disagreement over how much of a counterinstitution the co-op should be.[84]

Food co-ops were greedy consumers of labour power, which regularly threatened to scuttle their egalitarian democratic ideals. Volunteers with Karma II and Sunnyside Food Co-op began to resent the demands placed on them by less motivated members. Both Centennial Food Co-op and Etobico-op folded due to a lack of active participants. It was a malady that probably hit the handful of co-ops established by left-wing organizations, like the Parkdale Food Co-op and the Just Society Movement's food co-op, both of which were geared to working-class consumers. Projects such as the Regent Park Food Co-op also belied the institution's middle-class image. Quasi co-op consumerism in the form of "free stores" and tenant-run convenience stores existed in several Ontario Housing Corp. projects.[85]

In the mid-1970s many of the food-co-ops federated. Thanks to a LIP grant and loans from area churches, the Don Area federation transported food, arranged bulk purchases, and provided information for the six co-ops in its area. In 1975 this federation expanded and became the Toronto Federation of Food Co-operatives. It enhanced its viability by becoming a food supplier to co-op daycares and supporting organic agriculture in Ontario, which helped its co-ops compete with the U.S.-imported organics found in private health-food stores. Shortly after its founding, members of the Federation launched the Ontario Natural Foods Co-op, which developed a wide network for its fleet of refrigerated trucks.[86]

Food co-ops were supplemented by a renewed interest in community gardening and worker-based health-food collectives such as The Golden Ant and The Whole Earth Natural Food Store, which also viewed themselves as alternatives to the profit-based food industry. According to a *Telegram* reporter, they were provisioners "to their community of longhairs, freaks, radicals and undergrounders first and to straights second." A number of the "straights" who shopped at these hip collectives most likely did so because some of their product offerings would have been hard to find otherwise. Reflecting a contemporary-sounding range of gastronomical delights, a collective managing Rochdale College's cafeteria offered ten kinds of smoked meat, nineteen types of honey, and twenty-five varieties of coffee.[87]

After the government grant boom collapsed in the second half of the 1970s, new co-operative enterprises had a hard time finding money. The people who set up Carrot Commons (a supermarket-scale workers' co-op on Danforth Avenue) turned to the Bread and Roses Credit Union for a loan. Toronto had several long-standing credit unions, but activists complained that they operated largely like banks. The goal of Bread and Roses was social change. In contrast to the loaning criteria of its older peers, it was keen to lend money to collective projects deemed ecologically sound, non-sexist, non-racist, and socially useful. Its members extensively debated issues such as consensus vs. majority decision-making and were torn over the class politics of offering RRSPs. The Metropolitan

Toronto Women's Credit Union, which urged women to take their money out of male-dominated financial institutions, also favoured loans to co-ops.[88]

Food co-ops were just the most visible of a range of co-operative and community-controlled ventures set up in the 1970s. Projects ranged from a temporary help centre, set up by former day labourers to compete with for-profit employment agencies, to community parole organizations, which empowered former felons and supplanted the role of parole officers. Downtown Action was probably the most important of several projects dedicated to assisting such projects. It was a research-oriented advocacy organization providing detailed intelligence to tenant and other community organizers about their corporate adversaries; its staff believed that victories by the community-based struggles they assisted could create bases of support for longer-term social change.[89]

New left advocates of community-controlled health clinics saw similar mobilizing potential in the new roles and relationships these clinics encouraged as opposed to "traditional socialist" approaches to health care. *The Community Health Centre Handbook* presented these clinics as alternatives to "de-humanizing care" and stepping stones to a more just social order. They were cheaper, less bureaucratic, and friendlier than hospitals. But groups such as the Health Liberation Collective cautioned that every community clinic was not necessarily germane to broader social change. The Don District Community Health Centre, controlled by elected members from that community, was favourably contrasted to the Regent Park Community Health Centre, which had only token community participation. Art Moses, who helped launch South Riverdale's community-controlled health centre, wrote of the importance of people-controlled services from post-dictatorship Portugal, where he was investigating health clinics and residents' commissions. In central Toronto, experiments arising from the Rochdale Free Clinic, such as the Neighbourhood Health Centre, became committed to complete community control of its operations. Over at the Toronto Sure Free Youth Clinic, Dr. David Collins—a "hip"-looking man who disliked the title "Doctor," said the newspapers—distilled that clinic's kindred philosophy: "I'd like this place to become a model for future medical clinics, with community control, community sponsorship, and elimination of professional barriers and fees as the basic maxims."[90]

A similar new leftist spirit suffused Toronto's injured workers' movement, which from 1970 onwards sought to stand up for workers injured on the job. It was an interesting alliance of working-class Italian men, aspiring law students, and seasoned activists, which undertook to fight Ontario's notoriously cold-hearted Workmen's Compensation Board (WCB). In doing so, they generated a considerable social movement that staged countless demonstrations. One militant was even implicated in interfering with the opening of the Ontario legislature, when in a neck-to-waist plaster cast, he "slipped through the guards" and "threw himself . . . on the red-carpeted floor of the House in front of cabinet ministers," shouting "Workmen's Compensation, this is the way they treat you."[91] Those favouring a more collective, left-wing approach, as opposed to fighting each case as it came up, later formed the Injured Workers' Consultants. The Union of Injured Workers, launched in May 1974 by seasoned movement activists, was committed to a program based on four fundamental demands: full compensation or job security; cost of living increases; no WCB doctors; and improved and enforced occupational health and safety laws. It demonstrated time and again, sometimes violently—and it got results, in the form of greatly improved workers' compensation legislation, such as rulings that enabled many injured workers to receive supplements to their permanent pensions.[92]

The Canadian Medical Association was criticized for upholding corporate-style health care.

Guerilla, undated, 1971.

Something of the same ethos was turned in a more feminist direction by members of the Immigrant Women's Health Centre and the Healthsharing Collective. The Feminist Therapy Support Group, which viewed consciousness-raising as part of the therapeutic process, envisaged a "feminist therapy" in which "therapist and client are seen as equals in struggle, insofar as this is possible in a capitalist society." Militants belonging to the Women's Health Centre likewise believed that medicine was part of a capitalist, male-dominated system. They wanted to revolutionize it. Some were lesbians and others wanted to question the validity of Western medicine altogether, identifying the killing of germs with war, rape, and oppression. For some, the urgent needs of women trumped the desire to teach political lessons, but others suspected that the Women's Health Centre was applying band-aids to a sick system that they "wanted to destroy," for nobody could be truly healthy in an unhealthy society, "where everyone is oppressed by … dirty air, sexism, racism, or professionalism."[93]

It was a portrait not only of the complications of feminism but also of those attending all new left attempts to transform daily life: when did offering social services to society's oppressed start to mean palliating rather than terminating the sicknesses caused by capitalism? Radical medical projects moved to narrow this gap between reform and revolution by emphasizing preventative health care—seen as a way of highlighting class, gender, and racial barriers to health

A New Democratic Youth poster denouncing the imposition of the War Measures Act.

Courtesy Charles Dobie.

with a medically sound diagnosis and an anti-capitalist treatment. Here, some activists would undoubtedly have considered Chinese remedies. Several visiting speakers came to Toronto with first-hand accounts of China's preventative health-care system (living in communes was great for mental health), de-professionalization, and medicine by the people for the people ("barefoot" peasant doctors). It was a model of care that was cheek to cheek with many countercultural and new left ideas. Yet other aspects of Chinese Communist rule were hardly so congruent. When a legal activist suggested that developments in China showed there was no need for civil liberty advocates in post-revolutionary societies, he was swiftly hit with a typical new left rejoinder: "No one should put any more faith in the future 'socialist judges' and 'socialist constitutions' than in the capitalist ones."[94]

* * *

The precept that lawyers should serve the people and immerse themselves in social struggles can be traced back to the heyday of Yorkville in the 1960s. In 1967 the Diggers organized a group of University of Toronto law students and one lawyer into what became Canada's first storefront legal clinic, the Village Bar. This legal collective set up tables in front of Yorkville's famed coffee houses and published, in the thousands of copies, a booklet offering guidance to ordinary people about their legal rights. In the 1970s, new leftists distinguished their approach from this earlier form of "hip" or "radical" lawyering, which to them savoured of liberal do-goodism rather than revolutionary praxis. The Law Union emerged when lawyers defending people arrested at the May 1970 anti–Vietnam War demonstration transitioned from merely co-ordinating their activities to imagining how they and like-minded lawyers might change the world. Soon they launched a demonstration against the War Measures Act, established a Kensington Market law clinic geared to Portuguese immigrants, and set up no fewer than ten working groups. Yet, after only a year of activity, the Union was effectively dead—some said because of a split between those demanding a more cohesive group capable of fighting hard for the dictatorship of the proletariat, and those who favoured a Popular Front theory and were suspicious of vanguard parties. Even the renowned firm associated with Clayton Ruby and Paul Copeland split apart.[95]

***Guerilla* vendors sell copies of their Quebec-themed issue amidst the War Measures Act crisis; Oct. 17, 1970.**

Courtesy Charles Dobie.

A few years after the demise of the Law Union, it was successfully revived. Once more, social movements clamouring for legal help prompted young lawyers to do something. This time they were inspired by the 1974 Artistic Woodwork strike. The resurrected Law Union was founded by twenty lawyers and sixty law students for the purpose of changing society, transforming their profession, and providing a mutual support network. Membership rose to two hundred within months. No fewer than three hundred attended an inaugural conference, which opened with competing perspectives on how to be a lawyer and a revolutionary.[96]

In new left style, the Union's steering committee was voluntary with only member assemblies given the power to speak on behalf of the organization. As in the case of its predecessor, working groups would be the main outlets for practical activity. It was divided over its exact political basis. The decision as to whether the group would include liberals was formally left unresolved. An early editorial in *Law Union News* defined the group as reformist by nature, situating it somewhere between a vanguard formation and a younger civil liberties association. As in the Union's first incarnation, there was an ongoing tension between those two poles.[97]

Whether in the Law Union or outside it, young radical lawyers still felt obliged to help the oppressed in their battles with the legal system in the 1970s. Many gravitated to community law clinics, wherein legal activists sought to provide individual legal services to low-income people in tandem with encouraging collective action and community empowerment. As with many of the movements of the 1970s, clinic activists saw their organizing efforts as part of a broader struggle against the class system, but preferred to speak in the Aesopian language of community.[98]

Neighbourhood Legal Services, formed in 1971, drew from lawyer-militants already active in community organizing. As a mark of its singularity of new left purpose, the clinic took almost three years to get off the ground because its founders had insisted on 100 per cent community control. The clinic emphasized issues, such as unemployment and workers' compensation, that had an impact on the lives of the poor and working class, and it made helping community groups a core part of its mandate. Less than a year into its full-time operation, the clinic had already helped create Welfare Information Services and Roomers' Rights. In a likely knock at Parkdale Legal Services, the clinic's founders said they did not want the group to be dominated by a law school or any other outside organization.[99]

That Parkdale office, also founded in 1971, became perhaps the best-known legal clinic in the country. The "dynamic tension" that Shelly Gavigan refers to in her history of the clinic denotes the pulls that staff experienced between their respective roles as lawyers and community activists. There was political struggle as well, between clinic staff primarily concerned with social change and those most interested in training lawyers. In its first year of operation, students fought for and won an equal share in the office's management. Staff, students, and community residents at weekly office meetings and "town hall" forums debated issues ranging from the future of the clinic to the revolutionary overhaul of the entire Canadian legal system. In late 1971 one of those meetings unanimously voted to implement community control as soon as possible. Student Doug Ewart hoped that this move would push budding lawyers to become organizers rather than professionals in a "social service complex." He believed that community control would encourage poor people to organize and end the "absurdity" of middle-class professionals debating what the poor really wanted.[100]

But community control was not forthcoming. The clinic seemed to be clipping its radical ambitions, fearing backlash from the faculty of Osgoode Hall Law School and the Law Society of Upper Canada. There were also concerns about the weakness of neighbourhood community organizations and insufficient "community consciousness." Meetings became less frequent, community participation began to decline, and increasing the number of cases was emphasized. Ewart worried that the office had become little more than a "legal factory" or a "clinical training plant." Substantive change finally arrived in 1973 with a flurry of position papers considering the possible features of community representation. Debate centred on whether the community reps would have majority or 50 per cent control, but faculty opposition to the majority position settled the issue. Students won two of five "non-community" seats on the ten-person board, but gave up one of them so that lay advocates and secretaries could be represented.[101]

Deciding who would get the community seats was a stickier matter. The executive of the Parkdale Tenants' Association (PTA) criticized the clinic's broad definition of community, saying it amounted to an amorphous, geographic space without any social differentiation or political division. It argued that only groups that supported the office's new orientation should be invited. The PTA was certainly correct in noting that political divisions were factors in any community. But playing the "community game," with its dominant themes of consensus and unity, necessitated ignoring this fact in public. The Parkdale left did not want to confirm the clinic director's fear of a "left-wing takeover" by appearing under partisan labels. In open elections, a left-wing PTA slate—supported by Fire Hall Day Care, Parkdale Jobs Office, Parkdale Women's Group, St. Marks-Parkdale Group, Stop 400, and Sunnyside Food Co-op—romped to victory over representatives from more conservative community groups.[102]

The tenant movement was a prime beneficiary of the revamped clinic's largesse, with two community legal workers essentially becoming PTA organizers. Staff members were loaned to help organize a Federation of Metro Tenants conference. The clinic began providing free services to the Law Union and started taking the cases of gay activists, who often had difficulty finding lawyers to work on their behalf. An influx of new left-wing lawyers and community workers pushed the clinic further to the left. But activists continued to encounter resistance when seeking to endorse the actions and causes of other organizations. Something as innocuous as posting a grape boycott sign in the clinic's window would cause lengthy discussions in meetings of the steering committee, office committee, and board. From the perspective of the director, such moves risked jeopardizing the delicate balance between the practical needs (funding and authority) of the clinic and its radical needs (changing society and the legal profession). But its ties to York University and the cautious approach of a number of its leftists protected the clinic from some of the storms sweeping through other legal clinics. An influential Communist Party board member complained about the risky tactics of "ultra-leftists" at other legal clinics.[103]

Clinic workers nevertheless faced sanctions for "unprofessional" offences. The Law Society threatened to disbar a lawyer and to refuse to license an articling student because of the clinic's "unsuitable" location. A judge filed a complaint against an articling student because she wore a suit in his courtroom. Such moves were symptomatic of the radical lawyers' contradictory location, both within and outside their profession. They were conscious of transgressing professional standards and of thereby working to crack the myth of the neutral legal system. Picketing, marching, and leafleting were not only a blow against the Law Society's brand of professionalism but also, as legal activist Jeff House suggested, a means for lawyers to shed their internalized professionalism. Despite the important work they did in the courtroom, members of the Law Union believed that the key both to changing society and to reforming the law was organized and militant pressure from outside.[104]

Legal clinic radicalism flourished in the 1970s, but the following decade saw a turn away from the tactic. A small part of the reason had to do with activist burnout and a greater number of staff members viewing their jobs as a paycheque instead of a political project. But the unrelenting efforts of the provincial agency tasked with disbursing clinic funding were primarily responsible for the movement's quick decline. Decision-making powers were centralized; clinics were pressured to sever links with community organizations; the influence of lawyers increased; and new projects such as the Working Women's Clinic were denied funding. This greater surveillance and regulation discouraged the political organizing that had once been a cardinal trait of the clinics. When the provincial coalition of clinics refused not only to form a new board made up exclusively of lawyers but also to end its advocacy role and to redefine clinics as little more than vehicles for service delivery, the agency terminated its funding.[105]

* * *

Perhaps the most surprising contribution of the new left to the rise of democratic variants of professionalism came in the sphere of librarianship. Although Toronto enjoyed one of Canada's largest library systems, it exhibited only a few signs of change until the early 1970s, when its board voted to replace around two dozen neighbourhood libraries with a handful of "mega-libraries." That vision never came to pass.

Following the 1974 municipal election, hardline reformers were kept out of the housing, transit, and other planning committees they coveted and had to make do with influencing an area in which most aldermen had little interest—the library system. James Lorimer, Sherrill Cheda, a feminist librarian, and hardline alderman Dorothy Thomas were all appointed to the central Toronto Public Library Board. The following year this group, joined by Marian Engel, "author, feminist, nationalist," and Becky Kane, a library outreach worker described as a "civic activist, feminist," became a majority. The new board decisively rejected the mega-library system. After all, "the neighbourhood [was] the primary location of citizen participation."[106]

Just as he was joining the board, Lorimer pilloried the library system for its bogus calls for public participation after the properties needed to build the mega-libraries had already been expropriated. Under the new board, community groups and individuals organized area committees to advise and support the system. Activists with community-organizing experience filled out many of these new community library groups (the chairperson for the east end's influential group, for instance, was the vice-president of Forward 9). The hope was that library staff, in conjunction with such community groups, would jointly plan each branch's programming and budget allocations. To increase library access, the city hired LIP workers to bring the library to many who were unable to get there themselves. That spoke to the concerns of librarians worried that not enough residents were using their collections. Librarians at one branch identified the problem as a general perception of libraries being middle-class institutions. This dovetailed with the views of Lorimer, who believed that an emphasis on professional expertise often reflected a political judgment that reinforced libraries as domains of the white-collar middle class.[107]

Part of the solution was to have libraries acquire not only more popular materials, chiefly paperbacks, but also periodicals and playing records. Not everyone rejoiced in the new direction. Militants in a Friends of the Palmerston Library group believed that placing "popular culture" over "education" meant trading cultural treasures for comic books. One librarian condemned the inclusion of "trivial, escapist material" and appealed to leftists by declaring that members of the working class were attracted to libraries because they saw them as institutions for upward mobility and that working-class folk would turn away from libraries that emphasized popular materials. Another librarian, particularly upset by Harlequin Romances appearing on library shelves, extolled the educational role of libraries and "the fallacy of giving people what they want." While he allowed that broadening the library's holdings to dubious categories such as science fiction would "triple the statistics," such reforms under "the guise of permissiveness" would undermine the library's educational role.[108]

In the end the city's library board made sure that branches in working-class areas received spending budgets on par with those in more prosperous areas and gave branches autonomy to shape their individual holdings. In addition to new "popular culture" offerings, the system particularly encouraged the adoption of non-English materials. Some branches (such as Riverdale, which acquired a substantial Chinese-language collection) gained many new users because of this. The branches were also pushed to prioritize made-in-Canada materials (a big help to local new left publishers). A writer in *Emergency Librarian*, a Toronto-based feminist publication that, like *The Body Politic* and *This Magazine Is About Schools*, won renown for Toronto new leftism in a wider world, complained that even Margaret Atwood's *Survival: A Thematic Guide to Canadian Literature* (1972), a book that had attracted considerable public interest, was nowhere to be seen in the library system a year after its publication.[109] Co-edited by new library board member Cheda, *Emergency Librarian* fought against the bureaucratic patriarchy of the library system. All power to the readers!

Some library staff had mixed opinions about the library board's new direction. One librarian was cheered that "the *old boys' club* was definitely gone. As a matter of fact, there were only a few *boys* left; two thirds of the members were women." The librarian appreciated that board meetings were now public events held in branches and agreed with their general direction, but she saw a continuing problem in the role of "conservative" library administrators. Instead of being transferred to rank-and-file librarians, power was held by librarians at the overall co-ordinating level and by newly hired administrators who were "just as authoritarian as the old administrators." The board's changes provoked disgruntled librarians from both the left and the right to launch a union drive that prompted 80 per cent of library workers to sign union cards. The nature of worker participation was to be the defining issue of the campaign.[110] As in the case of health and legal clinics, the extent to which the empowerment of professionals in the library meant empowerment of the "community" was a lively, perhaps unresolvable, issue.

Mary Ann Wilson, a supporter of the board, celebrated what she saw as an assault on the "museum image" of libraries and their subsequent transformation into "a vital part of the community." Across North America the city's experience came to be upheld as profoundly instructive. A 1976 editorial in the premier U.S. library journal declared: "Public libraries in North America are indebted to the Toronto Public Library Board for boldly embarking on a management experiment that could prove or disprove many of our traditional concepts of library management, as well as some of our brand new ideas."[111]

* * *

Meanwhile, another new left eruption was underway in social work. Social workers, many of them educated in the University of Toronto School of Social Work, were numerous in the new left. For community-control theorist Buchbinder, social work in a capitalist society was an intrinsically contradictory phenomenon; its expressed commitments to human well-being were undercut by its institutional function, that is, legitimating the system. Wars on poverty in both the United States and Canada had accentuated this contradiction. In many eyes, at least the politicization of poverty by the state rendered redundant an older doctrine that professional social workers should not involve themselves in politics. Buchbinder believed it was significant that some students interested in social action had become socialists and went on to organize courses and seminars that challenged their program's limitations with topics such as the relation of capital to property. From 1969 to 1974 the Toronto-based academic journal *Social Worker* published many articles on the theme of social worker as social activist, and it pondered ways of empowering clients and debated whether social work was intrinsically reformist or potentially revolutionary. Many of the critics noted that an elitist social work common sense was being unsettled by more democratic models, which, at their limit, problematized the agency-client relationship.[112]

To this end, members of the Association of Social Service Workers—formed as a radical alternative to the professional provincial social work society—became highly active in four union-organizing drives while stepping up their own union involvement in already organized workplaces. These members did not ignore the interests of clients (or "consumers," as the Association preferred to call them). They could use the union structure to redistribute money and power within their workplaces, to de-emphasize the importance of university degrees (thus creating opportunities for "consumers" to become social service workers themselves), and to institute joint worker-"consumer" control over policies and services.[113]

The Association had, superficially, accomplished a major goal—unionization. Social workers enlisted in the union in large numbers. But in fall 1977, when several social service workers, all former members of the now largely defunct Association, met to assess the political utility of their efforts, all of them were decidedly underwhelmed. The union seemed to be an institution ill-suited for the time and energy that they, as socialists, had poured into it. Many of them had used the prospect of better services for clients as a rationale for unionization, but their experience now seemed to show that the goals were not tightly linked. Only two locals had narrowed the wage gap between lay and professional social workers, and their bargaining units did not include clerical workers. They noted that many social workers were middle-class people aspiring to a future in agency management. It remained an open question as to whether social workers wanting to build socialism should centre their efforts inside or outside of their workplaces. Many committed leftists who had led organizing struggles had become burnt out, and some had even been co-opted, during the long process of certification, which allowed liberal social workers to assume leadership in the new locals. In the future, critics were saying, socialists would be wise to save their energy for the campaign for a first contract. Involvement in leadership roles was now frowned on in favour of less-time-consuming and more grassroots efforts such as grievance committee work, the establishment of left-wing workplace caucuses, and city-wide efforts to co-ordinate and support socialist activism.[114]

The group came to believe that their very premise had been incorrect. Union certification did not politicize workers except in cases of particularly bitter opposition from management. They saw more "progressive" staff in the young independent unions they had favoured than in the established unions. They faulted the Canadian Union of Public Employees (CUPE) for not even entertaining the radical ideas favoured by their Association.[115]

Anti-poverty activism had been an important sector for these new left social workers. They were a substantial presence among the seventy-odd associate members of the Just Society Movement (JSM), a 1968–71 organization by the poor and for the poor that had hundreds of members. Its very name mocked the liberalism of Trudeau's "just society"—"A Just Society for the Capitalists," some of its activists said. Led by single mothers living in poverty, JSM's radical politics and strong commitment to non-hierarchical structures provide yet another example of a new leftism extending well beyond university campuses. Although some dedicated social democrats supported it, JSM spokespeople said the NDP would have to abolish its current structure and hand decision-making power to "the people" before they would consider embracing the party. JSM's organizing staple was its direct-action casework, which won rights and payments for countless welfare recipients. It did not win much love from social workers in targeted agencies—the president of an affected CUPE local complained that JSM attacked people for doing their jobs—but new left social workers applauded its tactics.[116]

As well as assisting with JSM's day-to-day activities, its social worker associates worked to "expose" and transform key social work programs and funders. Their first sustained target was the Toronto Social Planning Council. In this they were aided by a range of social movement allies as well as now-alderman Sewell, who suggested that the Council might be better off disbanding and dedicating its resources to anti-poverty organizing. Support also came from some older leftists on the board, such as social worker and anti-racist activist Wilson Head, who saw an opportunity to get rid of "ultra-conservative" members, and U of T professor John Crispo, who complained that until recently there had been strong opposition to even using the term "social animation" within the Council.[117]

Slates of radical candidates for Council positions were defeated, but they made minor inroads that convinced some conservatives to leave, complaining of a radical takeover. The turmoil was certainly good for the Council's membership numbers, which climbed from 700 to 1,500 and then 2,500 as duelling sides conscripted more allies to join them. The Council began to work more with left-wing community organizations and at the end of 1970 it voted to become a grassroots movement and fight for social change. There were even suggestions that it might give all its funding to community organizations. But the United Appeal, the source of most of the Council's money, was clearly unhappy with this new direction and pressured the Council to curb its new enthusiasm for all things grassroots.[118]

United Appeal's interference added to a litany of complaints from radicals about that organization. Activists had long been leery of the organization's strong ties to business and near exclusive support for professional social service agencies. JSM had previously accused it of interfering with the Ontario Welfare Council after its members helped convince that body to invite anti-poverty and student activists onto its board. JSM's influence later extended to the Canadian Welfare Council, which supported the principle of having welfare offices operated by welfare recipients and passed a resolution to investigate the real sources of poverty: "We have studied those people—the welfare recipient and the poor—who are suffering over and over again. Now we must study those who are causing this suffering." These efforts heightened the United Appeal's fear of the group.[119]

Not surprisingly, then, some JSM-affiliated social workers later formed Concerned Citizens About Social Policy to agitate against funding what was now being called the United Way. They argued that most of the money raised through its annual drives went to pay the salaries of professional service workers and that grassroots-based organizations were more worthy of funding. A leaflet, *I Didn't Give at the Office*—with some five thousand copies distributed—contained additional criticism. In a move labelled "disgusting" and "inexcusable" by *The Globe and Mail*, the new leftish Toronto Board of Education supported the group and refused to endorse the United Way campaign drive. It also voted to ensure that any school distributing United Way information would hand out opposition literature as well. Some of the United Way's defenders saw these interventions as cowardly acts. Supporting the United Way's annual drive was a "motherhood" issue for much of business and labour; and these social workers were arguing against a funding drive that benefited many of their colleagues. Though they failed in their stated aims, the insurgents created additional pressure to fund the kind of projects they supported.[120]

In January 1971 Toronto hosted the National Poor People's Conference, where five hundred anti-poverty activists from across the country debated strategy and attended four lively days of workshops. Government officials were barred despite the conference's state funding. Delegates approved dozens of resolutions, ranging from agreements to establish national tenant and poor peoples' organizations to calls for freeing U.S. militant philosopher Angela Davis. They also agreed to mount a national protest against the unjust distribution of wealth and power—the real cause of poverty. But despite predictions of a turnout as high as thirty thousand, the January 25 protest was a modest affair. The largest event was in Toronto, where less than a thousand turned up. A welfare office was "invaded" and a copy of the General Welfare Assistance Act was burned on the steps of the Ontario legislature. At the offices of Argus Corp., activists demanded a share of the conglomerate's profits to support daycare centres, community health clinics, and alternative education.[121]

Organizers of the Ontario Poor People's Conference, held the following January, stated that the government was reluctant to fund them because the Conference leaders refused to ally with poverty professionals or their organizations: "The professionals didn't want publicity because if anything is done to alleviate the plight of poor people they're out of jobs. They're the true parasites, not the poor." Continuing this theme, tenant activist and key organizer Mike Carson told delegates that most money meant to fight poverty was siphoned off for staff salaries and administration, operating, and capital costs. As in the previous year's conference, delegates supported several left-wing resolutions. A *Varsity* reporter detected "an obvious increase in the sentiments and rhetoric of anti-imperialism." But the proceedings as a whole seemed to have less of a new left air. Many of the motions centred on job creation via made-in-Canada cars, new hospitals, daycare centres, and low-income housing. By the end of the conference the 225 delegates voted to establish an ongoing group called the Ontario Anti-Poverty Organization (OAPO). Its executive, like the delegates themselves, was overwhelmingly Toronto-based. Its conference, held the following year and attended by 650 delegates, received government money to ensure better representation.[122]

Between conferences, OAPO demonstrated, lobbied, and tried to co-ordinate anti-poverty activism. The group ran into trouble after dozens of people employed under a LIP grant it had obtained were found to be engaging in activism instead of research. It might have done better by misusing its grant in a proper fashion—perhaps like the approach of the Ontario Housing Tenants' Association, which was accused of employing tenant organizers. Instead, OAPO's grant workers went door-to-door gathering signatures for a petition strongly supporting a guaranteed annual income (GAI). GAI promised liberation from invasive, benefit-denying "poverty professionals," and the only new left critique of it seemed to be that it would not abolish capitalism. By the early 1970s, prominent NDPers, Liberals, and Progressive Conservatives had all come on board and debates about GAI tended not to be about "if" but "how much?" An Ontario government pilot GAI project, announced to begin in mid-1973, promised payments somewhere between the figures suggested by federal Progressive Conservative opposition leader Robert Stanfield and the Communist Party.[123]

By the time of OAPO's 1974 conference, members sensed that their momentum had stalled. They were unable to attract many new people, and potential activists appeared to be uninspired: "I thought this afternoon would be more exciting, something like the Russian Revolution with people storming city hall and all," said one participant. "Instead, it's just the same old speeches." It had also become apparent that the government was no longer paying much attention to the movement. Politicians who had once demanded to be allowed into anti-poverty conferences were now avoiding them with apparent disinterest. A friendly politician suggested to OAPO that the government had moved beyond its earlier fear of the poor.

The ebbing of this perception would create difficulties for all sorts of community organizations in the mid-1970s. Fears of U.S.-style violence and riots had provided powerful rationales for public officials and politicians, from both the right and the left, to hand out money and support progressive reforms. The Riverdale Community Organization, for instance, had received government money in the belief that the donations would discourage violence. Certain organizations clearly benefited from this dubious perception. Some gestured towards such notional bodies as the Yorkville Liberation Front, which was expressly poised to launch a riot if the city refused to close a street and free up space for young people. One local politician, Margaret Campbell, strenuously argued that fostering participation was important if Toronto were to avoid the "long, hot summers" of violence plaguing U.S. cities. As Black activist Leonard Johnson observed: "Every time there's an eruption of violence down there we reap the benefits up here in the form of tokenism to blacks."[124]

Issues relating to poverty were often tied to fears of violence. Ted Mann, chair of the Sociology Department at York University and an NDP candidate for office, warned that Toronto's lack of affordable housing could prompt future riots: "Violence, at first would be sporadic but then when people started to organize, the demonstrations would become more militant and fierce." The Ontario Economic Council, an official advisory group, suggested that a guaranteed annual income could help steer poor people away from U.S.-style violence. The head of the National Council of Welfare warned that if welfare recipients were not granted greater autonomy and the working poor did not begin to receive government assistance, "The next few years will be violent, frightening and bloody ones." As a reporter warned, politicians had to act immediately to fight poverty because: "In this country the poor have not mobilized. They do not pose as immediate a threat to the very survival of the nation."[125] It seemed that once the spectre of violence had retreated, the anti-poverty movement lost momentum.

Adding to OAPO's 1974 malaise was criticism that women had been woefully under-represented in its executive positions. Women made up more than half of OAPO's membership—so why should they be content with only one seat on the conference's planning committee? Seemingly happy with many of OAPO's feminist-tinged policies, but dissatisfied with its "male-chauvinist" structure, a group of women from Alexandra Park launched the Women's Action Conference, out of which grew the Women's Action Group and the Mother-Led Union.[126] At its height, the Mother-Led Union claimed a couple of dozen Ontario "locals," including four in Toronto. Its mid-term goal was for at least a thousand mothers to go on strike for improved government benefit payments. This would be a real strike, its organizers hastened to add, and not some kind of token gesture. Mothers would leave their children at Queen's Park for the duration to generate leverage.

JSM's pioneering model, of direct-action-oriented, mother-led anti-poverty groups for social change, was replicated by a number of smaller organizations. The trend continued into the 1980s, when the Mothers' Action Group (est. 1981) became renowned for both its coalition-building and direct actions—going so far in some cases as to trap mice and cockroaches in their buildings and releasing them in welfare offices.[127]

* * *

Teachers found themselves being caught up in similar debates. A central argument of the Ontario government's Hall-Dennis Report was an individualistic empowerment of the teacher and principal, acting as a team and inspiring entire schools to achieve excellence. It was a vision that the report combined with its new left–sounding critique of urban alienation.[128] Yet, as new left teachers engaged with the system in the 1970s, they often encountered the different logic, which Hall-Dennis also supported, of high-tech educational television, brutalist architecture, and ever-more powerful and bureaucratic school boards. Like the social workers, they confronted the core problems of unionizing professionals from a new left perspective—that is, of determining the exact location of "community" power. Did the teachers run the schools, or the parents, or the students, principals, or administrators? If the right answer was, "They all do," how could this approach be reconciled with conventional collective bargaining involving just two parties, a system centred on wages and working conditions and with its own non-professionalized traditions of seniority?

Such issues boiled over from 1971 to 1978 as the School Board tilted further to the left. In Ward 6 two activist candidates, Dan Leckie, and Bob Spencer, based their campaigns on the ideal of community control over schools. A traditional trustee, they argued, saw himself as a "representative." They wanted a more direct democracy in which parents would challenge the narrow culture—WASP, middle-class, hierarchical—that prevailed in education. Another candidate, identified with the gay liberation movement, wanted Toronto schools to promote sexual liberation, but also demanded community control and action to counteract class and ethnic discrimination.[129] Frank Nagle, a former U of T student activist, contrasted his own vision of the role of trustee with the 1960s version of the same post, in which a trustee was just a manager of "the System." Trustee Jan Dorion expanded on this new left–influenced interest in direct and participatory, rather than indirect and semi-fictional, democracy:

> We must have a built-in political decentralization which brings local people into the decision-making process regularly. In other words, as George [Martell] says, "we must all be politicians." If we allow the experts, the bureaucrats, and the occasional reform politician to make most of our decisions for us, we weaken ourselves and our communities.[130]

Meanwhile, the provincial government, having opened the educational spending spigot in the 1960s, now decided to impose spending ceilings. Teachers fought back. In May 1973 they called in sick in large numbers—at Scarbor-

The inaugural convention of the Inter-Collegiate Student Council of North York. Created by administrators to sideline student radicalism, the Council later helped organize one of the largest student demonstrations in Canadian history; April 25, 1968.

Clara Thomas Archives and Special Collections, Toronto Telegram fonds.

ough's Mowat Collegiate to the extent that the school was effectively closed. What was even more worrying, from a professionalizer's perspective, was that teachers seemed to be forming anti-austerity alliances with their students. At Scarborough's Stephen Leacock Collegiate, 73 teachers and 150 students canvassed the neighbourhood in a campaign against educational spending ceilings; the next day, students from Thomson Collegiate and Midland Avenue Collegiate, chanting "end the ceilings," left their classrooms to march on the Board of Education. On November 1 the ad hoc Committee for Student Action, made up of both elected school council members and rank-and-file activists, held meetings to co-ordinate fourteen schools in a week of rotating one-day strikes to support the non-salary demands of the teachers. About 1,500 students from Harbord Collegiate, Central High School of Commerce, and Central Technical High School started off the week with a rally at Queen's Park. That week the North York Council of Student Presidents called for a two-day walkout the following week against the "deteriorating quality of education." It was to be, said its president, not so much a "pro-teacher" as a "pro-student" protest.[131]

On the Monday, a sizable demonstration protesting the budget ceilings at Queen's Park was backed by the Etobicoke Secondary School Presidents' Council.

The next day fifteen thousand Toronto students walked out of class, with about half assembling at Queen's Park. That impressive demonstration was trumped on Wednesday, when seventeen thousand North York students left class for a two-day strike. While there had been fear of expulsions, the massive number of students involved made any penalties "inconceivable" to school authorities. During the week of strikes, the students, teachers, and parents united to form the Metro Committee on Provincial Education Policy to further pressure the Ontario government.[132]

The largest university-based demonstrations of the 1960s and 1970s could not hold a candle to the approximately thirty-two-thousand high-school students who participated in protest action that week in 1973. Mobilizing and co-ordinating so many students proved an immense accomplishment. The concrete results of the strikes are hard to determine precisely. The minister of education did agree to meet a delegation of ninety-four students and introduced a watered-down student bill of rights in the legislature. An activist with the Committee of Student Action hoped that their actions contributed to the tentative agreement made with teachers on November 20 that decreased class sizes and increased teachers' pay.[133]

The 1974 School Board elections probably accelerated the degree and pace of change in Toronto education. This was when alumni from *Community Schools* and *This Magazine* began to increasingly shape the Board. "We were very much part of an international new left," one mid-decade trustee recalled. After the 1974 election and throughout the 1970s the Board of Education was sometimes an audaciously left body. Gay activist Tim McCaskell was employed at the Riverdale Intercultural Council when the Board contracted the Council to organize workshops on race for public-school students. He remembers the difficulty of trying to "convince a group of high-school kids that their problems were the result of capitalists trying to divide and conquer the working class." Later, recalling Lenin's words that "the heart and soul of Marxism" was "the concrete study of concrete conditions," McCaskell shifted to a more nuanced approach. Reflecting a growing concern among the trustees for more working-class-centric approaches, Dundas Public School launched a five-year experiment to come up with "curricula based upon the language and culture of working class children."[134]

The contract with the Riverdale Intercultural Council was not an anomaly. The hiring of administrative staff and consultants reflected the politics of the Board. Activists thought to be sympathetic to its left objectives were appointed to staff positions. As one former School Board administrator remembered: "If you think George Bush is harsh in naming a judge, you should see the way we chose consultants." One influential "independent" report from the 1970s, which helped reorient board policies in a leftward direction, was written by Karl Jaffary, well known in his prior life as a prominent left-wing alderman.[135]

At the same time, educational administrators reduced the concept of community schools to the proposition that schools might be open to the community after hours. In contrast, left-wing education activists demanding community control of schools called for tangible participation in everyday school decisions. They wanted community control over the selection of principals and school curriculum. Yet certain issues revealed how difficult it might be to determine whose voice should count in a given "community." In one case, students, parents, and teachers all had to vote on whether to establish a smoking area at a local high school. The result had a majority of students and parents supporting the measure, but because the teachers did not support it, the proposal was not implemented. Here was a concrete example of why some students demanded a student bill of rights that would give them exclusive control over an issue such as smoking.[136]

A centrepiece of the community school strategy was the creation of ward-wide councils to link the community councils based on individual schools. These larger councils would be vital conduits of information and, at least potentially, the key decision-makers when it came to the directions taken by area trustees. Contemporary sources suggest that these councils were not uniformly functional. The Ward 5 Educational Council seemed to be well-established and had its own newsletter. Some one hundred participants turned out at a meeting reported in *Community Schools*. Ward 7's council was called an Education Forum, but seemed similar in purpose.[137] For the 1976 elections, hundreds of activists in Ward 9 gathered to select candidates to run for city council and the boards of education on a platform hammered out by the "community conference."[138] The education platform centred on implementing a more progressive education tax, school-based daycares, decentralized decision-making and other community involvement schemes, anti-sexism and racism programs, and an end to streaming students based on social, economic, and cultural backgrounds (that is, vocational schooling). Candidates running against the community slate often spoke in the language of community as well, but were hostile to the direction being taken by the progressive School Board and community candidates. Marguerite Rea demanded "a halt to the epidemic of permissiveness," while David Moll specified that, although supporting community involvement, he was opposed to community control.[139] Nonetheless, the meeting elected three of the five candidates running on the community-control platform. They announced their first step: establishing a community council, charged with organizing and politicizing the ward, to which they themselves would be accountable.[140]

In the long march through educational institutions, activists discovered the complexity of a radical politics founded upon community. Although leftists were predictably pro-union, they did not always agree with trade unionists.

Some school councils took on issues that challenged the educational status quo across the city.

This Magazine Is About Schools, Fall–Winter 1971.

The teachers' unions were adamantly against involving the wider community in decision-making. The unions typically did not like student participation in the selection of principals and remained wary even of parents' involvement, arguing that parents were not interested enough to take part and that students would violate the proceeding's confidentiality. Ultimately, thanks in part to divisions among the leftists themselves, the students were left out of such deliberations. Even parent representatives had to demonstrate that they were supported by a substantial percentage of their fellow parents to get a seat at the table.[141]

Still, new leftists did achieve a remarkable victory in Toronto educational politics. As McCaskell suggests, the Toronto system paved the way for inclusiveness and an honest reckoning with racial divisions, to be followed by more enlightened policies with respect to sexual minorities—a testament to the victories that new leftists scored in Toronto schools in the 1970s.

For teachers struggling to combine their commitment to their profession with their new left sensibilities, the educational sphere represented both challenges and opportunities. Unifying teachers and parents was one significant challenge. Resistance to cuts, layoffs, and other aspects of austerity could bring parents and teachers together, as suggested by some of the larger demonstrations of the 1970s. But rival identifications—as ratepayers, members of traditional parties, or parents—could divide them. In 1976 School Board elections bore witness to a small conservative push-back against allegedly excessive spending, led by Trustee Dennis Colby, who was hailed by the *Sun* as a "maverick" standing up to the big spenders (his subsequent arrest on a charge of marijuana possession and attempt to turn his trial into an indictment of drug criminalization made him an unlikely hero for the right). A renewed progressive majority returned to the Board in 1978. Yet new fissures emerged between left trustees and the teachers' unions. The Toronto Ontario Secondary School Teachers' Federation did not like left trustees acting on the basis of their own agenda and called for the caucus of left-wing trustees to be disbanded. Yet even OSSTF officials must have been pleased with a huge demonstration of one thousand teachers and two thousand parents, orchestrated by the Board and its left-wing parent and teacher allies in 1979, which helped sway public opinion against education cutbacks.[142]

New left ideas strongly influenced professionals in law, library science, social work, and education, all of them increasingly found in contradictory class locations—for they were, at the same time, both white-collar proletarians answerable to bosses and without much capacity to determine the conditions of their working lives, and budding self-directed professionals answerable to their peers and calling out for respect and status from society. Even struggles defending their immediate interests were sometimes pushed in different directions—towards solidarity with a broader population of clients and students or towards defence of their particular interests in specific institutions. Many activists came to appreciate that militant public pressure could prove decisive, as in the case of the Law Union's struggle to fight deportation orders against refugees, which dramatized the refugees' plight in high-profile demonstrations rather than behind-the-scenes negotiations.[143] For all the particular circumstances that shaped their lives, Toronto's left-wing professionals exhibited a growing conviction that in order to safeguard the radical humanistic ideals they had learned about in university, they sometimes had to "act unprofessionally."

* * *

a lip-grant of selected communities
and a middle-class slum evict the poor

crew-cut white-painters have been
replaced by bearded sand-blasters

the committed take up urban scouting; learn to read
subway maps; practice rat-bite cures

sporty silver avantis and English racing bikes
are closely watched when cabbagetowners stroll by

communication and ultimate themes of the good life stand
mute when selecting a suburban school for the children

south of the st.jameston elevators
they believe in manifest destiny.[144]

Hans Jewinski's poem "Cabbagetown Renaissance," published in *Seven News*, captured some of the wider dilemmas of the eruption of the new left in civic politics. Some of the new left professionals intent on democratizing school boards and ward councils numbered among the white-painters he skewered. Each of them would have been aware of an accompanying rise in property values. In 1974 activists in a neighbouring ward estimated that a thousand properties a year were being bought from low- and middle-income residents, renovated, and then "flipped" to higher-income people.[145]

To combat the effects of both white-painters and corporate developers, new leftists helped to push through a series of measures, including rent controls, co-op and subsidized housing projects, and mechanisms forcing developers to build lower-cost units. The platforms of radical neighbourhood organizations discussed and occasionally noted further-reaching anti-capitalist solutions, such as the gradual takeover of all privately owned property by the municipal government. But a wider shift to the left was required before they could enact their most ambitious proposals. Failing that, some leftists feared that poor and working-class people would be forced to move en masse to the suburbs—a process underway today.[146]

Some of Jewinski's skepticism was spot-on. From Bill Davis's decision on the Spadina Expressway to Hall-Dennis's radical-seeming program for education, from the federal Local Initiatives Program and Opportunities for Youth to the absorption of many "soft-line" urbanists by city hall, from the food co-ops to the health centres: a liberal order clearly had a seemingly infinite absorptive capacity to entrap and enfeeble radical democrats, some of whom combined seemingly revolutionary rhetoric with white-painting gentrification. Indeed, especially when viewed from the disillusioned perspective of our own starkly class-divided neo-liberal age, the new leftists' quest for egalitarian political forms that anticipated a better world to come, and especially those that emphasized individual empowerment and community self-government, can be represented as so many instances of bourgeois individualism. Yet such a dismissive interpretation misses the point. In one new left experiment after another radicals sought to make of Toronto something much more than a stage for the performance of an abstract radicalism. They tried heartily—and in a surprising number of cases, successfully—to develop radically democratic counterinstitutions that, together, could be seen as a first draft of an alternative social order.

8

Without Walls—No Ceiling: A Cultural Revolution, 1971–78

NEW LEFT STUDENT Clark Akatiff was certain that his geography professor was an old leftist. William Bunge did not dig the sixties scene and probably seldom if ever listened to the Beatles. It was doubtful that he had any idea who the Grateful Dead were. He was definitely down on drugs—Bunge had figuratively hit the roof, and almost literally hit Akatiff, after the student advised him to chill out and drop some acid.[1] Yet despite such seemingly uncool opinions and an enduring attachment to the Communist Party, Bunge did become a new leftist, at least in the broad sense.

Bunge's unique brand of geography placed the discipline "in the service of the people." His penchant for "expeditions" focused on fostering local leadership and solving problems identified by the communities that he worked in (a component of his first project, in Detroit, was a university extension program to speed the admission of local Black residents). Bunge insisted that the "power of the expedition itself, who hires and fires, who writes cheques and so forth must be in the hands of the people being explored, risky as that sounds to academics." In 1969 the Wisconsin-born professor emigrated to Canada, landing a job first at the University of Western Ontario and then teaching, from 1972, at York University. In 1975, based on the research of his Toronto Geographical Expedition, he co-authored a book called *The Canadian Alternative: Survival, Expeditions and Urban Change.*[2]

The book included maps that might be expected in a left-wing urban geography project, like those showing park-deprived areas or absentee landownership. Yet many others were brilliantly unconventional, illustrating the use of front porches, the degree of friendliness to children on Halloween, the colours of painted brick houses (a sore point for some of Toronto's Anglo inhabitants), and the locations of "stoner" and male-only spaces. Projects such as mapping smiles might seem frivolous, but they underpinned a cohesive approach that aimed to identify the subtle and almost invisible ways in which human beings lived out class differences. Although Bunge confessed that capitalists could not be blamed for the lack of snowfall in the habitats of inner-city working-class children (vs. the quantities enjoyed by children in the more affluent suburbs), he considered the length of time that the snow remained on the ground to be a "class matter."[3]

He and his co-author devoted a good portion of the book to understanding Toronto's fast-changing cultural composition. "If the cultures of Canada cannot even be seen in Toronto; if the landscape tone of the city is forever Anglo-Saxon, then what does the policy of [a] multi-cultural state mean?" asked Bunge, who wanted the city's environment to reflect the cultures of all of its citizens. He argued for a recognition that everyone—even prejudiced "'just plain' Canadians"—belonged to distinct "urban nations."[4] Paralleling community-control ideals, Bunge wanted each "urban nation" to have the power to govern its own neighbourhood. As he honestly conceded, this formula led to difficulties, especially when it came to racialized minorities such as Black, Indigenous, and Québécois people who lacked the concentrated numbers to dominate a neighbourhood. Embracing Bunge's "people-defined regions," maps by the expedition's semi-autonomous Black component included impersonal surveys of the GTA's Black population but also, on a smaller scale, the "Dispersal of Grant Morris' Black Friends." The book imaginatively mapped where Indigenous peoples had lived in an earlier Toronto and where they were living in the mid-1970s. It also visualized a Toronto living in a "Native way," with pueblo-inspired rooftop gardens and grass-free lawns as well as more fundamental changes. Devised by the expedition's Indigenous associate, this future Toronto was positioned somewhere between a pre- and post-capitalist society, with the downtown business district contemptuously renamed and moved to what appears to be northern Scarborough.[5]

The book was clearly unusual, but it paled in comparison to some of Bunge's articles, which, though essentially geographic in subject matter, were written in the distinctive style of "gonzo" journalism. A few were part travelogue, with Bunge extolling sights and sounds, writing of people he met, and detailing emotional highs and lows. He often fashioned unexpected segues and made lengthy personal and political observations. His field report from the Dominican village of Coulibistrie ruminated on Black power (in favour), lesbian separatism (opposed), and methods of cadre development (extensive and unorthodox). The editor of the academic *Political Geography Quarterly* journal was amazed that anyone could consider such articles suitable for publication. Yet some of Bunge's troubles with editors only differed in degree from the travails of other new left geographers, who could also sometimes find themselves accused of "not" doing geography. Canada Customs officials once seized copies of the new left geography journal *Antipode*, charging that it was "mislabelled."[6]

Although left-wing geography fell under a variety of designations in the 1970s and 1980s—such as human geography, or critical geography—these were but varieties of "new left geography," as an article in the first issue of *Antipode* suggested. But Bunge's community-derived geography never did receive recognition as an academic genre. To a small degree, that failure was because many of the young academics of the time gravitated to Marxist analysis of British anthropologist and geographer David Harvey. Although the Toronto Geographical Expedition played a role in the formation of the Union of Socialist Geographers (a picture of its founders was taken in front of the expedition's headquarters on Brunswick Street to commemorate the occasion), at least one Harvey fan wanted the Union to tighten its structure to exclude "extreme feminism" and Bunge's "rambling and utopian thinking."[7]

Bunge sometimes bitterly clashed with geographers who sought more interventionist community-organizing models or saw the workplace as the main terrain of struggle. He insisted on the key importance of working-class communities ("the point of reproduction") and warned that an industrial focus could only create a "male trade unionist party." Although Bunge held that geography was a cause that had nothing to do with professionalism (amateurs were the true geographers, he argued, while professionals would say anything for a buck), he maintained that university-trained geographers nevertheless played a crucial role. Would any ordinary worker have been as effective as a doctor in Norman Bethune's field hospital? He worried that many new left geographers were turning their backs on geography in favour of activism or a thinly disguised political economy. In response some new left geographers drew a giant-sized Bunge walking through an impoverished community shouting, "What you people need are maps!" Left professionalism was still a form of professionalism.[8]

Bunge increasingly attacked "vanguard thinking," spoke of "many paths to socialism," and warned of a thin line between "vanguard" and "snot nosed snob." He slammed the Communist Party's schema of stages (anti-monopoly government followed by socialism followed by communism), likening it to the right-wing domino theory that posited the dreaded spread of communism from one country to another, with special reference to Southeast Asia. Drawing from geography the idea that people operated on different scales simultaneously, Bunge insisted that "links do not form a chain but rather a network."[9] In 1975 he turned his back on academia and became a cab driver, an occupation he had lionized as an ideal one for urban geographers. Some of his closest students dropped out to drive taxis, engage in community organizing, and promote non-academic community geography. The local Is Five Foundation, said to have pioneered Canada's first roadside, multimaterial pickup recycling operation (in the Beaches/east end area of the city), was one of their accomplishments. But the withdrawal of these renegade geographers further diminished Bunge's influence within academia. The former professor, for his part, continued his own geographical research while taking fares. In the early 1980s local buildings and hydro poles were festooned with Bunge's post-apocalyptic, anti-nuclear maps, a testament to his active involvement in the city's peace movement.[10]

What does this particular case suggest? For one thing, for many new leftists, intellectual pursuits were not focused on ways of making a living—they were *causes*, expressions of an underlying humanist radicalism irreducible to careerism on the one hand or "knowledge for its own sake" on the other. The upshot was a perpetually agonistic relationship with the very concept of professionalism.[11] It also showed how someone like Bunge had to fight a two-front struggle: against rulers within the academy, for whom Marxist scholarship was anathema; and also against more orthodox Marxists, for whom the industrial workplace and the working class, both narrowly defined, were far more significant than the processes of social reproduction to which Bunge devoted his attention.

In the academy new leftism meant paying attention to lived experiences and daily life, in ways that were difficult to square with top-down and objectifying accounts of the state or the abstract schemes of urban planners. Also, while it undoubtedly unfolded in Toronto, Bunge's Expedition in the city was always seen as taking place in one node in a transnational capitalist economy, as fully functional in Vancouver or Detroit as in Toronto. Finally, as suggested by the Expedition's decentralizing political thrust, a fine, at times invisible, line separated new left scholarship from political activism. When Bunge's former students followed his example and took to driving cabs, they did so to further the cause of community-based economic development and to go beyond mere criticism to constructive action.

* * *

One of the things that made the new left "new" was its greatly intensified focus on cultural questions. Rising up against the meaninglessness and cruelty of the world around them, many new leftists believed in the urgency of developing a radical humanistic praxis, a culture that would allow the ideals of national liberation, community, and self-management to blossom. For them, such a cultural revolution entailed a comprehensive resistance to capitalist alienation, with respect to both the development of egalitarian and non-capitalist cultural institutions and the diffusion of radical humanist messages. It was about creating places and forces in which the liberated future of tomorrow would be prefigured today. It not only meant popularizing a critique of commercialized popular culture but also entailed the prospective demolition of the distinctions between high and low culture upon which elite institutions such as art galleries, museums, theatres, and universities relied. It meant challenging corporate control of elite cultural institutions—which, as the soon-to-be-fired director of the Royal Ontario Museum put it in 1971, encouraged a conservative mentality, stifling the imagination necessary for culture to thrive in our "machine made, profit-oriented society."[12]

The cultural revolution also meant consciously struggling to reinvent the very idea of culture (conceiving of it as a revolutionary process) in the interests of working people (whose "use value," two Toronto artists explained in 1976, was appropriated by mainstream culture as well as by capitalist industry). For some, the shift entailed the quest to combine revolutionary form with progressive content. As dancer Brenda Neilson explained, truly revolutionary work meant transforming them both. Such new leftism would hardly rest content with cultural work aimed at a minority and dominated by the wealthy. Announcing his resignation from a national network of artist-run centres, Clive Robertson, who would go on to co-found *Centerfold/FUSE* magazine, reaffirmed his belief that art galleries were "irrelevant, unnecessary and literally counter-productive."[13]

Toronto's first major hub for countercultural artists and writers was the Bohemian Embassy, established in 1960 by a handful of CBC employees. Poetry and folk music were the mainstays of this coffee shop, but, anticipating later artist-run spaces, it also exhibited a multidisciplinary proclivity (experimental film, art exhibits, dance). The poets in the Allan Gardens free-speech fight were Embassy regulars. The artist-run co-op Artisans Shop later donated its space to the Student Union for Peace Action. Theatre Workshop Productions, a "group theatre" spearheaded by socialist director George Luscombe, launched its first collective creation in 1961 and tried to inject culture into the wider community—and also presaged later trends. Privately owned Coach House, a small publisher established in 1965, operated on co-operative principles and championed multidisciplinary art (one of its owners likened the camaraderie there to the sense of fellowship in the peace movement). The press later plugged into Rochdale College. Avant-garde and left-wing cultural revolutionaries flocked to these cultural experiments, which tended to have antagonistic relationships with longer established, state-financed institutions.[14]

These early experiments were dwarfed by the development of new left cultural forms in the 1970s, with dozens of projects springing up and aiming, across a vast spectrum of fields, to revolutionize cultural life. As Kenneth Coutts-Smith, one of the world's foremost experts on artist-run galleries, wrote, all art was political; to ignore that condition was to encourage "self-indulgent irrelevance." Yet to make

The Festival of Underground Theatre, held in 1970, attracted many of the city's radical cultural workers.

Guerilla, July 31, 1970.

art a force for progressive change, its production had to remain embedded within everyday life. "Once the creative event is taken out of the continuum of social relations," Coutts-Smith said, "once it is frozen into cultural history, once it is reified into a museum, it then ceases to be art to any active sense, and becomes transformed into mere property—into cultural property." Even abstract ideas could be possessed as property. There was nothing inherently revolutionary about avant-garde art, especially if it were subjected to reification in a market economy. The giant accounting firm of Price Waterhouse was perfectly comfortable with abstract art. What *would* be revolutionary were cultural producers who were not content to demand a larger share of the liberal order's pie—here Coutts-Smith detected the weakness of artists' unions—but resisted that order altogether, in part because they remained organically linked to subaltern groups. Although, certainly, not all left-wing cultural producers in Toronto were acolytes of Coutts-Smith, his views were by no means atypical of their time and place. Across many spheres, cultural producers were demanding "culture for the people," whether this meant embracing new media, new groups, new venues, or new institutions.[15]

A theme that runs through left-wing innovations in theatre, music, film, and dance in 1970s Toronto is the drive to perform revolution—to help people visualize both the necessity of revolutionary change and the processes and people that might lead to this transformation. In theatre this drive was to create a worker-run theatre that would attract a wide audience to progressive plays, often ones written not by one playwright but by an entire collective. The plays should be gutsy, controversial, and watchable—or, as Donald Bryden explained in a 1977 article calling for more popular theatre for the masses of ordinary people (who tended to stay away from Canadian theatre in droves), "more left-wing, more nationalist, more pacifist, more feminist, more four-lettered."[16]

In the 1970s revolutionizing theatre often entailed a concerted effort to reinvent the theatrical documentary, often with the idea of dramatizing social struggles—especially those originating in class, race, and gender. It also meant subverting the notion of "classical theatre" as a distant antique removed from the storms of the twentieth century, and instead dramatizing more contemporary events. Many of those events took place in Canada, for a major theme running through Toronto's experiments in revolutionary theatre in the 1970s was the anti-colonialist vocation of people's theatre in Canada.[17] In 1971 Joseph Addison's *Two Countries* indicted the foreign ownership of Canadian industry, conveying this political message by staging the play amid a huge montage made up of hundreds of logos from U.S. corporations active in Canada.[18]

That same year, Jeremy Gibson's *Late, Late Crisis,* produced at Global Village Theatre, responded directly to the recent War Measures crisis. "The essence of the play is political and provocatively in favor of the revolution," one reviewer noted, observing as well that the "youngish long-haired audience" was prone to shouting "Right On!" at suitable moments. Using a quiz-show format, the play depicted two opposing teams, "right" and "left," with a scoring system heavily biased in favour of the left. In Ward 7 the Theatre Second Floor put on *Leave It to Beaver Is Dead* in 1975; it depicted the dismaying transformation of a community health clinic into a for-profit business. Less blatantly partisan was *Far as the Eye Can* See, staged in 1977. This was the first substantial artistic depiction of Alberta's transformation by big oil. Opinions differed as to whether it was a path-breaking exploration of U.S. capitalism and Canadian docility or a soft-centred middle-of-the-road populist presentation suitable for moderate New Democrats.[19]

That play was the work of Theatre Passe Muraille (TPM), founded in 1968 out of Rochdale College. The theatre, seeking to eliminate the distinction between actor and spectator—its name translates to "theatre goes through walls"—attained a national reputation in the 1970s. It produced the first classic of the documentary genre, *The Farm Show,* in 1972. In preparation, the theatre troupe had lived on a farm and incorporated interviews with farmers and their experiences working as farm labourers into the play. The farming community not only provided the material for the play, but also served as its first audience. Other documentaries by the company included *Under the Greywacke* (1973), which took place in a former mining town, and Rick Salutin's *Adventures of an Immigrant* (1974), which focused on the Italian community in Toronto (the lead actress worked in a garment factory to prepare herself for the role).[20] Leftists debated the politics of TPM's productions, some of them complaining that the company merely held up a mirror to social relations without indicating how the structures might be transformed, but the presentations were generally in keeping with a new left sensibility. They validated the competence of local producers, treated Canadian experiences as suitable subjects for a theatre group, and subverted high/low cultural distinctions by presenting works that spoke to both working-class and elite audiences. In Salutin's *1837: The Farmers' Revolt* (1973), TPM recovered Ontario's leading revolutionary moment from the nineteenth century.

Open Circle Theatre (fd. 1973), the only theatre devoted entirely to the documentary, prided itself on its research and contacts with the community. The theatre went from documenting specific local problems, such as unemployment and pollution, to staging more general productions, such as a play on race relations in South Africa. The theatre, according to one critic, was the "dramatic equivalent of a monthly news magazine." In 1973, in the wake of a 1972 federal election campaign in which the NDP had excoriated "corporate welfare bums," Open Circle's *No Way, José* came to the defence of lowlier "welfare bums," often directly quoting from interviews with welfare recipients and highlighting such musical numbers as "Why Should I Work 9 to 5," "Money Is the Root of All Evil," and "I'm the Man (the Very Fat Man) Who Waters the Worker's Beer." The very titles suggest the play's anti-capitalist thrust.[21]

That approach, in some left-wing eyes, might be a problem. Such apparent realism could conceal the political choices inherent in any selection of theatrical material. In 1977, in the wake of the city's storms over race, Open Circle brought out *The Primary English Class*, a play that some thought promoted debate about racist jokes and others considered too didactic. Some critics delivered the same verdict with respect to the Theatre Company of Toronto's 1977 production *Comedians*, which depicted the "ugly side of comedy," although commentators also admired the ingenuity of a production that first encouraged audience members to laugh at bigoted jokes, only then to discover that they themselves were the butt of the playwright's scorn.[22]

Factory Theatre, founded in 1970, was the first of the new theatres to declare that it would exclusively produce Canadian plays. Overtly political offerings from its first season included *Two Countries*, which centred on a threatened U.S. invasion after some American-based industries had been nationalized, and *Branch Plant*, written with the help of laid-off workers, about the recent closure of Toronto's Dunlop factory (the issue that had mobilized Wafflers). Toronto Free Theatre was established in 1972 entirely on the basis of LIP grants. The name of the theatre bespoke its approach—of not choosing to stage proven hits and of offering free admission. A founding member noted, "It was a gesture against the notion of theatre as commodity."[23]

The first bloom of Black radical theatre had arrived in 1968, with the establishment of a short-lived group called The Communicators. Keith Barton, a member of Canadians for the National Liberation Front, wrote its first play, *The Carving*, a meditation on interracial romance, the limits of tolerance, and the plight of Caribbean immigrants. The play's director, Peter Robinson, an active member of the Afro-American Progressive Association and Black Liberation Front, cited noted playwright LeRoi Jones when speaking of the importance of Black power and Black theatre in correcting the loss of Black identity. Plays like *The Carving*

A poster advertising a play by Black Theatre Canada, 1975.

Author's collection.

were important correctives to the sugar-coated films of Black Hollywood actor Sidney Poitier, he opined, which were just as destructive as prejudice.[24]

That theatre company was the predecessor for the early to mid-1970s emergence of a larger milieu of Black cultural workers who appeared to mix the ideology of Black power with some of the forms favoured by the predominantly white new left cultural workers' movement. Those years saw the establishment of three different theatre companies. Black Theatre Canada, formed in 1973, stood for the principle that a social and political agenda should be infused in its plays and later initiated the Arts Against Apartheid Festival. Its members believed that establishing a Black, left-wing culture was pivotal to the success of the Black new left movement. A few of their plays, such as 1975's *Changes* and 1978's *Holes*—about a young revolutionary just released from jail after "a computer smashing incident" (with a resonance of the Sir George Williams affair)—discussed Black new left activists themselves.[25] Other Black experiments, although not as overtly linked to the new left, shared some of its cultural passions. The Afro-Caribbean Theatre Workshop, established in 1974, produced a collaboratively written play exploring the links between Blacks in the diaspora and native Africans. Theatre Fountainhead, founded in 1974, criticized the political nature of much of Black Theatre Canada's programming and did not share that theatre's collaborative approach. Instead it devoted itself to fostering a Black identity.[26]

Feminist theatre designed to raise the consciousness of women was no less prominent. The Redlight Theatre flourished mid-decade. In 1978 Theatre Workshop Productions hosted "*Fleck*"*xibility*, a benefit evening in aid of the Fleck Manufacturing plant strikers (*The Fleck Women*, a locally produced documentary, also exquisitely captured the struggle of these female autoworkers). The production highlighted such female performers as comedian-singer Nancy White, who spoofed the official "Ontario" theme song with her rendition of "Ontario, When It Comes to Confrontation, Is There Any Place You'd Rather Be?" True to the times, Charnie Guettel, author of *Marxism and Feminism* (1974), sang in a cabaret program dedicated to the problems of working women—a performance one sympathetic reviewer thought helped to redeem an evening prone to slip into a vague liberal feminism. It was a one-woman demonstration of how fluid the lines were between theoretical and cultural work in the 1970s left. The boundaries between cultural categories were equally fluid, as the Clichettes, an all-woman troupe that delighted in upending the conventions of popular culture, suggested.[27]

After infiltrating the 1970 Miss Canadian University Pageant, an activist from the Toronto Women's Liberation Group leapt upon the stage to denounce the proceedings. Judy Darcy, also on stage, but "posing" as Miss York University, yelled, "It's true, it's a meat market, and they do exploit women." Just a few months later, the 1970 Miss General Idea Pageant featured five contestants in bear costumes, singing and dancing, while a sixth contestant, Miss Honey, demonstrated her skills at a telex machine. Both "performances" critiqued the process and sexism of beauty pageants.[28] Were they acts in a theatre or political acts? Surely they were both.

Throughout the 1970s a debate occurred over how and why theatre should attempt to change the political outlook of its audience. New leftists all agreed that

The Fruits, seen here performing in the heart of the city's financial district, were part of a growing queer arts scene.

Courtesy Charles Dobie.

theatre should be organically connected with that audience, in both form and content, but predictably differed with each other over how explicitly audiences should be confronted with the socialist message. In any case, the wide breadth and vibrancy of new left theatre in Toronto confirmed once again that the forces of revolt did not swiftly decline after 1969. Instead, an opposite process occurred, with slender shoots from the 1960s blossoming into a veritable eco-system in the 1970s. A number of these theatrical projects endured for years—and, indeed, some are still proceeding.[29]

* * *

The new left similarly flourished in the visual arts. A striking feature of the 1970s was the creation of alternative—some said "liberated"—spaces removed from, and opposed to, the capitalist marketplace. For Susan Britton, a video artist writing in the late 1970s, it was imperative to "loosen the obnoxiously close relationship between artists and funding bodies.... I think artists should reinvent the art world rather than just fitting in where they can."[30]

For many left artists in Toronto, the Art Gallery of Ontario (AGO) typified what was stifling and even corrupt about the art world in a capitalist society. It had exerted centralized control over semi-autonomous spaces once curated by the city's various art societies; its increased funding and burgeoning staff meant that

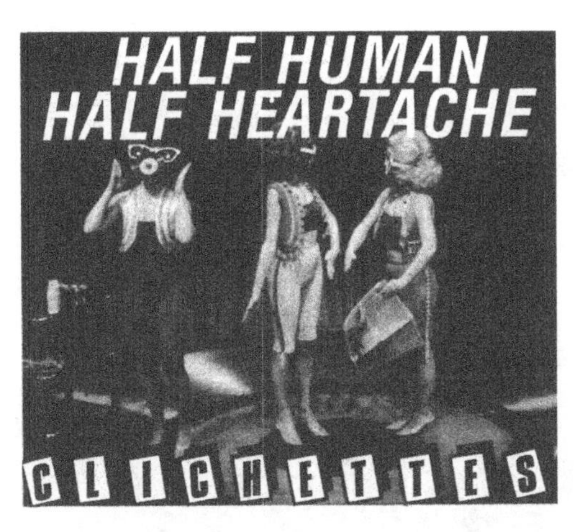

Comprising Louise Garfield, Janice Hladki, and Johanna Householder, the Clichettes became renown for combining art, politics, and entertainment.

Fireweed 11, 1981.

it behaved more and more like a capitalist institution; it declined invitations to foster experimental art; and its board of trustees, on which artists secured a minimal position in 1973, was dominated by the bourgeoisie.[31]

To the question raised at a 1968 AGO seminar, "Are art galleries obsolete?" left artists in the 1970s answered: "Yes, if they look and act anything like the AGO."[32] They regarded the institution's lavish state funding with suspicion. One artist-run gallery projected slides onto the front wall of the AGO, depicting an art director in a pinstriped suit alongside images of dollar signs. Left nationalists critiqued the appointment of American Richard Wattenmaker to the chief curator position, while feminist left nationalists organized pickets and information tables to protest the minimal presence of women in the gallery. Black activists picketed the AGO in 1974, demanding that it display more art by Black Canadians and Indigenous peoples.[33]

For leftists, Lily Eng's experience with the AGO in 1978 seemed sadly typical. When she was performing her solo performance piece, a security guard proclaimed that what she was doing was not art and tried unsuccessfully to remove her. Eng said to her audience: "Every time I come into this fucking place the security guards harass me. Well if you want to get me out you'll have to fucking come and drag me out." Prior to showing another experimental artist's videotape, an AGO trustee contacted the police department's morality squad, which resulted in the intervention of the Ontario Censor Board.[34] The AGO was not only oppressive and complicit in capitalism but also drearily conventional in its cultural proclivities.

General Idea was one of the most famous of the Toronto experiments to create a space for art liberated from the imperatives of a capitalist society and the AGO's bureaucratic regimentation. A collective founded in 1967 by artists Feliz Partz, Jorge Zontal, and A.A. Bronson, who were also the leading spirits of *FILE* magazine, General Idea took up the new left theme of cultural alienation and applied it to a diversity of cultural phenomena—beauty pageants, television shows, and mass media. In 1974 it established Art Metropole, which defied convention both by being non-profit and by championing mixed media. General Idea was plainly animated by the new left's radical ambition to critique and subvert the common sense of a capitalist culture; and the collective, in both its organization and content, similarly defied state boundaries, as its key figures operated in both Toronto and New York. Its conceptual art drew on the work of Marxist cultural critic Guy Debord, who theorized that the economy had colonized the totality of everyday life, hiding that condition and all social relationships behind a spectacle of images designed to induce passivity. Debord and his fellow "situationists" believed that the goal of left-wing cultural workers was to create situations contributing to the collapse of this spectacle: "We want to work not on the spectacle of the end of the world [a reference to Dada], but on the end of the world of the spectacle." General Idea sought to break the "image bondage" of that spectacle.[35]

Other artists looked even further afield, collaborating with unions and rank-and-file workers as they painted working-class subjects and displayed their work in union halls and other public venues.[36] In 1976 the two-day Partisan Art Festival drew fifty performing and visual artists with its call for arts that supported "working people; trade unions; women's, Native and civil rights groups; anti-pollution movements, etc." It featured a painting of "Winnipeg 1919," photos from the Texpack strike, a tape on wage and price controls, and a children's play about "Greedy Miller."[37] This was not art as conceived of by the Art Gallery of Ontario.

Toronto's first artist-run gallery grew out of the privately owned Nightingale Gallery, started in late 1968 by a U.S. draft resister. In 1970 it morphed into the collectively run A Space. Through the 1970s and early 1980s A Space remained a pole of creativity and debate. Under the leadership of Victor Coleman of Coach House, it became more interdisciplinary, adding dance, poetry, and music to its field of activities. In 1978 it embraced, controversially, the philosophy of a "gallery without walls," emphasizing works that were performative and site-specific. In the following decade a new board declared that it wanted to showcase artists from minority communities and take the gallery back from "independent curators."[38]

Partisan, which formed in the mid-1970s but only acquired its own space in 1980, was the only gallery devoted to left-wing, political art. Members of the Partisan collective included new leftists and "hip" CPCers. The seeds for Partisan gallery were sown in a discussion group established to explore films screened and distributed by the new leftish Development Education Centre (DEC), another collective (fd. 1971) that, besides distributing books and films across the country, did research and organized workshops with schools and unions.[39] The discussion group meetings in turn sparked a process of forums about the relationship between art and politics, with the aim of developing a nucleus for a community of progressive artists. Collective members hosted a wide range of left-wing exhibits, including one featuring the puppets, props, and banners used by activist artists in local demonstrations. The vibrancy of the gallery was diminished in 1983 when members of its women's collective split to form an organization centring on women's culture. A statement signed by thirty-nine women registered a series of complaints summarized as "manifestations of what we had all read about in 60's essays on sexism in so-called progressive organizations."[40]

In the same year that A Space was born, the Art and Communication collective was created; in the 1970s it became the Centre for Experimental Art and Communication (CEAC). From its inception, this gallery was closely associated with the gay and lesbian community—at one point, CEAC, *The Body Politic*, and Glad Day Books (fd. 1970) all shared the same quarters—and had much in common with the libertarian ethos of the gay movement. This tendency was evident in courses designed to liberate students from the "logical organization" of contemporary society and that relied on such autonomist-Marxist theoreticians as Bruno Ramirez, Mario Troni, and Silvia Federici, all associated with the journal *Zerowork*. In Toronto Amerigo Marras argued that it was essential for artists to confront capitalism directly, outside of the realm of cultural production, which he perceived to be the "trap" of the "alternative." Only those artist-run centres were of value that became instruments in "explicit communication and provocation in the class struggle."[41]

In 1978, to reflect its refusal to co-operate with the system, CEAC renamed its publication: from *Art Communication* to *Strike*. At the peak of its leftism, CEAC supported Italy's Red Brigades and espoused a new line in its campaign against the state: "Insult, New provocation. New Insult. Until their downfall!"[42] Channelling Lenin, Coutts-Smith discerned in CEAC "an infantile ultra-leftism, a totally uncritical and non-analytic anarchism, masquerading as 'socialism' which constitutes nothing other than egotistic and romantic posturing." Although Coutts-Smith believed that CEAC was seriously grappling with Marxism, he suggested that the group had ended up with an overly dogmatic reading of Marxist texts. CEAC's retort questioned Coutts-Smith's revolutionary credentials and implied that he was the equivalent of the obsolete Communists of Europe: "Countries like France or Italy have the Communist Party and Canada has Coutts-Smith."[43] Much of this fiery debate could have been transplanted holus bolus from similar discussions engulfing the new left in Europe.

* * *

Like their compatriots in galleries and theatres, a number of young Toronto filmmakers were attracted to the precept of self-management. "*Redpath 25*—Redpath for the manufacturer of sugar cubes, 25 from the formula for LSD—really was the movie that started it all," recalled Robert Fothergill, who along with David Cronenberg, Lorne Michaels, and Jim Plaxton co-founded the Canadian Filmmakers' Distribution Centre in 1967. Members of this underground-oriented co-op, which was located for a time in Rochdale College, produced a wide variety of films. The Toronto Filmmakers Co-op, also in Rochdale, was later critiqued by dissenting filmmakers who said it had become too service-driven, merely providing cheap facilities to what were in fact small businesses. More overtly political collectives included The Funnel (fd. 1977), a collective of specifically experimental filmmakers that had its own screening room, and production collectives, such as the Film League (established in 1978 with a focus on documenting workers' struggles), which produced socially engaged film. Trinity Square Video was a key hub for the creation and distribution of new left-influenced videos. DEC Films, as an integral part of the Development Education Centre, was not only a general distributor of politically engaged local cinema, such as Clarke Mackey's *A Right to Live: The Story of the Union of Injured Workers* (1977), but an outlet for hard-to-find progressive films from the Third World, Europe, and America.[44]

One of a number of local new left–inspired filmmakers was Laura Sky, whose works ranged from a focus on the early decade's community-building movement—*Tomorrow's Children* (1976, advocating for community schools), *Co-op Housing: The Best Move We Ever Made*, and *Co-op Housing: Getting It Together* (both 1975)—to the struggle against deindustrialization at the end of the decade (*Shutdown*, 1980). In new left style, Sky avoided "expert" narration in favour of showing how "everyday" people had their own knowledge, analysis, and strategy. Her "militant cinema" placed emphasis on how problems could be solved and avoided the guilt-driven approach of "liberal cinema."[45] In step with their academic comrades, new left filmmakers like Sky had little patience for pleas to be more objective: "It's my belief that the phoniest word in the English language is 'objectivity.' The word is a walking lie. Objectivity defines the bias of the people in power.... So-called objective filmmakers allow viewers to remain passive and apolitical."[46]

Some of Sky's films were produced in conjunction with Challenge for Change (c. 1967–80), an arm of the National Film Board credited for its "very special New Left corpus." A number of filmmakers associated with that program utilized a social realist style, replete with broad left messaging, in working-class areas of the city such as Cabbagetown and Riverdale.[47] Towards the late 1970s the racial diversity of Riverdale became an additional lens that independent left-wing filmmakers employed to view that community. Teacher Linda Schulyer, who made an early anti-racist film, *Between Two Worlds*, in conjunction with students at her Riverdale school in 1975, went on to produce other anti-racist videos in that community in partnership with Kit Hood. One of their short films, *Ida Makes a Movie* (1979), indicates that the new left–influenced quest for social realism and "authenticity" was not limited to documentaries. The movie centred on the ethical dilemma of a nine-year-old who made what she considered an environmental film, but an approving panel of judges mistakenly see it as an anti-war piece and on that basis accept it for entry into an NFB festival. That short film later became the first installment in CBC's celebrated *Degrassi* franchise. That Riverdale-situated series, lauded for its "Canadianness," more specifically reflected broad changes within the artistic, educational, political, and social context of Toronto during the 1970s.[48]

* * *

Music concerts and festivals often became sites that joyously upended the tidy conventions of traditional Toronto. Folk music remained the favourite of leftists nostalgic for the days of the Popular Front, some of whom had encountered it as Red-diaper babies in left-wing summer camps. Yet by 1973 one astute left critic, Robin Endres, believed that a quietly dying "counter-culture" from the 1960s no longer existed as a political force. She paid attention to the views expressed by members of the eclectic group Horn, whose spokesperson, David deLauney, argued that music, although hardly a replacement for political theory and action—it was difficult to turn "What Is to Be Done?" into a catchy tune—could still be a "guide to action." As an older youth culture succumbed to commodification and, as another group member said, drifted into "petit-bourgeois ideology and anarchy," the need for a revolutionary musical culture had not subsided. To argue for the subordination of such cultural issues to factory organizing suggested a "moralist kind of argument" out of touch with the realities of daily life.[49]

In 1978 CEAC's *Strike* magazine broadcast the advent of a new day with the headline: "New Wave: Kill Your Parents." Punk and new wave took hold in Toronto before catching on in most other American cities. Bands like The Clash proportionally sold more records in Toronto than they did elsewhere. The second half of the 1970s represented early days for this music, and fans believed that new wave would deal the death knell to stadium performances. This musical protest against the blandness of mainstream culture demanded smaller, more intimate settings.[50]

For most of the 1970s the labels "new wave" and "punk" were used interchangeably; and, until the end of the decade, the genres were forced onto the margins. When punk/new wave began to take off in 1976, Toronto radio stations were not willing to play it. Even managers at the famed El Mocambo, on Spadina Avenue, when asked if they were willing to book new wave bands, declined (it later became a renowned venue for this music).[51] Not much more sympathetic were some of the vanguard groups. The International Socialists' first take on punk was atypically "old mannish" for the organization. A writer explained that rock music in the 1960s had been generally progressive, positive, and reflected youth rebellion, while 1970s rock was reactionary, reflecting hopelessness, despair, and sexism. Left-wing critics saw Canadian punk as pushing this negative trend further. One of them attacked its subcultural nature—"It is fostering new adherents to the bizarre"—and described the music itself as "a primal grunt, representing as much inventiveness as a metronome." To explain why Toronto's all-women punk bands were also verboten, despite their lyrics about women's oppression, he explained that the typical punk form of their names and outfits pointed to their inner anger and degradation.[52]

Then, in a pattern that inadvertently confirmed the porous nature of the boundaries separating one left-wing cultural sphere from another, punk/new wave bands, which often emerged from Toronto's art scene, found venues in the galleries and bars in the neighbourhood of Queen Street West, which supplanted Yorkville as Toronto's little bohemia. As the former Ontario College of Arts students who formed the group Martha and the Muffins wrote, "Suddenly, everyone around O.C.A. and neighbouring Queen St. W. seemed to be starting a band or was in one already." Michaele Jordon of The Poles exchanged her paint brush for a microphone. The artistic new wave band The Time Twins consisted of two women who explored issues of gender. The Curse, whose songs often dealt with sex and exploitation, were Toronto's first female punk band. Their premier performance was at Crash 'n' Burn, a basement venue for the new music, in June 1977.[53] The group of OCA students who formed The Diodes performed at Crash 'n' Burn after being barred from other venues. CEAC released that band's first record under its own imprint (CBS issued the band's second record). And CEAC was not the only left-wing artist body invested in the punk/new wave scene. General Idea put out a record by The Dishes, and A Space occasionally acted as a venue for local punk (and was the location for the Talking Heads' first Toronto performance).[54]

Crash 'n' Burn, run by CEAC, was one of the most militantly new left of all Toronto's cultural experiments. From CEAC's theoretical perspective—that it was important for such Marxists to have a politically informed theoretical perspective on music went without saying—the Canadian punk scene, in contrast to Britain's, was not a response to working-class conditions, but to the homogeneous suburbs. Punk fans used their imagination and recycled goods to craft a form of expression that both played into, and subverted, consumer capitalism. CEAC hoped that punk and new wave would generate the energies for a new revolutionary initiative. Sure, punk, like its folk and rock predecessors, was swiftly commodified: investors "rush towards the cliché of fashion like flies to a mound of shit," noted an *Art Communication* editorial. But the sense of deep alienation it sought to address persisted.[55]

Under the aegis of CEAC, music and art were mixed together. While a plethora of punk bands played in CEAC's basement venue, performance art group SHITBANDIT performed upstairs in the gallery space. The performers, partially clad in pseudo-bondage, alternated between challenging each other and the audience. The audience became outraged after lit matches were thrown at them, on top of the performers' verbal and gestural provocations. Finally, audience members cut the performance short by hurling beer bottles into SHITBANDIT's performance area.[56] Left cultural producers faced a constant challenge: walking the fine line between provoking an audience to progressive reflections and outraging their sensibilities.

* * *

One of the less-studied aspects of the performance of revolution in Toronto is dance. Like many in theatre, new left-influenced dancers were often interested in questions of Canadian nationalism, though for them the focus was on funding indigenous talent. Calls to nationalism seldom entered the realm of content. Dancer Lily Eng agitated against artists from the United States obtaining Canada Council money because U.S. competitors would "be grabbing at that juicy piece of beef in your mouth." For similar reasons, Elizabeth Chitty decried the strong presence of Americans at AGO dance exhibitions.[57]

A key site for new left–influenced dancers like Eng and Chitty was the 15 Dance Lab, formed in the early 1970s by dancers unhappy with the bureaucratic structures of established dance companies. Members of this collective sought to control all aspects of their experimental and multidisciplinary performances—acts that dance companies in general, with concepts of "excellence" mirroring the function of "objectivity," did not see as being dance. Some collective members argued that their radical productions were intrinsically political because they emerged from a worker-controlled environment. Dances themselves did not necessarily have to contain distinct social or political messaging. Others maintained that dance had to be radical in both form and content. A small group of dancers, ideologically close to CEAC, appeared to combine the philosophies and styles of Maoism and punk.[58] Quoting the ideas of Gramsci via American cultural critic Susan Sontag, one 15 Dance Lab member suggested that the evocative and intellectually rich cultural environment that dancers were creating fell nicely within a larger strategy of social change: "The very overthrow of the bourgeois state must wait until there is first a nonviolent revolution in civil society. Culture, more than the strictly political and economic institutions of the state, is the medium of this necessary civil revolution."[59]

* * *

In some spheres of the high-growth world of post-secondary education, leftists scored equally lasting victories. It was true, as student (and budding journalist) Tom Walkom pointed out in 1973, that those paying attention to such things were seeing a decline in university radicalism. At the University of Toronto the struggle to achieve voting parity for students had not succeeded, in part because no one was quite sure what great goal parity was meant to accomplish.[60] Radicals, having learned that the university could not be so easily toppled, were retreating to the library. Yet there they busied themselves subverting the university's governing ideology. Walkom also underlined the significance of how university-trained radicals were mounting their own intellectual ventures, such as New Hogtown Press and the Women's Educational Press.[61]

Walkom had a good point. In 1973 U of T students were still sufficiently rebellious to stage an overnight occupation and rallies over an eleven-day period to protest the firing of professors in the Math Department—but they did not prevail.[62] Although in 1974 some panic-stricken professors viewed the campus Students for a Democratic Society as a menace—Kenneth McNaught thought them a "group of ruffians"—a forceful students' protest against Professor Edward Banfield, an American urbanologist and in their eyes a racist, impeded his seminar while earning suspensions for participants. McNaught himself learned, to his chagrin, that the Ontario Ministry of Education had, acting on the basis of an unidentified pressure group, removed textbooks from the curriculum after deeming them offensive: McNaught concluded that "our government will approve textbooks only if they are agreeable to the sentiments of Canadian Muslims." A fellow professor, who supported the imposition of the ban, thought the professor was overlooking the offending book's factual errors and cultural prejudice.[63]

That issue was just one sign of changes in the historical profession that troubled McNaught. He worried, for instance, about how Gregory Kealey, "leader of the more extreme wing of the student movement in Toronto," had managed to make his way into Ph.D. studies at the University of Rochester (and ultimately into a highly distinguished career as a university historian, administrator, and president of McNaught's own Canadian Historical Association).[64] His fellow historian Michael Bliss, once active in the progressive Student Christian Movement, shared McNaught's disdain for the "simple-minded and vulgar protestors who called themselves the New Left." He was disturbed by a session at Rochdale College on Canadian history, led by Stanley Ryerson, the Communist author of a "dogmatic, almost cartoonish history of Canada as the product of endless class struggle." He was also bothered by the sight of hundreds of students being harangued by Steven Langdon, "bullhorn in hand." The event made him think of

Nazi Germany. He was concerned about the abolition of the university's honour courses as a result of a report authored by U of T's eminent political economy professor C.B. Macpherson, who was purportedly pursuing the goal of "some misguided equality." The sight of a student occupation in 1971 over the parity question was equally vexing—he reported shouts of "Burn the Fucking University Down," "Let's Bomb the Place," and "Go to Hell All of You," and a leaflet calling the faculty opponents of parity "cretins," "anachronisms," and "senile." Here was a cohort intent on filtering "the absurdities of Marxism" through "the sophistries of Herbert Marcuse, with slogans by Mao Zedong." Their moral and political vacuity was underlined by the Banfield affair, in which the police arrived on campus and radicals turned the proceedings of the university's disciplinary body into "televised guerilla theatre." The university, in Bliss's opinion, was failing in its obvious duty to bring criminal charges against the radicals. Yet, fortunately, their movement was in its "final death-throes."[65]

Bliss exaggerates—Toronto's university students remained active through the 1970s. Sociologist William K. Carroll recalls: "Arriving at York—this is 1975—it was still very much a centre of new left activism and there was a very strong presence of the new left on campus." In his study of post–Second World War student activism, Nigel Moses found that students continued to struggle against increased tuition fees, including a 1972 fees strike, the occupation of the office of the president of the University of Toronto in 1978, and the formation of a Coalition Against Cutbacks. In 1978 some seven thousand students from the University of Toronto, Ryerson, and York University massed at Queen's Park in what was called the largest student protest in Canadian history, which became all the more dramatic with an attempted occupation of the legislature itself.[66] Yet he exaggerates a valid point. The new left's long march through the universities, having encountered fierce resistance from stalwarts of the existing institutions, took a new path: it surged into the disciplines themselves, some of which were entirely reconceptualized.

One of those disciplines claimed the attention of professors McNaught and Bliss. David Frank, yet another U of T leftist destined for a distinguished academic career, explored "Rewriting Canadian History" in 1971. He noted a still WASPish field's virulent anti-Quebec and anti-Indigenous biases, the relative neglect of protest and minority movements, and the disregard for class; yet he also underlined the emergence of different voices as exemplified in Leandre Bergeron's *Petit manuel d'histoire du Québec* (1974); the Corrective Collective's *She Named It Canada (Because That's What It Was Called)* (1971); *101 Year Rip-Off: The Real History of British Columbia* (1971); and *The People's History of Cape Breton* (1971), a project in which he himself had been involved (a Toronto collective predictably eschewed such regionalism in favour of a national people's history). All of them placed day-to-day struggles at the forefront of history. *Varsity* writer Wayne Roberts, a year later, deplored the "stale pedantry and eclecticism" of Canadian urban history, lamenting that at a time of intense urban controversies activists would look in vain to urban history for insights into these subjects. Like Frank, he hungered for "a people's history seen from the bottom up."[67] By decade's end and into the early 1980s, many radical scholars in Canadian history had brought out significant monographs. Bryan Palmer's *A Culture in Conflict* (1979) and Gregory Kealey's *Toronto Workers Respond to Industrial Capitalism* (1980) brought Marxist ideas into academic history writing. Both of them celebrated, in slightly different registers, the achievements of workers as they struggled for a more egalitarian society and their own self-emancipation.[68] The same years saw the consolidation of *Labour/Le Travail*, the flagship journal of what came to be called "working-class history."

A reason to read *She Named it Canada*.

Pedestal, December 1971.

Other radicals longed to hear about women, the "neglected majority" evoked in the title of an influential collection of essays in women's history that appeared in 1977. In 1975 a number of them established the Canadian Committee on Women's History, and what had been a dearth of content related to the history of women in Canada gradually constituted itself as a field of scholarship with scores of titles to its credit.[69]

Almost all the disciplines in the humanities and social sciences went through similar left-wing overhauls in the 1970s and 1980s, with new left ideals of self-determination and community being woven into a vast diversity of scholarly inquiries. In sociology, S.D. Clark, a pre-eminent figure at the University of Toronto, was as discombobulated as Bliss by the intellectual revolution in his discipline. He lamented sociologists who had taken up Marxism "with the fanaticism of the newly converted" and who misused the legacy of political economist Harold Innis to legitimate their own "alien" project: "I cannot help but think . . . that a good deal of sociology in Canada has moved too far in what might be described as a leftist direction."[70]

Many of the sociologists that Clark critiqued were moving in the direction of political economy, and their flagship journal—*Studies in Political Economy: A Socialist Review* (*SPE*)—was established in 1979 by an alliance made up mainly of political scientists and sociologists. Since 1975, under the initial leadership of Daniel Drache at York University, the Canadian Political Science Association had been maintaining a special section on political economy. Now these allied scholars undertook to establish a journal that, in words that have an emphatically "70s ring," declared their commitment "as socialists" to "contribute to the on-going and diverse activities of the left and the working-class movement; to be scholarly is also to be relevant in informing practice."[71]

In its early years, *SPE* intently focused on unravelling the complexities of the Canadian state, corporatism in Canada, the new French-Canadian bourgeoisie, labour in a staples economy, the always complicated relations of Quebec and English Canada, and the paradox of a country that was in some respects a colony of the United States and in others an imperialist power in its own right.[72] It was also keen to open Canada up to European left theory, as suggested in articles by or about such theorists as Nicos Poulantzas and Guglielmo Carchedi.[73] *SPE* was not headquartered in Toronto but at Carleton University in Ottawa; and York, by the late 1970s Toronto's premier left-wing campus, was the base for an expanding circle of Marxist scholars, a large and notable hub in a transnational network. The short-lived Marxist Institute of Toronto brought radical academics and activists together over a period of time to mount (according to the Institute's own book of lectures) "a series on the 'national question' in Canada." In 1977 Leo Panitch, then a professor at Carleton but destined for York, brought out his edited collection of articles, *The Canadian State: Political Economy and Political Power*. In 1978 Wallace Clement and Daniel Drache's *A Practical Guide to Canadian Political Economy* declared the reinvigorated field's commitment to helping scholars overcome their disciplinary boundaries and to discover a Marxist tradition that had been rejuvenated after years of wooden orthodoxy.[74]

Although many left academics, by choice or through necessity, turned to university presses as venues for their monographs, they also often favoured presses committed to scholarship as a form of activism. Hogtown Press had originated in 1968–69 as an outgrowth of the publication service of the Canadian Union of Students. A new group, with seed money from the Students' Administrative Council, came to the fore in 1972, renamed the project New Hogtown Press, and set it up as a non-profit corporation run by a volunteer collective.

Soon New Hogtown was bringing out a formidable array of left publications. The drive to bring workers and primary producers into the centre of Canadian history was marked by the publication of Gregory Kealey's *Hogtown: Working Class Toronto at the Turn of the* Century (1974), Russell Hann's *Farmers Confront Industrialism: Some Historical Perspectives on Ontario Agrarian Movements* (1975), Steven Langdon's *The Emergence of the Canadian Working Class Movement, 1845–75* (1975), and Pat Schulz on *The East York Workers' Association: A Response to the Great Depression* (1975). Responding to the feminist upsurge, New Hogtown published Margaret Bentson's widely celebrated *Political Economy of Women's Libera-*

tion (1970), Mickey and John Rowntree's six-page rejoinder, *More on the Political Economy of Women's Liberation* (1974), and Kathleen Gough's *The Origin of the Family* (1972) and *Women in Evolution* (1973). Although it maintained one foot in the world of practical activism—as suggested by the *Free School Handbook* (1973) and *Anti-Corporate Research Guide* (1975)—the press also targeted the academic disciplines, which were often depicted as craven boosters of the established order. In its first publication after a 1975 reorganization, Jesse Lemisch indicted his fellow U.S. historians in *On Active Service in War and Peace: Politics and Ideology in the American Historical Profession* (1975). The book came with an equally scathing introduction from Thomas Schofield that went after such Canadian historians as Donald Creighton, A.R.M. Lower, and Frank Underhill, figures in a profession that had blacklisted Stanley Ryerson for his dissident views while staunchly maintaining its own freedom from all ideology.[75]

An edition of Mickey and John Rowntree's popular pamphlet published by Toronto Women's Liberation and Hogtown Press, 1974.

As a feature in *The Varsity* explained in 1975, New Hogtown, although winning markets for its books among scholars and non-scholars alike, cherished the same activist goals that had originally inspired its founders. Still, its tactics had changed: "The large, activist movement of the sixties relied on confrontation and mass pressure, while the socialists of the seventies have had to retrench and devote themselves to laying the groundwork, through education, for another upsurge sometime in the future." It was a diagnosis of the "long march," whose gist was fully captured by the article's caption: "New radicalism is cuddly and loveable, unlike 60's version."[76]

A new leftist rejoinder might well have been that the new radicalism had successfully escaped from its predecessors' conceptual and social narrowness—as it increasingly addressed issues of interest to a far larger public and began to consolidate itself as a powerful tendency in Canadian scholarship. In this respect, New Hogtown was hardly alone. The Maoist NC Press brought out popularizations of Canadian history and was also especially hospitable to the writings of Black leftists. Between the Lines Press, a collective project jointly founded in 1977 by DEC in Toronto and Dumont Press Graphix, a typesetting and design collective in Kitchener, would make its way in the following decade by publishing such accessible but analytical titles as *Getting Doctored: Critical Reflections on Becoming a Physician* (1979) and *Acid Rain: The Silent Crisis* (1980). The books *Getting Started on Social Analysis in Canada* (1984) and *Case Critical: The Dilemma of Social Work in Canada* (1987) became favoured texts in sociology and social work courses across the country. The existence of the parent group, DEC, had apparently been sufficient to alarm the RCMP. A surveillance report, filed shortly before the press was launched, warned that many of its founders were "highly-political individuals who are predominantly Marxist." Toronto also had some collectively run layout and printing shops for activists who wanted to produce lighter materials such as posters and magazines; places where, as an advertisement for Muskox Press put it, "Progressives Gain Control of the Means of Production."[77]

Women-centred publishing houses contributed to the movement's visibility. The Women's Press, although sometimes accused of liberalism by other leftists and of Marxism by mainstream feminists, was unabashedly committed to a socialist restructuring of society. Operating at first on a LIP grant, the press featured eight paid employees, and in the beginning had no hierarchy: everyone helped on all facets of the work. Gradually it implemented a division of labour. By 1976 the Women's Press proudly reported that its sales were doubling every year. By the early 2000s the Women's Press and Between the Lines had each published over 150 books.[78]

Activists also poured their energy into creating progressive books for children, and by the mid-1970s the Women's Press could boast of its extensive selection of non-sexist children's books. Kids Can Press, established in 1973, was another collective committed to publishing books in which girls took on non-traditional roles. Like the Women's Press, this OFY and LIP-funded publisher tried to increase the racial diversity of the children it depicted. Some privately owned children's publishers, such as Groundwood Books, were also at first viewed as political projects by their leftist founders. All of these publishers featured stories that took place in local or Canadian settings. In a stark departure from the rareified environments of most mainstream children's books, some of the content was situated in working-class neighbourhoods and apartment buildings.[79]

Although new leftists were often organically tied to academic institutions, they had a truly conflicted relationship with them. The long march through those institutions meant, then, a radical rethinking of that site—and a drive to build a revolutionary counterpart.

* * *

Despite its manifold achievements, Toronto's new left cultural revolution had its limitations. As many left scholars were only too aware—especially those teaching in the new field of communications studies—the media in which the left flourished were not generally the media influencing the masses. While the spike in left-wing magazines and newspapers was remarkable, it was television that heralded the media future. It was an expensive medium, dominated by well-funded corporate and state networks by no means friendly to the new left's agenda (even though, at times, willing to publicize its more dramatic happenings). It was typical of Toronto in the 1970s, though, that left activists struggled energetically and with some success to carve out liberated spaces even in a televisual sphere that exemplified to perfection the "cultural industries" denounced by the likes of Herbert Marcuse. They were fortunate that the high point of their movement coincided with the transformation of cable televison from fringe entertainment to mass phenomenon.

Toronto cable subscribers, numbering a mere 17,000 in 1968, had jumped to 85,000 by 1969, and a quarter of all Toronto residents were plugged into cable by the end of 1970. Some said Toronto had more cable subscribers than anywhere else in North America. Enthusiasts foresaw a future in which people would be able to shop on TV through electronic catalogues and take university courses without leaving their homes.[80]

"The wired city is going to transform our society," proclaimed Stanley Burke, a member of the Intercommunity Television Organization. Popularly known as Intercom, this new group was committed to nationalizing the cable companies and vesting control over them in local areas. As an interim step, members focused on exploiting a new Canadian Radio-television and Telecommunications Commission (CRTC) regulation that, as of 1971, forced cable companies to provide a channel devoted to community programs.[81] Recognizing that the immediate prospects of a publicly owned cable system were slight, Intercom sought to decouple programming from private ownership and place it under community control. The group's thirteen-page manifesto outlined how communities would control all creative and technical aspects of these programs, for which Intercom would act as a quasi-union. Rather like new leftists in education, the cable activists imagined that television might be transformed into a cultural phenomenon that was democratically controlled—or, in Burke's words, "television by the people, rather than merely for the people."[82]

The cable companies proved predictably reluctant to endorse such communitarian leftism. After indicating a willingness to consider Intercom's proposal for decentralized programming, they then backtracked. A meeting called by Metro-area cable operators to hammer out a united response decided to create the Greater Toronto Cable Association to counter the efforts of the upstart group.[83] The Association quickly found an ally in Liberal MPP George Ben, who warned that activists were about to "charge into our livingrooms through our TV sets and take over." At least a dozen newspapers printed his allegations about a large-scale, radical infiltration of cable, and the cable companies themselves echoed his thoughts in a blood-chilling declaration:

> There is a new danger to everybody's political freedom. It is caused by the use of community cable television by groups who set themselves up arbitrarily as "citizens" or "community" groups but who have no real mandate from the communities concerned.... Responsible people must act immediately to stop this proliferation of access by those who have nothing to say but "Let us disturb and disrupt the status quo."[84]

Meanwhile, those intent on shaking up that status quo sprang into action. Intercom had announced its own plans to directly produce television programs, which included a late-night talk show with John Sewell as host, a weekly news broadcast, televised town halls, and teach-ins. They aimed to produce eight hours of television a day by the following year. (Two cable companies signed up for the news broadcast; none wanted an uncensored live talk show.)[85] When interest in television production threatened to overwhelm Intercom, members created a complementary organization, Downtown Community Television (DCT), to handle the programming side of things. Around thirty community representatives and at-large members formed the core of DCT, which boasted of making all decisions at public meetings and having no bureaucratic structures. A photo taken of the DCT committee shortly after its inception, showing an equal number of men and women who were both older and less white than the average new left-tinged group, suggests that the group had made an effort to represent the downtown.[86]

DCT's first on-air program in 1971 featured representatives from the Duke of York Mothers group, Park School Community Council, and Black activist Vera Cudjoe. "It's not just a straight talk show," suggested DCT co-ordinator Bruce Arnold. "A community documentary would be a better word."[87] When not bringing community agitators to its studio, DCT had its television crews go outside to conduct interviews and record many of the seminal activist events of the early 1970s. A dispute between renters, landlords, and police on Bleecker Street, which mainstream TV stations had to film outside the rental homes, was captured by DCT cameras *inside* the dwellings themselves. Wayne King of DCT expounded the far-reaching significance of this pattern: while the mainstream media might fall for landlords' claims that the houses were unfit for habitation, his camera crew was there to "show the community that the Bleecker and Ontario Streets houses were fit to be lived in—contrary to the landlord's claims. We could give the happening more time and show the community why the tenants are so angry." For King and his comrades, televisual objectivity was a chimera, especially when touted by commercial television stations. As one mainstream scribe put it, from the DCT perspective, a program should present "openly and blatantly, strong, one-sided points of view." Indeed, one member of DCT, who criticized the group for never airing the landlords' side of the story, complained that his plea for objectivity had been drowned out by laughter.[88]

In this highly politicized context, the lowly Portapak attained a status analogous to that of the cellphone today: as a device that could record bottom-up representations of top-down impositions. Community television activists preferred the Portapak because it was small, inexpensive, easy to operate, and mobile. Those keen to limit its use brought up questions of production quality and professionalism. Cable companies had technical reasons to prefer other video cameras, and used arguments about quality to push community groups to stay inside the studio and leave the technical aspects of production to "experts."[89]

True to Toronto form, this new left experiment received money from both LIP and OFY. It also aroused substantial interest and support from its supposed old left adversaries. Organized labour signed on to its vision of public ownership and community control of cable television. The Metro Labour Council and Ontario Federation of Labour both funded and sponsored Intercom workshops in television production. As many as one hundred people attended DCT meetings, drawn from organizations as diverse as the Earlscourt community project and the Union of Ontario Indians.[90]

Other members of DCT sought to go beyond content and radicalize how television was made. Some even said that they were not concerned about visual quality. It was more important, they argued, to guard against any "creeping professionalism" that would hide their message under layers of slick programming. Like many of the NFB's Challenge for Change filmmakers, DCT's Bruce Lawson thought that "the process which we go through is more important than the program. . . . The whole idea is to create community."[91]

A host of other examples of cable-centred activism came into being, although DCT was probably the largest of such ventures. A subset of community television was hyper-local, broadcasting only to a collection of large apartment complexes through closed-circuit systems from small television studios located in the High Park, St. James Town, and Thorncliffe Park areas. A small number of groups, such as the Thorncliffe Park Community Organization's television committee, produced television for and by tenants, with the Portapak their only camera. While the size of their potential audience was clearly a constraint, they had the libertarian advantage of not having to conform to broadcasting regulations until cable companies, complaining that closed-circuit TV was "unfair competition," convinced the CRTC to shut them down.[92]

DCT and other groups regularly clashed with the new CITY-TV station over control of community programming. They complained that CITY prevented them from editing their own programs, and never allowed them to go live on-air, and they alleged that community content was only being broadcast as an inexpensive means to meet Canadian content regulations. In frustration, about twenty community groups, including DCT, formed a "common front," Metro Community Media (MCM), to try to get a community-run studio.[93] But Intercom and MCM both failed when the cable companies and broadcasting stations refused to work through them, forcing their supporters to work directly with the companies to get their programs on-air. It was a sign that the dream of community-controlled TV as a fulfillment of a holistic cultural revolution was fragile in a society and city that still moved to the rhythms of the capitalist market.

* * *

The left's limited success in penetrating mass culture in Toronto revealed how sturdy were the cultural earthworks and trenches that made up the front lines of capitalism. The left launched an impressive series of raids on those trenches, and in spheres relatively autonomous from the market it achieved lasting victories. If time-travellers from the future were seized with the ambition of visiting a Canadian city in which they could find thousands of new leftists organized in scores of institutions, ranging from humble co-ops to revolutionary art galleries to independent Marxist journals to daycares, they could hardly do better than drop into Toronto in the 1970s. It was a place where people could live much of their lives surrounded, much of the time, by fellow leftists. Of course, the unceasing sense of crisis that seized so many leftists—who believed both that a new world was possible and that time was running out to achieve it—could be exhausting. In the feverish atmosphere of cultural hope and despair, many harsh words were spoken and destructive impulses indulged. Video artist Susan Britton, once determined to align her art with her Maoism, became disillusioned and produced such works as *Me$$age to China* (1979), which juxtaposed the slogans "the working class must organize itself" and "magnum ale is a new taste experience" in a couplet that suggested both their equivalent meaninglessness and China's rapid devolution as a site of socialist hope.[94]

The work of cultural revolutionaries in Toronto reveals the manifold scales upon which new leftists worked. First of all, for many of them Toronto was a generic site of modernity, indistinguishable in essence from New York, London, or Los Angeles: General Idea's situationism critiqued a global society of the spectacle, and CEAC's transnational imagery of the class struggle was not about specific issues unfolding in its neighbourhood but about the universal mission of a worldwide proletariat. Toronto was just one node, perhaps not an especially significant node, in a vast network of sites of capitalist production and consumption.

For others—cultural nationalists—Toronto, the location of so many publishers, broadcasters, and galleries, encapsulated Canada as a whole: a country whose character and destiny they had discovered and which they aspired to influence. Their Toronto was Canada, although as they launched themselves into that complicated place, their Toronto-centred perspectives roused resistance and were often transformed as a result.

A third tendency, evident in 15 Dance Lab and Theatre Passe Muraille, many of the alternative presses, and the Portapak-wielding radical broadcasters, sought to fuse these imagined Torontos in new forms of cultural praxis. The new left's sheer heterogeneity and diffuseness, the scales from the very local to the universal upon which the cultural revolutionaries worked, although in some respects a sign of their strengths, also made it difficult for them to share a unifying narrative with activists working in different spheres and on different scales. Many of their most striking innovations and achievements have not been remembered by succeeding cohorts of radicals. And with the rise and strengthening of identity leftism, many new leftists came to distrust any such unifying narrative.

Yet, from a twenty-first-century perspective, the new left achievements in 1970s Toronto were staggeringly impressive. To an extent only dreamt of in the 1960s, whole cultural spheres vibrated to the rhythm of left-wing images, ideas, and debates. Large and successful left-wing institutions in theatre and art and a sizable network of left-wing university intellectuals emerged over one short decade. The Toronto school system became a bastion of progressivism—and would remain so. Contrary to theses positing decline and nostalgia-fuelled elegies, many of the gains of this war of position were long-lasting. Even after the long decades of neo-liberalism that ensued after the 1980s, the achievements of Toronto's new left culture are discernible today, a permanent legacy from which future leftists should draw inspiration and lessons. The revolution did not succeed in overthrowing the system—such was never probable in one North American city—but, with surprising effectiveness, its partisans did create a striking first draft of the post-capitalist and emancipated cultural life that might well follow.

9

Subaltern Identities, Universal Truths, Transnational Complexities: The Rise of Identity-Based Resistance, 1971–78

THE BLACK rock band Crack of Dawn cranked up their amplifiers. The band was trying to drown out a member of the Western Guard who had seized a microphone and was fulminating about a Black takeover of his country. A crowd of about thirty white supremacists, many wearing brown shirts, swastika armbands, and false mustaches, went wild. They shouted "white power," gave Nazi salutes, threw bananas, and then took the stage, striking one of the musicians with a metal pipe. The band's nine-year-old singer was slapped in the face and the child's white aunt was kicked in the stomach. They said she was a "nigger-lover." A police constable, there to prevent potential disturbances, stood aloof and refused to intervene. It all happened live on CITY-TV.[1]

That was in June 1974. Leftists and people of colour had been long complaining that the police were allowing the Western Guard to get away scot-free. The group had committed dozens of brazen attacks in the daylight and spread terror with their bullets and Molotov cocktails at night. But outside of a few publications, including *Contrast*, the news media tended to treat the Guard as a trivial curiosity. After extended complaints about the CITY-TV invasion, the police did make a few arrests, but a judge determined that the identities of the attackers could not be confirmed beyond a reasonable doubt. When a member of Crack of Dawn and another Black musician were shot and injured a half-year later, speculation arose about the unknown gunman being motivated by racism. But the press quickly lost interest.[2]

In May 1975, fifteen-year-old Michael Habbib was walking across the parking lot at the huge Fairview Mall, in the city's northeast. He was on the way to his part-time job. A person unknown to him fired two bullets directly into his face, killing him instantly. A witness jotted down the shooter's licence plate, and a man named George Ryan was quickly apprehended. Ryan's father, described as a "company president," told reporters that his son had become obsessed with immigration and had spoken of an impending race war. Trial reportage depicted Ryan's racism as intensely personal—as being fired by the idea that young Black men were his romantic rivals. At the trial's conclusion Ryan was found not guilty by reason of insanity.[3]

Yet Habbib's shooting can hardly be understood as the work of an unhinged individual. In a larger sense, white supremacy was the culprit: racist views were increasingly being expressed openly in the mid-1970s. Some of the language that Ryan used was clearly reminiscent of Western Guard circulars; Ryan did confess to shooting the two musicians. *Contrast* was the only newspaper to link those shootings with the CITY-TV incident in the wake of Habbib's death. That they were random victims, as Ryan maintained, seems unlikely.[4]

After Habbib's death and the CITY-TV attack, *The Toronto Sun* depicted what it called the extreme right and the extreme left as equivalents, although, in the tabloid's usual fashion, it simultaneously argued that leftists and Black militants were more dangerous (and more racist).[5] *The Globe and Mail*, more subtly, dipped into similar waters. A feature article musing about race relations after Habbib's death claimed that only members of the white "Marxist fringe" and Black "zealots" demonstrated against racism. Journalists were covering up misdeeds by Black militants for fear of being called racist, it alleged, and this biased reporting had to stop:

> To take a random example from dozens at hand, there is a group called Black Theatre Canada, which produces plays by blacks acted by blacks and aimed at blacks. It raises not a peep from civil rights activists. Why not? Can you see a White Theatre Canada? And yet "black" theatre is covered by the drama critics of the papers and not by reporters with a bent for social pathologies. Why is this?[6]

After a *Globe* editorial used Rosie Douglas's reaction to the shooting as an additional reason to deport him, the Ontario Regional Director of Oxfam-Canada (one of many organizations to have their meetings attacked by the Guard) called the paper on it: "Rosie threatens that blacks in Toronto will defend themselves against racist attacks and warns white tourists that Caribbeans are aware of the attacks on their sisters and brothers here. With your 'in return,' you equate self-defence and warning with the racist murder of Michael Habbib."[7]

With stories like these, then, in the 1970s the new left was being transformed—from an almost wholly white movement to one encompassing a host of activists intent on contesting the city's and country's racial order. It was also being altered by the ever-growing presence of a women's movement and a strong gay and lesbian presence—both of them more and more distinct from the new left but continuing to champion its underlying precepts. By 1978 no one could describe Toronto leftism as a unified movement; nor, because leftists occupied so large a place in movements demanding new rights and recognition for subaltern identities, could it be described as inconsequential.

* * *

Mayor William Dennison's Toronto—in which the Orange Order wielded substantial political power, churches overflowed on otherwise quiet Sundays, and the "Belfast of North America" exuded a palpable British atmosphere—was fast fading in the closing years of his mayoralty. One Black activist newspaper recalled that, over the space of a few years in the 1970s, one high school went from 15 per cent to 40 per cent Black, prompting an outpouring of programs, liaison committees, and sensitivity-training exercises on the part of the educational system—and ultimately sustaining pro-Black activism among students and parents.[8]

Conversely, other groups historically associated with the left experienced a decline. These groups included Toronto's Jews, once the mainstay of both the social-democratic and communist left. As left-wing playwright and commentator Rick Salutin observed, a Jewish middle class bound for suburban prosperity was likely to produce a different consciousness than had its working-class predecessor.[9] Jews also became divided among themselves on the question of the State of Israel, once the darling of much of the left. Israel's treatment of the Palestinians gradually became an issue of central concern for many Toronto leftists. Although the new left boasted many Jewish supporters, members of the old left United Jewish People's Order complained that younger radicals were failing to embrace their Jewishness as an important political, or even personal, identifier.[10]

Black activism reflected some of the most dramatic indications of change on the left. Much of the existing literature dwells upon Toronto's response to the civil rights struggles in the U.S. South, with the implication that Toronto's patterns were simple spillovers from the experiences of U.S. cities. Although movements such as Student Nonviolent Coordinating Committee and the Black Panthers had enthusiasts in Toronto, and a recurrent trope in Black new leftism equated Canada with Alabama, "continental" readings risk missing what was more fundamentally transnational about Toronto's Black new leftists—the extent to which, like their counterparts in Montreal, many of them were intensively studying movements for decolonization and taking their cues from Third World leaders—and also risk overlooking how much Toronto's Black new leftism arose in response to homegrown racism, which by the mid-1970s was perceived to have reached crisis proportions.[11]

Was Toronto a racist city? One common knee-jerk response was denial, certainly in comparison, it was said, to analogous centres in the United States. Yet much commentary and reportage confirmed the charge. In the 1970s a front-page *Toronto Star* article shocked readers by reprinting, verbatim, racial slurs coming from the mouths of ordinary citizens. One housewife declared, "Everyone I know is against Pakistanis." Hundreds of people flocked to a demonstration to denounce the *Star*'s article. Mahmood Khan, chairman of the Pakistani Canadian Association, defiantly proclaimed, "We're not here to be grateful to anyone." Referring to calls for assimilation, he asked if the people making this demand wanted their boys to be hooligans and drug addicts. The *Star*'s managing editor defended the article, saying the comments were necessary to show that racism appeared to be growing in the city. The paper, he said, in no way endorsed those views.[12]

Moreover, there was no denying the prominence of far-right racist groups in Toronto. The Western Guard's founder Don Andrews was sentenced in 1975 to two years in jail for plotting arson and for possession of weapons and explosives. The Black community experienced weekly attacks from the Guard, which for its part warned of a creeping black majority in Canada. Black businesses, social organizations and homes were barraged with white power graffiti, arson, and bullets. Although viewed as irrelevant extremists by the mainstream press, the Western Guard was not regarded so casually by those upon whom they inflicted violence. For Bromley Armstrong, recently appointed to the Human Rights Commission, such groups had made Toronto "the North American capital for racism."[13]

Western Guard right-wing violence fed upon the uncertainties induced by the 1975 release of a federal Green Paper on immigration. This paper ostensibly welcomed ethnic and racial diversity, but emphasized the recruiting of immigrants who would match the needs of Canada's capitalist economy. It also implied that the state might require immigrants to settle in remote, underpopulated areas. Robert Andras, the minister responsible, conceded that the Green Paper had fed racial animosities, even as he pointed the finger at anti-racist groups for inflaming the discussion.[14] Certainly the Toronto hearings into the proposed Green Paper showcased the city's racial tensions. On the first day of the hearing, about four hundred people stood outside protesting the process, chanting "Deport Andras and Trudeau, all the racists got to go." Within the hearings, John Zimmerman of the Inter-Church Committee on Chile denounced discrimination against unionists, socialists, and communists. Steve Moore of the Committee to Oppose the Green Paper called for supporters of the Western Guard and others on the extreme right to be banned from entering the country. When, on the last day, the Western Guard was scheduled to present its brief, about fifty demonstrators stood up, shook their fists, and chanted "Fascists have no right to speak." They effectively drowned out the Guard's presentation.[15]

Police who responded to racist attacks were not, it seemed, particularly sympathetic. When suspected members of the Western Guard fired bullets through his bookstore window, Leonard Johnson called the police, only to be told, "There are a lot more of you people here now taking white people's jobs so you have to expect some trouble." This attitude meshed with the Western Guard's campaign for white jobs, which entailed sending one dollar to numerous members of the Black community accompanied by notes telling them that it was their last chance to leave Canada.[16] One CTV poll suggested that 70 per cent of Canadians wanted a return to a more discriminatory immigration system. Only one of ten white Torontonians interviewed by the *Star* declared for racial harmony. Some spoke of the sudden efflorescence of anti-Pakistani jokes. When a Jamaican diplomat criticized the Toronto police for their inaction in a string of racist assaults, he was lauded by many in the Black community. The Canadian government expressed its displeasure at what they saw as a violation of protocol, and the diplomat was forced to return to Jamaica. Before he left the country, someone sent him a stick of dynamite in the mail. Surveying the scene in 1975, one downtown detective sergeant prophesied, "There's real bad race trouble in Toronto. It's going to be a bad, bad summer."[17]

Although the news media acknowledged the existence of racism in Toronto, comparisons with the United States tended to trivialize local problems. In late 1975 NBC aired a documentary on race relations in Toronto that labelled the city "a racial time bomb." CBC ran a rebuttal called *The Many Faces of Black* (1977). That program's producer said that she did not want to look at problems faced by the Black community, but could not resist contrasting race relations in Toronto with the United States. All of the Black men and women shown in the documentary, when asked about their most pressing problem, said "The weather."[18]

Not all Black Torontonians shared that sanguine outlook. Black new left organizations proliferated from 1971 to 1978.[19] Black activists, who had long complained about the near invisibility of their community on Canadian television, created shows such as *Statements in Black* and *Black Focus* on cable TV.[20] Black student unions could be found on the city's college and university campuses—and were frequently in the news for their activism and the victimization of their members.[21] The Black Students Union of Ontario sought to give them a province-wide presence. The celebration of African Liberation Day on May 25, technically to honour the formation of the Organization of African

Waiting for the 1975 African Liberation Day march to get underway.

Fireweed 16, 1983.

Unity, was a moment in which a multitude of Black groups in Toronto, alongside leftists from official parties, could signal their presence and make claims to representativeness. By 1972 the Black Educational Project boasted both full-time and part-time staff people, a steering committee, and a new policy of accepting government money in its quest to challenge racism in the schools. In that same year over one thousand people attended the first African Liberation Day demonstration, which echoed to such slogans as: "What time is it? . . . Nation time!" and "What are we? . . . Africans!" As many people again came out in 1975 to protest against the murder of Michael Habbib.[22]

The Toronto chapter of the African Liberation Support Committee (ALSC) was in the early 1970s a significant player in Black politics across the continent, with Rosie Douglas occupying a position on its executive. It subsequently became a venue for strenuous fighting among sectarian groups. A pattern across this heterogeneous and complicated web of Black institutions was a growing interest in combining traditional socialist thought with the new insights of Frantz Fanon, Malcolm X, and Eldridge Cleaver. Although, as BEP's adoption of more formalized structures suggested, such Black organizations were gradually becoming more mainstream and bureaucratic, there is no denying the overwhelmingly new left atmosphere of virtually all of them. This tendency was particularly evident in *Caribbean Dialogue* magazine, which was published by Toronto's New Beginning Movement in collaboration with the U.K.-based *Race Today* collective. It was a transnational new leftism—one shaped by many recent immigrants from the West Indies in particular, in which such radical figures as Cheddi Jagan and Walter Rodney of Guyana and Michael Manley of Jamaica were connected to Toronto by many threads and respected by many people who were not drawn from these particular countries.

The Re-United African Peoples (RAP), a black coalition of Toronto high-school students, provides an excellent example of Black new leftism. Initiated in 1974 at the Harriet Tubman Centre in west-central Toronto, by February 1975 RAP had some two hundred members and was said to be active in nineteen schools, among other things pressing the case for a recognition of Black history.[23] In his recollections, Antiguan immigrant Clifton Joseph remembered RAP's inspirational presence at his high school, Bloor Collegiate, where the group attracted seventeen people who wanted to party and read Black history and political studies (including works by Rodney—especially his *How Europe Underdeveloped Africa* [1972]—C.L.R. James, Angela Davis, and the Black Panthers). They produced plays and even organized a track club. "Malcolm X called for a 'revolution of the mind' and Parliament Funkadelic sang 'Free your mind and your ass will follow,' and we listened to them both in a defiant mix of party & politics," Joseph said. It was an "ecstatic" time with an "electric" atmosphere. It was also a time of tense confrontations with the Toronto District School Board, which, in the eyes of some left critics, attempted to substitute a bland multiculturalism for a principled stand against racism.[24] For Joseph, the novel *To Kill a Mockingbird*, required reading in his high school, epitomized the problems that Black students confronted: "We didn't want to read [that] shit because we weren't reading anything positive about Black folks so we definitely didn't want to see them shucking & jiving, minstrelling, and all of that." Journalist-playwright-poet Lennox Brown, who lived in Toronto around that time, described the Black Students Union of Ontario and the Black Youth Organization: "Their racial pride and sense of community service have put the older selfish generation to shame," and "They are in fact the only genuine hope for a Black culture in Canada."[25]

Equally symptomatic of the time was the March 1971 conference held to "Fight Racism" in Canada and the ensuing Committee Against Racism (CAR), headed by Charles Roach, who came to be known across the city as a Black intellectual and activist. CAR, linked to the Canadian Party of Labour, held demonstrations against racist groups and discriminatory immigration laws, which Roach considered to be heavily implicated in racism; it also stood up for Jamaican domestic workers, women who were being threatened with deportation because to gain acceptance into the domestic worker program they had found it necessary to lie to authorities about not having children.[26] In addition to such pragmatic aims and concrete attachments, CAR's overall argument was that for racism to be ended, capitalism itself must be overturned. Such a movement could not be based on Blacks alone: CAR made anti-Asian discrimination part of its mandate. In 1975 it supported a demonstration in Chinatown, disrupted the meeting of the governing council at the University of Toronto, and fought the expulsion of one student from the medical school—a symptom in its eyes of the faculty's entrenched anti-Chinese racism.[27] Members of Students for a Democratic Society at the University of Toronto, also linked to the CPL, electrified the campus in 1974 with their struggle to prevent a professor they considered racist from speaking.[28] In the 1970s the issue of anti-racism became an all-pervasive theme in the Toronto Left, in part because it offered a way for various racialized minorities to make common cause against the Canadian state. The Revolutionary Marxist Group (RMG), one of Toronto's leading Trotskyist organizations, took the anti-racism struggle so seriously that it produced an *Anti-Racist Work National Circular*. Its internal documents provide rich insights into the extent to which various Marxist groups were involved in the movement, as well as penetratingly self-critical comments about the Marxist tradition's historic neglect of the "Race Question."[29]

Many activists lived and breathed in a Black community, still somewhat centred on a "Black belt" bounded by Queen Street West, Ossington Avenue, Bloor Street, and Huron Street, which was seething with ideas. So worrying to some was the sight of Black youths at the Bathurst subway station that the Black Youth Organization was able to use this concern as a pretext for a state-funded Black community centre.[30] *Black Voice, Spear*, and *Contrast* claimed many readers—as many as 30,000 in the case of *Contrast*—and, together with ample coverage of race issues in the daily press, contributed to the atmosphere of both fear and hope. It is a movement that is often underplayed in accounts of Canada's 1960s and 1970s, because the Black new left in Toronto generally eschewed Black Panther romanticism, frequently adopted united front organizing and alliances with more mainstream organizations, and was not tied in any way to SUPA or groups like the New Left Caucus. Yet Toronto's Black new left attained an influence within its core constituency that outrivalled anything attained by white new leftists, and it did so by linking transnational anti-racist thought with on-the-ground conditions. The spectre of racial unrest on the U.S. model caught many a Torontonian's attention: one riot in the United States had accomplished more for human rights than "one hundred years of academic surveys" and the academics' "forests of footnotes," Lennox Brown provocatively argued in 1972.[31] Yet in the relative absence of such riots, Toronto Black new leftists were able to challenge the systems oppressing them with more efficacy than shown by many of their American cousins.

Some of that success can be attributed to talented leaders. Horace Campbell, who had immigrated from Jamaica to Canada in the mid-1960s, wrote analyses of the racism inherent in Canadian immigration legislation and of the contradictions of the emergent "war on drugs," which he thought was characterized by strategies "typical of the liberal bourgeoisie," such as supervised heroin use, and which avoided, for instance, systemic attacks on unemployment and youthful alienation.[32] Campbell was credited with the formation of the Black People's Movement at York University and, as a graduate student at the University of Toronto, with the formation of a Black Students' Union and the Transitional Year Program. He was almost certainly amongst the small number of radicals who had private meetings with Angela Davis and other celebrated U.S. Black power figures during their visits to the city. At the decade's mid-point, Campbell was involved in several radical Black milieus, ranging from Pan-Africanist and vanguard groups to the Rastafarian Tacky Study Group.[33]

Rosie Douglas was another prominent figure. In speeches about the Caribbean and his native Dominica, he developed a "stagist" interpretation, in which the unity of all patriotic and democratic forces would achieve national liberation, seen as the crucial antecedent to economic liberation. A particular inspiration for Douglas was Amilcar Cabral of Guinea-Bissau, who was considered, along with Fidel Castro, a revolutionary who had combined grassroots nationalism with rigorous Marxist theory.[34] In a speech called "Racism in Canada" delivered to the "Vanguard Forum" in February 1975, Douglas told his mostly white audience that since Canada was founded on racism, progressives needed to make overturning it a priority; and they needed to understand that Canada was no mere "junior partner" to imperialism, but, in the Caribbean and elsewhere, an imperialist power in its own right. For Douglas, anti-racism in Toronto was no mere local issue; rather, it was one node in a transnational pattern of revolutionary resistance:

> My friends, you have a great responsibility. And that responsibility has to be tackled very seriously, very determinedly. We are doing our part in the Black community. But the problem of racism is embedded in the minds of white workers and it is your responsibility to help eradicate it. It is your responsibility to explain to them, and not in any half-hearted way, what racism is; what apartheid in South Africa is all about; what Zionism is all about—to explain that to be anti-Israel doesn't mean to be against the Jewish people. And as soon as people can begin to understand these things, I think the basis will be there for world revolution.[35]

For Douglas and his circle, a "narrow" nationalism—one taking race to be the fundamental factor—would lead to incorrect theory and reactionary practice.

Common struggle with whites was now obligatory. In 1975, still under threat of deportation because of his activities in the Sir George Williams computer centre episode, Douglas went across Canada setting up local "Alliances Against Racism and Political Repression," and large numbers of whites could be found marching under the banner of the "Ad Hoc Committee Against the Deportations." One evaluation from within the Revolutionary Marxist Group saw Douglas's anti-racism campaign as being hobbled by the activities of rival anti-racists in the vanguard parties: neither the Communist Party of Canada (Marxist-Leninist) nor the Canadian Party of Labour was willing to support his movement; and at one demonstration a Douglas supporter was physically forced to stop carrying a placard raised in his leader's defence.[36] A shrewd critic of the contradictions entailed in radical groups accepting government funding, Douglas was also emphatically new leftist in his demand for a movement developed, as Fanon had urged, from the bottom-up, building co-operative institutions, and developing its own infrastructure of food and clothing stores and housing co-ops, all first steps to the making of the revolution.[37] In December 1975 he presided over a "Four Days Against Racism" conference, which featured talks from Tariq Ali, Madeleine Parent of the Confederation of Canadian Unions, Waffler (and athlete) Bruce Kidd, and representatives from the Ojibway nation.[38]

Douglas was acutely aware of the dangers of the Black new left retreating to the defence of a narrowly construed Black culture. If that happened, the movement could not mount the hegemonic revolutionary challenge to capitalism of which he dreamed. If a core element of the Black new left in Toronto was the assertion of Black pride, another was the quest for a united front with other racialized minorities. In 1975 the founding meetings of the East Indian Defence Committee, partly in response to the racist violence of the Western Guard, echoed with Black Panther–like speeches favouring armed self-defence: "If we are attacked with words, we will fight with words. If we are attacked with fists we will fight back with fists and if we are attacked with guns, we will fight back with guns."[39] A dozen Black power activists were present at the founding of the East Indian Defence Committee, while the organization itself testified to its transnational radicalism by making a generous donation to a representative of the progressive forces in Zimbabwe. Subsequent meetings of the group drew as many as four hundred people.[40]

One of the local Black movement's staunchest Aboriginal allies was Vern Harper, a member of the Toronto Warrior Society (TWS), which was affiliated with the American Indian Movement (AIM). Harper was a regular speaker at the city's annual African Liberation Day celebrations, anti-racism rallies, and even Rock Against Racism concerts, where he evoked the need for unity amongst racial minorities and collaboration with white progressives. For much of the

1970s he was a Marxist-Leninist; as a participant in the 1974 Native Peoples Caravan to Ottawa he was regularly seen with a Mao button attached to his leather jacket.[41]

Estimations of the TWS membership vary enormously, from twenty active members to two hundred formal members. At mid-decade the organization, like Harper, appeared to be strongly oriented to the global communist movement. Many of the articles in its *Native Peoples Struggle* newspaper were emphatically anti-capitalist and internationalist, indicating, as Red Power scholar Scott Rutherford observes, both the pan-indigenous and firmly global perspectives held by these activists. Local members of AIM worked in solidarity with Indigenous peoples in other parts of Ontario and organized demonstrations in support of noted U.S. militant Leonard Peltier.[42] In late 1976 they carried out a five-day occupation of an office in the Royal Ontario Museum, demanding the immediate repatriation of a body recently dug up by a museum archaeologist near Grimsby, Ont. Although AIM had not been the first Indigenous organization to press for the protection of burial sites, it was undoubtedly because of that occupation that the Ontario government proceeded with new legislation governing archaelogical excavations. In an attempt to "put the shoe on the other foot," some of the occupiers later made headlines by threatening to dig up the bones of Sir John A. Macdonald.[43]

If Harper remained a Marxist-Leninist at the end of the decade, his socialism was by no means imported holus bolus from China or any of the new Leninist groups. In reflecting on his participation in the 1974 Native Peoples Caravan to Ottawa, in advocating for a distinct Indigenous socialism he made observations typical of a Black new leftist. He wrote about the important role of consciousness-raising in breaking down white conditioning, building up Native pride, and mitigating tribal differences. He strongly approved of braiding hair and other physical manifestations of a renewed Indigenous identity. He reflected on long discussions about what, exactly, was the "Native way." And—perhaps because he was writing at the end of the decade—he also referred to caravan participants grappling with gay and women's issues. Harper believed that Native people themselves would have to define the kind of socialism they would follow, suggesting that culture, environmentalism, spirituality, and transnationalism would be important elements.[44]

In addition to the hegemonic challenge of creating a formidable united front of racialized minorities, Black new leftists also wrestled with the question of forming alliances with whites. By the end of 1974 a certain momentum had begun to move towards white inclusion. It probably started when the Black African Liberation Solidarity Committee sat down with the largely white Toronto Committee for the Liberation of Portugal's African Colonies (TCLPAC) and decided to co-operate on a number of ventures. In founding the Black Workers

Alliance, Douglas in some respects situated the Black community as still within stage one of Amiri Baraka's process for revolution. As he put it, "The Black worker must first reach a position of strength so that he can deal on equal footing with the white worker." But the stages had become less rigid. Although Black cultural and political mobilization remained paramount, there was a feeling that this process could coincide with working with white-dominated organizations. Once again the Revolutionary Marxist Group's internal documents analyzed both the necessity and the difficulty of such bridge-building. Many Black organizations, it noted, had a deep-seated hostility to white left organizations and a preference for nationalist rather than Marxist formulations. When asked about this question, Walter Rodney remarked that he believed in no definitive rule; rather, alliances would develop according to the level of the struggle.[45] Alliance with the "white left" was easily imagined but difficult to realize—and that was especially so with the rise of new communist movements in the 1970s because many of them looked upon the insurgent anti-racist movements with possessive eyes. They were keen to monopolize the message, recruit its newly radicalized purveyors, and thwart the similar designs of rival vanguard groups.

The *Asianadian* magazine repeatedly aired the question of allying with whites to fight racism. Although a majority of its contributors were Chinese or Japanese, it also included members of the Filipino, Korean, Vietnamese, and South Asian communities. Reflecting its late 1970s start, the magazine immediately demonstrated an exceptional commitment to combating multiple oppressions in Canada. Numerous articles emphasized the interrelations of class exploitation, racialization, sexism, colonialism, and capitalism. The magazine strove to obtain gender parity in its collective and launched two issues dedicated specifically to women. The editors even devoted one issue to analyzing the gay Asian experience, highlighting how homophobia and racism operated in and outside Asian communities.[46]

From a distance it might seem that *Asianadian* could be placed comfortably within the left. After all, many of its collective members were influenced by Marxism.[47] Yet, in a manner not dissimilar to radical feminists and some gay liberationists—who by the late 1970s were discounting ties to the "male left" or the "straight left"—an article suggested that the "white" or "Anglo" left was an unsuitable partner for Asian activists:

> There will never be an alliance between the Left and the Asian community mainly because the Left is Anglo dominated. Because of this Anglo component, the racial question in the Left has been side-tracked to the back of the bus. . . . If a socialist order miraculously arrived, where would Asians, Blacks, and Natives be? It would be a socialism controlled by Anglos![48]

Protesters demanding justice for Albert Johnson.

Photographer: Carl Beveridge, *Centrefold*, October-November 1979, Thomas Fisher Rare Book Library.

The article's author allowed that Anglo "elites" were the prime purveyors of racism in Canada, but concluded that the white working class itself had been manipulated into becoming an arm of racism. Racism, he argued, had become an emotional facet of Anglo life that transcended all class lines. As to gay, feminist, or broader left movements, the author opined that they had little room for Asians because all three were dominated by Anglos and lacked awareness of racial oppression. Instead of involving themselves with these external movements, Asian activists would be far more productive organizing with their fellow Asians.[49]

At the same time, *Asianadian* acknowledged the need to influence more people than its immediate constituency. Members of the collective joined a powerful campaign against the CTV news show *W5*, which had broadcasted a feature called "Campus Giveaway" that alleged how foreign Chinese students were taking university slots that would otherwise have gone to Canadians.[50] In addition to its scaremongering and inaccurate statistics, the program's principal deficiency was its equation of Asian Canadians and foreign students: as the camera panned over Asian students one young white woman complained that an influx of foreign students had precluded her own admission to the University of Toronto's pharmaceutical program.[51] Yet there were no *foreign* students in the program—a point stressed by around two thousand demonstrators converging on the television station. In his remarks to the gathering, Mayor Sewell tied the "campus giveaway" hoax to the recent police shooting of Black youth Albert Johnson. Such incidents revealed that both the media and police had to change if people of all races were to feel at home in Toronto. There followed yet another attempt to create an anti-racist umbrella group for all of Toronto.[52]

* * *

The second great identity-based movement to enter the sphere of the new left was the feminist movement. As historian Joan Sangster observes, the manifestations of the feminist movement of the 1960s and 1970s would come to be systematically misrepresented in much of the subsequent literature, in which an extraordinarily diverse and creative movement has been routinely castigated as white, middle-class, homophobic, ableist, and even racist.[53] Ironically, in promoting such a one-dimensional and hostile interpretation of what came to be called the second wave, its critics inadvertently silenced the thousands of non-white, non-middle-class, and non-racist feminists of the day, who in Toronto and elsewhere enriched the movement and influenced its debates.

Like the Black new left, the feminist new left—that is, people who placed women at the centre of a politics of national liberation, personal authenticity and self-determination, community empowerment, and participatory democracy—was a movement of movements. Much of the new feminist energy came from recent immigrants. Many had fled their countries of origin after being subjected to politically motivated violence and imprisonment. In Canada they often threw themselves into immigrant women's movements, sometimes via workplace unions, exiled political parties, or an organization like the Black Educational Project.[54] Some were experienced left-wing activists by the time they reached Canada; others first encountered left-wing ideas in Toronto. Very few such women developed their socialist-feminist consciousness in the U of T student movement, the prior women's liberation movement that arose from SUPA, or the Waffle, a condition that highlights the danger of centring on such phenomena as decisive keys to the left activism of the period.

At least as important as the organizations were the publications. In magazines such as *Velvet Fist*, *The Other Woman*, *Bellyful*, and *Breakthrough*, left feminists debated each other and plotted their movement's forward march. Some of these periodicals claimed large circulations, The York University–based *Breakthrough*, which received indispensable seed money from a student council led by leftists, claimed four thousand readers in 1975, reaching a larger audience than many a conventional left-wing paper.[55] *The Other Woman* was the feisty successor to the stodgier, if more intriguingly named, *Velvet Fist*, and distinguished itself by candidly facing up to the question of lesbianism.[56] It continued to agree with Marxists that society required a revolutionary overhaul; but in contrast to most other socialist publications it placed its emphasis not on the socialization of the means of production but on the transformation of social reproduction. The egalitarian redesign of that sphere was already implicit in women-directed groups.

Moreover, other publications associated with the left, such as *This Magazine Is About Schools*, *Our Generation*, and *Canadian Dimension*, showed signs of their slow permeation by feminist consciousness. Pamphlet after feminist pamphlet came out of Toronto, with some of them rapidly taken up by feminists in New York and Chicago, just as ideas emerging from circles in those U.S. cities would quickly spread to Toronto. Many feminists came to see themselves as authentic agents of revolution. They debated with comrades, and also with themselves, over whether the women's movement needed to learn from the Marxist tradition. Book-length treatments by Canadian feminists Charnie Guettel and Dorothy Smith presented different takes on that tradition, oriented to the Communist Party of Canada and to Maoism respectively and arriving at slightly different conclusions.[57] The questions explored in temperate language in their books were approached more combatively in countless conversations. Voices were raised and relationships foundered in the highly polemicized "Marx vs. Feminism" debates, and they are recalled without nostalgia by some as moments of personal distress and even anguish.

Many of Toronto's transnational left feminists, a good many born, like both Guettel and Smith, outside Canada, were thus entirely "global," at home in debates taking place in New York, London, or Paris. Those who were recent immigrants often identified with national liberation struggles far removed from Canada. Yet they came to be as completely "local," generating in Toronto their own complex network of institutions. One of the most significant, and less-heralded, of those institutions was communal housing.

In the early 1970s an efflorescence of feminist-informed co-operative living arrangements appeared in Toronto. Now a woman could cook dinner once a week and expect to return home other days to a home-cooked meal. Both genders took on the collective responsibility of chores and parenting, and women could face criticism if it was thought that they had spent "too much" time caring for children.[58]

The lowly schedule proved to be an important tool for overturning the traditional household division of labour. Virtually all houses came to adopt one, even those that otherwise rejected traditional forms of order. The household chores that had provided the main source of conflict in earlier communal experiments became less contentious, and women, who had done most of the housework in "order-free environments," were the primary beneficiaries of the transition. The utopian communal promise of drastically reduced household labour time was finally being realized. In one study, sociologist Meg Luxton found that feminist consciousness had percolated into the very definition of what a commune or co-op was supposed to be: "As feminism was a fundamental part of communal ideology, to accuse someone of being a male chauvinist was to accuse him of violating communal philosophy. It was tantamount to saying that he should not be living in the group."[59] Other researchers, looking more broadly at thirty communes, twenty-two of them in Toronto, came to the same conclusion: many of the women were deeply involved in the women's movement, refused to be treated as "sex objects," and resisted any assumption that domestic chores were their responsibility. Even child-rearing was transformed, with youngsters growing up to be less dependent upon their mothers.[60]

Alongside the improved status of women in mixed houses came a substantive growth in women-centric co-ops and communes. One of the earliest was a commune on Euclid Avenue formed by radical feminists who had first come together in a consciousness-raising group. "We have to learn to trust our sisters and train for the revolution," explained a member. "We set up the house as a deliberate political act." The women pooled their savings over two years to buy their own house, and even hired a babysitter once a week to ensure equal participation in house meetings.[61] Many of the circa-1970s lesbian feminist activists studied by Becki Ross in her book *The House That Jill Built* continued to opt for communal living in houses on Garden Ave., Clinton St., Walker Ave., Spruce St., Gerard St. E., and Palmerston Blvd., or more institutional settings such as the McPhail Home for Women, Stop 158 hostel, or the mixed-gender Bain Co-op. Within these new households, radical women continued to experiment with creating an egalitarian women's culture and collaborating on political projects, whether through established social movement organizations or informal "zaps" that brought their burgeoning culture into the public realm—by public kissing, for instance, or by intervening when they saw sexual harassment on the streets, or even surprising patrons of local doughnut shops and laundromats by singing "A Is for Amazon" or "Leaping Lesbians."[62]

Later in the 1970s left feminism displayed its growing strength by invading community television channels. Feminists aired shows on birth control, welfare, and women's history. Viewers got to see programs produced by Liberation Media such as *Free Mum, Free Dad, Free Daycare*, *Women at Work*, and *Rape, Justice & Karate*. A number of feminist documentary filmmakers got their start on the medium. Nothing like these programs appeared on "regular" television, espe-

Feminists opposed the idea that cultural products could be divorced from everyday life.

Artist credit: Ann Pearson and Yvonne Klein; *Fireweed* 11, 1981.

cially since CBC management had cancelled a planned *All About Women* series after being deluged with calls and letters of complaint from a Christian group.[63]

From 1971 to 1979, lines of demarcation were continually being drawn and redrawn, not only separating socialist from radical feminists—but also separating both those camps from the liberal feminists increasingly catching the ear of Ottawa. Mary O'Brien's book *The Politics of Reproduction* captured international attention when it appeared in 1981,[64] but four years earlier she was already building the radical-feminist case that issues of gender oppression needed to be front and centre. In 1977 Toronto feminists were engulfed by a debate over the film *Snuff*, a low-budget effort made in Argentina that purported to show women being actually murdered. Although eventually exposed as a hoax, the film was sufficiently credible to persuade many people that it depicted actual violence against women. For feminists, whether that violence was "real" or "fake" was in a sense beside the point, which was to highlight the extent to which women were subject to the repressive acts and imaginations of men.

In Toronto, O'Brien recalled, the group Women Against Violence Against Women (WAVAW), organized in 1977, was already planning a demonstration against violence directed at women when *Snuff* opened; indeed, the movie house was on the planned route of the demonstration. Some women opted for direct action against the showing of the film and occupied the theatre, to be dispersed only by a police riot squad. Rather than saluting feminists for taking a strong stand against the film, the mainstream media judged that they had given it undeserved publicity. It was a case of "shrill women getting worse."[65] O'Brien's response was that the protesters were empowering themselves. Moreover, they had found a unifying cause—the cessation of violence against women—that had eluded previous feminists, who had proved incapable of uniting and expanding the movement on the basis of calls for wages for housework, free abortion on demand, and unionization of women workers. O'Brien drew a far-reaching conclusion from their experience:

> Many of the women who took part in the action are socialists of one kind or another, but serious Marxist women are increasingly coming to doubt that women can rely on class struggle to liberate them . . . and are recognizing that male dominance is pre-capitalist and supra-class. Instead of following "male supremacist ideologies," these women know that women must develop their own theory, practice and political forms and are rejecting the hierarchy and vanguardism found in "Marx-Engels-Lenin-Stalin-Trotsky-Mao-Castro-ISM."[66]

O'Brien was noticing a trend that attained ever-greater visibility in Toronto feminist circles from 1977 through to the mid-1980s: the split between two camps of left feminists, the "socialist feminists" and the "radical feminists," with the socialist feminists predominating in the International Women's Day Committee (IWDC), responsible for organizing the annual March event, and the radical feminists in both WAVAW and the Feminist Party of Canada (fd. 1979). If both camps still talked a language of "new leftism," the radical feminists, in vesting their hopes in women's struggle against men, were now thinking of revolutionary change from a post-Marxist position. Some conventional Marxists, including women, responded by seeing the campaigns against rape and violence against women as a mere "diversion." Its main outcome in the real world, they thought, would be more right-wing campaigns to "Clean Up Yonge Street."[67] The more alert orthodox Marxists gave the issue closer attention. Some were sufficiently self-reflective to muse that the question of rape was a "particularly thorny one," and that they had been delinquent in avoiding it.[68]

From the mid- to late 1970s, feminists of all descriptions, and not only radical feminists in pursuit of the movement's one unifying issue, highlighted violence against women. The struggle for women's shelters was intense and took place under the often mocking eyes of established opinion. Indeed, *The Toronto Sun*, noting the lack of any women's hostels at all in Toronto prior to the 1970s, took the opportunity to ruminate about a women's liberationist conspiracy. One of the better-known women's shelters in Toronto was the collectively run Nellie's, whose staff and supporters famously engaged in an "occupation" of their own building to protest its lack of funding. Yet shelter staff, like their compatriots in other "counterservices," sometimes danced to an awkward beat to maintain both their activism and their state funding. The director of Interval House pulled the plug when she learned that her staff members were going to appear at a press conference supporting WAVAW's demands, allegedly because she thought that organization's association with lesbians would harm the shelter's reputation.[69]

The campaign to change the law so that women rape victims were not browbeaten and pilloried in court was similarly intense. The issue of rape and the limits of progressive private practice came into focus when Maryka Omatsu, an articling student at Charles Roach's firm, refused to help defend a man against sexual assault charges and Roach fired lawyer Marilynne Glick for coming to Omatsu's defence. All three were members of the Law Union, which ultimately sided with Glick, who went on to win a wrongful dismissal suit.[70] Part of their reason for siding against Roach was a belief that rape, like racist attacks, was a political crime that served to keep down a subordinate group; and thus those accused of sexual assault charges should not be defended by members of the Law Union. An article in the *Law Union News* hints that Roach may have argued for the rights of the accused to a defence on the grounds that they could be victims of a frame-up or racialization, but a majority of members thought otherwise.[71]

The case was symptomatic of wider misgivings among some Black new leftists about the implications of the highly energized women's movement of the 1970s. A divisive question within the Black power new left was to what extent women should organize autonomously. Sylvia Searles argued that Black women had the double burden of being both Black and female and that salient points from the women's liberation movement had to be incorporated into the Black struggle. Pat Thorpe emphasized that women's liberation was not just for middle-class white women. She argued that women from minority groups were especially harmed by gender oppression. Like Searles, she argued for the incorporation of aspects of feminism into the Black liberation struggle, as opposed to building a new women's organization, and that an anti-imperialist and anti-racist ideology could not be sidelined. Marlene Green, director of the Black Educational Project, said the fight was more difficult for Black women because if they tried to develop independence they were accused of dividing their own community. Unlike the others, she believed that it was important for women to struggle independently because they faced problems that were distinctly different from those of men.[72]

A number of men in the Black power new left community were wary of feminist arguments, especially those vaunting women's autonomous organization. One author believed that the capitalist press gave women's liberation attention because it knew that if women could be taken out of the struggle, Black liberation would be weakened: "It is my feeling that the government, the man, is financing women's liberation to divert the struggle, and that women are falling for it just like they fell for the pill, like they are falling for abortion and all the little tricks that they come up with."[73]

Activists enjoying a 1974 picnic hosted by the Black Women's Organization.

Fireweed 16, 1983.

Some writers described what they believed were the counter-revolutionary consequences of taking suggestions from *Contrast*'s socially liberal advice columnist: "Not only do we need more people for the revolution, but Black families should be strengthened and not destroyed.... It's a very revolutionary thing to rear young black kids for the revolution."[74] Many Black feminists navigated the tricky relationship between the two left struggles in their own minds, although, significantly, few if any female activists appear to have left the male-dominated Black movement.

Yet as the 1970s progressed there was an unmistakable move towards recognizing the autonomy of Black women. Female members of the mid-decade Black Workers Alliance regularly spoke of their triple oppression as Black working-class women and formed their own organization, Black Women in Support of Revolutionary Change. A full-page cartoon published in *Black Labour* highlighted the sexist views held by some activist men (with one cartoon militant predictably saying that women's liberation would divide the struggle). The feature demonstrated a commitment by both male and female activists to give more prominence to issues of women's oppression. An article in *Reaching Out*, a local Black socialist-feminist publication, suggested that Black women were increasingly coming into their own as independent activists and theorists: "She was interested now in the action behind the power words, the follow up of the upraised clenched fist."[75]

If women had any trepidation about getting involved in white-dominated feminist groups, it was largely because this rising feminist consciousness remained coupled to the stagist idea that the first task was to form stronger Black communities:

> Once there is unity among black women in Canada we will be in a position to go into the international women's movement. We will enter as a united black women's movement, fully conscious or aware of our goals and fully intent on participating with other groups of women to change the present social order in Canada and in other parts of the world.[76]

Combining feminism with class-based movements could prove as difficult. Varda Burstyn, who worked intensively within the Waffle, credits that NDP faction with making socialist feminism a powerful current within the women's movement as a whole. Indeed, according to prominent Toronto feminist Judy Rebick, the resulting alliance of autonomous women's groups and women in labour unions forged in organizations like the Waffle was an important marker demarcating the U.S. and Canadian feminist movements. But Burstyn also remembers the intensity of the polemical debates that shook the Waffle in 1972, and the strain upon marriages constituted by the new politics. Counterbalancing such negative memories are those of "the exhilaration of the women's meetings: the laughter, the anger, the strategizing, the jokes—the sheer energy was a high I will never forget." She also recalls struggling to maintain her "dignity and political credibility" while explaining "the notion of sexual objectification" to a "leering, whooping room of . . . steel workers."[77]

For Burstyn and others like her, those steelworkers were potential allies temporarily swayed by a reactionary gender ideology. Some feminists were inclined to see hope in a "men's liberation movement"—which both *The Other Woman* and *Breakthrough* magazines publicized, and which in Toronto had a markedly socialist and pro-feminist orientation and adopted such long-standing techniques as consciousness-raising.[78] Other feminists regarded men in general as unredeemable and said so. The first issue of *The Other Woman* in 1972 included this bon mot: men resisting the coming feminist revolution would not suffer because their sexism harmed the class struggle or narrowed their own personhood. They would suffer because they would be "mowed down, killed, destroyed."[79]

* * *

Gays and lesbians, constituting the third large manifestation of identity leftism in Toronto in the 1970s, had first organized in the University of Toronto Homophile Association in 1969. The group's members set up information tables on campus, promoted education and discussion, and sought to combat "homophobia"—a recently coined term for the hatred of homosexuals. The Community Homophile Association of Toronto (CHAT) was formed in December 1970 (and incorporated in 1973) and in short order established its own office, spearheading efforts to provide legal, medical, and other supportive information to the gay and lesbian community.[80] From 1970 to 1977, under the directorship of George Hislop, CHAT was an influential presence in Toronto, with a Church Street centre that served as a regular venue for dances and meetings. It offered a help line for the distressed and a library for the inquisitive, and even a television show on cable TV. Most members of CHAT were not new leftists, but many of its initiatives fell within the precepts of community-building and personal autonomy, with an added emphasis on challenging pre-existing stereotypes and scientific theories with a grassroots approach to knowledge formation.

Toronto Gay Action (TGA, fd. June 27, 1971), was CHAT's somewhat unpredictable child, formed out of its activist caucus and made up largely of CHAT militants. As Peter Zorzi remembers in his invaluable memoir:

> There was a ferment of ideas about the personal and the political and about their intersection, and if we could just spread them among our own people then gay life would begin to open up and life itself would start to change for us. It wasn't all going to happen overnight, but it was gay people talking with gay people, that was the meaning of it and the glory of it. It was the taking into our own hands of our destiny.[81]

Soon friction arose between CHAT and the new caucus, which was inclined to a more confrontational style of new leftism. When the caucus decided to organize a national gay rights demonstration in Ottawa, the vast majority of CHAT's membership voted to support the protest, but a minority opposed it on the grounds that CHAT should stick to supplying social services. CHAT's bureaucratic roadblocks led to growing frustrations, and members of the caucus decided to operate separately.[82]

Thus it was TGA, via its organization of the August 28th Committee, which inspired the first national gay demonstration that summer. On Parliament Hill, a couple of busloads of Toronto gays and lesbians converged with smaller contingents from Kitchener-Waterloo, Montreal, and Ottawa. A speaker read from a "'We Demand' manifesto," which decried the inequality of the Criminal Code and demanded legislative changes.[83]

Such reforms were hardly the sum of the gay liberation program. Evoking the rationale behind the women's liberation parliamentary brief on abortion in 1967, Toronto gay activists indicated that the demands being raised were merely part of a larger radical strategy.[84] One TGA brochure outlined the group's vision of a "loving" society with a "non-materialist culture," proclaiming its commitment to a socialist government, a "truly pacifist government with *no* (0.00) defense budget," and "anarchy—in the sense of minimal government," with "most decisions made at the community level."[85]

Although the first formal meeting of TGA did agree to form a steering committee, it added substantive new left provisos to this concession to organizational efficiency: 40 per cent of the committee members were to be rotated out of office every two months. Following the Ottawa demonstration, decision-making was dramatically decentralized, the steering committee abolished, and even chaired meetings were declared a thing of the bureaucratic, hierarchical past.[86] (Such

The gay rights march passes by the new hydro building being built at College St. and University Ave., 1972.

Courtesy Charles Dobie.

experimentation was not all that unrealistic in a group with a formal membership of around fifty, about half of whom would attend the average meeting.)[87] TGA believed that gay liberationists could benefit from the insights of the women's movement, especially with respect to the power of consciousness-raising and the imperative to resist the "patriarchal" basis of society. It was no surprise that speakers at Toronto's first Gay Pride March in 1972 struck a strongly pro-feminist note.[88]

Like Black power and left feminism, gay liberation was suffused with the radical ambition to remake society. Many of Toronto's gay activists, like their feminist sisters, lived in communal housing. Discussions might flow easily from the editorial offices of *The Body Politic* collective to the kitchens and bedrooms of co-ops, a reality that some participants said contributed to cliquishness and that others valued as an indication of resistance to the system. Gay journalist Gerald Hannon believed that communal living provided the material foundation for the experiment in journalism: since *The Body Politic* magazine could never afford to pay more than a pittance to a couple of employees, the economies made possible by living together kept both those staffers and the publication's wider circle of volunteers alive. Certainly the militants of *The Body Politic*—founded in 1971, it would be a vibrant centre of new leftism for the rest of the decade—sought to "live otherwise" in Hannon's Marchmount Road house: income was pooled, food shared, and a joint bank account served the entire home. When food ran short, members might sometimes co-operatively shoplift from corporate—never community-owned—grocery stores.[89]

Often living lives outside the established social conventions, gay liberationists enjoined others to liberate themselves from their chains. "*PEOPLE—TAKE OFF*

Returning to Allan Gardens at the end of the march, 1972.

Courtesy Charles Dobie.

YOUR MASKS—DISCOVER YOURSELVES—BE FREE!" urged a TGA pamphlet.[90] The group favoured "zaps," in which unsuspecting night-clubbers were surprised by same-sex "dance-ins." It also demonstrated against biased media stories, protested the exclusion of sexual orientation from the Ontario Human Rights Code, and issued warnings to patrons entering places where washrooms were kept under police surveillance. It organized gay-identified contingents to march in large protests against nuclear testing and the Vietnam War. More controversially, it decided that no one supporting the war was welcomed as a member.[91]

Yet, although its vision was never limited to remaking the sexual order, gay liberation did consider the revolutionary transformation of sexuality a crucial step towards the wider emancipation of humanity. TGA militants sought a "sex-positive culture" that would not only free gays and lesbians, but also straights. Men would no longer be trapped by their masculinity, forced to repress their feelings of sensitivity and gentleness. Women could escape from the chains of femininity, which promoted passivity and dependence in a world in which men held all the power. All sexual roles, homosexual and heterosexual alike, were destructive. By destabilizing the labels, categories, and disguises to which most people were forced to conform, gay liberation, no less than Black power or left feminism, combined specific goals aimed at a subset of the population with an ambitious vision aimed at everybody: as the slogan had it, "Gay Liberation Is People Liberation."[92]

As Scott de Groot shows, gay liberation drew upon a diverse array of intellectual influences in a transnational network of activists and intellectuals, albeit one still generally bounded by linguistic barriers in an English-speaking world

Getting ready to march during Gay Pride Week in 1972.

Courtesy Jearld Mordenhauer.

in which the Toronto gays in particular played a surprisingly important role.[93] Early gay liberation in Toronto deployed a down-to-earth existentialism in its critique of the artificiality and hollowness of conventional morality. A revealing TGA leaflet of the early 1970s critiqued old-school Torontonians who, by long-standing tradition, thronged outside the Halloween drag show, often with the intent of harassing and assaulting the gays, lesbians, and trans people who made their sexual eccentricity visible:

> Many of you have come here tonight thinking that you are going to see someone else playing a role, someone else in costume, someone else wearing a mask.
>
> *But you're wrong.*
>
> You're the ones wearing the masks—masks that you wear every day of the year, not just on Hallowe'en ...
>
> Look again at the drag queens. They are laughing at *you*. They can see through your disguises. They are showing you how superficial those disguises are.[94]

Gay liberation contingents began joining some of the city's larger demonstrations, like this one organized to oppose the U.S. war in Vietnam.

Courtesy Jearld Mordenhauer.

Offering a down-to-earth anticipation of some of the insights that were later to be developed as queer theory, these gay activists suggested that even in the heart of a prospective gay-basher lurked an individual yearning to savour the true freedom of sexual liberation. Such a new leftish quest for personal authenticity often coexisted uneasily with the pragmatics of social service delivery and political lobbying, which was the path that CHAT often appeared to be taking. *The Body Politic* denounced both the mainstream path and those following it:

> CHAT can no longer be called a moderate organization. It is a reactionary organization, with political views ranging from conservative to non-existent. It is a Canadian Mattachine Society, but a Mattachine Society before gay lib erupted [into] view. It is anti-democratic and paternalistic. It is imbued with the aura of the comfortable closet.[95]

In addition to rallying to *The Body Politic*, such activists also pivoted towards the Gay Alliance Toward Equality (GATE), founded in July 1971 in Vancouver and by 1972 establishing a presence in other large Canadian cities. It devoted itself to political campaigning and kept spreading the message of freedom from oppression for all, with a particular emphasis on winning civil liberties for gays. Some of them soon found the group's atmosphere constricting. "To my mind if you put the civil service in charge of the gay movement that would be GATE," was Peter Zorzi's acerbic judgment. Yet *The Body Politic* and GATE shared office space, and with the collapse of the TGA, GATE assumed responsibility for organizing the Pride Parade, which in 1974 drew over one hundred people.[96]

For many observers *The Body Politic* was the most dramatic manifestation of the gay liberation movement. One of the few new left publications in Canada to attain a world-wide reputation, *Body Politic* was initiated by members of TGA along with activists attached to Toronto's chief underground newspaper, *Guerilla*. Zorzi, in his memoir "Queer Catharsis," recalls the names of a half-dozen members of the *Guerilla* collective who were among the magazine's founders. They had been successful in getting *Guerilla* to advertise and report on gay events and on one occasion convinced the collective to publish a gay manifesto. But they hit a roadblock when they wanted to expand gay coverage further and other members of the collective accused them of wanting to turn the paper into a gay publication. The activists eventually concluded, "Although there were strong gay connections with *Guerilla* and the paper was open to us, there was still only so much opportunity for the gay community to use it as a resource." An early fall 1971 meeting of TGA announced plans to proceed with a gay liberation paper.[97]

An unsigned article in the first issue of *The Body Politic*, which appeared to function as an editorial, heavily criticized TGA. It acknowledged that the group's "zaps" had been fun and had perhaps made a difference for some; but the efforts were small-scale, disorganized, and apolitical. What activists needed were more collective solutions and mass action—that is, "A movement composed of organizers, not a small band of crusaders." Several issues later, Brian Waite—both a TGA militant and Trotskyist, and credited by historian Tom Warner as being "one of the first to articulate the need to pursue a human rights strategy as a means of moving toward liberation"—suggested that fighting for the inclusion of sexual orientation in human rights legislation could provide a base for gay liberation's more far-reaching goals. He drew examples from the anti-war, abortion rights, and women's suffrage struggles. As Waite later acknowledged, he and other gay Trotskyists were extrapolating to the lesbian and gay struggle notions worked out in the League for Socialist Action.[98]

All the identity-based new leftisms encountered a similar contradiction in the 1970s—that of somehow combining the quest for rights with the revolutionary goal of subverting the political order that was being called on to grant those rights—but in this case, the links connecting different spheres of left identity politics were conscious and direct. One writer, coming like Waite from the Trotskyist movement, attributed TGA's problems to its countercultural orientation and lack

"Zaps" were sometimes decried for being too radical, but this early 1970s photo of one outside city hall might look banal to observers today.

Courtesy Jearld Mordenhauer.

of a campaign around a single issue. He agreed with Waite that changes to the human rights code should be that issue. And a majority of the *Body Politic* collective appeared to agree. A spring 1973 editorial sanctioned a focus on obtaining gay civil liberties as a first step to winning the maximum program of gay liberation.[99]

Yet, as was the case with the parallel single-issue focus of Trotskyists in the women's movement, the activists could never reach a consensus on this way of focusing gay liberation. Michael Lynch, who would emerge as an important figure, exclaimed in July 1979: "I want to burn police cruisers, bomb corporations and never again to deal with straights." For him, the "Human Rights" decade—exemplified by the 1975 formation of the Coalition for Gay Rights in Ontario—was over.[100] By then the debate over sexuality in Toronto had passed well beyond the "zap" stage. The moral panic aroused by the murder of shoeshine boy Emanuel Jacques on Aug. 1, 1977, the raid on the offices of *The Body Politic* on Dec. 30, 1977, and the bathhouse raids on Dec. 9, 1978, in which twenty-three men were arrested, all meant that when Lynch declared his impatience with a cautious rights-based incrementalism, he was doing so in the midst of a vast battle in which the very survival of his community was imperilled. The left cultural community rallied around, supporting *The Body Politic* with benefit events and demonstrations. Indeed, Lynch—who was himself quite willing to lobby Queen's Park and did not mock what had been achieved in bringing the question of gay rights to public consciousness—presented a more subtle historical analysis than implied in his proud declaration of gay autonomy. In many respects a program of "relentless reformism" was unavoidable, even for someone like Lynch, whose "radical gay vision" scorned "reformism."[101]

Such acute skepticism of reformism among gay and lesbian activists was strengthened by how the mainstream media covered them—which, in contrast to the more nuanced treatment of equality-demanding women—was almost always negative. Although the activists, organized in such bodies as the Gay TV Collective and fully alive to the potential of television, brought out such shows as *We Are the Gay People* and *This Program May Be Offensive to Heterosexuals*, the opportunities to speak out on their own behalf were infrequent and subject to the whims of commercial interests that had no interest in their cause. In cancelling the Gay TV Collective's *Gay News and Views*, the Maclean-Hunter cable company cited an on-air picture of two men kissing, the presence of a poster of Queen Victoria advertising a VD clinic, and materials about gay health and safety that had "crossed the line." To add insult to injury, it then explained that it was cancelling the show because it was worried that homosexuals were hurting themselves by speaking out:

> The material on the program is intellectually hostile, and disrespectful to the establishment heterosexual community. It does not project a better understanding of the gay community and is too militant. The program seems to admit that there is no hope for better understanding. This insulting attitude is not in the best interests of the gay community.[102]

The cancellation was of a piece with the increasingly repressive climate for homosexuals in the city, a context in which down-to-earth reforms, such as the right to privacy for bathhouse patrons and provisions to make police officers accountable, could only seem highly desirable. Yet, if they became the major focus of the movement, they risked becoming its end-goals, not its transitional demands. "In terms of a decade ago, the 'human rights strategy' has become the new 'homophilism,'" Lynch complained. "It seeks assimilation, legislation, and isolation—the isolation of this one issue from all the rest that concern us." Some rights for gays were:

> not much of a sop for a government to give, and the more we equate gay success with achieving them, the more we risk the fate of the abolitionist movement after the Emancipation, the feminist movement after the Franchise, the Black movement after the Civil Rights Act of 1964. To those American memories we may add the way the Quebec "sexual orientation" amendment lulled Quebec gays into a lethargy from which they have not yet fully recovered.[103]

Like Waite and Wilson, Lynch was keenly aware that gay liberation had emerged within a thicket of other left-wing movements, and could learn lessons from them. But he drew a very different lesson than did his predecessors: the "human rights decade" had run its course, and gay liberation, in its fullest new left meaning, seemed smaller as a result. Tim McCaskell, writing in *The Body Politic* in 1975, had sounded some of the same alarms: although Marxists had a great deal to teach gay liberation, and gay liberation could in turn offer Marxists much-needed assistance in addressing sexuality and repression, it was a mistake to parachute into gay politics "correct" formulations from the straight left. They could hardly substitute for the researches and activism of lesbians and gays themselves. Thus far, many of the tools that the conventional left had suggested for gay liberation were woefully inadequate: "We've been armed with a ripe banana and told to knock down the brick walls of capitalism and sexism."[104]

* * *

A paradox of Toronto left history in the 1970s is that the barriers erected by orthodox Marxists to ward off new left theorists and activists varied inversely in their impact with the extent to which traditional Marxist texts spoke to the identity in question. On questions of race and nationality, and to a lesser extent on those of gender, the tradition was replete with pertinent texts—and Toronto was home to a variety of people who sought to put them to work in the 1970s. Moreover, anti-racism and feminism could be ambitiously linked with Marxist political economy, as emerging and prolific scholarly literatures demonstrated. With respect to gay liberation, though, the Marxist tradition had almost nothing directly to say, and what little it did say seemed either offensive or pointless.

For McCaskell, one of the ripest bananas handed to gays was Engels, whose writings on the family, heavily flavoured with mid-Victorian anthropology, were still cited with considerable reverence in the 1970s. Gary Kinsman, coming from the Trotskyist tradition and leading both a course and a reading group on gay issues at the Marxist Institute, relied upon the writings of Wilhelm Reich, one of the very few important Marxist theorists who was preoccupied with sex, and who enjoyed an unusually elevated status among a number of Toronto new leftists.[105]

Moreover, apart from demanding human rights for all, activists found it considerably more difficult to connect gay liberation with Marxian political economy and working-class issues. An often voiced (if infrequently tested) assumption of many Marxists was that homosexuals and their goings-on were intrinsically offensive to working-class sensibilities. Even such a creative Marxist thinker as William Bunge waxed indignant when it emerged that a researcher on one of his "geographical expeditions" was gay. Why was it necessarily "bad manners" not to "be liberal

Cable companies agreed that the show might be offensive to heterosexuals, 1978.

Canadian Lesbian and Gay Archives.

toward homosexuals"? Why mount a defence of "homosexual permissiveness" when any such demand was foreign to the working-class agenda? "Any behaviour that seriously insults local norms," Bunge concluded, "is unacceptable." It did not seem to matter much that the offensive queer in question was himself a working-class taxi-driver involved in organizing his fellow workers into a union.[106]

Still, the influence of organized Marxist parties on gay liberation in Toronto was considerable, partly because gay activists sought to enter the left movement and enlist its (suitably chastened) members and partly because gay liberation seemed to undermine the activists' own "scientific" credibility on a question, sexuality, that was obviously on many Torontonians' minds as the 1970s unfolded.

Conflict within CHAT also proved important to the development of independent lesbian organizing. Its female members had chafed at the inordinate amount of time discussing male issues and the lack of women involved in the organization. In 1972 they demanded that half the seats on the executive be reserved for women, and the men largely agreed. But during the following year several female members formed an ad hoc group called CUNTS and left the organization: "As lesbians we are oppressed both as cunts and dykes. Until the gays of CHAT see the necessity of struggling against sexism, until the structure of CHAT is revolutionized, then CHAT will reflect the status quo through legalization and acceptance."[107]

Members of CUNTS, like those of TGA, had clearly grown impatient with the relatively respectable reformism of CHAT. But the split primarily reflected a growing realization that gay and lesbian interests were not wholly the same—as one lesbian put it, the men at CHAT tended to be "typical men"—and a desire for distinct lesbian-identified organizations.[108]

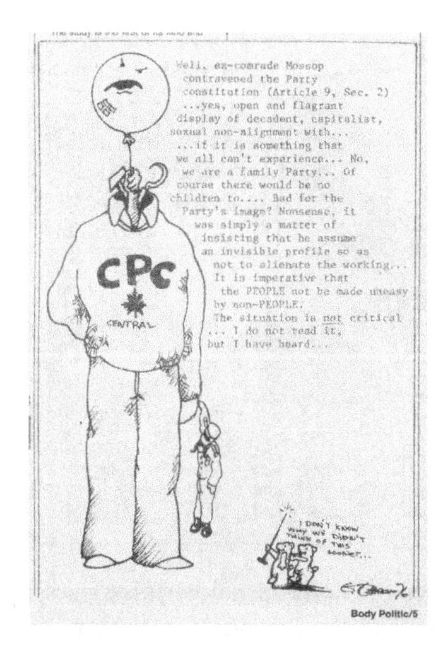

The Body Politic **lampooned the CPC after the party's expulsion of Brian Mossop.**

Body Politic, November 1976.

The split from CHAT roughly overlapped with the dissolution of the New Feminists, Toronto Women's Caucus, and Toronto Women's Liberation Movement, leaving a number of experienced activists without a political home. Some became involved in Women's Place, founded in mid-1972. Its Dupont Street address quickly became a clearing house for everything feminist. It boasted a bookstore, library, educational courses and forums, a speakers' bureau, legal and medical services, drop-in groups, and more. Everything was based on small collectives, linked together by a central administrative collective. A policy restricting the central collective's membership to those "not already belonging to a male dominated left political organization" was seen as a way of limiting the influence of Trotskyists.[109]

Lesbians initially encountered strong opposition to running lesbian-identified services, but that began to ebb as more lesbians came out. By early 1973 at least one member was complaining that straights were being made to feel guilty and that some women were staying away because Women's Place seemed more like Lesbians' Place. When a financial crunch uprooted Women's Place in 1974, some of its lesbian services relocated to Kensington Market (where they operated under the umbrella of the Amazon Workshop) and 342 Jarvis Street (in conjunction with other lesbian-dominated political organizations, services, and businesses).[110]

From some Marxist perspectives, what was wrong about gay liberation was that it was so patently the product of the new left. Apropos of the split between CHAT and TGA, one Marxian critique maintained:

> The gay movement, like most others has the problem of coming to grips with concepts adapted from the so-called "new" left, idealist and utopian notions such as "counterculture," "personal liberation" through head-changing, etc. In TGA these ideas comprise one of the most important ideological barriers to the advancement of the mass action perspective as a central strategy for gay liberation.[111]

Trotskyist critiques of gay liberationists for setting a higher bar for entry, as suggested by the policy refusing admission to Vietnam War supporters, proceeded from the assumption that the Leninists themselves, building as they did upon an established revolutionary praxis, knew best how lesbians and gays should organize.[112] It was a claim to authority weakened by the numerous splits in the Trotskyist movement, the profusion of many different lines about sexuality, and, perhaps most seriously, the lived experiences of the many former Trotskyists who went on to join the gay liberation movement. For Maurice Flood, the Vancouver-based inspirer of GATE who still considered himself a Trotskyist, the League for Social Action in particular offered, not inspiration, but a cautionary example of a movement "stranded on the shores of Ann Landers liberalism." Others argued that, after a year or so of creative energy, the LSA had stalled, prompting many who took the question seriously to leave.[113] Indeed, when the LSA did come forth with a position, its upshot was that gays and lesbians should struggle for their human rights and lend their support to other movements. Yet the organization also suggested that it might be better for both gays and lesbians, and the left as a whole, if they stayed in the closet. If the new stance suggested at least a timid acceptance of some of the demands of gay liberation, represented a lifting of a controversial ban on even discussing the issue in local branches, and freed Trotskyists to involve themselves on a more-or-less individualistic basis, it struck many gay liberationists as a manifestation of a movement less sympathetic to their cause than was the Democratic Party in the United States.[114]

Because so many gay liberationists were initially linked to Leninist movements, from which they had received their political education and with which they maintained sometimes productive and frequently tense relationships, Marxist ideas were debated with a zeal that must surprise anyone with a twenty-first-century impression of Toronto's gay and lesbian community. For Brian Mossop, one of the leading intellectual lights of *The Body Politic*, it was important in 1975 to refute, point by point, the political theses contained in two new books from the Trotskyist publishing houses Pathfinder and Pluto. One of those books repeated stale Marxist critiques of gay associational life as being contaminated by bars and bathhouses (which begged the question, said a partially sympathetic Mossop, of where one ought to go to agitate within the community); the other erred in the opposite direction, by simply championing a liberal-humanist politics of ending discrimination and forgetting the feminist and Marxist critique of the family. Here, said Mossop, were "revolutionary words but homophile content."[115] For many Maoists, who gained ground on the Trotskyists as the decade proceeded, gay liberation was more a symptom of capitalist decadence than a path to emancipation, and it thus received even shorter shrift.

From 1971 to 1978 gay liberation had emerged and evolved as a significant identification for a constituency in Toronto. *The Body Politic* had won wide renown, human rights advocates had pondered ways of safeguarding the lives of lesbians and gays, and left-wing organizations had given the perspective some airtime. Yet, of the three big "identity leftisms," it was the most vulnerable. Warner points to 1977 as the first year of a backlash against gays and lesbians—with homophobia surfacing in response to the Ontario Human Rights Code Review Committee's recommendation to include sexual orientation; the first of singer Anita Bryant's Canadian anti-gay tours; and continuing examples of police repression.[116] Fervent debates over sexuality in the Toronto District School Board foreshadowed the violent homophobia of Toronto's 1980 election, which brought defeat not only to gay candidate George Hislop—who was accused of being a "closet liberal" and condemned for his business connections—but also to progressive mayor John Sewell, blamed for having spoken out on behalf of his gay fellow citizens.[117]

Gay liberation had been beset by challenges shared by the other identity leftisms, such as judicial repressiveness, liberal strategies of co-option and absorption, battles with rival and well-established left authorities, and the often wayward energies of its followers—but it was also set apart from them by having a smaller demographic base upon which to build and a higher politico-ethical hill to climb, challenging as it was the understandings with which most people conducted their personal lives.

* * *

Each strand of identity new leftism revealed a paradoxical characteristic: it dwelt intensively upon the particular "we" to be mobilized against "them"—in such evocative binaries as "Black power against the white left," "socialist feminism against the male left," or "gay liberation against the straight left"—while constantly formulating positions that took in all of humanity. Blacks were not merely fighting for themselves, but for all victims of racial oppression; feminists stood not just for women, but for all people oppressed by sexism; gay liberation meant not just human rights for homosexuals, but freer, fear-free personal lives for all people. To the conflicts inherent in splitting away from established left institutions in the name of their particular struggles, these new leftisms added those of their conflicting universalisms: each of them, at their most ambitious, presented itself as a general remedy for human ills.

For left movements, one way of mitigating almost limitless fragmentation was to focus attention outside Canada. In the 1970s solidarity activism, with Latin America and South Africa looming large, attained a greater stature—though based to a degree on earlier foundations from the previous decade, such as the Fair Play for Cuba Committee. Recent scholarship has shown the depth and intimacy of Quebec's entanglement with Latin America, with such events as the coup in Chile in 1973 prompting leftists to rethink their strategies within Quebec itself.[118] The Toronto pattern has yet to receive the monographic attention it deserves, but an initial survey suggests both differences and similarities. That many Québécois shared Catholicism with Latin Americans was one significant difference. The salience of the national question, and the drive to see Quebec as a Third World nation striving for independence, was another.[119] Yet the contrast should not be pushed too far. David Sheinin observes that a progressive church movement in both English Canada and Quebec, one he considers Gramscian in much of its take on global politics, shaped Canadian perceptions of the Third World. In a reading of the letters and articles of Toronto-based solidarity activist John Foster, Sheinin observes the extent to which neo-Marxist assumptions shaped his world view, while less contentious concepts characterized his public statements.[120] As historian Sean Mills observes, in both "Canadas" the hopes aroused by the election of Chile's Salvador Allende in 1970 at the head of a Popular Unity government were dashed with Pinochet's coup of 1973, with its ensuing human rights abuses. The progressive churches had already held a conference on Chile in 1972; after the coup they redoubled their efforts to change Canadian immigration policy in favour of accepting Chilean refugees, with about six thousand of them arriving between 1973 and 1978, many settling in Toronto. He cites the memories of one of them, Patricia Godoy:

> Of course I was in the [Chilean] women's group here in Toronto.... I think all of us who arrived in that era got involved in everything. So I participated a lot with the Uruguayans, the Argentinians, we helped the *Madres de Mayo*, I was involved in all that kind of thing. We had fiestas, and through the fiesta we'd raise money to send to the countries.[121]

The "popular internationalism" of Chileans, in short, although focused initially on their own particular identity and challenges, eventually extended "far beyond the specific case of Chile."[122] Such sentiments would lead to substantial movements in Toronto on behalf of revolutionary movements in Nicaragua and El Salvador.

The path followed by Janice Acton might stand in for the one taken by hundreds of other Toronto new leftists. From 1972 to 1977, at Women's Press, Acton was impressed by the collective and the deep interpersonal connections that transnational solidarity fostered. She was particularly stirred by the attempt of the Women's Press to respond to the U.S. domination of the women's movement by emphasizing Canadian national themes (even though several of its founders were women from the United States). A major turning point for Acton, and for the collective, was the publication of Margaret Randall's work on Cuba in 1972. For Acton, the organized left was highly factionalized, prone to acute cynicism, and critical of everything; yet her milieu was simultaneously suffused with charged debates over the nature of Canada—imperialist, comprador, or colonized?—and the responsibilities of leftists to the larger world. Gradually, as a lapsed Protestant, she developed a greater affinity for progressive Christians—many of them already known to her through the anti-war movement. She gravitated to Connexions, made up mainly of Catholics interested in the new currents active in their church. They in turn were connected to similar circles in Mexico. Although never regaining her faith, she did come to appreciate the down-to-earth, compassionate style of Christian leftism. At the Centre for Spanish Speaking Peoples (CSSP), yet another "liberated" space run by a collective, she was brought in touch with a new cohort of Latin American women activists, many of them already leftists and sympathetic with established left parties, as part of a project whose founders emphasized the centrality of working-class issues such as daycare and wages for immigrant women.[123] In 1978 she became a member of the Latin American Working Group collective, which had earlier provided her with some of her most vivid experiences of "the blending of political agendas" and the "very rich learning opportunity" provided by down-to-earth struggles.[124]

Acton's journey into the transnational politics of solidarity in Toronto suggests many of the elements that impelled a good many new leftists to commit much of their adult lives to going along the same road. Moving in a circle of like-minded people—although herself wrestling with the personal and political challenges of acknowledging her own lesbianism—Acton found little that was politically or personally satisfying in the existing revolutionary parties. What drew her to Catholics and their version of social Christianity was not religious faith, but rather respect for their radical humanism and positive engagement with the lives of others. At a time when new leftists were often thought to be disconnected from labour, Acton saw in practical solidarity work ways of re-establishing connections, especially given the direct interest that many First World trade unionists had in issues of Third World oppression. It would be figures like Acton who helped shape local perceptions of the Nicaraguan Revolution, which came to a head in 1978–79 and would become, in the following decade, one of the local left's defining transnational issues.

Acton's apparent ease in moving from a feminist publishing project to work in transnational solidarity indicates, again, the flow of common values that new leftists shared over and above their many disagreements. Recalling her time at the Centre for Spanish Speaking Peoples, Jean Unda fondly mentioned its "collective but also communal" atmosphere, which for her exemplified "women's ways of working—very relational, working with systemic change in a way that created a liberated territory."[125] She spoke with the authentic accents of the new left, which actively sought to anticipate in the present world the egalitarianism and solidarity of an ideal future. Many such leftists experienced the warm emotions of working in transnational solidarity institutions as a relief from the rigours of ideological conflict in the broader movement.

In Toronto, groups such as LAWG, Development Education Centre, Inter-Church Committee on Human Rights in Latin America, Canadian News Synthesis Project, and Task Force on the Churches and Corporate Responsibility all worked hard to spread awareness of Canada's involvement in the global South. In this regard the left in general experienced strenuous debates, sometimes traceable back to the political realities of the countries from which immigrants had recently departed: a shared hatred of Pinochet, for example, was not enough to unify all the rival leftists who had both supported and critiqued Allende's government. The annual African Liberation Day witnessed persistent denunciations of South Africa's apartheid regime, but discussions about the African National Congress's turn to armed struggle against the white rulers or the Cuban military engagement in the former Portuguese colony of Angola generated less unanimity.

Solidarity leftism was nowhere more contentious than with respect to the State of Israel. In the Law Union, radical professionals disagreed with each other over the plight of the Palestinians. The issue came to the fore in the late 1970s when the Toronto steering committee refused to endorse a solidarity call from its Ottawa chapter, declaring that the motion was divisive and abstract and that the Union should only take stands on legal issues relating to Canada. Bryon Pfeiffer pointed out that much of this reasoning was inconsistent with the steering committee's support for the revolution in Nicaragua (with some complaining that the rebel Sandinistas were insufficiently revolutionary). Harry Kopyto, on his way to becoming one of Toronto's most celebrated left-wing lawyers, agreed with endorsing Palestinian self-determination, but not with supporting the Palestine Liberation Organization (PLO). He believed that some of his fellow lawyers were hypocritical in their willingness to overlook Israel's human rights violations. Others, following the direction of the United Jewish People's Order in 1976, took strong exception to characterizations of Zionism as racist.[126]

The *Canadian Jewish Outlook*, although lamenting what it thought was a rising tide of Jewish conformity and sometimes courting new leftists, publicized the opinions of one professor who thought young Jews who identified with the new left did so because of self-loathing and incipient anti-Semitism. Former Trotskyist Nathan Glazer made a similar argument, blaming the new left for moving young Jews away from their traditional occupations.[127] Rabbi W. Gunther Plaut, of the city's senior Reform temple, Holy Blossom, warned his congregation that the end of the Vietnam War meant additional Jewish children could fall into this trap:

> Be aware that under the guise of humanitarian impulses, the same forces of the Old and New Left which combined so successfully in the Vietnam enterprise, may be marshalled against Israel. Most likely the first focus of the anti-Israel campaign will be made to liberals. Probably a number of liberals in the Jewish community—especially among the youth—will become very uncertain and some may become disaffected publicly.[128]

Writing in *Canadian Jewish Outlook*, Rabbi Abraham Feinberg condemned the "anti-Jewish fulminations" of Black power advocates, which he linked to the *United Church Observer*'s critical coverage of the Palestinian question. Jews on the Toronto left increasingly found themselves to be living with a transnational dilemma—able neither to renounce Israel nor to shield their eyes from the enormities of the occupation of Palestine. They wanted to be a part of the broader left, yet that left was itself in the midst of a vast transnational sea change in which phenomena resembling the Western occupation of a Third World country, which was one way to see the Palestinian situation, would always be resisted.[129] Since the turn of the century Jewish identity and left-wing interests in Toronto had often converged, especially in the most dynamic years of the Communist Party; but now they seemed to be pulling in opposite directions.

On the other side of the issue were the new movements that identified strongly with the Palestinian cause. Within months of the defeat of the Arab states in the six-day April 1967 war came a new organization, the Canadian Arab Federation (CAF), formed in large measure to support the Palestinians. Some of its proponents proclaimed that pan-Arabism was more strongly displayed in Canada than in any place on the planet outside the Middle East.[130] Echoing (most likely inadvertently) similar comments in the left Black press—statements that condemned West Indian organizations for their supposed national blinkers and focus on entertainment rather than struggle—the editor of the CAF's *Arab Dawn* damned their Arab equivalents for only pursuing "'Hummus' and 'Tabboula.'"[131]

The CAF was not a leftist organization, but it did skew in that direction. It supported the PLO, conventionally seen as a radical left-wing group, and staunchly critiqued Western imperialism. It also opposed the October 1970 War Measures Act, condemned government inaction on unemployment, and supported Indigenous self-determination. The "WASP establishment" was criticized for its indifference to misery and hardship in both Canada and the Middle East.[132] Like so many other bodies in the 1970s, the CAF evinced a new leftism that was not part of its more politically amorphous official job description.

George Haggar, its leading theoretician and president from 1970 to 1972, was more overt in his radicalism. Formerly a student socialist in Lebanon, in 1960, while enrolled at the University of Toronto, he was elected leader of the campus

An early pro-Palestinian demonstration; Sept. 27, 1969.

Clara Thomas Archives and Special Collections, Toronto Telegram fonds.

CCF/New Party (the antecedent of the NDP) and championed its pragmatic liberalism.[133] Prior to the formation of CAF, Haggar had taken a keen interest in the Middle East, publishing papers on the Kurds, the situation in Algeria, and the role of the United States in the formation of Israel. He served as president of the Arab Community of Canada, which sent doctors from Canada to assist the Arab side during the 1967 war and was forthright in its opposition to the Canadian government's support for the Israeli side. It advised Arab states to cut their diplomatic relations with Canada, called Prime Minister Pearson "North America's staunchest Zionist mouthpiece," and referred to the media as a "cultural outpost of American imperialism."[134]

Later, now in a teaching post, Haggar was, like many new leftists, a radical critic of the post-secondary educational system that paid his salary. He referred to the university as "a place of slavery, a cave, a cage, a prison, a plantation where the profane is sacred, the destruct[ive] creative, the savage civilized, the effeminate manly, the servile liberated and the obsequious emancipated." The role of the university was to "produce robots to make the world safe for capitalism." The new tokenism of allowing students and professors to sit on governing boards would do nothing to change that.[135]

Haggar's enthusiasm for the new developments in the Middle East was boundless: "The revolution is engulfing the whole region and linking itself with the world revolutionary movements. Such historic feats will open a new epoch for mankind!" He believed that fallout from the 1967 war with Israel had discredited the autocratic Arab regimes and propelled the advance of "working class revolutionism." No less significant was the battle of Karameh the following year, in which he saw the PLO and Jordanian military smashing the myth of Israeli invincibility and proving that armed struggle was the only means of accelerating the drive to socialism. Haggar believed that mainstream Communist positions on the Middle East were obsolete and insufficiently anti-imperialist. He viewed with suspicion the "progressive" regimes that had undermined people's democratic rights, and hoped the Baath and Fateh parties might overcome their "bourgeois radicalism" in favour of more Leninist positions. He also emphasized Fanon's argument about the cultural significance of the shift to armed struggle, which he thought applied equally to Arabs in the Middle East and Blacks in North America. He had little patience for Black activists who emphasized building Black culture through non-violent forms of struggle. "You cannot create the new man except by the use of a gun," he thundered, when defending the tactics of the Black Panthers. It was a real shame, opined Haggar, that millions of Vietnamese were fighting the United States while millions of Black Americans were marching on Washington merely to sing "We Shall Overcome."[136] Like many a moderate social democrat of the 1960s, Haggar a decade later was more attuned to the revolutionary currents of his age.

Months after CAF's founding, Haggar lost his teaching job at Waterloo Lutheran University. It seems that his political views had rankled university administrators, as well as some of his colleagues. He insisted on talking about the political situation in the Middle East during otherwise cozy faculty meetings, aired his disagreements over the Vietnam War with visiting cabinet minister Paul Martin Sr., and was known to be a supporter of all kinds of student causes.[137] Since he was only on contract, the university was not obliged to provide the reasons for his dismissal. The Canadian Association of University Teachers ruled that the university was within its rights to terminate Haggar and suggested that he might have violated a clause in his contract that disallowed attacks on, or the disparagement of, Christianity. Despite ample student protest—and pleas from some of his colleagues to resign and save the university from negative publicity—Haggar's firing stuck and four hundred students left their classes to attend a funeral procession for academic freedom. After Waterloo, Haggar's pursuit of an academic job and his activist commitments continued to clash. At Southern University in Louisiana he was fired for joining students in a nineteen-day strike. The U.S. government ordered that he be deported to Lebanon, but Haggar somehow managed to escape and return to Toronto.[138]

Back in Toronto, Haggar appeared to devote his time to activism and his duties as CAF president, though he left the city a couple of times to meet with resistance leaders and organizations in the Middle East. One of his most notable achievements was his extensive interview with Palestinian activist Leila Khaled, which he turned into *My People Shall Live: The Autobiography of a Revolutionary*, published by NC Press in 1973. Haggar was one of the city's few non-white militants to take up the cause of Canadian nationalism. He served as secretary of the National Canadianization Committee and, along with Robin Mathews, a professor of English at Carleton University, led a march and held a sit-in at the Department of Manpower and Immigration to press for a moratorium on hiring foreign university professors.[139] As Haggar's biography suggests, the interests of new leftists and pro-Palestinians slowly converged. At the first major anti-Vietnam demonstration following the 1967 war, a contingent of Arabs marched, holding signs comparing the struggle in Vietnam to the situation in the Middle East. At a later pro-Palestinian rally, a *Globe and Mail* reporter suggested that the 250 protesters—a mix of radical students, people in traditional Arab dress, and men in business suits—made for an odd sight indeed.[140]

On the weekend after that rally, a crowd of five hundred people protested in front of Rochdale College against a conference of the Canadian Organization for the Liberation of Palestine being held there. Carrying picket signs reading "Jewish survival" and "Down with Arab imperialism," they listened as a philosophy professor asked why radicals fought for the freedom of everyone but Jews. When about half of the two hundred conference-goers marched to Queen's Park, shouting "Down with Zionism," "Escalate the people's war," and "Long Live Al Fatah," the Zionist counterprotesters responded with ironic chants of "Long live genocide." The acting chair of Students for Jewish Survival expressed his outrage that this "march of hatred" had been allowed to take place. After that weekend's events, the Jewish Defence League announced that it was immediately establishing a Toronto branch. Pro-Israeli activists mobilized to prevent Toronto from hosting a UN conference potentially attended by representatives of the PLO, a position supported by both Progressive Conservatives and New Democrats, with the governing Liberals citing the risk of disorder and the PLO's "divisive effect" on public opinion. While the Canadians Against the PLO group was non-committal about violence, in 1975 the Jewish Defence League promised that any Palestinian delegate showing up in Toronto would be killed.[141]

The PLO debate continued into fall 1975, when shouting Zionist students prevented Shafiq al-Hout, vice-chair of the PLO's UN delegation, from speaking to a meeting of one thousand at the University of Toronto. Paul Godfrey, chairman of Metro Toronto, had urged the university to rescind the booking; as it turned out before things could even begin the meeting room was besieged by hundreds of protesters. The event featured fist fights and the appearance of the Western Guard. The university's vice-president of Internal Affairs condemned the disruption as a violation of the right to free speech. A *Varsity* editorial complained that campus and municipal police had stood by, ignoring the disruption, and compared the administration's tepid response to its aggressive posture during the Banfield affair. The editorial was particularly incensed with the coverage of *The Globe and Mail*, which had featured a Western Guard member with a white-power T-shirt above the caption "PLO supporter." The meeting was rescheduled to a hotel, but again cancelled after the hotel received a number of threats. It did finally take place in a church, with police kept busy separating the Arab and Zionist demonstrators who remained outside.[142]

*   *   *

All of these distinct new leftisms, each a complicated movement of movements in its own right, shared an acute fear of co-optation and assimilation by the liberal order. For racialized minorities, the federal policy of multiculturalism presented both opportunities and perils, with leftists tending to emphasize the perils. Writing in *Spear*, Junior Anthony condemned the federally funded midsummer Caribana festival as "irrelevant, escapist, exploitative and racist," a reactionary exercise in "decadent nostalgia." Writing in the social justice magazine *Rikka*, Maureen McNerney argued that multiculturalism was divisive and worked to prop up traditional ethnic structures that subjugated women. Charles Roach considered multiculturalism a code word for pacifying minority demands for power. True, multiculturalism money had funded the ethnic press, but it did nothing to get racialized minorities into mainstream media. It thus encouraged people to believe that being separate was as good as being equal—a polite form of official apartheid.[143]

Worries over co-optation and assimilation were radically accentuated when identity groups turned to the vexed question of accepting government money. There was no easy answer. Turning down grant money meant turning your back on the needs of members of the community and indulging in puerile purism. Accepting it brought the risk of diluting revolutionary politics and being transformed into a service provider in the welfare state rather than being a radical movement devoted to its overthrow. In the Black Educational Project the shift to paid full-time and part-time staff by 1972 meant that decision-making shifted from volunteers to a steering committee. The following year that committee became a board of directors. Jumping on the government's money train transformed BEP from a social movement into a conduit through which parents could demand changes from the Board of Education. For Rosie Douglas, government spending on Black identity-building programs encouraged Blacks to fight amongst themselves and meant they had little incentive to challenge the values and perspectives of the dominant white community: "It is a device to force the black community ass-backwards into the Canadian mosaic. This we have to reject completely."[144] Such challenges were also faced, to a degree, by the women's and gay and lesbian movements, although only in the following decades would they start to fully draw upon, in women's shelters and front-line AIDS work, the resources of the Canadian state. In the 1970s the activists working at the Centre for Spanish Speaking Peoples, providing such services as English as a Second Language and assistance with refugee claims, sometimes went without pay to keep the place going, and even sheltered refugees in their own homes. Perhaps they came the closest to appreciating the contradictions of left institutions making the transition into quasi-state agencies.

The state-funding issue crystallized a more diffuse contradiction: were identity-based new leftists building movements that would work to defend their communities and safeguard past achievements, or were they seeking to challenge bourgeois hegemony through a more expansive campaign to transform the common sense of their society? Yet the implied distinction between an inward-looking defence system and outward-looking revolutionary activism was too rigid. Reality was more fluid and complex. The "wars of manoeuvre" experienced by groups besieged by the Western Guard could morph into "wars of position," as anti-racist militants struggled to defeat their opponents' views through tactics ranging from mass pressure to legislative change. It was obvious that, in the short term, apathy had succeeded outrage in the Black movement—with 1977 marking a nadir in terms of attendance at demonstrations, community groups becoming mere social service agencies, and the bankruptcy of the publication *Islander*, which had ended its acrimonious rivalry with *Contrast* by merging operations with the newspaper.[145] These ebbs and flows were inevitable in movements built by actual people, and these people in particular had passed through a year marked by violence and brutality from which they needed respite.

Moreover, what the orthodox Leninists tended to miss, because they still dreamt of a homogeneous movement answerable to a single vanguard, was the extent to which the new left had evolved more fluid attachments. Rather than joining one dominant party, activists could experience dozens of meaningful attachments with left institutions. They could begin to identify, if only as an ally, with a host of subaltern positions, not only their own. In 1974 over three hundred people rallied in Toronto to support the Native Caravan en route to Ottawa; they were advised by Larry Joseph, a militant from Cache Creek, that the struggles of Indigenous peoples in Canada were aligned with those of African and Latin American revolutionaries, and by Vern Harper that white-Native unity was essential.[146]

It was perhaps in the sphere of identity-based resistance that Toronto new leftists registered their most conspicuous and lasting achievements. Anti-racist activists managed not only to fight the particular outrages of Toronto's extreme rightists but also to transform the common-sense ways in which racism was generally understood—not as an individual malady but as an element within the socio-economic system; and this changed understanding influenced thinking at the highest levels of the state. As Toronto's women's liberation of the 1960s morphed into the socialist and radical feminism of the 1970s, it transformed conventional understandings of violence against women, upended repressive laws about contraception and abortion, and lastingly changed how many in trade unions and especially in the NDP regarded women activists. Gay and lesbian liberationists in Toronto built a publication and a movement that won international attention and, ultimately, transformed the legal position of same-sex relationships.

In all three cases, the local and the global were often effectively fused. On some balance sheets the rise of identity leftisms spelled the end of a new left imagined as a more unified movement of peace activists and students; but from our point of view, this phenomenon led to moments in which new left energies actually came to be integrated into practical on-the-ground struggles, with effects registered in Toronto, in Canada, and even around the world.

In 1972 activists within CHAT had imagined a new theory of revolution in which gays would unite with "other oppressed groups," such as Québécois, Indigenous activists, working-class Canadians, and everyone struggling against imperialism. For activist Bob Wallace, it was patently obvious that gay liberation on its own could accomplish little—"but in alliance with other revolutionary groups, it can accomplish a great deal."[147] For *The Body Politic*, one of the strengths of the Canadian gay liberation movement, in contrast with that of the United States, was that it had never pursued a narrow politics of defending only its own turf. Rather, it had supported lesbian autonomy, "urged gay men to consider yet again the devious, often sublimated, forms of their own sexism," and contributed to a "democratic coalition of diverse groups."[148] In what amounted to an emergent philosophy of intersectionality, the identity new leftists came to embrace a much more nuanced sense of their own role in the historical process. Rather than presenting race, sex, or class as *the* key to revolutionary politics, or conversely advocating a weak pluralism in which everyone minded their own political gardens, the most creative new leftists imagined a movement in which identities were more fluid and struggles more open to the interventions of allies and friends.

It was also a movement that sensed in its very being the importance of being transnational. Some activists who participated in all four movements favoured Canadian nationalism.[149] They also typically insisted that that nationalism must be detached from any ethnic or racial particularism and wide open to the world. It would be difficult to imagine a more porous movement than the Toronto left in the 1970s, wherein one could argue over which Guyanese social party to support, the rights of Chilean women, or the rights of gays and lesbians in Australia. Toronto new leftists saw themselves as citizens of the world—not the liberal order they had inherited from the past, but the far more egalitarian and democratic world they aspired to build in the future.

10

New Leninists and New Constellations: In Quest of the Revolutionary Party, 1971–82

IN MAY 1975 Reuben Samuels arrived in town. He was on a mission to whip a number of Toronto comrades into shape—to turn a bunch of "rotten new leftists" into hardened Bolsheviki.[1] Samuels, a dedicated lifelong Trotskyist, was a heavyweight representative of the International Secretariat of the Spartacist League, a Trotskyist organization based in New York. He had been responsible for assigning positions of responsibility when the New York office had founded a "satellite" organization called the Trotskyist League of Canada. Now, headquarters was sending him north to set things straight.

Local members of the Trotskyist League (TL) had split off from another formation, the Revolutionary Marxist Group, in 1974, and the two organizations were, not surprisingly, at odds. The TL specialized in denouncing competitors for departing from the views of Lenin and Trotsky. It created the impression that other vanguardists were mere opportunists, easily co-opted by less rigorous and more "new leftish" currents. From the TL perspective, the authentic left was tiny. The Trotskyist League's publication, *Spartacist Canada*, was always reminding its readers how one or another ostensibly revolutionary organization—"ORO" for short—had failed an "acid test for the left," proving themselves to be not only "fake Trotskyist" or "fake socialist" but "fake leftist" as well. Such fakirs were everywhere. They could be found in all the hip and liberal social movements, from the anti-nuclear and anti-working-class "eco-faddists" to the "liberal consciousness soothers" promoting boycott and disinvestment campaigns against apartheid South Africa.[2]

Dubbed the "Sparts" by their many opponents, members of the Trotskyist League became a highly visible presence on the Toronto left. Like other new Leninists, they claimed that their group was the only real revolutionary organization in town. But in a marked departure from most of the organization's rivals, their recruitment strategy focused on wooing the doctrinaire and disillusioned members of their adversaries. Trotskyist League members, selling copies of their *Spartacist Canada* newspaper, were ubiquitous at left-wing events, where they gained notoriety for persistently denouncing their many ideological enemies.

The minutes of Samuels's key meeting in Toronto read like field notes from an experiment designed to highlight the danger of obedience to unreasoned authority. A good deal of what Samuels had to say was highly personal, abusive, and free of political argument. He dismissed one member as "dense and dumb," and pointed out that her unreliability was confirmed by her sexual behaviour: "After she was discharged from the hospital she became engaged in a triangle all of whom contracted venereal warts. This triangle or VD clique became a source of anti-leadership, anti-exec grumblings." VD was becoming known throughout the Spartacist tendency as the "Canadian Disease," quipped Samuels, in one of his many pokes at the alleged Canadian nationalism and "Toronto Firstism" of local members (one of whom was criticized for having suggested that the Trotskyist League should have been founded in Toronto rather than New York). After a member was shot down for objecting to some of Samuels's criticism, the rest of those in attendance appeared to meekly accept his remarks. But even they became the butt of the New Yorker's scarcasm: "I confess to being a petty-bourgeois submenshevik new lefter," was his mocking paraphrase of one such confession. "Amen. I confess to being a Canadian nationalist and mistrusting IS [International Secretariat]. Amen . . ."[3]

The local leadership adopted the general thrust of Samuels's critique and strongly condemned new left–derived personalism. They then moved on to criticize and speculate upon the personal relationships of some of the group's newest members. The sad state of the Toronto branch might be helped by disciplining members for "violating Bolshevik morality." It might also be reformed by transferring members into and out of the city. The "weak elements," for instance, could go off to the San Francisco Bay Area for strengthening.[4]

The intervention by the American Samuels in Toronto is a particularly harsh example of a wider anti-democratic and even abusive trend in the politics of the new Leninist parties that came to the fore in the 1970s and held a certain sway into the 1980s. But it is by no means the whole story; some of the groups in that array of left activism enjoyed more democracy than that experienced in some new left organizations; and working together as a disciplined unit they were sometimes able to exert an outsized influence on the city's busy political terrain.

Activists sought this structured alternative to new left modes of organizing for a number of quite logical reasons. Many who rallied to Trotskyist and Maoist parties saw new leftism as an infantile phase of a revolution that they were called upon to organize in a different way. New Leninist models offered a remedy to the informal leadership and inertia that sometimes plagued new left organizations. In contrast to the new left's cornucopia of ideas, Leninism provided a cohesive—many would say battle-tested—theory of social change. Historic and contemporary examples of vanguard parties seizing power appeared to prove that those bodies represented a theory of action that could bypass ineffective circles of "petit-bourgeois radicals," connect to the working class, and bring "power to the people." Although most new Leninists recognized the problems inherent in certain historic Leninist models, they were able to attribute those failings to a mixture of personalities and objective conditions.

Vanguardist groups tended to adopt a policy of entering industrial workplaces—"industrializing," they called it—a tactic that testified to the relatively buoyant industrial economy of the 1960s and 1970s, when it was no great feat for a militant in search of employment to land a reasonable job in a factory. (It was always useful, for such a militant, to see that only an edited account of his or her past radical activities made it to prospective employers.) A modicum of centralization, professionalism, and specialization was hardly dangerous. Instead of being less than the sum of their parts—as some new left organizations undoubtedly were—vanguard parties and other groupings promised to maximize the energies of their activist memberships. As Lenin remarked, and vanguardists repeated, "The strength of the vanguard is ten times, a hundred times, more than a hundred times greater than its numbers."[5]

* * *

The plethora of vanguard parties of the late 1960s, 1970s, and early 1980s included not just the various and ever-changing Trotskyist and Maoist groupings but also the Communist Party of Canada; and in Toronto from 1971 to 1982 all of these groups were in an often bitter competition with each other—which meant that many meetings of the left were opaque to outsiders unfamiliar with the background of the groups.

Many participants spoke an arcane language that made sense only to people steeped in left history and comfortable with such left terms as opportunist, adventurist, sectarian, tailist, and ultra-leftist, none of which came with universally agreed upon definitions, and all of which were common terms in polemical warfare. Moreover, much of what was debated was the international history of the communist movement. Maoists and Trotskyists claiming the mantle of Lenin were intent on showing that the CPC had betrayed the revolution. Maoist organizations waged a constant battle over the history and future of the Chinese Revolution, a contest that became all the more bitter after 1972, when the signs coming out of Peking (Beijing) were so difficult to interpret. One of them, the Canadian Communist League (CCL, later the Workers' Communist Party, WCP), became notorious for declaring the Soviet Union to be the enemy of the revolution. In one polemic, it even praised the Canadian army's future role in standing up to the Soviets, in contrast to Americans said to be intent on appeasing the "Soviet Empire." Cuban fishing trawlers operating in Canadian waters were likened to the Caribbean country's military intervention in Angola. It was even possible that Canada's Progressive Conservatives were shrinking in the face of Soviet aggression because they were beholden to companies with a vested interest in Soviet trade.[6] The CCL was hardly the only group to blare forth with stark pronouncements on the world—because being authoritative on questions of the world revolution and being perfectly decisive in determining who locally was a friend and who an enemy were all part of the working description of a vanguardist in the 1970s.

Other factions arose with a rapidity that was both astounding and confusing. For much of the 1970s at the University of Toronto the CPC's Central Committee had to contend with two opposition currents: on one side, the Eurocommunists, wide open to new left influences and practices; on the other, CPCers calling for a hard line against those tendencies. Both sides jockeyed with a larger, more amorphous body of centrists. Among the Trotskyists at large, the League for Socialist Action, the Trotskyist League, and the Revolutionary Marxist Group were joined by yet another grouping, the International Socialists (IS). In addition to the Canadian Communist League, the Maoist formations included a group called In Struggle! (IS!) as well as the Communist Party of Canada (Marxist-Leninist) or CPC-ML, the Canadian Liberation Movement (CLM), the Canadian Party of Labour, and the Bolshevik Union, which tried to pick up disgruntled members from the other factions of the Maoist movement. Other groups that joined the fray, such as the New Tendency (NT) and Wages for Housework (W4H), also sought to overcome deficiencies in new left praxis, but were more difficult to pin down ideologically.

Writing in 1972 in *Transformations*, an intellectually rich magazine that straddled new leftist and new Leninist perspectives, Marjaleena Repo insightfully underlined a tendency in vanguard groups to zero in on one "primary contradiction." For example, the Canadian Liberation Movement, she said, had allowed its militants to declare their absolute support for Canadian trade unions—because the primary contradiction for all Canadian leftists was presented by the battle against U.S. imperialism—without pondering how democratic and emancipatory such unions would really be for rank-and-file workers. After establishing this "primary mystique," the groups would see other key issues—such as the oppression of women—as mere distractions or even threats to unity.[7] In vanguard groups with charismatic leaders or behind-the-scenes caucuses, determining the "primary contradiction" could vest a tiny minority with a great deal of power.

While factory work was popular during the 1970s for many young leftists—especially for those belonging to new Leninist groups—most found themselves employed in white-collar environs, an experience that occurred in tandem with the growing unionization of public-sector workers and the emergence of the Canadian Union of Public Employees as the largest union in the country. Reflecting the relative radicalization of this sector, the Civil Service Association of Ontario was transformed into the Ontario Public Service Employees Union at mid-decade. Hospital workers repeatedly engaged in illegal strikes during these years, and the Canadian Union of Postal Workers, which had embarked on its first major strike only in 1965, earned a reputation as a particularly strike-prone union. In 1980 members of the Public Sector Alliance of Canada conducted one of the largest strikes in Canadian history, temporarily halting all passenger service at what was then known as the Toronto International Airport.

But the vanguard parties were not all that interested in teachers or office clerks. Members in white-collar and service-sector occupations were often pressured to find more useful work. As far as the revolution was concerned, most public-sector workers had dead-end jobs.

Still, one thing the vanguard groups had in common was a view of the working-class revolution as the only avenue to human emancipation. Indeed, the key to correct thinking and action was an analysis of the working class and its interests—although, as Repo complained, for the new Leninists the human and alienated workers depicted by Karl Marx had been displaced by mythological creatures lacking interest in culture, sex, or anything beyond the workplace.[8] The "peculiarly narrow and limited human beings" portrayed by new Leninists were always male, often muscular, and seemed to have but one hobby: that of raising their fists.

> The worker is uncomplicated, brave, militant, ready for action—and always held back by "bad leaders." The worker is never young and scared about his/her future. The worker is never middle-aged, arthritic, obese, cancer-ridden. The worker is never old and defeated by his/her life experiences. The worker is never sexist and oppressive towards women. The worker is never a woman with too many children, and too little time to understand them. . . . The worker is never a bundle of unfulfilled hopes and dreams.[9]

In *Waking Up in the Men's Room*, a memoir of her 1970s activism, Catherine MacLeod recalls the liveliness of the Revolutionary Marxist Group, with some

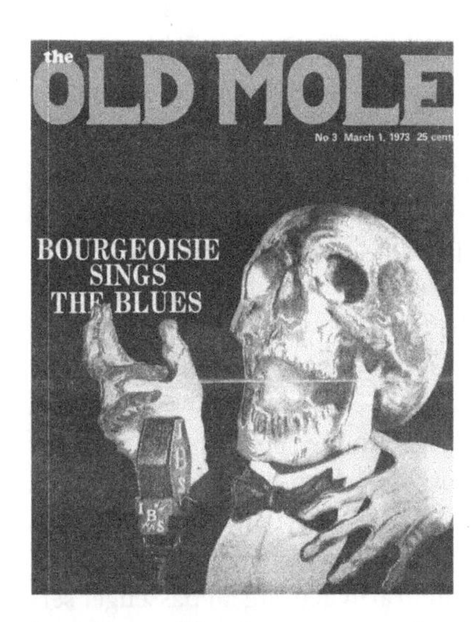

The RMG's *Old Mole* had more visual appeal than most new Leninist publications; March 1, 1973.

William Ready Division of Archives and Research Collections.

reservations about how the politics worked in practice. Although the RMG members had a distaste for the middle class and fetishized the working class, it struck working-class MacLeod that they tended to want the working class to rise up to their own level. They seemed disinclined to immerse themselves in a working-class culture that was not their own.[10]

RMG's documents themselves suggested the new complexities of doing class politics in the 1970s. The organization conceded that it could not reach most workers in a plant-by-plant campaign, but it still championed working within unions in order to "develop an exemplary practice in a few selected unions so as to demonstrate the RMG's capacity for effective mass action to the emerging vanguard." By the summer of 1973 RMG boasted a handful of members working at the post office, Douglas Aircraft, and Canada Packers. Militants could draw inspiration from Lenin's *What Is to Be Done?* (1902), which they interpreted as arguing that the development of a working-class base would not only pay off strategically but also ensure such a group's political integrity. In vivid contrast to such groups as the CPC-ML and the CPC, RMG initially did almost nothing to acknowledge the extent to which many workers were members of racialized minorities.[11] RMG engaged in polemics with the Trotskyists in the League for Socialist Action (LSA) in part because the RMG lined up behind the leadership of the United Secretariat of the Fourth International whereas the LSA backed the opposing forces associated with the U.S.-based Socialist Workers Party (SWP).[12]

Some vanguard tendencies looked more critically at the working class, at times recognizing that white male workers frequently won their victories at the expense of their less powerful comrades. One tendency in a group called Wages for Housework (W4H) maintained that each section of the working class had its own strengths and weaknesses, and "no one section has all the strengths sufficient to build the power of the whole class."[13]

* * *

If these vanguard parties had a disproportionate impact on the Toronto left in the 1970s, much of the secret for that phenomenon rested in their firm grip on members. Members who joined a party tended to be tithed, and their work for a given organization was intensively monitored. It often seemed that, if the "personal" was indeed the "political," in many a vanguard group this only meant that the personal had been colonized by the political. "Maybe interpersonal chemistry plays a role in social clubs or petit-bourgeois political organizations," argued a report endorsed by one Trotskyist political committee, "but not in organizations like ours."[14]

In the Maoist group In Struggle! many members, although drawn to a considerable extent from the middle class, lived below or at the poverty line. John Cleveland, a pioneering scholar of the Canadian far left, remarks that members lacking stereos or television sets before they joined were unlikely to acquire them afterwards. At the end of 1977, when In Struggle! recognized that it could not win masses of workers with its onerous dues regime, it put a new policy into place, but still suggested sacrifices on the part of its members: they could keep the first $150 of their weekly earnings but were urged to give In Struggle! 75 per cent of anything above that. The group also sought to structure its members' time, devising schedules with days divided into four-hour time blocks.[15] It had a preoccupation with questions of security, and many members did not even know the real or full names of people they worked with, or the identities of the party's leadership, under the understanding that members subjected to police interrogation would have little to tell. Long after the easing of these emergency measures—explicable enough in a Montreal-headquartered group whose members well remembered the October Crisis—the emphasis on "compartmentalization" continued to restrict communications among lay members. As Cleveland concludes, this limit on horizontal forms of communication increased the power of party full-timers and centralizing tendencies more broadly.[16]

Many new leftists, sometimes influenced by European denunciations of "Obsolete Communism," considered the Communist Party of Canada a grey monolith, but behind the scenes the CPC was home to more democracy and debate than found in many of the other vanguard groupings. The records of the University of Toronto Communist Club suggest the liveliness and freedom of many of its discussions. Some discussions turned on questions of direct interest to new leftists. What was the level of student consciousness? Did increasing student cynicism in the wake of the decline of student power signal possibilities for the left or the right? Should graduate students impose their more developed world views upon undergraduates? Is the NDP a writeoff or the next left's nucleus? Why are the many intellectual Marxists in political science—especially at York—so inactive when it comes to acting on actual issues? And what is the proper definition of the "left"?[17]

The Toronto Eurocommunists built upon the analyses of two Clarkes, Nelson and Phyllis, who assessed past Canadian Marxist thought critically and argued forcefully that any future socialist order in Canada must be pluralist. The left had to make provision for a variety of parties with an enshrined right to disent. From Nelson Clarke's perspective, it was absurd to expect young people, intent on democratizing all aspects of society, to support the policies of a party over which they exerted no control.[18] For his wife Phyllis Clarke, a member of the University of Toronto Club, the party centre had its own version of "me-tooism," which involved modelling itself holus bolus on other parties from other times and a concept of proletarian internationalism that was reduced to a carte blanche defence of the practices of "existing socialism." She advised the party to learn to work better with others, consider the merits of some external criticism, and build a united front against monopoly capital today, not in some indefinite future.[19]

Historian Stanley Ryerson was also a key figure in this milieu, and from his perspective it made no sense for Communists to treat new leftists as enemies and thereby throw away all chance of influencing or correcting them. It was all too easy for the CPC brass to dismiss the new left as petit-bourgeois, the very loose term it often applied to critics of centralism who were in search of more inner-party democracy. Charnie (Guettel) Cunningham, the future author of *Marxism and Feminism*, discerned a party leadership fearful of younger communists like herself, yet she distinguished between the "errors of growth" that such young Reds were bound to make and the leadership's "errors of decline," which were so often predicated on notions of preserving the party from impure mass movements.[20]

Contrary to stereotype, the University of Toronto CPC Club was strongly committed to freedom of speech as a fundamental precept of a full democracy: it even argued against banning anti-socialist propaganda in such a future society, because political censorship threatened to undermine such a society's very existence. On the U of T campus, Communists in general played a leading role in a wide assortment of student associations. Dues-paying members of the Communist Club numbered thirty-one in 1977, a respectable number for one campus, and—in the wake of controversies and departures over the previous two years—undoubtedly down from earlier times. A good number of U of T Communists remained outside the Club, but were plugged into other parts of the CPC's rather labyrinthine bureaucratic structure.[21]

In general the local CPC, hurt by Toronto's changing demographics in the 1960s and 1970s—as Jews migrated to the suburbs and anti-Communist East Europeans gravitated to the right—made efforts to recruit Italians, Greeks, and Portuguese, in large measure because of the influence of its sister parties in each national group's respective European homeland. Sometimes these efforts brought more conflict than agreement when the CPC's orthodox opinions and strategies collided with the policies and issues of the homeland organizations.[22]

By 1979 many in the Eurocommunist wing, having lost significant battles in the early 1970s against hard-liners and in the mid-1970s on gay and lesbian questions, believed the time had come to hang up on the Communist Party. In 1979, in a document he quietly circulated to selected party members, Nelson Clarke contemplated an alternative to the CPC. Echoing new left arguments, he drew attention to the extent to which the CPC theorists had never grasped the significance, in a modern age, of capitalism's superstructure; nor had CPC leaders internalized the imperative of forming a united front with like-minded groups in a Canada in which Communists remained a tiny minority of the population.[23]

What all this came down to was the conclusion that the party was unlikely to change. Like many "revisionists" with a long history in the party, Nelson Clarke had seen real promise for a more open and creative party up to the Soviet invasion of Czechoslovakia in 1968, but he now believed that change was so unlikely that the only plausible scenario was via a change in the Soviet party itself. He was not tempted to split off a faction from the CPC, believing that splinter groups had a record of failure and were viewed suspiciously by the broader left. Instead, he envisioned working outside the party's structures—taking up the goal of convincing movement activists of the importance of a new, leading party.[24]

He was influenced in this position at least partly by a reading of *Beyond the Fragments: Feminism and the Making of Socialism* (1979), an important collection edited by Sheila Rowbotham, Lynne Segal, and Hilary Wainwright—a text that also excited many a Maoist.[25] From this book, Clarke learned that socialist consciousness in the women's movement had often developed without (and sometimes in spite of) the intervention of vanguard-type groups. He quoted from a review of that book in the British publication *Marxism Today* to illustrate the kind of party that was now needed:

> The relationship between experience and consciousness does not therefore, in my view, abolish the need for a party, but it significantly alters its role. If consciousness comes more from the experience of struggle and less from the guidance of a revolutionary vanguard, <u>the party's legitimation no longer comes from its being separate from and above other movements, but from its knowledge of and involvement in them, its understanding of their similarities and differences. A different kind of orientation is needed, which is more open to dialogue on equal terms with other movements.</u>[26]

Clarke wanted to accelerate the development of that orientation by writing about the experiences of the tenants' movement, the establishment of the Ontario Association of Legal Clinics, and the building of ReforMetro, all of which he claimed had happened because of the decisive role played by "Creative Marxists" both inside and outside the party.[27]

* * *

For many years the CPC's primary opponents on the far left were the Trotskyists, whose largest and longest-established Toronto organization in the late 1960s was the League for Socialist Action/Young Socialists (LSA/YS)—which had played a key role in such groups as the Fair Play for Cuba Committee and Vietnam Mobilization Committee. Some militants, like Ross Dowson, could trace their involvement in revolutionary politics back to the 1940s. Fully caught up in the "Canada Question" debates of the early 1970s, the LSA hit a high point in 1973 with an impressive three-hundred-person-strong convention in Toronto, celebrated in its well-received publication *Labor Challenge*.[28]

The LSA was soon joined, first by the Revolutionary Marxist Group and then by the International Socialists, whose origins lay in a socialist study group at York University. The study group was a bit eclectic but strongly tended towards Trotskyism. In 1973–74 its members decided to become involved in the Waffle en masse in at attempt to influence the faction's political direction. Political Science professor David McNally, then of York University, recalls being struck by the extent to which the Waffle had developed a base among trade unionists, and how Waffle events had a different atmosphere than efforts orchestrated by student-dominated organizations. "There were steel workers, auto workers, health care workers, nurses and so on" in the midst of the Waffle, he says, with "many of them very well rooted trade union activists." While the Waffle tended to disappear from the historical radar after its split with the NDP, it continued through the early 1970s to be a substantial socialist organization, boasting a paper membership of six hundred, almost half of them spread among the organization's three Toronto branches.[29]

Although the pre-IS members were by no means Marxist-Leninists, some of their discussions reflected the "soft" Maoism of the time, with slogans or definitions authored by Mao creeping into their political vocabulary. An early document, defiantly casting the group as a formation that did not adhere to Moscow, Peking, or the Fourth International, nevertheless added: "Of the two major socialist powers, we recognize China as far more progressive than the Soviet Union." Casual references to Mao could also be found within the Waffle itself.[30]

Borrowing from Trotsky, members of the York study group considered the Waffle to be centrist, that is, as vacillating between reform and revolution, attracting people who might otherwise join a real revolutionary organization. The task for Trotskyists was thus to smash the "hegemony of centrism," even if this meant "splitting and destroying the Waffle." In pursuit of this goal, study group members placed Waffle members into three categories: potential recruits, the politically useless, and the dangerous. Members of the study group consciously saw themselves as a vanguard and acted accordingly.[31] In broad strokes, the main political difference setting it apart from the Waffle's leadership appeared to be the study group's open embrace of a revolutionary party. As the Waffle entered its terminal crisis, the militants argued that the faction provided a good negative example of a middle-class movement that had failed to implant itself in industry.[32]

In the end the study group decided to dissolve its Waffle connection in favour of a new revolutionary organization, which members at first called the Independent Socialists before quickly renaming it International Socialists. An initial step was to put into motion an earlier plan for implantation of members at targeted factories. Reluctant participants were pushed and told that timidity and lack of confidence were the main barriers to the party's growth. When some members left because they were opposed to, or reluctant to accept, the turn to industry, the International Socialists presented their departures as a positive development. The lack of democracy that the study group had complained about in the Waffle—it had, with some justification, criticized authoritarian tendencies within the Waffle leadership—had surfaced within this smaller group.[33]

The International Socialists' industrial turn ended a year later, in 1976, marked by the expulsion of the group's national chairman and the resignation of fourteen members, a number of whom had won elected union positions. Some subsequently formed the short-lived Militant Worker group. Departing members were accused of having tried to build a coalition of left-wing bureaucrats, rather than one of rank-and-file workers. Although one member had won the presidency of the union at the large Canada Packers factory, this activist was accused of then allowing the plant's rank-and-file caucus and newsletter to fall apart and moving to the right of even the union bureaucracy. Other members, including the president of an Ontario Association of Nurses local, were accused of having substituted *The Hospital Worker* newspaper for real rank-and-file struggle. This parting of ways reflected a larger international split, as the industrial-focused International Socialists in the United States and the International Socialists in the United Kingdom also parted ways, with remaining members of the local International Socialists siding with the U.K. party.[34]

Reflecting on the reasons for the International Socialists' industrialization program in the first place, one of its participants concluded: "We believed that the root of all our problems was our petty bourgeois social composition or in other words the problem was ourselves." Others recalled a theory that the IS would best be able to recruit by proving, through struggles in the workplace, that it provided the real leadership of the working class. Yet the desire to lead, many complained, led members to hide their revolutionary politics in favour of merely extolling a kind of militant unionism. Some believed it was because of industrialization that the organization had become much more centralist and less democratic. When members became frustrated with their lack of momentum, they charged, the leadership engaged in false triumphalism to uphold group morale. Each failure was seen as a step along the road to victory, and criticism was simply not permitted. One exception was "petty-baiting," whereby members not holding industrial jobs were called "petties" (short for petty-bourgeois) and encouraged to leave. Coupled with an anti-intellectual tendency to present whatever "workers" supported as being correct, a crisis atmosphere remained near-constant.[35]

In its subsequent "total turn outward," the IS prioritized sales of its *Workers' Action* newspaper. Emphasizing the superiority of organizing outside factories, the organization provided its membership with the same kind of exaggerations previously used to justify organizing inside factories. Thus sales of the *Workers' Action* at the Hamilton Steel Car factory were presented as being more important than the activity of members inside that plant. In contrast to the now officially dismal record of IS industrialization, a leaflet distributed outside another workplace was credited for having "almost sparked a wildcat strike." Members were told that "Lenin was an excellent factory agitator although he never worked in a factory." The IS leadership later claimed such exaggerations were necessary in order to wean the membership away from industrialization.[36]

* * *

The Trotksyists did not monopolize the field of vanguard groups and parties. The supposedly grassroots socialism of Chinese Communism excited many leftists in Canada, as an antidote to fossilized Soviet Marxism, tepid NDP-style democracy, and the hypercritical factionalism of the Trotskyists.

The Canadian Liberation Movement, with its five Toronto branches, was one of the more dynamic and original of the Maoist movements. While never publicly declaring itself a Marxist-Leninist group, it was largely run by a secretive executive called the Marxist-Leninist Caucus and was particularly keen on promoting the representation of Canadians on university faculties and establishing Canadian unions for Canadian workers.

Its Toronto East Club in particular, notwithstanding its Leninist commitment to providing a vanguard to the working class, became strongly committed to community organizing—affiliating itself to the Greater Riverdale Organization, for example. It joined a fight against air pollution at the local Canada Metal factory. Supported by a storefront office, members went door to door, built alliances with local organizations, organized car pools to transport children for lead-poisoning tests, and lauded working-class residents for standing up to a proposed expressway.[37] In an electoral campaign, the CLM focused on issues such as lead-poisoning, rent control, and overnight parking privileges. It called for a tax system that benefited small businesses over U.S. corporations. Multilingual propaganda touted the CLM candidate over his business-affiliated competitors, and more unexpectedly enunciated the CLM's opposition to shopping plazas as being distinctly American in both architecture and consumerist philosophy.[38] In all such moves, the CLM suggested its close adherence to creating a united front of all who might fight U.S. imperialism. It had drunk deeply from the well of Chairman Mao's writings on the "new democracy," which counselled Marxists to work in broad concert with others to achieve national liberation. By the end of 1973 it had adopted "Yankee go home!" as its official slogan, in a move condemned by some as racist and that ultimately led to members of the group facing prosecution under Canada's hate crimes legislation.[39]

CLM exemplified both the advantages and disadvantages of the vanguard approach. As its frontal attack on conservative labour unions in Toronto suggested, vanguardism implied a certain fearlessness in the face of entrenched opposition. In the mid-1970s, CLM created the Canadian Workers' Union (CWU) as a militant counterpart to the movement for independent Canadian trade unions. It succeeded in signing up at least 30 per cent of the workers at one factory and came close to winning certification at a major hotel. At another factory, CWU militants signed up an impressive 80 per cent of the workers, despite confronting a determined campaign from the Labour Council, Ontario Federation of Labour, Canadian Labour Congress, and the Ironworkers' Union. The CWU itself was finally certified, notwithstanding hearings described by a reporter as "tumultuous," with labour's established powers seeking to block the upstart union.[40]

Perhaps the CLM's most lasting accomplishment came with the establishment of New Canada Press, which by the mid-1970s (becoming known as NC Press) had grown from a $30,000-a-year operation to one pulling in $100,000 in sales. It published a small library of books upholding the left-nationalist position on Canadian working-class history.[41] All of these accomplishments were made possible by the selfless labour of committed militants. CLM members were kept extremely busy, both on special campaigns and in the everyday routine of selling newspapers, attending meetings, and party organizing. Although CLM's leadership recognized that overwork could constitute a problem—a January 1974 report noted that it was important for people to be able to join without committing themselves to organizing seven days a week—they appeared to have done nothing to alleviate this pressure. Indeed, they heightened it considerably. After plans to double membership in six months dramatically failed, members were told to increase their discipline and given a new target of tripling membership over the course of a year. CLM's chairman Gary Perly even intensified the pressure. "Workers are calling up at 2 AM in the morning demanding to know why we're not organizing," he exclaimed, channelling at least some of the spirit of new left voluntarism. "The Canadian people are ready willing and able to fight imperialism. They're crying out for leadership in the most literal sense." But CLMers were not up to this task, he complained. Before progress could be made they had to transform their movement and "change ourselves."[42] Something of a new left focus on achieving individual authenticity had also evidently survived the transition to vanguardism.

Perly's leadership of CLM also highlighted certain disadvantages of the vanguard model, chief among them a marked tendency to put Marxism-Leninism to work as a weapon in interpersonal conflicts within organizations. Applying the Chinese communist idea that left-wing movements tended to exhibit two lines of struggle (bourgeois and proletarian) that had to be strictly monitored and controlled, Perly announced that none other than the CLM's general secretary had been sabotaging the organization. She was accused of various crimes against the organization and her husband. Members voted to henceforth refer to this person as "the Poobah." It was not the first time such a campaign had been mounted against a member.[43]

In an earlier campaign a U.S.-born member produced a twenty-three-page self-criticism. Admitting that she had committed terrible crimes against the Canadian people and their movement, she identified her primary contradiction as being an "Anti-imperialist Canadian in words and Yankee 'progressive' conscious agent in deeds." She confessed to being a "rotten Yankee agent" who had tried to "split and wreck the movement." Many of her actions, she said, were blameworthy. She had thrown the Canadian flag on the floor of a closet while cleaning a communal sleeping space. She had believed Canadians to be dumb—and Americans smart. She had invited American friends and relatives to visit, thus intensifying the U.S. domination of Canada. Subsequent published elaborations of her sins suggested that she had been a police informant, drug pusher, strikebreaker—and even an enabler of the Central Intelligence Agency.[44]

The general secretary's self-criticism extended even to her days in high school, where she confessed to having failed to achieve solidarity with working-class students because of her upper-class background. Her fate—at least as it is described in three contemporary sources—was to spend a considerable period under the close surveillance of CLM members, which included living in a closet for about a month. She had to ask permission to leave, whether to go to work or use the washroom. She had scalding hot water and tea poured over her head on multiple occasions. She was ordered at least once to lie on her back and bark like a dog.[45]

Her case was extreme, and perhaps accentuated by this woman's past reputation as Perly's inquisitor-in-chief. But it was not unique. Eventually the whole of CLM joined in the crusade to combat the enemy within—reminiscent of the Moscow trials of the 1930s or, closer to home for Maoists, the vilification campaign from 1966 to 1969 against "capitalist-roader" Liu Shaoqi in China. Members working on NC Press were accused of "sabotage" and required to produce self-criticisms for infractions like delays or sloppy work. Problems in organizing unions were also attributed to sabotage. Members confessed that they had not recruited new members because they were, as selfish exponents of bourgeois values, keen to avoid the mass work that such an influx would portend, or remained averse to working-class struggles in principle.[46] Others in the CLM remembered a woman dissident being punished by being forced to stand outside in rainy weather without a coat.[47] Vanguardism could extract extraordinary feats of energy and self-sacrifice from ordinary members; it could also run roughshod over their democratic rights to speak their minds.

By 1976 the CLM was in the throes of a crisis. Early that year, members voted to set aside the planned agenda of their annual congress in favour of discussing their past and future. Their first item of business was discussing a paper on the "Role of Fascism in CLM," a charged topic on which no fewer than forty-three members spoke. The comprehensive document upon which they based their discussion traced CLM's problems to its very origins, when Perly had established himself as the group's sole intellectual. Rival intellectuals, such as Gary Teeple, and older and experienced activists, including Bill Spira, had eventually been driven out. The document noted that a small group of dissidents who left in 1970–71 had specifically criticized Perly's treatment of members (especially women). Shortly thereafter troublesome members from outlying parts of the country were brought to Toronto, where they were subject to Perly's "psychoanalysis." Things were getting so bad that they had difficulty recruiting new members because potential newcomers were turned off by the relentless criticisms occurring in CLM meetings. All of these signs of authoritarianism surfaced even before the most rigorous campaign against "bourgeois selfishness" had begun.[48] That campaign brought CLM's introversion to a whole new level. Husbands and wives were prevented from belonging to the same political clubs, heads were shaved in acts of humiliation, and dissidents were subjected to verbal and at times physical abuse. Members became isolated not only from society, but from each other, as bitterness, hatred, and mistrust took hold. Under Perly's thumb, those most dedicated to CLM became oppressed and tortured by their own organization. Major decisions seemed to be made, not by the members at large, but by an unelected and secretive clique called the Marxist-Leninist Caucus, made up of a handful of founding members. Then, said the document, "finally the mill ran out of grist."[49]

Members hoped they could salvage the CLM by expelling Perly, which by a resounding majority they decided to do. Yet some warned that the movement's problems ran deeper than that. What had prevented ordinary members from speaking out about his leadership style? Surely a top-down approach had become a sacrosanct element of proletarian organizing—and now called out to be superseded by more grassroots methods and a more nuanced understanding of the various identities and groups active on the left.[50] The annual meeting passed a flurry of motions anticipating such a radical-democratic future, but to no avail: weighed down by its heavy history, CLM was essentially finished by 1976.

Competing with that organization was the mainly Southern Ontario–based Canadian Party of Labour, which, like the CLM, had come out of the Canadians for the NLF organization and, like other vanguard parties, engaged in "industrializing" its members. An autobiography of one CPL member has him bounce from the U of T library to the Pilkington Glass factory, General Motors, Ford, Goodyear Tire, Greyhound, and Canadian Pacific Railway in the course of just a few years.[51]

In 1974–75 the CPL decided to "proletarianize" its anti-racist front, the Committee Against Racism, downgrade the community-oriented Workers' Action movement, and de-emphasize the sales of its paper, *The Worker*. Inspired by historical reconstructions of the Russian Revolution, CPL militants judged that activities outside the industrial workplace should be subordinated to activism within it. Factory cells, not broadly based coalitions, were the key to the revolution.[52] All CPL workers joined such cells, which met on a weekly basis to discuss political and workplace issues. Each cell had its own leader, who in turn attended larger meetings of cell leaders. With the CPL's redoubled turn to factories, a labour commission was added to this structure to oversee the work of the cells. A former member of the CPL complained that leaders on this body used it as a means to bully and browbeat rank-and-file members to step up their activity. Some of the cells put out workplace newsletters, such as *Inglis Worker* and *Government Housing Workers*. CPL militants often ran for, and some won, executive offices in union locals. Even after the CPL receded from view in the mid-1980s, some of these militants remained as local presidents.[53]

The CPL exemplified the democratic deficits characteristic of many vanguard groups—which were sometimes justified in terms of revolutionary continuity and excellent leadership. The decision-making powers of members were greatly diminished, and ultimately they were deprived of a chance to develop as individual leftists. A former member, David Owen, recalled only one party convention in his thirteen years of membership—and no elections at that one-off event. The CPL's national committee was instead chosen by the tendency's founding leader, Phil Taylor. In the 1980s members complained bitterly about the lack of discussions preceding a major change in the group's line. It did not help matters that Taylor was alleged to have had an affair with one-half of a prominent couple in the party. Owen remembered that five members of his teachers' cell—himself included—left the CPL at this time: "The party's organization, discipline, ideology, and leaders squeezed the joy out of the struggle for me."[54]

Of greater long-term significance than these early versions of Maoism was the Canadian Communist League (Marxist-Leninist), which many contemporaries simply called "The League." Based in Montreal, it grew to an organization of a thousand active members, larger than any of its rivals on the far left. It was capable of mobilizing as many as three hundred delegates to labour conventions in Quebec. In 1976 the Toronto group Workers' Unity—which presented an archetypal critique of the new left organization Red Morning as "a youth-culture-oriented, petit-bourgeois leftist organization which was totally divorced from the masses of people"—rallied to the League.[55] The substantial working-class base of the League was a standing rebuke to other far left groups, seemingly mired forever in the new left student and "petit-bourgeois" demographic. Inspired by a reading of Communist history, it focused especially on the establishment of workplace cells (of the sort recommended by the Bolshevization strategy in vogue from 1924 to 1935). "Each factory must be a fortress for communism," explained the League's publication, *The Forge*—in language that would have been quite conventional in 1931.[56]

Through its punchy graphics and fiercely polemical articles, often ending with a succession of slogans followed by exclamation marks, *The Forge* channelled the fervent militancy of the Communist Party from 1928 to 1935—the famous (or infamous) Third Period. It also functioned somewhat conspiratorially, with the membership only slightly aware of the identity of its leaders—and a good proportion of them turned out to be Anglophone in an overwhelmingly Francophone province.[57] In one of *The Forge*'s more energetic epistles against Trotskyism, it denounced them as verminous "agents of the bourgeoisie" and called upon loyal militants to "wipe them out." Perhaps it was merely repaying the Spartacists for judging members of the League to be "Running Dogs of the Bourgeois Army." Although the League as a whole was initially very dogmatic, sectarian, and isolationist, it had mellowed considerably by 1981, by which time it was known as the Workers' Communist Party. Still, it continued to maintain ties with China and remained more theoretically orthodox than its rival Maoists in En Lutte!/In Struggle![58]

When In Struggle! imploded in 1982, the WCP saw that party's failure not as a crisis in Marxism or party-building, but as a validation of its own ideology. Yet a flurry of letters in issues of *The Forge* immediately subsequent to that statement suggested otherwise. More letters, and eventually articles, appeared reassessing earlier views on culture and gender. Punk and new wave went from reactionary to exciting and progressive, as local rock musician Dan Kelly showcased some of the city's popular left-wing acts such as L'Etranger (with future writer and NDP MP Charlie Angus; Andrew Cash also became an MP), Mama Quilla II (some of its members, including Lorraine Segato, later formed The Parachute Club; members reunited to perform at Jack Layton's funeral), Young Lions (a fairly well known punk band), Truth and Rights (mostly reggae), and the more obscure Rude Awakening. Socialist realism was retired with little complaint. The Toronto branch's showing of the anti-porn film *Not a Love Story* (1982) led to discussions about the need for a more total assault against sexism and an acknowledgement that this problem extended to the left and the WCP.[59]

In mid-September 1981, the party criticized its past treatment of intellectuals and in early October several *Forge* writers—referring to the deluge of letters they had been receiving—outlined a host of criticisms, from a need to print more articles that went beyond workplace struggles to conducting more realistic political assessments. Their new desire to interview unaligned activists, to print articles by progressives who disagreed with their party, and to touch more on topics for which the party had not developed positions paralleled like expressions from the militants of In Struggle![60]

The revolution against WCP's orthodoxy continued to expand, including criticisms of the lack of gay and lesbian issues in the newspaper and a revisiting of the whole national question. The party acknowledged errors not only towards independent leftists but specifically vis-à-vis pro-independence forces. The party's allegiance to China was also panned, with a key article concluding that Chinese Communism and its Canadian adherents shared a similar negative dynamic to that of the much-criticized USSR and its Canadian enthusiasts. As these reassessments continued, signs of decline began to surface as Toronto shuttered its Norman Bethune Bookstore, partly because it was not serving the needs of the "progressive community," but mostly for financial reasons.[61] The very phrase "progressive community" would have struck Maoists five years earlier as a patent throwback to the communitarianism and spontaneism of the new left.

By the time the winter of 1982–83 had set in, the party was pretty much over. Members were heading for the exits, and internal criticism continued to expand as "Stalinist conceptions" came under attack and critics raised new issues such as "big city chauvinism." While a couple of expelled members were readmitted, the central committee was disbanded and a debate followed on whether or not WCP's former leaders themselves needed to be expelled. Amidst extensive criticism from women, a fleeting new leadership committee was structured to have gender parity. As would also be the case with In Struggle! all of these changes seemed to come too late, and WCP soon disappeared from view.[62]

In Struggle! was very much influenced throughout its life by its emergence in the early 1970s in working-class Montreal. In 1972, Charles Gagnon, former FLQ activist, brought out his pamphlet *For the Proletarian Party* (1972), in which he renounced his former Quebec nationalism and declared a commitment to mil-

A scene from a 1977 Marxist-Leninist conference sponsored by In Struggle!

Documents of the 2nd Conference of Canadian Marxist-Leninists on the Path of Revolution in Canada: Montreal, April 8-9, 1977 (Montreal: In Struggle!, 1977).

itant trade unionism. The same year, the newspaper *En Lutte!* began to promote Gagnon's ideas, and in 1974 it became the official publication of a group with the cumbersome name of Create the Marxist-Leninist Organization of Struggle for the Party. In 1976 the group, generally called In Struggle! by Anglophones, launched a bilingual theoretical journal, *Proletarian Unity*, and found supporters in Toronto, Halifax, Regina, and Vancouver. The organization's "strategic line" was that socialist revolution in Canada would be achieved through the establishment of a proletarian dictatorship, which required the defeat of the workers' two main enemies, the Canadian bourgeoisie and U.S. imperialism. Of those two enemies the first was the most important because Canada was an independent imperialist power in which the bourgeoisie held state power.[63] Rather like the RMG, In Struggle! drew in middle-class intellectuals and social activists, but until 1980 their voices were not easily audible to people outside the movement. In 1978 In Struggle! renamed itself the Marxist-Leninist Organization of Canada, In Struggle! and tried valiantly, but without success, to rally all Maoists to its side. In contrast to other vanguard groups, In Struggle! placed little emphasis on industrializing its members. In Toronto and elsewhere it attracted professionals into its circle—including the pre-eminent feminist sociologist Dorothy Smith.

In the same year as In Struggle!'s Canada-wide push came the emergence of the Bolshevik Union. The very title of its journal, *Lines of Demarcation*, declared its high-octane polemical level. From the Bolshevik Union perspective, with Lenin and Stalin already having made most of the important decisions for communists, the true revolutionary's goal simply lay in rallying Marxist-Leninists to these "authentic" positions. In this, as in other historically rooted questions, the international communist movement was presented as having the correct line, from which, from time to time, national components were prone to stray.[64] In its fierce loyalty to the concept of one unified Marxist-Leninist tradition, the Bolshevik Union even condemned Judy Darcy—the Maoist who headed up the library workers at the University of Toronto—because in one talk she used the phrase "Marxism and Leninism," thus qualifying the orthodox position that Leninism constituted the higher form of Marxism.[65]

BU played a satellite role within Maoist circles reminiscent of that performed by the Spartacists among Trotskyists. But neither of the rival vanguards would have countenanced any suggestion that they shared revolutionary goals in common. Although individuals migrated from Trotskyism to Maoism and vice versa, the organizations themselves believed that the chasm dividing them was unbridgeable. From the BU perspective, Trotskyism, based in the petite bourgeoisie and labour aristocracy, was part of a global ruling-class strategy of blocking popular acceptance of revolutionary politics. Yet in some respects BU was no less critical of fellow Maoists. It condemned engagement in any kind of mass action as premature and best reserved for the later stages of party-building. This position allowed it to pour scorn on the bridge-building exercises of its rivals, as in their frequent campaigns in union politics. From the perspective of its rivals, BU—especially in its role at three conferences aimed to produce a unified organization out of the galaxy of groups upholding Chairman Mao's politics—was nothing better than a bunch of saboteurs.[66]

The New Tendency group was distinctive in that it officially renounced the Leninist model of party-building. It also maintained close contact with a diversity of European intellectuals, including the Italian communist group Lotta Continua, and explored how a new, perhaps post-industrial, working class was emerging in the womb of industrial capitalism. Although its members tended to give priority to "colonizing" large-scale blue-collar workplaces, most agreed that "students, teachers, white collar workers, housewives etc have undergone a process of proletarianization which links them objectively to the working class and makes possible an unprecedented level of struggle."[67]

"Wages for Housework" was something different again—coming from a class-based feminist perspective that sought to liberate the most unwaged and powerless—with a struggle for wages for domestic labour. As advocate Judy Ramirez explained, the fundamental exploitation of women happened when they were called upon to perform unpaid labour in the home. The traditional left, in focusing so intently on the industrial workplace, thus overlooked the majority of working-class women.[68] A group of women who split from New Tendency (G1) credited the W4H perspective for helping them understand their experiences with women in the workplace, develop their feminism, and critique an assortment of left-wing practices they had formerly mistrusted only on a "gut level." Yet they also retained some of the autonomous ideas that they had learned in the New Tendency, emphasizing concepts like the struggle against work and the social factory. Their insistence on "local autonomy" would clash with the ideas of another group of women who adopted the W4H concept.[69] This group, (G2), had a preference for strong, centralized leadership, precluding any immediate merger between the two factions. G2 believed that while sectoral autonomy was acceptable—autonomous lesbian organizing, for instance—individual or local autonomy was not. Capital was international and thus the leadership of the fight against wagelessness also had to be international. By envisioning the international W4H network as only a space for "making links" between locally autonomous branches, G1 was accused of denying the internationalism of capital, trivializing W4H as a mere reform campaign or consciousness-raising exercise, and lacking a perspective for achieving true power. G2 was particularly aggrieved that members of the rival tendency had "attacked" W4H's international leadership—Selma James, Silvia Federici, and Toronto's Judy Ramirez (then Quinlan) in particular—and had accused them of operating the network along "male-leftist" lines reminiscent of the Trotskyist Fourth International.[70] As far as G2 was concerned, their local rival's undue suspicion of leadership, although perhaps conditioned by its partisans' fear of power and "housewife syndrome," was equally a holdover from the disorganized, liberal, and pluralist new left.[71] They argued that G1's stance amounted to having no leadership at all and rejected that tendency's proposal for a "representative" leadership structure, insisting that an integrated W4H must be led by those with the greatest ideological clarity and experience. In short, G2 would only accept unity on its own terms, with its "freedom to lead" unencumbered. Its partisans engineered the expulsion of G1 from the international network and named themselves the Wages for Housework Collective.[72]

W4H largely pioneered the idea of resistance against work as such. For one member, "Helen," who resented working as a typist and being a "cheerful cog in a cheerless machine," W4H meant the opportunity to do the things that made life worthwhile, to work as little as possible and to be able to put forward demands that could not be co-opted. Her burning desire was "not to bash a typewriter for capitalism, but to be part of the struggle to get rid of capitalism all together."[73] Spoken like a true new leftist, one might say—but her tendency followed a pattern of hammering out definite positions, for which the members argued militantly and controversially in many different settings, with a polemical rigour typical of Leninism. Numerous complaints came from gay and women's activists about the conduct of W4H and its allied organizations at conferences and protests, including criticisms targeting the group's supposed anti-gay sentiments.[74] Women's activists took umbrage at W4H's implication that long-standing feminist calls for abortion rights might be rooted in racism, although it was an allegation that did connect with some immigrant women.

* * *

In all their diversity, these vanguard groups—seventeen in total in Toronto in the 1970s—shared a unifying critique of the new left. It was petit-bourgeois, self-indulgently countercultural, infantilely undisciplined, spontaneist, and tendentially counter-revolutionary. At their most extreme, the vanguardists believed that new leftists were tools of the bourgeoisie, working to stop communists' revolutionary work by luring away potential followers into futile, self-absorbed, and self-infatuated exercises in consciousness-raising.

Much vanguardist energy was expended in the critique of new left lifestyles—equated with a penchant for drugs, rock 'n' roll, and sex. "How do you unite the people against the imperialist ruling class when the people are stoned?" ran one satire of this tendency by a new leftist: "Far out, man. I mean, far out."[75] Sartorial and musical choices had political consequences. The unkempt, long-haired men and indecorously dressed women of the new left were, in many a Leninist critique of the 1970s, exactly the kinds of people who turned off the working class and delayed the day of the proletarian revolution.

The Canadian Party of Labour waxed particularly eloquent on the subject. One writer graciously conceded that hippies and beatniks had once exemplified the crisis of the social order and had come up with some skeptical appraisals of the system. Yet his self-righteousness soon overcame such efforts at culturally complex analysis: he contrasted the Maoists' emphasis on "self-reliance and struggle" to the "same old bag" of "acid muzak or freaking out in Dorkville." His fellow party members related how interested people could find useful insights into the decadence of jazz music—in Albania.[76] When *The Worker* looked back on the sixties a decade later, it blamed the Beatles for diluting some of the more rebellious elements of popular music in order to sell themselves to the middle class. For a time, the Velvet Underground had apparently tried to fight against the attempts of psychedelic music to "divert anger against capitalism and Vietnam into harmless hash dreams," but that band too became "bogged down in perversity and decadence."[77]

Unsurprisingly, many Maoists regarded drugs with the utmost hostility. The CLM officially banned pot for its members, on the grounds that drug-taking put the group in legal jeopardy, did not complement political activities, contradicted the image of the selfless revolutionary, and was despised by the Canadian people.[78] From within the CLM, Michael Drache and Larry Haiven analyzed "youth culture" as at best an extension of bourgeois liberalism, at worst a New York–

induced force of reaction that drove a wedge between the working class and disaffected middle-class youth. The creed of the beatnik and hippie was individualism. They tended to disrespect their fathers' work. The poet Milton Acorn , one of the better-known supporters of the CLM, strongly backed the group's ban on pot and deemed the majority of pot smokers to be "definitely anti-struggle types." Evidently writing on the basis of his own personal experience, Acorn remarked that marijuana consumption induced mental confusion. If the CLM dropped its ban on drugs, Acorn would leave the group.[79]

The CPL saw drugs as an important tool in the capitalist arsenal that could only be eliminated when that social system was overturned. "Turning on" meant tuning out oppression and being unable to see that "we need unity and not divisive tactics like dope." CPL militants noted that pot flooded campuses amidst rising protests and contrasted getting stoned to fighting against the war in Vietnam. It was not just student activists who were being sidelined by drugs. One letter writer testified that dope was a big reason why workers in his factory were so passive.[80]

In general, sects and drugs did not pair well in 1970s Toronto. In one CCL/WCP analysis, drugs, alcohol, and other vices served to pacify the people on behalf of the bourgeoisie: "It tries to get us involved in pastimes that lead nowhere. For example, the bourgeoisie has legalized pinball machines. They are everywhere."[81] From the perspective of the Revolutionary Workers League (RWL), formed from a merger of the LSA and RMG, an indulgence in marijuana imperilled the group's commitment to "industrializing" itself. "No member may engage in the use of illegal drugs or remain in the presence of persons taking illegal drugs," the RWL leadership ruled. Members were called on to inform on any fellow members who violated this regulation; if they did not do so, they were declared a threat to the organization's existence.[82] The irony—that a Leninist vanguard group was in effect policing its members so that they would not fall afoul of the surveillance system established by capitalists—went unremarked.

* * *

Emerging as many of them did in the 1970s, almost all the vanguards in Toronto felt obliged not only to pronounce on the "Canada Question" or nationalism, but also to grapple with what were considered the outstanding issues of the period—women's liberation and feminism, race and racism and Indigenous rights, and the gay and lesbian movement. On all of these issues they embraced a stunning panorama of positions.

Among Trotskyists, nationalism was often linked to Stalin's "Socialism in One Country," and was rarely supported as such. The Canadian Party of Labour upheld the position that all nationalism was reactionary, and launched attacks not only on the English-Canadian nationalists of the Waffle and CLM, but also on backers of the FLQ and other nationalist movements in Quebec. The Bolshevik Union argued that the question of Canada and its role in the imperialist system had been settled by the Comintern in 1928; thus there was no further need to debate the issue. The Trotskyist League, having defined itself largely in opposition to the bourgeois nationalism infecting the Toronto left, made no concessions to the existence of Canadian national sentiment. For the RMG, Canadian nationalism was saturated with the values of the petty bourgeoisie—a declining class whose ideology had been appropriated by the ruling class and put to work to motivate the credulous majority.[83] RMG rejected every variety of Canadian nationalism as petty-bourgeois and firmly characterized Canada as an oppressor imperialist nation in its own right. Canadian nationalism was not only reactionary in and of itself, but was used by the ruling class to "crush the vanguard" and intensify the exploitation of the working class.[84]

Early on the League for Socialist Action had embraced Canadian nationalism, though not without reservations. In 1968 one member, with copious quotations from Lenin, argued that Canada was not a colony and noted that the Bolsheviks had never campaigned against foreign ownership.[85] In 1972–73 the party took up this early and isolated critique of Canadian nationalism as its "new line." The September 1972 issue of the LSA's *Labor Challenge* presented readers with the idea of a "United Socialist States of North America" in conjunction with a new critique of the Waffle's Canadian nationalism.[86] A new central committee resolution firmly placed Canada in the company of imperialist powers and suggested that Canadian nationalism was chiefly used to support oppression, war, and class collaboration. In October 1972 *Labor Challenge* informed its readers that the LSA's long-standing leader Ross Dowson (a strong supporter of progressive Canadian nationalism) had stepped aside to make it possible for a new generation to assume leadership.[87]

When a number of LSA members, including Dowson, eventually left the organization, nationalism was the primary reason for their departure; they promptly founded a new group, the Socialist League (SL). As the initial issues behind their mutual estrangement were magnified, political differences between LSA and SL members multiplied. For its part, the Socialist League attempted to justify Canadian nationalism as part of the Trotskyist tradition, highlighting the role of a "founding father" who had believed Canadian nationalism to be anti-imperialist and anti-capitalist back in the 1920s (which was, at best, a partially accurate assertion). The LSA responded that SL's nationalism had "inevitably" led that group to adopt racist and chauvinistic positions.[88]

The activist left of the 1970s was nearly unanimous in its support of Quebec's right to self-determination. But there were divisions, especially amongst the vanguard groups, on the issue. The most prevalent questions—whether to support independence and what stance to take on language policy—frequently became one of the many "lines of demarcation" between them. The Trotskyist League, for one, while joining the rest of the Toronto far left in recognizing Quebec's right to self-determination, vested considerable energy into showing how this position meant no truck or trade with nationalism. It was on the basis of this anti-nationalist reasoning that the TL, unlike the rest of the far left in Toronto, *opposed* the use of French in Quebec airspace: the central issue of the 1976 air-traffic controllers' strike. It was a position imposed upon its Toronto members, initially favourable to the Francophones, by their New York leaders, on the grounds that scientific evidence supported the danger of using French. To argue otherwise was to "tail" petty-bourgeois Quebec nationalism. Moreover, all good Marxists were in favour, in principle, of unilingualism among air-traffic controllers because they had grasped that the entire planet was en route to an English-speaking future: "The use of English as the lingua franca of air traffic control prefigures the development of a common world language under socialism."[89]

Among the Trotskyists, both the LSA and RMG believed that Quebec constituted an acceptable "acid test" of the revolutionary steel of Canadian Leninists. For the RMG, Quebec was "the front line of the struggle for a red North America." In its books, the isolation of the Canadian working class from their comrades in Quebec was the largest factor constraining the country's working-class and revolutionary movement.[90] Members believed that left nationalists, with their slogan "two nations, one enemy," were guilty of subordinating Quebec's nationalism to Canadian independence. The more recently established International Socialists hoped that rising working-class militancy and class consciousness across Canada would render the Quebec issue redundant. It urged electors not to vote in the 1980 referendum on Quebec's sovereignty because federalism and an independent capitalist Quebec were "false solutions."[91] Among the Maoists, the Quebec issue was bitterly contested ground, in part because the two largest of the new Leninist groups, the Canadian Communist League and In Struggle!, had both arisen in Quebec in the wake of the FLQ Crisis in 1970, and both rejected the idea that Quebec had been colonized by Canada.

Many of the Maoist groups were outliers in a Quebec left that was, by and large, in favour of independence. Initially, the Canadian Party of Labour believed that all nationalisms served to divide the working class and strengthen capitalism. Those crying out for self-determination would find out that they were just exchanging French bosses for English bosses—and, moreover, Quebec nationalism was anti–English Canadian and racist. The victory of the PQ in 1976 prompted the party to revise its position. True to form, it now branded opponents of Quebec's self-determination racist.[92] In 1978 the CPL's new position on Quebec led to an angry split with its U.S. parent, which continued to consider calls for self-determination pro-capitalist. It also led to fierce polemics with other vanguard parties, now accused of hiding the depths of Québécois national oppression from English-Canadian workers. For its part, the CLM, renouncing the possibility of organizing in Quebec, hoped for closer co-operation and solidarity between the Canadian and Quebec independence struggles.[93]

Of all the parties, the CPC, although committed since the mid-1940s to the recognition of French Canadians as a nation, long remained the closest to upholding the status quo in Quebec. When it reluctantly moved in 1965 to grant its Quebec wing semi-autonomous status, it did so in language expressly denying that the province was a colony calling out for national liberation, thus rationalizing what an official history of the party called its "vigorous campaign against separatism." The CPC was a reluctant partisan in the 1980 referendum campaign, although it ultimately came over to the "Yes" side, on the grounds that such a verdict would strengthen the hands of those who wanted a renewed Quebec-Canada relationship in a still-united Canada.[94]

Early on questions of race and racism were rarely debated. Although all the vanguards were against racism, some of them were not at all comfortable with ceding their authority on the question to the people who most directly experienced its impact. Nor, as a virtual civil war erupted among the groups in the mid-1970s for control of the anti-racism movement, did they want to cede control to other groups.

When CPC stalwart Sam Walsh responded to the revolt at Sir George Williams, his denunciation of the students' tactics—they "smash up and burn valuable equipment"—was reminsicent of that of the mainstream media. The CPC's young Black members, such as Pat Case, wanted the party to strike a commission looking into questions of racism. Toronto's burgeonining immigrant population of people of colour had changed the face of the city since the late 1960s. For Guyana-born Gail Teixeira (who later became an education minister in Guyana), it behooved the CPC to create Che-Lumumba clubs (named after Che Guevara and Patrice Lumumba) similar to those found in the United States.[95] The CPC proved unresponsive to her call.

For the Trotskyist League, Indigenous peoples offered a litmus test to distinguish revolutionaries who were true from those who were merely pseudo. Unlike their "pseudo-revolutionary" competitors, Trotskyist Leaguers were proud to avoid romanticizing the First Nations. Rather, they maintained that Indigenous peoples should be integrated into the "Canadian workforce." They endorsed even minor reformist steps calculated to achieve that goal. From the standpoint of the New York–based leadership, the land claims of Indigenous peoples should not be pressed so hard that they imperilled the oil and gas industry. True revolutionaries in the Trotskyist tradition realized that Indigenous peoples did not constitute nations. Such revolutionaries consequently opposed "the utopian call for 'self-determination.'" In what seemed a calculated poke at new left sensibilities, the TLers denounced the goal of First Nations self-government as a class collaborationist exercise, and Indigenous nationalism was likened to Zionism.[96]

The far left viewed the rising women's movement with both enthusiasm and trepidation—and in this regard the vanguard groups played a significant, though perhaps ironic, role. They provided feminists with their most powerful impressions of the imperious ways of the "male left." Still, contrary to legend, the Leninist parties debated women's liberation intensively—even though in some respects the vanguard groups and parties were an unlikely place to look for socialist-feminist thought. The CLM, CPL, and CPC-ML were all headed by larger-than-life male leaders, each of them the centre of fair-sized cults of personality. Yet the growth of less leader-centred groups coincided with the rise of the women's movement, and some of these organizations duly responded to the issue. Some of them did so with great originality and creativity.

From within the Communist Party, which had played a leadership role in the struggle for daycare at the University of Toronto, Charnie Guettel's widely discussed *Marxism and Feminism* sought to synthesize the two movements. Within the party, Guettel damned its leaders with faint praise for having at least caught up with other leftists in clarifying its line on abortion (which went from regarding it as a question between a woman and her doctor to demanding free abortion on demand). Yet she also noticed that Communists remained loyal to a world view in which every social question came down to class and tended to equate "female chauvinism" with "male chauvinism," as though they were equally powerful phenomena. Barbara Cameron argued that the CPC had failed to grasp the significance of women's new role in the workplace and had adopted a sectarian attitude towards women's groups. She complained that party leaders showed a tendency to see women as housewives and topics such as food prices as "women's issues." According to Cameron, the CPC's long-standing front group on the women's question, the Congress of Canadian Women, was two decades behind the times in its thinking. Communists were deluding themselves if they thought it was representative of the women's movement. Guettel was in general agreement with Cameron and angry at the CPC for treating gender politics as a topic that could perpetually be deferred until the next convention. She linked women's issues with those raised by homosexuality, since in her view many women saw parallels between the gay and women's movements.[97]

Other tendencies also weighed in. Articles in the RMG's *Old Mole* had initially spoken quite critically of the limited horizons of a women's liberation divided into small groups and seemingly incapable of raising theoretical issues. They critiqued their rival Trotskyists' single-issue focus on such questions as abortion, which often meant a "lowest-common-denominator" approach that in effect sidelined the linking up of issues demanded by a genuinely revoutionary project.[98] Uniquely amongst the vanguard groups, the RMG subsequently acknowledged that some radical feminists spoke in favour of socialism—they were fellow revolutionaries, not misguided liberals—but it critiqued them for their economic ignorance and casual stance towards the longed-for but undertheorized destruction of the nuclear family.[99] The *Old Mole* devoted a major review to Guettel's *Marxism and Feminism*, calling into question the author's pro-Sovietism, neglect of the housewife, inability to draw salient lessons from radical feminism, tendency to think in terms of historical stages, and her "fantastic" assumption that state daycares could be democratically controlled. A behind-the-scenes rejoinder in its *Internal Bulletin* indicated that the RMG's own women's commission was upset by the review. The writer, Rose LaCombe, believed that most of Guettel's analysis was correct and had been shamelessly misrepresented. Guettel had quite appropriately differentiated Marxism from radical feminism. Yet this more appreciative critic also demonstrated that, for many vanguardists, the question of Marxism and feminism was pitting groups against each other. "We must contend with CP militants at every . . . event," LaCombe proclaimed, clearly not wanting to cede Guettel the last word, even though seemingly agreeing with much of her analysis.[100]

The "Woman Question" played a central role throughout the history of the RMG, without ever yielding an answer satisfactory to those who wanted the group to champion a new order with respect to gender and sexuality. In a major "Women's commission document," most likely penned in 1974, RMG differentiated itself strongly from the "feminism" it associated with the new left. Such feminists had rejected theoretical analysis for the "politics of experience" and, like new leftists as a whole, had been unable to strategize a revolutionary seizure of power. Consciously or unconsciously following the lead of Herbert Marcuse, these socialist feminists harped on "participatory democracy," but in practice this meant male superstars, "with advantages of sex and class" seizing the limelight. The problem with new left women was that they were inclined to be ahistorical and seemed to imagine that a revolution could be organized only by working with women—or, just as nebulously, by uniting all oppressed women. Just how such a revolutionary union would take place or mount a struggle for state power was never explored concretely. The socialist feminists had clearly not learned from the impasse faced earlier by women's liberation. Signs of hope, such as the campaign for Wages for Housework, did exist, revealing that at least some women were open to Marxist theory and searching for "leadership and revolutionary practice." Gearing up for a "serious revolutionary intervention" into the movement, the RMGers hoped they could persuade all involved that socialist revolution was the precondition of women's liberation.[101] As one internal critique from 1976–77 noted, the RMG, when it dealt with groups such as W4H, tended to revert to a kind of "workerism" when speaking about women, as though women faced nothing but economic challenges. As the rival of LSA/YS, the RMG also tended to respond reflexively when it came up against the appearance of single-issue campaigns; its militants had been reluctant to involve themselves in a campaign to defend abortion crusader Henry Morgentaler or fully endorse calls for more powerful positions for women in the labour movement.[102]

In the New Tendency, acceptance of autonomous women's organizing was evident at a Windsor conference where, with one exception, the first round of workshops was organized strictly along gender lines, with separate meetings for men and women working in factories and men and women involved in community activism, and yet another for non-industrial women only. It was a stance that distinguished NT from many more well-established vanguard groups.[103] NT activists were among the most adventurous of leftists in arguing that the traditional left's fascination with the working class, narrowly defined—pursuing collective bargaining, women's right to work, and nationalization, for instance—obscured the need to transform the *content* of work. Moreover, labour power was not only stolen in the factory, but leached away while riding the subway, attending school, or doing housework.

Challenges to capital did not come about only through strikes, then—they could be found in worker absenteeism, single mothers struggling to get by, shoplifting, housing squats, and the evasion of streetcar fares. It was not only the traditional working class and youth who were refusing work: the gay movement's refusal of "masculine personality" and sexuality, struggles by Indigenous peoples against integration into waged work, and prisoners and psychiatric patients resisting against their rehabilitation as labourers were all components of a larger refusal of work. In the New Tendency it was considered a mistake merely to support a wildcat strike as opposed to seeing in such a strike a latent manifestation of the struggle against work itself.[104] One female member of NT, who had worked in a number of Toronto-area factories, told her comrades that women factory workers had shown a widespread interest in women's liberation, and they might even be best organized as *women* workers, not in conventional unions dominated by men. It would be best if this were done in ways that acknowledged that the working class was constituted, not just at the point of reproduction, but also in the sphere of social reproduction—in the family and in the community.[105]

For the International Socialists, anti-sexism had come to be seen as a militant's normal outlook, although they relied on a heavily economic reductionist view of women's liberation, as typified by the response of one *Workers' Action* reader to seeing a lingerie-clad model in a store window: "I was very angry about such an attempt to further divide the working class."[106] But during the following decade, the IS would even find some nuanced words for the Direct Action group, which had orchestrated a campaign of violence against Litton industries and B.C. porn shops. IS could not approve of such tactics, but it could understand them, given the sad ineffectiveness of the mainstream peace and women's movements.[107] IS was hostile to both leftists and the many women's movement activists who saw a patriarchal system at work. To them, the idea that all men benefited from sexism necessarily meant a failure to understand how sexism benefited the ruling class and the need for class-based struggle. A late 1977 article on rape marked a turning point in the organization, not so much because many socialists tended to downplay or even dismiss the need for anti-rape agitation, but because for the first time IS was emphasizing the role of an independent woman's movement as a solution instead of simply presenting the usual answer of socialism.[108]

Through most of the 1970s the Canadian Party of Labour was rather quiet on issues pertaining to the women's movement. It had a small, fleeting opposition caucus in the early 1970s dubbed "Bad Apple," which disagreed with the organization's characterization of gay and women's issues as divisive matters best settled after the revolution. Closer to mid-decade, members of the CPL were suggesting that women only took birth control and consented to abortions because of economic hardship: "I've never heard a woman say she didn't want a child simply because she didn't want one." All socialists supporting abortion were characterized as "Trotskyites"; critics of the Catholic Church's anti-choice stance were denounced as closet racists. The group eventually codified its position on contraception in a pamphlet, *The Scientific Killers*, which members hoped would entice working-class women to join them.[109] After having long absented themselves from the women's movement, CPL members cautiously engaged with it at the tail end of the 1970s. The CPL's writings on the "Woman Question" relied heavily on male authorities, notably Lenin, Stalin, and Albanian communist leader Enver Hoxha.[110]

The Canadian Communist League (CCL) enunciated a starkly go-it-alone stance with respect to International Women's Day (IWD). It refused even to attend a broadly defined IWD celebration in order to "demarcate [itself] from all the rotten ideological tendencies." Where was any statement or slogan calling upon women to resist the superpowers—conflict between which the League said was inevitable? Gradually, as the League morphed into the Workers' Communist Party, its stance became less isolationist, and by 1981, it was encouraging members to participate in Toronto's Take Back the Night event, a radical-feminist initiative.[111]

From the perspective of the Bolshevik Union, feminists were exploiting the women's movement "for the expression of their vilest, most intimate fantasies of petty-bourgeois individualism." No one could enter a feminist bookstore "without being assaulted by prominently displayed propaganda urging its readers into sexual seduction." In Struggle! wrestled powerfully with feminist issues in its closing year, with articles in the tendency's newspaper urging the group to "Feminize the entire organization" and calling women's liberation groups and services, once dismissed as divisive and reformist, "exciting experiments of women taking power."[112]

In Struggle! reimagines Marx as an overburdened housewife and mother; *Proletarian Unity*, March-May 1982.

Thomas Fisher Rare Book Library.

In general, when they responded to questions of race and gender, the vanguards almost invariably inserted them into models traceable back to Victorian Marxism. Only occasionally, as in the cases of Charnie Guettel and Dorothy Smith, did they countenance newer explorations—and both those authors remained committed to the proposition that feminists and communists shared common interests. The Marxism they advanced was one in which class struggle provided both fundamental historical perspectives and present-day projects. Their tragedy was that, especially as the 1970s rolled into the 1980s, workers were providing so few examples of struggles reminiscent of the *Communist Manifesto* (1848), and so many manifestations of the accommodations and divisions that Lenin had skewered in his *Imperialism: The Highest Stage of Capitalism* (1917). On only a few occasions would social reality and Marxist expectations be aligned.

Gay and lesbian issues posed even trickier problems for vanguards. In the first place, Marx and Lenin had had so little to say about those issues. Second, gays and lesbians inherently questioned the politics of reproduction that most communists had championed for years. The terrain conflicted with the macho muscle-bound proletarian image still cherished by many vanguard leaders, and the discussions often arrived complete with new left associations, arousing vanguard animosity against bohemianism and the counterculture. Queer issues also proved vexatious because some of the vanguard parties contained a disproportionate number of gays and lesbians, many of them powerfully influenced by the 1970s' other powerful liberation movements. Vanguardists found few Marxist authors to consult on the subject, even though some did attend to the sexological explorations of Wilhelm Reich, who validated the importance of sexuality to Marxist theory but also urged leftists to stand resolutely against homosexuality.[113]

The U of T Eurocommunists wrestled mightily with gay and lesbian issues. The countercultural atmosphere of the Communist Club at the University of

A demonstration held in conjunction with the Fourth Annual Gay Conference for Canada and Quebec; September 1976.

Courtesy Charles Dobie.

Toronto was widely noted. The Gramsci Club, also on campus, and the Young Communist League had many militants who felt ill at ease at social events hosted by their Eurocommunist comrades. In 1975 this tension erupted into a full-scale controversy and a letter from the central party that singled out "sexually aggressive dancing, flaunting homosexuality, and pot smoking" as particularly objectionable goings-on. In response, although the Club agreed that its members should dial down on their public pot-smoking, it announced (in an early and ironic use of the phrase) its unwillingness to enforce "politically correct" lifestyles.[114] In 1976 the top Communist Party officials worried about Club members sporting gay liberation buttons. The Club told those officials to back off and to submit the question of homosexuality to full discussion prior to the CPC's 1976 convention.[115]

As the debate unfolded, it became obvious that the Club had welcomed to its ranks a good sampling of gay men, who by the mid-1970s had read studiously about "Marxism and Sexuality." They doggedly called the party out on the slipperiness of its position on sexuality, since in one breath it seemed to support the civil rights of homosexuals, and in the next to suggest they all retreat to the closet and stop bothering the heterosexual majority with their off-putting public presence. If the party insisted that a person's sex life was his (or her) own affair, would that not actually work to insulate from critique the vanguard's resident homophobes, who could now, in the privacy of their own lives, be as discriminatory as ever? Did it not give the party permission to shove the issue to the margins? Such critics also noted how the party leadership tended to conflate the struggle for basic gay rights with more contentious claims for the inherent progressiveness of homosexuality or bisexuality.[116]

Although members of the CPC were not uniformly reactionary on gay and lesbian questions, gay militants in the party were given the sense that their comrades did not fully understand, or sympathize with, their politics.[117] The records of U of T's Communist Club record eloquent discussions between gay members, such as Dave Forman, who were fed up with the party's tepid support, and his comrade "Jennie," who said that even one openly gay member might prompt others to come out of the closet and fight to change the party, just as some feminist members had already done.[118]

The RMG rivalled the CPC as a political home for homosexuals and attracted such major figures as Gary Kinsman. In articles like "Smash All the Closets" in *Old Mole*, Kinsman posited that gay issues were fully compatible with revolutionary Marxism. The third national gay conference, in 1975, he suggested, showed the new prominence of the movement, with a left gay caucus and members from both Quebec and English Canada. The demonstration against the firing of jockey John Damien in October 1975—one of the biggest gay protests to that date in Canadian history—showed the RMG the importance of building alliances with other progressive groups. The demonstration was preceded by intensive leafleting in areas with "high concentrations of gay workers"; it was boosted by the attendance of a contingent from Montreal's Groupe homosexuelle d'action politique; and it had offered the RMG a great opportunity to present the message that gay liberation was only possible through a socialist revolution in which the working class would become fully engaged with the gay question. As so often within the RMG, the militants hoped that Canadians would learn from Europe, where there were much tighter links between gay liberationists and radical socialists. For Kinsman, the RMG distinguished itself for its relative sophistication. It did not imagine that the supposedly family-besotted working class could not grasp gay and lesbian questions. It avoided the argument that homosexuality was merely a morbid symptom of capitalism's decline. Even so, Kinsman eventually left the RMG after becoming disappointed with its handling of gay and lesbian issues.[119]

Catherine MacLeod recalls that RMGers "threw great parties," appreciated good food, and "liked to sing and dance and make music"—which is all reminiscent of a new left politics of personal authenticity and self-realization. "Some played in rock bands," she wrote. "They read poetry. They liked sex. New couples formed and disbanded almost weekly. It was not correct to be jealous and possessive, although everybody was." Yet the RMG's Women's Commission objected to the group's poor integration of women's perspectives and complained that too many comrades viewed such supposedly peripheral movements as a relic from

Seeking to normalize lesbian parenting, the Lesbian Mothers' Defence Fund emphasized that a child with two mothers could be healthy and happy.

Grapevine, Spring 1981.

the past and mere training grounds for the ultimate move to "the 'Big One"—the working-class revolution. Their critique was seconded by Charles Lang when he resigned from the group in 1977. Lang believed that the pro forma denunciations of sexism only went so far. RMG men steadfastly refused to internalize their anti-sexist message. Both women and gay men experienced themselves as being considered merely a "sideshow," in a group whose leadership had marginalized their politics.[120]

In their *Internal Bulletin*, RMG activists reported on their work with groups such as the Gay Alliance Toward Equality (GATE) and their campaign for law reform, which had drawn in other Trotskyists from the LSA/YS. Thus far on the revolutionary left, they said, apart from a long "dead-end discussion" in the LSA, the left had not seriously discussed gay and lesbian issues. The LSA had both helped the movement—in its articulation of a standpoint distinct from that of the CPC-ML, wherein homosexuality was held to be a disease—and limited it—in that it had tied gay Trotskyists to a narrow, depoliticizing single-issue formula and left a bad memory of manipulation in some minds. Then the Socialist Workers Party, with which LSA had close ties, turned against gay liberation in 1973; closer to the RMG, the influential Trotskyist economist Ernest Mandel had also enunciated a gay-unfriendly position. In this setting, the RMG confronted both the possibility of contributing to a radical movement and the danger of being drawn too close to the limited lifestyle politics of the ghetto, about which, as it said, *The Body Politic* expressed so little principled criticism.[121]

Vanguardists were never more forcibly confronted with the complexities of contemporary gender politics than they were with the rise of W4H. That group's whole perspective challenged vanguard fixations on male working-class struggles. In the group itself, some women directly critiqued the expectation that women conform to a certain body-type and endorsed "fatness" as a "refusal to do one part of the work expected of us."[122] The argument put forth simultaneously defied orthodox notions of the Marxian concept of the class struggle and conventional masculine expectations of what women should look like.

The related Wages Due Lesbians collective established a similar connection between the demand for wages and resistance to the patriarchy: wages for housework, it insisted, meant "wages *against* heterosexuality and *for* lesbianism."[123] Some former male NT members launched "Men Against the Family Allowance Cutbacks" to support W4H's family allowance campaign. The establishment of the Lesbian Mothers Defence Fund in 1978 mobilized mothers threatened with having children taken away and, in conjunction with the Lesbian Childcare Collective, provided such services as daycare.[124] It was difficult to dismiss such movements with conventional Leninist arguments against bohemian radicals who understood nothing of working-class life.

The International Socialists, having arrived relatively late on the Toronto scene, seemed to be in search of "larger ponds to swim in," which they found in the women's, gay, and anti-unemployment movements of the late 1970s.[125] After initially backing the drive to ban all pornography, in 1983 the IS shifted to a different position: that state censorship would open the doors for the censorship of gays, unions, ethnic associations, and other allies; not only that, it would work to the advantage of social conservatives and cause a worse problem, an underground porn industry. Instead, the party called for "popular censorship," that is, direct action to stop racist, sexist, or fascist images and ideas, including the boycotting of such things by progressives, even by the performers in the industry itself. As for sex workers, another of the hot-button issues raised by radical feminists, IS decided they should be unionized. Members should not fall into the trap of "woman-hatred." The linkage between combating pornography and the class struggle proved to be a trifle forced.[126]

The Maoist groups showed more resistance to gay and lesbian liberation, at least until the final years of the two largest vanguard formations. From the perspective of the Canadian Party of Labour, the defeat of Sewell in 1980 came about because, although in many ways an extraordinary mayor, he had made the mistake of pandering to the gay and lesbian community—even to the extent of launching his campaign at the office of a gay aldermanic candidate: "Workers, immigrants and particularly working women, had to take a back seat so John Sewell could go to bat on the liberal-glamour issue of homosexual rights."[127]

Within In Struggle! gay and lesbian liberation was not a priority until the group's closing days. The topic was not even broached, said one critic, until 1980.

In November 1980 Tim McCaskell wrote an influential letter to its newspaper advising the group to rethink its notion of homosexuality as a form of bourgeois decadence. By 1981 a gay and lesbian caucus had emerged within the group—which called, with a certain irony, for the revolutionary group to catch up with the Province of Quebec, which had already granted gays and lesbians human rights in its charter. The In Struggle! gays and lesbians thanked the women's movement for advancing their cause and demanded the right to caucus separately. Articles in the tendency's newspaper slammed revolutionary leaders for dismissing homosexuality as a merely personal issue, a dereliction of duty that strengthened the hold of conservative ideas in the working class.[128]

All of the Marxist-Leninist groups harboured socially conservative tendencies, but the Bolshevik Union proudly laid claim to an outlier position when it argued against having sex simply for pleasure, "without any productive value whatsoever." Casual sexual encounters were merely a form of prostitution. In the eyes of *The Body Politic,* the Bolshevik Union showed just how much a Marxist group could resemble Bible-thumping Christians, with "imperialism" taking the place of sin or Satan.[129] The gay liberationists may have underestimated just how much energy the Bolshevik Union had poured into this subject, for at a time when many other Leninists were rethinking their positions on gay and lesbian liberation, this group drew another "line of demarcation" that separated them from such backsliders. Homosexuality was linked to "decadent" bourgeois culture and associated with pacifism and long hair for men. More substantively, the Bolshevik Unionists suggested that homosexuality perpetuated the oppression of women by reinforcing antagonism and divisions between genders. Above all, it menaced the "proletarian family," corrupting and undermining the possibilities of proletarian revolution. Gays and lesbians were simply placed in the category of "pimps, Don Juans, [and] exhibitionists"—people who should never be defended by communists.[130]

Wages Due Lesbians, not surprisingly, was at the polar opposite of this discussion. Echoing some of the arguments of radical feminists, it complained that all left, gay male, and women's movements were hostile to lesbians. In its eyes, W4H was an acceptable "mixed" group because its autonomous affiliated organizations ensured that the concerns of lesbians, as well as Black women, would never be papered over.[131] W4H's ancillary organization, the Committee to Advance the Status of Housework (CASH), spoke in more moderate language with the official goal of promoting the recognition of housework as productive work; it even received funding from the federal and provincial governments, Oxfam-Canada, PLURA (a coalition of churches promoting justice), Doctors Hospital, and the Jackman Foundation.[132] Another W4H initiative, the Lesbian Mothers Defence Fund (fd. 1978), helped mothers threatened with having their children taken away, provided services such as daycare in conjunction with the Lesbian Child-care Collective, and also played a social role, arranging potlucks and other events so that lesbian mothers, some of whom had no support networks, could have an opportunity to talk with others in their situation.[133]

* * *

In the end the Leninists, although tending to be aggressively critical of the new left, often wound up validating many of its ideas. Perhaps the party that most closely reflected "new leftish" ideals was the Revolutionary Marxist Group.

For instance, in contrast to the soft-sell of the CPC, which highlighted the tragic sufferings of Vietnamese women and children, the RMG emphasized the slogan "Victory to the NLF," which it believed would sharpen the political understanding of advanced workers and students, the vanguard it sought to influence.[134] That the group had something of a "new left" atmosphere was the gist of criticism from the Bolshevik-Leninist Tendency, a caucus within the RMG, which accused fellow members of having adapted to a "left milieu" by capitulating to feminism, "studentism," "infantile" anti-authoritarianism, and Quebec nationalism. Exhibit A for this tendency was the RMG's high-school publication, *Jailbreak!*—its whose very name, echoing new left themes, was an appropriate disillation of its countercultural orientation.[135]

By 1977 the RMG had grown into a fairly considerable group. There were as many as fifty-five comrades in the Toronto branch, and the group employed two full-time and three part-time employees. The organization's documents suggest both its resistance against and its attraction to the new left. Here, remarked an internal document from 1973, was an "amorphous" radical milieu, "composed of individuals, various types of sectoral caucuses, publishing projects, research and study groups, etc.," which functioned "in the absence of any hegemonic left wing organizations." That milieu itself was just the most visible expression of a "molecular radicalization"—a process taking place in small groups or within individuals—that was influencing much of the petty bourgeoisie. When RMG threw itself into anti-racism work in 1975, which rivalled the post office as a site of its consistent interventions, it adopted a stance of "open immigration," partly on the basis of internationalist principle, but also with the hope that this would give the group ammunition against the Waffle, the RMG's *bête noire* for many of its early years.[136] From the RMG perspective, the Waffle was not so much a group of fellow socialists as a source of error and illusion, an "increasingly serious threat to the construction of a revolutionary party in Canada." As the RMG urged: "All our propaganda should be directed against the spontaneism, North American parochialism and Canadian nationalism, and workerism and economism which are the dominant ideological currents in our audience."[137]

When RMGers gazed around the University of Toronto campus in the early 1970s, they spotted the "stale leftovers"—cynical, passive, centrist—of "the left subculture."[138] Many of these leftovers had been student radicals. They had once played a "vanguard" role in the "peripheral radicalization" of the late 1960s and early 1970s, by which RMGers meant that their activities had been focused on struggles outside the industrial workplace, such as the students' and women's movements. But now, for RMGers, with the "collapse" of the new left, arose the question of the creation of a revolutionary workers' party—an organization reflecting revolutionary rigour and analytical clarity. No more crazed ultra-left adventures and no more attempts to buy working-class support by "handing out sandwiches and coffee at the factory gates." An end to a political practice that was "revolutionary in word and reformist in deed!" One could exit that swamp, writer Michael Kaufman proclaimed in *Old Mole*, and attain the highlands of Leninist clarity.[139]

The RMG's opening statements in 1973 disclose its drive to understand and overcome the conditions that had thus far led so many radicals and revolutionaries into North American dead ends. Since the disintegration of the radical student movement, which the RMG dated to 1969, Canadian socialists had been wrestling with a number of questions, such as: what was the best way to organize; how to relate to the working class; whether the NDP was an obstacle or an opportunity; and the manifold complications of Canadian nationalism. The result was a continuous process of "flux, splits, regroupments and realignments." In North America particularly, where leftists were tragically detached from an exciting and progressive Europe, the lack of strategic direction had led to a deadly "impasse," resolvable only through a resolute confrontation of geographical and cultural barriers. RMG realized it was but one revolutionary nucleus within a fragmented North American left and called upon other groups to initiate discussions with them.[140]

In some RMG analyses, such as that advanced in 1972 by Tina Craig, the "new left" was simply another form of petty-bourgeois populism, the expression of non-working-class students and youth. When it did coalesce in Canada, it was afflicted by Canadian parochialism and backwardness, the confusions of Canadian nationalism, and the incapacity of the RMG's Trotskyist rivals in the League for Socialist Action/Young Socialists. At their worst, new leftists had imagined substituting, for a revolutionary working class, a "coalition of sectors," each defined in terms of a specific type of oppression—a "theoretical shortcut" to nowhere and a cautionary tale about the perils of listening to left populists.[141] In 1973, writing about the student left, Wally Seccombe—later to become a major critical historian of the Western family—argued that students, unlike workers, were radicalized on the ideological, not the economic, plane. Unfortunately, student radicals could find no social force capable of making the revolution; their anti-authoritarian politics had no clear class correlate. The new left had wasted its most committed vanguard politics in senseless acts of ultra-leftism. Its collapse had left a legacy of atomization and demoralization—and in this conjuncture, it was the task of Marxists to remind all prospective leftists of the errors of their past.[142]

Yet RMG thinkers also realized that, in their drive to critique and remove the new left, some old and new Leninists had lived up to every hostile caricature that new leftists had broadcast about them. The CPC, CPL, CPC-ML ("the prophets of Peking")—none of them offered reassuring examples of the efficacy of the vanguard party. Yet if these self-selected and often feuding vanguards offered few models, neither did "the 'independent' left, repelled by its 'vanguardist' counterparts," which displayed "the worst features of spontaneism, including both practical ineffectiveness and opportunist adaptation towards mass movements and especially towards the workers' struggles." Thus honest revolutionaries were seemingly caught on the horns of a dilemma: either they aligned themselves with the vanguard parties, in all their incongruousness, or they contented themselves with a futile independence, with all its political impotence. RMG rejected the "ultra-democratic fetishes" of the new leftists, but then suggested that in its own variant of the vanguard party, many of the worries about authoritarianism would be set to rest. After all, the RMG's own founding conventions had seen the free expression of different viewpoints, with a full and open debate, even concerning the group's most fundamental beliefs.[143]

Perhaps the latter-day RMG never sounded more "new left" than it did on questions of culture, in which it not only esteemed cultural figures associated with the new left but articulated a doctrine of cultural autonomy fully in accord with new left libertarianism. Such was not always the case. In 1973 a piece on building the revolutionary party took shots at the "utopian reformist currents" at *This Magazine Is About Schools* and *Community Schools*. Yet in other phases, RMG's cultural commentary suggested that many of its writers sympathized with authors commonly adopted by the new left. In 1973 Carl Gardner published his reflections on John Berger's *Ways of Seeing* (1972), discerning in that book an exciting alternative to bourgeois notions of culture as entertainment and Stalinist reductions of art to propaganda. A co-authored piece by Seccombe and Graham Barker argued that past revolutions suggested there could be no easy correlation between political and cultural revolution. Cultural questions did not yield easily to "correct line" thinking, and the case of "socialist realism" illustrated the damage brought about by attempts to enforce cultural conformity. For Sheila Delaney, many of the received left-wing truths about cultural struggle were simplistic, such as the position that declared the isolated artist a thing of the past. "Come now!" she exclaimed. "Is there to be three to a canvas in the new workers state?" Delaney urged revolutionaries to familiarize themselves with the existing terrain of debate and to stop adopting a "smug, know-it-all position." In 1976, reviewing a blatantly left-wing Art Gallery of Ontario exhibition, artist Deirdre Gallagher declared, skeptically: "The emphasis on self-awareness, personal change, the declaration that the revolution is in your head, has accelerated to the point that any perception of social context is eradicated." She found herself unmoved by the artists' attempts to be political. "By trying to make their work conform to political requirements they impose limits on the special power of art—its ability to challenge reality, explode consciousness, liberate the imagination, etc. Art can effect perception, but it can't change the world. That's the job of politics."[144]

In 1976 several RMG members published *Revolutionary Art: A Toy; a Tool; and a Weapon*, which echoed Trotsky's position on the significance of art as a force that could prefigure the total liberation for which the left was fighting. Art should not become sloganeering or seek merely to follow the requirements of the liberation. Bob Smith was similarly skeptical of the revolutionary prospects of working-class poetry in Canada, which he said combined mediocre technique with rampant sentimentality. In such collections of proletarian poetry as Tom Wayman's *A Government Job at Last* (1975), he saw only a lot of proletarian heroes ("romantic, hard-drinking, idealized workers") drawn up according to the specifications of poets who had either inadvertently become working-class or longed to be so. Others, agreeing with Smith about the "vulgarity and hypocrisy" of the idealization of the working class, urged him to understand that poetry was intrinsically on the side of "unfettered desire, of revolution."[145]

From 1975 on, the RMG's internal debates—which attained an honesty that stands to the group's credit—raised doubts about whether the group had itself escaped what it had considered a new left cul-de-sac. In 1975 a document written to defend supporters of a minority tendency at a recent convention declared that their disquiet about the RMG's "debilitating social composition," that is, the predominance of petty-bourgeois militants, remained well founded. At a time when the class struggle had grown quiet, and more as a result of "psychology" than politics, those leftists had succumbed to the "political disease" of their class: sectarianism. Moreover, their individualistic lifestyles suffused RMG, turning it into an "unending series of free-lance initiatives, only some of which have ever gained official sanction."[146] Among those initiatives were the immersions in the women's movement and gay liberation—showing results that sometimes suggested that these new social movements had gained a purchase on members' loyalties equal to, if not greater than, their commitment to the Leninist group.

* * *

In some ways In Struggle! was for Maoists the counterpart of RMG for Trotskyists—in that a cadre drawn largely from the middle class surveyed the broader field of Marxism in Canada and tried to imagine how it might make a revolution on such a terrain.

Throughout much of its life from 1973 to 1982, In Struggle! presented a somewhat monolithic and unapproachable face to others on the left. It had emerged from the very different left milieu of Montreal, and its early pamphlets (*Against Economism*, 1975, and *Fight the Sectarianism of the CCL [ML]*, 1976) strictly projected its chosen strategic line. In early years the tendency's theoretical organ *Proletarian Unity* voiced extremely critical opinions on women's liberation, also known as "bourgeois feminism."[147] On other left-wing issues, In Strugglers judged "economistic" and "opportunistic" those projects and campaigns that proceeded from an evaluation of the immediate interests of workers and not from the urgent imperative to establish a proletarian dictatorship.

Much changed in 1980. Even veteran Trotskyist Ross Dowson wrote to *In Struggle!* to congratulate the newspaper for becoming "a welcome breath of fresh air in the oppressive and sterile sectarianism that cloaks and smothers the revolutionary left in Canada at this time." One editorial mused that, at a time when all left tendencies had apparently failed, it was time for a "real debate" about their future. Had an overreliance on foreign models blighted the prospects of Canadian Marxists?[148] Might there not be, mused the organization's general secretary in December 1980, problems with the vanguard model itself? A "vanguard can only exist," he remarked, "if recognized by those it's seeking to lead." Perhaps a study of more recent history would "teach us more than the reception of principles formed by great revolutionaries in the past. The danger of reformism should not scare us away from the struggle for reforms." The Montreal-based publication began to publish a number of articles looking at social movements in Toronto, even those whose views were not easily reconciled with Maoist opinion. One sang the praises of the Open Circle and Toronto Workshop Production theatres, the Development Education Centre's film distribution service, and the reggae band Third World—all manifestations of a dynamic Toronto movement.[149]

One in-depth *In Struggle!* article featured extensive comments by Himani Banerji and other women's activists, who could not say enough about the epochal significance of the feminist collection *Beyond the Fragments*.[150] It was remarkable how intensely the tendency responded to the book by Rowbotham, Segal, and Wainwright, which might be appropriately categorized as new left and quite out of keeping with vanguardism in general. August 1981 saw the emergence of a Women's Research Collective, which drew in fifteen In Struggle! militants from Toronto. Varda Burstyn sent the publication voluminous letters, in which she criticized Leninism and argued for the need for prefigurative forms of socialism.[151]

Vanguardism was itself under critical scrutiny in 1981. As a party document from that time observed, although Marxist-Leninist groups had arisen out of a reaction to the new left and dismissed it as "revisionist," they had also adapted "some of its basic tenets," such as the idea that revolution was on the immediate agenda and the importance of transforming men and women into people capable of living like true revolutionaries in the here and now. The Marxist-Leninists had tried to explain to the new left that a revolution would happen only if the correct line were applied. Yet it had since become clear that having a correct line was only one aspect of the revolutionary struggle. It was completely possible that revolutionaries in El Salvador were not entirely orthodox in theory or practice—but In Struggle! sent them $15,000 and declared its opposition to the notion that it should support only those Marxist-Leninist vanguards poised to establish a dictatorship of the proletariat.[152]

Other editorials took up the theme of "workers' control" (conceding that this favourite theme of new leftists, although problematic, merited more than the usual Marxist-Leninist diatribes) and the devolution of power and unity in other left groups (with the advice that members of the group should not be afraid to engage in public disagreements). At the start of 1982 the paper thought it possible that the "full and complete democratization of society" might be more important than any other aspect of the socialist program. Canadian workers were not interested in seeing a repeat of Chinese or Soviet communism. "We will never rally workers to a programme that promises less political democracy than exists under capitalism," the paper argued in an article that also pondered developing closer relationships with social democrats fighting for immediate objectives. The following month, as though to underline the point that the erstwhile critics of new leftism had wound up sounding exactly like new leftists, on issues ranging from the progressiveness of cultural experimentation to daycare to workers' control, members attending *In Struggle!*'s June 1982 congress voted 197-27 (with 12 abstentions) to dissolve their organization. The activists, having decided that the very idea of a vanguard party was flawed, and that a new way of conducting politics was necessary, deemed it untenable merely to renovate the organization.[153]

* * *

The early 1980s witnessed the crisis and collapse of many of the Leninist groups. In 1978 the RMG, LSA, and the Montreal-based Groupe Marxiste Revolutionnaire fused to form the four-hundred-member-strong Revolutionary Workers League, in some respects marking the high point of the Trotskyist project in Canada. Initially, the RWL seemed well positioned to defy the turn to the right of the 1980s. Having emerged from a painful period of discord, RWL went into the 1980s relatively unified. Many formerly troublesome members had left. The group's *Socialist Voice* was reporting success after success. Sure, there was some talk of a crisis of Marxism, and even allegations that the Leninist model of party-building had failed, but that was "only the crisis of certain individuals and organizations unable to cope with the big developments in the international class struggle." The collapse of In Struggle! carried no lessons for the RWL, it was said, because the now-defunct group had failed to grasp the logic of orienting itself to industry, which was where most of RWL's members could be found.[154] From the leaders' perspective, working-class consciousness was radicalizing at such a pace that the Trotskyists might find it hard to keep up. The group had earlier been sufficiently confident in itself that it felt capable of transferring at least twenty members from Toronto to branches in Edmonton, Hamilton, Regina, and Winnipeg.[155]

Rather like its Maoist rivals in the Workers Communist Party, the Revolutionary Workers League focused closely on the working class—so closely that, radically unlike the RMG, it declared its disinterest in movements that were not directly related to the class struggle. "The peace and disarmament movement is *not our movement*," the RWL proclaimed, referring to one of the era's most prominent protest campaigns. "It is *not our framework* for building an antiwar movement in this country." Declaring that this movement had "*nothing* in common" with the one against the war in Vietnam, it highlighted the predominance of professionals and students in it and contrasted such elite efforts to an anti-war movement led by "working class fighters in the plants." Increasingly integrated into the Socialist Workers Party, the RWL even disregarded the New Democratic Party, so long an object of entryism on the part of Trotskyists, but now hardly worth mentioning.[156]

In 1982, although signs of radical decay were everywhere, RWL leaders insisted that objective conditions were favouring them. "The theory of the leadership is that decline can be overcome if one places a *plus* sign wherever life presents a *minus*," complained one of the group's few remaining dissidents, on his way out the door. By that point the group had shrunk from 400 to less than 120 members. To cope with a loss of revenue and to maintain its top-heavy apparatus of seventeen staff (some of them in Toronto), the RWL leadership—much of it with roots in the LSA—began ratcheting up the pressure on members to pay weekly "sustainers" beyond their regular dues.[157] Newspaper-selling took on added significance. Factory-gate sales were projected as a verification of the group's political line. In time, newspaper-selling became an implicit substitute for other activity. A big mobilization to sell newspapers at a disarmament demonstration was proof that the RWL didn't just criticize from the sidelines, while during the U.S. invasion of Grenada in 1983, RWL explained, the "sales were a powerful act of solidarity with the people of Grenada and the Cuban internationalist workers who fought against the U.S. marines." Such desperate optimism barely concealed how, for Trotskyists, the early 1980s were almost as much of a disaster as they had been for Maoists.[158] Their numbers and influence declined, their groups split and split again, and the Fourth International's anticipated triumph had not materialized for an organization immersed in its own bitter conflicts.

Among the Maoists, to the demise of In Struggle! in June 1982 was added the collapse of the Workers' Communist Party in November. The year 1982, then, took on a certain historical significance as a turning point: it marked the demise of two of the 1970s' largest Leninist organizations, both of them Montreal-based but with significant memberships in Toronto. To some extent, they were unavoidably the victims of a changed conjuncture. In the looming age of austerity and right-wing politics, small morale-boosting victories in workplaces and community organizations were difficult to attain. The 1980–82 recession hit hard, and those who had fully imbibed the Marxist-Leninist position—according to which the correct line would lead to the construction of a revolutionary party and, in fairly short order, the rise of the proletariat to power—were in a poor position to evaluate a historical period in which no line, no matter how inventive, seemed capable of prevailing over capitalism's changing dynamics. For Maoists in particular, the revolutionary world from which they had drawn inspiration—above all Mao's China—was also undergoing its own mutations. As early as 1977, *In Struggle!* had announced its disenchantment with China and looked to form an official connection with Communist-run Albania, only to be turned down by the Albanian Party of Labour (which chose to align with CPC-ML). The Workers' Communist Party persisted in idealizing China, even into the era of Deng Xiaoping; but soon, as a group boasting a large contingent of working-class activists, it rallied to the support of the trade unionist Solidarity in Poland.

Much of the allure of the new Leninism was that it offered to connect "parochial" Canadian leftists with the transnational struggles remaking the world. Yet, over time, immersion in global politics could come to seem a mixed blessing. Trotskyist groups differed with the Communist Party of Canada over events that had happened in the Soviet Union in the 1920s and 1930s, for which it held present-day Communists—or "Stalinists," to use a term of which they rarely tired—fully responsible. The major Maoist groups argued incessantly, and in some cases came to blows, over China's "Three Worlds policy," which was parsed and re-parsed in their newspapers. The Canadian Party of Labour, In Struggle! and Revolutionary Workers League were all highly enthusiastic about the Islamic Revolution in Iran—thereby modifying an old left tradition of "defence of the Russian Revolution" into a new one of "defence of Revolution, period."[159]

Undeniably, then, it was an unfavourable economic and geopolitical conjuncture that did much to condemn Toronto's bumper crop of vanguardists to wither. Yet it would be unwise to place undue weight on exogenous factors when the endogenous ones were so emphatically highlighted by vanguardists themselves as they headed for the exits. The activists themselves pinpointed many of the reasons as to why the quest of the vanguard party or movement had proved so elusive.

One feature of the 1970s that made it radically unlike the 1930s, a romanticized version of which had entranced so many vanguardists, was so obvious that it might go unreported: there was in the earlier days a more or less unified Communist movement, inspired by the Russian Revolution and represented in Canada by a unified, relatively strong party.[160] It was possible, in other words, for a Toronto leftist of the 1930s and even 1940s to believe that "the Communists" offered wise strategic and tactical ideas, based on their revolutionary continuity with Lenin's Revolution and their conspicuous success in local as well as global politics, and that they did so with one voice. The position of such a leftist in the 1960s and 1970s was necessarily very different. Now such a leftist confronted not one conspicuous vanguard group or party but well over a dozen, each of them claiming the revolutionary tradition of Lenin and the scientific rigour of his mode of analysis. As they competed with each other, they inevitably focused on their rivals' limitations. "The closer an organization is to your politics," argued one RMGer in 1974, "the more relentlessly you should try to destroy it, because it confuses and often deflects the best militants from the proper course."[161] The difficulty was that, if each vanguard group wielded its bludgeon against all the others, and all did so, one wound up with an endless cycle of organizational rivalry and destruction—which is the impression some people, including veteran vanguardists, came away with from Toronto's far left in the 1970s. They were not anxious to revisit the days of running dogs and exterminable vermin.

It was axiomatic among new Leninists that new leftists had failed. They had abandoned the working class as the decisive revolutionary force. They had produced mere "fragments," settled for a cult of spontaneity, and increasingly drifted into lethargic inactivity.[162] Still, however much they might seek to overcome the legacy of the new left, vanguardists operated in a pluralistic setting in which their tendency, group, or party was required to defend its truth-claims before often highly unfriendly critics. They were often found preaching quasi-absolute truths in an inherently relativizing and specific milieu—one in which a faltering or unattractive line could lead to a diminished market share, declining revenues from tithes, and ultimate disappearance. Although vanguardists sometimes imagined themselves to be seated at the control panel of history, deftly navigating the revolution through the shoals and eddies of bourgeois reaction, and some groups exhibited considerable analytical skill in discerning underlying socio-historical patterns, the mechanisms they manipulated were often glaringly detached from the realities they hoped to influence. Even when it seemed that an effective mechanism had been located, it was difficult to be sure if deploying it would necessarily generate a revolutionary outcome. Did, for example, the slow and partial reform of Canada's abortion regime energize the entire women's movement, or did it sidetrack militants into a reformist struggle easily accommodated by the liberal order?

Added to this setting was the rise of new social movements that appeared to owe relatively little to the Leninist inheritance. No uniformity governed the vanguardists' stances on the women's question, which ranged from calls to venerate a romanticized "working-class family" to those that called for its revolutionary smashing. Among the numerous women who entered vanguard parties, debates over the theoretical and practical priority of gender over class, and the proper reading of the texts of Marx and Engels, often took place, not between rival tendencies, but within the heads of individual activists. If the quest for a revolutionary party was often also a quest for philosophical certainty, for many women vanguardists it led to a more and more refined sense of doubt about the underlying legitimacy of Marxist science with respect to a set of issues that mattered keenly to them. To this was added the gender-blind assumption of many vanguard parties that one could simply ramp up demands upon members without any consideration of the particularities of their lives—as brought out graphically in one widely circulated *In Struggle!* cartoon that pictured a house-bound Marx, with squalling children and a pile of ironing, implying that he would never have been able to finish *Capital*. Yet well into their sunset years, vanguard parties were reluctant to make any concessions to the specific burdens carried by women. They were even slow to "get" the significance of providing daycare for militants who happened to be mothers.

If Leninist women felt increasingly alienated from the groups and parties supposedly speaking in their name, gays and lesbians often had the even more alienating experience of being told to shut up. If socially conservative views among traditional Communists and trade unionists were predictable—on a materialist argument, they corresponded to the interests of many men in the movement—so too was it to be expected that young men and women contesting the sexual status quo would turn to movements seemingly devoted to its overthrow. On the whole, and with honourable exceptions in the RMG and Communist Party, their concerns, difficult to reconcile with the reductionist principles attributed to historical materialism, went unaddressed. Often they encountered scientific claims to a knowledge of their own position, and insight into society's "primary contradiction," that bore no relation to their own experiences or to a growing library of works validating contrary insights. While it appears that a disproportionate number of gays and lesbians entered vanguard groups in the 1970s, it also seems that they departed in great numbers from the mid-1970s on. (Some, especially in In Struggle! seem to have held on to the bitter end.)

The vanguard formations, in their push to be authoritative on questions as basic as family and sexuality, faced the dilemma more generally of justifying clear-cut, often absolute distinctions (reform/revolution, man/woman, science/superstition, materialism/idealism, us/them) that the society and culture of the 1970s were rendering more and more fluid and indistinct. To outsiders, especially those immersed in Toronto's seething avant-garde and community movements, such vanguardists, for all their claims to be on the cutting edge of history, could seem like the last holdouts of a "Victorian left." They were ill-equipped to handle a modernity in which all that had been solid was becoming fluid—or "melting into air," as the fine old phrase of Marx had it.

The new Leninists' resistance to community-focused activism and participatory democracy was, like their stances on gender and sexuality, neither uniform nor consistent. Still, it would have been an unusual vanguardist manifesto from the 1970s that did not take a poke at starry-eyed new leftists pursuing their communitarian utopias in defiance of the stern realities of the class struggle. Many documents internal to the groups suggest their almost visceral rejection of a new left they narrowly construed as the student and peace movements of the 1960s. And within many there was a conscious rejection of new left–flavoured experiments in consciousness-raising and participatory democracy. Democratic centralism was positioned in many groups as the professional antithesis of such amateurish and spontaneist new leftism. In practice, it placed considerable power in the hands of vanguard leaders, some of whom, like Hardial Bains and Gary Perly in Canada, or Gerry Healy in Britain, became veritable "Little Lenins" vested with considerable, and easily abused, powers over rank-and-file militants. It was often possible to divide and conquer members of one's own groups, or to discredit other groups, by making accusations about opponents being police agents (a tactic one RMG account associated with CPC-ML attacks on activists such as Louis Cameron and Rosie Douglas).[163]

Nevertheless, many members of vanguard parties did learn important skills in organizing and public speaking while in such organizations—a point underlined by some of the women interviewed in Judy Rebick's oral history of the women's movement.[164] Part of what they learned was to question authority, even when that authority was exercised by a revered Marxist channelling the even more revered legacy of the Russian Revolution.

Vanguardists, it might be said, were engaged in an arduous struggle to salvage that revolution from its many false friends and bourgeois enemies. They lived in a 1970s Toronto that was, to judge from many of their writings, little more than one small point on a continuum stretching from the Revolution of 1917 to the imminent great day of proletarian revolution in the West. They made few concessions to the reality that they lived in a time and place in which the vast majority of people were not fully engaged with the finer points of the Bolsheviks' history—a history that lived in their minds with an intensity that led them into almost endless quarrels with other vanguardists, even within their own tendencies. Although often involved in local struggles and proud of the accomplishments of their "industrialized" members, they always integrated such struggles and feats in an imagined master narrative of universal history. When they sought to engage with the more down-to-earth conditions of Canada—the demands of the women's movement, the rising up of Indigenous peoples, the resistance of gays and lesbians—they almost always did so with reference to a calculus that depended on criteria proceeding from a universal Leninist model. In their purest form, they had no interest in or loyalty to the particular city of Toronto or its inhabitants: their loyalty lay, rather, with the World Revolution, as they so variously and combatively construed it.

The vanguardists tended to begin the 1970s with forceful denunciations of new leftists, those petty-bourgeois, university-centred, peace-addled, distractable, and unrigorous folks whose weakness and disorganization cried out for the strong medicine of Leninist discipline. But they ended the 1970s, in many cases, rediscovering many of the issues that new leftists had traditionally emphasized. Undoubtedly they did damage to the new left, drawing away much of its energy and siphoning off some of its most competent leaders. Yet, in retrospect, it seems that new leftism, far from succumbing to its Leninist adversaries, succeeded instead in slowly drawing them back into its orbit.

Many former vanguardists certainly sounded like unreconstructed new leftists in the early 1980s, when, as though awakening from a dream, they re-engaged with the complicated society all around them. New leftism was never just the narrowly conceived, exclusively petty-bourgeois, countercultural foil against which so many of them had once railed—and in their partial and often mistaken estimations of this left formation, which had influenced the voluntaristic style of many of their organizations, resided many of the reasons why vanguardists so conclusively failed to establish themselves as significant and enduring political forces in the 1970s.

11

A Long, Ambiguous Goodbye, 1982–85

In Toronto in the 1970s or early 1980s a young left-wing woman or man might leave home in the morning and hasten to support a left-liberal reformist campaign, follow that with a communist-backed protest against a Third World dictatorship at noon hour, take in a consciousness-raising group focused on demolishing patriarchy and sexism in the afternoon, and attend a strategy meeting in the evening—perhaps all quite blissfully unaware of not being fully consistent in her or his politics. In those days many a leftist contentedly swam in currents that were both old and new left.

Although the boundaries of new leftism can be, however roughly, specified in theory, they were often less distinct in practice—a matter that renders questionable stark lines of demarcation separating the new left from its old left antecedents. The senses of spontaneity and eclecticism were precisely the characteristics that other leftists, particularly Leninists, firmly believed that new leftists needed to outgrow. In the long run, though, this new left was never quite outgrown, much less outlasted or vanquished. It was not so much simply brought to an end, but rather *aufheben*—to employ that German word with seemingly contradictory meanings: cancelled or abolished, simultaneously preserved, and yet also transcended—by a new constellation of forces.

In the early 1980s a revived student movement showed signs of the preservation of new left ideals. In 1980 an anti-racism committee at the University of Toronto won support from the student government and even publicly recalled the SDS activism that liberals had found so unsettling years before.[1] In 1982, after a visit to campus by Ralph Nader, a handful of students launched a local Public Interest Research Group (PIRG), which joined with similar campus organizations in Ontario to create the Ontario Public Interest Research Group (OPIRG). They also struggled and won funding for their group from the student government. In 1983 one hundred students occupied the library and three hundred disrupted a

Board of Governors meeting. Women fought for and won a women's centre on campus, an innovation the engineering students challenged on the grounds that the prospective centre was going to be operated as a collective. Female students also won the right to establish a Sexual Education Centre, which was duly challenged by the Catholic St. Michael's College as a bridgehead for contraception and abortion. Feminists regularly mounted guerrilla incursions on the engineers' biannual strip shows and "slave auctions."[2]

All of these occurrences would have warmed the heart of an earlier generation of activists, who would also have been thrilled by a university-centred demonstration of 3,000 people and a joint rally sponsored by the Canadian Federation of Students, Ontario Teachers' Federation, and Workgroup of Metro Parents, with 10,000 people in attendance—a turnout well in excess of almost any protest in the 1960s.[3] The radicalism of the 1970s was by no means swiftly succeeded by an apathetic early 1980s.

Yet the 1960s and 1980s also had signal differences. If the 1960s witnessed the mobilized expression of widespread alienation against the "meat grinder of education," militants in the 1980s were far more focused on making education affordable and accessible to more people. The aim was not so much to entirely overthrow institutions, or to revolutionize their governance through achieving parity between students and educationists, but to safeguard them from state budget cuts. Moreover, *The Varsity* and other student papers suggested that the environment in which such activism unfolded had also changed. When activists sounded "new leftish" in their resolve to wrap many issues into practical campaigns over funding, they were admonished for straying beyond a single-issue focus.

By 1985 almost no one in Toronto would have called herself or himself a new leftist. What many contemporaries had once seen as a coherent philosophical, political, and cultural current, albeit a formidably complicated one, now seemed to have been split into a diversity of disconnected movements, many of them keen to differentiate themselves not only from each other but also from the past history of the left. That history was increasingly not a source of inspiration but a fount of cautionary tales about what "progressive" movements should at all costs avoid. Yet, coinciding with this widespread "cancellation" of the new left was equally widespread evidence that many new left notions had proliferated so generally that they had become a kind of common sense. The once original new left formula for socialism—personal authenticity and self-determination, solidarity with national liberation movements, anticipatory egalitarianism and participatory decision-making, plus community empowerment—had set new leftists apart from many of the actually existing socialist parties and governments, even though the "lines of demarcation" could often be blurry and at times erased. But now variants of that formula were to be found everywhere. Yet they were at the same time preserved in radically altered form—transcended in new ways of seeing, above all predicated on socialist feminism and the peace movement, which in essence changed their function and meaning in politics. There was much about post-1980 left politics, for all that it still proclaimed the virtues of grassroots participation and solidarity with liberation struggles, that earlier generations of leftists would not have been able to recognize.

There was, in particular, a marked change in the vocabulary used to denote the society that would come *after* the anticipated triumph of the left. The sixties and seventies new leftists had no great difficulty in imagining that future to be "socialist." Their eighties counterparts were far less inclined to do so.[4] That was partly because the left was increasingly on the defensive and more apt to use vaguer terms, such as "social justice." But it was also because, for many current activists, the word "feminist" came to perform the same function once filled by "socialist," that is, as denoting their most fundamental values and allegiances. (For others, "anarchist" and "anti-racist" came to serve the same purpose.) This change in vocabulary coincided with a change in message and even audience. A lingering contingent of leftists continued to define themselves, and social reality, in strict class terms. But just as class, participatory democracy, and anti-imperialism had been trademarks of the left in previous decades, anti-racism and feminism surely became so for the 1980s.

By the early 1980s, feminism had become such a strong element on the Toronto left that it could reasonably be described as a "hegemonic" force capable of setting the basic terms of debate for the vast majority of leftists. Socialist feminists often spoke as if they had the historical responsibility to achieve a dynamic synthesis of gender, class, and race politics, and International Women's Day, both the March 8 event and the increasingly elaborate network of groups organized around it, served to some extent as a measuring rod for other leftists. Yet socialist feminists found themselves both divided and overburdened—divided between those still inclined to favour orthodox Marxist-oriented characterizations of reality and those moving to consider "radical-feminist" positions in which the patriarchal rule of men was their primary enemy; and overburdened by those who wanted feminism to be the main vehicle for the politics of peace and anti-racism.

The three themes of IWD in 1983 were the right to jobs, the right to choose, and women's right to peace—an emphasis, argued Mariana Valverde, that suggested new alignments with feminists and the peace movement. In the past, the International Women's Day Committee, which retained its new left support for national liberation and self-determination, had followed a different line than did feminist pacifists, but now such lines were blurring. Many pacifists did not condemn armed struggle in Nicaragua, and the peace movement had become much less abstract in its analysis. Some of its activists and theorists highlighted the link between rape and war, a theme that socialist feminists were only starting to explore.[5]

In neither the 1960s nor the 1970s had new leftists decisively broken with the ideal of *the party*, even if they routinely complained that actually existing parties travestied the great goal of participatory democracy. In the post-vanguardist 1980s, the "coalition" and the "network" came to replace the "party" and the "movement" in the left-wing lexicon. Activists Michael Riordan and Heather Ramsay lightheartedly captured some of this zeitgeist in a skit about the swampy aspects of coalition politics, which they presented to a workshop co-sponsored by Women's Action for Peace and the IWDC to build support for an upcoming march against war in Central America. It included such lines as "Your group lacks analysis" and "You should be in analysis." For Valverde, subsequently to be one of the most significant of Canada's socialist-feminist intellectuals and who represented IWDC on the Toronto Disarmament Network (TDN), the feminist vision of a "non-sexist, non-hierarchical world should be of concern to all peace activists, and can provide us with valuable guidance about how to organise ourselves so that we don't replicate authoritarian structures."[6] Her assumptions spoke to the times: if all new leftists would have agreed that it was a bad idea to replicate authoritarian structures, few before the 1980s would have argued that the women's movement enjoyed a privileged position, perhaps almost a vanguard position, in keeping those structures at bay.

A Socialist Network (SN) that emerged in 1984 was only one of many attempts to square the circle—that is, to have each group, organized to defend a particular identity, enjoy full autonomy as it expressed its standpoint to a wider world, while also uniting with other groups in something still familiarly called "the left." For Dorothy Smith, who had been closely involved with In Struggle! and was emerging as one of Canada's foremost feminist theorists, the fall of the vanguardist groups had freed many feminists from their gravitational pull and "sectarian distortions." Yet the results, she said, had been mixed. "Groups specialize; when they split, they split and there are no countervailing pressures; people can be working away politically in one part or sector of the city and simply not know what others are doing." With the vanguards' disappearance, there seemed to be "no one whose business it was to work for, and talk socialism and to build relations among socialists." Given that the mass media could hardly be relied upon to help leftists remedy this state of atomization, constructing an alternative could only arise from the creation of a new emphasis on "communications and networks." She looked forward to a "constellation of various groupings" coming together once or twice a year.[7]

Constellations typically require suns—and the sun of this prospective constellation was socialist feminism. The early to mid-1980s witnessed many attempts across the country to create new socialist groups—and particularly formations that would seek to integrate socialist feminism into their practice. These new socialist organizations discarded the new Leninist prescriptions for party-building that had been so conspicuous in the 1970s, and favoured a democratic pluralist model that sought to integrate feminism and anti-racism with class politics.

In English Canada these formations included the Socialist Organizing Committee in British Columbia, which produced the magazine *Leftwords*; a committee of socialists from the Atlantic provinces who held regional conferences in hopes of forming an integrated "network"; and a similar project in Saskatchewan. A multi-tendency formation called the Ottawa Committee for Labour Action (OCLA) was crucial to the eventual development of a network in Toronto. Members of OCLA had persevered through the collapse of the Waffle and Movement for an Independent Socialist Canada and in the early 1980 manifested their feminist beliefs through adopting a policy of gender parity.[8] In 1983 OCLA initiated an Ontario-wide conference with ambitious plans for a network of related organizations and paid staff. Although the assemblage numbered an impressive three hundred, Leo Panitch recalls that most attendees were over thirty-five, had families, and were in danger of burning out. From the outset, lacking the energy and time that they had enjoyed in earlier decades, the conference organizers seemed unlikely to succeed. Nonetheless, a caucus of attendees from Toronto volunteered to host a follow-up later in the year.[9]

The Toronto discussions were symptomatic of the 1980s. They revolved around frank explorations of where participants were coming from and where they wanted to go. The ghost of vanguards past haunted them throughout—which meant that they placed a maximum emphasis on the uncoerced freedom of groups to respond autonomously to the oppressions they sought to overcome. A women's caucus was the first event on the conference's agenda; a later session of the caucus was held in tandem with a "men's meeting." The conference led to a "Socialist Forum," which in turn evolved into the Socialist Network. The SN had an "animation committee," but the activists—some in neighbourhood-based units, many more in such spheres as education—were responsible for organizing their own meetings and communicating with the wider network.[10] The small groups were autonomous, and the Socialist Network took no formal role in running them or deciding who could participate. Their intimate setting was supposed not only to offer a ready and welcome distinction from the usual meetings that crowded an activist's calendar but also to draw more interest. Smith, favourably contrasting the SN's small groups to the leftist study groups that she herself had experienced, emphasized that the Network would have "no line" and its discussion would flow freely. Participants would be without risk of "coming out on the wrong side of a two-line struggle."[11]

The SN still had a new left atmosphere—its members distanced themselves from both social democracy and communism, and "power to the activists" could have been its unofficial mantra. It was a "network" and not a party. Animators were assuredly not commissars. Unity should never be achieved at the cost of removing activists from their existing struggles. The SN would not strive to have positions on everything. Debates would flourish, and different positions coexist. Controversy would never be censored. Some argued that the vanguard model was also inappropriate because the vast, dense, and subtle organization of current capitalism meant "Control cannot be grabbed."[12] In the eyes of Craig Heron, soon to become one of Canada's leading historians of the working class, an emancipated society would include a massive decentralization of economic activity and the preservation of small-scale market forces. Planning would be localized and community-based. Experts, professionals, and technocrats might advise—they would not govern. This socialism would promote a diversity of lifestyles and adopt more creative and exciting forms of culture than the ones favoured by the old left.[13]

In vivid contrast to In Struggle! and the Workers' Communist Party, at least before their final moments, the Network would place socialist-feminist values at its very core. Those involved appeared to agree that feminist analysis and processes had to be integrated into socialist theory and practice. But beyond a basic concern with eliminating both oppressive deeds and sexist language among individuals, it was never quite clear how that goal might be accomplished. Many members complained that they could not grasp the organization's central purpose. Discussions often seemed interminable and inconclusive. Some participants wanted a cohesive organization that could initiate its own projects, although they would never have called it a "party." Others wanted a network within which activists from a diversity of backgrounds could get to know one another. Some two years into the Network, which had grown to 150 members, this debate was still unresolved. In 1987, with fewer and fewer people doing the work and the number of members, especially women members, plummeting, the Network entered a death spiral.[14]

Both its emergence and its demise were signs of the times. It emerged when many leftists around the world were contemplating the "crisis of socialism." The SN's publication *Talking Socialism* was suffused with this sensibility, but so too were the magazines *Fuse*, *Mudpie*, and *Incite*, three new entrants into Toronto's already crowded left media scene. *Incite* distilled the early-1980s spirit exactly:

> We understand that the "crisis in socialism" is not just an internal debate within the left—the old "economic vs. ideology" theme. Rather, it is the failure

> of the left to seriously address the role of social relations in the revolutionary project. In particular these are questions of sexuality and sexism, minority rights and racism, the psychology of the individual and its relation to the social, as well as culture itself.[15]

It was impossible simply to go on with traditional left ideas and practices, and it also seemed impossible to define what exactly would take their place. Here were the years of the new left's painful and ambiguous goodbye—in which many of its democratic ideals and practices had apparently triumphed over its vanguardist critics and adversaries, yet did so in a way that called into question even the contours and possibility of "the left."

* * *

For many left-wing Torontonians, the network that mattered most to them was not the Socialist Network but the International Women's Day Committee. In many, largely unintended, ways, the IWDC—a discreet and amorphous body whose work for the annual event, through its March 8th Coalition, was closely scrutinized—took the place of a central organization, both as inspiration and target for activists. Did it stand for socialist or radical feminism? What about making IWD a women-only event? How well were the concerns of women of colour addressed? Or would it not be better if these women were separately organized—given the indifference shown their concerns by "white feminists"? What about gays and lesbians? Should they even be lumped together in one category, when many gay men were so conspicuously not part of a feminist common sense? What happened on the IWDC was taken to be a sign of which way the entire Toronto left was headed.

Thus the first coverage of International Women's Day by the newly established radical-feminist monthly *Broadside* slammed it as a male-dominated sellout lacking any real feminist content.[16] The IWDC revealingly conceded much of *Broadside*'s case. True, the magazine's complaints might have been rooted in its many connections with activists in Women Against Violence Against Women, who were demanding a women-only event. But the IWDC statement conceded that the committee had fumbled the question of lesbianism. It had since conducted extensive sessions of criticism and self-criticism and organized numerous educational sessions on the subject. The IWDC now felt it was properly equipped to bring the discussion of lesbian rights to schools, community groups, and unions.[17] The key features here are not only just the extent to which lesbian issues were accorded central significance, but also the IWDC's assumption that it had an almost party-like capacity to represent the interests of a broader left to the wider community.

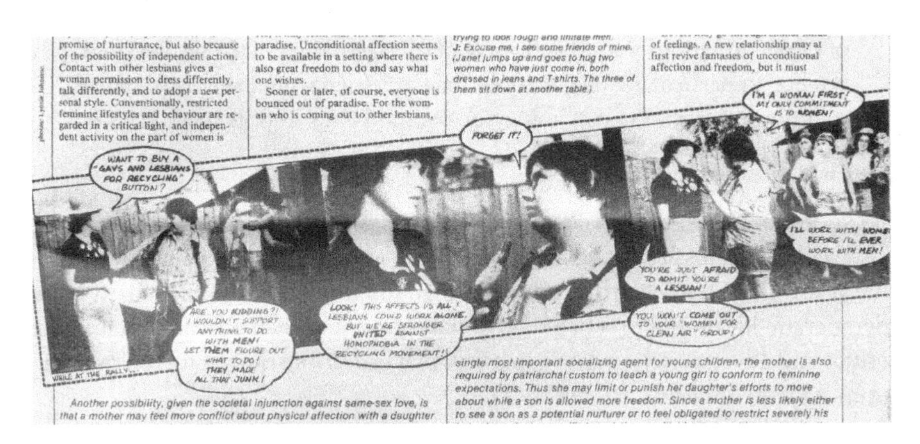

promise of nurturance, but also because of the possibility of independent action. Contact with other lesbians gives a woman permission to dress differently, talk differently, and to adopt a new personal style. Conventionally, restricted feminine lifestyles and behaviour are regarded in a critical light, and independent activity on the part of women is

paradise. Unconditional affection seems to be available in a setting where there is also great freedom to do and say what one wishes.

Sooner or later, of course, everyone is bounced out of paradise. For the woman who is coming out to other lesbians,

J: Excuse me, I see some friends of mine. (Janet jumps up and goes to hug two women who have just come in, both dressed in jeans and T-shirts. The three of them sit down at another table.)

of feelings. A new relationship may at first revive fantasies of unconditional affection and freedom, but it must

Another possibility, given the societal injunction against same-sex love, is that a mother may feel more conflict about physical affection with a daughter

single most important socializing agent for young children, the mother is also required by patriarchal custom to teach a young girl to conform to feminine expectations. Thus she may limit or punish her daughter's efforts to move about while a son is allowed more freedom. Since a mother is less likely either to see a son as a potential nurturer or to feel obligated to restrict severely his

Rosemary Barnes, with photographer Lynnie Johnson, had activists Chris Bearchell, Val Edwards, Amy Groves, Fay Orr, and Mariana Valverde enact a series of lesbian-feminist debates.

The Body Politic, October 1980.

The critique of IWDC was of a piece with the febrile atmosphere of the early 1980s in feminist circles. For some radical feminists, who attended especially to the writings of Catherine MacKinnon, Andrea Dworkin, and Robin Morgan, the networks and alliances blossoming everywhere on the Toronto left spelled the dangerous dilution of the identity and demands of women. Susan G. Cole, for one, feared a return to the days in which feminists were relegated to a "women's auxiliary of the left." A *Broadside* editorial observed that coalitions were dangerous places for feminists, for instead of constituting spaces of reciprocity and "two-way dialogue," they always meant women subordinating their interests in the name of some other, supposedly more urgent or important, issue, possibly aligning themselves with arch-enemies in the process. Even coalitions that did not directly sideline women's issues might be of limited representativeness and effectiveness—as in recent mobilizations against the Ku Klux Klan, allegedly boycotted by many Blacks because of the visible involvement of anti-racist lesbians and feminists.[18]

Lorna Weir speculated that the popularity of such coalitions stemmed from the growing prominence of the women's movement, which made everyone want to enlist it as a coalition partner. Many shared Sheila Rowbotham's urge to go "beyond the fragments," especially during the time of a resurgent right; and to many the women's movement seemed to be the place to do so—a place in which the values of national liberation, community, and self-management had survived the 1970s. "Feminism is for everybody," as bell hooks later put it. Yet working with men posed the danger of being co-opted and marginalized by the male left. Nonetheless, Weir thought the risk had to be run—for to do otherwise was to indulge "the sin of purism" and to risk isolating the women's movement. She hoped to see coalitions—dynamic, multi-issue, and long-term—that could take on the offensive against the right. Over time, she thought, such coalitions might gradually create a coherent ideology capable of synthesizing separate movements. Taking anti-racism as an example, Weir foresaw a creative coalition that would help the women's movement deal with racism in its own ranks while other components dealt with their own sexism. Her model of a coalition would surmount fragmentation and prefigure a more universal popular-democratic movement.[19] It was an attempt to square the circle—how to combine participatory democracy and the creation of a dynamic movement capable of pushing its demands upon a recalcitrant status quo.

Yet others, especially in the women's movement, were resistant to any such scheme. Mary O'Brien and Frieda Forman noticed what they saw as a continual erosion of feminist content in favour of class and more participation by male-dominated groups. With respect to IWD, O'Brien believed the inclusion of Spanish-language content and references to the plight of Central Americans to be superfluous. But what most alarmed many, and led them to swear off future involvement in the absence of change, was the insertion into IWD of the struggle in Palestine, "a highly divisive and deeply controversial issue," and not just in the March 8 parade but in the keynote workshop on "Women's Liberation, Disarmament and Anti-Imperialism." A woman had even been booed for trying to add "a feminist perspective" to the event.[20]

Lois Lowenberger, who was linked to the Committee Concerned about the Israeli/Palestinian Question and IWD, also believed the inclusion of the Palestinian issue to have been a diversion from the core IWD program. Feminists should only support liberation movements that stood for the rights of women. Imperialism stemmed from patriarchy, and any feminist analysis that equated patriarchal liberation movements with feminist ones was delusive. Provocatively, she argued that feminists should compare Israeli and Arab women, asking where their respective countries and nationalities stood on issues like polygamy, genital mutilation, unilateral divorce, abortion, and birth control.[21]

It was a sign of the times—not just in suggesting how hard it would be for a coalition to arrive at a coherent and unified position on questions of world politics, or in suggesting the extent to which some feminists now traced imperialism back to patriarchy rather than capitalism, but also in revealing a perception of the IWD as an important indicator of progressive opinion in Toronto, a significant emitter of signals for a far broader public. Was it merely offering lip service to feminist ideals, as Lowenberger alleged, or was it something more genuine?

Citing the analysis of Maria Teresa Larrain of Women Working with Immigrant Women (WWIW), IWDC's response noted how pertinent many of the issues confronting immigrants were to all Canadian women. It pointedly reminded *Broadside* that by pronouncing such issues as "peripheral," it was echoing many past polemics that had held out the lesbian critique of heterosexism as being "the peripheral issue par excellence in the women's movement."[22] Valverde expanded upon the point:

> As lesbians, we have had to be blatant about our sexuality in order to redress a historic imbalance, a historic silence. In being blatant, we may have indeed appeared to be acting in a "divisive" way, but the eventual result has been (in some places) to unify all women around an understanding of how heterosexism oppresses us all.[23]

Another participant in the debate critiqued Lowenberger's claim that a universal system of patriarchy underlay women's oppression, on the grounds that such a construction was at once simplistic and Eurocentric, and like Valverde she quoted Larrain: "How can we talk to women who are in fear of their lives, who are fighting political repression, who do not have enough food to eat or a decent place to live, how can we talk to these women about abortion, about pornography?"[24]

Although *Broadside*'s polemics about IWD gradually died down,[25] the discussion suggested the extent to which, by the early 1980s, socialist and radical feminists saw the world in strikingly different ways, with socialist feminists retaining much of the Marxist analysis of imperialism, and radical feminists arguing emphatically that the problems of all women, including immigrant women, were traceable back to a universal system of patriarchy.

At "Socialism 1984" workshops in February and March 1984, some participants argued that socialist feminism offered a broader conception of politics than traditional left models often allowed. As Dorothy Smith observed, "The old debates between reform and revolution have no meaning in contemporary contexts. We know in the women's movement how to work for concrete objectives in ways which expand and develop the powers and capacities of women to organize and work together."[26] Yet, as Joanne Kates remarked, the "new style of socialism" also presented challenges. As the experience of the recently collapsed major vanguard groups had suggested, the dynamics between socialist men and women could be complicated. Whether non-sexist working relationships should become the focus of socialist feminists was a controversial proposition. Many were "skeptical about a project aiming at bringing socialists together without any clear objective in sight," and many women in particular did not want to be a part of a mixed-gender group. Yet, if men and women went their separate ways, what possibilities remained for a socialist movement?[27]

Even the achievement of abortion rights, which had been such a major theme of the early 1970s, seemed in the 1980s to entail many complications. As a number of feminists argued in *Healthsharing* magazine, the early 1970s emphasis on abortion as a paramount issue meant that the issue was detached from the overall oppression of women. The Toronto Midwifery Collective pointed out that women-controlled birthing would liberate a central element of the politics of reproduction from the state. The "Case for Lay Abortion" was, similarly, that it would free women from undue reliance upon male professionals and state authority.[28]

Nancy Adamson and Susan Prentice agreed. They argued that a left reproductive politics overwhelmingly oriented to the struggle for "choice" had tended to narrow horizons by making abortion the overarching issue, rather than encouraging feminists to engage more broadly with midwives and health activists and in ways that subversively critiqued mainstream medical models. There was nothing intrinsically individualistic or bourgeois about moving outside the medical system and demanding, like the co-operative daycares of the 1970s, a more holistic approach to reproduction. Somehow the pro-choice movement had adopted a strategy of "near-total reliance on doctors and corresponding validation of the medical model," when many other spheres of reproductive health (such as midwifery, lay health care, and home birthing) were of direct interest to left feminists.[29]

The issue that most visibly, and painfully, divided socialist and radical feminists was pornography.[30] For some feminists, pornography was an integral part of patriarchal violence against women. For others, pornography was an integral part of a more emancipated sexual order, and calling upon the law to stop or restrict it sanctioned an attack on freedom. This debate divided the feminist world for two decades. Although the anti-pornography and anti-censorship camps did not map directly onto the division between the radical and socialist feminists, a rough correlation existed between the two. If the controversy reinforced the divide, it also suggested the fragility of the links tying feminism to gay liberation, whose partisans had been so recently fired up by the struggle to defend *The Body Politic*.

The Black power movement continued to contract from the late 1970s into the 1980s, as the declining visibility and disappearance of African Liberation Day celebrations suggested. *Contrast*, for instance, cut back on its publication schedule. But at the same time feminist ideas were attracting a substantial number of Black women. Ayanna Black had worked for the previous twelve years with the Times Change Women's Employment Centre, Metro Women's Credit Union, Toronto Women's Writing Collective, and Fireweed Collective, institutions that in themselves suggested the institutional richness and depth of Toronto's feminism. In looking back in 1986 she remembered consciousness-raising groups as being homogenously white and middle class in the early 1970s. Over time the movement had come to include out-of-the-closet lesbians, Francophones, the disabled, and housewives, but only rarely Black women. As she came to embrace feminism, she encountered resistance from "some socially and politically astute black men" who felt "that my involvement with feminism or what I called activism—was dividing the race."[31]

As the feminist movement came to be seen, by both partisans and opponents, as the universalizing movement of the left, it was also critiqued for failing to live up to its promise of emancipation for all. For Lorna Weir, the question raised by Black feminism went to the heart of how to think through the manifold contradictions present in the social order: "In the same way as the contradiction between men and women cannot be reduced to the contradiction between labour and capital, so too the contradiction between white and non-white, or colonizer and colonized, is not reducible to the contradiction between men and women." Yet what were the implications for feminists, if everyone—anti-imperialists and anti-racist activists, gays and lesbians, liberals and socialists—came to adopt "feminism"? Was there a risk of it becoming ever more difficult to see as a distinct movement? For Weir, inter-movement alliances carried a distinct risk of losing independence and devaluing principles—of working with men and "returning to the typewriters and coffee cups of the male left." Increasingly, the "male left" was distinguished from "us." When Chai Chu Thompson of the Visible Minority Women's Coalition attended a Voice of Women function she was startled by the extent to which, for those present, men had become the enemy. As she reported it, "We found their analysis 'extremist,' saying that wars are the responsibility of men, who are born war-like." Did not embracing this binary and defending the notion that women were by definition in struggle with men make it logical to pursue a politics more or less entirely separate from them? Weir remembered that "coalitions" had long been part of the women's movement, and for her the separatist option was unattractive. Many others disagreed with her.[32]

IWD especially found itself embroiled in debates traceable back to this core contradiction of a feminism established on the basis of the identity leftism of the 1960s and 1970s and that at the same time wanted to be perceived as the solution to the fragmentation and partiality of left politics in general. Feminists who wanted to go "beyond the fragments"—to make their movement the carrier of the general project of human liberation—thus found themselves caught up in debates that earlier feminists would not have immediately identified as pertaining to "women's issues." Jobs, hunger, anti-imperialism, access to health care: all could and should be addressed by the feminist movement. Yet—on the basis of what logic?

Some feminists seemingly worked comfortably within conventional middle-class notions of the world. When in 1979 Susan G. Cole depicted the trying time that a progressive middle-class family had experienced with the sexist attitudes of a Vietnamese refugee family, the content of her article seemed to question admitting refugees with such retrograde attitudes. Amanda Hale took a rare position on the left, advocating the adoption of a "melting pot" approach to immigrants because violence against women was "more explicit" in immigrant communities. Adrienne Rich complained that socialist feminists often relied for their analysis of racism on a strategy of simply tacking "race" on to conventional class analysis and to regard both racism and sexism as illusions or false consciousness, rather than as practices with real and damaging material consequences.[33]

Such discussions about race and feminism became even more heated later in the 1980s, when a storm erupted over the racial composition of the Toronto Women's Bookstore.[34] The controversy became particularly acute when the planners of the 1986 IWD decided to organize the event around a similar issue: racism. The rallying cry was "Women say no to racism, from Toronto to South Africa." From the perspective of the Black Women's Collective (BWC), the decision was presumptuous. In a statement read at a March 8th Coalition meeting on Feb. 5, 1986, the Black Women's Collective voiced a dissatisfaction with the decision-making process used by the Coalition:

> The Coalition in our point of view has organized white women over the last ten years. In selecting this theme perhaps it was not fully aware of the step it was taking. Simply, it was seeking to organize Black women! Did the Coalition consider how it would have to change in order to do so? What matters it would of necessity discuss and how that would change the very face of the women's movement?[35]

It seemed, the Collective charged, that Black women had been marginalized in an event organized, ironically enough, to fight racist oppression. The Collective recommended that white feminists, who alone could free themselves, conduct their own closed workshops. It was not the BWC's job to educate them about racism. Nor should the white women imagine that they could organize Black women.[36] From the perspective of Chai Chu Thompson, the feminist movement in the 1980s faced fundamental challenges with respect to race. The steering committee of her Visible Minority Women's Coalition was made up of representatives from several racialized groups; they had decided that white women would be allowed to attend meetings but not to join the Coalition. White women, she believed, had a harder time understanding that in much of the world, wars of national liberation provided the only path to peace.[37]

Members of the BWC and the Native Women's Resource Centre (NWRC) rejected the March 8th Coalition planning. They complained that Coalition members had empowered themselves to shape the day in any way they saw fit, from the order of contingents in the march, to the topics at the fair's workshops, to the kind of music played at the dance, all without accountability to racialized women. The move sparked the question of who spoke for women of colour and a sense that the decision had betrayed longer-standing members of the Coalition. Black women who had fraught relations with BWC objected to that organization being assigned this key role. Members of the Latin American Women's Collective, who had come to recognize themselves as oppressed by race as well as by class and gender, dropped out of active participation in the Coalition when the NWRC defined them as white oppressors.

The integration of an anti-racism perspective within feminism was not smooth. The fallout from that International Women's Day included both back-and-forth accusations of racism and heartfelt attempts to grapple with its personal and institutional dimensions. In the immediate aftermath, instead of becoming more diverse, IWDC became less so. The IWDC's existing women of colour caucus disintegrated, while the hopes for a fruitful relationship with BWC and NWRC appeared to be dashed, with the Native women sending an audio recording to explain that to avoid wasting their own time and energy they would have no further involvement.

The mid-1980s thus resounded with calls for a feminist anti-racism with many repercussions. A leading figure at Women's Press reported in 1986 that, prompted by the Lesbians of Colour group, it was conducting a regular anti-racism workshop. Some found off-putting the new emphasis on white and Black women meeting separately, and Black women sitting separately from white women at meetings. There was widespread acceptance among left-wingers of the principle of autonomous organizing.[38] On some readings, white-only workshops provided safe places for some feminists to think through the politics of racism and anti-racism, and grasp, in the words of Michèle Paulse, why "certain dynamics come up between white women and women of colour who are working together." As another activist explained:

> We're hoping that from now on we're building a new women's movement—one which recognizes that the struggle against racism is the same struggle which women have been fighting against oppressive companies and governments. A new women's movement requires not only the participation, but the leadership, of women of colour.[39]

Yet, was it the *same* struggle? Or was it a *related* struggle? If the first, then it might make sense to imagine a united feminist movement providing central direction for the waging of *the* struggle. But if feminism and anti-racism, Third World solidarity, and the struggle against homelessness were *distinct* struggles, who or what should relate them with each other—and on what basis? There was no organization, or body of opinion, vested with the authority to adjudicate such a question. The organized "movement" of the 1960s, the "parties" in the 1970s—these were no longer there. In some respects, the mid-1980s saw both the full flowering of basic new left principles of organizing and the eclipse, in an "Age of Fracture," of the possibility of there being any one big movement wherein these principles, or any others, could be realized.[40]

The mid-1980s crisis of the IWDC, in some respects a late standard-bearer for the core new left values, suggested not just the challenges awaiting feminist anti-racism but also an emergent existential crisis for the left as such. Many were the voices distancing themselves from it. Sandy Steinecker—who had been involved in the organization of Interval House, some of the largest mid-1970s feminist demonstrations, and IWDC—had gradually become less and less engaged by the scene, in part because of political differences and in part because of the demands of single parenthood. She experienced IWDC politics as akin to being on a treadmill because experienced militants were perpetually obliged to bring new recruits up to speed and keep their analyses bare-bones and accessible. "We couldn't seem to use what we had learned over the years and give that to them. In fact there was a real taboo against that." She often felt that she was obliged to pull back from who she was and what she really thought. The taboo was reinforced by the prevailing post-vanguardist aversion to hierarchy. On her analysis, neither the IWDC nor the many left coalitions were free of elitism. "Instead, we created informal structures which were worse, and harder for new women to get into because they weren't formal or acknowledged." Even a small group like the IWDC could feel somewhat cliquish. Leaders were needed, and they existed—but they could not be acknowledged. For all their grievous weaknesses, the traditional left groups had displayed one unmistakable virtue—people did not join them as a token gesture.[41]

In 1984 Nancy Adamson delivered a letter of resignation to the IWDC, expressing some of the same sentiments. She believed the group was not going anywhere. She found herself angered and frustrated by the lack of discussion surrounding important questions and was convinced that the group refused to deal with "issues of politics, purpose, leadership or accountability." Activists Marie Lorenzo, Christina Mills, and Linda Yanz struck a similar note when they resigned from IWDC that same year. They complained that the Committee offered little serious discussion and debate over fundamental issues, and that although IWDC had come to have a less and less coherent practice and identity, it still adopted a rather sectarian attitude towards other groups and people.[42]

* * *

Similar debates roiled gay liberation, which, though initially a movement claimed by both gay men and lesbians, had been articulated as part of the left; certainly, vanguardists had often credited it with the potential to unsettle their parties and undermine the proletarian family. Its most radical ambition was to create a sexual realm of freedom, distinct from and even opposed to the conventional bourgeois family—a term combining class and gender analysis that feminists and gay liberationists could share.

Like feminists, many gay liberationists hoped in the early 1980s to join forces with like-minded progressives in coalitions and alliances. During the early 1980s, left-wing gay activists strongly supported the movements for national liberation in Central America. But they were not prepared to leave their sexual politics at the door and organized gay liberation contingents for larger solidarity protests. These activists attacked the homophobia of not just the El Salvador government (a junta in the midst of a civil war) but also the ruling Nicaraguan Sandinistas (victorious in the 1978–79 revolution), suggesting that in such revolutionary versions of sexual politics, the left called out for transformation almost as much as the right. Yet, in the early 1980s, there was exuberance in the sense that connections might flourish outside the narrow confines of the gay community. Referring to a contingent of twenty gays and five lesbians at an El Salvador benefit dance, Michael Riordan confessed that it had been a long time since many of them had been participants in "such a spectacularly hetero scene." Although a few straight participants told organizers they were leaving because of same-sex dancing, these isolated instances of homophobia, combined with gay and lesbian persistence, convinced a group of Latin Americans at the dance to set up their own, specifically Latin American, gay organization.[43] Their answer to the gay activist predicament seemed to be working:

> It's a dilemma shared by women and gay people who want to be active in communities and movements for change other than feminism and gay liberation. Does one battle have to take precedence over another? Do we always have to wait until "the revolution is secure"? When we've done so in the past we've always lost.[44]

Riordan joked that he had mixed feelings about chanting "We will not, we will not be cruised" at rallies against the cruise missile, but such were the ironies and pleasures of bringing a gay presence to a wider audience. As in their Central American solidarity efforts, gay liberationists believed it important to maintain an independent gay identity. They formed, for instance, the Gay-Lesbian Action for Disarmament. Gary Kinsman argued that homosexuality and militarism, as opposing forces, were "incompatible," that gay liberation taught men not to be "agents of warfare," but "to be playful, erotic, loving of each other, which breaks down the homophobic values of patriarchal militarism." His fellow activist Walter Davis hoped to see a "renewed gay movement" that could "speak to issues of racism, sexism, authoritarianism, elitism and class." Remembering the links made between opposition to the Vietnam War and gay liberation in the pages of *The Body Politic* during the early 1970s and lamenting the subsequent "straight jacket of the equal rights strategy," Davis wanted gay liberationists to join young people in a "peace culture," something "more than the sum of the individual marches, public meetings, letter writing and so on." He saw the movement as "a social force of people seeded throughout society with visions broader than their local issues."[45] Here again was a call to move "beyond the fragments."

A demonstrator, standing next to an abandoned police cruiser, surveys the large crowd angered by the bathhouse raids.

North American Anarchist, March-April 1981.

Yet the question was how to do so without sacrificing the identity that had been so painstakingly constructed and defended in the previous decade. Many new leftists had rallied behind gay activist George Hislop's unsuccessful run for aldermanic office in 1980.[46] En masse, they also supported the campaign of John Sewell, who had stood with gays through the bathhouse raids and supported Hislop. Yet both Hislop and Sewell had been defeated in a campaign strongly influenced by the police association. Sewell was replaced by Art Eggleton, who kept up the traditional distinction held by the media and many politicians, arguing that closeted gays should be protected if discovered, but not those who were already out of the closet (and thus guilty of "promoting" homosexuality). In the wake of their defeat, many New Democrats in Toronto seemed even less sympathetic than usual to the gay and lesbian community. "Look what Sewell did for gays and what it got him," was the message they took away from 1980. Sewell was a "romantic anachronism" from an earlier time, argued one prominent New Democrat, although party dissidents, including the chair of the Ward Six Community Organization, thought otherwise. With the demise of ReforMetro and its local components, gay, tenant, and other activists complained that it was much easier and safer for the NDP to ignore their demands.[47]

The New Democrats were being opportunistic, but they were not necessarily out of touch with political realities. If feminist demands could be put forward as those of the majority, and as such at least potentially those of an emancipated humanity, gay positions could be similarly universalized only if they were construed as offering radically new ways of organizing human sexual life. Asking liberals and social democrats to support civil rights for homosexuals was one thing; asking them to revolutionize their thoughts about sexuality was something else.

Questions arose especially when "family values" intersected with the identities of ethnically or racially marginalized groups. In that case gay men themselves could become seen as the elite, the potentially dangerous "Other" to "community."

In the 1980s criticisms of *The Body Politic*'s libertarian politics erupted once again. In 1983 a significant left-wing, feminist, and anti-racist campaign arose after two *Body Politic* decisions: to carry an ad for Red Hot Video and subsequently to defend the company after an anarcho-feminist-inspired bombing of one of its Vancouver outlets; and to print racist personal ads, later justified in an article that complained that whites too could be victims of racism.[48] While many of the forty women who signed a Rape Crisis Centre letter against *The Body Politic*'s handling of the Red Hot Video issue had probably never been great fans of the magazine, the fifty-plus signers of another protest letter included a number of socialists of both genders, and many of them had been its past supporters. They accused *The Body Politic* of pitting "good feminists," that is, those involved in pro-choice activism and IWDC, like many of the signers, against "bad feminists," that is, those who made anti-pornography activism a central element of their politics; and they interpreted its stance on the Vancouver bombing to be an attack on the women's movement in general. Others targeted the narrowness of *The Body Politic*'s focus, which had allowed for such insensitivity. One letter summarized both instances as examples of the magazine's "single-issue preoccupation with censorship and 'freedom of the press.'"[49]

The 1983 debate returned with a vengeance in 1985 after a decision by a majority of collective members to run a personal ad from a white man requesting a Black man for a "houseboy." It was printed over the objections of a handful of members, including the collective's only person of colour. In a subsequent meeting between *The Body Politic* and three small gay and lesbian groups in which people of colour predominated, some saw anti-racism and gay liberation as working at cross purposes, whereas others defended the classic new left libertarian position that expressions of sexual desire were not to be policed. Historian David Churchill underlines a generational pattern in the debate—with the younger *Body Politic* supporters more alert to the wider ramifications of the issue than their older counterparts—but ideological change was also a factor, with the libertarians at *The Body Politic* prevailing over beyond-the-fragments socialist feminists.[50] Some two years of debate had ensued, without noticeable changes of opinion on either side. The impasse testified to the feelings of negativity and exhaustion arising from a clash between two key components of new leftism: personal authenticity and autonomy on the one hand, and community on the other. That some left gay liberationists departed for other publications (such as *Pink Ink* and *Rites*) also suggested a diminished sense that one publication, set of leaders, or movement could represent such a heterogeneous and conflicted group of people, with the term "community" appearing to be ever less apposite. For gay liberationist and theorist Brian Mossop, who rejected any conception of gay liberation as a subordinate component of feminism, such events in the 1980s were a cue to downplay the search for allies and emphasize instead a radical, lifestyle-centred approach, which he jokingly called "hedonistic socialism."[51] For all his firm disavowal of seeing gay liberation as an echo of feminism, it is difficult to overlook the parallels between his path and the separatism articulated by many radical feminists. On both sides, initial enthusiasm for going into a wider-ranging politics of association had led to frustration. Soon gay liberationists would be wrestling, to a great extent on their own, with the AIDS epidemic.

* * *

For many in the 1980s, the peace movement was paramount. The end of détente in the era of Ronald Reagan's presidency, the seemingly endless proliferation of nuclear weapons, the coming to Canada of cruise missile testing under the auspices of the federal government, the calamitous "proxy wars" fought out between the superpowers: all of these prompted a peace movement revival—and within it new left themes and tactics were front and centre. Yet there were indications that this peace movement was the swan song of Toronto's new left.

The peace demonstrations in the first half of the 1980s were enormous. In June 1982 the turnout was estimated at 15,000 in a general march for peace; the following year, in February, 5,000 turned out for a more specific march to "refuse the cruise." In October 1983, estimates of the crowd at a Metro Toronto rally ran from 17,000 (police) to more than 30,000 (the organizers). Even in October 1985, after Prime Minister Brian Mulroney said no to Reagan's "Star Wars" missile defence system, organizers claimed that 10,000 marchers took part in an anti-nuclear rally.[52]

Substantial media coverage was also a factor in the large size of the demonstrations. *The Toronto Star* in particular ran extensive coverage in the lead-up to major demonstrations, so that interested readers would know when and where to go. The newspaper provided regular updates on many of the decade's inter-city "peace walks," often accompanied by lists of upcoming educational workshops and protests. A survey of first-time peace demonstrators indicated that a substantial number had learned of the protest through the media.[53] The numbers at their largest demonstrations—those at the 10,000 to 30,000 mark—were substantially larger than at any peace or anti-war protest in Toronto from the 1960s or 1970s. Yet, in testament to the power of the image of the 1960s, even supportive reporters, in commending the turnouts as impressive, frequently declared them to have been the largest since the 1960s or since the end of the Vietnam War.[54]

Even more impressive than the numbers of people willing to turn out, even in the winter, to protest for peace, was the movement's institutional grounding. The Toronto District Labour Council, the executive committee of city council, and the Toronto District School Board were all supportive. The School Board even organized a "Thinking and Deciding in a Nuclear Age Advisory Committee" that organized conferences and workshops for teachers and put together curricular materials on nuclear and ecological issues. In November 1985 *The Toronto Star* reported that as many as forty high-school peace clubs had been formed. Members of Educators for Nuclear Disarmament, which grew out of one of those workshops, encouraged classes and school assemblies devoted to nuclear issues, attended demonstrations, and lobbied the government. In the Catholic system, Teachers for Social Responsibility did the same. Parents for Peace provided resource kits for parent-run meetings, distributed its newsletter to home and school associations, and, with help from the Toronto district of the Ontario Secondary School Teachers' Federation, also created teaching materials. In 1985 the Association for Canadian Studies *Bulletin* devoted eight pages to "Peace Research and Studies in Canada." Professors joined with teachers to form the Canadian Peace Educators Network.[55] The Toronto Board of Health told citizens that no bomb shelters could save them in the event of nuclear war—and advised city council to pressure Ottawa to push for nuclear disarmament. It also asked school boards to develop a curriculum on nuclear war and the promotion of peace and opposed the production of components for nuclear systems. At the behest of the Board, the city agreed to publish a pamphlet on how to survive nuclear fallout. Its core message to the public: take political action before it was too late.[56] On Jan. 31, 1983, city council voted to declare Toronto a nuclear-weapon-free zone, making the city the first in North America to do so; for its part, in February 1985, Ward Six resolved to ask its peace committee to erect signs advising citizens and visitors that they were entering a no-nukes area.

Toronto had a staggering variety of peace organizations in the early 1980s. The NDP had its Anti-War Committee, the Labour Council formed a Peace and Disarmament Committee, and the Ontario branch of the Canadian Federation of Students started its Peace and Disarmament Committee. Faith-based peace groups included the Christian Movement for Peace and the Shalom Disarmament Group, and others linked to specific denominations and even single churches. In addition to an assortment of neighbourhood peace groups, more regionally based bodies sprang up, such as East End Peace Action and North York Action for Disarmament. The peace movement even trickled into suburbs outside the Metro area, with the Peel Peacemakers, a Mississauga-based group claiming seventy-one members, and Markham Citizens for Nuclear Disarmament boasting of having grown to 150 "families."[57]

Occupation-based peace groups were formed, some of them due to 1960s and 1970s activists finding themselves now ensconced in careers: Library and Information Workers for Peace, Scientists for Peace, Lawyers for Social Responsibility, Nurses for Social Responsibility, Physicians for Social Responsibility and Psychologists for Social Responsibility. Many of them held conferences, printed newsletters, and had substantial memberships. The Arts for Peace and the city's Performing Artists for Nuclear Disarmament branch also had larger memberships.[58] It was the sort of movement that the SUPA-connected Peace and the Professions group of the mid-1960s had envisioned but never came close to realizing.

Many of these phenomena can be validly interpreted as indications that new leftists were having an impact in their long march through institutions. The School Board, for instance, appeared to be thronged with educators who interpreted the world through a critical, left-wing lens; and the emerging network of peace institutions exhibited an unmistakeable new left atmosphere. The Cruise Missile Conversion Project (CMCP), formed at the beginning of the 1980s, provides a good example. Members of the CMCP became best known for following a philosophy of non-violent, direct action in mass acts of civil disobedience carried out in front of the Litton factory, which produced components for cruise missiles. Members constantly urged the labour and peace movements to embrace each other's issues and regularly waited at plant gates to initiate discussions and distribute the latest issue of *Jobs and Peace* to workers. Although CMCP urged Litton plant workers to unionize, they also advertised their long-term vision of worker-owned companies and generalized worker self-management.[59]

As the name of its newsletter implied, CMCP emphasized that ditching military production did not have to mean unemployment, and it devoted substantial resources to envisioning a weapons-free economy. Members told Litton workers that violence meant not just the missiles produced at the plant, but issues like the denial of guaranteed collective bargaining rights and sexual harassment. In line with a focus on class and organized labour, CMCP activists took inspiration from past battles such as the 1919 Winnipeg General Strike and the 1978 strike by female Fleck auto-part workers as important examples of non-violent resistance. Although CMCP stuck to "peace issues," it consistently emphasized the connections between a myriad of phenomena, from militarism to the "domination of maleness."[60]

The Alliance for Non-Violent Action (ANVA) adopted a very different approach. It critiqued a "narrow" focus on cruise testing. It thought, rather, that many issues should be woven into the peace movement. This group was founded in the spring of 1982 after activists from two poorly attended peace meetings at Toronto's Bathurst United Church decided to merge their gatherings and discovered they had similar concerns about the movement's direction. Ken Hancock of the Coalition of Lake Ontario Against the Cruise was particularly adamant that more people would come out if the focus became a broader struggle against militarism. A gathering in Kingston at the end of May formally launched ANVA as a province-wide coalition. An early proposal for ANVA envisioned it becoming "the direct action arm of the movement in this country," and direct action became its calling card. Its Remembrance Week campaign in 1983, for example, included a woman-only civil disobedience protest (and a "liberation struggles solidarity" civil disobedience protest) among its more general direct actions against militarism. The program of the week's scheduled events was careful to draw connections to additional issues, including gay and lesbian struggles.[61] ANVA's *Civil Disobedience Campaign Handbook* emphasized this multi-issue approach, going beyond information on peace and tactical advice—some drawn from labour history—to include sections on feminism and anti-racism. The handbook emphasized that integrating feminism and anti-racism into its analysis was part of a long-term vision for a non-oppressive and exploitative world: "Only through dismantling oppressive power relationships and building alternative models of community living will militarism be abolished."[62]

ANVA's structure, like its analysis, was heavily influenced by other social movements and reflected the early 1980s return to emphasizing egalitarian and democratic organizational values. Adopting the statement of unity from a Toronto Men Against Sexism collective as an organizational template, it decided on a form of consensus decision-making in which any members seeking to block consensus had to argue convincingly that their objections were more consistent with the group's basis of unity than was the favoured proposal. Here, one member observed, was the same process that had been used by groups ranging from the Vietnamese fighting U.S. imperialism to feminist collectives.[63]

In striving for a decentralized structure, the alliance encouraged the formation of smaller internal bodies to aid in discussion and decision-making. Its attentiveness to decentralized democracy was particularly noteworthy at its provincial meetings, where decision-making was a lengthy process involving a number of strategies: members pairing off to discuss their emotions; larger fishbowls (non-hierarchical discussions); constructive criticism sessions; affinity groups; and caucus and collective sub-meetings. Gender-based meetings took place via both men's and "wymyn's" caucuses. Women's Action for Peace, a fully autonomous public group, held its own separate meetings.[64]

These two organizations—along with about one hundred others—were part of a larger coalition called the Toronto Disarmament Network (TDN). After its first two years, the Network tightened its structure, established membership dues and permanent committees, and implemented provisions for voting when unanimity through more consensual means could not be reached.[65] At a December

1983 TDN conference, the connection between the disarmament movement and the Central American anti-intervention movement was a major focus of debate. A large majority believed that the disarmament movement should be part of anti-intervention activities, although others wanted to stick with the single-issue orientation. Matthew Clark, a member of TDN's co-ordinating committee, argued that disarmament could not be a single issue: "If we eliminate nuclear weapons, all other relationships within that system will change. Conversely, changing the system may aid our efforts to eliminate nuclear weapons.... By opposing nuclear weapons, we are removing one of the tools of intervention; by opposing intervention, we are removing a justification for the nuclear arsenal." In response to arguments that abandoning their single-issue approach would dampen effectiveness and alienate some supporters, Clark acknowledged the risk, but evoked the movement against the war in Vietnam as an example of how successful a multi-issue struggle could be. "We should not be a movement for peace in the north only, or for whites only," Clark declared. "We should be a movement for peace." One militant, referring to the barrier dividing peace protesters from armaments makers, added, "For many of us, the revolution begins at the fence."[66]

If new left ideals of participatory democracy, community, and national liberation were omnipresent in the peace movement in the 1980s, so too were archetypal new left tactics. At Queen's Park in 1983, a "peace camp" demonstrated against war for two months, before moving on to Liberal Party headquarters. Just hours before the first cruise missile test, ACT for Disarmament (ACT), a youthful, anarchist-leaning peace group, staged a mock funeral procession from Bloor and Yonge streets to a die-in in front of the Eaton Centre.[67] Most dramatically, a group called Direct Action—which turned out to be based in British Columbia—bombed the same Litton factory that had been the site of many of the peace movement's protests. The Oct. 14, 1982, bombing injured several and cost millions in property damage. Like the 1968 bombings directed at war-industry executives, this one sparked police raids on the homes and offices of peace activists. Most activists condemned the bombing, and some speculated that it had been carried out by police or other state forces to discredit the peace movement. Others suggested that the bombing might bring more attention to the struggle against the cruise. A minority of anarchists were exceedingly vocal in their support for the action and strongly condemned activists who were not. They praised Direct Action for "raising the spirits of those who share their anger and rage without having their courage."[68]

Yet, although the bombing campaign suggested the extent to which a vanguard group could dramatize issues of peace and war, it seemed patently obvious that no such actions could create a lasting change in Canadian foreign or defence policy. Indeed, the anti-war campaigns of the 1980s provided unfavourable terrain for most vanguard groups, especially those still wedded to *Communist Manifesto* schemas of class analysis. The International Socialists, for example, at first insisted on focusing on the key role of atomic workers in anti-nuclear agitation. Yet the group seemed to be swayed by a prominent English member of its still heavily British tendency who advised against wasting time and energy on such a "CND-style" movement, that is, an organization so prone to moralism and resistant to the scientific insights that a vanguard might supply.[69]

If in the 1960s and 1970s, mass demonstrations might be likened to the tips of icebergs—portending social movements more deep-seated and well-supported than the numbers suggested—in the 1980s the reverse was the case. Although a sizable segment of young people joined with movement veterans and accomplished much, the peace movement of the 1980s ultimately failed to inspire an activist cohort on the scale of the one forged in the late 1960s and early 1970s. For continuing new leftists who hoped that the peace movement would provide a fulcrum for a general society-changing movement, a number of significant obstacles arose.

One was the amorphousness of the issue. One might oppose the Liberal government's acquiescence in cruise missile testing, but a Liberal prime minister (Trudeau) also embarked upon an ambitious international peace quest that won him headlines both in Canada and around the world. Ontario premier Bill Davis himself declared his support for disarmament. Some privately funded groups, one with Conrad Black on its board, said they wanted the same thing.[70] Declaring opposition to thermonuclear war did not necessarily require signing on to a more searching critique of the social order that made such war conceivable. It might—but in many cases, it did not.

Another obstacle, for new leftists, was that by the 1980s the "Other" of the peace movement had, for many, changed identities. Writing in *Broadside*, Juliet Huntley of the anti-nuclear Toronto Mobilization for Survival declared, "The days of single-issue politics are over!" She then outlined how human rights and economic issues fit within an anti-nuclear stance. Men and the ruling classes did not want peaceniks to make these connections. *Broadside*, incidentally, had featured a nuclear reactor on its inaugural cover in 1979. From the *Broadside* perspective, struggling against war and struggling against men were two sides of the same coin.[71] In vanguard style, *Broadside*'s editors declared the superiority of feminist analysis over that of "old time" anti-war activists: "The fact that feminists are prepared to examine the motivations that could take their countries to war, means that women are the most likely candidates for leadership in the anti-war movement of the eighties."[72] Rejecting the calls of some men for an overarching strategy for the anti-nuclear movement, Gay Bell of Women Against Nuclear Technology remarked: "We all have to organize in our own milieux." In her case, this meant organizing with other women around anti-nuclear issues. Rather than a new left "participatory democracy" model, then, this approach to the peace movement came closer to a notion of separate groups organizing separate campaigns in their separate ways. On Bell's line of analysis, given the investment all men had in the making of war, it was unlikely that many of those groups would be made up of men. Some feminists sought a framework that was less dichotomizing. Debra Curties argued that separatists restricted themselves to explicitly women-related issues and refused to organize with men, while autonomy allowed them to work in non-women-specific struggles and with men—"on our own terms." Activist Anne Cameron, critical of the radical feminists who would not support working with men to oppose nuclear war, quipped: "Well, I hope their feminist ovaries protect them from radiation." But then she went to a benefit concern in support of anti-nuclear activism and was shocked with the sexist songs and remarks made by the performers. Although that did not alter Cameron's stance that it was wrong to boycott mixed-gender events, it was also a reminder that social movement organizing in the 1980s could hardly close its eyes to sexism.[73]

Young activists were sometimes skeptical of sixties movement veterans, as represented in this work by artist Marian Lydbrooke.

Graphic Feminism: Graphic Art of the Ontario Women's Movement, 1970-86.

Some feminists complained there was little organized feminist presence at late 1970s-early 1980s demonstrations against the Darlington nuclear reactor, just outside Toronto, which had attracted thousands of youthful protesters and kicked off a renewed interest in civil disobedience. Although over half the protesters at one of the major demonstrations were women, there were complaints that no one addressed the crowd on the question of patriarchy. Indeed, the only visible presence of the feminist movement was Witches Against Nuclear Technology, which had formed a circle to gather and direct the Earth's energy against the nuclear plant. Women would have to put more work into increasing their visible presence in the future.[74]

The feminist presence was much more visible at Women for Survival's occupation at Ontario Hydro headquarters, where fifteen of their members were arrested and charged with trespassing. But although Judy Liefshultz, their spokesperson, had previously condemned nuclear power for embodying the patriarchal characteristics of violence and aggression, mainstream press accounts did not reveal any distinctly feminist message implicit in the women's demands to halt construction at Darlington, phase out nuclear energy and install pollution control devices at coal energy plants.[75]

Focusing on making the links with other areas of feminist activity, one Women for Survival event included a panel with Pat Schulz (Action Daycare), Laura Rowe (Rape Crisis Centre), and Sue Genge (CUPE Local 1582 and IWDC). They held parallel workshops, Men Against Violence Against Women for men, along with a women's only session on "Women's Survival—Patriarchy and the Nuclear Mentality," which connected women's immediate survival needs with the threat posed by nuclear war. With the more established Voice of Women and Congress of Canadian Women, they hosted "Women, War and the Nuclear Nightmare."[76]

Women for Survival's knack for making the links and alliance-building led to a conference on Grindstone Island that sought to analyze the relationship between women and militarism and its meaning for the peace movement. A strategy session led to the formation of Women's Action for Peace (WAP), whose statement of unity emphasized themes from the Grindstone conference. Associated with the ANVA, WAP stressed education that tied the oppression of people from the Third World and labour issues to their main themes and pacifist action.[77]

Members of WAP believed there was an "undeniable clear connection between the bomb-making militarism of this male-dominated society and the oppression of women everywhere." Non-violence was at once antithetical to patriarchy, tied into the "personal is political," and linked to "living otherwise."[78] As member Margaret Hancock explained:

> You have to see that in order to change that structure radically, you have to treat other people and other groups of people in an equal, just way. Otherwise, you will just perpetuate the same power structure. So if you are talking about radical social change I don't see that you can really use any other technique.[79]

To Hancock, not having children, being an open lesbian, and opening an abortion clinic or a rape crisis centre were all in some way acts of civil disobedience. Yet they did not result, as frequently, in arrests. Janice Williamson, one of twenty-nine women arrested during a WAP action at Litton, believed that the process of being arrested and going through the courts and all that entailed could in itself be a politicizing experience. It certainly was for Williamson, who credited the idea for her book on the history and issues of women's peace activism in Canada to her time in the courtroom.[80]

Thus, although new left precepts were plainly at work, anti-war activism in the 1980s was increasingly influenced by feminism—and often, in its arguments about the intrinsically war-like nature of men, radical feminism. Marusia Bociurkiw sounded very much like a new leftist from a decade before when in 1985 she proclaimed the urgent need, in a left that was often indifferent to cultural work, to "get rid of the artist/activist split, to explore where the needs and skills of artist and activist intersect." Yet a decade had made a considerable difference. She was creating "women's pictures" and was an activist with the Women's Media Alliance, which sought to link feminism and peace.[81]

* * *

New leftists thus often found in the feminist movements of the 1980s activists who seemed quite familiar—with their owns ways of approaching self-determination, national liberation, and democratic participation—yet who also turned these ideals in new, women-centric directions. At least for some scholars, feminism, both socialist and radical—which had its own distinctive theories of the essential features of the social order, its own notions of the patriarchal Other, and its own imagined future destination—constitutes a fifth left formation, related to but not the same as the new left. And it was in the early 1980s that this new formation largely overshadowed its predecessor.[82]

Such new leftists might also have experienced the same feelings of both recognition and unfamiliarity when they regarded the emergent anarchist movement in Toronto. Once again, one can speak of preservation—the self-determination ethos of the new left, now taken to what some thought was its logical conclusion in the demand for the abolition of the state itself. There had been a small Toronto Anarchist Group (TAG) in 1968, and the publication *Liberation*, associated with the near-legendary Attilio Bortolotti, once a close associate of Emma Goldman. At the University of Toronto, a branch of the Industrial Workers of the World briefly flourished, and Professor Graeme Nicholson tried to reconcile anarchism with Canadian nationalism. After the 1970s, however, anarchism became something much bigger, in large measure because of the growing hegemony of radical feminism.[83]

The radical lesbians of the Toronto Women's Anarchist Group, who joined with others in seizing the stage of the Miss Canada pageant in late 1975, were an early outlier. In 1978 Pat Leslie, an influential editor of *Other Woman*, joined the half-dozen male members of TAG and began organizing women-only anarchist meetings. Subsequently a number of members of the Lesbian Organization of Toronto (LOOT) began to identify as anarchists. One penned an essay identifying the new left underpinnings of past women's liberation activity—from the Abortion Caravan through to Women's Place—as distinctly anarchist. Anarcha-feminism itself appeared not to be entirely distinct from radical feminism, as another essay explained that the raison d'être of anarcha-feminism was to challenge all hierarchy by attacking sexism, and creating a "countersystem" of collectives to challenge society.[84]

A key development for both local and North American anarchism was the founding of the Anarchist Communist Federation (ACF) in 1978. The ACF arose out of the Social Revolutionary Anarchist Federation, a loosely knit continental organization. Members of ACF wanted a tighter network, which would exclude tendencies like anarcho-capitalism and allow for the ideological cohesion necessary to move from debate to action. The Toronto Anarchist Group, which became the ACF's local branch, was particularly influential, in part because it was responsible for publishing the federation's newspaper. The ACF made no bones about declaring its main enemies: government, capitalism, and patriarchy.[85]

The late 1970s were pivotal in shaping the trajectory of anarchism, and the ACF had a role to play in how it unfolded. ACF came to represent the rebirth of an "anarcho-communist" pole that in later decades would be represented by groups such as Love and Rage Revolutionary Anarchist Federation and North Eastern Federation of Anarchist Communists. It also became a foil for the distillation of rival tendencies. Members of ACF engaged in polemics with the noted anarchist John Zerzan, controversially critiqued the social ecology of Murray Bookchin, and were slammed for their "workerism" by Jason Quinn (later editor of *Anarchy: A Journal of Desire Armed*) and iconoclast Bob Black, who also criticized the ACF's "leftism."[86] Exchanges between the ACF's Steve Ellams and Jim Campbell—after Campbell refused to join an ACF-organized contingent for Toronto's 1980 IWD march—reflected the divide between ACF and the philosophical outlook of other anarchists. Campbell criticized ACF for its strategy of "winning" people to anarchism, "infiltrating" the women's movement, and its copious reports of strikes and workplace politics, none of which emphasized the struggle against work itself. This, Campbell thought, was indicative of vanguardism and an attempt to move the anarchist movement towards the socialist-identified left. Lamenting the orthodox lives lived by many anarchists, some ACFers undoubtedly among them, Campbell hinted that anarchism's constituency might never be the "workers of the world": "We are the mad-ones, the outsiders, the runaways, the malcontents, the poets and the prophets. Anarchy is the highest level of disorder and not order."[87]

Ellams, for his part, believed that only those who centred on the political and economic components of the class struggle could legitimately call themselves anarchists. Situating himself firmly within the tradition of the classical anarchists Bakunin, Kropotkin, and Malatesta, he wrote that Campbell and other anarchists hostile to founding revolutionary groups were merely "'lifestyle' anarchists," unwilling to pursue the centralized co-operation necessary to seriously challenge

An Anarchist Communist Federation banner, at a spring 1980 demonstration against nuclear power, suggested that more revolutionary demands were needed.

North American Anarchist, June-July 1980.

the state. He did not agree with the emphasis Campbell placed on youth-oriented countercultures, or with the idea that anarchism would advance organically through the building of alternative communities.[88]

Based on strong local collectives, ACF was only around for a few years before fracturing. Its contribution to the development of anarchist politics was chiefly through its newspaper—claimed to be the most regularly issued and largest-circulated anarchist publication in North America—and pamphlets on feminism and self-management, and against the strategy of terrorism (*You Can't Blow Up a Social Relationship*). In late 1981, by which time ACF had disintegrated, members of the former Toronto collective began publishing *Strike!*, which devoted more attention to workplace struggles.[89]

The first half of that decade saw a stunning proliferation of anarchist organizations. One anarchist ventured that the city had around twenty-five such groups.[90] Their new infrastructure included an anarchist bookstore and a host of publications, including the *Anti-Authoritarian News Network Bulletin*, *Reality Now*, *Up from the Ashes*, and *HEART: The Central Organ of the Anarchist Party of Canada (Groucho-Marxist)*. But *Kick It Over* (*KIO*) was probably the most significant.[91]

There was much here, then, to gladden the heart of a new leftist from the 1960s—yet also much that he or she would also have found disconcerting. Members of the *KIO* collective extricated themselves from "the left," which they saw as ignoring "the politics of everyday life." The "official left," they alleged, did not talk about freedom from patriarchal and family control, which had radicalized many members of the *KIO* collective, nor did it really discuss issues pertaining to quality of life, sexuality, community, or identity. Instead of reactively railing against right-wing politics, *KIO* members would talk about their desires and help form an "alternative" community.[92] *KIO* seemed to publish articles on every sort of oppression baring that of a strictly class or economic nature. For a time, one of the most common subjects within its pages was pornography, reflecting both anarchism's attachment to radical feminism and the affiliation of female members of the *KIO* collective with Women Against Violence Against Women. *KIO* women called on all revolutionaries to study feminism and integrate it into their praxis and criticized the previous generation of anarchists for having ignored pornography and rape. Many appeared to agree with a WAVAW statement affirming that class, race, and national divisions were all products of "masculinist ideology."[93] There was a signal confluence of radical feminism and anarchism in Toronto in the 1980s that constituted the simultaneous preservation, cancellation, and transcendence—in that fifth left framework—of new left themes.

* * *

If the left was increasingly divided between two formations, one of which was ceding place to the other, it was also beleaguered as rarely before by a self-confident and aggressive new right politics. While in Canada the full achievement of new right hegemony awaited the twenty-first century—notwithstanding many a left critique pinpointing the dangers of Mulroney, Thatcher, and Reagan—it is also the case that, through the course of the 1980s, policies that presupposed free-market fundamentalism became increasingly common. A 1980 speech by economist Milton Friedman to a conference on the role of government spoke of the danger of collectivism and the virtues of lower taxes. Mel Watkins, the former Waffle leader, characterized Friedman's views as "not pre-Keynesian but pre-Cambrian—a retreat back into the Stone Age." Chilean refugees offered a sobering vision of how Friedman's "laboratory" had worked out in their homeland.[94] Yet views that seemed antediluvian in 1980 came to be almost orthodox by the next decade, when a right-wing revolution left nothing in Toronto unchanged. So hegemonic was this neo-liberal transformation that, when a historian looks back on Toronto from 1958 to 1985, and at the radical ambition of its succeeding cohorts of new leftists, it is with the elegiac sense of recovering a lost continent of political hope—one whose recovery in memory may prefigure its return as an indispensable source of warnings, insights, and inspirations for the left formation emerging all around us.

* * *

The new left in Toronto from 1958 to 1985 constituted one of the largest and most successful countercapitalist movements in Canadian history. Thousands of militants in scores of movements touched, directly or indirectly, the lives of hundreds of thousands of Torontonians. Its core values of personal freedom, solidarity with national liberation, and real-world democracy could be found mobilizing a vast swath of the city's inhabitants. It constitutes the last time in which revolution was palpably in the air. In contrast to earlier left formations—and its communist and social-democratic predecessors were those against which new leftists measured themselves most insistently—this configuration was, despite the best efforts of vanguardists, never captured by a dominant party or organization, which means that any assessment of its overall strength and influence must be based on debatable inferences drawn from a myriad of data.

New leftism was shaped by the socio-economic conditions of post-1945 Canada, and specifically by the realities of the postwar compromise that undergirded the Keynesian welfare state. Many new leftists lived and breathed in a Canada in which the state sector had expanded dramatically. While the first formation of Canadian leftists found many of its supporters in outdoor extractive industries—mining, farming, forestry—and the second and third formations (communism and social democracy) drew from both there and mass manufacturing industries, the fourth formation, which included the new left, was shaped by a more white-collar work world (albeit still one in which the traditional sectors of the working class were far from quiescent). It was also shaped by many young people who found that world to be the alienating denial of their dreams. Class still mattered to most new leftists—especially down to the late 1970s—but it was increasingly supplemented by race, gender, and sexuality as key categories of analysis and activism.

New leftism was in part a refusal of older patterns of leftism, whose obsolescence in the new postwar world was widely asserted. Yet this did not equate in Canada, as it reportedly did in other countries, with a total, generation-based rejection of those older traditions. Satisfying as it might be to draw a tidy "line of demarcation" separating new leftists from communists and social democrats, to do so risks purchasing analytical clarity at the cost of empirical inexactitude. Rather, many people who came out of or related to those older formations—even those, as we have seen, in the supposedly moribund Communist Party of Canada, and even many members of the NDP—took up the new left dream of a genuinely democratic revolution. Moreover, the vanguardist attempts to bring new leftists to heel and enrol them in new communist movements, although they undoubtedly influenced legions of urban leftists, did not ultimately succeed. For all their sound and fury, they left a diminutive historical footprint, whereas new leftism, operating on many fronts at once, left a much more tangible legacy.

The evidence provided by the records of the CCF-NDP, the Communist Party, left-leaning Liberals, Trotskyists, and Maoists suggests that all of these parties and organizations responded vigorously to what they perceived to be a tangible threat from new leftism. It also suggests that many of their members were deeply shaped by the new leftism they were officially sworn to oppose. In focusing so intently on creating a cultural revolution, new leftists offered the entire left a body of theory and an imperative to activism that seemed far more appropriate to a fast-changing modern world than did many of the antecedent progressive traditions. New left ideas did not just "drop from the sky," to paraphrase Chairman Mao. Many of them were born in the minds of old leftists grappling with the socio-political conditions of the postwar period.

Previous socialist formations in Canada had been manifestations of global patterns and were often keenly aware of their status as nodes in wider transnational networks. None was an exercise in Canadian isolationism. Still, Toronto new leftism provides an unusually clear-cut case of a consciously transnational leftism. Whether it was resistance to the war in Vietnam and imminent nuclear war, whole-hearted identification with people's power in Chile and Nicaragua, or direct involvement in struggles against racism in both the United States and Canada, new leftists were acutely conscious of living at a time of global revolutionary change. New leftism was forged amidst the global proliferation of national liberation struggles. For many in this left-wing generation, the war against the war in Vietnam remained, for their entire lifetimes, an abiding call to arms and politics. Black radicals saw themselves as part of a transnational liberation movement that connected the decolonization of Black peoples in the Western world to African liberation movements. White radicals spoke of decolonizing everyday life and linked the independence of Canada to global national liberation movements. For some new leftists, national liberation was so important that it became a synonym for socialism itself.

Because of their historically specific class location, political precepts, and differentiation from older left traditions, Toronto new leftists placed a particular emphasis on "community." Sometimes they used the term in a conventional way—as an identifiable set of people living in a particular area. But more often they were thinking of collectivities pursuing, through projects of local control and social action, unalienated, free, and democratic lives. No less substantively, "community" referred to everyday life outside the workplace. It was the central sphere of social reproduction and ideological struggle. A core new left insight was that culture and community were not mere reflections of the industrial "workplace," of minor interest to people concerned with revolution, but the spheres in which fundamental change could be pursued and achieved. Notwithstanding much theorization of "workers' control," it was in community that participatory democracy, that *sine qua non* of new leftism, would be achieved. If it was (roughly) true that many new leftists commenced their pursuit of free and democratic community in educational institutions—high schools, community colleges, and universities—it was also true, from Wacheea onwards, that they hardly ended there. By 1980 a vast network of community health and law clinics and libraries testified to the new left drive to realize the ideal of self-regulating and unalienated community.

Self-determination, which like community and national liberation had been consigned to the margins of old left praxis, also became a dominant tenet. Never content to relegate individual freedom to some future socialist society, new leftists insisted upon having it in the here and now. Revolution Now!—it was more than a slogan, it was an imperative. If workers were treated as things in their workplaces, if students were treated as receptacles for knowledge in their schools, if women were objectified in their relationships and demeaned in the public sphere, if racialized minorities were stigmatized and confined to demeaning jobs, if gays and lesbians suffered both subtle psychic wounds and unsubtle violence merely for expressing their sexuality—then none of them was living freely in a genuinely "democratic" society. Each and every one of them was called upon to rise up against their oppression and overturn the social order responsible for it. Whether talking about the Asian-Canadian community, a nation or neighbourhood, a health clinic, or a woman's body, self-determination was, to invoke a favourite new left term, a "non-negotiable demand." New leftists who had been transformed, in demonstrations and consciousness-raising groups, into self-activating free people would not often submit quietly to fellow leftists who, quoting Marx, Lenin, Stalin, and Mao, thought they should simply follow the leader. Much of the story of the far left in the 1970s was one of trying to talk fellow travellers into doing so—with results that revealed just how profoundly and permanently a new left sensibility had penetrated a wide swath of the population, including, ironically enough, many new Leninists themselves.

Socialism, new leftists said (and it remained, until the 1980s, the preferred term for the future for which they fought), was not something to be achieved on the great (but distant) day of the revolution. Its promised egalitarianism and democracy were to be lived in the here and now. The ends did not justify the means—which for some vanguardists meant that the egalitarian end justified authoritarian means. In a genuinely socialist praxis, ends and means were interwoven. Hence the huge drive, from 1958 to 1985, to *live* the revolution—to put one's body on the line in demonstrations, to live in collectives and communes free from the mindless compulsion of bourgeois materialism, to broadcast the possibilities of *actual freedom* in books, magazines, films, art, theatre—indeed, throughout the entire cultural sphere. Socialism was to be lived, and it was to be performed. No leader could, at the end of the day, be counted on to do that for you: rather, in order to authentically prefigure the freedom of future humanity, you yourself had to grasp the underlying patterns of your life and *change* them. The new left was after a *total revolution*—one that promised (and risked) transforming every individual caught up within it, along with the political and social order that had hitherto confined them to lives of abject meaninglessness. Each moment of this revolution, no matter how big and small—a commune here, a strike there, a piece of street theatre somewhere else—was seen as a partial fulfilment of this overarching objective.

Today's historians have not forgotten those years of struggle, but with the post-1985 decline of the left—even of the very idea of "the left" as a systematic alternative to bourgeois society—the movements that flourished in them have tended to be separated off, placed in specific historiographical silos. Black power is certainly remembered, as are second-wave feminism and gay liberation: a fate that is certainly far better than historical oblivion. Yet what has largely been minimized is the more general new left context within which those movements took place. They attain a posthumous and near-absolute separateness that departs from a historical record that shows, over and over again, how activists in each of these movements were shaped by the overall context of a left to which they almost all proclaimed their allegiance. That, of course, did not make the history of the Toronto left a happy and harmonious one—for the absence of an amiable compartmentalization of distinct struggles led to fierce struggles for hegemony over the entire movement. As the 1970s turned into the 1980s, these conflicts gradually spelled a systemic transformation of the formation as a whole.

The history of the Toronto new left has not been widely remembered for other reasons as well. One is that a principal beneficiary of the changing shape of left-wing Toronto was the New Democratic Party. Until the 1980s the NDP had always managed at best a precarious base in the city. In the 1950s David Lewis had held the federal York South seat for its predecessor, the CCF, before the entire city turned Conservative in 1958. The NDP gained two federal seats in 1962 and rose to four in 1968, but its electoral success remained traditionally confined to eastern Toronto British working-class ridings and the heavily Jewish population of York South. Provincially in 1981 the party won seven Toronto seats in such areas as Etobicoke and Dovercourt as well as in its more secure fortresses in Riverdale and York South. The limited successes of the "Metro New Democratic Party," an attempt to introduce party politics to municipal and school board elections, came largely in the downtown core and culminated in the unsuccessful effort to elect Jack Layton as mayor in 1991.

Many new leftists flowed in and out of the NDP. Some echoes of new leftism were certainly heard when Bob Rae, a University of Toronto radical back in the 1960s, became Ontario leader in early 1982. In one speech Rae condemned the ruling Conservatives' vision of Ontario as "Toryland"—as "essentially a country club in which women and people of colour were not welcome."[95] The vibes of feminism and anti-racism allowed some leftists to hope that the provincial NDP would set about to transform Ontario in a fundamental way, but then Rae steered the party into an accord with the minority Liberals in 1985 before winning a surprising victory in 1990 (helped by a massive vote swing in the Greater Toronto Area that brought the party no fewer than sixteen seats). Having raised hopes and drawn upon the energies of many leftists, the Rae government turned out to be a conventional provincial government with the prime goal of attempting to stay in power during an economic downturn. It was turfed out in June 1995, having alienated vast swaths of the labour and progressive movement, including organized workers angered by the government's "Social Contract" legislation and gays and lesbians dismayed by the party's opportunistic refusal to press for recognition of their human rights.

Rae, a Liberal before and after his stint as a New Democrat, epitomized in some ways the political fluidity of the age; the debacle of his government deepened cynicism on the left towards the NDP and added to a widespread public alienation from politics in general. Containing a fair number of new leftists and sometimes sounding as though it were genuinely interested in furthering new left values, the Rae regime tarnished the movement in the eyes of many. Social democracy as anything more than a temporary electoral expedient—voting for the least bad option, in a sense—has yet to recover. If indeed the very notion of the "left" as representing the possibility of systemic egalitarian change waned noticeably in post-1990s Toronto, the Rae regime had a good deal to do with that trend. It revealed that left-wing activists mouthing left-wing phrases might, when they achieved power, not make much of a difference.

Another reason as to why the Toronto new left has not been widely remembered as a coherent movement is because it operated on so many spatial scales, ranging from the very local ("Defend Marlborough Avenue against Developers!") to the universal ("Smash Patriarchy!"). Given the absence of a unifying organization, the integration of those scales in an effective historical bloc capable of imposing itself upon collective memory was intermittent at best. Many new leftists were in, but not of, Toronto. In their imaginations they were transforming not a particular place, but the planet. This breadth of radical imagination was their glory—no one could accuse most of them of isolating themselves from the wider world—but it could also be their grief. It led some of them to develop slender ties with the actual people around them, who had little choice but to live in particular contexts. Despite moments in which Toronto new leftists integrated themselves effectively into wider struggles, a strong possibility always existed for a disconnect between new left analyses and any potential mass audience in Toronto.

In the maelstrom that is capitalist modernity, any sense of "belonging" to Toronto is complicated by the city's ceaseless economic and demographic transformations. The inhabitants of the "Toronto" that we usually speak of in this book—occupants of the old City of Toronto—were by 1981 a minority in "Metropolitan Toronto." The number of industrial workers in the city had declined, even as the number in the wider metropolitan area rose and the value of industrial production skyrocketed. In such a pattern of industrial capitalism, the Marxist expectation that working-class communities would over the generations develop their own cultural resources to be used in battling capitalism was frustrated by the sheer volatility of capitalism itself. By 1981 the "foreign-born" made up almost 40 per cent of the population of the Central Metropolitan Area. Many of these new arrivals make up a good portion of the city's working class. In general, the potential mass constituency for left-wing movements in this megalopolis is vast, but so too are the challenges inherent in addressing it. For all the admitted porousness of the term "new left," the most question-begging word in the phrase "The Toronto new left" may well be "Toronto." Time will tell if a next left, sensitive to the many spatial scales upon which any modern movement of resistance must operate—and that it must integrate—can find a language and practice of modernity that will bring anti-capitalist insights to such a hyper-capitalist milieu.

It is tempting to conclude with an elegy for lost hopes and dashed dreams. The new right took a lesson from the new left about the centrality of cultural struggle, and arrived with the odds heavily stacked in its favour. Much of the business class repudiated the welfare state. Liberals increasingly orchestrated a passive revolution that transformed into anodyne "rights and freedoms" the world-changing and personality-changing transformations that new leftists had imagined. The city returned to corporate normalcy. The moment passed, certainly, but it left behind more than fond or bitter memories: it left a treasury of tactical and strategic wisdom, a drive to democratic practice, both of which can inform contemporary left-wing struggles. Today's radical who imagines a post-capitalist world free of oppression is at one with a legion of new leftists who in their own time made the city resound with their claim for a redeemed and revolutionized humanity—the pith and substance of their radical ambition.

Notes

1. Toronto: Capital of Capitalist Modernity

1 Peter Gzowski, "The Righteous Crusaders of the New Left," *Maclean's*, 15 Nov. 1965.

2 Jennifer L. Bonnell, *Reclaiming the Don: An Environmental History of Toronto's Don River Valley* (Toronto: University of Toronto Press, 2014), 165, xv, xvii, xvi–xvii. We closely follow her masterful account.

3 Richard Harris, *Creeping Conformity: How Canada Became Suburban, 1900–1960* (Toronto: University of Toronto Press, 2004), 138, points out that Don Mills was preceded by Hamilton's Westdale.

4 Bonnell, *Reclaiming the Don*, 139, 171, 147, 167, 171.

5 Ibid., 145, 147, 171, 165.

6 Ben Bradley, "By the Road: Fordism, Automobility, and Landscape Experience in the British Columbia Interior, 1920–1970," Ph.D. thesis, Queen's University, 2012, abstract.

7 Mark Kingwell, "Tabula Rasa," in *The Ward: The Life and Loss of Toronto's First Immigrant Neighbourhood*, ed. John Lorinc et al. (Toronto: Coach House Press, 2015), 281. Frank Lloyd Wright also dismissed the towers, remarking that they reminded him of gravestones and predicting that future generations would say, "This marks the spot where Toronto fell." Cited in Andrew Levine, *Toronto: Biography of a City* (Madeira Park, B.C.: Douglas and McIntyre, 2014), 241.

8 Donica Belisle, *Retail Nation: Department Stores and the Making of Modern Canada* (Vancouver and Toronto: UBC Press, 2011), 6. See also Steve Penfold, *The Donut: A Canadian History* (Toronto: University of Toronto Press, 2008), 8; James Lemon, *Toronto Since 1918: An Illustrated History* (Toronto: James Lorimer and Company, National Museum of Man, and National Museums of Canada, 1985), 198.

9 See Levine, *Toronto*, 241. Trefann Court was located near Regent Park South; the Trefann saga played out over a number of years.

10 Drawing upon Ian McKay, "Modernity: In Search of a Critical Definition," unpublished manuscript, 2010.

11 Edward Relph, *Toronto: Transformations in a City and Its Region* (Philadelphia: University of Pennsylvania Press, 2014), 1.

12 Relph, *Toronto*, 43, 4; Fulford quoted in Relph, *Toronto*, 1; Amy Lavender Harris, *Imagining*

Toronto (Toronto: Mansfield Press, 2010), 17; Francis Pollock, *Jupiter Eight* (Toronto: Thomas Nelson & Sons, 1936), 49, https://archive.org/stream/jupitereight00polluoft#page/48/mode/2up/search/rube.

13 Gregory S. Kealey, *Toronto Workers Respond to Industrial Capitalism 1867 to 1892* (Toronto: University of Toronto Press, 1992).

14 Keith Walden, *Becoming Modern in Toronto: The Industrial Exhibition and the Shaping of a Late Victorian Culture* (Toronto: University of Toronto Press, 1997), 4; Eaton's in Belisle, *Retail Nation*, 30, 52, 209–10.

15 Richard Harris, *Unplanned Suburbs: Toronto's American Tragedy 1900 to 1950* (Baltimore and London: Johns Hopkins University Press, 1996), 33; Relph, *Toronto*, 4; Harris, *Unplanned Suburbs*, 34.

16 Kevin Brushett, "Blots on the Face of the City: The Politics of Slum Housing and Urban Renewal in Toronto, 1940–1970," Ph.D. thesis, Queen's University, 2001, 3.

17 Sean Purdy, "'Ripped Off' by the System: Housing Policy, Poverty, and Territorial Stigmatization in Regent Park Housing Project, 1951–1991," *Labour/Le Travail*, 52 (Fall 2003), 46.

18 Harris, *Creeping Conformity*, 130–31, 138; Paris cited in Levine, *Toronto*, 206.

19 Stephen Maynard, "'Horrible Temptations': Sex, Men, and Working-Class Male Youth in Urban Ontario, 1890–1935," *Canadian Historical Review*, 78, 2 (June 1997), 1–26; "Through a Hole in the Lavatory Wall: Homosexual Subcultures, Police Surveillance, and the Dialectics of Discovery, Toronto, 1890–1930," *Journal of the History of Sexuality*, 5, 2 (October 1994), 207–42.

20 Elise Chenier, "Sex Work and the Ward's Bachelor Society," in *The Ward*, ed. Lorinc et al., 263; Peter Hobbs and Cate Sandilands, "Queen's Park and Other Stories: Toronto's Queer Ecologies," in *Urban Explorations: Environmental Histories of the Toronto Region*, ed. L. Anders Sandberg et al. (Hamilton, Ont.: L.R. Wilson Institute for Canadian History, 2013), 76, 90.

21 Harris, *Unplanned Suburbs*, 25, 49.

22 See William J. Smyth, *Toronto, The Belfast of Canada: The Orange Order and the Shaping of Municipal Culture* (Toronto: University of Toronto Press, 2015), 196–97; Brian Clarke, *Piety and Nationalism: Lay Voluntary Associations and the Creation of an Irish-Catholic Community in Toronto, 1850–1895* (Montreal and Kingston: McGill-Queen's University Press, 1993).

23 See the outstanding discussion of Ruth Frager, *Sweatshop Strife: Class, Ethnicity, and Gender in the Jewish Labour Movement of Toronto 1900–1939* (Toronto: University of Toronto Press, 1992).

24 Levine, *Toronto*, 201. See also Ester Reiter, *A Future Without Hate or Need: The Promise of the Jewish Left in Canada* (Toronto: Between the Lines, 2016); and Gerald Tulchinsky, *Joe Salsberg: A Life of Commitment* (Toronto: University of Toronto Press, 2013).

25 For Yorkville, see Stuart Henderson, *Making the Scene: Yorkville and Hip Toronto in the 1960s* (Toronto: University of Toronto Press, 2011).

26 Greg Marquis, "Confederation's Casualties: The 'Maritimer' as a Problem in 1960s Toronto," *Acadiensis*, 39,1 (Winter/Spring 2010), 89, 90, 91.

27 Marquis, "Confederation's Casualties," 84, (alderman) 91.

28 Harris, *Imagining Toronto*, 190 (as she notes, the claim is investigated at length and debunked in Michael Doucet, "The Anatomy of an Urban Legend: Toronto's Multicultural Reputation," Working Paper no.16, CERIS, Toronto, 2001); Clarke cited in Harris, *Imagining Toronto*, 194.

29 Relph, *Toronto*, 17–18.

30 Ibid., 18–19. This discussion relies heavily on the extremely useful distillation of his chapter 2, "Confused Identities." The population of the GTHA—that is, the Greater Toronto-

Hamilton Area, a term that reflects the new, increasingly unified megalopolis on Lake Ontario—is an estimated 6,954,433.

31 Daniel Cohn-Bendit, *Obsolete Communism: The Left-Wing Alternative* (New York: McGraw-Hill, 1968). See, in particular, Maurice Isserman, *If I Had a Hammer: The Death of the Old Left and the Birth of the New Left* (New York: Basic Books, 1987). Our position is essentially the same as his—that there were substantial and enduring bridges between the "two lefts," with the Toronto case suggesting that this thesis not only holds but understates the degree of continuity.

32 Marshall Berman, *All That Is Solid Melts into Air: The Experience of Modernity* (London: Verso, 2010), 7.

33 See Josh Cole, "Children, Liberalism and Utopia: Education, Hall-Dennis and Modernity in Ontario's Long 1960s," Ph.D. thesis, Queen's University, 2015.

34 Scott de Groot, "Out of the Closet and Into Print: Gay Liberation across the Anglo-American World," Ph.D. thesis, Queen's University, 2015.

35 Harris also notes a 2007 documentary, *Let's All Hate Toronto*, and a 1956 satire of the same name; Harris, *Imagining Toronto*, 20; citation at 16.

36 See especially Sean Mills, *The Empire Within: Postcolonial Thought and Political Activism in Sixties Montreal* (Kingston and Montreal: McGill-Queen's University Press, 2010).

37 A theme explored in Ian McKay, "Sarnia in the Sixties (or, the Peculiarities of the Canadians)," in *New World Coming: The Sixties and the Shaping of Global Consciousness*, ed. Karen Dubinsky et al. (Toronto: Between the Lines, 2009), 24–35.

38 "Prince Edward Viaduct," https://en.wikipedia.org/wiki/Prince_Edward_Viaduct (accessed December 2017).

39 Ryan O'Connor, *The First Green Wave: Pollution Probe and the Origins of Environmental Activism in Ontario* (Vancouver and Toronto: UBC Press, 2015).

40 Cited in O'Connor, *First Green Wave*, 43.

41 Ibid., 134.

2. A Slow, Cautious Hello: First Stirrings of a Movement

1 "Police Tell Soap Box Poets They'll Get Summons," *Toronto Star* (*TS*), 30 July 1962.

2 "Poets, Police Play Return Match," *Globe and Mail* (*GM*), 6 Aug. 1962; "Police Tell Soap Box Poets They'll Get Summons"; "Allan Gardens Poetry," *GM*, 23 July 1962.

3 "Police Silence Poets in Allan Gardens," *TS*, 16 July 1962.

4 "Anti-Nuclear Zealot Arrested, Bailed Out; Says Police Beat Him," *GM*, 31 July 1961; "Sounding Off in Park Is a Right—Judge," *TS*, 30 Aug. 1961.

5 "Crowds Browse While Poets Rhyme in Park," *GM*, 9 July 1962; "Allan Gardens Poetry," *GM*, 23 July 1962; "Poets, Police Play Return Match," *GM*, 6 Aug. 1962; "Bohemian Bards in Allan Gardens," *TS*, 9 July 1962.

6 Editorial, "Freedoms in Toronto Parks," *TS*, 2 Aug. 1961; editorial, "Make Way for Soapbox Orators," *TS*, 15 Aug. 1961; editorial, "Park Oratory Re-affirmed," *TS*, 30 Aug. 1961; editorial, "Poetic Justice," *TS*, 27 July 1962; editorial, "Sunday in the Park," *GM*, 28 July 1962; Allan Gardens Poetry," *GM*, 23 July 1962.

7 "Soviets Reject War, Rally for Peace Told," *GM*, Sept. 7, 1962.

8 Victor Huard, "The Canadian Peace Congress and the Challenge to Postwar Consensus, 1948–1953," *Peace & Change*, 19-1(January 1994), 25–26, 30–42; "Delegate's Seat Refused Member of Peace Council," *GM*, May 19, 1952.

9 "Union Leftists Lose Argument," *TS*, 10 Nov. 1960; "Claims Reds Led Rent Control Bid," *GM*, 21 April 1954; "Charges Owners Used Tactics of McCarthy," *GM*, 27 April 1954; "Unionists Attack City Hall Ouster as Dictatorship," *GM*, 15 June 1954; editorial, "Communism and Controls," *GM*, 19 June 1954; editorial, "'Class War' Is Communism," *GM*, 29 Nov. 1951; editorial, "The Class Warriors," *GM* 13 Oct. 1959; "Motion to Bar Communists Voted Down by City Council," *GM*, 30 Oct. 1951; "Bid to Ban Reds Fails; Massey Hall Tax Urged," *GM*, 5 Feb. 1952; "Calls Moral Decay Greatest Threat," *GM*, 24 April 1952.

10 Len Scher, *The Un-Canadians: True Stories of the Blacklist Era* (Toronto: Lester Publishing, 1992), 34–35, 39–40, 47–48, 53–54, 189–94, 206–7, 215; "Wouldn't Hire Teachers Loyal to Foreign Land," *GM*, 6 April 1951; "Professor Agrees Red Teachers Must Be Fired," *GM*, 15 April 1953; "Make Life Unbearable for Reds, MP Urges," *GM*, 5 July 1954; "Unionists Attack City Hall Ouster as Dictatorship," *GM*, 15 June 1954.

11 "Letter Claims Varsity Curbs Political Views," *GM*, 8 Jan. 1953; "Denies Writing for Varsity Bar to Entering US," *GM*, 25 Nov. 1953; "Students Burn Effigy of McCarthy," *GM*, 2 Nov. 1953; "Advocate of Thought Control, Varsity News Editor Quits," *GM*, 5 Nov. 1953; "Leader of PCs at U of T Held at Palm Beach," *GM*, 4 Jan. 1954; "Ottawa Intervenes, Gets Two Students Released in Florida," *TS*, 4 Jan. 1954; "Toronto Students Quick to Protest Detention," *TS*, 5 Jan. 1954; "U.S. Closes Case, Varsity Boys on Way to Canada," *TS*, 5 Jan. 1954; "Varsity Pair Freed, Blame Name Mix-Up," *GM*, 5 Jan. 1954.

12 "Vera Brittain Asks Nuclear Disarmament," *GM*, 25 March 1958.

13 "Plan City Session of Peace Mission," *GM*, 28 Oct. 1950; "Church Brief," *GM*, 16 Dec. 1950; "'True Peace' Church Goal Offset Reds, Is Mission Aim," *TS*, 16 Jan. 1951; "Christian Ideal Best Defense, Clerics Declare," *GM*, 20 Jan. 1951; "Church Briefs," *GM*, 29 Aug. 1953; "Church Briefs," *GM*, 12 June 1954; "Church Briefs," *GM*, 26 March 1955.

14 "Parade Banners Demand End to H-Bomb Test," *GM*, 7 April 1958.

15 "Rally to Oppose Nuclear Tests Joined by Foes, Unsought Allies," *GM*, 12 May 1958; "300 Rally to Protest A-Arms Test," *TS*, 12 May 1958; "Marchers Urge Paraders Join in Nuclear Ban," *TS*, 7 April 1958.

16 "1,800 at Peace Rally Give $1,574," *TS*, Feb. 8 1960; "Mrs. Jagan Jokes on Red Tag, Dodges Query," *GM*, 12 March 1962. See also Huard, "Canadian Peace Congress and the Challenge to Postwar Consensus," 25–26, 30–42; "Delegate's Seat Refused Member of Peace Council," *GM*, 19 May 1952. See also Ian McKay and Jamie Swift, *Warrior Nation: Rebranding Canada in an Age of Anxiety* (Toronto: Between the Lines, 2012); and Stephen Endicott, *James G. Endicott: Rebel Out of China* (Toronto: University of Toronto Press, 1980).

17 "No Pamphlet Bar," *GM*, 3 May 1958.

18 Bruce Michael Douville, "The Uncomfortable Pew: Christianity, the New Left, and the Hip Counterculture in Toronto, 1965–1975," Ph.D. thesis, York University, 2011, 116; "Rabbi Urges All Support U of T against A-Test," *GM*, 28 Nov. 1959; Irene Howard, *The Struggle for Social Justice in British Columbia: Helena Gutteridge, the Unknown Reformer* (Vancouver: UBC Press, 1992), 254–56.

19 "Pastor Explains Stand On Red-Front Groups," *GM*, 16 Feb. 1953; "The Rev. Gordon Domm," *TS*, 12 Sept. 1959.

20 Edward Mann, *A Mann for All Seasons: A Memoir* (Toronto: Lugus Publications, 1996), 2–25, 89–117.

21 "Ask Committee to Press Ban on Atom Tests," *GM*, 19 June 1959; "Launch Fight Here against Atom Tests," *GM*, 19 June 1959. TCD went through a couple of name changes; here we will continue to identify the organization as TCD.

22 In this context, *The Globe and Mail* tried to discredit the emerging movement by printing the first of at least six editorials linking it to the pacifist movement of the 1930s, which in the paper's view had led to the appeasement of Hitler and the Second World War. *The Toronto Star* was quietly supportive, although it was also concerned to separate the respectable protesters from those it considered subversive. See, for *The Globe and Mail*, "Pacifism Marches Again," 8 April 1958; editorial, "Between the Extremes," 27 Nov. 1959; editorial, "Pacifism Run Wild," 10 Oct. 1960; editorial, "The Middle Ground," 13 June 1960; editorial, "No Room for Hysteria," 23 March 1961; editorial, "Demonstrations for Peace or War?" 19 Sept. 1961. For *The Toronto Star*, see editorial, "Dissent Is Not Disloyalty," 6 Feb. 1961.

23 "The Bomb-Banners Rally," *GM*, 18 April 1959; "From Alberta, a Sane Fight to Ban the Bomb," *GM*, 15 Aug. 1959; "Spectators on Bloor Form Easter Parade," *GM*, 30 March 1959; "Quakers Are Pleased to Be Called Pacifists," *GM*, 27 June 1959.

24 "Rev. J.M. Finlay Begins Ministry at Carlton United Church," *GM*, 6 Aug. 1938; "Archdeacon Frank Honored for 25 Years of Service," *GM*, 22 Oct. 1960; "Jobless 106 Give First Aid to Themselves," *GM*, 24 Nov. 1938; editorial, "Frank's House an Example," *GM*, 16 Feb. 1939; "Jobless Mass Protest Planned by Pastors," *GM*, 18 May 1939; "Leadership League Backed by Clergy, Attacked by Buck," *GM*, 27 Feb. 1939; "Foster-Home System for Inaccessible Areas Planned as Creche Adjunct," *GM*, 22 March 1939; "Small Vote Returns Old Control Board; Left Makes Gains," *GM*, 2 Jan. 1943; "All CCF Defeated; Conboy Returned," *GM*, 3 Jan. 1944; "Flock Upholds Pacifist Cleric," *GM*, 18 June 1940; "Shall Intimidation Undermine Our Symphony?" (ad), *TS*, 13 Sept. 1952; "Longer Controls of Rents," *GM*, 4 Feb. 1954.

25 Abraham L. Feinberg, *Storm the Gates of Jericho* (Toronto: McClelland and Stewart, 1964), 62–77, 142–45, 251, 264–66, 292–314; editorial, "A Deplorable Proposal," *GM*, 5 Dec. 1950.

26 Feinberg, *Storm the Gates of Jericho*, 139–42, 219–37, 240–44.

27 "Comics, Coddling, Poor Equipment, Says Feinberg," *GM*, 15 March 1957; "Council Head Bars Mixing Politics, Art Interests," *GM*, 2 Feb. 1953; Feinberg, "Will Abortion Be Upheld as a Safeguard against Overpopulation?" *GM*, 6 Oct. 1961; Abraham L. Feinberg, *Sex and the Pulpit* (Toronto: Methuen, 1981), 315.

28 "Document Stresses Urgency," *GM*, 23 Nov. 1959; "U of T Movement to Ban A-Weapons Said Spreading," *GM*, 26 Nov. 1959; "Dief Gets U of T Petition," *TS*, 14 Dec. 1959.

29 Douglas K. Campbell, "A History of the Ban-the-Bomb Movement: Toronto, 1959–61 (Part 1)," 5, 15, Nelson and Phyllis Clarke fonds, Baldwin Room, Toronto Public Library, 41–43; "Students Plan Protest French Nuclear Blast," *Varsity*, 10 Feb. 1960; "Atom Trek Stirs Police," *Varsity*, 15 Feb. 1960; "Students Start New Group to Promote World Peace," *Varsity*, 19 Feb. 1960; "New Group for Peace Begins Its Activities," *Varsity*, 4 March 1960.

30 "Rabbi Asks Students Act for Disarmament," *GM*, 17 March 1960; Abraham L. Feinberg, "A Requiem for Radicalism," *Varsity*, 25 March 1960.

31 "Students Stage Protest March," *GM*, 26 March 1960; "Boycott Goods of South Africa, Students Urge," *GM*, 15 April 1960; "Students Plan South African Protest March," *GM*, 25 March 1960; "Students' March Will Protest South Africa," *Varsity*, 25 March 1960; Pierre Berton, "South Africa and the Commonwealth Myth," *TS*, 18 April 1960; "2,500 at Toronto Rally Condemn Africa Policy," *TS*, 25 April 1960.

32 "Pacifism Marches Again," *GM*, 8 April 1958; editorial, "Between the Extremes," *GM*, 27 Nov. 1959; editorial, "Pacifism Run Wild," *GM*, 10 Oct. 1960; editorial, "The Middle Ground," *GM*,

13 June 1960; editorial, "No Room for Hysteria," *GM*, 23 March 1961; editorial, "Demonstrations for Peace or War?" *GM*, 19 Sept. 1961; editorial, "Dissent Is Not Disloyalty," *TS*, 6 Feb. 6, 1961; "Demands Frost Okay the Charter," *TS*, 25 April 1960; "Frost Okays Charter for Africa Committee, Overrules Roberts," *TS*, 26 April 1960; "'Hypocrisy for Canada to Condemn South Africa'" (letter), *TS*, 5 May 1960.

33 "Clergymen Oppose Missile Base," *TS*, 24 Feb. 1960; "Anti-H-Bomb Petition Sparks Chain Reaction," *Workers Vanguard* 5-1 (mid-December 1959); Campbell, "History of the Ban-the-Bomb Movement," 3, 5–7; Michael Maurice Dufresne, "'Let's Not Be Cremated Equal': The Combined Universities Campaign for Nuclear Disarmament 1959–1967," in *The Sixties in Canada: A Turbulent and Creative Decade*, ed. M. Athena Palaeologu (Montreal: Black Rose Books, 2009), 24–25.

34 Campbell, "History of the Ban-the-Bomb Movement," 6–7.

35 "Province Said Able to Enforce CD Drills," *GM*, 15 July 1960; "Pickets Boost Shelter," *GM*, 11 Aug. 1960; Campbell, "History of the Ban-the-Bomb Movement," 6–8; "Picket 'Diefenbaker's Coffin,'" *TS*, 4 July 1960; "Protest Bomb," *GM*, 6 Aug. 1960.

36 "Young, Elders Clash in Arms Ban Group," *GM*, 9 Aug. 1960; Campbell, "History of the Ban-the-Bomb Movement," 8.

37 "Ban-Bomb Petition Barred from CNE," *GM*, 27 Aug. 1961; Campbell, "History of the Ban-the-Bomb Movement," 13; "Everything from Big Cars to Brief Bikinis," *TS*, 24 Aug. 1961.

38 "Shelter Drama Falls on Its Face as Pickets Protest Nuclear Arms," *Workers Vanguard*, Mid-September 1961; Andrew Paul Burtch, *Give Me Shelter: The Failure of Canada's Cold War Civil Defence* (Vancouver: UBC Press, 2012).

39 Gary Moffatt, *History of the Canadian Peace Movement until 1969* (St. Catharines, Ont.: Grape Vine Press, 1969), 134; Campbell, "History of the Ban-the-Bomb Movement," 23–24.

40 Moffatt, *History of the Canadian Peace Movement*, 134; Campbell, "History of the Ban-the-Bomb Movement," 4, 11.

41 Moffatt, *History of the Canadian Peace Movement*, 134; Campbell, "History of the Ban-the-Bomb Movement," 25; "500 Paraders Planning Nuclear Arms Protest," *TS*, 30 March 1961; "Hecklers Join Ranks in Ban Bomb March," *TS*, 3 April 1961; "Duty to Wipe out Enmity, Not an Enemy, Feinberg Tells Peace Marchers at City Hall," *GM*, 3 April 1961.

42 Campbell, "History of the Ban-the-Bomb Movement," 27–31; Moffatt, *History of the Canadian Peace Movement*, 134–35.

43 Moffatt, *History of the Canadian Peace Movement*, 135. For more about the U.K. Committee, see Samantha Jane Carroll, "'Fill the Jails': Identity, Structure and Method in the Committee of 100, 1960–1968," Ph.D. thesis, University of Sussex, 2010; for some of Daniels's experiences as a CPC member in the 1950s, see Dan Daniels, *Paranoia and Dirty Feet* (Montreal: White Dwarf, 1995); "Police Carry Away Ban-the-Bomb Sitters," *GM*, 29 March 1962; "Ban Bombers Picket IBM, Get on TV," *TS*, 19 June 1962.

44 Moffatt, *History of the Canadian Peace Movement*, 137–38; "Were We Civilized at the Don Jail?" *TS*, 11 Dec. 1962; "150 Rush Police after Lucas, Turpin Hang," *TS*, 11 Dec. 1961.

45 "Fisher Hangs at Don Jail," *TS*, 27 June 1961; "Killed Woman, Fisher Hanged at Midnight," *GM*, 27 June 1961; editorial, "Punishment and Crime," *Toronto Telegram* (*TT*), 11 Dec. 1962; "Picketers at Executions—Crusaders or Egotists," *TT*, 12 Dec. 1962.

46 "Anti-Nuclear Zealot Arrested, Bailed Out; Says Police Beat Him," *GM*, 31 July 1961; Gary Moffatt (letter), *TS*, 5 Aug. 1961; "Ban-the-Bombers Follow Poets into Allan Gardens," *TS*, 3 Aug. 1962; "Ban-bomb Speakers Draw Crowd of 175 at Allan Gardens," *GM*, 3 Aug. 1962; "Ban Bombers Are Convicted for Park Talk," *GM*, 13 Feb. 1963; "Police Take Names of Speakers at

Allan Gardens Bomb Meet," *GM*, 15 April 1963; "Park Orators in Toronto Win Victory," *GM*, 6 April 1963.

47 "21 Youths Arrested as Police Break-up Anti-Nuclear Demonstration," *GM*, 24 Dec. 1962; "Demonstrators Mock Arrest of Youngsters," *GM*, 7 Jan. 1963; "The 'Riot' That Was Never a Riot," *TS*, 4 March 1963; "17 Ban Bombers Brought to Justice," *TS*, 21 Jan. 1963; "Teacher Inferior to Docker?" *TS*, 31 July 1963.

48 "Toronto Calendar," *Sanity*, 2 (1962); Moffatt, *History of the Canadian Peace Movement*, 136, 138–39.

49 Moffatt, *History of the Canadian Peace Movement*, 103–4; Benjamin Isitt, "Tug-of-War: The Working Class and Political Change in British Columbia, 1948–1972," Ph.D. thesis, University of New Brunswick, 2008, 282; Larry Gambone, *The Comox Project 1965* (Nanaimo, B.C.: Red Lion Press, 2007).

50 "Inter-Branch Memo," 15 Sept. 1961, William Ready Division of Archives and Research Collections, McMaster University Library, Combined Universities Campaign for Nuclear Disarmament (CUCND) fonds, 1-1; "Secretariat Minutes," 16 June 1963, CUCND fonds, 1-6.

51 Orie Loucks, "J. Roger Bray and Gwendolyn Struik," *Ecological Society of America*, esa.org/history/bray-j-roger (accessed 12 Aug. 2016); "Anarchist Advocates Abolition of Authority; General Strike to Restore Social Ownership," *Varsity*, 20 Jan. 1961. When asked if exams would be abolished, Bray said "Naturally." He explained that he would give all of his students a base grade of 80 per cent and use a computer to randomly generate the remaining 20 per cent.

52 Roger Bray, "To Start Wagging and Stop Tampering," *Anarchy*, November 1962. Due to the ecological underpinnings of this future socialist society, Bray cautioned that speech would have to be kept to a minimum: "To be always talking is against nature. Even about disarmament."

53 *Sanity*, July 1964.

54 Christopher William Powell, "'Vietnam: It's Our War Too': The Antiwar Movement in Canada: 1963–1975," Ph.D. thesis, University of New Brunswick, 2011, 344.

55 "Move to Oust Reds from CUCND Fails," *Varsity*, 30 Sept. 1960; Harvey L. Shepherd, "Hey Buddy, Wanna Buy a Bomb," *Varsity*, 9 Nov. 1960.

56 "Punch Your Nose Says Communist Leader at Disarmament Meeting," *Varsity*, 27 Jan. 1961; "Daniel Goldstick—Campus Communist," *Varsity*, 14 Nov. 1960.

57 "Daniel Goldstick—Campus Communist," *Varsity*, 14 Nov. 1960; letter, Judith Claivar (Corresponding Secretary of CUCND-Toronto) to Dimitri Roussopoulos, 1 Nov. 1961, CUCND fonds, 1-8; "Goldstick Still CUCND Member Following Attempted Expulsion," *Varsity*, 29 Sept. 1961; "CUCND President Resigns from Executive after Defeat in Nuclear Testing Controversy," *Varsity*, 1 Nov. 1961; "Anti-Bomb Leader Quits over Red's Membership," *GM*, 2 Nov. 1961.

58 Letter, Dimitri Roussopoulos to Judith Claivar, 10 Nov. 1961, CUCND fonds, 1-1; letter, CUCND Toronto to Dimitri Roussopoulos, n.d. [1961], CUCND fonds, 1-1; "CUCND Executive Expels Communist Head as Detrimental to Disarmament Movement," *Varsity*, 8 Nov. 1961; "Goldstick Must Go—CUCND Assembly," *Varsity*, 15 Nov. 1961.

59 Letter, Judith Claivar to Dorothy Thompson (UBC Nuclear Disarmament Club), 19 Nov. 1961, CUCND fonds, 1-8.

60 Stuart Robinson Henderson "Making the Scene: Yorkville and Hip Toronto, 1960–1970," Ph.D. thesis, Queen's University, 2007, 10, 63, 83, 86, 137.

61 Art Silver and John Cowan, "When It Hits Home May This House Be Safe from Tigers," *Varsity*, 15 Feb. 1961; Len Shifrin, "Why the CUCND's Present Image May Bring Canada Nuclear

Weapons," *Varsity*, 16 Oct. 1961; *Ryersonian*, 22 Oct. 1965; *Ryersonian*, 15 Nov. 1965; "Open Letter to Vietniks," *Ryersonian*, 5 Dec. 1965.

62 "Foes of A-Arms Begin 3-Day Protest March," *GM*, 12 April 1963; Mary Jane Miller, "CUCND," *Varsity*, 8 Nov. 1963; "SCM Strives to Produce Intelligent Action," *Varsity*, 8 Jan. 1964; *Sanity*, February 1964.

63 While the Leninist theory of the United Front sought to unite all workers and left-wing organizations against the bourgeoisie, the later concept of the Popular Front—first evoked in the face of the fascist menace of the 1930s—sought a broader unity amongst "the people," including sections of the bourgeoisie. The music of Pete Seeger is considered emblematic of Popular Front culture.

64 Catherine Gidney, *A Long Eclipse: The Liberal Protestant Establishment and the Canadian University, 1920–1970* (Montreal and Kingston: McGill-Queen's University Press, 2004), 185; "Pete Seeger Sings in the JCR," *Varsity*, 17 Feb. 1958; "Hey Buddy Wanna Buy a Bomb," *Varsity*, 9 Nov. 1960; Moffatt, *History of the Canadian Peace Movement*, 148; "Song of Survival," CUCND collection 1-4; "10,000 Folkniks Have a Ball," *GM*, 13 Aug. 1962; "Coffee Set to Honor Speakers," *TS*, 14 Sept. 1962; "Hootenanny—CUCND Style," *Varsity*, 18 Oct. 1963.

65 "He's Working His Way—with Gags," *TS*, 15 Aug. 1963; "Beards and Sneakers in Protest Parade," *GM*, 18 Oct. 1965.

66 Bryan D. Palmer, *Canada's 1960s: The Ironies of Identity in a Rebellious Era* (Toronto: University of Toronto Press, 2009), 324–25.

67 Editorial, "Mr. Gordon Hits Back," *GM*, 22 Nov. 1962; editorial, "Quebec and the CNR," *GM*, 4 Dec. 1962; editorial, "Gordon's Not for Burning," *TS*, 6 Dec. 1962.

68 Bruce Lewis, "Viewpoint," *Varsity*, 4 Jan. 1963; Wilf Day, "New Democrats," *Varsity*, 25 Sept. 1963.

69 Editorial, "A Chance to Act," *Varsity*, 13 Nov. 1963; "Movement to March on Queen's Park Gains Support from SAC and Students," *Varsity*, 15 Nov. 1963; Jim Laxer, "A Moderate Must Act," *Varsity*, 20 Nov. 1963.

70 "3000 Students Demonstrate Concern for Confederation at Queen's Park," *Varsity*, 25 Nov. 1963; "Text of Ward's Speech at Queen's Park," *Varsity*, 25 Nov. 1963.

71 "Discuss Row over CJBC Switch," *TS*, 30 Dec. 1963; "The CJBC Tempest," *GM*, 20 Dec. 1963; "Join the Battle," *GM*, 30 Dec. 1963; "Toronto-Area MPs Considering Legal Action to Keep CJBC English," *TS*, 27 Feb. 1964; "The Symbolic Sacrifice of One Radio Station," *TS*, 30 Dec. 1963; "Public Hearing on CJBC Move Asked by MP," *GM*, 6 Jan. 1964; "Pickersgill Denies Pressure on CJBC," *GM*, 14 Dec. 1963; "MP Asks Probe of CJBC Switch, Fears Rise of Anti-Quebec Feeling," *GM*, 23 Dec. 1963; Jim Laxer, "Pourquoi je suis separatiste anglais," *Varsity*, 4 Oct. 1963.

72 "200 March in Protest over Racial Bias Here," *TS*, 22 June 1963; "Freedom Marchers at U.S. Consulate," *TS*, 29 Aug. 1963; "200 in Toronto Hold Civil Rights March," *GM*, 29 Aug. 1963; "This Candidate Knows First Hand about Unemployment, Discrimination," *TS*, 9 Sept. 1963; "Housewife to Lead Protest March," *GM*, 22 June 1963; "Race Bias Here Only Little Less Than in U.S.: Rabbi," *GM*, 24 June 1963; "Colorblindness Will End War of Races: Rabbi," *GM*, 27 July 1964.

73 "Anti-Wallace Protest Aim of 18 Groups," *GM*, 4 July 1964; Letter from Mildred Lynch to Martin Luther King, 25 Nov. 1967, thekingcenter.org/archive/document/letter-mildred-lynch-mlk (accessed 27 May 2013); "Urge Banning of Law Segregating Negroes," *TS*, 11 Feb. 1964. Activists who ran the 1950s newspaper *Canadian Negro* formed the core of the committee.

74 Editorial, "Free Country," *GM*, 4 July 1964; "Toronto Labor Condemns Visit by Alabama Governor," *GM*, 3 July 1964; advertisement, "Welcome Governor Wallace," *TS*, 8 July 1964.

75 "250,000 Roar Approval at Lions' Best Ever Parade," *TS*, 8 July 1964; "Rights Fund to Canvass during Visit of Wallace," *GM*, 8 July 1964; "1,000 March at Gardens to Protest Wallace Visit," *TS*, 9 July 1964; "Wallace Closely Guarded as Crowds Jeer," *GM*, 9 July 1964; "Wallace Slams Civil Rights Law," *TS*, 10 July 1964; "Toronto Pickets US Racist," *Workers Vanguard* 9-3, Mid-July 1964; editorial, "Wallace's Non-Political Speech," *TS*, 10 July 1964; "'Feed Wallace to the Lions!'" *Young Socialist*, Summer 1964.

76 Walter D. Young, *The Anatomy of a Party: The National CCF, 1932-1961* (Toronto: University of Toronto Press. 1969), 124–37; Dan Azoulay, "'This March Forward to a Genuine People's Party'? Rivalry and Deception in the Founding of the Ontario NDP, 1958–61," *Canadian Historical Review*, 74-1 (March 1993), 46.

77 Dan Azoulay, *Keeping the Dream Alive: The Survival of the Ontario CCF/NDP, 1950–1963* (Montreal and Kingston: McGill-Queen's University Press, 1997), 187, 205, 212, 217.

78 "Need for Nationalization Declining Says Professor," *Varsity*, 26 Oct. 1960; "New Party's Sole MP Speaks, Says Socialism a Dirty Word," *Varsity*, 7 Dec. 1960.

79 "Soul Searching Fails to Define CCF Economic Stand," *Varsity*, 5 Feb. 1961; "Caplan Attempts to Sell NATO to Doubting NDP Party Meeting," *Varsity*, 4 Oct. 1961.

80 "Goldstick Must Go—CUCND Assembly," *Varsity*, 15 Nov. 1961; "CUCND," *Varsity*, 8 Nov. 1963; "Christianity in Academic Communities," *Varsity*, 9 Jan. 1961.

81 Jeremy Milloy, "A Battle Royal: Service Work Activism and the 1961–1962 Royal York Strike," *Labour/Le Travail*, 58 (Fall 2006), 19; "Shapiro's Pinkies to Aid Hotel Strikers," *Varsity*, 25 Oct. 1961; "U Toronto Star Graduates Picket Dinner at Royal York," *GM*, 27 Oct. 1961; Jim Laxer and Manuel Helzel, "A Close Look at the Royal York Strike," *Varsity*, 18 Oct. 1961; letter from Ian to Peter, 8 Aug. 1964, CUCND fonds, 2-5; Sally F. Zerker, *The Rise and Fall of the Toronto Typographical Union 1832–1972: A Case Study in Foreign Domination* (Toronto: University of Toronto Press, 1982), 278–314.

82 Michael Oliver, ed., *Social Purpose for Canada* (Toronto: University of Toronto Press, 1961).

83 Kenneth McNaught, *Conscience and History: A Memoir* (Toronto: University of Toronto Press, 1999), 166–67; Abraham Rotstein, ed., *The Prospect of Change: Proposals for Canada's Future* (Toronto: McGraw-Hill, 1965); Peter Russell, ed., *Nationalism in Canada* (Toronto: McGraw-Hill, 1966). The word "Reformation" in ULSR was later changed to "Reform."

84 National Council Meeting, YCL of CDA, 17–18 Feb. 1962, NAC, CPC fonds, reel 1618; T.D., "New Times—New Role?" *Bulletin*, no. 2, February-March 1963, NAC, CPC fonds, reel 1618.

85 YCL, "Report of the National Executive to the 16th National Convention, 1963," NAC, CPC fonds, reel 1618.

86 Young Communist League, *Look Around: Youth, the Future, the Challenge* (Toronto: Young Communist League, 1965), 4; Bill Clause, "Decadence of Canadian Culture," *Discussion Bulletin*, no. 5, Socialist Youth League, April 1960, NAC, CPC fonds, reel 1618; Rae Murphy, "Youth in a Changing World," *Marxist Quarterly*, Spring 1963, 37; "Up Beats, Down Beats, or Off Beats?" *Scan* 3-3, May-June 1967.

87 "Up Beats, Down Beats, or Off Beats?" *Scan* 3-3, May-June 1967; "The Non-Violent Approach," *Scan* 1-3, May 1965; "NDY: A Look Ahead," *Scan*, July-August 1967; Myrna Wood, "These Boots Were Made for Walkin'. . ." *Scan*, February-March 1968.

88 "Canada and the Peace Struggle," *Canadian Tribune* (*CT*), 19 Aug. 1963; "Organizers, Promoters to Blame for 'Rowdyism' at Folk Festival," *CT*, 26 Aug. 1963; "Four Working Lads from Liverpool," *CT*, 7 Sept. 1964; "Teach-In," *CT*, 24 May 1965; "Radicals on Campus," *CT*, 14 Feb. 1966.

89 Ernest Tate, *Revolutionary Activism in the 1950s and 60s: A Memoir—Volume 1, Canada 1955–1965* (London: Resistance Books, 2014), 23, 39–42.

90 Ibid., 30, 85, 131, 146, 207, 215, 235.

91 Ibid., 62, 82, 114, 212.

92 "Teen-agers Boo, Hiss as Rabbi Feinberg Called Liar, Pro-Red," *GM*, 24 Oct. 1960; "Crowd Backs Arms Ban Speakers," *GM*, 9 Dec. 1960; "Student Group Wants Canada to Leave Nato," *GM*, 19 Dec. 1960; "Students Back Holy Loch Demonstrators," *GM*, 6 March 1961; "Ferment on Toronto Campus, *Workers Vanguard*, Mid-October, 1961; "CSND High School Paper," *Young Socialist*, December 1963; "High Schools Hit Cadet Training," *Young Socialist*, April-May 1964; *Young Socialist*, September 1964.

93 "Cuba's New Schools Belong to Students," *Young Socialist*, February 1964; *Young Socialist*, October 1964; "A Left Separatist View," *Young Socialist*, November-December 1964; "Ont. YND Left Gains," *Young Socialist*, November-December 1964.

94 "Ferment on Toronto Campus," *Workers Vanguard*, Mid-October 1961.

95 Dufresne, "'Let's Not Be Cremated Equal,'" 29–33, 38, 53; Bruce Douville, "Project La Macaza: A Study of Two Canadian Peace Protests in the 1960s," in *Worth Fighting For: Canada's Tradition of War Resistance from 1812 to the War on Terror*, ed. Laura Campbell, Michael Dawson, and Catherine Gidney (Toronto: Between the Lines, 2015), 161–62, 170–71.

96 Letter, Mike to Dimitri, 16 Aug. 1961, CUCND fonds, 1-8; letter, Mike to Dimitri, 27 July 1961; "U of T CUCND Will Present Own Resolutions," *Varsity*, 8 Nov. 1963; "CUCND Votes in Favour of Withdrawal from NATO," *Varsity*, 15 Nov. 1963. "Mike" denied an inference that Toronto was the only branch opposing withdrawal from NATO; Dufresne, "'Let's Not Be Cremated Equal,'" 36.

97 See, for instance, Dimitri Roussopoulos, "Canada: 1968 and the New Left," in *1968: Memories and Legacies of a Global Revolt*, ed. Philipp Gassert and Martin Klimke, *Bulletin of the German Historical Institute*, Supplement 6, 2009, 39.

98 "CUCND's Constitution Ratified with Much Mudslinging at UWO," *Varsity*, 8 Jan. 1962.

99 Moffatt, *History of the Canadian Peace Movement*, 53; ad, "C.U.N.C.D. Seminars," *Varsity*, 3 Dec. 1962; Ian Gentles, "Non-Violence and the Negro Revolution," *Varsity*, 23 Oct. 1963.

3. A Movement Emerges, 1965–67

1 "SNCC Will Try Again at U of T," *Varsity*, 2 Oct. 1964; "Rightists Assail Rabbi," *Varsity*, 2 Nov. 1964; "Vigil Turnout Taken as Mandate for Peace Study," *Varsity*, 13 Nov. 1964; Michael Maurice Dufresne, "'Let's Not Be Cremated Equal': The Combined Universities Campaign for Nuclear Disarmament 1959–1967," in *The Sixties in Canada: A Turbulent and Creative Decade*, ed. M. Athena Palaeologu (Montreal: Black Rose Books, 2009), 33, 41–42; Bryan D. Palmer, *Canada's 1960s: The Ironies of Identity in a Rebellious Era* (Toronto: University of Toronto Press, 2009), 253.

2 Palmer, *Canada's 1960s*, 259–60; Dufresne, "'Let's Not Be Cremated Equal,'" 42–43, 45.

3 "CUCND to Parade for Peace in Vietnam," *Varsity*, 16 Dec. 1964; "The Police-Made Law That Censors Signs," *Toronto Star* (*TS*), 27 Oct. 1964; "The Police-Made Laws They Won't Reveal," *TS*, 10 Dec. 1964; "Marchers to Defy Sign Law," *TS*, 18 Dec. 1964; "Peace Paraders Defy Law, Wave Un-OK'd Placards," *TS*, 19 Dec. 1964; "Toronto Youth Will Ask to Be Arrested," *Canadian Tribune* (*CT*), 18 Jan. 1965; untitled, *Young Socialist*, February 1965.

4 "300 Protest Bombing; 200 Protest Protest," *Varsity*, 10 Feb. 1965; "Engineers Are Different But How and Why?" *Varsity*, 22 Feb. 1965; "To Blitz Campus for Protest Petition," *Varsity*, 10 Feb. 1965.

5 David S. Churchill, "SUPA, Selma, and Stevenson: The Politics of Solidarity in Mid-1960s Toronto," *Journal of Canadian Studies*, 41 (Spring 2010), 46.

6 Ibid., 46–47; Myrna Kostash, *Long Way from Home: The Story of the Sixties Generation in Canada* (Toronto: James Lorimer and Company, 1980), 9–10; Gary Moffatt, *History of the Canadian Peace Movement until 1969* (St. Catharines, Ont.: Grape Vine Press, 1969), 162–63; Palmer, *Canada's 1960s*, 269. SCM and SUPA were officially acting on behalf of the Friends of SNCC.

7 Churchill, "SUPA, Selma, and Stevenson," 33, 48; Judy Pocock, interview, 16 Oct. 2011, Toronto; "Canadian Students Protest," *Canadian Weekly*, 24 April 1965; "Bearded Canadian's Vow: 'I'll Catch 1st Bullet at Selma,'" *TS*, 20 March 1965.

8 Gary Cristall, Presentation, Outstanding Alumni Event, Simon Fraser University, Sept. 13, 2017, https://vimeo.com/233928088; email from Gary Cristall, Sept. 27, 2017.

9 Kostash, *Long Way from Home*, 10; "Students Demand Rights, Trustees Won't Let Students Speak," *TS*, 16 March 1965; *Young Socialist*, Summer 1965.

10 Burnley "Rocky" Jones and James W. St. G. Walker, *Burnley "Rocky" Jones: Revolutionary* (Halifax; Winnipeg: Roseway Publishing, 2016), 9, 12, 27–29, 40, 44–45, 50–51, 56.

11 Ibid., 58–60.

12 "Canadian Students Protest," *Canadian Weekly*, 24 April 1965; "Leading Sask. Radicals Join Young Socialists," *Young Socialist*, September 1970; Judy Pocock, interview.

13 Tony Hyde, "The Student Union for Peace Action: An Analysis-History of the Organization," n.d., William Ready Division of Archives and Research Collections, McMaster University Library, Revolutionary Marxist Group (RMG) fonds, 4-16; letter to Cathie and Brewster Kneen, 9 March 1965, CUCND fonds, box 15, folder: SUPA and RIPP national . . . ; "Jazz, Poetry to Aid Malcolm X Widow," *TS*, 10 March 1965; "U of T Protesters Bed Down for Night," *Globe and Mail* (*GM*), 11 March 1965; "NDP Delegates Protest U.S. War in Viet Nam," *TS*, 15 July 1965.

14 Churchill, "SUPA, Selma, and Stevenson," 52–53; Moffatt, *History of the Canadian Peace Movement until 1969*, 161, 165.

15 Kostash, *Long Way from Home*, 15–17; "SUPA Demands Total Involvement," *Varsity*, 15 Oct. 1965.

16 "SUPA Demands Total Involvement," *Varsity*, 15 Oct. 1965.

17 Federal Council Minutes, Sept. 9–12, 1965, CUCND fonds, 1-18; Palmer, *Canada's 1960s*, 261–67.

18 Linda Seese, "SUPA as Seen by an Outsider," *SUPA Newsletter*, no. 9, 1965; Jim Harding, "SUPA at Saskatoon: An Evaluation," *SUPA Newsletter*, 27 Jan. 1966.

19 "A Step Towards a Movement in Canada," *Freedom Now*, 1 June 1965; "New SNCC Group Organized," *Young Socialist*, Summer 1965.

20 "Why Consensus," *Freedom Now*, 1 June 1965; "Consensus Strikes Again," *Freedom Now*, 1 June 1965; "New SNCC Group Organized," *Young Socialist*, Summer 1965.

21 Barry O'Neil, *SUPA Newsletter*, 30 Aug. 1965; Harvey Shepherd, "SNCC in Canada," *SUPA Newsletter*, 30 Aug. 1965.

22 "Vietnam Action Committee Report, no. 3," CUCND Collection, 7-Worklist, 1965.

23 Margaret Daly, *The Revolution Game: The Short, Unhappy Life of the Company of Young Canadians* (Toronto: New Press, 1970), 37.

24 Marvin Ross, "Quits SUPA: Charges Disorganization," *Varsity*, 14 Nov. 1965; Denis Kennedy, "Why I Left SUPA," *Varsity*, 29 Nov. 1965; Harvey L. Shepherd, "Still More on SUPA" (letter), *Varsity*, 8 Dec. 1965.

25 Gary Teeple, "Last Notes of a Paranoid," *SUPA Newsletter*, 12 Dec. 1965.

26 Christopher William Powell, "'Vietnam: It's Our War Too': The Antiwar Movement in Canada: 1963–1975," Ph.D. thesis, University of New Brunswick, 2011, 149–58.

27 Ibid.

28 Palmer, *Canada's 1960s*, 218, 223; Ian Milligan, *Rebel Youth: 1960s Labour Unrest, Young Workers, and New Leftists in English Canada* (Vancouver: UBC Press, 2014), 38–41; "Farmers May Mount Quebec-style Roadblock," *GM*, 13 April 1966; "Where Will the Tractors Strike Next?" *TS*, 25 June 1966; "600 Tractors Back; Expect Same Today," *GM*, 26 July 1966; "Tractors Roll Toward Metro," *TS*, 26 July 1966; "Irate Farmers Mob Queen's Park," *GM*, 28 July 1966; "Irate, Empty-Handed, Farmers Trek Home," *TS*, 28 July 1966; "Tractor Farmer: 'What Did We Get? A Big Fat Nothing,'" *TS*, 28 July 1966.

29 Jim Mayor, "Report of SUPA's Eastern Canada Study Conference—May 11–16, 1966 or Laxer's 30 Year Plan to Free Canada," *SUPA Newsletter*, 15 June 1966.

30 Henry Tarvainen, "Peace Groups" (letter), *GM*, 29 Sept. 1965; Powell, "'Vietnam: It's Our War Too,'" 137–38.

31 "Marchers Seek End to War in Vietnam," *GM*, 19 April 1965; Powell, "'Vietnam: It's Our War Too,'" 138–39; Ross Dowson, "Dear Comrades," 18 Oct 1965, Ross Dowson Resource Website, rossdowson.com/corr/1965/1965-10Oct18.jpg (accessed 7 May 2014).

32 Middleton had led a student delegation to Cuba the year before and in 1963 had served as an NDP candidate. Ernest Tate, *Revolutionary Activism in the 1950s and 60s: A Memoir*, vol. 1, *Canada 1955–1965* (London: Resistance Books, 2014), 161; "Suggests Sabotage of Plants Aiding U.S," *GM*, 18 Oct. 1965; "Man, 36, Is Charged after Guard Killed, Three Jets Blown Up," *GM*, 29 Jan. 1965.

33 "Overflow Crowd Plans for Two Viet Nam Marches," *Varsity*, 22 Feb. 1966; Powell, "'Vietnam: It's Our War Too,'" 160–62; Malcolm Fast and Cathie Kneen, "Federal Council," *SUPA Newsletter*, 15 March 1966.

34 Powell, "'Vietnam: It's Our War Too,'" 133–34, 161, 164–65; Moffatt, *History of the Canadian Peace Movement until 1969*, 181.

35 Cited in Powell, "'Vietnam: It's Our War Too,'" 165.

36 Moffatt, *History of the Canadian Peace Movement until 1969*, 184; Powell, "'Vietnam: It's Our War Too,'" 196.

37 "What about the Future?" *CT*, 4 April 1966; "Passion for Peace," *GM*, 1 Oct. 1966.

38 Powell, "'Vietnam: It's Our War Too,'" 194, 200–1; "Notes on the Anti-War Movement," *LSA Internal Discussion Bulletin*, July 1967.

39 "5,000 Anti-War Protesters March down Yonge St.," *TS*, 23 Oct. 1967; "Toronto Protest March Draws 4,000," *Varsity*, 23 Oct. 1967; "100 Hawks Jeer, Jostle 3,000 Marching Doves in Metro War Protest," *GM*, 23 Oct. 1967.

40 "5,000 Anti-War Protesters March down Yonge St.," *TS*, 23 Oct. 1967; "Toronto Protest March Draws 4,000, *Varsity*, 23 Oct. 1967; "100 Hawks Jeer, Jostle 3,000 Marching Doves in Metro War Protest," *GM*, 23 Oct. 1967; Moffatt, *History of the Canadian Peace Movement until 1969*, 129; Kostash, *Long Way from Home*, 50; Powell, "'Vietnam: It's Our War Too,'" 207–9.

41 "Dow Job Interviews Provoke Protest," *Varsity*, 20 Nov. 1967; "Students, Professors Besiege Dow Recruiter," *GM*, 21 Nov. 1967; Laurel Limpus, "Why I Sat In . . ." *Varsity*, 22 Nov. 1967;

Bob Bossin, "Notes on a Sit-in, SAC, Dow, etc . . ." *Varsity*, 24 Nov. 1967; "Dow Protesters Prepared for Encore," *Varsity*, 4 Dec. 1967; "Sit-in Sparks SAC Debate on Employment Recruiting," *Varsity*, 22 Nov. 1967; "Vietnam War Suppliers Not Welcome at U of T: SAC," *Varsity*, 24 Nov. 1967; Powell, "'Vietnam: It's Our War Too,'" 210–11.

42 Editorial, "An Example to their Elders," *GM*, 2 Dec. 1967; "St. Michael's Council Condemns Sit-in," *Varsity*, 24 Nov. 1967; Arthur Kruger, "Academic Freedom" (letter), *GM*, 23 Nov. 1967; Natalie Zemon Davis, "The Wrong Method" (letter), *Varsity*, 22 Nov. 1967.

43 Paul Hoch, "Civil Libertarians and Campus Protest," *Varsity*, 5 Jan. 1968.

44 "Voice of a Woman?" *Pro Tem*, 19 Dec. 1963; Linda Light, "Further Critical Evaluation" (letter), *Pro Tem*, 4 Feb. 1965; "Let's Meet Again . . . Soon," *Pro Tem*, 15 Oct. 1965; editorial, "On Protests," *Pro Tem*, 11 Feb. 1965; editorial, "Demonstration: A Case of Diminishing Returns," *Pro Tem*, 18 March 1965; Harry Kopyto, ". . . and Radicalism," *Pro Tem*, 5 Nov. 1965.

45 Linda Light, "Better Red than Dead: A Fallacy" (letter), *Pro Tem*, 11 Feb. 1965; Linda Light, "York University," *SUPA Newsletter*, no. 11, 1965.

46 "Low Turnout Mars March," *Varsity*, 29 Oct. 1965; "2400 Protest Ontario Student Aid Program," *Varsity*, 30 Sept. 1966.

47 "900 Marchers at Protest," *Ryersonian*, 6 Oct. 1966; "Davis 'Out to Lunch,'" *Ryersonian*, 6 Oct. 1966; "Well Done Marchers! But . . . No Leader in Sight," *Ryersonian*, 7 Oct. 1966; [untitled photo] *Ryersonian*, 14 Oct. 1966.

48 Nigel Moses, "All That Was Left: Student Struggles for Mass Student Aid and the Abolition of Tuition Fees in Ontario, 1945–1975," Ph.D. thesis, University of Toronto, 1995, 32, 79, 386–88, 400–1; Roberta Sharon Lexier, "The Canadian Student Movement in the Sixties: Three Case Studies," Ph.D. thesis, University of Alberta, 2009, 76–86; 145, 150, 152–54.

49 Kathe Anne Lemon, "Agent of Social Change: A History of Canadian University Press," M.A. thesis, Ryerson University and York University, 2004, 1, 12, 22–23, 30, 36.

50 "They Sit for 'The Queen,'" *TS*, 8 Sept. 1960; "Native Sons Won't Play 'Queen,' Controllers Walk out of Banquet," *GM*, Nov. 24, 1958; "O Canada Nice Song, She Says," *GM*, 29 Nov. 1958; "Plan Public Meeting on National Anthem," *GM*, 1 Dec. 1958; "'The Queen' or 'O'Canada,'" *TS*, 25 Nov. 1958; "Liberals to Press for Canadian Flag," *TS*, 16 Dec. 1958; "Flag-Anthem Action Asked by Quebec PC," *GM*, 23 Dec. 1958; "We're Not Anti-British, All We Want Is Our Own Flag," *TS*, 3 Jan. 1959; "Sons Abandon Plan to Label House Members," *GM*, 13 Jan. 1959; "Flag Debate," *GM*, 19 Jan. 1959; "'O'Canada' Gains as National Anthem," *TS*, 26 Feb. 1959.

51 John Manley, "'Communists Love Canada!': The Communist Party of Canada, the 'People' and the Popular Front, 1933–1939," *Journal of Canadian Studies*, 36,4 (Winter 2002); F.W. Park, *The Power and the Money* (Toronto: Progress Books, 1958).

52 Stephen Azzi, *Walter Gordon and the Rise of Canadian Nationalism* (Montreal & Kingston: McGill-Queen's University Press, 1999), 64, 69, 89–90; L.C. and F.W. Park, *Anatomy of Big Business* (Toronto: Progress Books, 1962).

53 "Socialism Revised: Free Enterprise Need Acknowledged by CCF," *GM*, 3 Aug. 1956; "Argue Protests U.S. Ownership Of Canada Firms," *GM*, 18 Feb. 1959; "NDP Leader Praises End, Assails Methods on Flag," *GM*, 17 June 1964; Peter Russell, ed., *Nationalism in Canada* (Toronto: McGraw-Hill Ryerson, 1966).

54 "Petition Scores Arrow Decision," *Varsity*, 26 Feb. 1959; "Send Letter," *Varsity*, 27 Feb. 1959.

55 Jennifer Lynn Hunter, "'Is It Even Worthwhile Doing the Dishes?' Canadians and the Nuclear Threat, 1945–1963," Ph.D. thesis, McGill University, 2004, 130–31; Moffatt, *History of the Canadian Peace Movement until 1969*, 82; James M. Minifie, *Peacemaker or Powder-Monkey:*

Canada's Role in a Revolutionary World (Toronto: McClelland & Stewart Ltd., 1960); "The Roaring Mouse," *SOS: Survival or Suicide?* October 1960.

56 Don Roebuck, *U.S. Ownership and Control of Canadian Industry* (Toronto: RIPP, n.d. [written c. 1964].

57 Letter, Art Pape to Oglesby & Booth, Lynd, and Dellinger, "Worklist," CUCND fonds, 7-Worklist, 1965; Dimitrios R. [Roussopoulos], "A Proposal for Building the Movement," Worklist, Nov. 16, 1965, CUCND Collection, 7-Worklist, 1965.

58 *SUPA Newsletter*, 12 Dec. 1965; "Vietnam Action Committee Report, no. 3," CUCND Collection, 7-Worklist, 1965; "Reverse the Lament," *Varsity*, 2 March 1966.

59 Jim Mayor, "Report of SUPA's Eastern Canada Study Conference—May 11–16, 1966 or Laxer's 30 Year Plan to Free Canada," *SUPA Newsletter*, 15 June 1966.

60 Philip Resnick (book review), "Horace B. Davis, Nationalism and Socialism . . ." *Our Generation*, September 1967.

61 Harvey L. Shepherd, "Playing the Game in Ottawa," *SUPA Newsletter*, 15 June 1966; James Laxer, *Red Diaper Baby: A Boyhood in the Age of McCarthyism* (Vancouver and Toronto: Douglas & McIntyre Ltd., 2004), 171–72, 176.

62 [Roussopoulos], "Proposal for Building the Movement."

63 Dufresne, "'Let's Not Be Cremated Equal,'" 25; Lisa Makarchuk, "Exhilaration, Hope and Inspiration: The Sixties in Cuba through a Canadian's Eyes," in *Cuba Solidarity in Canada: Five Decades of People-to-People Foreign Relations*, ed. Nino Pagliccia (Victoria, B.C.: Friesen Press, 2014), 31; "Pro-Kennedy Demonstrators Counter Cuban Supporters at United States Consulate," *Varsity*, 24 Oct. 1962; "Here and Now," *Varsity*, 5 Nov. 1962; "Here and Now," *Varsity*, 2 Oct. 1963.

64 Cynthia Wright, "Between Nation and Empire: The Fair Play for Cuba Committees and the Making of Canada-Cuba Solidarity in the Early 1960s," in *Our Place in the Sun: Canada and Cuba in the Castro Era*, ed. Robert Wright and Lana Wylie (Toronto and Buffalo: University of Toronto Press, 2009), 96, 103–4; Tate, 148, 151–54.

65 Wright, "Between Nation and Empire," 106–9, 114; Tate, 163–64; Kostash, *Long Way from Home*, xxxv.

66 Latin American Working Group (LAWG), "Background to September 1969," Latin American Working Group fonds, Clara Thomas Archives and Special Collections, York University, 1-2; Meeting of the Working Committee on International Affairs, 9 Oct. 1966, LAWG fonds, 1-12.

67 Meeting of the Working Committee on International Affairs, 9 Oct 1966, 1-12; LAWG, "Background to September 1969."

68 Hugh Miller, "Some Notes on the Founding of NACLA," Chicago, 5–6 Nov., LAWG fonds, 1-10.

69 Linda Seese, "Ideas for the Latin American Working Group in Toronto for the Next 10 Mo.," LAWG fonds, 1-7.

70 "Notes for L.A.W.G.," 11 Aug. 1967, LAWG fonds, 1-7.

71 B. [Brewster] Kneen, "Some Comments in Response to Those of Linda Seese," 7 Aug. 1967, LAWG fonds, 1-7.

72 Norm Laverty, "Dominican Republic Project: Introduction and Progress Report," December 1967, LAWG fonds, 1-12; Kneen, "Some Comments in Response to Those of Linda Seese"; LAWG, "Background to September 1969."

73 Laverty, "Dominican Republic Project"; Kneen, "Some Comments in Response to Those of Linda Seese"; LAWG, "Background to September 1969."

74 "Canadian Women: The Issue of Equality," *Marxist Quarterly*, Summer 1962; Aileen Hall, "Are Women Treated Like 2nd-Class Citizens?" *Ryersonian*, 12 Sept. 1966.

75 Heather Dean, "On Passing Two Whores and a Nun," *Random*, October 1966.

76 Ibid.

77 "Campus Suffragettes, Arise" (letter), *Varsity*, 18 Nov. 1966; "Hart House Bounces Women," *Varsity*," 9 Dec. 1966; "Women Continue Their Fight," *Varsity*, 16 Dec. 1966.

78 "Five Women Successfully Defy Hart House," *Varsity*, 13 Jan. 1967; "Five Co-eds Integrate Hart House Debates Room," *Varsity*, 20 Jan. 1967.

79 "SAC Supports Hart House Protest," *Varsity*, 9 Dec. 1966; "New Campus Party Enters SAC Race," *Varsity*, 4 Feb. 1966; "Student Democratic Union Candidates," *Varsity*, 23 Feb. 1966; "New Active and Bold Blood for SAC," *Varsity*, 25 Feb. 1966; Laurel N. Limpus and Paul K. Hoch, "Maligning Bissell an Ominous Note" (letter), *Varsity*, 28 Sept. 1966; Laurel Limpus, "Do Courses Stifle Individual Creative Thought?" *Varsity*, 12 Oct. 1966; Laurel Limpus, "Sex View Labelled Mid-Victorian," *Varsity*, 5 Dec. 1966. NDPers were known to have been active in the Student Democratic Union.

80 Laurel Sefton, "Women Not the Same but Equal" (letter), *Varsity*, 7 Dec. 1966.

81 Bruce Michael Douville, "The Uncomfortable Pew: Christianity, the New Left, and the Hip Counterculture in Toronto, 1965–1975," Ph.D. thesis, York University, 2011, 188; Powell, "'Vietnam: It's Our War Too,'" 113; "Organized Student Action Topic of NDP Seminar Here," *Varsity*, 14 Dec. 1964; "Radicals Ignore New Issues: CUCNDer," *Varsity*, 4 Jan. 1965; Heather Dean, "Vote Labour for Bigger Genitals," *Varsity*, 5 Nov. 1965.

82 Dean, "Vote Labour for Bigger Genitals."

83 Ibid; "McCarthyism Looms as Vietniks Labelled 'Commy,'" *Ryersonian*, 3 Dec. 1965.

84 "Student Concern" (letter), *GM*, 23 March 1965.

85 Franklin Bialystok, "Neo-Nazis in Toronto: The Allan Gardens Riot," *Canadian Jewish Studies*, 4-5 (1996–97); Donna Rosenthal, "'Live-In' at Allan Gardens," *SUPA Newsletter*, 6 June 1965.

86 Rosenthal, "'Live-In' at Allan Gardens."

87 Andre Beckerman, "A Critical View of SUPA," *SUPA Newsletter*, 23 June 1965; Ken Drushka, "SDS-ERAP Conference," *SUPA Newsletter*, 23 June 1965.

88 Letter, Art Pape to Robert Nichols, 3 April 1964, CUCND fonds 3-4; letter, Ian to Peter, 8 Aug. 1964, CUCND fonds 2-5.

89 Linda Light, "York University," *SUPA Newsletter*, no. 11, 1965; "Clarke Calls for Revolt," *Varsity*, 26 Nov. 1965; "A Violent Peace Movement," *SUPA Newsletter*, 12 Dec. 1965; Doug Ward, "Community Organizing: Some Questions for Radicals," *SUPA Newsletter*, 21 Dec. 1965; letter, Ian to Peter, 8 Aug. 1964; letter, Art Pape to Oglesby & Booth, Lynd, and Dellinger.

90 Stuart Henderson, *Making the Scene: Yorkville and Hip Toronto in the 1960s* (Toronto: University of Toronto Press, 2011); Michael Boudreau, "'The Struggle for a Different World': The 1971 Gastown Riot in Vancouver," in *Debating Dissent: Canada and the Sixties*, ed. Lara Campbell et al. (Toronto, Buffalo, and London: University of Toronto Press, 2012); Lawrence Aronsen, *City of Love and Revolution: Vancouver in the Sixties* (Vancouver: New Star Books, 2010); Marcel Martel, *Not This Time: Canadians, Public Policy and the Marijuana Question* (Toronto: University of Toronto Press, 2006); Doug Owram, *Born at the Right Time: A History of the Baby Boom Generation* (Toronto: University of Toronto Press, 1996), 232; Palmer, *Canada's 1960s*, 280; *Sanity*, November 1965; *Sanity*, February 1966; "Diminishing Resources, Natives and Integration—Which Way," *Sanity*, March 1966; "A Question of War and Peace," *Sanity*, April 1966; "Human Society and the Natural Economy," *Sanity*, April 1966; *Sanity*,

May 1966; "Economic Exchange and Social Relations," *Sanity*, May 1967; "The Free Gift," *Sanity*, June 1967.

91 *Sanity*, Summer 1966; "The City: The Ultimate in Human Habitation?" *Sanity*, September 1966; "The Mythology of Wage Labor," *Sanity*, April 1967.

92 "Social Change as PLAY," *Sanity*, July/August 1967; "Where We Are Going," *Sanity*, November 1967; "Mythology of Wage Labor."

93 Jim Laxer, "Where Has the Student Movement Gone?" *Varsity*, 24 Jan. 1966; Harvey L. Shepherd, "SUPA Dissolved; NL Comm. Formed," *New Left Committee Bulletin* (*NLC Bulletin*), October 1967; Peter Warrian, "Waterloo U," *SUPA Newsletter*, n.d. [probably January 1967; that issue was devoted to reflections on SUPA's December 1966 Waterloo conference]; "Why Pot Threatens Canada's New Left," *TS*, 16 Nov. 1966.

94 "SUPA: What It Accomplished," *Varsity*, 2 Oct. 1967.

95 From Allan Marks to Don Roebuck (Oct. 17), 7-F-SUPA, Worklist, 1965–1967, CUCND fonds.

96 Heather Dean to Alan Marks (Oct. 19), 7-F-SUPA, Worklist, 1965–1967, CUCND fonds.

97 Ibid.

98 Tony Hyde to Allan Marks (Oct. 19), 7-F-SUPA, Worklist, 1965–1967, CUCND fonds.

99 From Jim Best to Tony Hyde (Oct. 21), 7-F-SUPA, Worklist, 1965–1967, CUCND fonds.

100 Donald McKelvey, "To Montreal and Toronto Comrades," 11 Dec 1966, 7-SUPA Worklist, 1965–1967, CUCND fonds.

101 Ibid.

102 Worklist, 5 April 1967, CUCND collection, box 7-F-SUPA, Worklist, 1965–1967; letter, Don McKelvey to Stan Gray, 8 April 1967, CUCND collection, 7-SUPA, Worklist, 1965–1967; list of participants in SUPA general membership conference, 5–10 Sept. 1967, 16a-7.

103 *SUPA Newsletter*, 21 July 1965; "School for Social Theory," *SUPA Newsletter*, 30 Aug. 1965; *SUPA Newsletter*, 26 Oct. 1965; Milligan, *Rebel Youth*, 79.

104 Kostash, *Long Way from Home*, 25; Myrna Wood, interview, John Cleveland Interviews with Toronto Feminists, University of Ottawa Archives and Special Collections, Canadian Women's Movement Archives fonds, 1984.

105 Kostash, *Long Way from Home*, 168.

106 Cyril Levitt, *Children of Privilege: Student Revolt in the Sixties; A Study of Student Movements in Canada, the United States, and West Germany* (Toronto: University of Toronto Press, 1984), 106–7.

107 Harvey Shepherd, "Thoughts on Women," *NLC Bulletin*, December 1967.

108 "Winston Gereluk interviews Peggy Morton," *Alberta Labour History Institute*, www.labourhistory.ca/Uploads/ALHI_TRANSCRIPTS/PDFs/MortonP.pdf (accessed 13 May 2005); Richard Harris, *Democracy in Kingston: A Social Movement in Urban Politics, 1965–1970* (Kingston: McGill-Queen's University Press, 1988), 56–57.

109 Myrna Wood, interview.

110 Ibid.; Harris, *Democracy in Kingston*, 72.

111 Email from Linda Seese, 5 April 2015; Jared E. Leighton, "Freedom Indivisible: Gays and Lesbians in the African American Civil Rights Movement," Ph.D. thesis, University of Nebraska, 2013, 64–86, 185–87; Linda Seese, "SUPA as Seen by an Inside-Outsider," *SUPA Newsletter*, no. 9, 1965; Myrna Wood, interview.

112 Myrna Wood, interview; phone conversation with Judith Bernstein, 4 April 2016; "Chicago: JOIN Project," *Studies on the Left*, 5, 3 (1965).

113 Phone conversation with Judith Bernstein; Jennifer Frost, *An Interracial Movement of the Poor: Community Organizing and the New Left in the 1960s* (New York: New York University Press, 2001), 166.

114 This passage and lines in the following paragraph draw closely on Ian McKay, "A Different Place in the World: A Reconnaissance of Socialist Feminism in Canada, 1965–1990," unpublished paper, 2003, 46.

115 Ibid., 47–51, 59.

116 "Winston Gereluk interviews Peggy Morton."

117 McKay, "Different Place in the World," 47, 49–50, 54, 59. Mitchell's article was subsequently reprinted in *New Left Committee Bulletin*: Juliet Mitchell, "Women: The Longest Revolution," *NLC Bulletin*, February 1968.

118 CUCND collection, 7-SUPA, Manifesto 1967; Kostash, *Long Way from Home*, 18; Harris, *Democracy in Kingston*, 69; Tony Tugwell, "A Counter-Community," *SUPA Newsletter*, 10 Aug. 1965; Myrna Wood, interview.

119 Peter Gzowski, "The Righteous Crusaders of the New Left," *Maclean's*, 15 Nov. 1965.

120 Harvey L. Shepherd, "SUPA Dissolved; NL Comm. Formed," *NLC Bulletin*, October 1967; "Elected New Left Committee," n.d., CUCND fonds, 16a-7; "Statement of the New Left Committee—October 1967," *NLC Bulletin*, October 1967.

121 "Statement of the New Left Committee—October 1967," *NLC Bulletin*, October 1967.

122 Harvey L. Shepherd, "SUPA Dissolved; NL Comm. Formed"; Rowan, summary of discussions held by some Toronto people with Jonathan Bordo, Jan 24–25, 1968 (copies to Bordo, Morton, Roebuck, Seese, Skinner and Wood), box 7-F-New Left Committee minutes, etc., CUCND fonds; Linda Seese, "To Subscribers," *NLC Bulletin*, March 1968.

123 Owram, *Born at the Right Time*, 221.

4. Out of the Meat Grinder: Confronting the Educational Leviathan, 1968–71

1 "Boycott Continues at OCA—March May Follow," *Varsity*, 26 Feb. 1968; editorial, "OCA Makes a Start," *Varsity*, 28 Feb. 1968; Heather Moore (letter), "Ontario College of Art," *Globe and Mail* (*GM*), 24 Feb. 1968; "No Authority at OCA, Davis Says," *GM*, 27 Feb. 1968; "600 Protesting Students Paralyze Art College," *Toronto Star* (*TS*), 24 Feb. 1968.

2 "Rebellious Art Students Get Backing of 5 Outside Colleges," *TS*, 23 Feb. 1968; "Art Students Approve Daily Sit-ins to Get Two Instructors Reinstated," *GM*, 23 Feb. 1968.

3 "600 Angry Arts Students Back Two Fired Teachers," *Toronto Telegram* (*TT*), 22 Feb. 1968; "OCA Students March on Queen's Park Today," *Varsity*, 29 Feb. 1968; "OCA Student Protest Gains More Options," *GM*, 1 April 1967; "Art College Reinstates Two Fired Teachers," *TS*, 1 March 1968.

4 "Art Students Leary of Power," *TS*, 13 March 1968; "Principal to Consider Complaints," *GM*, 18 March 1968; "Give Students a Voice, Report on Art College Urges," *TS*, 16 Oct. 1968; "Davis Promises Law to Seat Students on Art College Board," *TS*, 19 Oct. 1968; "The Artist Who Triumphed along with Student Power," *TS*, Oct 23, 1968; "MPP Backs Student Governors," *TS*, 7 Jan. 1969.

5 Editorial, "OCA Makes a Start," *Varsity*, 28 Feb. 1968.

6 "The Toronto Student Movement and the SAC," n.d., Canadian Liberation Movement (CLM) fonds, 22–13, William Ready Division of Archives and Research Collections, McMaster University Library, Hamilton.

7 "Student Tears up Diploma at U of T Presentation," *TT*, 1 June 1968; "Bissell Attacks Student Apathy," *TT*, 17 Sept. 1978; "Students Jeer Their 'Token' U of T Vote," *TT*, 5 Oct. 1968; Michiel Horn, *York University: The Way Must Be Tried* (Montreal and Kingston: McGill-Queen's University Press, 2008), 108; "Collegians Boo 'Nigger' Picket Signs," *TT*, 3 Sept. 1968.

8 "Must Liberate Minds Says Nigger Author," *Chevron*, 4 Oct. 1968.

9 "Bissell, Radical Scuffle on Stage at Museum Melee," *TT*, 6 Feb. 1969.

10 "Kerr's Second Lecture Tranquil," *TT*, 7 Feb. 1969; "Fiery Young Radicals New Militants and Self-Critics," *TT*, 8 Feb. 1969.

11 Ulli Diemer, interview, 20 July 2011, Toronto.

12 Ibid.

13 Ibid.

14 Ibid.; Daniel Cohn-Bendit, *Obsolete Communism: The Left-Wing Alternative* (New York: McGraw-Hill, 1968).

15 "Modes: The First Successful Classroom Revolt," *Excalibur*, 18 Sept. 1969; York Student Movement (YSM), "Structure of the Learning Situation," *Excalibur*, 23 Oct. 1969; YSM, "Content of the Learning Situation at York," *Excalibur*, 30 Oct. 1969; "YSM's 'Guerrilla Theatre' Disrupts Winters' Teach-in," *Excalibur*, 18 Sept. 1969.

16 Eric Mann, untitled, *Excalibur*, 18 Sept. 1969.

17 Judy Darcy, "Don't Dismiss the Radicals So Quickly," *Excalibur*, 6 Nov. 1969.

18 "Council Defends Itself at Protest," *Excalibur*, 14 Nov. 1968; "Referendum Approves Campus Recruiting," *Excalibur*, 12 Dec. 1968.

19 "Ryerson Sets Pattern in OUS Resolutions," *Ryersonian*, 3 Oct. 1967; "CUS, and Us: Vietnam, Pot, Protests Are Issues," *Ryersonian*, 10 Sept. 1968; "Great 'Red' Conspiracy Aired," *Ryersonian*, 21 Sept. 1967.

20 "Ryerson Students Vote 2-1 against 'Free School' Idea," *TS*, 3 Oct. 1968; "Student Power Dead at Ryerson," *Ryersonian*, 18 Oct. 1968; "The Letter," *Eyeopener*, 26 Sept. 1969.

21 "I Quit . . . Whoopee Shit!" *Eyeopener*, 11 July 1969; "On Threats and the Integrity of the Institute," *Eyeopener*, 16 Jan. 1970; *Eyeopener*, 10 April 1970.

22 "Mordell Shows Mettle, Cools Protest Mob," *Ryersonian*, 26 March 1970; "1,000 Back English 5," *Ryersonian*, 2 April 1970; "No Apathy," *Ryersonian*, 3 April 1970.

23 "Chairman Claims Violence Threats," *TT*, 4 March 1968; J. Ridpath (letter), *GM*, 11 Dec. 1968.

24 Editorial, "For the Fascist Few—Violence," *GM*, 29 Nov. 1968; "Threat of Sit-in Fades, U of T to Debate Brief," *GM*, 30 Nov. 1968; "The Time Has Come to Counter Student Violence, Bissell Says," *GM*, 28 Feb. 1969; Claude Bissell, "Campus Freedom and Student Rebels," *GM*, 5 March 1969; "Sword Urges Campus Rules to End Violence," *GM*, 23 May 1970; John M. Rist, "Student Activists" (letter), *GM*, 6 Dec. 1968.

25 F. Paul Fromm, "Vietnik Tricks and Violence," *Varsity*, 30 Oct. 1967; *TT*, 25 May 1968; "Campus Rebels No. 1 Threat to Canada—Rights Chief," *TT*, 2 Dec. 1968; Zink, "Our Violent Minority Needs Discipline," *TT*, 2 Dec. 1968; editorial, "Student Disorder," *TT*, 3 Dec. 1968; untitled cartoon, *TT*, 3 Dec. 1968.

26 "$10,000 Offered in Bombings," *TT*, 24 Sept. 1968; "Leaflets Threaten Continued Terror," *TT*, 25 Sept. 1968. Humphrey is famed as the author of the first draft of the United Nations' Universal Declaration of Human Rights.

27 "Leaflets Threaten Continued Terror," *TT*, 25 Sept. 1968; "Police Comb Photos for Student Suspects," *TT*, 25 Sept. 1968; "Police Call on Anti-War Groups," *TT*, 26 Sept. 1968; "FBI Agents Join Bombing Probe," *TT*, 27 Sept. 1968; "Metro Police Fear New Bomb Terror by Anti-War Groups," *TT*, 13 Dec. 1968.

28 Peter Worthington, "Anti-War Agitators Bombing Suspects," *TT*, 25 Sept. 1968.

29 David Austin, *Fear of a Black Nation: Race, Sex and Security in Sixties Montreal* (Toronto: Between the Lines, 2013), 131–37, citation at 137; "Students Accuse Canadian Papers of Inviting Violence on Campus," *GM*, 20 Sept. 1968; "All Protests Not Alike, Student Debaters Say," *GM*, 23 Jan. 1969; Bruce Michael Douville, "The Uncomfortable Pew: Christianity, the New Left, and the Hip Counterculture in Toronto, 1965–1975," Ph.D. thesis, York University, 2011, 365; Christopher William Powell, "'Vietnam: It's Our War Too': The Antiwar Movement in Canada: 1963–1975," Ph.D. thesis, University of New Brunswick, 2011, 244–45.

30 Harry Crowe and Douglas Fisher, "A New Barbarism," *TT*, 2 Oct. 1968; Crowe and Fisher, "Bitter Students," *TT*, 18 Oct. 1968; Crowe and Fisher, "Our Hitler Youth," *TT*, 14 Feb. 1969; Fisher and Crowe, "Bissell's views," *TT*, 12 March 1969; Crowe and Fisher, "Riding Student Tigers," *TT*, 28 Oct. 1968; Fisher and Crowe, "Order on the Campus," *TT*, 24 Sept. 1969; Fisher and Crowe, "Propaganda U," *TT*, 25 March 1969.

31 Kenneth McNaught, *Conscience and History: A Memoir* (Toronto: University of Toronto Press, 1999), 4–20, 93, 28, 123, 52.

32 Ibid., 149–59, 165, 179.

33 Ibid., 190.

34 "Support for Wallace Sick Society Symbol," *TS*, 15 Oct. 1968; "Labor Will Never Join Those New Left Students," *TS*, 24 Feb. 1969

35 Julius Grey, "The Paradox of Stanley Gray," *Canadian Dimension*, October-November 1969; G. David Sheps, "The Apocalyptic Fires at Sir George Williams University," *Canadian Dimension*, February 1969; Phil Resnick, "Exchange," *Canadian Dimension*, July 1969.

36 "Students Strike for a Smoking Lounge," *TT*, 27 Sept. 1968; "Students Plan Protest," *TT*, 3 Oct. 1968; "Metro Students March," *TT*, 26 Sept. 1968; "Student Gives In, Gets Haircut," *TT*, 25 Sept. 1968; "Principal Blames Agitators in Hair Row," *TT*, 8 Oct. 1968; "Student Walkout over Hair, Skirts," *TT*, 17 Oct. 1968; "100 Suspended over Danforth Tech Protest," *TT*, 18 Oct. 1968.

37 "Student Power: Alive and Well . . . in Toronto," *TT*, 16 Nov. 1968; "Student Scraps Valedictory Speech in 'Pressures' Protest," *TT*, 16 Nov. 1968.

38 "Teachers Ask Public to Support School Principals," *TS*, 15 Oct. 1968; "Youths Part Trustees down the Middle," *TT*, 4 Oct. 1968; "Board May Lay Charges over Rebels," *TT*, 8 Oct. 1968; "Student Power Lowers Its Sights," *TT*, 28 Feb. 1968; "Principal Blames Agitators in Hair Row," *TT*, 8 Oct. 1968; "Student Walkout over Hair, Skirts," *TT*, 17 Oct. 1968.

39 "Dress of No Concern to Principals—Poll," *TT*, 16 Oct. 1968; "Youths Part Trustees down the Middle," *TT*, 4 Oct. 1968; "Strap Stays in Scarboro, Board Rules," *TT*, 28 Jan. 1969; "Teachers Angry over Ad," *TT*, 25 Oct. 1968; "Teacher's Plan to End Blow-Ups," *TT*, 8 Oct. 1968.

40 "Student Walkout Threat over Longer School Year," *TT*, 13 Dec. 1968; "No Mass Student Walkout," *TT*, 16 Dec. 1968; "Labor May Aid Students in 2nd Protest March," *TT*, 19 Dec. 1968; "High School Students in Longer Term Protest," *TT*, 4 Feb. 1969.

41 Sarah Spinks, "An Interview with Judy Dexter," *This Magazine Is About Schools*, Autumn 1969; [caption from picture], *TT*, 29 April 1969; "Brace for Student 'Hits,' Trustees Told," *TT*, 9 May 1969; "Forest Hill—Focus of New Social Forces or a Prank?" *TT*, 3 May 1969; Forest Hill Suspends 2nd Student, *GM*, 30 April 1969.

42 "Forest Hill . . . A Paper Revolution?" *TT*, 1 May 1969; "Forest Hill 'Greatest' to U.S. Students," *TT*, 2 May 1969; "Father of Suspended Girl at Forest Hill Won't Talk Politics," *TT*, 6 May 1969.

43 Spinks, "Interview with Judy Dexter"; "Students and Staff Agree on Formula to End Sit-in," *GM*, 1 May 1969; "Bill of Rights Is Adopted in Forest Hill," *GM*, 2 May 1969; "Sit-in Students Leave, Return; Hope Dims for Reinstatement," *GM*, 3 May 1969; "3 Forest Hill Students Re-Admitted," *GM*, 7 May 1969.

44 "Student Article Sparks Faculty Argument," *TT*, 11 June 1969; "Principal's Assembly Criticized," *TT*, 12 June 1969.

45 "Student Councillors Learning How to Lead," *TT*, 3 July 1969; "Schools Ready for Student Unrest," *TT*, 20 Aug. 1969; "Student Fracas at Board Meet," *TT*, 14 April 1970; "Vietnam War Assemblies Urged," *TT*, 12 May 1970; "Students Win Right to Discuss Touchy Issues in School," *TT*, 14 May 1970; "Motion 'Nonsense' to Anti-Viet Pupils," *TT*, 26 May 1970.

46 "Student Group Wants to Overturn a 'Bankrupt' System," *TT*, 22 Oct. 1970; "Students Organized against the System," *TT*, 30 April 1970; "Ho-Hum," *TT*, 23 Nov. 1968; "Two Barred for Criticizing Teachers," *TS*, 27 April 1970; [untitled], *TT*, 18 Nov. 1969.

47 "Student Leaders Call May 3 Strike," *TT*, 28 April 1971; "Rebel Students" (letter), *GM*, 22 May 1971; "Cafeteria Boycott Success," *TT*, 24 Sept. 1970; "Welch Denies Inferior Trend in Education," *TT*, 5 May 1971; "150 Students Protest Prices in Cafeteria," *GM*, 8 May 1971; "Pupils Strike at 2 Schools over Food Cost," *GM*, 11 May 1971; "Students Eating Less after Price Increase," *GM*, 15 April 1971.

48 "500 Students Protest Spending Limits," *TT*, 4 May 1971; "High School 'Vigilantes' Clash with Protesters," *TT*, 18 May 1971; "2,000 High School Students Protest Higher Lunch Prices," *TS*, 18 May 1971; "Strike Committee Calls on Students to March on Legislature Today to Protest Budget Cuts," *GM*, 18 May 1971; "600 Students in March against Cuts," *TT*, 19 May 1971.

49 Editorial, "Where Oh Where Is HALL-DENNIS?" *Third Eye*, April 1970.

50 Adam Josh Cole, "Children, Liberalism and Utopia: Education, Hall-Dennis and Modernity in Ontario's Long 1960s," Ph.D. thesis, Queen's University, 2015, 1, 4–8.

51 Debra L. O'Rourke, "Defining and Defending a Democratic Public Education Site," M.A. thesis, York University, 2009, 23, 43, 52–55.

52 Bob Davis, *What Our High Schools Could Be . . . : A Teacher's Reflections from the 60's to the 90's* (Toronto: Our Schools/Our Selves Education Foundation and Garamond Press, 1990), 41–45; George Martell, "Cabbagetown," in *This Book Is About Schools*, ed. Satu Repo (New York: Random House, 1970), 272–73.

53 Martell, "Cabbagetown"; Davis, *What Our High Schools Could Be*, 57–77.

54 "25,000 Educations 'Sacrificed,'" *TT*, 19 Feb. 1969.

55 Cole, "Children, Liberalism and Utopia," 43, 204–7.

56 O'Rourke, "Defining and Defending a Democratic Public Education Site," 94–97, 117–19, 137; "Trustees Finally Closed the Generation Gap," *TT*, 21 March 1969.

57 "School Funds to Be Sought," *GM*, 29 Dec. 1969; "Those No-Rule Schools Are Staggering to Success," *TS*, 7 April 1969; Dorothy I. Frice, "Super-Schools" (letter), *GM*, 28 Dec. 1971; "The Mothers Who Want to Change the School System," *GM*, 25 Aug. 1969; O'Rourke, "Defining and Defending a Democratic Public Education Site," 100, 116.

58 Using a Smear on Mrs. Nelson," *TT*, 28 March 1969; "Secondary School Teachers Vote No-Confidence in Board," *TT*, 12 March 1969; "After Four Editorial," *TT*, 12 March 1969; "Fiona Returns after Apology," *TT*, 11 April 1969; "Record Secret, Fiona Quits," *TT*, 3 June 1969.

59 "Parents Ginger Group Bucks the 'Senile' System," *TT*, 25 Nov. 1969.

60 Ibid.; "Ginger Group Makes Bid for School Board Control," *TT*, 7 Nov. 1969; "Youth Support, Teacher Power Bring New-Look to City Trustees," *TT*, 2 Dec. 1969; "A Mid-Term Report on Your Trustees," *TT*, 4 April 1970.

61 "Most Slow Learners from Poorer Families—Report," *TT*, 22 Dec. 1970; "Children Aged 3 for '72 School Project," *TT*, 15 Sept. 1971; "Trustees Won't Consider Busing Students," *Toronto Sun* (*Sun*), 17 May 1972; "The Candidates," *TT*, 28 Nov. 1969; "School Board Ends Prayer, Just Meditates," *TS*, 20 Feb. 1970.

62 Ernest E. Barr, *My Encounter with Education* ([Toronto?]: R.H.I. Publishers, 1973), 40, 92, 122, 134–38.

63 Ibid., 104–8, 117, 7, 124; bold in original.

64 R. Val Scott, *Living and Learning without Schools: A Survey-Report to the Chairman and Members of the Board of Education* (Toronto: Board of Education for the Borough of North York, 1971), 8–15, 18–28, 38; Val Scott, "Former Colleague of Tommy Douglas Says NDP Falls Far Short of Its Original Promise," *The Canadian*, www.agoracosmopolitan.com/home/Frontpage/2007/12/03/01967.html (accessed 22 Nov. 2012).

65 O'Rourke, "Defining and Defending a Democratic Public Education Site," 115–19, 129–41.

66 Ibid., 143–46.

67 "This Magazine Was About Schools: An Interview with George Martell," *This Magazine*, January-February 1977; *This Magazine Is About Schools*, Winter 1971; "From the Board," *Community Schools*, January 1972; *Community Schools*, June 1971; Loren Jay Lind, *The Learning Machine: A Hard Look at Toronto Schools* (Toronto: Anansi Press, 1974), 230, 223.

68 George Martell, "Community Control of the Schools," *This Magazine Is About Schools*, Summer 1970; editorial, "On This Magazine," *This Magazine Is About Schools*, Summer 1971.

69 Political groups Blamed for School Discontent, *TT*, 24 Aug. 1970; "School System Said in Jeopardy," *TT*, 15 Oct. 1970; "Metro School Chief Hits at Left Wingers," *TT*, 1 Oct. 1971.

70 "Trustees Assailed over Bremer," *GM*, 3 June 1970; "How Secrecy Cost 'Reform' Trustees Their Man," *GM*, 8 June 1970; "New Education Head Urged to Quit Post by Reformist Group," *GM*, 9 June 1970.

71 Loren Lind, "The Politics of Subterfuge," *This Magazine Is About Schools*, Winter 1971; "School Involvement Sought," *GM*, 23 April 1971.

72 "5 Teachers Convicted on Marijuana Count in 2 Years, Only Clow's Certificate Not Affected, Welsh Reveals," *GM*, 29 Jan. 1970; "Educators Meet on School Dispute," *TS*, 17 Dec. 1971.

73 "700 Pack School to Urge Rehiring Teacher Suspended over Marijuana," *TS*, 20 Oct. 1971; editorial, "Marijuana and Change," *GM*, 20 Oct. 1971; editorial, "The Puritans Return," *GM*, 4 Dec. 1971; editorial, "A Second Penalty to Pay," *GM*, 21 Jan. 1972; editorial, "Caught between Laws," *GM*, 19 July 1972; editorial, "Double Jeopardy," *TS*, 20 Oct. 1971; editorial, "Penalty Enough," *TS*, 1 Dec. 1971.

74 "Why We Oppose the Community School in Don Mills" (letter), *TS*, 12 Jan. 1972; "A Divided School: Who Will Run It?" *TS*, 22 Dec. 1971; "'I Wonder What You're Doing in a School,' Judge Told Teacher Who Had Marijuana," *TS*, 29 Oct. 1971.

75 "Educators Meet on School Dispute," *TS*, 17 Dec. 1971; "Mao Teachings at Don Mills School, Liberals' President Protests Grants," *Sun*, 18 Jan. 1972.

76 "Clow Shouldn't Teach, Teachers Tell Province," *TS*, 4 Dec. 1971.

77 Mark Golden, "Taming the Teachers," *Community Schools*, January 1972.

78 "Clow's Future Cloudy as North York Teacher," *GM*, 22 Jan. 1972; "Clow's Future Now up to

North York Board," *TS*, 21 Jan. 1972; "Parents Ask Say in Decision on Teacher's Job," *TS*, 24 Jan. 1972; "Brian Clow Fired—But Only If He Gets Another Job," *GM*, 25 Jan. 1972.

79 "Clow Resigns Research Position," *GM*, 28 April 1973; "5 Teachers Convicted on Marijuana Count in 2 Years, Only Clow's Certificate Not Affected, Welsh Reveals," *GM*, 29 Jan. 1970; "Clow's Future Now up to North York Board," *TS*, 21 Jan. 1972; "MP Backs Don Mills Grant for Community School Plan," *Sun*, 20 Jan. 1972.

80 Editorial, "Get Ready Now," *TS*, 12 May 1971. For youth hitchhiking, see Linda Mahood, "Hitchin' a Ride in the 1970s: Canadian Youth Culture and the Romance with Mobility," *Histoire sociale/Social History,* 47,93 (May 2014), 657–58. As reasons for this phenomenon, Mahood cites the baby-boomer bulge, a move to the workforce delayed with schooling, the generational consciousness of young people, a search for authentic experiences, adventure, freedom, personal growth, intersection with subcultures, a chance to see the world/country, and unspecified global factors.

81 "Tent City Is Dead, But the Spirit That Fought for It Will Carry On," *TS*, 29 May 1971.

82 "Grass Roots: How It All Began and What It Wanted," *TS*, 22 July 1971.

83 "Tent City Is Rejected by Council," *GM*, 17 May 1971; "Trustees Back Tent City Plan for Youths," *GM*, 21 May 1971; "Labor Council Endorses Tent City," *GM*, 4 June 1971.

84 "Grass Roots Refuses to Abandon Program," *GM*, 24 June 1971; "Tent City Is Dead, But the Spirit That Fought for It Will Carry On," *TS*, 29 May 1971; "Concert to Back Tent City Attended by 500," *GM*, 5 July 1971.

85 "Injunction Sought If Wacheea Not Closed," *TT*, 29 July 1971.

86 "U of T Will Aid Transients in Finding Site for Tent City," *TT*, 12 July 1971; "Wacheea Can Happen," *CT*, 14 July 1971; "The 200 Young People Who Live in Those Tents," *TT*, 16 July 1971.

87 "U of T Will Aid Transients in Finding Site for Tent City," *TT*, 12 July 1971; "U of T Campus Squatters Vote to Defy Quit Order," *TT*, 16 July 1971; "Tent City Ignores Injunction and Stays on U of T Campus," *TS*, 17 July 1971.

88 "150 Evicted from Tent City Rally to Seek New Home," *TT*, 19 July 1971; *Guerilla*, no. 4, 1971; "Grass Roots: How It All Began and What It Wanted," *TS*, 22 July 1971; "Grass Roots and Wacheea: A Basic Change in Approach," *GM*, 24 July 1971; "Wacheea," *Red Morning*, Summer 1971.

89 "How Cops Smashed Youth Tent Colony," *CT*, 21 July 1971.

90 "Tents Unfold Despite Protests," *TT*, 22 July 1971; "Wacheea: The Radicals Claim a Victory," *TT*, 14 Aug. 1971; "Tent City Planners Hope a Picnic Will Soothe Angry Neighbours," *TS*, 31 July 1971; "The Greening of Wacheea," *GM*, 25 July 1971; Wacheea Neighbours Organize Rally to Assess Sentiment for Ousting Young Tent Community," *GM*, 26 July 1971; "Grant Not Spent on Site, Says Tent City," *TT*, 16 Aug. 1971.

91 "Stop Tent City Group Considers Legal Action," *TT*, 22 July 1971; "Tents Unfold Despite Protests," *TT*, 22 July 1971.

92 "Wacheea Criticism Termed Premature," *GM*, 30 July 1971; "Stop Tent City Group to Urge Wacheea Eviction," *TT*, 27 July 1971; "Parkdale in Crossfire of Tent War," *TT*, 28 July 1971; "Get Out or Be Evicted, City Tells Wacheea," *TT*, 30 July 1971; "Citizen Committee Won't Act to Oust Tent City," *TT*, 4 Aug. 1971.

93 "How to Get to Wacheea," William Ready Division of Archives and Research Collections, McMaster University Library, Revolutionary Marxist Group (RMG) fonds, 4-19; "Tent City 'Picnic' Attracts Neighbours Bearing Gifts," *TS*, 2 Aug. 1971; "Wacheea: The Radicals Claim a Victory," *TT*, 14 Aug. 1971.

94 "Grass Roots: How It All Began and What It Wanted," *TS*, 22 July 1971; "Grant Not Spent on Site, Says Tent City," *TT*, 16 Aug. 1971; editorial, "All Friends Together," *GM*, 10 Sept. 1971.

95 *Guerilla*, no. 10, 1971; "Wacheea: The Radicals Claim a Victory," *TT*, 14 Aug. 1971; "Grass Roots and Wacheea: A Basic Change in Approach," *GM*, 24 July 1971.

96 "Wacheea Tents Fold, Youths Plan to Set up Home in Warehouse," *TS*, 10 Sept. 1971; "U of T Handbook Attacked by Press," *Varsity*, 15 Sept. 1971; "SAC May Demand Sword's Resignation," *Varsity*, 15 Sept. 1971; "Faculty Set up Reform Group," *Varsity*, 15 Sept. 1971; "Campers Evicted from U of T; 21 Are Arrested," *GM*, 19 July 1971.

97 Most of the details in this discussion on Rochdale College are drawn from Stuart Henderson, "Off the Streets and into the Fortress: Experiments in Hip Separatism at Toronto's Rochdale College, 1968-1975," *Canadian Historical Review*, 92, 1 (March 2011), 107–33.

98 Howard Adelman and Dennis Lee, eds., *The University Game* (Toronto: Anansi, 1968).

99 Quoted in Henderson, "Off the Streets and into the Fortress," 120.

100 Ibid., 114, 121n.

101 See, for instance, Paul Axelrod, *Values in Conflict: The University, the Marketplace, and the Trials of Liberal Education* (Montreal and Kingston: McGill-Queen's University Press, 2002).

5. Bringing the Revolution Home: Black Power, Feminism, and Turning the Local into Global, 1968–71

1 "Football Star: 'Racial Discrimination in Ottawa,'" *Toronto Star* (*TS*), 6 Dec. 1967.

2 Myrna Wood, Peggy Morton, and Linda Seese, "Women Arise—We Have Nothing to Lose!!" 20 Nov. 1967, McMaster University Library, Combined Universities Campaign for Nuclear Disarmament (CUCND) fonds, 16a-7; "Subversive Canadian Group, W.L.F. Exposed," *New Left Committee Bulletin*, November 1967; Women's Liberation Group, "Brief to the House of Commons Health and Welfare Committee on Abortion Law Reform," n.d., 117-Toronto Women's Liberation Movement, Canadian Women's Movement Archives (CWMA) fonds, University of Ottawa Archives and Special Collections.

3 Van Gosse, *Rethinking the New Left: An Interpretative History* (New York: Palgrave Macmillan, 2005), 5.

4 "Football Star: 'Racial Discrimination in Ottawa,'" *Toronto Star* (*TS*), 6 Dec. 1967.

5 "Another Rebuff for Muhammad," *Globe and Mail* (*GM*), 4 March 1966; "Toronto, the Tolerant," *GM*, 10 March 1966; "Smythe Adamant about Resignation," *GM*, 10 March 1966; "Smythe Stirs Write Brigade," *GM*, 15 March 1966; Dick Beddoes (untitled column), *GM*, 18 Oct. 1968.

6 "Discrimination? Yes? But Why the Surprise?" *Toronto Telegram* (*TT*), 7 Dec. 1967; "The Watkins Furor Picks up Steam," *TT*, 7 Dec. 1967.

7 "Watkins Calls Canada 'Lesser of Two Evils,'" *GM*, 3 Jan. 1968; Gary Dunford, "The Dapper Young Negro—Who Hates Whites," *TS*, 5 Jan. 1968.

8 Dunford, "Dapper Young Negro"; "Life with Ticats Easier Than at Ottawa: Watkins," *GM*, 6 Dec. 1967; Austin Clarke, *The Confessed Bewilderment of Martin Luther King and the Idea of Non-Violence as a Political Tactic* (Burlington, Ont.: Al Kitab Sudan Publications, 1968).

9 "Fear for Family in Canada, Watkins Shot in California," *West Indian News Observer*, June 1968; "Star Ticat End Slain in Hold-Up," *TS*, 3 June 1968; "Brother of Slain Ticat Sues Clerks," *TS*, 5 June 1969; "Watkins: Police Rule Self Defence," *TT*, 4 June 1968.

10 "Watkins: Police Rule Self Defence," *TT*, 4 June 1968; "Called Racist by Black, White Radicals Cheer," *GM*, 14 Dec. 1968; "Time to Get off Our Backs, Black Panther Tells Canadians," *TS*, 14 Dec. 1968; untitled, *GM*, 10 June 1968.

11 "Allan McEachern Says Action of Ted Watkins No Concern of League," *GM*, 8 Dec. 1967; "Need Czar to Control Outbursts: O'Quinn," *GM*, 7 Dec. 1967; "Football Star: 'Racial Discrimination in Ottawa,'" *TS*, 6 Dec. 1967.

12 "A Global Vision for Black Cats," *GM*, 15 April 1967; editorial, "Fuelling the Fires of Race Hate," *TS*, 16 Oct. 1968; "The Mind and Faith of Black Power," *TS*, 20 Jan. 1968.

13 William J. Smyth, *Toronto, the Belfast of Canada: The Orange Order and the Shaping of Municipal Culture* (Toronto: University of Toronto Press, 2015), 205–12, 229, 247; "Outlaw Discrimination by Licensed Businesses," *GM*, 30 May 1950; "Council's Solid Front Falls Apart in Passing No Discrimination Bill," *GM*, 27 July 1950; editorial, "Africa Is Booming," *GM*, 27 Feb. 1948; editorial, "Egypt's Threat to Peace," *GM*, 19 Dec. 1951; editorial, "The Problem of Kenya," *GM*, 23 Oct. 1952; editorial, "Color Lines in the United Nations?" *GM*, 26 Sept. 1960; editorial, "Mischief at the UN," *GM*, 23 June 1962; editorial, "The Black Man's Burden," *GM*, 21 Feb. 1961.

14 "Book; What Lies behind the Mau Mau" (ad), *GM*, April 24, 1953; "Crowd Cheers Attack On Policy of British in Handling Mau Mau," *GM*, Apr 25, 1953; Tarah Brookfield, "Protection, Peace, Relief and Rescue: Canadian Women's Cold War Activism at Home and Abroad, 1945–1975," Ph.D. thesis, York University, 2008, 137–51; Carla Marano, "'We All Used to Meet at the Hall': Assessing the Significance of the Universal Negro Improvement Association in Toronto, 1900–1950," *Journal of the Canadian Historical Association*, 25,1 (2014), 144–48, 157, 164–65, 168.

15 "Negroes Seek Change in Immigration Laws," *GM*, 14 Feb. 1955; editorial, "No Place for Threats," *GM*, 16 Feb. 1955.

16 Burnley "Rocky" Jones and James W. St. G. Walker, *Burnley "Rocky" Jones: Revolutionary* (Halifax; Winnipeg: Roseway Publishing, 2016), 50–51.

17 "Now Toronto Gets Black Power," *TS*, 2 March 1968; "A Tolerant People? Nice to Believe. We're Really Just Polite Racists," *GM*, 15 Feb. 1969.

18 "Inter-Race Violence Inevitable in Canada Says Ted Watkins," *TS*, 26 Feb. 1968; "Black Nationalism in Canada," *West Indian News Observer*, March 1968; John Doig, "Now Toronto Gets Black Power"; Diana L. Braithwaite, interview with Leonard Johnson, 24 Nov. 1981, tape 3 of 3, Multicultural History Society of Ontario.

19 "'Burn, Kill,' Cry Black Radicals in Protest at U.S. Consulate," *TS*, 8 April 1968.

20 "A Tolerant People?"; "Statement of Purpose," *Harambee*, May 1968; "Toronto's Tribute to Malcolm X," *Harambee*, May 1968; "A Call for Unity," *Harambee*, May 1968, *Harambee*, May 1968.

21 Huguette Casmir, interview with Leonard Johnson, 3 Aug. 1978, tape 1 of 1, Multicultural History Society of Ontario; Keith S. Henry, *Black Politics in Toronto since World War I* (Toronto: Multicultural History Society of Ontario, 1981); Diana L. Braithwaite, interview with Leonard Johnson; "Rally to Hail Garvey's Birthday," *Contrast*, August 1970.

22 "A Tolerant People?"

23 "Called Racist by Black, White Radicals Cheer," *GM*, 14 Dec. 1968; "Panthers Warn of Race War," *Ryersonian*, 19 March 1970; "History and Objectives [of the] Black Liberation Front of Canada," *Black Liberation News*, July 1969; "Blacks Demand Board to Study Police Conduct," *TS*, 26 July 1969.

24 "Gang Battles Police, Shouts Black Power Slogans," *TS*, 18 July 1969; "Policemen Beaten in

City 'Black Power' Riot," *TT*, 18 July 1969; "Blacks Want Board to Watch over City Police," *GM*, 28 July 1969.

25 "200 Mill on Street, Armed Man Arrested in Race Clash Area," *TS*, 19 July 1969; "Kensington Residents Blame the Police," *TT*, 19 July 1969; "Blacks Want Board to Watch over City Police."

26 "Canada—1969," *Black Liberation News*, September 1969.

27 "BLFC Seminar Demands Citizens Control of Police," *Black Liberation News*, August 1969; "U.S. Racism Runs off on Canada, Negro Says," *TS*, 27 Feb. 1969; "Black Power Just the Start—Jones," *TT*, 27 Feb. 1969.

28 "A Tolerant People?"; "Black-Indian Coalition," *TT*, 22 Feb. 22, 1969; *Contrast*, 7 March 1969.

29 Jan Carew, "Don't Shift the Blame," *GM*, 15 Feb. 1969.

30 "Blacks Demand Sir George Inquiry," *TS*, 3 Nov. 1969; "Black Liberation Struggle Today," *Black Labour*, August 1975; "Black Organizations and the Crisis in Schools in Toronto," *Caribbean Dialogue*, March 1976.

31 "Black Organizations and the Crisis in Schools in Toronto"; "What B.Y.O Wants," *Black Voice*, November 1970, "To All Our Readers," *Black Voice*, November 1970; "Black Man's Role Discussed," *TT*, 3 March 1969.

32 "Marcus Garvey: Black Internationalist," *Black Liberation News*, October 1969.

33 "Article Disturbs Workers," *Contrast*, 24 Sept. 1972; "The Black Education Project 1969–1976," n.d., 1-4, Multicultural History Society of Ontario, Black fonds, box 2.

34 "A Tough-Talking Bunny Girl Seeks a Better Deal for Black Children," *TS*, 31 Oct. 1970; Dionne Brand and Krisantha Sri Bhaggiyadatta, *Rivers Have Sources, Trees Have Roots: Speaking of Racism* (Toronto: Cross Cultural Communication Centre, 1986), 175.

35 "Tough-Talking Bunny"; "Darts and Laurels," *TS*, 9 Oct. 1970.

36 "Blacks Assail Rights Group for Inaction," *GM*, 5 April 1971; letter, "Human Rights Commission," *GM*, 20 April 1971.

37 Harold Hoyte, "Horace Campbell Looks Back," *Contrast*, 29 Sept. 1972; "Metro's Blacks: Uncle Tom Lives in Bramalea," *TT*, 15 May 1971.

38 William Cameron, "Three Toronto Blacks Worry about Long, Hot Summer," *TS*, 18 June 1970; J. Ashton Brathwaite, *Niggers, This Is Canada* (Toronto: 21st Century Book, 1971); for *Born Black*, directed by Lennie Little-White, see Kass Banning, "Conjugating Three Moments in Black Canadian Cinema," in *North of Everything: English-Canadian Cinema Since 1980*, ed. William Beard and Jerry White (Edmonton: University of Alberta Press, 2002), 85–88.

39 Stanley Grizzle, "Black Canada Talks Unity," *West Indian News Observer*, November 1969; "Blacks Want 'No Strings' Aid," *TT*, 20 Oct. 1969; "Canadian Black Groups Divided," *TT*, 24 Oct. 1969.

40 "National Black Coalition: Whose Baby Is It Really?" *Black Liberation News*, November 1969; "National Black Coalition," *Contrast*, October 1969; "Second Anniversary—Sir George Williams University—A Statement," *Contrast*, 6 March 1971; "Rosie Douglas; Call for Halt in Exploitation of Africa," *Contrast*, 20 March 1971; *Contrast*, 23 Jan. 1971.

41 John Harewood, "NBCC Leaders: Wills and Clarke," *Contrast*, 31 Oct. 1975; "Planning Time for the NBCC," *Spear*, November 1973; Myrna Kostash, *Long Way from Home: The Story of the Sixties Generation in Canada* (Toronto: James Lorimer and Company, 1980), 160; Rosie Douglas, *Black Liberation and World Revolution: A Prison Interview with Rosie Douglas* (Notre Dame de Grace: Mondiale Publishers, n.d.), 6; "Emergency Meeting of NBCC," *Contrast*, 2 April 1976; Peter Paul, "Letter to the Black Community," *Contrast*, 12 May 1977.

42 Harold Hoyte, "Horace Campbell Looks Back," *Contrast*, 29 Sept. 1972; Errol Hasfal, "Rosie Speaks," *Contrast*, 4 July 1970; "Whites Walk Out," *Contrast*, 6 March 1971.

43 Lyba Spring, "Rally May 20 with Rosie Douglas: The Sir George Williams Affair," *TWLM Newsletter* [Toronto Women's Liberation Movement], May 1971; "Toronto Rally Launches Black Student Defense," *Labor Challenge*, June 1971.

44 Errol Hasfal, "An Analysis of Panther Politics," *Contrast*, 1 Dec. 1970; Errol Hasfal, "Rosie Speaks," *Contrast*, 4 July 1970.

45 "Panthers Speak in Toronto," *Contrast*, 4 April 1970; Malcolm X cited in George Elliott Clarke, *Odysseys Home: Mapping African-Canadian Literature* (Toronto: University of Toronto Press, 2002), 29.

46 "National Black Conference," *Black Voice*, November 1970.

47 "We Remember Malcolm X," *Black Voice*, November 1970.

48 Chris Harris, "A Gramscian Historical-Materialist Analysis of the Informal Learning and Development of Black Working-Class Organic Intellectuals in Toronto, 1969–1975," M.A. thesis, University of Toronto, 2005.

49 "Black People's Conference," *Guerilla*, no. 19 (1971); "Meet the Dynamic Young Woman behind the Big Conference: Sister Akousa," *Contrast*, 20 March 1971.

50 "25 White Leftists Rise up Angry, Stalk from Meeting," *TT*, 22 Feb. 1971. A separate group of fifteen whites stayed in their seats.

51 "Time to Get off Our Backs, Black Panther Tells Canadians," *TS*, 14 Dec. 1968; "Imamu Amiri Baraka," *Contrast*, 20 March 1971; Hogan (column), *Contrast*, 18 Oct. 1974; "Black Woman, White Woman and the Black Man," *Contrast*, 14 Nov. 1976; Xiaoping Li, *Voices Rising: Asian Canadian Cultural Activism* (Vancouver: UBC Press, 2007), 53–54; Ruth Magaly San Martin, "Picking up the Thread: The Oral History of the Latin American Women's Collective in Toronto, 1983–1990," Ph.D. thesis, University of Toronto, 1998, 72–73.

52 Gosse, *Rethinking the New Left*, 188. In his original, Gosse has "American" rather than "North American."

53 "She Didn't Wear a Bikini," *GM*, 27 Jan. 1969; Judy Rebick, *Ten Thousand Roses: The Making of a Feminist Revolution* (Toronto: Penguin Canada, 2005), 10–11.

54 Laurel Limpus, as told to Sherry Rochester, "The History of the Toronto Women's Liberation Movement," mimeo, Toronto, February 1971, CWMA, Toronto Women's Liberation Movement, 4; "Equality for Working Women," CWMA, 117-Toronto Women's Liberation Movement; Cathy Pike and Barb Cameron, "Collective Child-Care in a Class Society," 1971, CWMA, 117-Toronto Women's Liberation Movement.

55 Women's Liberation Campus Community, Cooperative Daycare Centre, *Handbook, 12 Sussex Daycare Centre* (Toronto: Hogtown Press, 1971), 1.

56 Ibid., 1–3; Latin American Working Group fonds 1-13; Rebick, *Ten Thousand Roses*, 61.

57 Rebick, *Ten Thousand Roses*, 62–65.

58 Pike and Cameron, "Collective Child-Care in a Class Society."

59 Rebick, *Ten Thousand Roses*, 35–43; "'How We Differ,' Vancouver, June 1970," in *Canadian Women's Issues*, vol. 1, *Strong Voices*, ed. Ruth Roach Pierson et al. (Toronto: James Lorimer and Company, 1993), 43–45.

60 Rebick, *Ten Thousand Roses*, 40–43.

61 Barb Cameron and Frances Gregory, "A Critical Look at the Conference," *TWLM Newsletter*, May 1971; Carolyn Egan, Maureen Hynes, and Lyba Spring, "Building the Movement,"

TWLM Newsletter, May 1971; *Women Unite! An Anthology of the Canadian Women's Movement* (Toronto, Canadian Women's Educational Press, 1972), 11.

62 *Women Unite!* 7.

63 Maureen Hynes, interview, 5 Aug. 2011, Toronto; Mary Bolton, "Sisterhood at the Conference," *TWLM Newsletter*, May 1971.

64 Bolton, "Sisterhood at the Conference"; "Nov 26 Educational on Sexual Fantasy and Lesbianism," *TWLM Newsletter*, December 1970; "Lesbian Educational," *TWLM Newsletter*, April 1971; "Educational Report," *TWLM Newsletter*, April 1971; Hynes, interview.

65 "General Information on the Women's Liberation Movement in Toronto," *TWLM Newsletter*, December 1970.

66 Ibid.; Hynes, interview; "Working Women Collective Report," *TWLM Newsletter*, February 1971; "Working Women Report," *TWLM Newsletter*, March 1971.

67 "Quebec Collective and the Committee for a Free Quebec," *TWLM Newsletter*, December 1970.

68 "Women's Culture," *TWLM Newsletter*, April 1971; "Coordinated Political Struggle Minutes: Feb. 6," *TWLM Newsletter*, February 1971; "Women's Coordinated Political Struggle Group Minutes, March 15," *TWLM Newsletter*, March 1971.

69 Barb Cameron, Charnie Cunningham, Lynn Lang, Ruth McEwan, Cathy Pike, Judy Skinner, and Leslie Towers, untitled statement, 23 Oct. 1971, CWMA, Toronto Women's Liberation Movement.

70 Bonnie Kreps, "The 'New Feminist' Analysis," *New Feminist*, 8 Dec. 1969; "New Women's Liberation Group Formed by the Disenchanted, the Disapproving," *GM*, 3 Sept. 1970; Liz Angus, Pam Dineen, and L. Robertson, "Toronto Women's Caucus: A Two-Year Experience in a Cross-City Women's Liberation Group," LSA (League for Socialist Action) IDB (Internal Discussion Bulletin), no. 23, December 1972.

71 Limpus, "History of the Toronto Women's Liberation Movement"; Lynne Teather, "The Feminist Mosaic," in *Women in the Canadian Mosaic*, ed. Gwen Matheson (Toronto: Peter Martin Associates, 1976), 330; "The Wave of Feminism Opposes Motherhood, Marriage," *GM*, 1 May 1969; "The Feminists," *TT*, 5 Sept. 1969; "In Toronto: Three Groups Fight to Arouse Women," *TS*, 31 Jan. 1970; Bonnie Kreps, "The 'New Feminist' Analysis," *New Feminist*, 8 Dec. 1969; "Clenched Fist Posters Overlook New Feminist Drop-In Centre," *TT*, 30 April 1970.

72 "Wave of Feminism Opposes Motherhood, Marriage"; "The Feminists"; Kreps, "'New Feminist' Analysis"; "Clenched Fist Posters Overlook New Feminist Drop-In Centre"; Bonnie Kreps, "Radical Feminism 1," in *Women Unite!* 71; "Beyond Sisterhood," *GM*, 2 April 1977.

73 Kreps, "Radical Feminism 1," 75.

74 "The Feminists"; Kreps, "'New Feminist' Analysis."

75 "The Feminists"; "'What Am I Going to Do?' Mother Asks," *GM*, 16 April 1970; "The Feminist Iceberg," *GM*, 23 April 1970; "Clenched Fist Posters Overlook New Feminist Drop-In Centre"; on "cells," see "Metro Women's Groups Don't Back U.S. Action, Plan City Hall Rally," *GM*, 26 Aug. 1970; and letter, Val Perkins, Corresponding Secretary, New Feminists, to Dawn Haites, Women's Liberation Movement Toronto, January 1971.

76 Quoted in "Report on Last Educational Feb. 4: Feminism Today," *TWLM Newsletter*, February 1970.

77 Letter, Val Perkins, Corresponding Secretary, New Feminists, to Dawn Haites, Women's Liberation Movement Toronto, January 1971; "Integration at the Royal York Hotel," *New Feminist*, January 1971; "Judge Remands Feminist's Case," *GM*, 29 April 29, 1971; "Feminism:

A New Logic," *TT*, 27 April 1970; "Complaints, Defacing Lead to Removal of Some Printing House Subway Posters," *GM*, 7 Feb. 1973.

78 Becki L. Ross, *The House That Jill Built: A Lesbian Nation in Formation* (Toronto: University of Toronto Press, 1995), 25; "Beyond Sisterhood," *GM*, 2 April 1977.

79 "Lesbian Educational," *WLMN Newsletter*, April 1971. Political differences within NF were probably facilitated by the group's small cell-based structure.

80 Ross, *House That Jill Built*, 25; "Beyond Sisterhood," *GM*, 2 April 1977.

81 Angus, Dineen, and Robertson, "Toronto Women's Caucus"; "New Women's Liberation Group Formed by the Disenchanted, the Disapproving"; "Metro Women's Groups Don't Back U.S. Action, Plan City Hall Rally," *GM*, 26 Aug. 1970; "Women Tell Their Story Despite Heckling and Jeers," *GM*, 27 Aug. 1970.

82 "Toronto Women's Caucus," n.d., CWMA, 107-Toronto Women's Caucus; "T.W.C. and the Women's Movement as a Multi-Level Struggle," n.d., CWMA 107-Toronto Women's Caucus; Angus, Dineen, and Robertson, "Toronto Women's Caucus."

83 Corileen North and Yvonne Trower, "Letter to Toronto Women's Caucus and/or Women's Liberation Movement as a Whole," Canadian Student Social and Political Organizations, 8-4, William Ready Division of Archives and Research Collections, McMaster University Library.

84 *Guerilla*, no. 5, 1970; "Man the Enemy Is Downtown," *TT*, 1 May 1970; Corileen North (letter), *Guerilla*, no. 9, 1970.

85 "Socialists and Women's Liberation," *Labor Challenge*, 13 April 1971; Angus, Dineen, and Robertson, "Toronto Women's Caucus."

86 "Toronto Women's Caucus," CWMA, Toronto Women's Caucus; Liz Angus, "The Next Step in the Evolution of the Velvet Fist," CWMA, Toronto Women's Caucus.

87 Unsigned, "Reply to the Discussion Paper by Liz Angus on the Next Step in the Evolution of the Velvet Fist," CWMA, Toronto Women's Caucus; Christabelle Sethna and Steve Hewitt, "Clandestine Operations: The Vancouver Women's Caucus, the Abortion Caravan, and the RCMP," *Canadian Historical Review*, 90,3 (September 2009), 470.

88 Liz Angus, "A Reply to the 12-Point Paper Presented by Pat Leslie, Gail Mathias, Gail Arthur, Karen Train, Jill Thompson, Andree Roy, Mary Ellen Clark," CWMA, Toronto Women's Caucus.

89 Angus, Dineen, and Robertson, "Toronto Women's Caucus."

90 Pat Schulz, "Submission to the 1973 LSA/LSO Convention on Women's Liberation: A Counter Document," LSA IDB, no. 32, 11 March 1973.

91 Ibid.

92 Ibid.

93 Ibid.

94 Angus, Dineen, and Robertson, "Toronto Women's Caucus."

95 Ellen, "Infiltration of the Women's Movement by the YS/LSA," *Other Woman*, November-December 1973.

96 Ibid.

97 "Minutes of the General Meeting—October 12," *TWLM Newsletter*, October 1971; "A Paper from the Leila Khaled Collective," in *Feminist Organizing for Change: The Contemporary Women's Movement in Canada*, ed. Nancy Adamson, Linda Briskin, and Margaret McPhail (Toronto: Oxford University Press, 1988), 265–68.

98 "Minutes of the General Meeting—October 12," *TWLM Newsletter*, October 1971.

99 Ibid.

100 Peggy Morton, *They Are Burning, They Are Burning Effigies: Why, Why, Why, Effigies?* (Toronto: Hogtown Press, n.d.); Peggy Morton, "Women's Work Is Never Done ... or the Production, Maintenance and Reproduction of Labour Power" [essay dated January, 1970], in *Women Unite!* 46–68; "A Paper from the Leila Khaled Collective," in *Feminist Organizing for Change*, ed. Adamson, Briskin, and McPhail, 265–68.

101 Sandy Stewart and Anne Darcy, "Report from York University Day Care Centre," October 1970, McMaster University, Ontario Union of Students fonds, 42-women folder.

102 Barb Cameron and Frances Gregory, "A Critical Look at the Conference," *TWLM Newsletter*, May 1971.

103 "New Women's Liberation Group Formed by the Disenchanted, the Disapproving"; "In Toronto: Three Groups Fight to Arouse Women"; "The Feminist Iceberg"; "Man the Enemy Is Downtown"; "Just Jo: Liberation Is Call of Beauty," *GM*, 20 July 1970; "Feminism: A New Logic."

104 Ian Milligan, *Rebel Youth: 1960s Labour Unrest, Young Workers, and New Leftists in English Canada* (Vancouver: UBC Press, 2014), 88; "The Women's Movement Must Not Bar Men," *Varsity*, 4 Oct. 1971; Kathie Johnson (letter), "Women Must Organize without Men Present," *Varsity*, 8 Oct. 1971.

6. Obsolete Communism and Conflicting Visions? Wafflers, Liberals, and New Leninists, 1968–71

1 "Hundreds Climb Fences, Fight Police at Rock Fest," *Toronto Star* (*TS*), 27 June 1970; "Calm Settles on Rock Festival after Violent Start," *TS*, 29 June 1970; "Festival Express: Bashed Heads and Bad Trips," *Globe and Mail* (*GM*), 29 June 1970; "Clashes Don't Faze CNE Chiefs, Willing to Hold Another Festival," *Toronto Telegram* (*TT*), 29 June 1970.

2 "2 Days of Rock Will Cost You $16," *TS*, 24 June 1970; "Music Takes Back Seat to Politics at Festival," *GM*, 29 June 1970.

3 "Leftist Groups Mounting Opposition to Rock Festival," *GM*, 25 June 1970; "2 Days of Rock Will Cost You $16."

4 EATON-WALKER (RIP-OFF) FESTIVAL IS FREE FREE FREE (Yeah) IF WE TAKE IT TAKE IT TAKE IT (Dig It)," poster, McMaster University Archives, Student Social and Political Organizations, 5-17; "New Left Group Calls Festival a 'Rip-Off,'" *GM*, 24 June 1970; "Leftist Groups Mounting Opposition to Rock Festival"; "2 Days of Rock Will Cost You $16"; *Festival Express*, dir. Bob Smeaton and Frank Cvitanovich (2003; Fox Video, 2004), DVD.

5 "Metro Police Cool off Rock Festival Gate-Crashers," *TS*, 29 June 1970; "Calm Settles on Rock Festival after Violent Start," *TS*, 29 June 1970; "Festival Express: Bashed Heads and Bad Trips," *GM*, 29 June 1970; "... and 2,000 Enjoy Free Concert," *TT*, 29 June 1970.

6 *Festival Express*; "Called 'Scum' by Mayor, Promoter Says," *GM*, 11 Nov. 1970; "Rock Festival Reduces Maclean-Hunter Profit," *GM*, 29 July 1970; "Mariposa Crashers Raise Fear of Death for All Mass Concerts," *TS*, 28 July 1970.

7 Abraham L. Feinberg, *Rabbi Feinberg's Hanoi Diary* (Don Mills, Ont.: Longmans, 1968); "An Aged Rebel and the Voice of Youth," *TT*, 23 June 1970; "Feinberg Named Church Rabbi, Backs Angela," *GM*, 14 March 1972; "Hearst Kidnap of 'Great Value': Rabbi Feinberg," *Toronto Sun* (*Sun*), 20 Feb. 1974; "Profile: Chandler Davis," *Random*, February 1967; "A Rough Guide to the

Old Left: How the Co-opted White Bourgeois Swingers Are Finding Their Way Back to the True Path," *Random*, 18 Dec. 1967.

8 "NDP Policy Echos Demands of New Left," *GM*, 10 June 1966; "Lewis Father-Son Team Split as Renwick Elected NDP Head," *TS*, 5 July 1967; "NDP to Emphasize the Rights of Individuals," *TS*, 20 June 1967.

9 Ed Broadbent, *Beyond the Welfare State* (Edmonton, Alta.: Confrontation Publications, n.d. [1969?]).

10 John Bullen, "The Ontario Waffle and the Struggle for an Independent and Socialist Canada: Conflict within the NDP," *Canadian Historical Review*, 83,2 (June 1983), 193–94.

11 "The Waffle Manifesto: For an Independent Socialist Canada (1969)," http://www.socialisthistory.ca/Docs/Waffle/WaffleManifesto.htm (accessed 10 May 2018).

12 Robert Hackett, "Pie in the Sky: A History of the Ontario Waffle," *Canadian Dimension*, October-November 1980.

13 Ibid.; Bullen, "Ontario Waffle," 193–96.

14 Ibid.

15 "NDP to Start Marching and Protesting," *TT*, 30 Jan. 1970; Bullen, " Ontario Waffle," 196–97.

16 Bullen, "Ontario Waffle," 197; Hackett, "Pie in the Sky," 26.

17 Bullen, "Ontario Waffle," 198–200.

18 Ibid., 201; "NDP May Try to Forge Links with Grassroots Groups, Protesters," *GM*, 26 Sept. 1970; "Nationalize Refineries: NDP," *GM*, 3 Oct. 1970.

19 Bullen, "Ontario Waffle," 202–5; Hackett, "Pie in the Sky," 7–8; "Labour in Ontario," July 1970, Gordon Laxer fonds, Clara Thomas Archives and Special Collections, York University, 2009/043/002 (8).

20 Hackett, "Pie in the Sky," 10–13; "Interview with Mel Watkins," *Guerilla*, no. 4, 1971; Reg Whitaker, "Introduction," *Studies in Political Economy*, 32 (Summer 1990), 167; Gregory Albo, "Canada, Left-Nationalism, and Younger Voices," *Studies in Political Economy*, 33 (Autumn 1990), 162.

21 Jackie Larkin, interview, Gordon Laxer fonds, 2009-043/003 (12); Jim Laxer, "Strategy for Organizing in the New Movement," in Ontario Waffle, "Towards a Movement for an Independent Socialist Canada," 1972, Gordon Laxer fonds, 2009-043/00.

22 Paul Craven, Fay McLeod, Norm McLeod, and Joey Noble, "Organizing for Socialism and Independence—The Role of Social Animation," in Ontario Waffle, "Towards a Movement for an Independent Socialist Canada"; Ralph Cook, "Community Organizing," in Ontario Waffle, "Towards a Movement for an Independent Socialist Canada."

23 Jim Littleton, interview, Gordon Laxer fonds, 2009-043/003 (12); "A Student's Garden of Politics," *Varsity*, 18 Sept. 1972.

24 Ulli Diemer, interview; "Parity More Than Just a Liberal Cause" (letter), *Varsity*, 20 Oct. 1971; Linda McQuaig, "U of T Student Radicalism Hits New Low," *Varsity*, 29 Oct. 1971; Ulli Diemer, "Keep Smiling as You Smash the State," *Varsity*, 5 Nov. 1971; Ulli Diemer, "Notes from Underground or Where is the Old Mole?" 14 Nov. 1971, Revolutionary Marxist Group (RMG) Collection, 4-25; Our Generation, "Labour Day Weekend Annual Meeting," 3–5 Sept. 1972, Howard Buchbinder fonds, Clara Thomas Archives, 10–25.

25 "Manitoba Waffle Debates NDP Civic Platform," *Labor Challenge*, 26 July 1971; "NDP Debate Sets Tasks for Party's Left," *Labor Challenge*, 21 Sept. 1970.

26 Cy Gonick, "Revolutionary Reformism: A Strategy," [n.d., probably 1970], Gordon Laxer fonds, 2009-043/005 (10). The document's theoretical underpinnings relied heavily on André Gorz.

27 "How the Left Intervened in the NDP Election Campaign," *Labor Challenge*, 8 Nov. 1971;

"Rally NDP Ranks, Waffle Challenged," *Labor Challenge*, 31 Jan. 1972; editorial, "Where Is Waffle Going?" *Labor Challenge*, 28 Feb. 1972.

28 William Stewart, "Unite to Defeat Tories," *Canadian Tribune* (*CT*), 17 March 1971; William Kashtan, "Some Thoughts on the NDP Convention," *CT*, 5 May 1971.

29 "Petty-Bourgeois Revolutionism and Reformism," *Communist Viewpoint*, May-June 1970; "Professor's Version of Labor History," *CT*, 10 May 1972; "'Democracy on the Job,'" *CT*, 12 March 1975.

30 "Are Students So Special," *CT*, 6 Nov. 1968; Don Currie, "Need Sober Analysis of Student Movement," *CT*, 2 Jan. 1969; Stanley Ryerson, "For Broader Approaches," *69 Convention* [discussion bulletin], 26 Feb. 1969, Clarke fonds, 2-18; Sam Walsh, "Three Points of Difference with Comrade Stanley Ryerson," *69 Convention*, 14 March 1969, Clarke fonds 2-18.

31 Communist Party of Canada, *Canada's Party of Socialism: History of the Communist Party of Canada, 1921–1976* (Toronto: Progress Books, 1982): 239–41, 237, 242–43.

32 "...Towards Trudeau's Participatory Democracy," *Obiter Dicta*, 9 Oct. 1968.

33 "Great 'Red' Conspiracy Aired," *Ryersonian*, 21 Sept. 1967; "Janet Weir Is Alive in Etobicoke, Engaged, Teaching," *Ryersonian*, 5 Nov. 1968; "Sty on Eyeopener," *Ryersonian*, 23 Sept. 1970.

34 "Student Liberals Split on Involvement," *TT*, 22 Feb. 1969; "Young Liberals Want Senior Party Vote at 14," *TT*, 13 Jan. 1969; "Youth Increases Party Hold," *TT*, 27 Jan. 1969.

35 "Student Pull-Out Threat over 'Disenfranchised,'" *TT*, 3 Nov. 1969; "OSL to Help Poor," *Ryersonian*, 7 Nov. 1969.

36 "Student Pull-Out Threat over 'Disenfranchised.'"

37 Tim Reid and Julyan Reid, eds., *Student Power and the Canadian Campus* (Toronto: Peter Martin Associates, 1969); "OSL to Help Poor," *Ryersonian*, 7 Nov. 1969; "Young Liberals: 'We Give a Damn!'" *Ryersonian*, 7 Nov. 1969; "Visions of the Future," *Random*, 30 Nov. 1967.

38 "Clarkson Sees Priority Need for Transit," *TT*, 14 Oct. 1969; "Clarkson Challenged on His 'Silence' over Expropriation," *TT*, 7 Nov. 1969; "Choice between People or Cars, Says Clarkson," *TT*, 10 Nov. 1969.

39 "Charting the Path of Party Power," *GM*, 26 Aug. 1969.

40 "Trudeau to Face Angry Student Liberals," *TT*, 5 Feb. 1970; "Thanks to All, Campus Liberals Had a Bad, Bad Day," *TT*, 2 March 1970.

41 "Student Liberals Call for Legal Pot," *TT*, 7 July 1970; "Toronto Liberals Want Legal Marijuana," *TT*, 18 Sept. 1970.

42 "Toronto Liberals Want Legal Marijuana"; "City Liberals Back Student's Jail Reform Plans," *TT*, 18 Sept. 1970; "City Liberal Delegates Push Economic Nationalism," *TT*, 21 Nov. 1970.

43 "Toronto Liberals Attack Ottawa," *TT*, 19 May 1971; "City Liberals Protest Party Platform," *TT*, 30 Jan. 1971.

44 "Peace March Ends in Fight with Rightists," *TS*, 29 April 1968; "Clash at U.S. Consulate," *TT*, 29 April 1968; "Nine Arrested during Demonstrations on Vietnam," *GM*, 29 April 1968.

45 "Nine Arrested during Demonstrations on Vietnam."

46 Editorial, *CNLF Bulletin*, May 1968.

47 Peter Rosenthal, "What Happened on April 27?" *CNLF Bulletin*, May 1968; Tom DeCastro, "Trotskyite Betrayal on April 27th: A Personal Account," *CNLF Bulletin*, May 1968; PST, "The 'Vanguard' and 'Tribune' Comment on the 27th ... and a Slight Reply," *CNLF Bulletin*, May 1968; "The Bogs of Opportunism," n.d., Canadian Liberation Movement (CLM) fonds, 15-6, William Ready Division of Archives and Research Collections, McMaster University Library; "Our Tactics in the Past Year," n.d., CLM fonds, 16-4. Fanon's best-known work is *The*

Wretched of the Earth, trans. Constance Farrington (New York: Grove Press, 1968), first published in French as *Les Damnés de la Terre* in 1961.

48 Bryan D. Palmer, ed., *A Communist Life: Jack Scott and the Canadian Workers Movement 1927–1985* (St. John's: Committee on Canadian Labour History, 1988): 158–59, 161.

49 "Canadian Workers Reject Agents of American Nazis," *Left Leaf*, 1 July 1965.

50 Ibid.; Mance Mathias, "The Auto Parts Pact," *Left Leaf*, October 1965; R. Kiner, "The Man Who Had to Hang," *Left Leaf*, October 1965; "Birds of a Feather," *Left Leaf*, Winter 1966.

51 Palmer, *Communist Life*, 161; "Leftist Groups Demonstrate over Viet Nam, Race Riots," *TS*, 16 Aug. 1965; "Left-Wing Radicals Picket Communists," *GM*, 23 May 1966; "Trade Union Experiences in PWM," CLM fonds, 15-6.

52 "Trade Union Experiences in PWM." For a different version of this event, see *Kevin Hendley's A Life Full of Lies* website: kevinhenley.blogspot.ca/2012/08/a-socialist-in-toronto-next-summer-i.html (accessed 3 April 2014).

53 *CNLF Bulletin*, 17 Nov. 1967; *CNLF Bulletin*, 1 Jan. 1968; *CNLF Bulletin*, April 1968; *CNLF Bulletin*, September 1968.

54 After CNLF formed, the PWM branch appeared to split, with a strong majority hewing closer to the political line of the Progressive Labor Party (PLP), a U.S.-based party that had formerly been allied to the Canadian group.

55 *CNLF Bulletin*, June 1968; "Notes toward a Working Paper for C.N.L.F.," *CNLF Bulletin*, June 1968.

56 "A Review of Two CNLF Seminars," *CNLF Bulletin*, July 1968; Steve Moore, "The Poor People's Campaign," *CNLF Bulletin*, July 1968.

57 *CNLF Bulletin*, September 1968; "Canadian Independence Movement Formed," *CNLF Bulletin*, October 1968.

58 Chandler Davis, "Canada Is Not Vietnam," *CNLF Bulletin*, September 1968; Bill Lewis, "A Worker's Reply," *CNLF Bulletin*, September 1968.

59 "Bogs of Opportunism."

60 Ibid.

61 Ibid.

62 "Police Block Yonge St. March," *TS*, 28 Oct. 1968; "34 Arrested Protesting Vietnam War," *GM*, 28 Oct. 1968; "Why We Are Holding Our Own Demonstration," *CNLF Bulletin*, October 1968; "Political Opportunism on Oct. 26," *CNLF Bulletin*, November 1968.

63 "The NLF Is Coming to Toronto," *CNLF Bulletin*, November 1968; "In This Issue," *CNLF Bulletin*, February 1969; "C.P. Goons Try to Oust N.L.F. Flags," *CNLF Bulletin*, February 1969.

64 "Students: Don't Sell Them Short," *Canadian Worker*, 1-2, 1969; "It Pays to Fight," *Canadian Worker*, 1-1, 1969. *Canadian Worker* was officially monthly (although it never had twelve issues a year). At some point in 1973 it was rebranded *The Worker* (maintaining the prior newspaper's volume and issue number sequence).

65 "The Party and Student Struggle," n.d., CLM fonds, 15-6; "Wernick & Co Do Their Thing to TSM," *Canadian Worker*, October 1969.

66 "The Student 'Leader' as Uncle Tom," *CNLF Bulletin*, October 1968; Steve Moore, Tony Leah, and Paddy Ryle, "The Wiener Strike," n.p., n.d., CLM fonds, 23-14; Perry Anderson, *Components of the National Culture* (Toronto: Canadian Labour Party [Marxist-Leninist], n.d.); Robin Blackburn, *Inequity and Exploitation* (Toronto: Canadian Labour Party [Marxist-Leninist], n.d.); André Gunder Frank, *Functionalism, Dialectics and Synthetics* (Toronto: Canadian Labour Party [Marxist-Leninist], n.d.).

67 Moore, Leah, and Ryle, "Wiener Strike"; "Women's Liberation and Class Politics," n.d., CLM fonds, 15-6.

68 "Wernick & Co Do Their Thing to TSM"; Bill Johnson, "Bad Marx for 'New Left,'" *Canadian Worker*, October 1969; "Campus Workers, Students Unite!" *Canadian Worker*, February 1970; "New College Struggle Continues," *Canadian Worker*, March 1970; "Students Ally with Hospital Workers," *Canadian Worker*, March 1970; "Students: Don't Sell Them Short, *Canadian Worker*, 1-2, 1969; "End of an Era," *Canadian Worker*, May 1969; "Imperialism and the University," n.d., CLM fonds, 15-6.

69 Bill Johnston, Bob Dewart, and Steve Moore, "The Student Movement and Class Politics," *Canadian Worker*, October 1969.

70 "Easy Rider," *Canadian Worker*, August 1970; "Joe, an Oscar for Fascism," *Canadian Worker*, December 1970; "MASH Is Anti-Worker Trash," *Canadian Worker*, November 1970; "Class View of Movie 2001," *Canadian Worker*, May 1969; "How the Movies Are Fixed," *Canadian Worker*, December 1970; "Goin' Down the Road: A Dead End," *Canadian Worker*, September 1970.

71 "U of T Students Fight for Daycare," *Canadian Worker*, May 1970.

72 "4000 Vote to Strike," *Canadian Worker*, March 1971.

73 "Workers Struggles Grow, Nationalists a Shambles," *Canadian Worker*, November 1971; *Canadian Worker* (letter), May 1970; "A Greek-Canadian Worker, Our Struggle Is Here," *Canadian Worker*, July 1970; "Capitalism and the Immigrant Worker (Part 3)," *Canadian Worker*, September 1971.

74 "Language Classes," *Canadian Worker*, August 1971; *Canadian Worker*, November 1971; "Western Strike Victory against Racism," *Canadian Worker*, August 1972; "Straight from the Boss's Mouth," *Canadian Worker*, August 1970; "Workers Steal Show from NDP Phonies," *Canadian Worker*, May 1970; "Left-Wing Boss-Unionism," *Canadian Worker*, August 1970; "May Day March for Jobs," *Canadian Worker*, April 1971; "Laxer Less 'Independent' and 'Socialist,'" *Canadian Worker*, July 1972; "NDP Brass Gets Tough with Waffle; Laxer, Watkins Wage Half a Fight," *Canadian Worker*, August 1972; "Laxer, Watkins Flop as Red-Baiters," *Canadian Worker*, October 1972; "Laxer, Watkins Set Course for Nationalist Socialist Canada," *Canadian Worker*, December 1972.

75 Canadian Workers Project Century: 2, "Principles and Draft Program," n.d., 15, 24, 27, 54, 61, CLM fonds, 15-24; "Requiem for Liberal Radicalism," *The Nationalist*, August 1969; "Beyond Strawberry Fields," *The Nationalist*, 22 Aug. 1970.

76 Principles and Draft Program," 22, 25, 29, 46, 51, 56.

77 Ibid., 60.

78 "The Struggle for a Canadian Conscience," *The Nationalist*, 22 Aug. 1970; "Requiem for Liberal Radicalism, Part II," *The Nationalist*, December 1969.

79 "Requiem for Liberal Radicalism, Part II."

80 "Protesters Fight, Shatter Windows during Downtown Toronto Chase," *GM*, 11 May 1970; Poster, Canadian Student Social and Political Organizations, 5-17, William Ready Division of Archive and Research Collections; "Policeman Knocked Down," *TS*, 15 May 1970.

81 "Protesters Fight, Shatter Windows during Downtown Toronto Chase"; "U.S. Agitators Had Key Role," *TT*, 11 May 1970; "8-Block Area Was Storm Centre," *TT*, 11 May 1970.

82 "Metro's Militant Reds Aiming at 'People's Rule,'" *TT*, 12 May 1970; "May Fourth Movement, Student Social and Political Organizations," 5-17, William Ready Division of Archives and Research Collections, McMaster University Library.

83 "M4M Organizes Locally," *Chevron*, 12 June 1970; *Red Morning*, no. 2; *Red Morning*, no. 4 (early spring 1971); Judy Pocock, interview, 16 Oct. 2011, Toronto.

84 *Red Morning*, no. 2; "A Message to the People from Red Morning on Why Youth Will Make the Revolution," *Red Morning*, no. 6 (Summer 1971); Dennis Corcoran (letter), *Guerilla*, no. 5, 31 (July 1970); "We Live in the Cities," *Red Morning*, no. 2.

85 *Guerrilla*, no. 12 (11 Nov. 1970); "Speed," *Red Morning*, no.3; "We Live in the Cities," *Red Morning*, no. 2.

86 "The Angry Sounds of Protest," *GM*, 4 March 1971; "Taking It to the Streets," *Red Morning*, no. 4 (Early Spring 1971).

87 Pocock, interview; "Red Morning: What We're About," *Red Morning*, no.6 (Summer 1971).

88 Interview with Gerald Dunn, Toronto, 16 Sept. 2011.

89 Peggy Morton, *They Are Burning, They Are Burning Effigies: Why, Why, Why, Effigies?* (Toronto: Hogtown Press, n.d.), 1.

90 Ibid., 1, 11, 25–26. In line with RM's approach of encouraging full-time revolutionaries, Morton wrote that daycare struggles were only useful if victories allowed revolutionary cadre to devote themselves to organizing and not waste time on some foggy conception of building a mass movement. Women, she argued, should not waste their time and energy in the workforce, even if part of that time was spent organizing a union. In North America most struggles were outside the workplace and youth and women, rather than white male industrial proletarians, were "in the vanguard of the struggle to barbeque the imperialist hog." See Ibid., 9, 23–26.

91 *Red Morning*, no.2; *Red Morning*, no.3; Pocock interview.

92 "Demonstrators Break 15 Display Windows at Department Store," *GM*, 18 Oct. 1971; "Eaton's Windows Smashed by Rioters," *TS*, 18 Oct. 1971; "Red Morning at Eatons," *Guerilla*, no. 2-19.

93 *Guerilla*, no. 2-20.

94 "Jim K.'s Self Criticism," RMG fonds, 4-21.

95 Hardial Bains, *Thinking about the Sixties: 1960–1967* (Toronto: The New Magazine Publishing Company, 2006): 47, 54–59, 67.

96 Ibid., 81–90. Aspects of the SUPA conference that had troubled Bains surfaced within the Internationalists, as their formerly staid conferences and weekend retreats devolved into "instruments of pleasure" replete with drugs and "other forms of degeneration." Bains and his followers appeared to then disassociate themselves from the Vancouver group. See Bains, *Thinking about the Sixties*, 95.

97 Ibid., 100–3, 111–12, 116–17, 132–33; Communist Party of Canada (Marxist-Leninist), *Documents: Political Report 1970; Political Report 1973* (Communist Party of Canada [Marxist-Leninist], 1976), 15.

98 Hardial Bains, *Necessity for Change* (Ottawa: Communist Party of Canada [Marxist-Leninist], 1998 [first edition 1967]), 27–31, 54.

99 Ibid., 56–60, 63. This view of Marxists did not apply to anti-imperialists in the global South.

100 Ibid., 31, 35–36, 39–40, 45–48, 61–62.

101 Ibid., 19, 14.

102 Organization of Communist Workers (Marxist-Leninist), *The Movement for the Party* (n.p., 1976), 40; citation from *Mass Line*, 13 March 1971.

103 "Introducing the Necessity for Change Institute of Ideological Studies," *Literature & Ideology*, Fall 1969; Pauline Kogan, "Two Lines in the Teaching of Macbeth," *Literature & Ideology*, Fall 1969.

104 "Denounce U.S. Imperialist 'Youth Culture,'" CLM fonds, 17-16; "Summing up the Resistance Movement," *People's Canada Daily News*, 9 Oct. 1970.

105 "The Maoists," *TS*, 30 May 1970.

106 "Here and Now," *Varsity*, 1 Nov. 1968; "Here and Now," *Varsity*, 10 Jan. 1969; Andy Wernick, "A Guide to the Student Left," *Varsity*, 24 Sept. 1969.

107 "Maoists, Police Clash in Ottawa; 16 Arrested," *GM*, 20 April 1970; "War Theme at Peace Rally," *TT*, 2 March 1970; "1,500 Peace Marchers Clash with Maoists," *TT*, 2 March 1970; "The Maoists," *TS*, 30 May 1970.

108 "'Revolution Will Start in the Streets,'" *TS*, 30 May 1970.

109 *The CPC(ML): A Revisionist Organization of Agent-Provocateurs* (Montreal: In Struggle, 1978), 110; "Hospital Dishwasher on Hunger Strike," *TT*, 4 March 1970; "Charge Laid over Dishwasher," *TT*, 5 March 1970; "Girl, 22, Is Arrested for Row at Hospital," *GM*, 26 March 1970; "Remand Dishwasher on Vagrancy Charge," *GM*, 1 April 1970; "Hospital Hunger-Striker Given Day in Court, Fires Lawyer, Denies All," *TT*, 18 April 1970.

110 "In Hamilton: Comrades Robert A. Cruise and Tom Bates on 'Trial,'" *People's Canada Daily News*, 28 Aug. 1970.

111 "300 Who Seek the Revolution," *GM*, 7 Aug. 1970.

112 Ibid.; *People's Canada Daily News*, 11 Oct. 1970; "'Blood Debts Will Be Repaid in Blood!'" *People's Canada Daily News*, 9 Oct. 1970; "Hamilton, Ontario, an Armed Camp," *People's Canada Daily News*, 16 Oct. 1970.

113 "In Hamilton: Upsurge in Support of R.A. Cruise," *People's Canada Daily News*, 14 Oct. 1970; "Hamilton, Ontario, an Armed Camp."

114 "Hamilton, Ontario, an Armed Camp"; "Summing up the Resistance Movement," *People's Canada Daily News*, 9 Oct. 1970.

115 Daniel Goldstick, "The Student Left To-day," *Canadian Jewish Outlook*, December 1969. Lennon and Ono's statement was that "War is over if you want it."

116 Ibid.; "300 Who Seek the Revolution." See the chapter on the Internationalists in Roger Laurence O'Toole, "The Sociology of Political Sects: Four Sects in Toronto in 1968–1969," Ph.D. thesis, University of Toronto, 1972.

117 "Demonstrators Fiercely Resist Fascist Police," *People's Canada Daily News*, 22 Sept. 1970; Communist Party of Canada (Marxist-Leninist), *On Unity of Marxist-Leninists* (Communist Party of Canada [Marxist-Leninist], 1976), 13; *Documents: Political Report 1970; Political Report 1973*, 118.

118 "Denounce Indira Gandhi's 'Visit' to Canada," *North American News Service*, 28 May–17 June 1973.

119 "Hindustani Ghadar Party Formed!" *Chingari*, 1970. HGP gave political and material support to the Communist Party of India (Marxist-Leninist.) That party had become virtually synonymous with the Naxalite movement, a popular term for the armed guerrilla struggle in India. HGP acted as the international arm of CPI-ML; its followers were essentially considered members of the Indian party.

120 See Jim O'Brien, "American Leninism in the 1970s," *Radical America*, November 1977/February 1978; Charles Sarkis, ed., *What Went Wrong: Articles and Letters on the US Communist Left in the 1970s* (New York: United Labor Press, 1982); Jean-Philippe Warren, *Ils voulaient changer le monde: le militantisme marxiste-léniniste au Québec* (Montreal : VLB éditeur, 2007); Pierre Milot, *Le paradigme rouge : l'avant-garde politico-littéraire des années 70* (Candiac: Éditions Balzac, 1992).

121 An early activist history of the new left in Canada stated that it had been "absolutely permeated" with Maoist ideas. See Tina Craig, "A Brief History of the Canadian New Left," *Old Mole*, 13 Sept. 1972.

7. "We Must All Be Politicians": Community Concerns and Urban Resistance, 1971–78

1 Danielle Robinson, "'The Streets Belong to the People': Expressway Disputes in Canada, c.1960–75," Ph.D. thesis, McMaster University, 2012, 32.

2 Ibid., 44–45.

3 Ibid., 43. The expressway was eventually built only as far south as Eglinton Avenue.

4 Ibid., 65, 69.

5 Ibid., 42–43.

6 Paul Weinberg, "The Praxis Affair: There's a Reason We Put limits on Spying within Canada," *CPPA Bulletin*, 1 March 2015.

7 Ibid.; "New Paper Hit by Fire," *Contrast*, 27 April 1978; "Play about Chile Gets Burned Out," *Toronto Sun* (*Sun*), 6 Nov. 1974; "Communist HQ Levelled," *Canadian Tribune* (*CT*), 30 June 1980; "Arson at Arab Centre," *Arab Dawn*, February 1975.

8 Michael S. Cross, "In Search of Ideology: Opposition Politics in Toronto," *Canadian Forum*, May 1972; Alan Powell, "Toronto City Politics: Making Strange Bedfellows," *Canadian Forum*, April-May 1975.

9 Graham Fraser, *Fighting Back: Urban Renewal in Trefann Court* (Toronto: Hakkert, 1972); James Lorimer and Myfawny Phillips, *Working People: Life in a Downtown City Neighbourhood* (Toronto: James Lewis & Samuel, 1971); John Sewell, *How We Changed Toronto: The Inside Story of Twelve Creative, Tumultuous Years in Civic Life, 1969–1980* (Toronto: James Lorimer & Company, 2015), 67.

10 Kevin Brushett, "Blots on the Face of the City: The Politics of Slum Housing and Urban Renewal in Toronto, 1940–1970," Ph.D. thesis, Queen's University, 2001, 619, 479–80; "800 E. York Tenants Protest Angrily over Rising Rents," *Toronto Star* (*TS*), 22 Feb. 1968.

11 "Pro-Spadina Group Protests Traffic Flow," *Toronto Telegram* (*TT*), 1 Oct. 1971; [untitled picture], *TT*, 18 Oct. 1971; "Hint of Bus Routes for Spadina," *Sun*, 16 Dec. 1971; "Parkway Blockade Urged," *Sun*, 13 Oct. 1972; "Approval of Spadina Expressway Was the Beginning of the Highway to Nowhere," *TS*, 21 Oct. 2016.

12 "Some Design Work Already Done on the Scarborough Expressway," *Globe and Mail* (*GM*), 5 April, 1972; "Scarborough Expressway Plan Won't Be Cut Back, Cass Says," *GM*, 27 July 1973; "Ward 9 Residents Ask for Public Study of Gardiner Extension," *GM*, 11 March 1971; "New Route Would Save 600 Homes," *GM*, 9 Aug. 1973.

13 "Scarborough Expressway Foes Say They'll Fight," *TS*, 7 Sept. 1973; "Expressway Would Ruin Riverdale, Pastor Says," *TS*, 21 Nov. 1973; "Will People in the East End Trust the Planners?" *GM*, 23 Feb. 1970; "GRO 'Declares War' on Godfrey over Expressway," *GM*, 11 Sept. 1973.

14 "Plans to Build Scarborough Expressway Fade Away as Former Boosters Switch to Ranks of Opponents," *GM*, 10 Sept. 1973.

15 "Godfrey Sent Regrets, Expressway Opponents Confront Him at Home," *GM*, 30 Aug. 1973; "Godfrey Bans Expressway Vote," *GM*, 7 Sept. 1973; editorial, "Where Have All the Support-

ers Gone?" *TS*, 21 Nov. 1973; "Godfrey Supports Soberman Stand on Killing Freeway," *TS*, 9 March 1974.

16 Editorial, "Fast Road Links Are Essential," *TS*, 15 June 1972; editorial, "One Spadina Folly Is Quite Enough," *TS*, 10 May 1973; editorial, "Road through the Eastern Gate," *TS*, 3 July 1973; editorial, "Don't Cut Back on Pickering Plans," *TS*, 23 Oct. 1973.

17 *Ward 8 News*, 14 Dec. 1979; Himani Bannerji, "New Film Is Mindless, Sentimental, Commercial," *Ward 8 News*, 17 Aug. 1978.

18 Tom Walkom, "What to Do with the *Clarion?*" February 1977, Toronto Clarion fonds, 1287, series 552, box 144469, Toronto Public Library Archives.

19 Editorial, "Voting: Love It or Leave It," *Toronto Clarion*, November 1978; editorial, "Vote NDP. But Real Change Comes from Our Own Organizing," *Toronto Clarion*, 16–29 May, 1979.

20 Jennifer Marguerite Keck, "Making Work: Federal Job Creation Policy in the 1970s," Ph.D. thesis, University of Toronto, 1995, 140, 201–2, 169, 186, 207–9; "Youth Program Has 'Farm for Street Freaks,'" *TT*, 17 June 1971; "Brand-New Community Paper in Ward 8," *Ward 8 News*, 28 Feb. 1978; see Erna Koffman, *The Big Rip-Off* (Toronto: SAANNES Publications, 1972).

21 Keck, "Making Work," 140, 202–2, 169, 186, 207–9; "Community Groups Scramble for Funds," *Seven News*, 18 June 1977; "About This Issue," *City Magazine*, March 1977.

22 Paul Weinberg, "Toronto Elections: The Choice Is Clear," *Pro Tem*, 29 Nov. 1972.

23 Ibid.

24 George Martell, "Community Control of the Schools," *This Magazine Is About Schools*, Summer 1970, 25.

25 See Jack Granatstein, *Marlborough Marathon: One Street Against a Developer* (Toronto: James Lewis & Samuel, 1971).

26 Howard Buchbinder and Gerry Hunnius, "The Politics of Change," Buchbinder fonds, Clara Thomas Archive, York University, 1994-026/007-9, ch. 1, 2–5, 8–11, 23. [Each chapter of this book manuscript has its own pagination.]

27 Ibid., ch. 2, 1–12; ch. 3: 1, 18–20; ch. 4: 1–7, 13–19, 26, 36, 51.

28 Ibid., ch. 5, 4–5, 18–19.

29 Howard Buchbinder, "Participation, Control and the E.P.O.," *Our Generation*, September 1971; "Community Action and the Workplace: A Strategy for Change," *Our Generation*, 8,3 (1972); Dimitrios Roussopoulos, "A Community Control Strategy," *Our Generation*, 9,1 (1973); "Howard Buchbinder Replies," *Our Generation*, 9,1 (1973).

30 Sara Rothschild, "Grass-Roots Cells, Devil's Architects Defend Communities" (book review), *Varsity*, 2 Feb. 1973; "Participation Described as Liberal Buy-Off," *Varsity*, 5 Feb. 1973, reporting the views of Lorimer; James Lorimer, "Canada's Urban Experts: Smoking out the Liberals," *City Magazine*, October 1974; Wayne Roberts, "The Limitations of the Reformers," *Varsity*, 1 Dec. 1972; Warren Magnusson, "Metropolitan Reform in the Capitalist City," *Canadian Journal of Political Science*, 24,3 (September 1981), 557–58; "The Myth of Citizen Control," *Seven News*, 26 May 1972.

31 Eric Blair, "Suburbs Overshadow Crombie," *Last Post*, October-November 1974.

32 John R. Graham, "A History of the University of Toronto School of Social Work," Ph.D. thesis, University of Toronto, 1996, 179–80; Brian Wharf, ed., *Social Work and Social Change in Canada* (Don Mills, Ont.: Oxford University Press, 1999), 17–18.

33 See R. Schechter, "Conflict Resolution: A Participant Observation Study of the Provisional Committee of the Cowan Avenue Firehall in Parkdale," n.d., Parkdale Library Community

Collection, Book IV; "Commie hangout" in "Aldermen Defy People's Democratic Decision," *Parkdale Tenant*, 21 Feb. 1976.

34 Meg Luxton, "A Study of Urban Communes and Co-ops in Toronto," M.A. thesis, University of Toronto, 1973, 66, 69–70, 76.

35 Ibid., 26–27, 30–31, 66, 69–70, 76.

36 Ibid., 5, 13, 15; "Commune on McCaul St.: The Warm Alternative," *TT*, 23 Jan. 1971; Maureen Hynes, interview, 5 Aug. 2011, Toronto; Norman Rogers, interview, 27 Sept. 2011, Toronto.

37 "Pigpens? The Lady Was Uninformed," *TT*, 23 Jan. 1971.

38 Luxton, "Study of Urban Communes and Co-ops in Toronto," 16, 43–47.

39 Rogers, interview.

40 Myrna Kostash, *Long Way from Home: The Story of the Sixties Generation in Canada* (Toronto: James Lorimer & Company, 1980), 18; Margarida Marquez, untitled, Toronto Women's Liberation Movement, Canadian Women's Movement Archives (CWMA) fonds, University of Ottawa Archives and Special Collections; "In Toronto: Three Groups Fight to Arouse Women," *TS*, 31 Jan. 1970; *Alternative to Alienation*, no. 5 (January-February 1975).

41 Judy Pocock, interview, 16 Oct. 2011, Toronto; "Red Morning: What We're About," *Red Morning*, 6 (Summer 1971); Dunn interview.

42 "Report of the Co-ordinating Committee to the Second Annual Convention of the Movement for Municipal reform," Toronto Public Library, Clarke Collection, 27, ReforMetro folder.

43 "Woman, 85, on Front Line of Apartment Rent Picket," *TT*, 2 April 1970; "Allow Anti-Landlord Sign but Tenants Can't Collect Rent," *GM*, 5 May 1970; "Tenant Threat over Saunas," *TT*, 23 March 1970.

44 "Rent Strike Is Renewed," *Varsity*, 16 Nov. 1970; "Residents Become Guerrillas," *Varsity*, 16 Dec. 1970; "OSHC Says No to Tenants Association," *Varsity*, 12 March 1971; [untitled], *Varsity*, 26 March 1971; "All Quiet on the Married Front," *Varsity*, 22 Oct. 1971.

45 Steven Langdon, "Tenants Try for Participatory Democracy," *TS*, 11 Feb. 1970.

46 David Smiley, interview, 20 Sept. 2011, Toronto.

47 "Metro-Wide Tenant Group," *TT*, 9 July 1969; "End the Small Landlord: Tenants," *TT*, 12 Jan. 1970.

48 "U of T Man Heads Ontario Tenants," *TT*, 30 June 1969; "Rent Strike New Sign of the Times," *TT*, 14 Feb. 1969; "Judge Calls Rent Strike 'Revolution,'" *TT*, 20 March 1969.

49 "400 'Tenant Power' Marchers Boo Randall," *TT*, 4 Oct. 1969; "NDP Organized Tenant March, Randall Charges," *TT*, 7 Oct. 1969; "'Obscene' Poster Passed to Police," *TT*, 12 Oct. 1969.

50 "Head of Tenants' Group Quits in Huff," *TT*, 1 March 1971. Young Socialist Dick Fidler and future *Ward 7 News* editor Norman Browne were the other MTA members on the OTA executive.

51 "Rent Strikers Plan March," *Labour Challenge*, 5 Oct. 1970; "OHC Bows to Protesting Regent Park Marchers," *TT*, 29 Jan. 1970; "OHC Tenants Storm Randall's Office, Win Probe into Complaints," *TT*, 4 Feb. 1970; "The Struggle of Tenants to Share in Management," *GM*, 2 Feb. 1970; "How Far Will the Tenant Participation Inquiry Go?" *GM*, 16 March 1970; "Angry Blake St. Tenants Plan OHC Sit-in," *TT*, 30 May 1970; "The Community Organizers," *Riverdale Review*, 11 June 1970; "Fence off OHC 'Instant Slum,' Bain Ave. Asks," *TT*, 26 May 1970; "The Bain Ave. Iron Curtain Hurts," *TT*, 28 May 1970.

52 "Tenants Attack OHC Attitude," *TT*, 18 June 1970.

53 Editorial, "Why Not Tenants on the Board?" *TT*, 29 May 1971; editorial, "Tenants on the

Board," *TT*, 9 Sept. 1971; Crombie Blows Stack at Eviction Hearing, *Toronto Clarion*, 9–23 Feb. 1977; Ottawa Fancies Tenant-Landlords, *Sun*, 15 July 1977.

54 "Metro Tenants' Group Bids to Force Rent Controls," *Sun*, 6 June 1973; "Campaign Launched for Action on Rent Controls," *CT*, 20 June 1973; "Citizens' Committee Wants Ontario Legislation to Control Rents," *GM*, 28 March 1974; "Tenants Plan March to Get Rent Freeze," *Sun*, 20 June 1974; "Toronto Wants to Restrict Rents to 5% Maximum Annual Increases," *GM*, 21 March 1975; "Make Landlord Justify Eviction, Tenants Demand," *GM*, 17 May 1975; "Growing Pressure for Rent-Control," *GM*, 24 May 1975; "Tenants' Task Force Faces Council's Knife after Alderman's Memo," *GM*, 12 June 1975; "Rents Board Proposed," *Sun*, 19 June 1975; "Tenants' Group Not Fooled by 'Pre-election Gimmick,'" *Sun*, 1 Aug. 1975.

55 Steve Amsel (letter), *CT*, 24 May 1976; "Tenants Organize New Association," *CT*, 31 June 1974; Federation of Metro Tenant Associations (FMTA), Annual Meeting, 21 Oct. 1977, FMTA "Archive" (unlabelled and unsorted boxes); FMTA, Membership List, c.1987, FMTA "Archive."

56 Toronto Community Press Service, "Co-operative Housing May Lower Inner City Shelter Costs," *Seven News*, 25 Nov. 1972; Virginia Smith, "Housing, Education . . . The Forgotten Issues," *Toronto Clarion*, 1 June 1977.

57 Janice Dineen, *The Trouble with Co-ops* (Toronto: Green Tree Publishing Company, 1974), 47, 49.

58 "New Housing Co-op Seeks CMHC Funding," *Seven News*, 28 July 1973; "Forward 9 Elections," *Ward 9 Community News*, 3 July 1973; "New Housing Co-op for Main-Gerrard," *Ward 9 Community News*, 24 Sept. 1974; "Local People Form Ward Housing Co-op," *Ward 9 Community News*, 8 May 1973; "Co-ops: Problems and Promise," *Toronto Clarion*, 4 Jan. 1978.

59 Dineen, *Trouble with Co-ops*, 55, 23, 34, 135, 140.

60 Ibid., 89–103, 107, 112.

61 "A Landlord's Tactics: Blaming Tenants for Rent Increases," *Seven News*, 28 April 1973; "Bain Avenue Tenants Fight Condominium Proposal," *Seven News*, 23 March 1974; "City Buys Bain Ave. Project for Tenants," *Seven News*, 4 May 1974.

62 "Bain Co-op Hit by Rent Strike," *Seven News*, 12 Feb. 1977; "Bain Co-op OK's Evictions," *Seven News*, 26 Feb. 1977; "Bain Gets Control," *Seven News*, 17 Dec. 1977; "If You Can't Beat Them Change the Rules!" *Bain Avenue Tenant's Voice*, May 1977.

63 Michael Goldrick, "The Anatomy of Urban Reform in Toronto," *City Magazine*, May-June 1978.

64 Jon Caulfield, *The Tiny Perfect Mayor* (Toronto: James Lorimer & Company, 1974), viii, 4, 22–24; Sewell, *How We Changed Toronto*, 67.

65 Rae Murphy, "The 'Greening' of Toronto . . . and the Paving of Ontario," *Last Post*, March 1973; James Lorimer, "Canada's Urban Experts: Smoking out the Liberals," *City Magazine*, October 1974.

66 K. Crooke, Interview with William Dennison, 1975, Woodsworth Memorial Collection, box 59, Thomas Fisher Rare Book Library; "11 Candidates Backed by Labor Elected to 23-Man City Council," *GM*, 6 Dec. 1966; editorial, "The Fretful Candidate," *GM*, 19 Oct. 1966; "Dennison Lacks Courage to Admit Tax Truths, Givens Says," *GM*, 25 Nov. 1966; "Two Candidates Back Sunday Liquor Serving," *GM*, 26 Nov. 1966; "A Political Son of Snake River," *GM*, 27 Sept. 1966; "The Crumbling of a Legend," *TT*, 6 Nov. 1969; "That Amazing Change of Heart," *TT*, 30 July 1969.

67 "Dennison's Refusal to Wear Party Label Nearly Ruins NDP Campaign in Toronto," *GM*, 8 Sept. 1969; "Dennison Shocked 'Hardly Believing,'" *TT*, 4 June 1971; "Dennison Scorns 'Bike-City'

Idea," *TT*, 3 Nov. 1970; "We Need Cash for Expressways, Not Subway: Mayor," *TT*, 29 June 1971; "Lampy Won't Oppose Mayor Dennison, Will Run for Alderman," *GM*, 19 Sept. 1969; "The Crumbling of a Legend," *TT*, 6 Nov. 1969; editorial, "No Toronto Wall," *TT*, 27 Jan. 1971; editorial cartoon, *TT*, 27 Jan. 1971; "Who Is the Basic Torontonian?" *GM*, 21 May 1969.

68 "Too Much Citizen Power a Threat to City—Mayor," *TT*, 2 May 1970; "City Refuses Grants to 2 Groups," *TT*, 22 Oct. 1970; "Riverdale: Alive and Well and Working," *GM*, 31 Dec. 1971; "Is the Mayor Afraid of Violence in Riverdale?" *GM*, 13 July 1970; "The Mayor Replies" (letter), *GM*, 18 July 1970; "Can Ottawa Help the People Bring down City Hall?" *GM*, 27 March 1971; "Switching from Radical to Mayor," *GM*, 11 Jan. 1972; "Mayor to Crack down on Hippies," *TT*, 12 July 1968; "Move to Convert Rochdale into Senior Citizens Home," *Sun*, 6 March 1972; "We Get a Lot More LIP," *Sun*, 6 June 1972.

69 "Ward Seven Council," *Seven News*, 16 April 1971; "Ward Six Council Meeting"; "Objectives of the Ward Six Council," Dan Heap fonds, Toronto Public Library, 138439-14.

70 "8 Ratepayer Groups Unite," *TT*, 1 Aug. 1969; "35 Metro Ratepayer Groups Link Up," *TT*, 12 March 1970; "Will CORRA Control City Hall?" *Varsity*, 7 March 1973; "Reform Slate: A Victim of Reality," *GM*, 13 April 1971; "CORRA Asks for City Control over U of T Expansion," *GM*, 12 Nov. 1969; "Groups Cheer Spadina Decision as a Victory for the People," *GM*, 4 June 1971; "Grass-Roots People Power Means Public Participation," *TT*, 21 Nov. 1970.

71 Nelson Clarke, "Coalition Being Formed," *CT*, 5 May 1971; "Trapped as the Rents Rise," *GM*, 6 July 1973; "'Public Be Damned!' Say City 'Fathers,'" *CT*, 3 May 1972; "Students Accuse Metro Police of Rough Treatment," *Varsity*, 13 March 1972; "CORRA Plea for 'Turned-on' Council," *TT*, 27 Nov. 1970; "CORRA Asks Council to Support the Activities of Citizens' Groups," *GM*, 10 Nov. 1970; "The Rabbit Button Aimed at Mayor," *GM*, 27 Nov. 1971; "Professor Will Head Ratepayer Groups," *GM*, 6 Jan. 1973; "CORRA: What Is It All About?" *Sun*, 22 May 1973; "CORRA Brief Claims 'Cop-out,'" *Sun*, 4 June 1973. See James T. Lemon, "Toronto: Is It a Model for Urban Life and Citizen Participation?" in *Community Participation and the Spatial Order of the City*, ed. David Ley (Vancouver: Tantalus Research, 1974); James T. Lemon, "The Urban Community Movement: Moving Toward Public Households," in *Humanistic Geography: Prospects and Problems*, ed. David Ley and Marwyn S. Samuels (Chicago: Maaroufa Press, 1978); CORRA, "Goals, Priorities and Objectives of City Council," [1976], Toronto Public Library.

72 "An Announcement to All Reform Citizens . . ." Clarke Collection, box 27, ReforMetro folder; "Citizens' Federation Formed in Toronto," *CT*, 11 June 1975; "New Movement for Metro Reform," *Varsity*, 15 Oct. 1975; "Reform Movement May Be in Its Grave, but Its Caucus Marches On," *GM*, 14 June 1976.

73 "Report of the Co-ordinating Committee to the Second Annual Convention of the Movement for Municipal Reform (Reform Metro)," n.d., Clarke Collection, box 27, ReforMetro folder; "Torontonians Oppose TTC Hike," *CT*, 8 March 1976; "Parliament Opens to Angry Protest," *Varsity*, 10 March 1976; "Making Racist Remarks Grounds for Dismissal Meeting Demands," *CT*, 1 April 1979.

74 "Voter Apathy Equals Myopia," *GM*, 12 April 1976; "Sewell Urges Tax Rise to Save Social Services," *TS*, 3 March 1976; Diana Fancher, "Press and NDP Off-Base," *Toronto Clarion*, December 1978; E. Phillips, "NDP Distrusts ReforMetro," *Toronto Clarion*, November 1978; "Reformers Optimistic," *GM*, 3 April 1978.

75 John Sewell, "Where Have All the Fireworks Gone?" *Seven News*, 3 Dec. 1977; "Is Don Vale Association Going to the Dogs?" *Seven News*, 18 Dec. 1976; "Is Community Participation Dead in Riverdale?" *Seven News*, 9 Oct. 1976.

76 "People Day on May 29th," *Seven News*, 21 May 1971; John Hagan, *Northern Passage: Amer-*

ican Vietnam War Resisters in Canada (Cambridge: Harvard University Press, 2001), 83; [photos with captions], *Riverdale Review*, 10 Aug. 1972; "Anti-Poverty Festival a Warm Up for Queen's Park March June 15th," *Seven News*, 9 June 1972.

77 "Meeting Sparks Revival of GRO," *Seven News*, 26 Oct. 1974; "Grape Boycott Committee Formed," *Seven News*, 26 Oct. 1974; "Ward Sports Council Formed," *Seven News*, 6 April 1974.

78 "Mothers in Traffic-Jam Protest," *TT*, 9 Sept. 1968; "The Crosswalk Mothers Carry on the Fight," *TT*, 10 Sept. 1968; "100 in Black Armband Blockade," *TT*, 12 Nov. 1968; "300 Protest on Metro Road Where Girl of 9 Killed," *TT*, 23 Nov. 1968; "Mothers Win School Fight," *TT*, 6 June 1969; "Picketing Moms Win Crossing Guard," *TT*, 14 Sept. 1970; "Crosswalk Protest," *TT*, 15 Sept. 1970.

79 "Mothers Win School Fight"; "Picketing Moms Win Crossing Guard"; "Crosswalk Protest"; "Barricade by Grandmothers to Save Park," *TT*, 18 July 1969.

80 "Barricade by Grandmothers to Save Park"; "They Played a New Game," *TT*, 27 Jan. 1970; "Rally to Save Ramsden Park," *TT*, 2 June 1969; "The Community Organizers," *Riverdale Review*, 11 June 1970.

81 "500 Hold Plant-in, Start People's Park on University Land," *GM*, 1 June 1970; "People's Park at Sussex and Spadina," *Guerilla*, 1-1; "Only Clay in the People's Park," *GM*, 15 July 1971; "People Make Own Park," *Seven News*, 21 May 1971.

82 Don Mitchell, *The Politics of Food* (Toronto: James Lorimer & Company, 1975), 223–24; People's Food Commission, *The Land of Milk and Money: The National Report of the People's Food Commission* (Kitchener: Between the Lines, 1980), 70–72, 78–81; "Local Comic Book Attacks Food Industry," *Seven News*, 15 June 1974.

83 "Shopping Co-op Store Stretches Food Dollar," *Ward 9 Community News*, 21 Dec. 1976; "Karma II Is a Successful Food Co-op," *Seven News*, 14 April 1973. "Community Is Critical of New Karma II Food Co-op," *Seven News*, 24 March 1973; "Feeding the People to Death," *This Magazine*, Fall 1972; "Food Co-ops on Increase," *TS*, 13 Dec. 1973.

84 "Country Living, Yoga Style," *GM*, 24 Aug. 1972; "Food Issues Report," *Karma Kronicle*, July 1981; Bob Melcombe and Maria Lester, "Co-op Bakery," *Karma Kronicle*, 16 Sept. 1982; Carolyn Lemon, "Lettuce Boycott on Again," *Karma Kronicle*, February 1980; "Farmworkers and the Multinationals," *Karma Kronicle*, February 1982; "Boycott: A Way of Trading Profits for Beliefs," *TS*, 30 Nov. 1985; Irene Whittman, "A Review of the Membership Policy vis-a-vis Low Income Members," *Karma Kronicle*, 1981; Howard Kaplan, "Dear Fellow Karma members," *Karma Kronicle*, June 1981; Jonathan Rudin, "To the Editor," *Karma Kronicle*, July 1981; Audrey Dyer, "Final Board Report 1980–1," *Karma Kronicle*, September 1981.

85 "The Food Co-operative Revolution: A Good Neighbour Policy and a Fair Shopping Deal," *GM*, 3 May 1975; "Achieving a Sense of Community," *Parkdale Citizen*, March 1974; "Centennial Co-op Seeks Members," *Seven News*, 9 Nov. 1974; "Ward and Area Food Co-operatives," *Seven News*, 29 Nov. 1975; "Food Co-ops Feed Members Cheaply," *Toronto Clarion*, 24 Aug.–21 Sept. 1977; "Faltering Food Co-ops Move in New Direction," *TS*, 6 Sept. 1980; "Food Co-op Should Beat Higher Prices," *Parkdale Citizen*, September 1972; "Concerned Mothers Set up Food Co-op," *Seven News*, 6 April 1974; "Free Store Makes Money Obsolete," *Seven News*, 1971; "Why Free Stores?" *Ontario Tenant*, 24 March 1972; "No Store at Orton Park," *Ontario Tenant*, 24 March 1972.

86 "Food Co-op Federation Gets LIP Grant," *Seven News*, 13 Dec. 1975; Neil Rothenberg, "Local Food Co-ops Get New Truck," *Seven News*, 6 March 1976; Keith Wallace, "Food Co-ops Feed Members Cheaply," *Toronto Clarion*, 24 Aug.–21 Sept. 1977; Beverly Biderman, "Co-ops Prosper," *Toronto Clarion*, 21 March–2 April 1979; "Ontario Natural Food Co-op," www.onfc.ca/index.php (accessed April 6, 2010).

87 "Allotments Gardeners—Unite!" *Ward 9 Community News*, 22 Jan. 1974; "The Natural Food Trip Becomes the New High," *TT*, 11 Dec. 1970; Robin Barry Simpson, "What We Got Away With: Rochdale College and Canadian Art in the Sixties," M.A. thesis, Concordia University, 2011, 93.

88 "Bread and Roses Preserves Credit Union Traditions," *GM*, 11 March 1985; "New Credit Union," *Toronto Clarion*, 21 Dec. 1977; "Co-ops and Credit Unions: An Uneasy Marriage," *Toronto Clarion*, 4 April 1979; "Here's a Different Credit Union, *Seven News*, 26 Aug. 1978; "Bread and Roses Credit Union Newsletter," *Connexions*, connexions.org/CxLibrary/CX2153.htm (accessed 2 Sept. 2017); "Women's Credit Union," *Other Woman*, December/January 1976; "Caught in the Squeeze: Women's Credit Union," *Broadside*, February 1981; "Toronto Women's Credit Union: Merging Ahead?" *Broadside*, June 1981.

89 "4U: An Untypical Employment Agency," *Seven News*, 6 March 1976; "Community Parole: A New Concept in Prison Reform," *Seven News*, 28 July 1972; "The Workers, Co-op Info Centre," *Community Newsline*, April 1972; editorial, *Downtown Action*, March 1976; "Toronto under Attack!" *Downtown Action*, March 1976; "The American Urban Industrial Complex," *Downtown Action*, August 1976.

90 "Che Was a Doctor. Live Like Him!" *Varsity*, 11 Dec. 1970; "Health Liberation Attacks Medical 'Conspiracy,'" *Varsity*, 1 March 1974; ad, *Varsity*, 6 March 1974; "Community Health Centres: Who Will Control Them?" *Seven News*, 30 June 1973; "Don Vale to Set up Own Health Clinic," *Seven News*, 20 Oct. 1973; "Lisbon Has Health Problems Too," *Seven News*, 21 Feb. 1976; "Rochdale Med-Clinic Proposal," *Seven News*, 22 Sept. 1973; "A Clinic Where You Don't Need an Appointment—or Money," *TT*, 24 Sept. 1970.

91 Robert Storey, "'Their Only Power Was Moral': The Injured Workers' Movement in Toronto, 1970–1985," *Histoire sociale/Social History*, 41, 81 (2008), 99–131, citations at 105.

92 See, in addition to Storey, "'Their Only Power Was Moral,'" P. Biggin, O. Buonastella, M. Endicott, H. McKinnon, S. Spano, and D. Ublansky, "Justice for Injured Workers: The Struggle Continues," *Journal of Law and Social Policy*, 41 (1995).

93 Working Women Community Centre, *Making the City: Women Who Made a Difference* (Black Point, N.S.: Fernwood Publishing, 2012), 34, 42; "Feminist Therapy," *Healthsharing* (Winter 1982); "Women's Health Centre," *Other Woman*, Fall 1974; "Women and Medicine," *Other Woman*, July 1974.

94 "Doctors Need Marx, Mao Students Told," *Varsity*, 22 Oct. 1971; "Revolutionary Medicine in China Praised," *Varsity*, 3 Dec. 1971; "Traditional Medical Training—Is It Necessary?" *Varsity*, 29 March 1972; "Alternatives to Western Scientific Medicine Discussed," *Varsity*, 2 Dec. 1974; "Chinese Legal System: 'Unparallelled Public Involvement,'" *Law Union News*, June 1978; "Lest We Rely on Promises . . ." *Law Union News*, December 1980.

95 "Why a Left Wing Lawyer Needs the Law Union," *Law Union News*, August 1974; "Yorkville Gets Hip to the Law, but No Key on Beating Vagrancy," *GM*, 27 May 1967; "The Birth and Growth of the Law Union," *Law Union News*, September 1985; "Law Society Wants Hippie Helpers off Street," *TS*, 30 May 1968; "Yorkville Pamphlet Advises Hippies How to Get Along with Policemen," *TS*, 11 April 1968.

96 "Why a Left Wing Lawyer Needs the Law Union"; "Report on the Founding Convention of the Law Union," *Law Union News*, 3 June 1974; "For Law Students," *Law Union News*, August 1974; "A Good Start for the Law Union: The September Conference," *Law Union News*, 30 Oct. 1974.

97 "Report on the Founding Convention of the Law Union," *Law Union News*, 3 June 1974; editorial, "The Political Underground of the Law Union," *Law Union News*, 3 June 1974; "A Starting Point: Do We Avoid Politics?" *Law Union News*, January 1978.

98 Vera Chouinard, "State Formation and the Politics of Place: The Case of Community Legal Aid Clinics," *Political Geography Quarterly*, 9,1 (January 1990), 28; Chouinard, "Challenging Law's Empire: Rebellion, Incorporation, and Changing Geographies of Power in Ontario's Legal Clinic System," *Studies in Political Economy*, 55 (Spring 1998), 69, 74.

99 "Neighbourhood Legal Services Hires Staff," *Seven News*, 15 March 1975; "Neighbourhood Legal Services," *Seven News*, 31 Oct. 1975.

100 Shelley A.M. Gavigan, "Twenty-Five Years of Dynamic Tension: The Parkdale Community Legal Services Experience," *Osgoode Hall Law Journal*, 35,3 (1997), 449; "Parkdale Community Legal Services—A Dream That Died," *Obiter Dicta*, 13 June 1972; S. Ronald Ellis, "The Ellis Archives—1972 to 1981: An Early View from the Parkdale Trenches," *Osgoode Hall Law Journal*, 35,3 (1997), 569; Ewart quoted in "Parkdale Community Legal Services: Community Law Office, or Law Office in a Community?" *Obiter Dicta*, 30 Sept. 1971.

101 "Parkdale Community Legal Services—A Dream That Died"; "The Cake without the Icing: True Story of Community Law Revealed," *Obiter Dicta*, 9 Dec. 1971; ""Parkdale Community Legal Services: Community Law Office"; "Parkdale Gets Eviction Notice," *Obiter Dicta*, 29 March 1973; "Parkdale—Is It Creating Radical Lawyers?" *Obiter Dicta*, 12 Oct. 1972; "Parity Approved for Parkdale," *Obiter Dicta*, 4 Oct. 1973.

102 Letter, executive of PTA to PCLS, Oct. 3, 1973, box 1, Folder: Steering committee minutes, 1972–74, Parkdale Community Legal Services fonds; letter, Nelson Clarke to Parkdale executive, Jan 10, 1974, Nelson Clarke Collection, 6-6; "Parkdale: Legal Education and Community Service," *Obiter Dicta*, 1 Oct. 1974; community election, 29 Jan. 1976, Parkdale Community Legal Services fonds, box 1985-002/004-information kit folder.

103 Minutes, 23 Sept. 1974, PCLS fonds, box 1, Folder: Steering committee minutes, 1972–74; Office Committee Minutes, 4 Feb. 1976, PCLS fonds, 1985-002/002, Office committee folder; 1 Oct. 1975 minutes, PCLS fonds, box 2, 1985-002/002, Office committee folder; 6 Aug. 1974 minutes, PCLS fonds, box 1, Folder: Steering committee minutes, 1972–74; 20 Aug. 1973 minutes, PCLS fonds, box 1, Folder: Steering committee minutes, 1972–74; Ellis, 571-2, 568; BOG meeting, 27 Aug. 1975, and steering committee, 19 July 1975, from box 1; office committee, 28 July 1975, 1985-002/002; Lina Chartland, response to Ron Ellis, box 6, folder: Flynn-Parkdale History 1972–78; memo, 9 Sept. 1976, box 2, Folder: Memos re: office reorganization 1976–77; 28 March 1977, box 2; Office Committee, OC 7 April 1976, box 2; office committee, 19 May 1977, box 2; letter, Nelson Clarke to William Kashtan, 27 Aug. 1977, box 4, folder 10.

104 Chouinard, "Challenging Law's Empire": 70; "Parkdale: Legal Education and Community Service," *Obiter Dicta*, 1 Oct. 1974; John Liss, "Artistic Woodworker Strike: Different Perspectives," *Law Union News*, 3 June 1974; Jeff House, "Law Union Strategy Criticized," *Law Union News*, April 1975; "How to Change the Laws: The Example of Workmen's Compensation," *Law Union News*, 1,4 (1974); "Bold Refugee Strategy Succeeds," *Law Union News*, February-March 1979.

105 Chouinard, "Challenging Law's Empire," 75–83; Chouinard, "State Formation and the Politics of Place," 34.

106 John Marshall, "Background—The Library Context," in *Citizen Participation in Library Decision-Making: The Toronto Experience*, ed. John Marshall (Metuchen, N.J.: Scarecrow Press, 1984), 53–55, 58–59; James Lorimer, "New Library Planned for Danforth Area," *Seven News*, 6 April 1974.

107 "Library Committee Seeks Help," *Seven News*, 24 Jan. 1976; "Meetings Called on Uses for Library," *Seven News*, 4 Oct. 1975; "Forward 9 Wants to Keep a Finger on Community Pulse," *Ward 9 Community News*, 8 Sept. 1975; "Library Outreach Program Helps Elderly Citizens," *Seven News*, 3 April 1976; James Lorimer, "The Coming Crunch for Public Libraries at City

Hall: Why Public Libraries Have to Reform Themselves to Survive the Next Five Years," *Emergency Librarian*, September-December 1978.

108 "Comic Books in Libraries Stir up Controversy," *Seven News*, 16 July 1977; Leonard Wertheimer, "Feedback," *Emergency Librarian*, January-April 1979; David Aylward, "Feedback," *Emergency Librarian*, May-August 1979. Another dissident librarian complained that the library board had been turned into "a band of Sixties-style activists." See "Pop Seen Menace to the Library," *GM*, 17 March 1978.

109 "East End Libraries Ask Equality and Seek Changes," *Seven News*, 12 Feb. 1977; Marshall, "Background—The Library Context," 58–59; Freyda Geirsson, "150 Books: A Review," *Emergency Librarian*, 1-3.

110 An Insider, "TPL Unionizes," *Emergency Librarian*, September-October 1976; Meyer Brownstone, "The Political Economy of Citizen Participation," in *Citizen Participation in Library Decision-Making*, ed. Marshall, 261–264.

111 East End Libraries Ask Equality and Seek Changes," *Seven News*, 12 Feb. 1977; editorial, "Toronto's Brave Experiment," *Library Journal*, July 1976.

112 Howard Buchbinder, "The Implications for Social Work of a Radical Analysis," 24 Oct. 1975, 2–6, Buchbinder fonds, 1996-018/012-16; John Barnes, "Remnants, Bags and Elites—The Social Welfare Role of Social Work Critic," *Social Worker*, May 1970; "Urban Community Development and Social Planning—A Viewpoint," *Social Worker*, July 1970; Blaine Nethune, "Action and Reaction," *Social Worker*, July 1970; Reul S. Samuel, "Action and Reaction," *Social Worker*, July 1970; Bernard Schikowski, "Self-Determination and Welfare Rights Groups," *Social Worker*, November 1970; "Will Gannon and How He Got That Way," *Social Worker*, February 1972; "Placards, Pens and Odd Thoughts—Social Action and Professional Responsibility in Canada," *Social Worker*, February 1972; Stephen Hagarty, "Revolution and Evolution: The Therapeutic Community as a Dimension of Social Democracy," *Social Worker*, Spring 1973; "Social Action in a Professional Social Work Association," *Social Worker*, Spring 1974; Eldon Green, "The Proper Role of a Professional Association," *Social Worker*, Spring 1974; Ben Carniol, "A Framework for Community Organization Practice," *Social Worker*, Summer 1974; "Unbecoming a Bureaucrat," *Social Worker*, Fall-Winter 1974.

113 "Introduction," Buchbinder fonds, 1996-018/018.

114 Ibid.

115 Ibid.

116 "UA Ignores Poor, Says Just Society," *TT*, 28 Oct. 1969; "The Vibrations Go out from 373 Huron St.," *TT*, 24 Jan. 1970; "Trudeau Magic Woos CNE," *TT*, 16 Aug. 1969; Margaret Hillyard Little, "Militant Mothers Fight Poverty: The Just Society Movement, 1968–1971," *Labour/Le Travail*, 59 (Spring 2007); "Militant Poor Group Denounced," *TT*, May 7, 1970.

117 "Ballot Chaos at Welfare Meeting," *TT*, 18 March 1970; "Power Struggle Looms between Welfare Groups," *TT*, 18 April 1970.

118 "Landlord, Tenant Act Pamphlet Is Multilingual," *TT*, 11 July 1970; "Daycare Pressure Group to Push for Better Facilities," *TT*, 29 Sept. 1970; "Major Win for Welfare Activists," *TT*, 17 Dec. 1970; "The 'Radicalization' of an Establishment Organization," *TT*, 18 Dec. 1970; "Soup for 'Men Only,'" *CT*, 6 Jan. 1971; "Social Planning Council Asked to Justify Support," *TT*, 2 Feb. 1971; "Activist Slate Beaten by Social Planners," *TT*, 29 April 1971.

119 "UA Ignores Poor, Says Just Society"; "United Appeal: A Small Purse with Many Strings," *Excalibur*, 20 Nov. 1969; "Father of 8 Attacks United Appeal Staff, *TT*, 22 May 1970; "United Appeal: Treating Individuals, Not Root Causes," *Varsity*, 6 Nov. 1972; "Welfare Offices in Street Proposed," *TT*, 20 June 1970.

120 "Campaign to Crimp United Appeal Fund," *Sun*, 9 May 1973; "12 Who Don't Give," *GM*, 1 Oct. 1973; "Two Citizen Groups in Battle over Role of the United Way," *TS*, 5 Oct. 1973; "Toronto Trustees Refuse to Back United Way Drive," *TS*, 21 Sept. 1973; editorial, "Still the Best Way," *GM*, 2 Oct. 1973; editorial, "One Last Hearty Push," *GM*, 3 Nov. 1973; "United Way Pledges Funds to LIP Groups," *GM*, 10 Oct. 1973.

121 "Divided Poor Call for Unity," *TT*, 11 Jan. 1971; "Poor People Planning Mass Protest against the 'Unjust Society,'" *TS*, 11 Jan. 1971; "Canada's Poor People Call for Demonstrations against Trudeau's 'UnJust Society,'" *CT*, 13 Jan. 1971; Poor People's Conference Plans Mass Jan. 25 Protest," *Labor Challenge*, 18 Jan. 1971; "Poor People Can Hold Their Heads High," *TT*, 20 Jan. 1971; "Canada's Poor Are Asked to Stage Protests Jan. 25," *GM*, 11 Jan. 1971; "Poor Invade City Welfare Office but Turnout Far Below Estimate," *TT*, 26 Jan. 1971; "Demonstrating Poor Invade Argus Offices, Keep Metro Welfare Staff Working Overtime," *GM*, 26 Jan. 1971.

122 "Poor Can Now Afford to Meet," *Sun*, 30 Dec. 1971; "Poor People Want Jobs, Assured Decent Income," *CT*, 19 Jan. 1972; "Poor People's Conference? No! They're Anti-Poverty," *Sun*, 17 Jan. 1972; "Poor Form Lobby Group to Seek Unity, $128 Minimum Wage," *GM*, 17 Jan. 1972; "Poor People Part II: Putting the Cart before the Horse, and the Train on the Track," *Varsity*, 21 Jan. 1972; "Ontario Grants $12,000 to Poor for Conference," *GM*, 25 Jan. 1973; "Poor Want Rent Controls, More Houses," *GM*, 19 Feb. 1973; "Poverty Fights Plan Protest at Queen's Park," *Sun*, 19 Feb. 1973.

123 "Thousand Take Part in Anti-Poverty Festival," *CT*, 31 May 1972; "Ontario Cabinet Hears Anti-Poverty Program," *CT*, 21 June 1972; "LIP Grant Balance Frozen Until Gov't Sees the Books," *Sun*, 4 May 1972; "Anti-Poor Money Not for Petition—Admits Carter," *Sun*, 5 May 1972; "LIP Probe 'a Whitewash,'" *Sun*, 16 May 1972; "Make It $26,000," *GM*, 7 Feb. 1966; "Two Non-Confidence Motions Challenge Pearson Government," *GM*, 2 April 1966; "Pay All Housewives a Wage, NDPer Says," *GM*, 22 June 1966; "Liberals Ask Study of Guaranteed Annual Income," *GM*, 13 Aug. 1966; "Critics Seek Ontario View on Income Plan," *GM*, 22 May 1968; "Income Guarantee Misinterpreted: Stanfield," *GM*, 13 June 1968; "Attitudes Changing toward Poverty Problem," *GM*, 17 June 1972; "Election '72—Campaign Briefs," *CT*, 3 Oct. 1972.

124 "A Lot of Talk about Poverty but Poor Want Action, Not Words," *Sun*, 15 Oct. 1973; "Anti-Poverty Coalition's Efforts Too Diffuse, Resolutions Are Easily Ignored," *GM*, 18 Feb. 1974; "Politicians Didn't Show," *Sun*, 17 Feb. 1974; Fran Klodawsky, "Accumulation, the State, and Community Struggles: Impacts on Toronto's Built Environment, 1945 to 1972," Ph.D. thesis, Queen's University, 1985, 361–62; "'Planning Prevents Violence,'" *TT*, 10 May 1971; Donald R. Keating, *The Power to Make It Happen: Mass-Based Community Organizing, What It Is and How It Works* (Toronto: Green Tree Pub., 1975), 75; "A Warning of Youth Bloodshed," *TT*, 25 April 1969; "Yorkville Groups Aim to Promote Violence, City Committee Told," *GM*, 9 June 1970; "Toronto Blacks Unite to Squelch That Ghetto Image," *TS*, 26 Dec. 1970.

125 "Warning of Low-Income Riots," *TT*, 5 June 1968; "Economic Council Wants Pilot Projects as Test of Anti-Poverty Programs," *GM*, 17 Dec. 1969; "'Bloody Years' If Poor Ignored: Welfare Chief," *TT*, 11 Aug. 1969; "Mr. Stanfield Signs on the Dotted Poverty Line," *TT*, 11 May 1968.

126 "Anti-Poverty Coalition's Efforts Too Diffuse"; Politicians Didn't Show, *Sun*, 17 Feb. 1974; "Women's Action Group," *Other Woman*, July 1974. OAPO had emphasized the need for equal pay for equal work and other feminist-tinged demands in its briefs and strongly supported universal daycare as a means to end poverty, but did not appear to be criticized for its political demands. See "What Can Be Done about Poverty," *CT*, 6 June 1973; Lesley Anne Towers and Barbara Cameron, *The Case for Universal Daycare* (Toronto: Ontario Anti-Poverty Organization, n.d.).

127 Cheryl Hawkes, "Beware the Mother Led Union," "Mother Led Union," and Joan Clark, "Women's Action Group Annual Report," 30 June 1975, all from Mother-Led Union folder, Canadian Women's Movement Archives (CWA) fonds, University of Ottawa Archives and Special Collections; "A Woman's Rich Life Working on Welfare," *Now*, 19 Sept. 1985.

128 Adam Josh Cole, "Children, Liberalism and Utopia: Education, Hall-Dennis and Modernity in Ontario's Long 1960s," Ph.D. thesis, Queen's University, 2015.

129 "New Look in Toronto's School Board," *Sun*, 5 Dec. 1972 ; "Ward 6 Trustee Candidates Offer Voters . . . Radical and Traditional Education Views," *Varsity*, 29 Nov. 1972.

130 *Ward 6 News*, 1 Sept. 1976; "Do You Know This Man?" *Ward 6 News*, 30 April 1975; Joan Dorion, "Let's Take Democracy Seriously," *Ward 6 News*, February 1979.

131 "4,000 Scarborough Students Walk Out, 49 Teachers 'Sick,'" *TS*, 18 May 1973; "High School Students Plan Series of Rotating Walk Outs," *GM*, 2 Nov. 1973; "1,500 Students March to Support Teachers," *TS*, 5 Nov. 1973; "Farmer Student Protests Overlap," *TS*, 9 Nov. 1973; "North York Students Organize Boycott," *GM*, 8 Nov. 1973; "17,000 Students in North York Boycott High Schools in Protest," *GM*, 15 Nov. 1973.

132 "Students Rally at Queen's Park," *GM*, 13 Nov. 1973; "City's Elementary Teachers Endorse OSSTF Staffing Call," *GM*, 16 Nov. 1973; "200 Students March in Spending Protest," *TS*, 9 Nov. 1973; "City's Elementary Teachers Endorse OSSTF Staffing Call," *GM*, 16 Nov. 1973; "No Penalty for Students in North York Boycott," *TS*, 15 Nov. 1973; "Teachers, Parents, Students Forming a United Front," *TS*, 15 Nov. 1973.

133 "Wells Refuses to Raise School Spending Ceilings," *GM*, 20 Nov. 1973; "Wells Tells Students Fads Waste Money," *TS*, 20 Nov. 1973; "Wells Unveils Education Bill Listing Parent, Student Rights," *GM*, 1 Dec. 1973; "New Respect for Students Gained after Work-to-Rule," *TS*, 26 Nov. 1973; "Tentative Agreement for Teachers: More Pay, Fewer Pupils," *TS*, 20 Nov. 1973.

134 Jane Gaskell, Laura-Lee Kearns, and Katrina Pollock, "Approaches to Poverty in the Toronto School Board, 1970–1990: No Shallow Roots," *Journal of Comparative Policy Analysis: Research and Practice* (December 2009), 437; Tim McCaskell, *Race to Equity: Disrupting Educational Inequality* (Toronto: Between the Lines, 2005), 15, 25–26; Doug Barr and Gord Cressy, "Experimental Programs Part of 1975 School Highlights," *Seven News*, 13 Dec. 1975.

135 Gaskell, Kearns, and Pollock, "Approaches to Poverty in the Toronto School Board," 438; Doug Barr and Gord Cressy, "Experimental Programs Part of 1975 School Highlights," *Seven News*, 13 Dec. 1975.

136 "Up in Smoke," *Community Schools*, April 1973; *Community Schools*, June 1971; "You Don't Know What's Happening, Do You, Mr. Jones?" *Community Schools*, October 1971; H.A. Scott, "To Us: 'Community Schools—the Voice of Misguided Extremism,'" *Community Schools*, November 1971.

137 Editorial, "The Need for Community School Councils," *Community Schools*, September 1971; Lionel Zelniker, "How to Set up a Community Council," *Community Schools*, February 1972; Maryann Griggs, "Grassroots Democracy: Ward Five Council," *Community Schools*, June 1972; Gord Cressy, "The Education Scene," *Seven News*, 24 Feb. 1973.

138 "Letters Column for You," *Ward 9 Community News*, 25 Oct. 1976.

139 "Trustees—They Spend Almost Half of Tax Dollars," *Ward 9 Community News*, 9 Nov. 1976.

140 "Wardle the Winners," *Ward 9 Community News*, 21 Dec. 1976; "The Great Flip Flop," *Ward 9 Community News*, 8 Feb. 1977.

141 "Parents Help Choose Principals," *Seven News*, 17 Dec. 1977.

142 "Tremors at the Board: Toronto's Reform Coalition Trustees," *Mudpie*, September 1980;

"Trustee Demands Educators Quit," *Sun*, 17 March 1976; "Dennis Colby: Maverick Trustee," *Sun*, 18 March 1976; "Trustee Guilty on Pot Charges Wants New Law," *Sun*, 14 Jan. 1977.

143 "Bold Refugee Strategy Succeeds," *Law Union News*, February-March 1979; "Left-Wing Chilean Refugee Stays as Immigration Backs down Again," *Law Union News*, June 1979.

144 Hans Jewinski, "Cabbagetown Renaissance," *Seven News*, 1 Feb. 1975.

145 Ward 6 Community Organization, "Issues Presentation," 10 April 1974, Dan Heap fonds, City of Toronto Archives, 138439-11.

146 William Bunge and R. Bordessa, *The Canadian Alternative: Survival, Expeditions and Urban Change* (Toronto: York University, Atkinson College, 1975), 116–19; J. David Hulchanski, *The Three Cities within Toronto: Income Polarization among Toronto's Neighbourhoods, 1970–2005* (Toronto: Cities Centre Press, University of Toronto, 2010).

8. Without Walls—No Ceiling: A Cultural Revolution, 1971–78

1 Clark Atatiff, "'Then, Like Now . . .': The Roots of Radical Geography, a Personal Account," Antipode Foundation, antipodefoundation.org/2012/09/04/then-like-now-the-roots-of-radical-geography-a-personal-account (accessed 9 Sept. 2016).

2 Derek Stephenson, "The Aim of Geographical Expeditions Is to Practice Geography, Not to Organize Communities," *USG Newsletter*, 1,1 (1975); Andy Merrifield, "Situated Knowledge through Exploration: Reflections on Bunge's 'Geographical Expeditions,'" *Antipode*, 17,1 (1995), 54–55; William Bunge and R. Bordessa, *The Canadian Alternative: Survival, Expeditions and Urban Change* (Toronto: York University, Atkinson College, 1975).

3 Bunge and Bordessa, *Canadian Alternative*, 19, 32, 113, 146–47, 152, 184, 188, 267–68.

4 Ibid., 148, 155.

5 Ibid., 19, 21, 153–58, 221, 316, 264, 350–58, 375–78; William Bunge, "Regions Are Sort of Unique," *Area*, 6,2 (1974), 95–96.

6 William W. Bunge, "Exploration in Guadeloupe: Region of the Future," *Antipode*, 5,2 (May 1973); William Bunge, "The Cave of Coulibistrie," *Political Geography Quarterly*, 2,1 (January 1983); *City Magazine*, May-June 1978.

7 J. Richard Peet, "New Left Geography," *Antipode*, 1,1 (1969); Tom Scanlon, "The Toronto Geographical Expedition and Service to the People," *USG Newsletter*, 1,1 (1975); Hector Giroux, "'Antipode': A Radical Journal of Geography," *USG Newsletter*, October-November 1977.

8 William Bunge, "The Point of Reproduction: A Second Front," *Antipode*, 9,2 (September 1977); "Dr. Bunge and the Vancouver Geographical Expedition: Expletives Undeleted," *USG Newsletter*, May 1977; William Bunge, "Geographical Expeditions: An Analysis," *USG Newsletter*, Summer 1976.

9 Bunge, "Point of Reproduction"; Bunge, "Cave of Coulibistrie."

10 Bunge, "Point of Reproduction"; William Bunge, "Geography Is a Field Subject," *Area*, 15,3 (1983), 209; Tom Scanlan and Derek Stephenson, "Explorers as Cab Drivers," *USG Newsletter*, 1,1 (1975); Judy Stamp, "Toward Supportive Neighbourhoods: Women's Role in Changing the Segregated City," *USG Newsletter*, December 1977-January 1978; Tom Scanlon, "Neighbourhood Geography," *USG Newsletter*, December 1977-January 1978; Susan Wismer and David Pell, *Community Profit: Community-Based Economic Development in Canada* (Toronto: Is Five Press, 1981); Tom Scanlon, *Exploring Your Neighbourhood* (Toronto: Is Five Press, 1985); Ryan Ernest O'Connor, "Toronto the Green: Pollution Probe and the Canadian Environmental

Movement," Ph.D. thesis, University of Western Ontario, 2010, 254–60; "Union of Socialist Geographers—Seminar in Marxist Geography," *Antipode*, 17,1 (1975), 84; William Bunge, *Nuclear War Atlas* (Oxford and New York: Blackwell, 1988).

11 Bunge, "Geography Is a Field Subject," 209.

12 *Readings on the Governing Boards of Arts Organizations* (Ottawa: Information Services, Canada Council, 1971), 22–25; Susan Crean, *Who's Afraid of Canadian Culture?* (Don Mills, Ont.: General Publishing, 1976), 140.

13 Peter Dunn and Loraine Leeson, "The Present Day Creates History," *Art Communication*, 6 (July 1977); Brenda Neilson, "Eight-Legged Dancing," *Spill*, December 1976; *Readings on the Governing Boards of Arts Organizations*, 22–25; Crean, *Who's Afraid of Canadian Culture?* 140; Clive Robertson, "Clive Robertson Resigns," *Parallelogramme*, 4,1, n.d..

14 Don Cullen, *The Bohemian Embassy: Memories and Poems* (Hamilton, Ont.: Wolsak and Wynn, 2007); *SUPA Newsletter*, 21 July 1965; Neil Carson, *Harlequin in Hogtown: George Luscombe and Toronto Workshop Productions* (Toronto: University of Toronto Press, 1995), 3, 29, 43, 73, 197; Dennis Reid, "'The Old Coach House Days,'" *Open Letter*, Spring 1997, 23–24; Nicky Drumbolis, *10four Between the Tweny 20 Lines: Extenuating Impressions of a Back Lane Community of Mindless Acid Freaks* (Toronto: Letters, 1991); "Listings," *Harbinger*, 19 July–8 Aug. 1968; Victor Coleman, "A Writer in the Arts Community: An Emotional Memoir—1964–1984," *Artsviews*, Winter 1987–88; "A Letter from the Publisher," *Centerfold*, April 1978; David McKnight, *New Wave Canada: The Coach House Press and the Small Press Movement in English Canada in the 1960s* (Ottawa: National Library of Canada, 1996), 80.

15 Kenneth Coutts-Smith, "Political Content in Art," *Centerfold*, April-May 1979; Coutts-Smith, "Art and Social Transformation," *Centerfold*, April 1978.

16 Donald Bryden, "What's New with LULU?" *Toronto Theatre Review*, February 1977.

17 See Brian Freeman, "Bafflegab from Ronald Bryden: Monsieur n'est pas arrivé," *Toronto Theatre Review*, October/November 1978.

18 "Theme: Canada vs. U.S.," *Canadian Tribune* (*CT*), 24 March 1971; "Crisis Is Political and Provocative," *Toronto Telegram* (*TT*), 4 June 1971.

19 "Theme: Canada vs. U.S."; "Crisis Is Political and Provocative"; "Theatre in the War," *Seven News*, 1 March 1975; "Far as the Eye Can See," *Toronto Theatre Review*, Summer 1977.

20 Denis Johnston, *Up the Mainstream: The Rise of Toronto's Alternative Theatres, 1968–1975* (Toronto: University of Toronto Press, 1991), 34, 120–22, 125, 129.

21 Ibid., 223, 226–29; "In Defence of 'Welfare Bums,'" *CT*, 18 April 1973.

22 "Horovitz in Toronto: Open Circle's the Primary English Class," *Toronto Theatre Review*, April 1977 ; "The Ugly Side of Comedy," *CT*, 6 Dec. 1977.

23 Johnston, *Up the Mainstream*, 74, 84, 171, 191.

24 "Black Theatre Underlines Negro Identity Search," *Toronto Star* (*TS*), 7 Aug. 1968; "The Colonial Mind on the Make," *CNLF Bulletin*, September 1968.

25 Robin Breon, "Black Theatre Canada: A Short History," *Canadian Theatre Review*, Spring 2004, 25–27; "BTC Provides Cultural Weapon," *Contrast*, 20 June 1975; "Flaw in Holes but Play Worth Seeing," *Contrast*, 1 June 1978.

26 "Play Examines Basis for Black Unity," *Contrast*, 6 June 1975; Jeff Henry, "Black Theatre in Montreal and Toronto in the Sixties and Seventies: The Struggle for Recognition," *Canadian Theatre Review*, Spring 2004.

27 "Fleck'xibility," *CT*, 26 June 1978; *The Fleck Women*, dir. Kem Murch, video, Canada, 1978; "The Clichettes," *Artviews*, Summer 1987; Johanna Householder, "For the Re-Materialization

of Objectional Art," in *Performance au Canada, 1970–1990*, ed. Alain-Martin Richard and Clive Robertson (Quebec: Editions Intervention, 1991), 191.

28 Judy Rebick, *Ten Thousand Roses: The Making of a Feminist Revolution* (Toronto: Penguin Canada, 2005), 10–11; Fern Bayer, *The Search for the Spirit: General Idea 1968–1975* (Toronto: Art Gallery of Ontario, 1997), 46.

29 There continue to be regular local revivals of popular left-wing plays first produced by radical theatres in the 1970s. The play *The Drawer Boy* (1999), which features the research and development leading to *The Farm Show*, was made into a film in 2017. A number of the theatres continue in operation, with TPM celebrating its fiftieth anniversary in 2018 and Nightwood its fortieth in 2019. Lacking the relatively generous grants of the 1970s, contemporary radical theatre companies tend not to have their own brick and mortar theatres. Praxis Theatre has notably followed the 1970s radical tradition of featuring plays about past left-wing movements: *Tim Buck 2* (2009), *Section 98* (2010), and *Jesus Chrysler* (2011).

30 Susan Britton, "Videoview 1," *Centerfold*, April 1978. On the vexed question of funding artists, see also Karl Beveridge, "Colonialist Chic or Radical Cheek?" *Centerfold*, June/July 1979; Judith Doyle, "Cold City/Public Access: Toronto Art Distribution Tactics," *Parallelogramme*, April-May 1987.

31 For the controversies at the AGO and the left's often perceptive criticisms, see E.P. Taylor Research Library and Archives, Art Gallery of Ontario, Board of Trustees Meeting, 25 Feb. 1969, B2.8.3; Director's Report, 3 March 1970; "A Strange, Costly Quest," *File*, May-June 1972; Karl Beveridge, "A.G.O. Union Drive: 'Robots Don't Take Coffee Breaks,'" *Centerfold*, October-November 1979; Jennifer Oille, "A Question of Place 2," *Vanguard*, November 1981.

32 See Duncan F. Cameron, ed., *Are Art Galleries Obsolete?* (Toronto: Peter Martin Associates, 1969).

33 Oille, "Question of Place 2"; Richard and Robertson, eds., *Performance au Canada*, 116; Randi Spires, "Feminism and Art in Toronto: A Five Year Overview," *Artsviews*, Spring 1987; *New Canada*, January 1975.

34 Peter Dudar, "I Don't Know If You Believe This Could Actually Happen in the Art Gallery of Ontario," *Strike*, January 1978; "A Letter from the Editor," *Centerfold*, September 1978.

35 Kenneth Coutts-Smith, "General Idea," *Artscanada*, February-March 1978; Anselm Jappe, *Guy Debord* (Berkeley and Los Angeles: University of California Press, 1999), 4–19, 68–69.

36 Judith Doyle, "Cold City/Public Access: Toronto Art Distribution Tactics," *Parallelogramme*, April-May 1987; Peter Hill and Michael Balfe, *Locations: Outdoor Works by Toronto Artists, May 15 to June 30, 1980* (Toronto: Mercer Union, 1980), 3.

37 Mike Constable, "Partisan for People," *CT*, 22 March 1976.

38 Diana P.C. Nemiroff, "A History of Artist-Run Spaces in Canada, with Particular Reference to Vehicule, A Space and the Western Front," M.A. thesis, Concordia University, 1985, 202–3, 209; Elizabeth Chitty, "Dance Axe Grinding," *Spill*, February 1978; Clive Robertson, "Publisher's Note: The A Space 'Takeover,'" *Fuse*, January/February 1983.

39 Robert Clarke, *Books Without Bosses: 40 Years of Reading Between the Lines* (Toronto: Between the Lines, 2017), 3.

40 "PARTISAN in Action," *CT*, 28 June 1976; "Partisan," *Art Communication*, no. 5 (1977); "Partisan Art for the People," *CT*, 12 May 1980; *CT*, 10 Jan. 1983; "In the Streets with Partisan," *Fuse*, May-June 1982; "Public Statement from the Women's Perspective Collective, July 19, 1983," *Fuse*, September/October 1983.

41 Amerigo Marras, "On Organization," *Strike*, January 1978; "The Day the Woodsman Split Open the Wolf's Guts," *Strike*, October 1978; *Art Communication*, 7 (1977); "CEAC School," *Strike*, January 1978; *Strike*, May 1978.

42 "Buggery and Battery in Grannie's Bed," *Strike*, October 1978; "Day the Woodsman Split Open the Wolf's Guts"; "'Snuff,'" *Strike*, October 1978.

43 Kenneth Coutts-Smith, "CEAC and Non-Associates," *Centerfold*, September 1978; Kenneth Coutts-Smith, "It Would Have Been Easy to Throw Lenin Back at Them," *Centerfold*, February-March 1979; Strike Collective, "Coutts-Smith Was in Toronto So We Met," *Centerfold*, February-March 1979.

44 Robert Fothergill, "Canadian Film-Makers' Distribution Centre: A Founding Memoir," *Canadian Journal of Film Studies*, 3,2 (1994), 81, 83; Film League, "Up from the Bargain Basement," *Fuse*, July-August 1980; "1,000 People at Video Festival," *TS*, May 21, 1973; Janine Marchessault, "Amateur Video and the Challenge for Change," in *Challenge for Change: Activist Documentary at the National Film Board of Canada*, ed. Thomas Waugh et al. (Montreal: McGill-Queen's University Press, 2010), 259; "Injured Worker Film Portrays Struggle to Change Laws," *Toronto Clarion*, 23 Feb.–8 March 1977; Margaret Cooper, "Talking to the D.E.C. Films Collective: 'We Don't Have Films You Can Eat,'" *Jump Cut*, 28 (April 1983); Mike Hoolboom, *Underground: The Untold Story of the Funnel Film Collective* (Ottawa: Canadian Film Institute, 2016).

45 Elizabeth Woods, ed., *Co-op Housing* (National Film Board of Canada, 1975); "After All, That Jazz," *Broadside*, June 1980; "New Images on Film," *Canadian Jewish Outlook*, March 1984; *Organizing Tenants* and *Fighting for Equal Ground: A Look at Rent Review*—both produced by Debbie Littman and Terry McGlade—portrayed the tenant side of the housing movement. See "Films for Tenants," *FMTA Newsletter* (Federation of Metro Tenants' Associations), February 1977.

46 "New Images on Film." For insight into Sky's background, see "I Am Not Objective: Filmmaker Laura Sky Talks with Fireweed about Her Work," *Fireweed*, 8 (Fall 1980).

47 Waugh et al., eds., *Challenge for Change*, 5–7; Peter K. Wiesner, "Media for the People: The Canadian Experiments with Film and Video in Community Development," in Waugh et al., eds., *Challenge for Change*; Kalli Paakspuu, "In Praise of Anomaly: Le bonhomme and Rose's House," in Waugh et al., eds., *Challenge for Change*.

48 "TV Show Claims Racial Strife Eroding Toronto," *TS*, 1 Jan. 1977 (about the production of *Between Two Worlds*); "The Fashions of Racism," *Ward 8 News*, 23 March 1979. Hood and Schuyler's work was produced under the auspices of their privately owned company Playing with Time Inc. In contrast to Schuyler and Hood's work, the Riverdale-centred *If You're Brown, Turn Around* was more forthrightly political and left-wing. For *If You're Brown . . .* see "Riverdale Show Examines East-Indian Life in Toronto," *Ward 8 News*, 22 Dec. 1978.

49 Robin Endres, "Horn: 'You Can Grab the Things People Are Aware of and Make Links,'" *CT*, 18 April 1973; "Cultural Meet Lacking in Ideas," *CT*, 28 Feb. 1973; Stuart Henderson, *Making the Scene: Yorkville and Hip Toronto in the 1960s* (Toronto: University of Toronto Press, 2011); Ester Reiter, *A Future Without Hate or Need: The Promise of the Jewish Left in Canada* (Toronto: Between the Lines, 2016).

50 "New Wave: Kill Your Parents," *Strike*, October 1978; David Livingstone, "New Wave: No-Star Rock," *Maclean's*, 7 April 1980.

51 Livingstone, "New Wave"; Bob Segarini, "Toronto! Take a Shot at Being No. 1 on the Pop Scene," *TS*, 5 Aug. 1978.

52 "The Music of Despair," *Workers Action*, September 1977. By the mid-1980s their estimation of punk and heavy metal had risen, largely because their audiences were believed to be alienated and rebellious working-class youth and thus considered superior to the hippy subculture of the 1960s. See "This Is Spinal Tap," *Workers Action*, June-July 1984; "Music Mags: Rebellion or Big Business," *Workers Action*, September 1984.

53 Martha and the Muffins, Band History, http://www.marthaandthemuffins.com/home_set.htm (accessed 8 May 2009); David Livingstone, "New Wave: No-Star Rock," *Maclean's*, 7 April 1980; Alan O'Connor, "Local Scenes and Dangerous Crossroads: Punk and Theories of Cultural Hybridity," *Popular Music*, 21,2 (2002), 229.

54 O'Connor, "Local Scenes and Dangerous Crossroads," 230, 234; Peter Goddard, "Raw-Boned Punk Rock Band an Intellectual Phenomenon," *TS*, 28 Jan. 1977; Clive Robertson, "The Travel Section: If You Lived Here You'd Be Home Now," *ArtViews*, July/August/September 1989.

55 "Spanking Punk: Latest Rebellious Form for Toronto's Youth Scene Media Coverage," *Art Communication*, 6 (July 1977); "If Anarchy Succeeds Everyone Will Follow," *Art Communication*, no. 9 (1977); "No Butter, No Butter, No Butter..." *Strike*, January 1978.

56 Dot Tuer, "The CEAC Was Banned in Canada," *C Magazine*, 9 (1987), 28.

57 Lily Eng (letter), *Spill*, December 1975; Elizabeth Chitty, "Random Editorial," *Spill*, no. 7 (1977).

58 Peter Graham, "The New Left Cultural Front: A Lens on Toronto Arts and 15 Dance Lab," in *Renegade Bodies: Canadian Dance in the 1970s*, ed. Allana C. Lingren and Kaija Pepper (Toronto: Dance Collection Danse, 2012), 197–204.

59 "The Social and Political Role of the Artist in Society (statements presented at the Dance in Canada Conference, July 1, 1979)," 15 Dance Lab Portfolio, Box 2 [no folder], Dance Collection Danse. Dragu similarly suggested that culture had a singular role to play in overthrowing the system: "We're not going to become communists, that's an old cause. We need something new, something focused around media." Yet this was not, she emphasized, an excuse to forfeit activism beyond the stage: "We have to be more than artists." See "Margaret Dragu: Honky Tonk Philosopher Queen," *Fanfare*, 14 June 1978.

60 Even in departments in which parity had been won, not enough students were willing to endure the frequent and lengthy committee meetings required to make it work after early enthusiasm waned.

61 Tom Walkom, "The New Radical Literature," *Varsity*, 19 Oct. 1973.

62 "Students Rally to Defence of Soon Jobless Professor," *Varsity*, 23 Feb. 1973; "Let Profs Do Hiring: Math Head," *Varsity*, 9 Feb. 1973; *Varsity*, 26 Feb. 1973; "Occupation Continues," *Varsity*, 28 Feb. 1973; "Greene Praises Open Math Meetings," *Varsity*, 9 March 1973; "All-Faculty Body to Study Math Dept," *Varsity*, 14 March 1973.

63 Kenneth McNaught, "A Challenge to U of T: Right of Dissent in Peril," *TS*, 15 July 1974; McNaught, "Muslim Group Took Books off List," *Varsity*, 27 Oct. 1976; "Caricatures of Muslims Demeaning," *Varsity*, 17 Nov. 1976.

64 Kenneth McNaught, *Conscience and History: A Memoir* (Toronto: University of Toronto Press, 1999), 191; Michael Bliss remembers Kealey as "one of the most menacing and blustering of the student radicals," who when Bliss hired him to work on editing a collection of labour history documents could only be consulted in the Don Jail, where he was serving a sentence for his activities in a demonstration outside the U.S. consulate. See Michael Bliss, *Writing History: A Professor's Life* (Toronto: Dundurn Press, 2011), 145.

65 Bliss, *Writing History*, 120, 123, 124, 129, 145, 155.

66 Elaine Coburn, "'Pulling the Monster Down': Interview with William K. Carroll," *Socialist Studies*, 6,1 (Spring 2010), 75; Nigel Roy Moses, "Forgotten Lessons: Student Movements against Tuition Fee Hikes in Ontario in the 1960s and 1970s," *Trans/forms: Insurgent Voices in Education*, 7,8 (2004), 143; "Twelve Decide to Take over Evans' Office," *Varsity*, 13 March 1978; "Occupiers Stay—Evans Refuses to Cancel Classes," *Varsity*, 15 March 1978; "Sit-in Breaks up for Demonstration," *Varsity*, 17 March 1978; "Biggest Student Demo Ever," *Varsity*,

17 March 1978; "York Occupation Begins," *Varsity*, 27 Sept. 1978; "Protest Continues at York University," *Varsity*, 29 Sept. 1978; "Unions to Rally for York," *Varsity*, 2 Oct. 1978; "York Staff Strike Ends," *Varsity*, 4 Oct. 1978. A number of professors refused to cross the staff picket line. See Michiel Horn, *York University: The Way Must Be Tried* (Montreal and Kingston: McGill-Queen's University Press, 2008), 164–65.

67 David Frank, "Rewriting Canadian History," *Varsity*, 10 Nov. 1971; Pat Bird, *Of Dust and Time and Dreams and Agonies: A Short History of Canadian People* (Willowdale, Ont.: Canadian News Synthesis Project, 1975); Wayne Roberts, "Stale Pedantry and Eclecticism: The State of Urban History," *Varsity*, 1 Dec. 1972.

68 See Bryan Palmer, *A Culture in Conflict: Skilled Workers and Industrial Capitalism in Hamilton, Ontario* (Montreal and Kingston: McGill-Queen's University Press, 1979); Gregory S. Kealey, *Toronto Workers Respond to Industrial Capitalism 1867*–1892 (Toronto: University of Toronto Press, 1980). For reflections on this historiographical moment, see Bryan Palmer, "Listening to History Rather than Historians: Reflections on Working Class History," *Studies in Political Economy*, 20 (1986).

69 Susan Mann Trofimenkoff and Alison Prentice, eds., *The Neglected Majority: Essays in Canadian Women's History* (Toronto: McClelland and Stewart, 1977). For reflections, see Joan Sangster, *Through Feminist Eyes: Essays on Canadian Women's History* (Edmonton, Alta.: Athabaska University Press, 2011).

70 S.D. Clark, "Sociology in Canada: An Historical Over-View," *Canadian Journal of Sociology*, 1,2 (Summer 1975), 233; S.D. Clark, "The Changing Image of Sociology in English-Speaking Canada," *Canadian Journal of Sociology*, 4,4 (Autumn 1979), 401.

71 "Editorial Statement," *Studies in Political Economy: A Socialist Review*, 1,1 (Spring 1979), iv, vi.

72 Leo Panitch, "Corporatism in Canada," *Studies in Political Economy*, 1 (1979); Jorge Niosi, "The New French-Canadian Bourgeoisie," *Studies in Political Economy*, 1 (1979); Patricia Marchak, "Labour in a Staples Economy," *Studies in Political Economy*, 2 (1979); Pierre Fournier, "The New Parameters of the Quebec Bourgeoisie," *Studies in Political Economy*, 3 (1980); William Coleman, "The Class Bases of Language Policy in Quebec, 1949–1975," *Studies in Political Economy*, 3 (1980); David McNally, "Staple Theory as Commodity Fetishism: Marx, Innis and Canadian Political Economy," *Studies in Political Economy*, 6 (1981); Anne Legare, "Towards a Marxian Theory of Canadian Federalism," *Studies in Political Economy*, 8 (1982).

73 George Ross, "Nicos Poulantzas 1936–1979: On the Loss of a Colleague and Comrade," *Studies in Political Economy*, 2 (1979); Guglielmo Carchedi, "Authority and Foreign Labour: Some Notes on a Late Capitalist Form of Capital Accumulation and State Intervention," *Studies in Political Economy*, 2 (1979).

74 *Imperialism, Nationalism, and Canada: Essays from the Marxist Institute of Toronto*, with Introduction by John Saul and Craig Heron (Toronto and Kitchener, Ont.: New Hogtown Press and Between the Lines, 1977), 7; Leo Panitch, *The Canadian State: Political Economy and Political Power* (Toronto: University of Toronto Press, 1977); Wallace Clement and Daniel Drache, eds., *A Practical Guide to Canadian Political Economy* (Toronto: James Lorimer, 1978). In 1975 the Committee on Socialist Studies had 96 members in Toronto, many of them attached to unions, community colleges, and activist projects, with the University of Toronto by far the dominant university of affiliates. By the end of the decade, York, where socialists had won in elections in 1975–76, was plainly becoming the "go-to" place for Toronto leftists, especially those interested in women's studies. See "Left Sweeps York Elections," *Forward*, Mid-April 1975; "Student President Interviewed," *Forward*, December 1975; "Left Slate Defeated at York University," *Labor Challenge*, 12 April 1976; "York U Left Gains," *Forward*, April 1977; "Breakthrough: Women Publish," *Breakthrough*, November 1977. Though the

Socialist League played a disproportional role in the united left slate, the alliance encompassed a variety of left-wing perspectives.

75 Thomas Schofield, "Introduction," in Jesse Lemisch, *On Active Service in War and Peace: Politics and Ideology in the American Historical Profession* (Toronto: New Hogtown, 1975).

76 "New Hogtown Press: After Retrenchment, a Few Steps Forward," *Varsity*, 31 Oct. 1975.

77 Clarke, *Books Without Bosses*, 4; advertisement, *Toronto Clarion*, 2 July 1982.

78 Christine Kim, "The Politics of Print: Feminist Publishing and Canadian Literary Production," Ph.D. thesis, York University, 2004, 316–25; Clarke, *Books Without Bosses*, 43. After beginning its life as The Women's Educational Press, the house later changed its name to Women's Press.

79 "Publishing by Women," *Breakthrough*, April 1976; Roy MacSkimming, *The Perilous Trade: Book Publishing in Canada, 1946–2006* (Toronto: McClelland & Stewart, 2003), 287–91.

80 "Why Everyone Wants to Plug into the Cable TV Boom," *TS*, 3 Jan. 1970; "New Group Aims at Cable Programming Control," *Globe and Mail* (*GM*), 25 Oct. 1970; "Cable-TV Has Brought about a Television Revolution," *TS*, 24 April 1971; "Cable TV's Future Is Endless," *TS*, 3 Jan. 1970.

81 "Community Programming in Cable TV Sparks Lively Debate at Centre," *TS*, 18 Sept. 1970; "Public Forum Criticizes Metro Cable Operators," *TT*, 18 Sept. 1970.

82 "Public Forum Criticizes Metro Cable Operators"; "Cable Group Shows Teeth," *TT*, 4 Sept. 1970; "New Group Aims at Cable Programming Control," *GM*, 25 Oct. 1970; "Metro Group Aims to Provide Cable TV Programming," *TS*, 25 Aug. 1970.

83 "A Welles-Like Scare Show on the CBC," *GM*, 27 Aug. 1970; "55 North Maple Usually Good," *TS*, 4 Sept. 1970.

84 "The Use of Cable-TV as a Community Force and Its Problems," *TS*, 27 April 1971; "Ben's Claims That Group Political 'Lies'—Official," *TT*, 17 May 1971; "Some Not So New Faces and Voices," *GM*, 7 Sept. 1970; "Participation and Dialogue," *Riverdale Review*, June 1971.

85 "Participation and Dialogue"; "A Welles-Like Scare Show on the CBC," *GM*, 27 Aug. 1970.

86 "Peoples TV in Downtown T.O.," *Riverdale Review*, June 1971.

87 "Grassroots TV Program Is Part of Ward 7's 'Communications Revolution,'" *GM*, 18 March 1971.

88 "Neighbourhood TV: A New Way to Build Community Spirit," *TS*, 25 Jan. 1972; "All Around the Town with a TV Camera," *GM*, 9 Nov. 1972; "Man at the Top Has Lots of Waste at the Start," *GM*, 29 Dec. 1971.

89 Earl Rosen and Reg Herman, "The Community Use of Media for Lifelong Learning in Canada," in *Access: Some Western Models of Community Media*, ed. Frances J. Berrigan (Paris: United Nations Educational, Scientific and Cultural Organization, 1977), 130, 134, 138. Toronto activist Marty Dunn, who had given up trying to produce programs for community cable because of this kind of cable company pushback, but continued to engage in community video production, shared Lawson's prioritization of process over product.

90 "LIP Grants Used—to Get More LIP Cash," *Sun*, 7 March 1972; "155 Metro Projects in $11.8 Million Youth Program," *TS*, 8 May 1972; "Community Control, Ownership of Cable TV Is Project of OFL," *GM*, 2 Nov. 1970; "The Use of Cable-TV as a Community Force and Its Problems," *TS*, 27 April 1971; "'Let Ordinary People Run Cable-TV,'" *TS*, 20 March 1971; Elizabeth G. Baldwin, "Community Radio: The Development of a Voluntary Organization," M.A. thesis, McMaster University, 1975, 45–47.

91 "Neighbourhood TV." To get away with such "unprofessional" experimentation and left-wing partisanship, DCT was aided by the decentralized responsibility inherent in its conception of

community and the reputable image of its public leadership. Burke, a York University professor, once posed DCT as a triumph of co-operation over confrontation; a "move beyond Saul Alinsky." Lawson, a member of CORRA and the NDP as well as the first executive director of CIC, explained the bias using the apolitical rubric of the "generation gap." DCT was also legitimized by the NFB, whose pamphlet *Community Cable TV and You* explained the impetus for community TV as a desire for social change and a new meaning of community. "Participation and Dialogue," *Riverdale Review*, June 1971; "All Around the Town with a TV Camera"; "Some Not So New Faces and Voices," *GM*, 7 Sept. 1970; "Canadian Independence Group Seeks 100,000 Recruits," *TS*, 17 Sept. 1970; "Most Roads Lead to CORRA," *TS*, 25 Dec. 1972; "NFB Handbook Urges Community TV," *TT*, 8 March 1971.

92 "Neighbourhood TV"; "'People TV' Near Bankrupt," *Sun*, 13 Feb. 1973.

93 "Rip Off? CITY-TV Fears 'Iron law of Oligarchy' [;] Lawson Corrects 'Inaccuracies'" (letter), *Seven News*, 11 Nov. 1972; Bruce Lawson, "Community TV: How to Stop the Media Rip-Off," *Seven News*, 30 Sept. 1972. Keeble Cable was able to minimize its reliance on community-based television groups by setting up booths with recording equipment and offering the public an opportunity to record themselves, a technique later replicated by CITY-TV's *Speaker's Corner* series. See "Hart and Lorne: A Winner at Last," *GM*, 25 June 1971.

94 Britton, "Videoview 1"; Beveridge, "Colonialist Chic or Radical Cheek?"

9. Subaltern Identities, Universal Truths, Transnational Complexities: The Rise of Identity-Based Resistance, 1971–78

1 "Nazi-Saluting Brown Shirts Stop CITY-TV Talk Program," *Toronto Star* (*TS*), 17 June 1974; CITY-TV Asks Why No Charges Laid in Studio Ruckus, *TS*, 18 June 1974; "Warrants Issued in CITY Fracas," *Globe and Mail* (GM), 26 June 1974; "Western Guard Head Denies Hating Blacks," *GM*, 29 Jan. 1975.

2 "Western Guard Leader Is Acquitted of Assault," *GM*, 30 Jan. 1975; "2 Musicians Wounded by Shots outside Yonge Street Tavern," *TS*, 28 Jan. 1975.

3 "Youth Shot to Death, Police Wound Suspect," *TS*, 7 May 1975; "Father Says Son on Trial for Killing Planned Race War," *TS*, 14 April 1976; "Jury Finds Man Insane in Slaying of Black Youth," *GM*, 15 April 1976.

4 *Contrast*, 16 April 1976; "Man Charged in Shooting of Musicians," *TS*, 18 Dec. 1975.

5 Editorial, "Is It Hate?" *Toronto Sun* (*Sun*), 18 June 1974; "Activists," *Sun*, 18 June 1974; editorial, "Racism," *Sun*, 12 May 1975; editorial, "Rum Jamaican," *Sun*, 15 May 1975; "The Swing to Violence," *Sun*, 3 Aug. 1975.

6 "Face of Fear: Racism in Canada," *GM*, 28 June 1975.

7 Paul Puritt, "Rosie Douglas" (letter), *GM*, 26 June 1975.

8 "The Question of Socialist Strategy" (editorial), *Caribbean Dialogue*, March 1976.

9 Michael Bodemann, "A Response to Rick Salutin," *Canadian Jewish Outlook*, April 1982.

10 See David Chud, "'Encounter' Proved Relevant," *Canadian Jewish Outlook*, August-September 1972; Sherri Bergman, "Responses to 'Encounter,'" *Canadian Jewish Outlook*, October 1972; Lynne Heller, "Responses to 'Encounter,'" *Canadian Jewish Outlook*, October 1972; Michael Bodemann, "Does the Jewish Left in Canada Have a Future?" *Canadian Jewish Outlook*, March 1981; Michael Bodemann, "What Place for Progressives?" *Canadian Jewish Outlook*, October 1981.

11 Małgorzata Kierylo, "'Equality Now!': Race, Racism and Resistance in 1970s Toronto," Ph.D. thesis, Queen's University, 2012.

12 "Metro Told to 'Keep Cool,'" *TS*, 10 May 1975; "Racism: Is Metro 'Turning Sour'?" *TS*, 10 May 1975; "250 Pakistanis in Metro Protest Star Story on Racism," *TS*, 20 May 1975.

13 "Racism: Is Metro 'Turning Sour'?"

14 "Immigration: Racism Issue Stalls Debate," *TS*, 31 May 1975.

15 "Immigration Panel Is Urged to Open Canada's Door Wider," *TS*, 10 June 1975; "Screams, Yells, Stall Hearing on Immigration," *TS*, 12 June 1975.

16 "Third World Books," *Contrast*, 27 Feb. 1976.

17 Davia K. Stasiulis, "Minority Resistance in the Local State: Toronto in the 1970s and 1980s," *Ethnic and Racial Studies*, January 1989; Claudio Lewis, "Blacks May Be Victims of Unemployment," *Contrast*, 22 July 1976; *Contrast*, 29 Aug. 1975; "bad, bad summer" in "Racism: Is Metro 'Turning Sour'?" In a 1976 study the Canadian Civil Liberties Association found that 11 of 15 employment agencies they surveyed were willing to screen out non-whites if asked by an employer.

18 *Contrast*, 6 Jan. 1977; Claudio Lewis, "'Many Faces of Black' Missed the Issues," *Contrast*, 20 Jan. 1977.

19 For an insightful overview of Black leftism with a particular focus on Montreal, see David Austin, *Fear of a Black Nation: Race, Sex and Security in Sixties Montreal* (Toronto: Between the Lines, 2013). For the Black student movement, see especially Ruramisai Charumbira, "'I Am Definitely Not Leaving without a Degree': A View from the Crossroads of Informal and Formal Learning—The Transitional Year Program at the University of Toronto," Research Report, 2001, https://nall.oise.utoronto.ca/res/72charumbira.pdf (accessed 21 May 2018).

20 "Women's Frustration to Be Aired on T.V. Channel 10," *Contrast*, 14 Nov. 1975; "Black Media Project," *Contrast*, 15 July 1976.

21 As in the case of the founder of the Black Student Union at Humber College, who was deported back to Nigeria in June 1975. *Old Mole*, June 1975.

22 "Canadian Blacks Demonstrate," *Labour Challenge*, 5 June 1972; "Anti-Racist Forces Unite—It's Only the Beginning," *Old Mole*, June 1975.

23 "Toward Social Consciousness," *Spear*, February 1975.

24 Clinton Joseph, "Recollections," in *Being Black*, ed. Althea Prince (London: Insomniac Press, 2001), 17; Karen Alcock, "Cover-Up Job," *Young Socialist Forum*, September-October 1975.

25 Joseph, "Recollections," 19; Lennox Brown, "A Crisis: Black Culture in Canada," *Black Images*, 1,1 (January 1972).

26 Paras Ramoutar, "CAR to Agitate for Realistic Policies through Political Action," *Contrast*, 31 Oct. 1975; "Group to Protest Mother's Deportation," *Contrast*, 6 Oct. 1977.

27 "CAR Chinatown Demonstration Supports Henry Fong, *Canadian Worker*, 21 Feb. 1975; "Reinstate Fong," *Canadian Worker*, 20 March 1975; "Letter from Members of the East Asian Studies Student Union," *Varsity*, 15 Oct. 1975; "Fight Mounts against Racist U of T—Fong Appeal," *Canadian Worker*, 17 Jan. 1976; "Angry Protesters Disrupt Meeting," *Varsity*, 27 Feb. 1976. Supportive societies ranged from the East Asian Studies Student Union to the Tai Chi Association.

28 See "Banfield Lecture Provokes Scuffling Incident," *Varsity*, 13 March 1974; "Classes Cancelled to Discuss Free Speech," *Varsity*, 27 March 1974; "Melee Outside: Gov Council Adjourns," *Varsity*, 29 March 1974; "The Caput Summer Follies," *Varsity*, 18 Sept. 1974.

29 Revolutionary Marxist Group (RMG), *Anti-Racist Work National Circular* (Toronto, 1975),

William Ready Division of Archives and Research Collections, McMaster University Library, Revolutionary Marxist Group (RMG) fonds, 1-1.

30 William Cameron, "Three Toronto Blacks Worry about Long, Hot Summer," *TS*, 18 June 1970; J. Ashton Brathwaite, *Nigger, This Is Canada* (Toronto: 21st Century Books, 1971); "Bathurst: What Is the Answer?" *Contrast*, 2 March 1972.

31 Lennox Brown, "A Crisis: Black Culture in Canada," *Black Images*, 1,1 (January 1972).

32 Horace Campbell and Selwyn Henry, letter to the editor, *TS*, 18 Jan. 1972; "Questions: Horace Campbell Looks Back," *Contrast*, 29 Sept. 1972.

33 "Davis Urges Whites to Join Blacks," *Varsity*, 25 Nov. 1974; "Contrast Takes Rough With Smooth as Blacks Seethe," *Contrast*, 20 June 1975; "Materialist Conception of History Urged—Horace Campbell," *Contrast*, 21 Feb. 1975. In 1975, in a period of increased friction between *Contrast* and young radicals, the newspaper denounced Campbell as "an itinerant champion of any community cause without a rebel." The Tacky group took its name from the leader of a Jamaican slave revolt of 1760.

34 Rosie Douglas, "My Objective in Dominica," *Caribbean Dialogue*, June-July 1976. See also Rosie Douglas, "A Look into the Future," *Spear*, September 1974. For Cabral in general, see Patrick Chabal, *Amilcar Cabral: Revolutionary Leadership and People's War* (Cambridge: Cambridge University Press, 1983).

35 Rosie Douglas, "Racism in Canada," *Labor Challenge*, 10 Feb. 1975.

36 "Anti-Racist Forces Unite," *Old Mole*, June 1975; "Racism Mounts; Left's Response Falters," *Old Mole*, January 1976.

37 Rosie Douglas, "Blacks in a Canadian Environment," *Spear*, August 1974.

38 Debbie Field, "Chalk up Two for the Good Guys," *Old Mole*, January 1976.

39 "Attacks on Black Community: Defence Force Set Up," *Black Voice* [Montreal], 25 May 1972; Claudio Lewis, "Adamson Raps Militants," *Contrast*, 27 Jan. 1977; "Hundreds Cheer as Indian Defence Group Launched," *Contrast*, 6 June 1975.

40 Jennifer Simmons, "East Indians Organize Self-Defense against Racist Attacks," *Old Mole*, May 1975. A recurrent issue surrounding the East Indian Defence Committee was its link with the CPC-ML, which limited its ability to work with other ant-racist forces.

41 "African Liberation Day," *Contrast*, 28 April 1976; "Let's Build Ties Rosie Started, Says Native Leader," *Contrast*, 9 March 1978; "Government Policy Attacked at Racism, Immigration Meeting," *Canadian Tribune* (*CT*), 7 May 1975; "Rally Attacks Racism 'Cancer,'" *Toronto Clarion*, 17-30 Oct. 1979; "Rally Reply Misses Mark," *GM*, 25 Oct. 1979; "200 Rock against Racism," *In Struggle!* 8 Jan. 1980; "Maoists Were Known and Accepted Part of Indian Caravan, Party Spokesman Says," *GM*, 9 Oct. 1974. Referring to a political divide in early 20th-century Russia, Harper opined that support for Native self-determination separated contemporary Bolsheviks and Mensheviks. See "Letter of Support from Vern Harper," *Lines of Demarcation*, July-August 1976.

42 "Canadian Indian Movement Rejects Help from Marxist-Leninists," *GM*, 7 Oct. 1974; Vern Harper, *Following the Red Path: The Native People's Caravan* (Toronto, NC Press, 1979), 43; *Native Peoples Struggle*, July 1975; Scott Rutherford, "Canada's Other Red Scare: Rights, Decolonization, and Indigenous Political Protest in the Global Sixties," Ph.D. thesis, Queen's University, 2011, 82, 179; "Indians Give Ottawa Ultimatum to Solve Mercury Pollution Issue," *GM*, 1 Oct. 1975; "Credibility: Closing the Gap on Mercury," *GM*, 4 Oct. 1975; "100 March in AIM Protest," *Sun*, 23 Jan. 1977; "AIM Wants New Peltier Trial, Investigation into Extradition," *CT*, 11 July 1977.

43 "Museum Sit-in Protests Taking of Indian Bones," *TS*, 1 Dec. 1976; "Indians End 1-Day Sit-in, Graves Will Be Protected," *TS*, 2 Dec. 1976; "Ontario Promises End to Removal of Indian

Bones," *GM*, 2 Dec. 1976; "Indians Warn of Angry Spirits," *TS*, 4 Dec. 1976; "Indians End ROM Sit-in: Ritual Calms Spirit of the Neutral Indian," *GM*, 4 Dec. 1976; "Indians Plan Their Own 'Museum' by Digging up White Pioneers," *GM*, 19 Dec. 1978; "Won't Dig up Sir John A., Indians Decide," *GM*, 28 July 1979.

44 Harper, *Following the Red Path*, 19, 27, 31, 39–44, 89–90. By the early 1980s Harper was working at Wandering Spirit School, a local alternative school for Indigenous children. See "Do the Schools Really Serve Our Different Communities?" *Mudpie*, June 1981; "Wandering Spirit School Extends Native Family," *Now*, 21 April 1983.

45 "New Direction," *Contrast*, 17 Jan. 1975; Arnold Auguste, "Why a Black Workers' Alliance," *Contrast*, 17 Jan. 1975; RMG, *Anti-Racist Work National Circular*; "Family Meeting with Rodney," *Black Labour*, 24 May 1975.

46 Xiaoping Li, *Voices Rising: Asian Canadian Cultural Activism* (Vancouver: UBC Press, 2007), 45–46. *Rikka*, a collectively produced Toronto journal founded prior to *Asianadian*, had a general social justice orientation informed by the pacifist politics of its founder George Yamada. For a brief political biography of Yamada, see "Activist Has 'a Passion for Justice,'" *TS*, 15 Dec. 2000.

47 Li, *Voices Rising*, 287.

48 T.T. Mao, "Asianadian and the Anglo Left," *Asianadian*, Winter 1979-80.

49 Ibid. In an exchange with an Asian activist who identified as being part of the "Anglo left," the author emphasized that he was not speaking for the wider collective and "The destiny of Asians in Canada can only be made by Asians." See Khurshed Wadud (letter), *Asianadian*, Spring 1980; "Mr Mao Speaks," *Asianadian*, Spring 1980.

50 Earlier in the decade a related controversy about the admission of Chinese Canadians to the medical school also demonstrated how many Canadians, including such prominent people as Bette Stephenson of the Canadian Medical Association and Morton Schulman, maverick NDP MPP and *Sun* columnist, harboured suspicions that Canadian students were being victimized by their foreign-born counterparts, even though most of the "Chinese students" in question were Canadians. "Foreign Medical Students Can't Talk to Patients: Shulman," *GM*, 22 March 1975; "Bad Old Days Are Still Too Close for Toronto's 50,000 Chinese," *GM*, 2 Aug. 1975; "Henry Fong Needs Help to Fight U of T Racism," *Varsity*, 8 Oct. 1975; "Evidence Uncovered in Fong Appeal Reveals Underlying Racism in Meds," *Varsity*, 10 Nov. 1975.

51 "W5 Angers U of T Community," *Varsity*, 10 Oct. 1979; "CTV 'Gives Away' Nothing," *Varsity*, 24 Oct. 1979; "W5 Producer Stands by Show," *Varsity*, 4 Feb. 1980.

52 "W5 Producer Stands by Show"; "2000 March on CTV," *Varsity*, 28 Jan. 1980; "'New Start' for Chinese," *Varsity*, 13 Feb. 1980; "Chinese Canadians Found National Council for Equality," *Forge*, 25 April 1980; "Forum on Racism: Both the Subtle and Not-So-Subtle," *Ward 8 News*, 21 Sept. 1980; "Racism Examined—the Other Conference," *Ward 8 News*, 14 March 1980; "200 Participate in Successful Rally for Albert Johnson Committee," *IS!* 4 March 1980; "300 at Rally for 'Firm Equality between Nations,'" *Forge*, 16 May 1980; "550 March against Klan," *Varsity*, 6 Oct. 1980.

53 Joan Sangster, "Radical Ruptures: Feminism, Labor, and the Left in the Long Sixties in Canada," *American Review of Canadian Studies*, 40,1 (February 2010), 1–21.

54 Working Women Community Centre, *Making the City: Women Who Made a Difference* (Black Point, N.S.: Fernwood Publishing, 2012), 13, 25, 28, 34, 36, 42, 49, 65, 72–74.

55 Lynn McFadden and Janet Patterson, "Breakthrough: Women Publish," *Breakthrough*, November 1977. The origins of the paper could be traced to militants previously active in Harbinger and the Women's Workshop on the York campus.

56 As pointed out by *Emergency Librarian* co-editor Sherill Cheda in *Other Woman*, 1,2 (September 1972).

57 Charnie Guettel, *Marxism and Feminism* (Toronto: Canadian Women's Educational Press, 1974); Dorothy E. Smith, *Feminism and Marxism—A Place to Begin, A Way to Go* (Vancouver: New Star Books, 1977).

58 Meg Luxton, "A Study of Urban Communes and Co-ops in Toronto," M.A. thesis, University of Toronto, 1973, 37, 80, 127.

59 Ibid., 37, 50–52, 58, 71, 117, 137.

60 Saul V. Levine, Robert P. Carr, and Wendy Horenblas, "The Urban Commune: Fact or Fad, Promise or Pipedream?" *American Journal of Orthopsychiatry*, 43,1 (January 1973), 150, 156. These authors did fret that children were allegedly receiving "early political . . . indoctrination."

61 Luxton, "Study of Urban Communes and Co-ops in Toronto," 35–36, 49, 110, 112, 115, 123.

62 Becki Ross, *The House That Jill Built: A Lesbian Nation in Formation* (Toronto: University of Toronto Press, 1995), 96–100. Some activists she interviewed left the city entirely, heading to British Columbia or rural areas of Ontario to further their experiments in living otherwise.

63 "Women Launch Media Group," *Varsity*, 2 Oct. 1972; Robin Barry Simpson, "What We Got Away With: Rochdale College and Canadian Art in the Sixties," M.A. thesis, Concordia University, 2011, 80–83; "You Would Have Liked to Meet These Women" (letter), *TS*, 7 June 1972. Like a number of projects Liberation Media came armed with a LIP grant and was also assisted by its cheap office rent at Rochdale.

64 Mary O'Brien, *The Politics of Reproduction* (London: Routledge & Kegan Paul, 1981).

65 Mary O'Brien, "At School on the Street," [n.d. but early 1978], OISE WAVAW, vertical file: 1-3; "Protests Bring Large Audiences and Box-Office Receipts to Snuff," *GM*, 10 Nov. 1977; "Horror Film Horrible Rip-Off," *TS*, 8 Nov. 1977; "Shrill Women Getting Worse," *GM*, 16 Nov. 1977.

66 O'Brien, "At School on the Street," 6, 11.

67 This dismissive opinion surfaced especially during negotiations between the LSA and the RMG over a possible merger. See Joanna Rossi, "Correct the Errors in Our Women's Liberation Work," *RWL/LOR PanCanadian Preconvention Discussion Bulletin*, 2-19, April 1979.

68 This was especially the case in the Revolutionary Workers' League, whose internal documents credit the *Snuff* protests with sparking discussion on the issue. "Morgan" wrote an interesting "Report on the Rape Question," RWL, *Appendix to the English Canadian National Bureau*, minute no.10, RWL and RMG boxes, Canadian Women's Movement Archives (CWMA) fonds, University of Ottawa Archives and Special Collections.

69 "Nellie's Still at War for More $$$ to Give Troubled Women a Hand," *Sun*, 13 Sept. 1976; "Nellie's Needs More," *Toronto Clarion*, 15 Oct. 1976; minutes, Tuesday, 1 Nov. 1977, WAVAW file, CWMA fonds. The two shelters were documented by the cultural front via TPM's play *Dreamgirls*, which was inspired by Interval House, and Teri Chmilar's film *Nellies*. See "Loser in War, Peace," *CT*, 22 Jan. 1979; letter, Judith, "Dear Sisters," 15 Dec. 1978, Toronto IWDC box, folder: Reports, speeches, flyers and other material, re: basis of unity, 1978, CWMA fonds; Teri Chmilar, dir., *Nellies*, video, 1981.

70 Robin Martin, "The Birth and Growth of the Law Union," *Law Union News*, September 1985.

71 Phillip Zylberberg, "The Rapist: Your Kind of Client?" *Law Union News*, February 1976.

72 Sylvia E. Searles, "Feminine Liberation," *Spear*, August 1976; Pat Thorpe, "The Black Woman and Woman's Lib," *Contrast*, 26 April 1974; Gregory Regis, "Black Women Urged to Fight Alone," *Contrast*, 5 Dec. 1975.

73 "Women's Lib Is an Outgrowth of a Bad Seed," *Contrast*, 14 Nov. 1975.

74 "Black Genocide?" *Contrast*, 1 Feb. 1974; "Birth Control," *Contrast*, 10 May 1974.

75 "Perspectives on the Women Question," *Black Labour*, 24 April 1975; B.W.S.R.C., "Perspectives on the Woman Question," *Black Labour*, 24 May 1975; "Perspective on the Woman Question: Women's Employment Centre Launched," *Black Labour*, August 1975; "Black Women in Struggle," *Black Labour*, August 1975; Valarie Braithwaite, "Changing Times," *Reaching Out*, 1.1 [n.d. probably mid-1970s].

76 Cynthia D. Jordan, "Social Participation and Social Change," *Reaching Out*, 1.1, n.d.

77 Varda Burstyn, "The Waffle and the Women's Movement," *Studies in Political Economy*, 33 (Autumn 1990), 175–84, citations at 176, 180; Judy Rebick, *Ten Thousand Roses: The Making of a Feminist Revolution* (Toronto: Penguin Canada, 2005), xii.

78 Bill Robinson, "Men and Liberation," *Other Woman*, December 1975; "The Other Side: Men's Lib," *Breakthrough*, October 1975.

79 "Collective Ramblings," *Other Woman*, 1,1 (May 1972).

80 Tom Warner, *Never Going Back: A History of Queer Activism in Canada* (Toronto: University of Toronto Press, 2002), 9–10, 59–60.

81 Peter Zorzi, "Me and the Bars and Charlie and TGA," http://www.onthebookshelves.com/tga.htm (accessed 6 Aug. 2016).

82 John Bannon and Brian Bennett, "A Perspective on Gay Liberation," LSA (League for Socialist Action) IDB (Internal Discussion Bulletin), no. 2, June 1972.

83 Letter, Brian Waite and Cheri DiNovo, 21 Aug. 1971, Canadian Lesbian and Gay Archives (CLGA), 28 Aug. folder; conversation with David Newcome, 28 Aug. 1971 folder, CLGA; Scott Frederick de Groot, "Out of the Closet and into Print: Gay Liberation across the Anglo-American World," Ph.D. thesis, Queen's University, 2015, 240. Maurice Flood suggests that a couple of members of Vancouver's new left–dominated gay liberation front—a group he referred to as "the Vietcong of Gay Liberation"—appeared at the demonstration in "revolutionary drag" and had no interest in TGA's brief to the government; see Maurice Flood, "For a Full (Not Limited) Intervention in Gay Liberation," LSA IDB, no. 16, 1972.

84 De Groot, "Out of the Closet and into Print," 240.

85 Toronto Gay Action, "What Is Gay Liberation?" n.d., CLGA, box 3, CAN 5618.

86 Minutes of Toronto Gay Action Meeting, 4 July 1971, CLGA, MAM folder; Bannon and Bennett, "Perspective on Gay Liberation"; TGA, Executive Meeting—May 29, 1972, minutes, accounts, membership lists folder, CLGA. TGA later backtracked and returned to a more traditional structure.

87 Toronto Gay Action, Membership List, CLGA; Bannon and Bennett, "Perspective on Gay Liberation." Maurice Flood in 1977 returned to vintage new left themes in "A Proposal," *Body Politic*, May 1977, in which he urged a gay liberation movement without a "specialized priesthood," with no presidents and a minimum of hierarchy.

88 Toronto Gay Action (TGA), *What Is Gay Liberation?* (Toronto: n.d. [c.1971]), CLGA, box 3, CAN 5618; Hugh Brewster, *Letter to Dear Sisters and Brothers* (July 1972), 28 July 1972, CLGA, box 3, CAN 5618; *On Our Own—Gay Consciousness* (reprinted from a New York-based gay liberation group), n.d., CLGA, box 3, CAN 5618.

89 de Groot, "Out of the Closet and into Print," 148.

90 Toronto Gay Action, *Take Off Your Masks* (Toronto: n.d. [early 1970s]), CLGA, file "TGA."

91 "A Program for Gay Liberation," *Body Politic*, November/December 1971; TGA, "What Is Gay Liberation?"; untitled, *Body Politic*, January/February 1972; Bannon and Bennett, "Perspective

on Gay Liberation"; untitled, CLGA, TGA folder (with Ian Young's signature at the top of the list of names); John Bannon, "Some Further Notes on Gay Liberation," LSA IDB, no. 24, December 1972. The Vietnam Mobilization Committee, Young Socialists, and Toronto women's groups were also invited to the first Pride Parade.

92 TGA, *What Is Gay Liberation?*; TGA, *Take Off Your Masks*; TGA, "Dear Student Council" (Toronto: 1972), CLGA, file "TGA." It would be many years before equally important issues or language usages, such as trans, non-binary, two-spirited, queer and questioning, and intersex—and usage of "they"—came to the fore.

93 De Groot, "Out of the Closet and into Print."

94 TGA, *Take Off Your Masks*.

95 Editorial, "Gone 'Fission,'" *Body Politic*, Winter 1973. The editorial dismissed CHAT as a Canadian equivalent to NAACP (recalling Toronto Black liberationists who had equated NBCC to NAACP) and suggested that CHAT's LIP grant had helped to defuse dissent.

96 Warner, *Never Going Back*, 70; Zorzi, "Me and the Bars and Charlie and TGA"; "Spirited March Launches Gay Pride Week," *Body Politic*, September/October 1974.

97 De Groot, "Out of the Closet and into Print," 51; Peter Zorzi, "Queer Catharsis," http://onthebookshelves.com/qcmenu.htm (accessed 13 July 2011). Zorzi writes that most members of the initial *Body Politic* collective were members of TGA.

98 "A Program for Gay Liberation," *Body Politic*, November/December 1971; Warner, *Never Going Back*, 71; Brian Waite, "Strategy for Gay Liberation," *Body Politic*, March/April 1972; Gary Kinsman and Patrizia Gentile, *The Canadian War on Queers: National Security as Sexual Regulation* (Vancouver; Toronto: UBC Press, 2010), 273–74.

99 John Wilson (letter), *Body Politic*, July/August 1972; editorial, "Never Going Back," *Body Politic*, Spring 1973.

100 Michael Lynch, "The End of the 'Human Rights' Decade," *Body Politic*, July 1979.

101 Ibid. For Lynch's biography, see Ann Silversides, *Aids Activist: Michael Lynch and the Politics of Community* (Toronto: Between the Lines, 2003).

102 "Media," *Body Politic*, December/January 1978; *Body Politic*, December/January 1979; "Rights of Access," *Body Politic*, November 1977; "Maclean Hunter Cancels Gay T.V.," *Body Politic*, June/July 1978.

103 Lynch, "End of the 'Human Rights' Decade."

104 Tim McCaskell, "The Political Perspective" (review), *Body Politic*, October 1975; McCaskell, "Heterosexual" (review), *Body Politic*, September 1976.

105 McCaskell, "Heterosexual"; Amy et al. (including Gary Kinsman), "On 'Gay Liberation in Canada, A Socialist Perspective': A Critique of the Recent Publication of the League for Socialist Action," RWL *Joint Internal Bulletin*, no. 15, July 1977; "Lesbian and Gay Liberation and the RMG," RWL box, CWMA fonds.

106 "Dr. Bunge and the Vancouver Geographical Expedition: Expletives Undeleted," *USG Newsletter*, May 1977. The context for Bunge's comments was a later expedition in Vancouver, but it seems reasonable to infer Bunge's attitudes on this question would have been similar in the Toronto context.

107 Ross, *House That Jill Built*, 34–35.

108 Ibid., 33–36.

109 Nora Ruck, "Liberating Minds: Consciousness-Raising as a Bridge between Feminism and Psychology in 1970s Canada," *History of Psychology*, 18,3 (2015), 299; agenda, 12 Oct. 1972, box 141, CWMA fonds; Policy Meeting, 4 Feb. 1973, box 141, CWMA fonds.

110 Ruck, "Liberating Minds," 300; Collective Meeting, 9 Feb. 1973, CWMA fonds, 141; Ross, *House That Jill Built*, 48–50.

111 Bannon and Bennett, "Perspective on Gay Liberation."

112 Toronto Trotskyists were themselves acting on the basis of a long history. Dowson believed that socialists should nurture an enlightened attitude towards sexuality; that he himself was gay meant that the Canadian movement did not blindly follow the path of their American counterparts, some of whom described homosexuality as a symptom of a society in decay. See Ernest Tate, *Revolutionary Activism in the 1950s and 1960s*, vol. 1, *Canada 1955–1965* (London: Resistance Books, 2014), 14.

113 Maurice Flood, "Gay Liberation Is That Important," *Body Politic*, November/December 1974; Kinsman and Gentile, *Canadian War on Queers*, 274 (citing John Wilson).

114 Bannon and Bennett, "Perspective on Gay Liberation"; Flood, "For a Full (Not limited) Intervention in Gay Liberation"; Bannon, "Some Further Notes on Gay Liberation."

115 Brian Mossop, untitled review, *Body Politic*, December 1975.

116 Warner, *Never Going Back*, 134–40.

117 For analysis of the election, see "We Lost," *Body Politic*, December/January 1981.

118 Nik Barry-Shaw, "Reve/cauchemar: Allende's Chile and the Polarization of the Quebec Left in the 1970s," M.A. thesis, Queen's University, 2014.

119 Sean Mills, "Popular Internationalism: Grassroots Exchange and Social Movements," in *Canada and the Third World: Overlapping Histories*, ed. Sean Mills, Scott Rutherford, and Karen Dubinsky (Toronto: University of Toronto Press, 2015).

120 David Sheinin, "Cuba's Long Shadow: The Progressive Church Movement and Canadian-Latin American Relations, 1970–87," in *Our Place in the Sun: Canada and Cuba in the Castro Era*, ed. Robert Wright and Lana Wylie (Toronto and Buffalo: University of Toronto Press, 2009), 124–25.

121 Cited in Mills, "Popular Internationalism," 260.

122 Ibid.

123 Ana Alberro and Gloria Montero, "The Immigrant Woman," in *Women in the Canadian Mosaic*, ed. Gwen Matheson (Toronto: Peter Martin Associates, 1976), 143–45, 147–48.

124 Janice Acton, interview with self, July 1993, Central American Solidarity Activists fonds, William Ready Division of Archives and Research Collections, 1-1.

125 Working Women Community Centre, *Making the City*, 36–39.

126 Bryon Pfeiffer and George Biggar, "Should the LU Take a Position on the Palestinian Question?" *Law Union News*, June 1979; Harry Kopyto, "Duty to Take a Position," *Law Union News*, April 1980; Shalom Schachter, "Can't Be Armchair Radicals," *Law Union News*, April 1980. For the position of the United Jewish People's Organization, see "UJPO Statement on Road to Peace in the Middle East," *Canadian Jewish Outlook*, January 1976.

127 Enoch Michael, "Deliberate Distortion of Problems Confronting the Jewish Community," *Canadian Jewish Outlook*, July-August 1974; "New Left's Effect on Jews Described," *GM*, 17 May 1969; "U.S. Jews Concerned by New Left Hostility to Israel," *GM*, 18 Aug. 1970.

128 George Lewis, "Rabbi Plaut—Harbinger of Doom," *Canadian Jewish Outlook*, April-March 1973.

129 Abraham Feinberg, "For Me, to Be a Jew Means to Be a Radical," *Canadian Jewish Outlook*, July 1972. For an interesting commentary, see Laura Doliner, "Dilemmas of a Jew on the Left," *Canadian Jewish Outlook*, December 1982; Esther Reiter and David Rapaport, "Jewish Identity, Socialist Commitment: A Debate on Left Anti-Semitism," *Canadian Jewish Outlook*,

October 1981. Cy Gonick of *Canadian Dimension* was particularly unhappy with the comparison between Israel's conduct in the Middle East and that of the Americans in Vietnam. On the other hand, as early as 1961, George Haggar, future leader of the CAF, was condemning those who claimed Israel had been carved out of the wilderness, whom he likened to Canadian Tories.

130 "The Canadian Arab Federation," *Arab Dawn*, October 1968; Jim Peters, "Arab Nationalism Abroad," *Arab Dawn*, August 1970. The federation was founded in November 1967.

131 Editorial, "Canadians, Arabs, Lebanese or Nothing," *Arab Dawn*, July 1969.

132 "FACS Convention," *Arab Dawn*, June-July 1971; "Abu-Lughod on Palestinian Revolution," *Arab Dawn*, June-July 1971; "Canadian Arab Federation Convention," *Arab Dawn*, February 1975; editorial, "One Failure of Arab Propaganda," *Arab Dawn*, September 1969. On the other hand, an *Arab Dawn* editorial suggested that voters give the Progressive Conservative's Robert Stanfield a try because the Liberals and NDP were seen to be more pro-Zionist. See "Stanfield Deserves a Chance" (editorial), *Arab Dawn*, Winter 1973.

133 "Soul Searching Fails to Define CCF Stand," *Varsity*, 5 Feb. 1961. Haggar diverged from his otherwise pragmatic liberalism by suggesting that companies with more than ten employees should be nationalized.

134 Flora Roy, *Recollections of Waterloo Lutheran University 1960–1973* (Waterloo, Ont.: Wilfrid Laurier University Press, 2006), 125; "30 Doctors Volunteer for Middle East," *GM*, 7 June 1967; "Canadian Arabs Ask for Diplomatic Break," *GM*, 20 June 1967. Haggar lamented that he would have liked to help those wanting to enlist in the general military effort as well, but that he had to turn away such volunteers, fearing they would lose their Canadian citizenship.

135 "Student Radicalism" (letter), *GM*, 18 Sept. 1969; Roy, *Recollections of Waterloo Lutheran University*, 127; George Haggar, "Academic Freedom and All That," *Canadian Dimension*, September-October 1968. The context was Haggar's firing from WLU.

136 George S. Haggar, *Imperialism and Revolution in the Mideast* (Toronto: Tahrir Press, n.d.), 7–9, 13, 18, 19–22, 27; "Black Radicals Clash on Nationalism," *Toronto Telegram* (*TT*), 16 March 1970. Haggar traced the changes in the USSR to the Communist Party's 1956 congress.

137 Roy, *Recollections of Waterloo Lutheran University*, 125–27. While teaching at Waterloo he ran for city council on a platform opposing land speculation and supporting community organizations, among other things.

138 "Arab Spokesman Accuses 5 Universities and Colleges of Bias," *GM*, 15 Sept. 1969; Roy, *Recollections of Waterloo Lutheran University*, 127; "Pro-Arab Professor Is Backed by Students in Dismissal by WLU," *GM*, 16 Jan. 1968; "400 Skip Class for Firing Inquiry," *GM*, 18 Jan. 1968.

139 "More Foreign Faculty Said Required by 1975," *GM*, 8 April 1972; "Demonstrators Ejected," *GM*, 27 Jan. 1971; Dee Knight, "Canadian Nationalism: Fighting Imperialism," *Alive*, March-April 1971. Robin Mathews was the editor, with James Steele, of *The Struggle for Canadian Universities* (Toronto: New Press, 1969), raising the issue of "the rapidly diminishing proportions of Canadians on . . . university faculties."

140 "Pro-Arabs Demonstrate against Zionists," *GM*, 3 April 1967; "The 'Vanguard' and 'Tribune' Comment on the 27th . . . and a Slight Reply," *CNLF Bulletin* [Canadians for the NLF], 1, 5 (May 1968); "Arabs Hold Rally to Mark Mosque Burning, Told to End War with Israel 'by God and Gun,'" *GM*, 25 Aug. 1969; "City Arabs Protest Mosque Fire," *TT*, 23 Aug. 1969. Press coverage highlighted a Canadian Jewish Congress statement depicting the rally as part of an international propaganda campaign of anti-Semitism and racism.

141 "Students Protest Pro-Arab Conference," *TS*, 26 Sept. 1969; "Anti-Arab Students March on Rochdale," *TT*, 26 Sept. 1969; "Students Protest Pro-Arab Conference," *TS*, 26 Sept. 1969;

"Arab-Jewish Clash Averted by 4 Police at Queen's Park," *TS*, 29 Sept. 1969; "Arabs Toss out Protesting Jews," *TT*, 29 Sept. 1969; "Militant Jewish Group Plans Toronto Branch," *TS*, 3 Nov. 1969; "PLO Uproar Grows, but Ottawa Still Pussyfoots," *Sun*, 11 July 1975; "Are You Going to Postpone Olympics?" *Sun*, 23 July 1975; "Arafat Called the Perfect Criminal," *Sun*, 17 July 1975.

142 "Zionists Curb PLO Tongue," *Varsity*, 21 Nov. 1975; "Fights, Shouts, Force Arabs to Cancel PLO Speaker," *Sun*, 20 Nov. 1975; "Banfield Revisited?" (editorial), *Varsity*, 21 Nov. 1975; "Threats Stop Arab Talks," *Sun*, 23 Nov. 1975; photo caption, *Sun*, 24 Nov. 1975.

143 Junior Anthony, "Caribana Follies: Is the Festival a Cop Out?" *Spear*, July 1974; Maureen McNerney, "Multiculturalism: Myth and Reality," *Rikka*, Spring 1980; Charles Roach, "Canadian Apartheid? *Rikka*, Winter 1981.

144 "The Black Education Project 1969–1976," n.d., Multicultural History Society of Ontario, Black, box 2, 5–7; Rosie Douglas, "Interview," *Old Mole*, December 1974. For an earlier critique, see Horace Campbell, "OFY-LIP: Liberal Rip-Off Continues (Or: What I Didn't Do during My Summer Holidays), *Varsity*, 15 March 1972.

145 "Black Apathy," *Contrast*, 14 April 1977; "Contrast and Islander to Merge," *Contrast*, 11 Aug. 1977.

146 "Native Caravan Arrives in Ottawa," *Old Mole*, October 1974.

147 "Proposed Program for an Activist Caucus within CHAT," CLGA, TGA I folder; Bob Wallace, "Wheat and Women: The Failure of Feminism in the West," *Body Politic*, Spring 1973.

148 "On Diversity and Diversion" (editorial), *Body Politic*, Autumn 1972.

149 For example, writers in *The Other Woman* likened Canada itself to a woman dependent upon her American man and drew a parallel between Canadians' acceptance of second-class treatment and women's acceptance of inferior status in their relationships. See Eva Zaremba, "USA & Canada," *Other Woman*, March 1973; Susan Crean, "Can Canadian Feminists Be Patriots?" *Other Woman*, August 1973.

10. New Leninists and New Constellations: In Quest of the Revolutionary Party, 1971–82

1 "Resignation from the Canadian RMG," *Workers Vanguard*, 2 Aug. 1974; "Draft Tasks and Perspectives, Canadian Ctte. of the International Spartacist Tendency," *IDB* (*Internal Discussion Bulletin*), 1, 4, July 1975.

2 "No-Nuke Reaction," *Spartacist Canada*, June/July 1979; "No Phoney Cultural Boycotts, But Militant Labor Solidarity!" *Spartacist Canada*, April 1977.

3 "Canada Report Based on Visit of 23-27 May 75 by George C and 23-30 May 1975 by Reuben S., Canadian Ctte. of the International Spartacist Tendency," *IDB*, 2, 30 July 1975.

4 "On the Tasks and Perspectives of the CCIST, Canadian Ctte. of the International Spartacist Tendency," *IDB*, 2, 30 July 1975; "Political Bureau Minutes of the TLC," 8, 27 Sept. 1975, 1996-022/011(05), Libby Scheier fonds, Clara Thomas Archives and Special Collections; "Canada Report Based on Visit." Some Trotskyist Leaguers were assigned to "security" positions that necessitated keeping their membership secret, probably with the objective of obtaining information about rival Trotskyist organizations. See "Comment on D's Document; Effects of the Security Situation," 1996-022/012(62), Libby Scheier fonds.

5 Cited in "Party Grows Stronger through Its Leadership of Struggles," *Forge*, 27 April 1978.

6 "In Struggle Now Turns to Direct Attacks on Socialist China," *Forge*, 2 Sept. 1977; "Cuban Trawlers with Russian Captains . . . Caught by Surprise in Canadian Fishing Zone," *Forge*, 18 Nov. 1976; "US Yields to Rise of USSR," *Forge*, 20 May 1976; "Appeasement: Green Light for Soviet Aggression," *Forge*, 6 Oct. 1978; *Forge*, 8 Feb. 1980; *Forge*, 24 April 1980; "Tories Soft on Soviet Aggression," *Forge*, 25 Jan. 1980. CPC-ML published similar attacks on the USSR.

7 Marjaleena Repo, "The Impoverishment of the Canadian Left," *Transformation*, Summer 1972.

8 Ibid.

9 Ibid.

10 Catherine MacLeod, *Waking up in the Men's Room* (Toronto: Between the Lines, 1998).

11 "RMG Second Convention," *Old Mole*, May 1975; "Building the Revolutionary Party in Canada," *IDB*, 1,3, 29 Aug. 1973; *Old Mole*, 7, May 1974.

12 After Trotsky and his supporters were kicked out of the parties that formed the Moscow-led Third International, they founded the Fourth International (in 1936, in Paris) to rally like-minded revolutionaries from around the world.

13 Toronto Collective, "Toronto Collective Statement," June 1976. Per Connexions: connexions.org/CxLibrary/Docs/CX19183-Autonomy&PowerWithinWorkingClass.pdf. (accessed 20 May 2018).

14 "Party Discipline, Loyalty and Security," *RWL Information Bulletin*, October 1982; "Forging the Proletarian Marxist Leadership of the Revolutionary Workers League," *RWL Information Bulletin*, March 1983.

15 John Cleveland, "The Political Is Personal: Why Women in the Canadian Marxist Group In Struggle Changed from Opposing to Supporting the Feminist Ideology of the Autonomous Women's Movement," M.A. thesis, Simon Fraser University, 1983, 144, 193, 138. One member, whose marriage to a non-party member was on the cusp of unravelling, received special, albeit reluctant permission—"revolutionary work is incompatible with a normal couple's life"—to decrease time spent on party work in an attempt to salvage the relationship. Under these circumstances the member only had to work for the party three nights and one week-end day a week in addition to attendance at cell plenary meetings; ibid., 197.

16 Ibid., 46–47. CCL/WCP's security measures were similar. See Judy Pocock, interview, 16 Oct. 2011, Toronto.

17 Minutes, 4 Sept. 1976, NPC (NPC) fonds, 6-4, Baldwin Room, Toronto Public Library; minutes, 15 Oct. 1976, NPC fonds, 6-4.

18 Clarke, "Building the Unity of the Left," *Discussion*, no. 2 (26 Feb. 1969), NPC fonds, 2-19. As the minutes of the Communist Party's Central Executive Committee (CEC) from the period reveal, either one of the two internal factions—the Eurocommunists or the hard-liners—might appeal to the "silent majority" in the centre in order to undercut the other—even to the extent of demanding the opponent's dissolution on the grounds of factionalism, a charge that could easily boomerang on those who made it. CEC minutes, 4 Nov. 1970, NPC fonds, 2-24.

19 Phyllis Clarke, "Need to Fight Sectarianism," *Discussion*, 14 March 1969, NPC fonds, 2-19.

20 Stanley B. Ryerson, *The Open Society: Paradox and Challenge* (New York: International Publishers, 1965); Ryerson, "For Broader Approaches," *Discussion*, no. 2 (26 Feb. 1969), NPC fonds, 2-19; Charnie Cunningham, "Why Bureaucratic Paralysis?" *Discussion*, no. 4 (25 March 1969), NPC fonds, 2-19.

21 Untitled, NPC fonds, 2-7; minutes, 4 Sept. 1976, 7 March 1977, 4 Sept. 1976, NPC fonds, 6-4; UT Club, 10 Aug. 1974, 10 Sept. 1974, NPC fonds, 6-2; minutes, 18 April 1977, NPC

fonds, 6-2; minutes, 13 Sept., 20 Sept. 1976, NPC fonds, 6-4. See University of Toronto Club, "Proposals on Program Amendments," *Discussion*, 14 March 1969, NPC fonds, 2-19.

22 "Build the Party and Its Influence amongst New Immigrant Groups," 12-14 Oct. 1974, NPC fonds, 3-7; 3 Oct. 1976, 14 Oct. 1976, NPC fonds, 6-4; CEC minutes, 31 Aug. 1972, NPC fonds, 3-1; CEC minutes, 14 Aug. 1979, NPC fonds, 3-23; CEC minutes, 28 Aug. 1979, NPC fonds, 3-23; CEC minutes, 11 Sept. 1979, NPC fonds, 3-23.

23 Clarke, untitled, NPC fonds, box 8, criticism of C.P.C. folder.

24 Ibid., 13, 8–10, 12, 14.

25 Sheila Rowbotham, Lynne Segal, and Hilary Wainwright, *Beyond the Fragments: Feminism and the Making of Socialism* (London: Merlin Press, 1979).

26 Clarke, untitled, NPC fonds, box 8, criticism of C.P.C. folder, 14. Underlining added by Clarke.

27 Ibid.

28 "Canadian Revolutionists Meet," *Labor Challenge*, 7 May 1973.

29 "Study Group on Historical Questions," Study Group, no. 1 folder, Abbie Bakan collection (her personal papers); "Membership Report," *Advance*, November 1973; Murray Cooke, "To Interpret the World and to Change It: Interview with David McNally," *Socialist Studies*, 7 1/2 (Spring/Fall 2011), 5. At this time the Waffle was formally called the Movement for an Independent and Socialist Canada (MISC) nationally but maintained the name Ontario Waffle provincially.

30 "Lenin on the Party," n.d.; untitled, n.d.; 13 Jan. 1973 minutes; "Structural Weaknesses of the Waffle," n.d.; "Preamble," all Bakan collection; and "A Movement Strategy," *Advance*, October 1973. For an atypically extensive engagement with Mao's ideas within the Waffle, see Robert Laxer, "National and Class Struggles in English Canada and Quebec," *Advance*, April 1974.

31 Abbie Bakan and Philip Murton, "Origins of the International Socialists," *Marxism: A Socialist Annual* (2004), 58–60; "Lenin on the Party," n.d., Bakan collection; "General Orientation to Work in the Waffle" [clipped piece of paper says June 1974], Bakan collection.

32 Bonnie Benedict et al., "Revolutionary Socialist Programme," author's personal collection; Bonnie Benedict et al., "Strategy for Waffle," *Advance*, September 1974. Members of the study group tussled with a new left–influenced tendency in the Waffle that preferred a "counter-hegemonic" strategy to the status quo of emphasizing workplace struggles, party-building, and Canadian nationalism. See Brian Smith et al., "A Letter of Resignation to all Ontario Wafflers," n.d., author's personal collection; D. Lake et al., "Reply to West Metro 'Letter of Resignation,'" *Advance*, 13 Nov. 1973.

33 "Transformation Tactics and Details," 1975, Bakan collection; "Organizing for I.S. Work," personal collection; "Toronto Branch Reports," personal collection; "Assessment of Practices in Waffle," Bakan collection.

34 "Industrial Policy Evaluation," personal collection; untitled joint resignation statement, personal collection; "Open Letter to Comrades in the Canadian I.S.," personal collection.

35 Taylor, "A Critique of the 'Immediate Turn' Document," *RWL Preconvention Discussion Bulletin*, February 1979; Executive Committee, "Tasks and Perspectives for I.S. Canada," August 1976, Bakan collection. There were also complaints that industrialization led IS to ignore socialist movements outside the workplace and to ignore or disparage women activists. See also "Amendments to the Tasks and Perspectives Document" (submitted by women's commission and passed), August 1976, Bakan collection.

36 Executive Committee, "Tasks and Perspectives for I.S. Canada"; "The Agitational Tasks of a Propaganda Group," 11 Dec. 1976; "Industrial Perspectives," August 1976, Bakan collection.

In criticizing its past practice, IS's executive committee suggested that York graduate students had been the worst "petty-baiters."

37 "Toronto Area Committee Report," Canadian Liberation Movement (CLM) fonds, 24-Congress 1975 folder, William Ready Division of Archives and Research Collections, McMaster University Library; "Toronto Area Report, Quarterly meeting," October 1974, 7-6.

38 "Toronto Area Committee Report"; "Larry Haiven for Alderman, CLM fonds, 4-28; "Toronto Area Report, Quarterly Meeting, October 1974," 7-6. A report notes that the chair of GRO lent support to their election campaign.

39 See the November and December 1973 issues of CLM's newsletter for the debate; ML Caucus, "On Yankee Go Home," *CLM Newsletter*, December 1973; "Police Should Worry about Racists, CLM," *Contrast*, 4 July 1975.

40 "Victory for CWU in Controversial Ballot," *Sun*, 13 Jan. 1976; "Unions Draw up Plans to Fight Rival," *Sun*, 11 March 1975; "CLM Labour Organizer's Report—March 1975," CLM fonds, 3-42. Though members of CLM's Hamilton branch lent assistance to one local certification drive, its chairman was criticized for refusing to mount a CWU campaign at his steel factory; "Victory for CWU in Controversial Ballot"; "Union Supporter Wins Job Back," *Sun*, 19 Aug. 1976. The fired vice-chair of CWU also had a victory at the board, which concluded he had been fired for union-organizing.

41 ML Caucus, "Let Us Unite and Go Forward," CLM fonds, 3-30.

42 "Paper on Sectarianism," *CLM Newsletter*, 3-1, January 1974; "General Secretary's Report," CLM fonds, 4-18; "Minutes of the Quarterly Meeting, 26–27 Oct. 1974," box 7, Quarterly Meeting, Oct. 26 folder, CLM fonds.

43 "Minutes of the Quarterly Meeting, 26–27 Oct. 1974."

44 "Self-Criticism—Betty Bower (CLM)," 1974, CLM fonds, 3-17; "Warning," *CLM Newsletter*, 1974.

45 Untitled document, 5-Lord, Gail folder, CLM fonds; Larry M., "It Is Time for a Reckoning"; untitled, 7-24; Errol Sharpe, "Regarding Gary Perly," 3-27, all CLM fonds.

46 "Special Supplement to Newsletter," *CLM Newsletter*, December 1975; "How Bourgeois Selfishness Sabotaged the Implementation of the New New Canada Plan," *CLM Newsletter*, 3,2; "Toronto Area Committee Report," CLM fonds, 24-Congress 1975 folder; "Toronto East Club Political Report," CLM fonds, 24-Congress 1975 folder; "Toronto Area Report," CLM fonds, 8-6. Some self-criticisms—around care of an air-conditioner or kitchen cleaning—suggest many members lived communally, extending proscribed penance to all aspects of life. It was also an opportunity for mutual surveillance, as criticizing the conduct of another member was sometimes seen as a step forward in an individual's self-criticism process. See Lord, Barry, self-criticism folder, CLM fonds 5-56; Haiven, Larry, self criticism folder, CLM fonds 5-26.

47 Untitled, 7-24, CLM fonds; "It Is Time for a Reckoning."

48 Motions of the CLM Congress, 28, 29 Feb. 1976, CLM fonds, 4-29; Greg Keilty, "Some Opinions on the Role of Fascism in the CLM," CLM fonds, 5-21. The author branded some members as anti-baby, anti-parent, and anti-people circa 1973.

49 Keilty, "Some Opinions on the Role of Fascism in the CLM."

50 Keilty, "The Caucus within the Caucus," CLM fonds, 4-6.

51 David A. Owen, *My Confession: The Making of a Militant* (Toronto: On the Edge Press, 2005), 59, 61, 67, 93–94.

52 "Establish Communist Leadership in the Factories," *Worker*, 17 Jan. 1976.

53 Owen, *My Confession*, 67, 93, 97–98; *Worker*, 6 March 1976; "CPLer for Teachers' President,"

Worker, 11 June 1976; "CPLer Wins Two at Inglis," *Worker*, 9 July 1976; "We Need Red-Led Unions," *Worker*, 19 Nov. 1976; "New Leaders but Old Line from OSSTF," *Worker*, 19 April 1978; "Inglis Militants Nail Wavering Hacks," *Worker*, 31 May 1978; "Rally of 700 Backs Sandinista," *Worker*, 5 July 1980.

54 Owen, *My Confession*, 100, 143–44, 155–57. Owen's autobiography disguises the names of CPL members, using Tim Philips for Phil Taylor and Danny L for David DePoe.

55 See Canadian Communist League (Marxist-Leninist), "Workers' Unity (Toronto) Rallies to the Canadian Communist League (ML): Statement and Self Criticism by Workers' Unity (Toronto)," Encyclopedia of Anti-Revisionism On-Line, https://www.marxists.org/history/erol/ca.secondwave/workersunityrallies/wuselfcrit.htm.

56 "Each Factory Must Be a Fortress for Communism," *Forge*, 11 March 1976.

57 See François Moreau, "Balance Sheet of the Quebec Far Left," 1986, Socialist History Project, http://www.socialisthistory.ca/Docs/History/Bilan-Moreau-English.htm.

58 *Forge*, 27 April 1977; *Spartacist Canada*, 8 Sept. 1976; "Violence against Women on the Rise," *Forge*, 20 Feb. 1981; "Take Back the Night!" *Forge*, 6 Aug. 1982.

59 "Does In Struggle's Demise Reflect on the Validity of Marxism[?]" *Forge*, 11 June 1982; "Marxism Must Be Abolished as a Dogma" (letter), *Forge*, 13 Aug. 1982; "Questions Also Concern the WCP," *Forge*, 20 Aug. 1982; "What Does the WCP Propose?" (letter), *Forge*, 27 Aug. 1982; "Democracy and Socialism," *Forge*, 27 Aug. 1982; Dan Kelly, "The Progressive Side of New Music," *Forge*, 6 Aug. 1982; "Brecht Questioned Socialist Realism," *Forge*, 27 Aug. 1982; "Evolution of Cultural Policies in the USSR from 1917 to 1932," *Forge*, 27 Aug. 1982; "On Socialist Realism" (letter), *Forge*, 24 Sept. 1982; "Private Screenings Only," *Forge*, 3 Sept. 1982; Judy Darcy, "Report on Film Didn't Go Far Enough" (letter), *Forge*, 10 Sept. 1982.

60 "Recognizing the WCP's Errors with Intellectuals," *Forge*, 17 Sept. 1981; "Taking a Look at the Forge," *Forge*, 1 Oct. 1982. Two weeks after the suggestion of encouraging non-party writers with conflicting views, historian Bryan Palmer was telling *Forge* readers why WCP's stance on the issue of peace was flawed. See Palmer, "Peace and the Russian Question," *Forge*, 15 Oct. 1982.

61 "Concerning Homosexuality" (letter), *Forge*, 22 Oct. 1982; "Serious Errors of Chauvinism in WCP," *Forge*, 19 Nov. 1982; "Discussions Under Way..." *Forge*, 19 Nov. 1982; "The Crisis of the Crisis of Socialism Poses Fundamental Questions," *Forge*, 19 Nov. 1982; "Norman Bethune Bookstore in Toronto Closes Down," *Forge*, 5 Nov. 1982.

62 "WCP in Quebec Holds Crucial Conference," *Forge*, December 1982; "Rehabilitation of Two Expelled Party Members," *Forge*, December 1982; "Different Opinions Expressed," *Forge*, December 1982; "Delegates Speak Out," *Forge*, December 1982; "Report from Congress," *Forge*, April 1983; "Should the Organization Continue?" *Forge*, April 1983; "Should the Ex-Leaders Be Expelled?" *Forge*, April 1983.

63 See "The Canadian Marxist-Leninist Group In Struggle! A Brief Presentation of Its History and Political Line" (1977), https://www.marxists.org/history/erol/ca.secondwave/ishistory.htm.

64 "Certain Features of the Historical Development of Canadian Revisionism: The Question of Imperialism," *Lines of Demarcation*, 9-10, n.d., 4–9.

65 "A Reply to Workers' Unity (Toronto)," *Lines of Demarcation*, no. 1 (July-August 1976); "'Marxism and Leninism'[:] The Trade Union Work of Workers' Unity (Toronto)," *Lines of Demarcation*, no. 1 (July-August 1976).

66 "Unmask the Imposters! Denounce the Bolshevik Union!" *In Struggle!* 29 Sept. 1977.

67 "Elements for a Political Perspective," *The Newsletter*, no. 3, n.d.

68 Judy Ramirez, "Introduction," *Women in Struggle*, February 1975.

69 Wages for Housework Group II, Untitled, W4H box, W4H manuscript material folder, Canadian Women's Movement Archives (CWMA) fonds, University of Ottawa Archives and Special Collections. The concept of "local autonomy" probably owed more to the new left's suspicion of hierarchical organization and sympathy for decentralism than to the Italian autonomist movement per se.

70 "Statement of Political Differences with Wages for Housework Group I," Statement of Political Differences ... 1975 folder; Ruth Hall, "Why We Expelled Toronto Wages for Housework Group I" (1975), Statement of Political Differences ... 1975 folder, CWMA fonds.

71 "Housewife syndrome" was a malady causing women to jealously protect what little power they had, at the expense of greater power through collective action. G2 wrote that autonomism, Leninism, and libertarianism all shared a rejection of working-class leadership, either viewing it as a "capitalist evil" or as something wielded by another class. The G2 members' realization that they were the working class rather than external actors was a significant milepost in their political development and informed their view of leadership.

72 G1's "fundamental differences" with the W4H perspective all revolved around this question of leadership.

73 Helen, "Why I Want Wages for Housework," *Women in Struggle*, 1.

74 Ken Popert, "Bryantism and Wages Due: Recruiting within Our Movement," *Body Politic*, September 1979.

75 Andrew Wernick, "The Return of the Empire Loyalists," in *Visions 2020: Fifty Canadians in Search of a Future*, ed. Stephen Clarkson (Edmonton, Alta.: M.G. Hurtig, 1970), 23.

76 Mike Nevin, "Murray the K on CHUM-FM—A New Groove in Toronto or the Same Old Bag?" *CNLF Bulletin* [Canadians for the NLF], August 1968; "Revisionists Corrupt Youth," *Canadian Worker*, August 1970.

77 Punk Rock Reactionary? *Worker*, 28 Dec. 1977. In stark contrast to the CPL's approach, IS believed that a movie's success as entertainment should be considered in tandem with political concerns, and readers frequently wrote to complain when this awareness was not in evidence. The newspaper, refreshingly, did not imply that there was one correct way to look at cultural works; rather, the political meaning embedded in a work arose out of a process of debate. Regular complaints against movies were not so different from what one might find reading the socialist press today: ignoring struggle, presenting problems only in individual terms, showing symptoms but not causes, and failing to offer alternatives to the status quo. IS members could hold starkly contrasting views on popular entertainment. Was *Apocalypse Now* (1979) racist and imperialist drivel—or was it a magnificent film that encompassed an anti-nationalist perspective? Did Madonna glorify the oppression of women or was she "a working class hero," who talked about one woman's survival in her own words? See, for example, "Space Debris," *Workers Action*, August 1977; "Star Wars Review 'Terrible'" (letter), *Workers Action*, September 1977. Also, "Tracing the Roots of Oppression," *Workers Action*, March 1977; "Woman under the Influence," *Workers Action*, 15 April 1975; "'All That Glitters' Doesn't Shine," *Workers Action*, July 1977; "One Flew over the Cuckoo's Nest," *Workers Action*, 1 Feb. 1976; "Telling It Like It Wasn't," *Workers Action*, November 1979; "Apocalypse When?" (letter), *Workers Action*, December 1980-January 1981; "Madonna: Selling a Narrow Oppressive Image of Women," *Workers Action*, June-July 1985; "Readers Debate Madonna," *Workers Action*, August 1985.

78 *New Canada*, November-December 1972.

79 M.A. [Milton Acorn], "Again, Again and Again on the Bloody Obvious," *CLM Newsletter*, n.d.

80 "Bosses behind Dope Pushing," *Canadian Worker*, December 1971; "Bosses Are the Real Dope Pushers," *Canadian Worker*, August 1971; *Canadian Worker*, September 1971.

81 "Folklore: A Vibrant Expression of the People's Culture," *Forge*, 20 Jan. 1977; "A New Record of Revolutionary Songs by the CCL (ML)," *Forge*, 14 April 1977; "Films Which Divert the People's Struggles," *Forge*, 3 March 1977; "In Praise of Economism," *Forge*, 31 March 1977; "Young People Have 'a Very Great Role to Play in the Revolution,'" *Forge*, 27 June 1977.

82 "RWL Security Policy on the Use of Illegal Drugs," *RWL Information Bulletin*, 4-1, September 1981.

83 Wally Matlowe, "The Petit Bourgeois Class in Canada," *Old Mole*, 13 Sept. 1972.

84 Hazel Woods, "Nationalism and Revolution," *Old Mole*, 5 May 1973.

85 A. Engler, "Nationalism and Anti-imperialism—a Counter Position to U.S.-Canada Relations," *LSA IDB*, 1968. Engler was later kicked out of LSA for having essentially adapted a more new left ideology. Different LSA members compared Engler (who was accused of "centrism") and his co-thinkers to infamous renegades from the LSA's sister organization, the SWP (Schactman, Burnham, and the Cochranites). In a display of democratic centralism that portended future developments, the group labelled ten members who abstained on a vote to have no further personal contact with Engler and co. as being disloyal. See "Forward," *LSA IDB*, June 1970 and other documents in that volume.

86 "MISC—a Dead-End Strategy," *Labor Challenge*, 11 Sept. 1972; "Ont. NDPers Launch Left Caucus," *Labor Challenge*, 9 Oct. 1972; CC, "Political Resolution," *LSA IDB*, no. 5, July 1972.

87 "Central Committee Statement on Canadian Nationalism," *LSA IDB*, no. 12, 1972; "Does U.S. 'Energy Crisis' Spell Ruin for Canada?" *Labor Challenge*, 19 March 1973; "LSA-LSO Elects New Exec," *Labor Challenge*, 9 Oct. 1972. Internally, Dowson rehashed opposition to the 1968 *Internal Bulletin* piece by Engler and tried to suggest that the new central committee resolution only pertained to bourgeois nationalism rather than the progressive nationalism he supported. See Ross Dowson, "A Step Backward Instead of Forward," *LSA IDB*, no. 18, November 1972.

88 "An Immigration Policy for Labor?" *Labor Challenge*, 4 Aug. 1975.

89 "Language Controversy in Quebec," *Workers Vanguard*, 2 April 1974; "The Language Controversy and the National Question," *Spartacist Canada*, November-December 1975; "Bilingual Air Traffic Control Disputes Rocks Canada," *Spartacist Canada*, September 1976; "RMG Consecrates Quebec Nationalism," *Spartacist Canada*, September 1976; "Quebec Nationalism and the Class Struggle," *Spartacist Canada*, January 1977.

90 "Quebec: Acid Test for Revolutionaries," IB, 7-9, 1 April 1977; "Theses on Perspectives and Orientation," IB, 2-8; The Changing of the Mole, *Old Mole*, September 1976.

91 "Quebec: A Socialist Perspective" (July 1977 convention), Bakan collection; "Separation? It's up to the People of Quebec," *Workers Action*, November 1976; "Nothing to Gain in PQ Referendum," *Workers Action*, November 1978.

92 "Laxer and Levesque: Nationalists Unite," *Canadian Worker*, March 1971; "Workers Struggles Grow, Nationalists a Shambles," *Canadian Worker*, November 1971; "Capitalism and the Immigrant Worker (part 3)," *Canadian Worker*, September 1971; Owen, *My Confession*, 115; "CPLers Challenge OFL Brass," *Worker*, 14 Dec. 1977.

93 "Support Quebec's Right to Self-Determination," *Worker*, 14 June 1978; "Nationalism Equals Capitalism," *Worker*, 9 Aug. 1978; "Trots and Maoites Join Anti-Quebec Chorus," *Worker*, 9 Aug. 1978; "Paper for Policy Discussion on Quebec," CLM fonds, 7-QUE paper for discussion folder. It saw their meetings with progressive Québécois and the distribution of literature on Quebec to the rest of Canada—especially Léandre Bergeron's *The History of Quebec: A Patriot's Handbook* (Toronto: NC Press, 1971)—as a modest means towards those ends.

94 Communist Party of Canada, *Canada's Party of Socialism: History of the Communist Party of Canada, 1921–1976* (Toronto: Progress Books, 1982), 256, 263–64; "The Quebec Referendum," *Canadian Tribune* (*CT*), 18 Sept. 1978; "Social Policy, National Question Main Focus of QFL Conference," *CT*, 12 Nov. 1979; "CP Urges Yes Vote in Referendum," *CT*, 5 May 1980. See CEC Minutes, "Re: The Referendum in Quebec and the Need for a Shift in Tactic," 26 Aug. 1980, NPC fonds, 3-23; untitled, NPC fonds, 2-7; Brian Mossop, "The Right of Quebec to Self-Determination," *Discussion*, no. 4, 19 Nov. 1971, NPC fonds, 2-6. An internal party document suggests that the change in line might have been initiated in Toronto by the party's leader, William Kashtan, who kicked off a series of meetings on the subject with a divided central committee. The backing of the yes side by the union federations was indeed a key factor in the final decision, but so too was an end to worries that a yes position would result in a split from the Quebec party and a fear of appearing responsible in the likely event that the corporate-backed no side won.

95 Sam Walsh, "Three Points of Difference with Comrade Stanley Ryerson," *Discussion*, 14 March 1969, NPC fonds, 2-19; Pat Case, "Roots of Racism," *Convention 74*, no. 4 (5 April 1974), NPC fonds, 3-5.G; Gail Teixeira, "Build a Struggle against Racism," *Convention 76*, no. 3 (24 Sept. 1976), NPC fonds, 3-5.

96 "AARPR Conference Flops," *Spartacist Canada*, January 1976; Philip Richards and Susan Carlson, "Native People in the N.W.T.: A Marxist Analysis," *Spartacist Canada*, January 1976.

97 Charnie Cunningham, "For a More Concrete Analysis of the Working Class," *Discussion*, no. 4 (19 Nov. 1971), NPC fonds, 2-26; Barbara Cameron, "Communist Work among Women," *Convention 74*, 28 March 1974, NPC fonds, 3-5; Cameron, "Building a Mass Democratic Women's Movement," *Convention 76*, no. 4 (30 Sept. 1976), NPC fonds, 3-13; Charnie Guettel, "Lessons of the Mass Movement," *Convention 76*, no. 3 (24 Sept. 1976), NPC fonds, 3-13.

98 Margot Henderson, "Strategy and Tactics of Women's Liberation," *Old Mole*, 15 Jan. 1973.

99 Morri Charbot, "Women and Revolution," *Old Mole*, 13 Sept. 1972.

100 "Guettel's Marxism and Feminism," *Old Mole*, May 1974; Rose LaCombe, "Review of the Review: Guettel's *Marxism and Feminism*," *IB*, 2-11, William Ready Division of Archives and Research Collections, McMaster University Library, Revolutionary Marxist Group (RMG) fonds, 2-6.

101 "Women's Commission Document," *IB*, 2-9, RMG fonds, 2-6.

102 Julie and Nadja, "Orientation," RMG fonds, 1-17.

103 "Leadership, Collective Practise and the New Tendency," *The Newsletter*, no. 3, n.d.

104 Ford et al., "Statement on the Dissolution of the New Tendency," March 1975, RMG fonds, 4-22, 7–9. The context was a recent wildcat strike of postal workers.

105 "Women, Unions and Workplace Struggles," *The Newsletter*, no. 3, n.d.

106 Ibid.; letter, "A Disgusting Surprise," *Workers Action*, November 1976. The IS considered "erotic clothing" itself to be a form of pornography. See "Pornography and 'Freedom of Choice,'" *Workers Action*, October 1976.

107 "Litton Bombing—Misguided Elitism," *Workers Action*, November 1982; "Heat Put on Red Hot Video," *Workers Action*, December 1982–January 1983.

108 "Little Party on the Prairie," *Workers Action*, April 1983; "Rape—A Crime of Violence," *Workers Action*, November 1977.

109 "A Student's Garden of Politics: Left, Right, and Centre," *Varsity*, 18 Sept. 1972; "Pro-Abortionist Attacks CPL" (letter), *Varsity*, 15 Feb. 1974; D.H., "Capitalism, Not Children, Is Our Problem" (letter), *Worker*, 30 Sept. 1976. Even though the 1976 letter was written by a working member of CPL, the editor of *Worker* advertised it as "Steelworkers wife writes," indicating the party's lack of enthusiasm for women's liberation and focus on strategic industries.

110 "The Party Organizer," *Worker*, 28 Feb. 1979; "Confused Line Cost Sewell Election," *Worker*, November 1980.

111 "Mar 8 Supplement: Celebrate March 8, International Women's Day," *Forge*, 26 Feb. 1976; "Criticism of En Lutte's Position," *Forge*, 26 Feb. 1976; "First League Meeting in Toronto: Oppose the Two Superpowers!" *Forge*, 1 July 1976; "Toronto Militant Criticizes March 22 Tract," *Forge*, 22 April 1976; "Violence against Women on the Rise," *Forge*, 20 Feb. 1981; "Take Back the Night!" *Forge*, 6 Aug. 1982.

112 Bolshevik Union, *The Woman Question: Imperialism, the Highest Stage of the Oppression of Women* (Montreal: Lines of Demarcation, 1979), 156, 167; "Exciting Experiments of Women Taking Power," *In Struggle!* 12 Jan. 1982; "Feminize the Entire Organization," *In Struggle!* 12 Jan. 1982.

113 For one such endorsement of Reich, see Marjaleena Repo, "The Impoverishment of the Canadian Left," *Transformation*, Summer 1972.

114 Minutes, 27 May 1975, NPC fonds, 6-2. The following year the club adopted a proposal to have the party include sex discrimination as grounds for disciplinary action. See 30 Aug. 1976, NPC fonds, 6-4. This libertarian stance might have made it difficult for the group to act on complaints about "pawing" and other sexist activities, which it had in essence ruled to be in the private sphere.

115 Minutes, 30 Aug. 1976, NPC fonds, 6-4.

116 UT Club, "Communist Morality," *Convention 76*, no. 3 (24 Sept. 1976), NPC fonds, 3-13. A separate contribution by a club member complained that the central committee's directive, stating that individuals publicly displaying homosexuality or openly advocating it could be subject to discipline, was typical of the lack of democracy in the party because it was implemented without any discussion or debate. See Andrew Stanley, "Against Routinism," *Convention 76*, no. 3 (24 Sept. 1976), NPC fonds, 3-13.

117 For example, during the agitation around the firing of jockey John Damien, strictly on the grounds of his homosexuality, a cause célèbre of the 1970s, the CPC's Metro chairman appeared at a rally on his behalf. When party candidates gave notice that they were going to attend a GATE-sponsored all-candidates meeting, they were instructed to speak in favour of gay rights. UT Club, "Communist Morality."

118 UT Club minutes, union section meeting, 23 Feb. 1977, NPC fonds, 6-4.

119 Gary Kinsman, "Smash All the Closets," *Old Mole*, July-August 1975; Kinsman, "Gays, Women and All Workers Unite!" *Old Mole*, October 1975; Kinsman, "Defeat Sexual Reaction!" *Old Mole*, November 1974; Deborah Brock, "'Workers of the World Caress': An Interview with Gary Kinsman on Gay and Lesbian Organizing in the 1970's Toronto Left," *left history*, 9,2 (Spring/Summer 2004).

120 MacLeod, *Waking up in the Men's Room*, 83; Women's Commission, "On the Necessity for a Document and Discussion on Women at the Convention," *IDB*, no. 6, 14 Aug. 1974, RMG fonds, 2-6; Charles Lang, letter of resignation, 15 Feb. 1977, RMG fonds, 2-6.

121 "Gay Revolution and Revolutionary Marxism," *IB*, 2-10, n.d.

122 Untitled, W4H manuscript material folder, CWMA fonds; Lorna Boschman, "Fat Women's Liberation from a Wages for Housework Perspective," W4H manuscript material folder, CWMA fonds.

123 Wages Due Lesbians, "Lesbian Autonomy and the Gay Movement," *Body Politic*, August 1976. Simultaneously, the W4H movement was able through its auxiliary organization CASH to attract considerable funds from foundations and governments in its promotion of housework as productive work. CASH vertical file, Canadian Lesbian and Gay Archives (CLGA).

124 Toronto Collective, "Toronto Collective Statement," June 1976. Per Connexions: connexions.org/CxLibrary/Docs/CX19183-Autonomy&PowerWithinWorkingClass.pdf. (accessed 20 May 2018); "The LMDF Is Three Years Old!" *Grapevine*, Spring 1981; "Sharing the Caring," *Grapevine*, Spring 1983.

125 Susan Waterson and Richard Collins, "Workers Action: Broadening Our Audience," 25-26 February 1978, national meeting, Bakan collection.

126 "Popular Control," *Workers Action*, March 1983; "No State Censorship!" *Workers Action*, April 1983; Ron Rosenthal, "The Importance of the Gay Struggle to Revolutionaries," I.S. Political Bulletin, no. 4, February-March 1978, Bakan collection; Susan Tybourne, "Lesbian and Gay Perspectives," 1978 convention, Bakan collection.

127 "The Party Organizer," *Worker*, 28 Feb. 1979; "Confused Line Cost Sewell Election," *Worker*, November 1980.

128 "It's Time for Gays and Lesbians to Speak Out," *In Struggle!* 26 Jan. 1982; Tim McCashell [McCaskell], "How Can the Socialist Movement and the Gay Movement Work Together?" *In Struggle!* 11 Nov. 1980; Gay/Lesbian Caucus, "Our Resolution for In Struggle's Congress," *In Struggle!* 4 May 1981; *In Struggle!* 8-15 Sept. 1981.

129 Bolshevik Union, *Woman Question*, 36, 43; Bolshevik Union, *On the Question of Homosexuality: Reply to the Body Politic Collective* (Montreal: Lines of Demarcation, 1981), 58.

130 Bolshevik Union, *On the Question of Homosexuality*, vii, 2–4, 7, 13–14, 40–42, 50; Bolshevik Union, *Woman Question*, 159.

131 JR, "Introduction," *Women in Struggle*, 3 (December 1976); JR, "Is Abortion the 'Right to Choose'?" *Wages for Housework Campaign Bulletin*, Fall 1977; Wages Due Lesbians, "Lesbian Autonomy and the Gay Movement," *Body Politic*, August 1976; "Conference Explores Lesbian Autonomy, *Body Politic*, September 1976; CB, "The Wages of Disunity," *Body Politic*, September 1977; Heather Ramsay, "Motherhood, Lesbianism, and Child Custody" (review), *Body Politic*, November 1977; Dorothy Kidd, "Wages Due Responds" (letter), *Body Politic*, March 1978.

132 Wages Due Lesbians, "Lesbian Autonomy and the Gay Movement," *Body Politic*, August 1976; CASH vertical file, CLGA.

133 "The LMDF Is Three Years Old!" *Grapevine*, Spring 1981; "Sharing the Caring," *Grapevine*, Spring 1983.

134 "NLF on to Saigon," *Old Mole*, 13 Sept. 1972.

135 "Bolshevik-Leninist Tendency Statement," RMG Collection, 2-6-IDB, 2-12, RMG fonds, 2-6 (in pen, 3 Jan. 1975).

136 See RMG, *National Newsletter*, 2 (19 Nov. 1974), RMG fonds, box 1, National Office, 1, "Waffle Perspectives Document" folder; "Anti-Racist Balance Sheet," 23 Dec. 1975, RMG fonds, Box 1, "RMG Anti-Racist Work" folder, 11; Clive Lloyd and Frank Rooney, "Whither Waffle? Or Waffle Withers," *Old Mole*, December 1974.

137 *IDB*, 2, 14 Jan. 1974.

138 "Draft for Chess Club Perspectives," National Office, RMG fonds, 1-1.

139 "Build the Revolutionary International," *Old Mole*, 1 March 1973; Michael Kaufman, "Lenin and the World Revolution," *Old Mole*, 1 March 1973.

140 "Statement of the Political Committee," Revolutionary Marxist Group, *Old Mole*, July-August 1973.

141 Tina Craig, "A Brief History of the Canadian New Left," *Old Mole*, 13 Sept. 1972.

142 Wally Seccombe, "Social Nature of the Student Milieu," *Old Mole*, September 1973.

143 "Democratic Centralism and the Leninist Organization: Founding Convention of the RMG," *Old Mole*, November 1973.

144 Carl Gardner, "Ways of Seeing," *Old Mole*, 15 Jan. 1973 (review reprinted from *Red Mole*); Graham Barker and Wally Seccombe, "Culture and Revolution," *Old Mole*, November 1973; Sheila Delaney, "Culturevolution," *Old Mole*, December 1973; Deirdre Gallagher, "It's Still Privileged Art," *Old Mole*, 20 Feb. 1976.

145 *Revolutionary Art: A Toy, a Tool, and a Weapon* (Toronto: A March Midnight, 1976), RMG fonds, 3-2; Bob Smith, "A Government Job at Last and The Great Canadian Poetry Annual" (review), *Old Mole*, July-August 1976; Colette Malo and Gary Penner, "Letter to the Editor," *Old Mole*, September 1976.

146 "In Defence of the Supporters of the Ex-Minority Tendency," 26 Dec. 1975, RMG fonds, 2-6.

147 See "Feminism, the Bourgeoisie's Standard," *Proletarian Unity*, February-March 1979.

148 Ross Dowson, "I Read In Struggle! Because," *In Struggle!* 16-23 Dec. 1980; "The Canadian Left: It's Time for a Real Debate," *In Struggle!* 16-23 Dec. 1980.

149 "Interview with In Struggle's General Secretary," *In Struggle!* 9-16, December 1980; "Behind the Scenes," *In Struggle!* 5-12 May, 1981; "In Struggle! and Cultural Work," *In Struggle!* 5-12 May 1981.

150 "Beyond the Fragments: The Debate Continues," *In Struggle!* 14-21 April 1981; see also "Avoid Defensive Reaction in Debate on Women," *In Struggle!* 21-8 April 1981. Some comrades thought the praise for the book extreme, but contextualized it by noting how long *IS!* had ignored the women's movement. For discussion, see Cleveland, "Political is Personal." Varda Burstyn led off a lengthy, reportedly tense discussion about *Beyond the Fragments* in August 1981.

151 "The Women's Research Collective Gets Down to Work," *In Struggle!* 18 Aug. 1981; Varda Burstyn, "What Parts of Leninism Should Be Retained?" *In Struggle!* 1 Dec. 1981; "Women, Democracy and the Party," *In Struggle!* 8 Dec. 1981.

152 "Towards In Struggle!'s Fourth Congress," *In Struggle!* 8-15 Sept. 1981; "Big or Small, It Makes a Difference," *In Struggle!* 21-28 April 1981.

153 "Who's Afraid of Workers' Control?" (editorial), *In Struggle!* 13 Oct. 1981; "In Struggle! Must Make Serious Changes," *In Struggle!* 13 Oct. 1981; "For a More Materialist Approach to the Struggle for Socialism," *In Struggle!* 15 Dec. 1981-12 Jan. 1982; "Building a Majority Consensus: Final Congress Resolutions," *In Struggle!* 18 May 1982; "In Struggle! No Longer Exists," *In Struggle!* 22 June 1982; "Evaluation of Certain Aspects of In Struggle's Past," *In Struggle!* 22 June 1982.

154 "Is Socialist Revolution Possible in Canada?" *Socialist Voice*, 18 April 1983; "Class Polarization, Working Class Radicalization and Party Building Opportunities Today," *RWL Information Bulletin*, November 1982; "Lessons from Our Work in Industry," *RWL Information Bulletin*, September 1981; "The Proletarianization of World Politics, the Creation of Revolutionary World Leaderships, and the Contribution of the Fourth International Today," *RWL Information Bulletin*, March 1983; "Forging the Proletarian Marxist Leadership"; "Building a Bi-National Proletarian Party: Our Role and Strategy in the Industrial Working Class," *RWL Information Bulletin*, May 1983.

155 "Tasks and Perspectives," October 1977, box 2, folder 4, RMG fonds, 7-2; Fortier, "Transfers," RMG fonds, 7-2; *Preconvention Discussion Bulletin*, 2-14, March 1979; "Statement of the National Bureau on the Situation in the Organization," *RWL Information Bulletin*, 3-3, July 1980; "Open Letter to the PC on the Closing of the Saskatoon Branch," *RWL/LOR Discussion Bulletin*, 3-13, December 1979; "Report to the Political Bureau on the Closing of the Saskatchewan Branches," *RWL/LOR Discussion Bulletin*, 3-22, February 1980. Members of the Toronto

branch—who composed over half the league's initial membership—were also prominent in a "flood of imported English Canadian cadres" to Montreal before RWL de-emphasized the Québécois struggle. Members of the RWL's tiny successor organization, the Communist League, later consolidated all of its active members in Toronto before closing that branch and decamping en masse to Montreal.

156 "Building an Antiwar Movement in the Working Class," *RWL Information Bulletin*, 6-1, February 1983; "Class Polarization, Working Class Radicalization"; "Forging the Proletarian Marxist Leadership." For an extensive, but chronologically and ideologically limited, critique of the direction of the SWP, see Paul Le Blanc, ed., *In Defense of American Trotskyism: Rebuilding the Revolutionary Party* (New York: Fourth Internationalist Tendency, 1990); Paul Le Blanc, ed., *In Defense of American Trotskyism: Revolutionary Principles and Working Class Democracy* (New York: Fourth Internationalist Tendency, 1992); Sarah Lovell, ed., *In Defense of American Trotskyism: The Struggle Inside the Socialist Workers Party 1979–1983* (New York: Fourth Internationalist Tendency, 1992).

157 *RWL Information Bulletin*, October 1982; "The Next Steps in Building the Revolutionary Workers League," *RWL Information Bulletin*, September 1981; "Building the Section of the Fourth International in the Canadian State," *Preconvention Discussion Bulletin*, November 1978; "Lessons from Our Work in Industry," *RWL Information Bulletin*, September 1981.

158 "Building an Antiwar Movement in the Working Class"; "RWL Discusses Central America, Quebec-BC Workers' Fightback, Labor's Struggle for Power," *Socialist Voice*, 30 Jan. 1984. Although a handful of Trotskyist groups survived the wreckage of the RWL, none appeared able to meet the challenges of the 1980s. IS, the largest, had noticeably declined and only external intervention had prevented its demise. The Alliance for Socialist Action, formed in 1985 from dissidents fleeing the RWL, focused extensively on feminism. The Socialist League increasingly slipped from view as it entered further and further into the NDP. The small Spartacist League continued to air its disagreements with all other Leninists at demonstrations and meetings, yet a split in its ranks created the International Bolshevik Tendency. Canadian International Socialists—1986 Faction Fight Documents, web.archive.org/web/20071123032558/http://www.etext.org/Politics/International.Socialists/86FIGHT.TXT (accessed 21 May 2018); "Alliance for Socialist Action," *Socialist Challenge*, 1 May 1986 (the newspaper's subtitle was "for socialist and feminist action"); "The Robertson School of Party Building," *1917*, Winter 1986; "The Necessity of Revolutionary Organization," *1917*, Winter 1986. In contrast to LSA members in the early 1960s, who participated in civil disobedience actions and aided activists pursuing that strategy, the Alliance resurrected the LSA's later mass movement line. Thus, with respect to anti-G8 summit activism in Toronto, it favourably counterposed the "many excellent speeches" at a Queen's Park rally to the "barely 3,000" who created a "spectacle of adolescent self-indulgence" by employing civil disobedience on the streets surrounding the summit. "Summit Protest Was Mixed Bag," *Socialist Challenge*, September 1988.

159 Editorial, "Revolution and Religion," *Worker*, 12 April 1979; "CPL: Next Year Mecca?" *Spartacist Canada*, June-July 1979; "US Interventions in Iran Denounced at Tehran Conference," *Worker*, June 1980; "A Struggle against Civilization?" *In Struggle!* 23 Jan. 1979; "Interview with an In Struggle! Militant Back from a Trip to Iran," *In Struggle!* 2 Oct. 1979; "SWP/RWL: You Wanted Khomeini! You Got Him!" *Spartacist Canada*, April 1979.

160 Even after 1928, when a Trotskyist opposition had emerged and recruited some Canadian supporters, it characteristically positioned itself as the Communist International's loyal opposition; even after the founding of the Fourth International in 1938, this perception persisted in the movement's loyal defence of the Soviet Union, in such moments as the Russo-Finnish War.

161 "Appendix One," *IDB*, 5, 2 July 1974, RMG fonds, 2-6. When RWL's political committee recognized that IS! was beginning to question Maoist tenets and that it had become the only Marxist-Leninist group willing to discuss politics with them, it decided that the League would henceforth target IS! and try to prevent it from recruiting. See "Our Policy toward Other Political Groups," *RWL Information Bulletin*, 2-6, June 1978.

162 "Canadian Left in Crisis," *Workers Action*, March 1983; "Little Party on the Prairie."

163 "Racism Mounts; Left's Response Falters," *Old Mole*, January 1976. In addition to the reports of abuse emanating from the CLM, a fuller account of this aspect of vanguardism would do well to pay careful attention to François Moreau's charge that within the Workers' Communist Party leaders built up an internal police force, kidnapped children, covered up at least one rape, and forcibly detained members under investigation for disloyalty to the group. See François Moreau, "Balance Sheet of the Quebec Far Left," 1986, Socialist History Project, http://www.socialisthistory.ca/Docs/History/Bilan-Moreau-English.htm.

164 Judy Rebick, *Ten Thousand Roses: The Making of a Feminist Revolution* (Toronto: Penguin Canada, 2005).

11. A Long, Ambiguous Goodbye, 1982–85

1 "SAC Starts Anti-Racism Committee," *Varsity*, 15 Sept. 1980; "Racism at the University: A Cause for Concern," *Varsity*, 23 Feb. 1981. In 1981 the issue of banning the Ku Klux Klan from the campus sparked another battle between liberals who did not want to ban even objectionable speech and leftists who did not think the Klan had a right to a voice on campus. Leo Casey, "Between License and Censorship," *Varsity*, 25 Feb. 1981.

2 "Nader's Raiders Won't Fade Away," *Varsity*, 8 Feb. 1982; "OPIRG to Go Ahead with Grad Vote," *Varsity*, 8 March 1982; *Varsity*, 31 March 1982; "Angry Students Occupy Sig Sam Library," *Varsity*, 23 March 1983; "300 Protestors Disrupt GC Meeting," *Varsity*, 30 March 1983; "Engineers Resist Women's Centre," *Varsity*, 17 Jan. 1985; "Abortion: Debate Starts," *Varsity*, 11 Feb. 1980; "Rebick Calls for Choice," *Varsity*, 5 Oct. 1983; "Sex Ed Controversy Resolved," *Varsity*, 7 Nov. 1983; "Engineering Society Drops Slave Day Strippers," *Varsity*, 20 Jan. 1984.

3 "3000 Brave Rain to Protest," *Varsity*, 12 March 1982; "Rally Attacks Bill 127," *Varsity*, 8 Oct. 1982.

4 The word "socialist" was frequently retained as an adjective, but rarely used with the precision that characterized the term in the 1930s. As Dorothy Smith put it, "socialist" was "what people want to make of it. We don't define it." Dorothy Smith, "Socialist Network Growing," *Cayenne*, 2 (February 1985).

5 Mariana Valverde, "Why Peace Now?" *IWDC Newsletter*, February 1983.

6 Ramsay and Riordan cited in "Coalition Politics: A Workshop," *IWDC Newsletter*, November 1982; Mariana Valverde, "Women's Way to Peace," *Peace Calendar*, March 1984.

7 Smith, "Socialist Network Growing."

8 *Leftwords*, 1980; "Maritime Socialist Conference: Many Voices, a Common Cause," *In Struggle!* 22 June 1982; "Progressives from Four Atlantic Provinces Hold Socialist Conference," *Forge*, 30 April 1982; Murray Dobbin, "Saskatchewan Socialists Meet," *Talking Socialism*, 2,1 (May 1986); Leo Panitch interview, 22 Sept. 2005, Toronto. Panitch recalls that members initially voted to call the Ottawa group "NDP (ML)."

9 Panitch, interview. This was not OCLA's first foray beyond Ottawa. In addition to maintaining relationships with broadly similar groups in British Columbia and Saskatchewan, members had encouraged the formation of the mainly student Kingston Socialists as well as a more worker-based group in London. "Toronto Socialist Network—A Chronology," author's personal collection. Panitch says attendees were "stepping on glass not to be sectarian."

10 "Dear Friend," 25 Aug. 1983, author's personal collection; "Toronto Socialist Network"; Stephen Douglas, "Report from the Computer Group," *Talking Socialism*, 1,2 (July 1985); *Talking Socialism*, 2,1 (May 1986); Marion Endicott, "Report from the 'Chocolate Digestive Biscuit' Group," *Talking Socialism*, 1,3 (November 1985).

11 Dorothy E. Smith, "Meeting in Small Groups," *Talking Socialism*, 1 (March 1985).

12 Editorial, "A Fresh Start," *Talking Socialism*, 1 (March 1985); Howie Chodos, "What Is the Socialist Network?" *Talking Socialism*, 2 (March 1985); editorial, "Are We Up to It?" *Talking Socialism*, 1,2 (July 1985); David Stewart, "From Here to There," *Talking Socialism*, February 1986.

13 Craig Heron, "Rethinking the Socialist Alternative," *Talking Socialism*, March 1985.

14 "Socialists and the Current Struggle for Reproductive Rights," *Talking Socialism*, November 1985; editorial, "A Fresh Start," *Talking Socialism*, 1 (March 1985); "Steering Committee Remarks," n.d. (c. 1984), author's personal collection; "Proposal by 5," author's personal collection; David Stewart, "The Network's First General Meeting," *Talking Socialism*, 2,1 (May 1986); "Building a Network of Socialists," *IWDC Newsletter*, September 1984; Animation Committee, "Will the Network Survive?" *Talking Socialism*, 2,3 (February 1987).

15 Editorial, *Incite*, July 1983.

16 Zaremba, "Now You See It, Now You Don't . . ." *Broadside*, May 1980.

17 "IWDC" (letter), *Broadside*, 1,1 (1979).

18 Cole, "Fair's Fair," *Broadside*, 2,6 (April 1981); editorial, "Coalition Politics," *Broadside*, 2,9 (July 1981). *Broadside* speculated, for example, about an anti-nuclear coalition that would embrace both feminists and anti-abortionists.

19 Lorna Weir, "Tit for Tat: Coalition Politics," *Broadside*, 3,4 (February 1982); bell hooks, *Feminism Is for Everybody: Passionate Politics* (Cambridge, Mass.: South End Press, 2000).

20 Mary O'Brien and Frieda Forman (letter), *Broadside*, 4,6 (April 1983).

21 Lois Lowenberger, "IWD: Lip Service to Feminism," *Broadside*, 4,6 (April 1983). Lowenberger also raised the issue of balance and counterposed the support for Third World liberation movements to working-class and racially oppressed women in Canada. She took a multipronged approach to argue against the inclusion of the Palestinian struggle, first focusing on an argument identifying three tiers of anti-imperialist struggle whose relevance to IWD was in descending order: (1) those with feminist goals (like Nicaragua); (2) those without, but who are working towards a better society that she, as a leftist, supports (including Cuba and El Salvador); (3) pure nationalists (IRA and PLO). A smaller issue in the debate had been criticism of the use of Spanish-language slogans at IWD events, which Forman later contrasted with using French, linking up with Quebec feminists and devoting attention to the struggles of Indigenous women. See Forman (letter), *Broadside*, 4,8 (June 1983). For a view accusing the IWD speakers of adopting a traditional male attitude towards violence, see Reva Landau, "Choosing Sides Wisely," *Broadside*, 5,1 (October 1983).

22 *Broadside*, 4,7 (May 1983).

23 Mariana Valverde (letter), *Broadside*, 4,7 (May 1983).

24 Shannon Bell, "More Than a Rhetorical War," *Broadside*, 4,8 (June 1983).

25 By 1984 *Broadside* was praising IWDC, even to the point of suggesting that its socialist-

feminist orientation had led to useful contacts between feminists and other political constituencies. In its comments on IWD in 1985, *Broadside* did not even target the presence of male alongside female Eaton's strikers at the head of the march. Editorial, "IWD: Turning Out Again," *Broadside*, 5,5 (March 1984); editorial, "Still Ain't Satisfied," *Broadside*, 6,5 (March 1985).

26 Dorothy Smith, "Socialist Women and the Peace Movement," *IWDC Newsletter*, May 1984.

27 "Talking about Socialist Feminism," *IWDC Newsletter*, March 1984.

28 Connie Clement, "The Case for Lay Abortion," *Healthsharing*, Winter 1983.

29 Nancy Adamson and Susan Prentice, "Toward a Broader Strategy for Choice," *Cayenne*, May-June 1985.

30 For the views of socialist feminists, see Varda Burstyn, ed., *Women Against Censorship* (Vancouver and Toronto: Douglas & McIntyre, 1985); Burstyn, "The Left and the Porn Wars: A Case Study in Sexual Politics," in *Who's on Top? The Politics of Heterosexuality*, ed. Howard Buchbinder, Varda Burstyn, Dinah Forbes, and Mercedes Steedman (Toronto: Garamond Press, 1987).

31 Ayanna Black, "Working With Collectives," *Tiger Lily*, 1,1 (November-December 1986).

32 "Two Wings of the Same Bird," *IWDC Newsletter*, September 1984; Weir, "Tit for Tat."

33 Susan G. Cole, "Sharing the Wealth?" *Broadside*, 1,1 (1979) (she took pains to distance her position from those who wanted to bar refugees for racist reasons); Amanda Hale, "Violence Begins at Home," *Broadside*, 5,5 (March 1984); Adrienne Rich cited in "Fighting Racism Is a Feminist Issue," *IWDC Newsletter*, Summer 1985.

34 "Toronto Women's Bookstore," *Rebel Girls Rag*, November/December 1987.

35 Ingrid MacDonald, "Conditions of Coalition," *Broadside*, 7,6 (April 1986).

36 "Statement of the Black Women's Collective," *Cayenne*, June-July 1986.

37 "Two Wings of the Same Bird."

38 Ayanna Black, "Working with Collectives, II," *Tiger Lily*, 1,2 n.d. (1987).

39 Ingrid MacDonald, "Conditions of Coalition," *Broadside*, 7,6 (April 1986).

40 Daniel T. Rodgers, *Age of Fracture* (Cambridge, Mass. and London: Belknap Press of Harvard Press, 2011).

41 "Talking to Socialist Feminists," *IWDC Newsletter*, September 1984.

42 Nancy Adamson, "Letter of Resignation," *IWDC Newsletter*, September 1984; Marie Lorenzo, Christina Mills, and Lynda Yanz, "Our Side of the Story," *Cayenne*, November-December 1984.

43 TM, "Sex and Sandinismo," *Body Politic*, May 1981; Michael Riordan, "A Space for Ourselves," *Body Politic*, July/August 1981.

44 Riordan, "Space for Ourselves."

45 Michael Riordan, "Cruising for Peace," *Body Politic*, March 1983; "Remembrance Day 1982 at Litton," *Body Politic*, March 1983; "Cruising for Peace: Demo Targets Missile," *Body Politic*, December 1982; Walter Davis, "Gay Perspectives on Peace," *Pink Ink*, July 1983.

46 New leftists were also important to the election of Canada's first open lesbian to public office in Vancouver. See "Sue Harris: Entering the Political Mainstream," *Body Politic*, February 1985.

47 "Rights Hearings Debate Gay Rights," *Now*, 10 Sept. 1981; "John Sewell's Back in City Politics," *Now*, 10 Sept. 1981; editorial, "The Price of Betrayal," *Body Politic*, May 1981; "NDP Forces Other Leftists out of Ward 6 Race," *Body Politic*, March 1984.

48 Editorial, "Arson, Abortion and Freedom," *Body Politic*, January 1983; "Race, Moustaches and Sexual Prejudice, *Body Politic*, June 1983; editorial, "Pornography and Solidarity," *Body Politic*, July/August 1983.

49 Debbie Parent et al. (letter), *Body Politic*, September 1983; Nancy Adamson et al. (letter), *Body Politic*, July/August 1983; Eng K. Ching (letter), *Body Politic*, September 1983; Richard Fung (letter), *Body Politic*, September, 1983; Mair Morton et al., *Body Politic*, September 1983; Board of Directors for Gays of Ottawa (letter), *Body Politic*, October 1983.

50 David S. Churchill, "Personal Ad Politics: Race, Sexuality and Power at The Body Politic," *Labour/Le Travail*, 8,2 (2003), 114, 116–18.

51 Brian Mossop, "The Classified Debate," *Body Politic*, June 1985; "Gay Men's Feminist Mistake," *Body Politic*, October 1980; "Dancing by Yourself," *Body Politic*, July 1984.

52 "Metro Rally Draws Estimated 17,000," *Toronto Star* (*TS*), 23 Oct. 1983; "Thousands Take Part in Anti-Nuclear Rallies," *TS*, 27 Oct. 1985. Police estimates were much lower.

53 "Peace Marchers Star in Town's Parade," *TS*, 29 May 1982; "20,000 in Metro Expected to Join Anti-Nuke Rally," *TS*, 21 Oct. 1983; "Who Are These People?" *Peace Calendar*, September 1984.

54 The closest antecedent of the large peace mobilizations of the 1980s was the 1971 Amchitka protests, when nationalists, environmentalists, and anti-war protesters rallied across the country to oppose U.S. nuclear testing in Alaska. Turnouts in mid-sized cities were particularly impressive, and the large proportion of high-school students involved was exceptional. Thousands of demonstrators closed international border crossings by occupying bridges in Niagara Falls, Sarnia, and Windsor. But protest attendance in Toronto was comparatively modest and failed to crack 10,000. See "The US-Canada Rift . . . A Border Closed by Protest . . . and a 'Continuing Trade Row,'" *Windsor Star*, 4 Nov. 1971; "2,500 Sing O'Canada and Chant in Amchitka Protest at Niagara Falls," *Globe and Mail* (*GM*), 4 Nov. 1971; "Two Windows Are Broken at U.S. Consulate as Thousands Protest Amchitka Nuclear Test," *GM*, 4 Nov. 1971; "4,000 in Metro Protest Aleutian A-blast," *TS*, 4 Nov. 1971; "Amchitka and Vietnam: Biggest Student Upsurge Ever," *Young Socialist*, November-December 1971.

55 "40 High School Clubs Form Network to Show They're Serious about Peace," *TS*, 26 Nov. 1985; "School Peace Groups," *Peace Calendar*, 1,4 (May 1983); "Peace Studies Moving Along," *Peace Magazine*, February-March 1987; "What's Going on in the Canadian Peace Movement Today?" *Peace Magazine*, October-November 1987. Peace studies also entered the universities.

56 "Nuking North York," *Now*, 25 March 1982; "City to Put out Nuclear Booklet," *Now*, 8 April 1982.

57 "70 Active Groups Are Promoting Peace," *TS*, 16 Oct. 1983; "Peace Group Continues Fight for World Nuclear Arms Ban," *TS*, 8 May 1984; "Jewish Community Tackles Nuclear Issue," *TS*, 17 Sept. 1985; "New Peace Activists in Pinstripe Suits March against War," *TS*, 7 Oct. 1985.

58 "Artists Form New Group," *Peace Calendar*, 1,9 (October 1983); "70 Active Groups Are Promoting Peace," *TS*, 16 Oct. 1983; "Peace Group Continues Fight for World Nuclear Arms Ban"; "New Peace Activists in Pinstripe Suits March against War."

59 Paula Rochman, "Introduction," in Cruise Missile Conversion Project, *A Case for Non-Violent Resistance* (Toronto: The Project, n.d. (c.1985), 3; Rose-Marie Colterman, "Converting Litton: The History of the Cruise Missile Conversion Project," in Cruise Missile Conversion Project, *A Case for Non-Violent Resistance*, 4; David Colins, "Conversion Planning," in Cruise Missile Conversion Project, *A Case for Non-Violent Resistance*, 8; Donald M. Wells, "Politics and the Economic Conversion of Military Production in Canada," *Studies in Political Economy*, 27

(Autumn 1988), 115, 133. Despite CMCP's best efforts, the failure of a unionization drive at Litton was blamed on labour's association with the peace movement.

60 Tom Joyce, "Organized Women Win Strike for Union Security," in Cruise Missile Conversion Project, *A Case for Non-Violent Resistance*, 14–17; Wayne Roberts, "The Winnipeg General Strike and Peaceful Conversion," in Cruise Missile Conversion Project, *A Case for Non-Violent Resistance*, 10–14; Rochman, "Introduction," 3. CMCP's emphasis on non-violent resistance, as both a philosophy and plan of action, did not appear to prevent it from supporting the Sandinistas in their war with the Contras. See Len Desroches, "Violence and Non-Violence: Nicaragua and Canada," in Cruise Missile Conversion Project, *A Case for Non-Violent Resistance*, 27–28.

61 "Random Notes of an Abortive attempt by C. Hal . . . to Write a History of A.N.V.A." [appears to have been replicated from notes taken sometime in 1984–85], 1–5, We-Peterborough: World Emergency Centre for Assertive Non-Violence fonds, Trent University Archives, 2-3; "To Remember Is to Resist," 1983, We-Peterborough fonds, 2-6. Members of ANVA occasionally made reference to "social direct action," which appeared to encompass actions such as building alternate communities. See "From Ken Hancock to the Alliance Meeting in September [1983]," We-Peterborough fonds, 2-1.

62 ANVA, *Civil Disobedience Campaign Handbook*, n.d., We-Peterborough fonds, 2-6. Feminism was a particularly strong influence within ANVA, and it was a rare educational tract that did not include a critique of patriarchy.

63 "Proposal for an Alliance for Non-Violent Structure," n.d., We-Peterborough fonds, 2-1. The proposal was probably authored by Ken Hancock and appears to have been largely adopted by the alliance. The unity statement it was based on agreed to carry out anti-racist, anti-homophobic, anti-sexist, and anti-capitalist work.

64 Ibid.; Sept. 24-25 meeting, We-Peterborough fonds, 2-1; July 1983 meeting, We-Peterborough fonds, 2-1; 13-14 Aug. 1983 minutes, We-Peterborough fonds, 2-1. Concerns about "Toronto Imperialism" were aired at the August meeting, which included delegates from Guelph, Hamilton, Kingston, Ottawa, and Peterborough.

65 "Toronto's Network Reorganizes," *Peace Calendar*, 1,4 (May 1983).

66 Matthew Clark, "The Third World and the Third World War," *Peace Calendar*, 2,1 (February 1984); Janice Williamson, "A Power We Have Been Taught to Bury," in *Up and Doing: Canadian Women and Peace*, ed. Janice Williamson and Deborah Gorham (Toronto: Women's Press, 1989), 175.

67 "'Peace Camp' Protestors Moving to Liberal Party Headquarters," *TS*, 17 July 1983; "Fight against Cruise Missile Tests Goes On, Peace Groups Vow," *TS*, 7 March 1984.

68 Sunday Harrison (letter), *Broadside*, 4,10 (August/September 1983); editorial, "Property, Violence and Morality," *Toronto Clarion*, 5 Nov. 1982; "Nuke Fight Shifts to Ottawa," *Now*, 21-27 Oct. 1983; "Critique of the Critique of the Litton Bombing," *Kick It Over*, February 1983; "Vanguard Terror vs. State Terror," *Kick It Over*, February 1983; "Introduction," *Bulldozer*, Winter 1983; "Introduction," *Bulldozer*, 6, 1983; "Introduction," *Bulldozer*, Spring 1984; "Introduction," *Bulldozer*, Summer 1985. For a personal account, see Ann Hansen, *Direct Action: Memoirs of an Urban Guerrilla* (Toronto: Between the Lines, 2001).

69 "No Nukes!" *Workers Action*, October 1979; "Hell No! We Won't Glow!" *Workers Action*, April 1980; "Wanted: An International Movement," *Workers Action*, June 1980; Colin Barker (letter), *Workers Action*, September 1982; "Peace Movement: Can It Win?" *Workers Action*, June/July 1984. Circa 1984 IS still advocated that the peace movement prioritize acts of working-class solidarity and ties with organized labour. That its members had little positive to say

and rejected all peace groups as either too bureaucratic or too disorganized suggests their absence from that decade's largest social movement.

70 "MPPs Plan to Hold Vote Today on Declaring Nuclear-Free Zone," *GM*, 24 Nov. 1983 (Davis made his statement while insinuating Bob Rae's links to the Soviet Union); "Many in Canada Staunchly Defend Testing of Missile," *TS*, 23 Oct. 1983. New groups like the Canadian Centre for Arms Control and Disarmament were built up through private funding. The Dove for Peace Foundation also hoped to grow from business donations. Al Rycroft, "How Much Has Changed?" *Peace Calendar*, 2,6 (July 1984); "Bringing Business into the Movement," *Peace Calendar*, 2,8 (September 1984). However, the Business Council on National Issues, composed of the CEOs of 150 major corporations, called for Canada's involvement in Star Wars and an 80 per cent increase in defence spending, to be financed by cutbacks in other government programs. "Business Leaders Call For 'More,'" *Peace Magazine*, March 1985.

71 Introductory issue, *Broadside*, May 1979; Juliet Huntley, "Candu: Cheap at Twice the Price," *Broadside*, November 1979. The newly organized Feminist Party of Canada also saw these connections and established as its second principle of unity the "Protection of the quality of the environment and all living species from industrial, military and technological exploitation." See "Feminist Party of Canada: First Principles," *Broadside*, May 1980.

72 "Silence Is Consent," *Broadside*, 1,5 (March 1980).

73 Gay Bell, "A Voice at the Back of the Hall," *Broadside*, 1,2 (November 1979); Debra Curties, "Feminist Fall-Out," *Broadside*, 1,9 (July/August 1980); Anne Cameron, "Acts of Folly," *Broadside*, 1,8 (June 1980). A number of local feminists active in the peace movement were inspired by the lengthy anti-nuclear agitation and occupation carried out by the women of the Greenham Common Women's Peace camp in the United Kingdom.

74 George Yamada, "Stop Darlington," *Rikka*, Spring 1979; "3,000 Descend on Nuclear Site," *Canadian Tribune* (*CT*), June 11, 1979; "117 Charged in Protest at Darlington Nuclear Site," *CT*, June 16, 1980; Judy Liefschultz, "Nuclear Power: Child of the Patriarchy," *Broadside*, 1,9 (July/August 1980).

75 Liefschultz, "Nuclear Power"; "Police Drag Women from Hydro Protest," *TS*, 31 March 1981.

76 *Broadside*, April 1981; *Broadside*, December 1981/January 1982.

77 "A Peace of the Action—An Interview with Margaret Hancock," *Broadside*, August/September 1983.

78 Ibid. For a critique of positions portraying peacemakers as female and war-makers as male, see Tana Dineen and Lori A. McElroy, "Blaming the Boys," *Peace News*, December 1986-January 1987.

79 Ibid.

80 Williamson, "Power We Have Been Taught to Bury," 12, 183–85.

81 Marusia Bociurkiw, "Making Women's Pictures," *IWDC Newsletter*, February 1985.

82 Ian McKay, *Reds, Rebels, Radicals: Rethinking Canada's Left History* (Toronto: Between the Lines, 2005), 206–10.

83 *Libertarian*, May 1968; *Libertarian*, July 1968; Mike Hargis, *Notes on Anarchism in North America 1940–1996* (Chicago: [No publisher] 1998), 13; "The Black Flag of Anarchism Is Flying Again," *GM*, 4 July 1970.

84 "The Other Woman Speaks to the Miss Canada Pageant Protesters," *Other Woman*, December/January 1976; Toronto Anarchist League (letter), *Varsity*, 20 Feb. 1978; "Transcription of Nov. 8th/78 Anarcha-Feminist Meeting at I.S.C.," Canadian Women's Movement Archives, Toronto Anarchist Group file; "Anarcha-Feminism," Toronto Anarchist Group file, Canadian Women's

Movement Archives (CWMA) fonds, University of Ottawa Archives and Special Collections. Although members associated with TAG sometimes used other monikers, TAG was the most consistently used. Despite their name they also spoke in terms of "libertarian socialism."

85 "Anarchists Take New Tack," *Open Road*, Fall 1977; "ACF Declaration," *North American Anarchist*, October/November 1979; "For Starters," *North American Anarchist*, October/November 1979. Neighbouring ACF affiliate Totally Eclipsed was also responsible for the federation's newsletter, which was produced with technical assistance from the *Toronto Clarion* collective. Of ACF's initial ten affiliates, three were Canadian.

86 "Against Naive Realism," *North American Anarchist*, August-September 1980; John Zerzan (letter), *North American Anarchist*, May-June 1981; "Theological Ecology," *North American Anarchist*, October-November 1980; "For Starters," *North American Anarchist*, January-February 1981; Jason Quinn (letter), *SRAFederation Bulletin*, no. 73, n.d.; Bob Black (letter), *SRAFederation Bulletin*, no. 74, n.d. Quinn was specifically attacking the *North American Anarchist*'s successor *Strike!*

87 *Ideas for Setting Your Mind in a Condition of Dis*ease* (Kitchener: Black Thumb Press, n.d.): 7, 15, 19. Campbell did not share Black's anti-feminism and told Ellams that anarchists could learn more from feminism than vice versa.

88 Ibid., 8–14.

89 "ACF's 6th Conference," *North American Anarchist*, August-September 1980; "ACF Conference," *North American Anarchist*, March/April 1981; "For Starters," *Strike!* August/September 1981.

90 Robin Isaacs, "Living My Life," *Upping the Anti*, May 2007, 38; Sam Wagar (letter), *SRAFederation Bulletin*, no. 87, n.d. Wagar claimed that there were more than forty groups if one-person operations were taken into account. For Wagar's foray into Toronto's anarchist scene (and extensive details about left-wing paganism), see Samuel Wagar, *I Know Where the Bodies Are Buried: A Memoir*, 1956–2011 (Edmonton: Obscure Pagan Press, 2014).

91 *Ecomedia* may have been more influential than *Kick It Over* in the second half of the 1980s.

92 Editorial, "Force of Circumstances," *Kick It Over*, September 1983; "What We Believe," *Kick It Over*, February 1985; Ron Hayley, "The Politics of Ego or How I Joined a Cult Instead of a Community," *Kick It Over*, February 1985.

93 Women of the KIO Collective, "Editorial: The Political Is Personal," *Kick It Over*, May 1983; "WAVAW Reaffirms Radical Feminism," *Kick It Over*, May 1983; Devon, "What Is AnarchaFeminism?" *Kick It Over*, February 1985; Bob Black (letter), *SRAFederation Bulletin*, no. 85, n.d.; S.E. (letter), *Kick It Over*, May 1983. The WAVAW statement claimed that leftists subordinated sexual oppression to class, racial, and national liberation struggles.

94 "Prophet of Monetarism Deplores the Erosion of Freedom," *GM*, 11 July 1980; "Friedman Offers Cure; Some Prefer Disease," *GM*, 11 July 1980; "Vintage Friedman Irks, Delights," *TS*, 11 July 1980.

95 Bob Rae, From *Protest to Power: Personal Reflections on a Life in Politics* (Toronto: Viking/ Penguin Books, 1996), 84–85.

Reading Further

1. Toronto: Capital of Capitalist Modernity

To situate Toronto's history against a background of capitalism and modernity, we can recommend five outstanding books: Donica Belisle, *Retail Nation: Department Stores and the Making of Modern Canada* (Vancouver and Toronto: UBC Press, 2011); Richard Harris, *Unplanned Suburbs: Toronto's American Tragedy 1900 to 1950* (Baltimore and London: Johns Hopkins University Press, 1996); Greg Kealey, *Toronto Workers Respond to Industrial Capitalism 1867 to 1892* (Toronto: University of Toronto Press, 1992); James T. Lemon, *Liberal Dreams and Nature's Limits: Great Cities of North America Since 1600* (Eugene, Ore.: Wipf and Stock, 2008); and Keith Walden, *Becoming Modern in Toronto: The Industrial Exhibition and the Shaping of a Late Victorian Culture* (Toronto: University of Toronto Press, 1997).

Useful general introductions to Toronto's geography, culture, and history include Amy Lavender Harris, *Imagining Toronto* (Toronto: Mansfield Press, 2010); Derek Hayes, *Historical Atlas of Toronto* (Vancouver and Toronto: Douglas and McIntyre, 2008); J. David Hulchanski, *The Three Cities within Toronto: Income Polarization among Toronto's Neighbourhoods, 1970–2005* (Toronto: Cities Centre Press, University of Toronto, 2008); James T. Lemon, *Toronto since 1918: An Illustrated History* (Toronto: James Lorimer and Company, National Museum of Man, and National Museums of Canada, 1985); Allan Levine, *Toronto: Biography of a City* (Madeira Park, B.C.: Douglas and McIntyre, 2014); Patricia McHugh and Alex Bozikovic, *Toronto Architecture: A City Guide* (Toronto: McClelland and Stewart, 2017); Edward Relph, *Toronto: Transformations in a City and Its Region* (Philadelphia: University of Pennsylvania Press, 2014); and Richard White, *Planning Toronto: The Planners, The Plans, Their Legacies, 1940–80* (Vancouver and Toronto: UBC Press, 2016).

For assessments of Toronto's environmental history, see Jennifer Bonnell, *Reclaiming the Don: An Environmental History of Toronto's Don River Valley*

(Toronto: University of Toronto Press, 2014); L. Anders Sandberg, Stephen Bocking, Colin Coats, and Ken Cruikshank, eds., *Urban Explorations: Environmental Histories of the Toronto Region* (Hamilton: L.R. Wilson Institute for Canadian History, 2013).

For an understanding of automobility and Toronto's phenomenal suburban growth, see Dimitry Anastakis, *Auto Pact: Creating a Borderless North American Auto Industry 1960–1971* (Toronto: University of Toronto Press, 2005); Cameron Bevers, "The King's Highway 401," http://www.thekingshighway.ca/Highway401.htm; Timothy J. Colton, *Big Daddy: Frederick G. Gardiner and the Building of Metropolitan Toronto* (Toronto: University of Toronto Press, 1980); Robert Fulford, "Fred Gardiner's Specialized City," in Fulford, *Accidental City: The Transformation of Toronto* (Toronto: Macfarlane and Ross, 1995); Ian Milligan, "'This Board Has a Duty to Intervene," *Urban History Review* 39,2 (Spring 2011), 25–39; Steve Penfold, "'Are We to Go Literally to the Hot Dogs?' Parking Lots, Drive-ins, and the Critique of Progress in Toronto's Suburbs, 1965–1975," *Urban History Review* 33,1 (Fall 2004), 8–23, and Penfold's more general study *The Donut: A Canadian History* (Toronto: University of Toronto Press, 2008); John Sewell, *The Shape of the Suburbs: Understanding Toronto's Sprawl* (Toronto: University of Toronto Press, 2009); John G. Shragge, "Highway 401—the Story," https://web.archive.org/web/20071224113717/http://www.roadscholar.on.ca:80/lateststory.html; Lawrence Solomon, *Toronto Sprawls: A History* (Toronto: University of Toronto Press, 2007); Patrick Vitale, "A Model Suburb for Model Suburbanites: Order, Control, and Expertise in Thorncrest Village," *Urban History Review* 40,1 (Fall 2011), 41–55; and Randall White, *On the Road in the GTA: An Eclectic Guide to the Exurban Sprawl of Greater Toronto* (Toronto: Eastendbooks, 2003).

For an early study of the Spadina Expressway controversy, see David Nowlan and Nadine Nowlan, *The Bad Trip: The Untold Story of the Spadina Expressway* (Toronto: New Press/House of Anansi, 1970); and also Danielle Robinson, "Modernism at a Crossroad: The Spadina Expressway Controversy in Toronto, Ontario, ca. 1960–1971," *Canadian Historical Review* 92,2 (June 2011), 295–322 and her excellent overview, "'The Streets Belong to the People': Expressway Disputes in Canada, c.1960–75," Ph.D. thesis, McMaster University, 2012.

The city's transition from Anglo seat of Empire to Canada's epicentre of multiculturalism can be explored through Franca Iacovetta, *Such Hardworking People: Italian Immigrants in Postwar Toronto* (Montreal and Kingston: McGill-Queen's University Press, 1993), and her *Gatekeepers: Reshaping Immigrant Lives in Cold War Canada* (Toronto: Between the Lines, 2006), much of which focuses on Toronto; John Lorinc, Michael McClelland, Ellen Scheinberg, and Tatum Taylor, eds., *The Ward: The Life and Loss of Toronto's First Immigrant Neighbourhood* (Toronto: Coach House Press, 2015); Michael Ornstein, *Ethno-Racial Groups in*

Toronto, 1971–2001: A Demographic and Socio-Economic Profile (Toronto: Institute for Social Research, York University, 2006); William J. Smyth, *Toronto, the Belfast of Canada: The Orange Order and the Shaping of Municipal Culture* (Toronto: University of Toronto Press, 2015); and Robert Vipond, *Making a Global City: How One Toronto School Embraced Diversity* (Toronto: University of Toronto Press, 2017).

Toronto's post-1945 labour history has yet to stimulate a synthetic treatment. For certain aspects of it, see Stefano Agnoletto, *The Italians Who Built Toronto: Italian Workers and Contractors in the City's Housebuilding Industry, 1950–1980* (Bern: Peter Lang, 2014); Ian Milligan, "'The Force of All Our Numbers': New Leftists, Labour, and the 1973 Artistic Woodwork Strike," *Labour/Le Travail* 66 (Fall 2010), 37–71; Peter McInnis, "Hothead Troubles: 1960s-Era Wildcat Strike Culture in Canada," in *Debating Dissent: Canada and the Sixties*, ed. Lara Campbell, Dominique Clément, and Gregory S. Kealey (Toronto: University of Toronto Press, 2012), 155–70; and Sally F. Zerker, *The Rise and Fall of the Toronto Typographical Union 1832–1972: A Case Study of Foreign Domination* (Toronto: University of Toronto Press, 1982). For two contemporary titles, see Stuart Jamieson, *Times of Trouble: Labour Unrest and Industrial Conflict in Canada, 1900–66* (Ottawa: Task Force on Labour Relations, 1968); and Marc Zwelling, *The Strikebreakers: The Report of the Strikebreaking Committee of the Ontario Federation of Labour and the Labour Council of Metropolitan Toronto* (Toronto: New Press, 1972).

Fascinating primary sources on suburbanizing Toronto from 1958 to 1985 include S.D. Clark, *The Suburban Society* (Toronto: University of Toronto Press, 1966); and Phyllis Brett Young's period novel *The Torontonians* (Montreal and Kingston: McGill-Queen's University Press, 2007 [1960]).

On Marshall McLuhan as an interpreter of modernity, see Philip Marchand, *Marshall McLuhan: The Medium and the Messenger* (Toronto: Vintage Canada, 1989); for contemporary appraisals of him from the left, see G. David Sheps, "Utopianism, Alienation and Marshall McLuhan," *Canadian Dimension* 3 (September-October 1966), 23–26; Sidney Finkelstein, *Sense and Nonsense in McLuhan* (New York: International Publishers, 1968).

For far-ranging general statements regarding the global revolts of the 1960s–1980s, see Tariq Ali, *Street Fighting Years: An Autobiography of the Sixties* (New York: Citadel Press, 1987); Wini Breines, *Community and Organization in the New Left, 1962–1968: The Great Refusal* (New Brunswick, N.J., and London: Rutgers University Press, 1989), which is excellent on the centrality of prefigurative politics and the new left; Fredric Jameson, "Periodizing the 60s," in Jameson, *The Ideologies of Theory: Essays, 1971–1986*, vol. 2., *Syntax of History* (Minneapolis: University of Minnesota Press, 1988), 178–208; also in Sohnya Sayres, Anders Stephanson, Stanley Aronowitz, and Fredric Jameson, eds., *The 60s Without Apology* (Minneapolis:

University of Minnesota Press in co-operation with *Social Text*, 1984), 178–209, on the problem of periodization, for which see also George Katsiaficas, *The Imagination of the New Left: A Global Analysis of 1968* (Boston: South End Press, 1987); and Arthur Marwick, *The Sixties: Cultural Revolution in Britain, France, Italy, and the United States, 1958–1974* (Oxford and New York: Oxford University Press, 1998), who argues for the "Long Sixties." See Cal Winslow, ed., *E.P. Thompson and the Making of the New Left* (New York: Monthly Review Press, 2014), for the writings of one of the period's most influential English-speaking new left intellectuals. Daniel Cohn-Bendit, *Obsolete Communism: The Left-Wing Alternative*, trans. Arnold Pomerans (Harmondsworth, U.K.: Penguin, 1969), was for many a seminal text on why leftists had to transcend the existing Communist tradition.

For especially significant titles on the global context of radicalism in the 1960s–1980s, see Karen Dubinsky, Catherine Krull, Susan Lord, Sean Mills, and Scott Rutherford, eds., *New World Coming: The Sixties and the Shaping of Global Consciousness* (Toronto: Between the Lines, 2009). Also of interest: Tariq Ali and Susan Watkins, *1968: Marching in the Streets* (New York et al.: Free Press, 1998); David Caute, *The Year of the Barricades: A Journey through 1968* (New York: Harper Row, 1988); Rebecca Clifford, "Emotions and Gender in Oral History: Narrating Italy's 1968," *Modern Italy* 17,2 (May 2012), 209–21; Gerard J. DeGroot, *The Sixties Unplugged: A Kaleidoscopic History of a Disorderly Decade* (Cambridge, Mass.: Harvard University Press, 2008); Niall Ferguson, Charles S. Maier, Erez Manela, and Daniel J. Sargent, eds., *The Shock of the Global: The 1970s in Perspective* (Cambridge, Mass. and London: Belknap Press of Harvard University Press, 2010); Carol Fink, Philipp Gassert, and Detlef Junker, eds., *1968: The World Transformed* (Cambridge: Cambridge University Press and the German Historical Institute, 1998); Ronald Fraser, ed., *1968—A Student Generation in Revolt: An International Oral History* (New York: Pantheon, 1988); Philipp Gassert and Martin Klimke, eds., *1968: Memories and Legacies of a Global Revolt*, Supplement no. 6, *Bulletin of the German Historical Institute* (Washington, D.C.: The Institute, 2009); G.-R. Horn, *The Spirit of '68: Rebellion in Western Europe and North America, 1956–1976* (Oxford: Oxford University Press, 2007); Martin Klimke, Jacco Pekelder, and Joachim Scharloth, eds., *Between Prague Spring and French May: Opposition and Revolt in Europe, 1960–1980* (New York and Oxford: Berghahn, 2011); Martin Klimke, *The Other Alliance: Student Protest in West Germany and the United States in the Global Sixties* (Princeton, N.J.: Princeton University Press, 2009); Mark Kurlansky, *1968: The Year That Rocked the World* (New York: Random House, 2005); Jeremy Varon, *Bringing the War Home: The Weather Underground, the Red Army Faction, and Revolutionary Violence in the Sixties and Seventies* (Berkeley: University of California Press, 2004); and Richard Vinen, *The Long '68: Radical Protest and Its Enemies* (New York: Allen Lane, 2018). A period text widely read in Canada was Patrick Seale and Maureen McConville, eds., *French Revolution 1968* (Harmondsworth, U.K.: Penguin, 1968).

Of the many books covering the European 1960s and 1970s, especially insightful are Geoff Eley, *Forging Democracy: The History of the Left in Europe, 1850–2000* (Oxford and New York: Oxford University Press, 2002), Part IV; Kristin Ross, *May '68 and Its Afterlives* (Chicago: University of Chicago Press, 2002); and Luisa Passerini, *Autobiography of a Generation, 1968* (Middletown, Conn.: Wesleyan University Press, 1996).

Among the books covering Great Britain, especially helpful are Celia Hughes, *Young Lives on the Left: Sixties Activism and the Liberation of the Self* (Manchester, U.K.: Manchester University Press, 2015); Michael Kenny, *The First New Left: British Intellectuals after Stalin* (London: Lawrence and Wishart, 1995); and Duncan Thompson, *Pessimism of the Intellect? A History of the New Left Review* (Monmouth, U.K.: Merlin Press, 2007). See also Lin Chun, *The British New Left* (Edinburgh: Edinburgh University Press, 1993); Michael Kenny, *The First New Left: British Intellectuals after Stalin* (London: Lawrence and Wishart, 1995); Michael Newman, *Ralph Miliband and the Making of the New Left* (London: Merlin and New York: Monthly Review Press, 2002), and Sheila Rowbotham, *Promise of a Dream: Remembering the Sixties* (London: Penguin, 2000). David Widgery, ed., *The Left in Britain, 1956–1968* (Harmondsworth, U.K.: Penguin, 1976), provides an accessible collection of documents on the far left.

From the United States, see especially Dan Berger, ed., *The Hidden 1970s: Histories of Radicalism* (New Brunswick, N.J. and London: Rutgers University Press, 2010); Van Gosse, *Rethinking the New Left: An Interpretive History* (New York: Palgrave Macmillan, 2005); Maurice Isserman, *If I Had a Hammer: The Death of the Old Left and the Birth of the New Left* (New York: Basic Books, 1987); Simon Hall, "Protest Movements of the 1970s: The Long 1960s," *Journal of Contemporary* History 43,4 (2008), 655–72; and John McMillian and Paul Buhle, eds., *The New Left Revisited* (Philadelphia: Temple University Press, 2003). Also noteworthy are Paul Buhle, *History and the New Left: Madison, Wisconsin, 1950–1970* (Philadelphia: Temple University Press, 1990); David Farber, *Chicago '68* (Chicago: University of Chicago Press, 1988); Buhle, ed., *The Sixties: From Memory to History* (Chapel Hill: University of North Carolina Press, 1994); Buhle, *The Age of Great Dreams: America in the 1960s* (New York: Hill and Wang, 1994); Andrew Hunt, "How New Was the New Left?" in *New Left Revisited*, ed. McMillian and Buhle, 139–55; James Miller, *Democracy in the Streets: From Port Huron to the Siege of Chicago* (Toronto: Simon and Schuster, 1987); Abe Peck, *Uncovering the Sixties: The Life and Times of the Underground Press* (New York: Pantheon, 1985); Doug Rossinow, *The Politics of Authenticity: Liberalism, Christianity, and the New Left in America* (New York: Columbia University Press, 1998), which focuses on Austin, Texas; Irwin Unger and Debi Unger, *The Movement: A History of the American New Left, 1959–1972* (Lanham, Md.: University Press of America, 1988 [1974]); and Jeremy Varon, Michael S. Foley, and John McMillian, "Time Is an Ocean: The Past and Future of the Sixties," *The Sixties: A Journal of Contemporary History* 43,4 (2008), 655–72. Todd Gitlin's *The Sixties: Years of Hope, Days of Rage* (New York: Bantam Books, 1987), is worth reading simply because so many people have since taken issue with its narrow perspective and declensionist narrative.

For useful documents, see Alexander Bloom and Wini Breines, eds., *'Takin' It to the Streets': A Sixties Reader*, 2nd ed. (New York and Oxford: Oxford University Press, 2003); Tom Hayden, ed., *The Port Huron Statement: The Visionary Call of the 1960s Revolution* (New York: Thunder's Mouth Press, 2005); Van Gosse, *The Movements of the New Left, 1950–1975: A Brief History with Documents* (London: Bedford/St. Martins, 2004); Peter B. Levy, *America in the Sixties—Right, Left, and Center: A Documentary History* (New York: Praeger, 1998); Sayres et al., eds., *60s Without Apology*; and Massimo Teodori, *The New Left: A Documentary History* (New York: Bobbs-Merrill, 1969).

The Canadian literature is growing quickly. See especially, for its innovative methodology and catholicity of approach, Sean Mills, *The Empire Within: Postcolonial Thought and Political Activism in Sixties Montreal* (Montreal and Kingston: McGill-Queen's University Press, 2010). Jean-Marc Piotte, *La communauté perdue: Petite histoire des militantismes* (Montreal: VLB éditeur, 1990) is an unjustly neglected classic. Still unrivalled as an accessible account is Myrna Kostash, *Long Way from Home: The Story of the Sixties Generation in Canada* (Toronto: James Lorimer and Company, 1980).

In addition to Dubinsky et al., eds., *New World Coming*, which contains an array of Canadian articles, Alvin Finkel, *Our Lives: Canada after 1945* (Toronto: Lorimer, 1997), provides an innovative postwar survey. Useful overviews are provided by Bryan D. Palmer, *Canada's 1960s: The Ironies of Identity in a Rebellious Era* (Toronto: University of Toronto Press, 2009), and Jean-Philippe Warren, *Une Douce Anarchie: Les Années 68 au Québec* (Montreal: Boréal, 2008), who both maintain a narrow temporal focus. François Ricard, *La génération lyrique: Essai sur la vie et l'oeuvre des premiers-nés du baby-boom* (Montréal: Les Éditions du Boréal, 1994), and Doug Owram, *Born at the Right Time: A History of the Baby Boom Generation* (Toronto: University of Toronto Press, 1996), place their bets on a generational interpretation, as did Cyril Levitt in his now superseded *Children of Privilege: Student Revolt in the Sixties: A Study of Student Movements in Canada, the United States, and West Germany* (Toronto: University of Toronto Press, 1984). Ian Milligan, *Rebel Youth: 1960s Labour Unrest, Young Workers, and New Leftists in English Canada* (Vancouver and Toronto: UBC Press, 2014), reveals the extensive working-class contribution to the radical upsurge.

Revealing studies of particular Canadian places include Lawrence Aronsen, *City of Love and Revolution: Vancouver in the Sixties* (Vancouver: New Star, 2010); Michael Boudreau, "Hippies, Yippies, the Counter Culture, and the Gastown Riot in Vancouver, 1968–71," *BC Studies* 197 (Spring 2018), 39–65; Joel Belliveau, *Le 'moment 68' et la reinvention de l'Acadie* (Ottawa: Presses de l'Université d'Ottawa, 2014); and Gordon Hak, *The Left in British Columbia: A History of Struggle* (Vancouver: Ronsdale Press, 2013).

Important collections of articles include Dimitry Anastakis, ed., *The Sixties: Passion, Politics, and Style* (Montreal and Kingston: McGill-Queen's University Press, 2008); Campbell, Clément, and Kealey, eds., *Debating Dissent*; and M. Athena Palaeologu, ed., *The Sixties in Canada: A Turbulent and Creative Decade* (Montreal: Black Rose Books, 2009). From the period itself, one can consult Dimitri Roussopoulos, ed., *The New Left in Canada* (Montreal: Black Rose Books, 1970); Roussopoulos, ed., *Canada and Radical Social Change* (Montreal: Black Rose Books, 1973); and Roussopoulos, ed., *Quebec and Radical Social Change* (Montreal: Black Rose Books, 1975). For more contemporary reflections from the same author, see Dimitri Roussopoulos, "Canada: 1968 and the New Left," in *1968: Memories and Legacies*, ed. Gassert and Klimmke, 39–46.

Useful collections of primary sources include Pierre Berton's hyperventilating *The Cool Crazy Committed World of the Sixties: Twenty-One Television Encounters* (Toronto: McClelland and Stewart, 1966); and Cy Gonick, ed., *Canada since 1960: A People's History—A Left Perspective on 50 Years of Politics, Economic and Culture* (Toronto: James Lorimer and Company, 2016), a superb distillation of articles from one of Canada's leading left magazines.

Memoirs and first-person reflections include A. Alan Borovoy, *Uncivil Obedience: The Tactics and Tales of a Democratic Agitator* (Toronto: Lester Publishing, 1991); Burnley 'Rocky' Jones with James St. G. Walker, *Burnley 'Rocky' Jones: Revolutionary* (Halifax and Winnipeg: Roseway Publishing, 2016); Douglas Fetherling, *Travels by Night: A Memoir of the Sixties* (Toronto: Lester Publishing, 1994); Fetherling, *Way Down Deep in the Belly of the Beast: A Memoir of the Seventies* (Toronto: Lester Publishing, 1996); James Harding, "Still Thinking Globally about the Sixties," *Canadian Dimension* 22 (November-December 1988), 16; and Pierre Vallières, *Nègres blancs d'Amérique* (Montreal: Parti pris, 1968), which became "the voice of a generation" in Quebec. It was widely read in English Canada under the title *White Niggers of America* (Toronto: McClelland and Stewart, 1971) and was reprinted in a later new French edition, "corrigée et augmentée" (Montréal: Éditions TYPO, 1994).

In general, the Canadian field has not yet generated many attempts to theorize about the new left formation as a whole, but see John Cleveland, "New Left, Not New Liberal: 1960s Movements in English Canada and Quebec," *Canadian*

Review of Sociology and Anthropolgy 41 (February 2004), 67–84; Ian McKay, *Rebels, Reds, Radicals: Rethinking Canada's Left History* (Toronto: Between the Lines, 2005), ch. 5; Palmer, *Canada's 1960s*; and Norman Penner, *The Canadian Left: A Critical Analysis* (Scarborough: Prentice-Hall, 1977), ch. 7.

2. A Slow, Cautious Hello: First Stirrings of a Movement, 1958–64

Odd Arne Westad, *The Cold War: A World History* (New York: Basic Books, 2017), following up on his *The Global Cold* War (Cambridge: Cambridge University Press, 2005), is an important revisionist account suggesting that the Cold War was far more widespread and long-lasting in its impact than the previous literature had indicated. Carole E. Fink, *The Cold War: An International History* (New York: Westview Press, 2017), presents a more accessible and distilled version focused on Soviet sources. For a global treatment of resistance to nuclear weapons, see Lawrence S. Wittner, *The Struggle against the Bomb*, vol. 1, *One World or None: A History of the World Nuclear Disarmament Movement through 1953* (Stanford, Cal.: Stanford University Press, 1993), and his more focused "The Nuclear Threat Ignored: How and Why the Campaign Against the Bomb Disintegrated in the Late 1960s," in Carol Fink, Philipp Gassert, and Detlef Junker, eds., *1968: The World Transformed* (Cambridge: Cambridge University Press and the German Historical Institute, 1998), 439–58. Canada's often confusing policies are tracked in Patricia McMahon, "The Politics of Canada's Nuclear Policy, 1957–1963," Ph.D. thesis, University of Toronto, 1999.

Reg Whitaker and Steve Hewitt, *Canada and the Cold War* (Toronto: Lorimer, 2003), provides an accessible introduction to the period; Gary Marcuse and Reginald Whitaker, *Cold War Canada: The Making of a National Insecurity State, 1945–1957* (Toronto: University of Toronto Press, 1997), provides much more detail. General insights into Canada's foreign policy during the Cold War can be found in Greg Donaghy, *Tolerant Allies: Canada and the United States, 1963–1968* (Montreal and Kingston: McGill-Queen's University Press, 2002); Peter T. Hayden, *The 1962 Cuban Missile Crisis: Canadian Involvement Reconsidered* (Toronto: Canadian Institute for Strategic Studies, 1993); Asa McKercher, *Camelot and Canada: Canadian-American Relations in the Kennedy Era* (New York: Oxford University Press, 2016); Asa McKercher and Galen Perras, eds., *Mike's World: Lester B. Pearson and Canadian External Affairs* (Vancouver and Toronto: UBC Press, 2018); Don Munton and David A. Welch, *The Cuban Missile Crisis: A Concise History* (New York: Oxford University Press, 2007); Stephen J. Randall, "Great Expectations: America's Approach to Canada," in

Transnationalism: Canada-United States History into the Twenty-First Century, ed. Michiel Behiels and Reginald C. Stuart (Montreal and Kingston: McGill-Queen's University Press, 2010); Erika Simpson, *NATO and the Bomb: Canadian Defenders Confront Critics* (Montreal and Kingston: McGill-Queen's University Press, 2001); Kevin Spooner, *Canada, the Congo Crisis, and UN Peacekeeping, 1960–1964* (Vancouver and Toronto: UBC Press, 2009); Denis Stairs, *The Diplomacy of Constraint: Canada, the Korean War and the United States* (Toronto: University of Toronto Press, 1974); and John Herd Thompson and Stephen J. Randall, *Canada and India in the Cold War World, 1946–76*, 4th ed. (Montreal and Kingston: McGill-Queen's University Press, 2008). Of particular interest to the left was Canada's position with respect to Cuba, for which see John M. Kirk and Peter McKenna, *Canada-Cuba Relations: The Other Good Neighbor Policy* (Gainesville: University Press of Florida, 1987); Robert Wright, *Three Nights in Havana: Pierre Trudeau, Fidel Castro and the Cold War* (Toronto: HarperCollins, 2007).

A recent trend has been to reconceptualize Canada in the world in two respects: first, to critically probe its heavy involvement in colonialism and imperialism; and, second, to broaden the focus from diplomats exchanging memos among themselves and with their political superiors to an emphasis on other actors in civil society and the general impact of broad ideological patterns. With respect to the first position, John Warnock, *Partner to Behemoth: The Military Power of a Satellite Canada* (Toronto: New Press, 1970), Victor Levant, *Quiet Complicity: Canadian Involvement in the Vietnam War* (Toronto: Between the Lines, 1986), and Jamie Swift and the Development Education Centre, *The Big Nickel: Inco at Home and Abroad* (Toronto: Between the Lines, 1977), were pioneering texts. In the twenty-first century they have been followed up by the work of Alain Deneault and William Sacher, *Imperial Canada Inc.: Legal Haven for the World's Mining Industries* (Vancouver: Talonbooks, 2012); Yves Engler, *The Black Book of Canadian Foreign Policy* (Halifax and Winnipeg: Fernwood Publishing, 2009), and Engler, *Canada in Africa: 300 Years of Aid and Exploitation* (Halifax and Winnipeg: Fernwood Publishing, 2015); Todd Gordon, *Imperialist Canada* (Toronto: University of Toronto Press, 2014); Gordon, *Blood of Extraction: Canadian Imperialism in Latin America* (Halifax and Winnipeg: Fernwood Publishing, 2016); and Lisa North, Timothy David Clark, and Viviana Patroni, eds., *Community Rights and Corporate Responsibility: Canadian Mining and Oil Companies in Latin America* (Toronto: Between the Lines, 2006). New left themes of anti-imperialism and solidarity with the global South are far from played out.

With respect to the second, see especially Brandon R. Dimmel, *Engaging the Line: How the Great War Shaped the Canada-US Border* (Vancouver and Toronto: UBC Press, 2016); Laura Madokoro, Francine McKenzie, and David Meren, eds.,

Dominion of Race: Rethinking Canada's International History (Vancouver: UBC Press, 2017); Sean Mills, *A Place in the Sun: Haiti, Haitians, and the Remaking of Quebec* (Montreal and Kingston: McGill-Queen's University Press, 2016); Ryan Touhey, *Conflicting Visions: Canada and India in the Cold War World, 1946–76* (Vancouver and Toronto: UBC Press, 2015); David Webster, *Fire and the Full Moon: Canada and Indonesia in a Decolonizing World* (Vancouver and Toronto: UBC Press, 2009); and Robert Wright and Lana Wylie, eds., *Our Place in the Sun: Canada and Cuba in the Castro Era* (Toronto: University of Toronto Press, 2009).

The rise of the Cold War security state has generated an impressive corpus of research work. See in particular Steve Hewitt, *Spying 101: The RCMP's Secret Activities at Canadian Universities, 1917–1997* (Toronto: University of Toronto Press, 2002); Hewitt, "'Information Believed True': RCMP Security Intelligence Activities on Canadian University Campuses and the Controversy Surrounding Them, 1961–1971," *Canadian Historical Review* 81,2 (June 2000), 191–228; Mark Kristmanson, *Plateaus of Freedom: Nationality, Culture and State Security in Canada, 1940–1960* (Toronto: Oxford University Press, 2003); Greg Kealey, *Spying on Canadians: The Royal Canadian Mounted Police Security Service and the Origins of the Long Cold War* (Toronto: University of Toronto Press, 2017); Gary Kinsman, Dieter K. Buse, and Mercedes Steedman, eds., *Whose National Security? Canadian State Surveillance and the Creation of Enemies* (Toronto: Between the Lines, 2000); Christabelle Sethna and Steve Hewitt, *Just Watch Us: RCMP Surveillance of the Women's Liberation Movement in Cold War Canada* (Montreal and Kingston: McGill-Queen's University Press, 2018); Christabelle Sethna, "High School Confidential: RCMP Surveillance of Secondary School Activists," in *Whose National Security?* ed. Buse, Kinsman, and Steedman; and Reginald Whitaker, Gregory S. Kealey, and Andrew Parnaby, *Secret Service: Political Policing in Canada from the Fenians to Fortress America* (Toronto: University of Toronto Press, 2012).

The earlier twentieth-century background to anti-war movements in the 1950s and 1960s in Canada can be traced in Victor Huard, "Armageddon Reconsidered: Shifting Attitudes Towards Peace in English Canada, 1936–1953," Ph.D. thesis, Queen's University, 1995; and Ian McKay and Jamie Swift, *The Vimy Trap: How We Learned to Stop Worrying and Love the Great War* (Toronto: Between the Lines, 2016); Barbara Roberts, '*Why Do Women Do Nothing to End The War?*' *Canadian Feminist-Pacifists and the Great War* (Ottawa: Canadian Research Institute for the Advancement of Women, CRIAW Papers, 1985).

For the women's peace movement in the early 1960s, see Christine Ball, "The History of the Voice of Women/La Voix des Femmes: The Early Years," Ph.D. thesis, University of Toronto, 1994; Frances Early, "Canadian Women and the International Arena in the Sixties: The Voice of Women/La voix des femmes and the Opposition to the Vietnam War," in *The Sixties*, ed. Anastakis, 25–41; Tarah

Brookfield, *Cold War Comforts: Canadian Women, Child Safety, and Global Insecurity* (Waterloo, Ont.: Wilfrid Laurier University Press, 2012); Marie Hammond-Callaghan, "Bridging and Breaching Cold War Divides: Transnational Peace-Building, State Surveillance, and the Voice of Women," in *Worth Fighting For: War Resistance in Canada from the War of 1812 to the War on Terror*, ed. Lara Campbell, Michael Dawson, and Catherine Gidney (Toronto: Between the Lines, 2015), 133–45; Kay Macpherson and Meg Sears, "The Voice of Women: A History," in *Women in the Canadian Mosaic*, ed. Gwen Matheson (Toronto: Peter Martin Associates, 1976); Kay Macpherson, *Persistent Voices* (Toronto: Lawson Memorial Fund, 1987); Kay Macpherson with C.M. Donald, *When in Doubt, Do Both: The Times of My Life* (Toronto: University of Toronto Press, 1994); Ian McKay, "Margaret Ells Russell, Women Strike for Peace, and the Global Politics of 'Intelligent Compassion,'" in *Worth Fighting For*, ed. Campbell, Dawson, and Gidney, 119–132; Cheryl Osborn, "Speaking Their Peace: Feminist Pacifists in the Nuclear Age, the Voice of Women, 1960–1972," M.A. thesis, Concordia University, 1999; Barbara Roberts, "Women's Peace Activism in Canada," in *Beyond the Vote: Canadian Women and Politics*, ed. Linda Kealey and Joan Sangster (Toronto and Buffalo: University of Toronto Press, 1989), 276–308; and Marilyn Sweet, "Purls for Peace: The Voice of Women, Maternal Feminism, and the Knitting Project for Vietnamese Children," M.A. thesis, University of Ottawa, 2007.

For the early Canadian resistance to nuclear weapons, see Bruce Douville, "Project La Macaza: A Study of Two Canadian Peace Protests in the 1960s," in *Worth Fighting For*, ed. Campbell, Dawson, and Gidney, ch. 12; Michael Maurice Dufresne, "'Let's Not Be Cremated Equal': The Combined Universities Campaign for Nuclear Disarmament 1959–1967," in *Sixties in Canada*, ed. Palaeologu, 9–63; Jennifer Lynn Hunter, "'Is It Even Worth Doing the Dishes?' Canadians and the Nuclear Threat, 1945–1963," Ph.D. thesis, McGill University, 2004.

For responses on the left to the Cuban Revolution, see especially, for the U.S., Van Gosse, *Where the Boys Are: Cuba and the Cold War, and the Making of the New Left* (London; Verso, 1993), and for Canada, Cynthia Wright, "Between Nation and Empire: The Fair Play for Cuba Committee and the Making of Canada-Cuba Solidarity in the Early 1960s," in *Our Place in the Sun*, ed. Wright and Wylie, 96–20. Canadian primary sources include Jack Scott, *A Second Look at Cuba* (n.p. [Vancouver], n.d. [1963]), which gathers together articles that appeared in the *Vancouver Sun* from 28 May to 7 June 1963; Fair Play for Cuba Committee, *Canadian Students in Cuba* (Toronto, 1965), which collects contributions from Canadian students who visited Cuba for two months during the summer of 1964; *The Real Cuba as Three Canadians Saw It* (Toronto: Fair Play for Cuba Committee, 1964) (which includes the impressions of Michel Chartrand, Vernel Olson, and John Riddell); and Al Purdy, *A Canadian Poet: and the Pilón Raid* (Toronto: Fair Play for Cuba Committee, 1964). The FPCC also published Che Guevara, *Socialism and Man* (Toronto: Fair Play for Cuba Committee, 1966). Che Guevara, *Guerrilla Warfare* (Harmondsworth, U.K.: Penguin, 1969 [first published in English by Monthly Review Press, 1961]), was read and admired by many Canadian new leftists, some of whom sought to apply its tactical insights to Canada.

For the role of radical Christians, see Catherine Gidney, "Poisoning the Student Mind? The Student Christian Movement at the University of Toronto, 1920–1965," *Journal of the Canadian Historical Association* 8,1 (1997), 147–63; for the stirrings of a "counterculture," see Stuart Henderson, *Making the Scene: Yorkville and Hip Toronto in the 1960s* (Toronto: University of Toronto Press, 2011); Bruce Michael Douville, "The Uncomfortable Pew: Christianity, the New Left, and the Hip Counterculture in Toronto, 1965–1975," Ph.D. thesis, York University, 2011.

3. A Movement Emerges, 1965–67

The war in Vietnam—a turning point for the Canadian new left—has generated a large international literature, much of it focused narrowly on the crisis it sparked in the United States. For a somewhat balanced U.S. appraisal, see Gerald J. De Groot, *A Noble Cause? America and the Vietnam War* (London: Pearson, 1999). For less U.S.-centric approaches, see Pierre Asselin, *Hanoi's Road to the Vietnam War, 1954–1965* (Berkeley: University of California Press, 2013), which draws in part on Canadian sources; Pierre Broucheux, *Ho Chi Minh: A Biography* (Cambridge: Cambridge University Press, 2011); Christopher E. Goscha and Christian F. Ostermann, *Connecting Histories: Decolonization and the Cold War in South East Asia 1945–1962* (Stanford: Stanford University Press, 2009); and Christopher E. Goscha, *Contesting Concepts of Space and Place in French Indochina* (Copenhagen: Nordic Institute of Asian Studies Press, 2012). Andrew Preston, "Balancing War and Peace: Canadian Foreign Policy and the Vietnam War, 1961–1965," *Diplomatic History* 27,1 (2003), 73–111, looks at the war through the eyes of Canadian state policy-makers. For Lester Pearson, see John English, *The Worldly Years: Life of Lester Pearson 1949–1972* (Toronto: Random House, 2011), and the refreshingly critical Yves Engler, *Lester Pearson's Peacekeeping: The Truth May Hurt* (Halifax and Winnipeg: Fernwood Publishing, 2012).

In addition to the classic studies of Warnock, *Partner to Behemoth*, and Levant, *Quiet Complicity*, see, for general resistance to the Vietnam War, Lara Campbell, "'Women United Against the War': Gender Politics, Feminism, and Vietnam Draft Resistance in Canada," in *New World Coming*, ed. Dubinsky et al., ch. 34; Christopher William Powell, "'Vietnam: It's Our War Too!': The Antiwar Movement in Canada, 1963–1975," Ph.D. thesis, University of New Brunswick, 2011;

and Matthew Roth, "Crossing Borders: The Toronto Anti-Draft Programme and the Canadian Anti-Vietnam War Movement," M.A. thesis, University of Waterloo, 2008. A significant primary text from the period is Charles Hanly, *Revolution and Response* (Toronto: McClelland and Stewart, 1966), which emerged from a University of Toronto teach-in.

A particular focus of the literature on resistance to the Vietnam War has been the immigration to Canada of U.S. war resisters and draft dodgers. An interesting U.S. discussion of the gender dynamics of draft resistance appears in Michael S. Foley, "The 'Point of Ultimate Indignity' or a 'Beloved Community'? The Draft Resistance Movement and New Left Gender Dynamics," in *New Left Revisited*, ed. McMillian and Buhle, 178–98. For Canada, see especially David Churchill, "An Ambiguous Welcome: Vietnam Draft Resistance, the Canadian State, and Cold War Containment," *Histoire sociale/Social History* 37,73 (May 2004), 1–26; Churchill, "Draft Resisters, Left Nationalism, and the Politics of Anti-Imperialism," *Canadian Historical Review* 93,2 (2012), 227–60; John Hagan, *Northern Passage: American Vietnam War Resisters in Canada* (Cambridge, Mass.: Harvard University Press, 2001); Frank Kusch, *All American Boys: Draft Dodgers in Canada from the Vietnam War* (Westport, Conn.: Praeger Press, 2002); Kathleen Rodgers, *Welcome to Resisterville: American Dissidents in British Columbia* (Vancouver and Toronto: UBC Press, 2014); Jessica Squires, *Building Sanctuary: The Movement to Support Vietnam War Resisters in Canada* (Vancouver and Toronto: UBC Press, 2013); and David Surrey, *Choice of Conscience: Vietnam Era Draft and Military Resisters in Canada* (New York: Praeger, 1982). For primary texts, see Kenneth Fred Emerick, *War Resisters in Canada* (Knox: Pennsylvania Free Press, 1972); Renée Kasinsky, *Refugees from Militarism: Draft-Age Americans in Canada* (New Brunswick, N.J.: Transaction Books, 1976); Byron Wall, ed., *Manual for Draft-Age Immigrants to Canada*, 5th ed. (Toronto: House of Anansi, 1970); and Roger Neville Williams, *The New Exiles: American War Resisters in Canada* (New York: Liveright Publishers, 1971).

The rise of English-Canadian nationalism is discussed in broad terms in José Igartua, *The Other Quiet Revolution: National Identities in English Canada, 1945–71* (Vancouver and Toronto: UBC Press, 2006); and in Palmer, *Canada's 1960s*. Particularly insightful are the analyses of Ryan Edwardson: see especially "Kicking Uncle Sam out of the Peaceable Kingdom: English-Canadian New Nationalism and Americanization," *Journal of Canadian Studies* 37,4 (Winter 2002), 339–56; "Of War Machines and Ghetto Scenes: English-Canadian Nationalism and The Guess Who's American Woman," *American Review of Canadian Studies* 33,3 (2003), 339–56; and *Canadian Content and the Quest for Nationhood* (Toronto: University of Toronto Press, 2008). See also Jeffrey Cormier, *The Canadianization Movement: Emergence, Survival, and Success* (Toronto: University of

Toronto Press, 2004). For left analyses, see James Laxer, "The Americanization of the Canadian Student Movement," in *Close the 49th Parallel Etc.*, ed. Ian Lumsden (Toronto: University of Toronto Press, 1970); and Al Purdy, ed., *The New Romans: Candid Canadian Opinions of the US* (Edmonton: Hurtig, 1968).

On the Company of Young Canadians, see Kevin Brushett, "Making Shit Disturbers: The Selection and Training of Company of Young Canadian Volunteers 1965–1970," in Palaeologu, ed., *Sixties in Canada*, 246–69; "Combler le fossé entre les deux solitudes: Animation sociale, développement communautaire et la Compagnie des Jeunes Canadiens, *1965–1975*," *Bulletin d'histoire politique* 23,1 (automne 2014), 62–81; and, from the period, Margaret Daly, *The Revolution Game: The Short, Unhappy Life of the Company of Young Canadians* (Toronto: New Press, 1970). For the equally significant Canadian University Service Overseas (CUSO), see especially William Langford, "'Helping People Help Themselves': Democracy, Development, and the Global Politics of Poverty in Canada, 1964–1979," Ph.D. thesis, Queen's University, 2017.

For an important new work on SUPA, see Victoria Campbell Windle, "'We of the New Left': A Gender History of the Student Union for Peace Action from the Anti-Nuclear Movement to Women's Liberation," Ph.D. thesis, University of Waterloo, 2017.

4. Out of the Meat Grinder: Confronting the Educational Leviathan, 1968–71

For classic North American studies of youthful alienation, see Paul Goodman, *Growing Up Absurd: Problems of Youth in the Organized System* (New York: Random House, 1960); and Edgar Z. Friedenberg, *The Vanishing Adolescent* (New York: Dell, 1959). For the notorious contemporary text, see Jerry Farber, *The Student as Nigger* (New York: Contact Books, 1969); for a more complete representation of Farber's views, see *The Student as Nigger: Essays and Stories by Jerry Farber* (New York: Contact Books, 1969), http://soilandhealth.org/wpcontent/uploads/0303critic/030301studentasnigger.html/.

Leading studies of the Ontario "Educational Leviathan" include Paul Axelrod, *Scholars and Dollars: Politics, Economics and the Universities of Ontario 1945–1980* (Toronto: University of Toronto Press, 1982); Adam Josh Cole, "Children, Liberalism and Utopia: Education, Hall-Dennis and Modernity in Ontario's Long 1960s," Ph.D. thesis, Queen's University, 2015; Robert Gidney, *Inventing Secondary Education: The Rise of the High School in Nineteenth-Century Ontario* (Montreal and Kingston: McGill-Queen's University Press, 1990); and Gidney, *From Hope to Harris: The Reshaping of Ontario's Schools* (Toronto: University of Toronto Press, 1998).

For general studies of Canadian post-secondary education, see especially Paul Axelrod and John Reid, eds., *Youth, University and Canadian Society* (Montreal and Kingston: McGill-Queen's University Press, 1989); Robert Stamp, *The Schools of Ontario, 1876–1976* (Toronto: Ontario Historical Series for the Government of Ontario, 1982); and Catherine Gidney, *A Long Eclipse: The Liberal Protestant Establishment and the English-Canadian University Campus, 1920–1970* (Montreal and Kingston: McGill-Queen's University Press, 2004); Gidney, *Tending the Student Body: Health, Youth and the Rise of the Modern University, 1900–1960* (Toronto: University of Toronto Press, 2015); and Gidney, "Shaping Student Bodies and Minds: The Redefinition of Self at English-Canadian Universities, 1900–1960," in *Bodily Subjects: Essays on Gender and Health, 1800–1960*, ed. Tracy Penny Light, Barbara Brookes, and Wendy Mitchison (Montreal and Kingston: McGill-Queen's University Press, 2014), 100–19.

For leading period statements from progressives about education, see Howard Adelman and Dennis Lee, eds., *The University Game* (Toronto: House of Anansi, 1968); James Harding, "From the Midst of a Crisis: Student Power in English Canada," in *Student Protest*, ed. Gerald McGuigan (Toronto: Methuen, 1968), 90–104; George Martell, ed., *The Politics of the Canadian Public School* (Toronto: J. Lewis and Samuel, 1974); T. Reid and J. Reid, *Student Power and the Canadian Campus* (Toronto: Peter Martin Associates, 1969); Satu Repo, ed., *This Book Is About Schools* (New York: Pantheon, 1970); and Sarah Spinks, "Participatory Bureaucracy and the Hall-Dennis Report," *This Magazine Is About Schools* 2 (Autumn 1968), 137–49.

For radical university politics in the 1960s in Canada, in addition to Levitt's dyspeptic *Children of Privilege*, see Hugh Johnson, *Radical Campus: Making Simon Fraser University* (Vancouver and Toronto: Douglas and McIntyre, 2005); Leila Lee, "'From the Liberal to the Critical University': C.B. Macpherson's Case for Higher Education from 1960–1980," M.A. Cognate Essay, Queen's University, 2015; Roberta Lexier, "Dreaming of a Better World: Student Rebellion in 1960s Regina," *Past Imperfect* 10 (2004), 79–98; Lexier, "To Struggle Together or Fracture Apart: The Sixties Student Movements at English-Canadian Universities," in *Debating Dissent*, ed. Campbell, Clément, and Kealey, 81–96; Lexier, "'The Backdrop Against Which Everything Happened': English-Canadian Student Movements and Off-Campus Movements for Change," *History of Intellectual Culture* 7,1 (2007), 1–18; Lexier, "Transformer les universités ou la société: les mouvements étudiants dans les années soixante dans les universités canadiennes-anglaises," *Bulletin d'Histoire Politique* 16,2 (hiver 2008), 117–32, all of which build on her "The Canadian Student Movement in the Sixties: Three Case Studies," Ph.D. thesis, University of Alberta, 2009; Marcel Martel, "'Riot' at Sir George Williams: Giving Meaning to Student Dissent," in *Debating Dissent*, ed. Campbell,

Clément, and Kealey, 97–114; James Naylor, "Rebelling Youth: Universities and Students," in *Canada since 1960*, ed. Gonick, 257–71; James M. Pitsula, *New World Dawning: The Sixties at Regina Campus* (Regina: Canadian Plans Research Center, 2008); and Dionysios Rossi, "Mountaintop Mayhem: Simon Fraser University, 1965–1971," M.A. thesis, Simon Fraser University, 2003.

On the University of Toronto specifically, see Catherine Gidney, "War and the Concept of Generation: The International Teach-Ins at the University of Toronto, 1965–1968," in Paul Stortz and E. Lisa Panayotidis, eds., *Cultures, Communities, and Conflict: Histories of Canadian Universities and War* (Toronto: University of Toronto Press, 2012), 272–94; Thomas N. Trenton, "Left-Wing Radicalism at a Canadian University: The Inapplicability of an American Model," *Interchange* 14, 2 (1983), 54–65, who studies student radicals at the University of Toronto and concludes they diverged markedly from the privileged brats emphasized by many U.S. authors. His article is based on "Canadian Identity and Nationalism among University Students: An Exploratory Analysis of the Applicability of Current Theory on Student Protest," Ph.D. thesis, University of Toronto, 1976. For a 1960s critique of left student politics from a U of T student, see Andrew Wernick, "The Student Government Left, Syndicalism, and the Search for Strategy," *Praxis* 2 (March 1969), 17–21.

For the radical Canadian Union of Students, see Robert Clift, "The Fullest Development of Human Potential: The Canadian Union of Students, 1963–1969," M.A. thesis, University of British Columbia, 2002; Doug Nesbitt, "The 'Radical' Trip of the Canadian Union of Students, 1963–69," M.A. thesis, Trent University, 2010.

For Rochdale College, see especially Stuart Henderson, "Off the Streets and into the Fortress: Experiments in Hip Separatism at Toronto's Rochdale College, 1968–1975," *Canadian Historical Review* 92,2 (March 2011), 107–33; other treatments include Brian J. Grieveson, *Rochdale* (Hamilton: Charasee, 1991); Lynn Lunde, "Rochdale College: A 1960s Adult Education Experiment as Viewed through Situated Learning Theory," M.Ed. thesis, University of Alberta, 1996; Henry Mietkiewica and Bob Mackowycz, *Dream Tower: The Life and Legacy of Rochdale College* (Scarborough, Ont.: McGraw-Hill Ryerson, 1988); David Sharpe, *Rochdale: The Runaway College* (Toronto: House of Anansi, 1987); and Ralph Osborne, *From Someplace Else: A Memoir* (Toronto: ECW Press. 2003). For period sources, see Dennis Lee and the Canadian Union of Students, *Notes on Rochdale* (Ottawa: Canadian Union of Students, n.d. [1967]); Peter Turner, ed., *There Can Be No Light without Shadow* (Toronto: Rochdale, 1971).

For RCMP surveillance of university campuses, see Steve Hewitt, "'Information Believed True': RCMP Security Intelligence Activities on Canadian University Campuses and the Controversy Surrounding Them, 1961–1971," *Canadian Historical Review* 81,2 (June 2000), 191–228; and Hewitt, *Spying 101*.

5. Bringing the Revolution Home: Black Power, Feminism, and Turning the Local into the Global, 1968–71

Reflections on global patterns of left solidarity movements include Ian Birchall, "'Vicarious Pleasure'? The British Far Left and the Third World, 1956–79," in *Against the Grain: The British Far Left from 1956*, ed. Evan Smith and Matthew Worley (Manchester, U.K.: Manchester University Press, 2014), 190–208; and Arif Dirlik, "The Third World in 1968," in *1968*, ed. Fink, Gassert, and Junker, 295–317. In the Canadian context, the leading monograph is Mills, *Empire Within*, which shows how a panoply of social and political forces in Montreal adopted the discourse of liberation movements from the global South; see also Mills, "Popular Internationalism: Refugee Movements from the Global South and the Transformation of Canada's Immigration Framework," in *Canada and the Third World: Overlapping Histories*, ed. Karen Dubinsky, Sean Mills, and Scott Rutherford (Toronto: University of Toronto Press, 2016), 246–66. For reflections on one important Canadian leader's life in solidarity activism, see John S. Saul, *Revolutionary Traveller: Freeze-Frames from a Life* (Winnipeg: ARP Books, 2009).

Allison McMahon, "From Charity to Solidarity: Liberation Theology, Dependency Theory, and Narratives of Parallel Struggle in the Canadian Nicaraguan Solidarity Movement, 1979–1990," unpublished paper, Queen's University, 2012, looks at a cause dear to many leftists in the late 1970s and 1980s. Other important studies of international solidarity movements in Canada include Janice Acton, "Witnessing Hope in the Long Learning of Solidarity," M.A. thesis, Saint Francis Xavier University, 2003; Kofi Hope, "In Search of Solidarity: International Solidarity Work between Canada and South Africa 1975–2010," Ph.D. thesis, Oxford University, 2011; and Carolina Palacios, "Social Movements as Learning Communities: Chilean Exiles and Knowledge Production in and beyond the Solidarity Movement," Ph.D. thesis, University of British Columbia, 2011.

For an important period book hailing the advent of a new, anti-colonialist international, see John Gerassi, ed., *The Coming of the New International* (New York and Cleveland: The World Publishing Co., 1971). For Frantz Fanon, read in Toronto as a leading theoretician and spokesperson for Third World insurgency, see Christopher Lee, *Frantz Fanon: Toward a Revolutionary Humanism* (Athens: Ohio University Press, 2015); David Macey, *Frantz Fanon: A Biography*, 2nd ed. (London: Verso, 2012); and Leo Zellig, *Frantz Fanon: The Militant Philosopher of Third World Revolution* (London: I.B. Taurus, 2016). For his most famous works, see *The Wretched of the Earth* (New York: Grove Press, 2005); *Black Skin, White Masks* (New York: Grove Press, 2008).

The American Civil Rights and Black movements were highly influential in Toronto, and an abundance of literature focuses on them. For the man who popularized the slogan Black power, see Stokely Carmichael, *Ready for Revolution: The Life and Struggles of Stokely Carmichael [Kwame Ture]* (New York: Scribner, 2003); a contemporary title announcing the new turn is Stokely Carmichael and Charles V. Hamilton, *Black Power: The Politics of Liberation in America* (New York: Random House, 1967). Another figure highly influential in Canada, C.L.R. James, is anthologized in *C.L.R. James and Revolutionary Marxism: Selected Writings of C.L.R. James, 1939–1949*, ed. Scott McLemee and Paul Le Blanc (Chicago: Haymarket Books, 2018); particularly apposite among his many writings are *A History of Pan-African Revolt* (Oakland, Cal.: PM Press, 2012); *Beyond a Boundary* (Durham, N.C.: Duke University Press, 2013); and *World Revolution 1917–1936: The Rise and Fall of the Third International* (Durham, N.C.: Duke University Press, 2017). For important Canadian contributions to the literature on James, see David Austin, ed., *You Don't Play With Revolution: The Montreal Lectures of C.L.R. James* (Winnipeg: AK Press, 2009); and Alfie Roberts, *A View for Freedom: Alfie Roberts Speaks on the Caribbean, Cricket, Montreal, and C.L.R. James* (Montreal: Alfie Roberts Institute, 2005).

Historical studies from the United States include Simon Hall, *Peace and Freedom: The Civil Rights and Antiwar Movements in the 1960s* (Philadelphia: University of Pennsylvania Press, 2006); Robin D.G. Kelley, *Freedom Dreams: The Black Radical Imagination* (Boston: Beacon Press, 2002); Peniel E. Joseph, ed., *The Black Power Movement: Rethinking the Civil Rights–Black Power Era* (New York and London: Routledge, 2006); "The Black Power Movement: A State of the Field," *Journal of American History* 96,3 (December 2009), 751–76; Charles Payne, *I've Got the Light of Freedom: The Organizing Tradition and the Mississippi Freedom Struggle* (Berkeley: University of California Press, 2007); Brenda Gayle Plummer, *In Search of Power: African Americans in the Era of Decolonization, 1956–1974* (Cambridge: Cambridge University Press, 2013); Robyn C. Spencer, *The Revolution Has Come: Black Power, Gender, and the Black Panther Party in Oakland* (Durham, N.C., and London: Duke University Press, 2016); Kimberly Springer, "Black Feminists Respond to Black Power Masculinism," in *The Black Power Movement*, ed. Joseph, 105–18; William L. Van Deburg, *New Day in Babylon: The Black Power Movement and American Culture, 1965–1975* (Chicago: University of Chicago Press, 1992); and Cornel West, "The Paradox of the Afro-American Rebellion," in *60s Without Apology*, ed. Sayres et al., 44–58. For a history of the pejorative word that so many radicals of the 1960s used with such abandon, see Randall Kennedy, *Nigger: The Strange Career of a Troublesome Word* (New York: Vintage Books, 2003).

In Canada, much attention has been focused on Montreal. See David Austin, "All Roads Lead to Montreal: Black Power, the Caribbean, and the Black Radical Tradition in Canada," *Journal of African-American History* 92,4 (Fall 2007), 513–36; and Austin, *Fear of a Black Nation: Race, Sex and Security in Sixties Montreal* (Toronto: Between the Lines, 2013). The Sir George Williams revolt generated a considerable literature at the time—see Dorothy Eber, *The Computer Center Party: Canada Meets Black Power* (Montreal: Tundra, 1969); and Dennis Forsythe, *Let the Niggers Burn: The Sir George Williams University Affair and Its Caribbean Aftermath* (Montreal: Black Rose Books, 1971)—and has become an object of scholarly inquiry: see Mills, *Empire Within*. For more general analyses, see Roseanne Waters, "A March from Selma to Canada: Canada and the Transnational Civil Rights Movement," Ph.D. thesis, McMaster University, 2015; and Peter Stamadianos, "Afro-Canadian Activism in the 1960s," M.A. thesis, Concordia University, 1994. The city of Halifax has also drawn attention: James W. St. G. Walker, "Black Confrontation in Sixties Halifax," in *Debating Dissent*, ed. Campbell, Clément, and Kealey, 173–92. To date Toronto has not received as much notice, but see David Churchill, "SUPA, Selma and Stevenson: The Politics of Solidarity in Mid-1960s Toronto," *Journal of Canadian Studies* 44,2 (Spring 2010), 32–69; and Chris Harris, "Canadian Black Power, Organic Intellectuals and the War of Position in Toronto, 1967–1975," in *Sixties in Canada*, ed. Palaeologu, 324–39. For a look at anti-racist organizing in Toronto during the late 1970s and early 1980s, see Julian Sher, *White Hoods: Canada's Ku Klux Klan* (Vancouver: New Star Books, 1983).

Women's liberation from the mid-1960s to the early 1970s has generated an enormous volume of literature internationally, some of which is useful in Canada. For general U.S. statements, see Susan Brownmiller, *In Our Time: Memoir of a Revolution* (New York: Delta, 1999); Alice Echols, *Daring to Be Bad: Radical Feminism in America, 1967–1975* (Minneapolis: University of Minnesota Press, 1989); S.M. Evans, *Personal Politics: The Roots of Women's Liberation in the Civil Rights Movement and the New Left* (New York: Knopf, 1979), and Evans, "Sons, Daughters and Patriarchy: Gender and the 1968 Generation," *American Historical Review* 114,2 (2009), 331–47; Betty Friedan, *It Changed My Life: Writings on the Women's Movement* (Cambridge, Mass.: Harvard University Press, 1998); and Ruth Rosen, *The World Split Open: How the Modern Women's Movement Changed America* (New York: Penguin Books, 2001). Elizabeth E. McGory, *The Challenge of Local Feminisms: Women's Movements in Global Perspective* (Boulder, Col.: Westview Press, 1995), is a welcome attempt to get beyond U.S.-centrism.

Contemporary U.S feminist books and pamphlets known to have been influential in Canada from 1968 to the early 1970s are readily available: see Bloom and Breines, eds., *'Takin' It to the Streets'*, ch. 8, "'She's Leaving Home': The Women's Liberation Movement," 388–463; Judith Brown and Beverly Jones, "Toward a Female Liberation Movement," in *Voices from Women's Liberation*, ed. Leslie Tanner (New York: New American Library, 1971); Shulamith Firestone, *The*

Dialectic of Sex: The Case for Feminist Revolution (New York: William Morrow, 1970), some of which was written in Halifax; Jo Freeman, "The Tyranny of Structurelessness," (1970), http://struggle.ws/pdfs/tyranny.pdf, a highly influential critique of actually existing prefigurative democratic politics; Jo Freeman, "The Revolution Is Happening in Our Minds," in *The New Feminism in the Twentieth Century*, ed. June Sochen (Lexington, Mass.: D.C. Heath and Company, 1971), 149–60; Carol Hanisch, "The Personal Is Political," in *Notes from the Second Year: Women's Liberation, Major Writings of the Radical Feminists*, ed. Shulamith Firestone and Anne Koedt (New York: Radical Feminism, 1970), reprinted in *Radical Feminism: A Documentary Reader* (New York: New York University Press, 2000), 113–17 (the author herself felt her statement was often completely misinterpreted in a wholly individualistic manner); Anne Koedt, "The Myth of the Vaginal Orgasm," in *Notes from the Second Year*, ed. Firestone and Koedt; Marge Piercy, *Grand Coolie Damn* (Boston: New England Free Press, 1969); Gayle Rubin, "Woman as Nigger," in *Masculine/Feminine: Readings in Sexual Mythology and the Liberation of Women*, ed. Betty Roszak and Theodore Roszak (New York: Harper and Row, 1969), 230–40; Betsy Warrior, "American Radicalism: A Diseased Product of a Diseased Society," in *No More Fun and Games: A Journal of Female Liberation*, 1,2 (1969); and Naomi Weisstein, *Woman as Nigger* (Pittsburgh: Know Inc., 1969), reprinted in *Voices from Women's Liberation*, ed. Tanner, 296–303.

British and European influences were also significant. Juliet Mitchell's "The Longest Revolution," *New Left Review* 40 (December 1966), 11–37, later developed into *Women: The Longest Revolution* (New York: Pantheon, 1984), was picked up almost immediately. Sheila Rowbotham's *Hidden from History: 300 Years of Women's Oppression and the Fight Against It* (London: Pluto Press, 1973), was also significant; for a discussion and interview, see Bryan D. Palmer, "Bread and Roses: Sheila Rowbotham, an Introduction, an Appreciation, and an Interview," *left history* 2 (spring 1994), 119–38. The most frequently cited French author was Simone de Beauvoir, whose *Le Deuxième Sexe* (*The Second Sex*) was published in a faulty translation by Knopf of New York in 1953; it was retranslated in 2009. See Nancy Bauer, *Simone de Beauvoir: Philosophy and Feminism* (Columbia University Press, 2012); and Elizabeth Fallaize, *Simone de Beauvoir: A Critical Reader* (London: Routledge, 1998).

For the background to 1960s feminism in Canada, see especially Julie Guard, *Radical Housewives: Price Wars and Food Politics in Mid-Twentieth-Century Canada* (Toronto: University of Toronto Press, 2018); Valerie Korinek, *Roughing It in the Suburbs: Reading* Chatelaine *in the 1950s and 1960s* (Toronto: University of Toronto Press, 2000), which documents the emergence of feminist themes in the magazine well in advance of its U.S. counterparts; Ester Reiter, *A Future without*

Hate or Need: The Promise of the Jewish Left in Canada (Toronto: Between the Lines, 2016); Joan Sangster, *Dreams of Equality: Women on the Canadian Left, 1920–1950* (Toronto: McClelland and Stewart, 1989); Sangster, *Regulating Girls and Women: Sexuality, Family, and the Law in Ontario, 1920–1960* (Toronto: Oxford University Press, 2001); Veronica Strong-Boag, "Home Dreams: Women and the Suburban Experiment in Canada, 1945–60," *Canadian Historical Review* 72,4 (1991), 471–504; Brian T. Thorn, *From Left to Right: Maternalism and Women's Political Activism in Postwar Canada* (Vancouver and Toronto: UBC Press, 2016); and Jill Vickers, "The Intellectual Origins of the Women's Movements in Canada," in *Challenging Times: The Women's Movement in Canada and the United States*, ed. Constance Backhouse and David Flaherty (Montreal and Kingston: McGill-Queen's University Press, 1992), 39–60.

In Canada the most accessible general survey remains Judy Rebick's *Ten Thousand Roses: The Making of a Feminist Revolution* (Toronto: Penguin Canada, 2005), based on oral interviews. Some three decades on, Nancy Adamson, Linda Briskin, and Margaret McPhail, *Feminist Organizing for Change: The Contemporary Women's Movement in Canada* (Toronto: Oxford University Press, 1988), still stands as a trailblazing attempt to develop a general theoretical framework for the history of the movement. See also Nancy Adamson, "Feminists, Libbers, Lefties, and Radicals: The Emergence of the Women's Liberation Movement," in *A Diversity of Women: Ontario, 1945–1980*, ed. Joy Parr (Toronto: University of Toronto Press, 1995), 252–80. Joan Sangster, "Radical Ruptures: Feminism, Labor, and the Left in the Long Sixties in Canada," *American Review of Canadian Studies* 40,1 (March, 2010), 1–21, assesses the relationship of feminists with the working-class movement. Roberta Lexier, "How Did the Women's Liberation Movement Emerge from the Sixties Student Movements: The Case of Simon Fraser University," *Women and Social Movements in America, 1600–2000* 13,2 (Fall 2009), looks at women's liberation from a student perspective.

Margaret Little, "Militant Mothers Fight Poverty: The Just Society Movement, 1968–1971," *Labour/Le Travail* 49 (Spring 2007), 179–97, studies an important Toronto-based movement. Joan Sangster, "Invoking Evidence as Experience," *Canadian Historical Review* 92,1 (March 2011), 135–61, discusses private letters written to the Royal Commission on the Status of Women; for more on that, see also Kimberly Marie Speers, "The Royal Commission on the Status of Women: A Study of the Contradictions and Limitations of Liberalism and Liberal Feminism," M.A. thesis, Queen's University, 1994.

The struggle over reproductive rights has been analyzed by Janis Lundman and Nancy Nicol, *Abortion Caravan: The Struggle for Choice* (Toronto: Toronto Horizontal Forest Productions, 1986); Beth Palmer, "'Lonely, Tragic, but Legally Necessary Pilgrimages': Transnational Abortion Travel in the 1970s," *Canadian*

Historical Review 92,4 (December 2011), 637–74; Christabelle Sethna, "The Evolution of the Birth Control Handbook: From Student Peer-Education to Feminist Self-Empowerment Text, 1968–1975," *Canadian Bulletin of Medical History* 23,1 (2006), 89–118; Sethna, "The University of Toronto Health Service, Oral Contraception, and Student Demand for Birth Control, 1960–1970," *Historical Studies in Education* 17,2 (2005), 265–92; Sethna, "All Aboard? Canadian Women's Abortion Tourism, 1960–1980," in *Gender, Health, and Popular Culture*, ed. Cheryl Krasnick Warsh (Waterloo, Ont.: Wilfrid Laurier University Press, 2011), 89–108; Shannon Stettner, "'We Are Forced to Declare War': Linkages between the 1970 Abortion Caravan and Women's Anti-Vietnam War Activism," *Histoire sociale/Social History* 46,92 (November 2013), 423–41; Shannon Stettner and Christabelle Sethna, "Reassessing the Abortion Caravan," http://activehistory.ca/2015/05/reassessing-the-abortion-caravan; Ann Thompson, *Winning Choice on Abortion: How British Columbian and Canadian Feminists Won the Battles of the 1970s and 1980s* (Vancouver: Trafford Publishing, 2004); and Frances Jane Wasserlein, "'An Arrow Aimed at the Heart': The Vancouver Women's Caucus and the Abortion Campaign, 1969–1971," M.A. thesis, Simon Fraser University, 1990. For period sources, see Eleanor Wright Pelrine, *Abortion in Canada* (Toronto: New Press, 1971); Pelrine, *Morgentaler: The Doctor Who Couldn't Turn Away* (Canada: Gage Publishing, 1975). Janine Brodie, Shelley A.M. Gavigan, and Jane Jenson, *The Politics of Abortion* (Toronto: Oxford University Press, 1992), offers an overview.

For state surveillance of women's liberation, see Sethna and Hewitt, *Just Watch Us*, which builds on "Sex Spying: The RCMP and Women's Liberation Groups," in *Debating Dissent*, ed. Campbell, Clément, and Kealey, 134–35; and Sethna and Hewitt, "Clandestine Operations: The Vancouver Women's Caucus, the Abortion Caravan, and the RCMP," *Canadian Historical Review* 90,3 (September 2009), 463–95.

The heyday of women's liberation from 1968 to the early 1970s witnessed an unprecedented outpouring of grassroots writing by and for radical women. Women's liberationists in Canada and especially Toronto soon started generating their own literature, some of which found readers across North America and beyond. One of these transnational texts was Laurel Limpus, *Liberation of Women: Sexual Repression and the Family* (Boston: New England Free Press, n.d.). Vancouver-based Margaret Benston's, "The Political Economy of Women's Liberation," *Monthly Review* 21 (September 1969), 13–27, became a much-discussed classic; it was reprinted as a pamphlet: *The Political Economy of Women's* Liberation (Toronto: Literature Committee, Toronto Women's Liberation and Hogtown Press: n.d. [1970]), and in Edith Hoshino Altbach, ed., *From Feminism to Liberation* (Cambridge, Mass. and London: Schenkman Publishing, 1971), 199–210.

She is remembered in Meg Luxton and Pat Armstrong, "Margaret Lowe Benston, 1937–1991," *Studies in Political Economy* 35 (Summer 1991), 7–11, and in Palmer, *Canada's 1960s*. Judi Bernstein, Peggy Morton, Linda Seese, and Myrna Wood, "Sisters, Brothers, Lovers . . . Listen . . . ," the famous manifesto generated within SUPA in 1967, was reprinted in Roszak and Roszak, eds., *Masculine/Feminine*. For Seese's later reflections, see "You've Come a Long Way, Baby—Women in the Movement," in *The New Women: A Motive Anthology on Women's Liberation*, ed. Joanne Cooke and Charlotte Bunch-Weeks (New York: The Bobbs-Merrill Company, 1970).

Charnie Guettel's *Marxism and Feminism* (Toronto: Canadian Women's Educational Press, 1974) came from a militant in the U of T daycare movement and remained in print for decades. Peggy Morton, another manifesto author, brought out *A Woman's Work Is Never Done or the Reproduction, Maintenance and Reproduction of Labour Power* (n.p. [Toronto]: n.d. [c.1970]), which then appeared in *Leviathan* 2,1 (May 1970), 32–37 and in Altbach, ed., *From Feminism to Liberation*, 211–27, and was later translated into Spanish—*Trabajo de la mujer nunca se termina*—in Mirta Henault, Peggy Morton, and Isabel Larguia, eds., *Las mujeres dicen basta* (Buenos Aires: Ediciones Nueva Mujer, c.1972). Morton also brought out, with Heather Jon Maroney, *Women's Liberation: An Introductory Paper* (n.p. [Toronto]: n.d. [1969]), and *They Are burning, They Are Burning Effigies: Why, Why, Why Effigies?* (Toronto: Hogtown Press, n.d. [1969]).

The poet and activist Sharon Stevenson, whose tragic suicide haunted many of her contemporaries, published *Stone* (Vancouver: Talonbooks, 1972) and *Golden Earrings: Select Poetry* (Vancouver: Pulp Press, 1984); she is remembered in James Doyle, *Progressive Heritage: The Evolution of a Politically Radical Literary Tradition in Canada* (Waterloo, Ont.: Wilfrid Laurier University Press, 2002).

Myrna Wood, one of the authors of the 1967 *Manifesto*, was the co-author, with Kathy McAfee, of "Bread and Roses," one of the most widely reprinted statements of women's liberation. It can be found as Kathy McAfee and Myrna Wood, "Bread and Roses," *Leviathan* 1,3 (June 1969), 8–11, 43–44; in Altbach, ed., *From Feminism to Liberation*, 21–38; as *Bread & Roses* (Detroit: Radical Education Project, n.d. [1969]); and as a New Hogtown pamphlet. For her other writings, see Kathy McAfee and Myrna Wood, *What Is the Revolutionary Potential of Women's Liberation?* (Boston: New England Free Press, n.d. [1970]), and Myrna Wood, *We May Not Have Much, but There's a Lot of Us* (Detroit: Radical Education Project, n.d. [1970]), which was billed as a "Discussion . . . between Myrna Wood, a member of the Women's Liberation Movement, and a woman who lives in a small city of Eastern Ontario, Canada."

Cathy Pike and Barb Cameron, *Collective Child-Care in a Class Society* (Toronto: Toronto Women's Liberation, 1971); and Kathleen Gallagher Ross, ed., *Good Day Care: Fighting for It, Keeping It* (Toronto: Women's Press, 1978), are period publications about one of women's liberation's key achievements. The child-care struggle in British Columbia is covered in Lisa Pasolli, "'Talkin' Day Care Blues': Motherhood, Work, and Child Care in Twentieth-Century British Columbia," Ph.D. thesis, University of Victoria, 2012, which formed the basis of her *Working Mothers and the Child Care Dilemma: A History of British Columbia's Social Policy* (Vancouver and Toronto: UBC Press, 2016).

Interesting attempts at on-the-fly analyses are Laurel Limpus, as told to Sherry Rochester, "The History of the Toronto Women's Liberation Movement," mimeo, Toronto, 1971, which can be consulted in the Toronto Women's Liberation Movement Fonds, Canadian Women's Movement Archives, box 117, University of Ottawa; and Francie Ricks, George Matheson, and Sandra Pike, "Women's Liberation: A Case Study of Organizations for Social Change," *Canadian Psychologist* 13,1 (January 1972). Margaret Fulford, ed., *The Canadian Women's Movement, 1960–1990: A Guide to Archival Resources* (Toronto: ECW Press, 1992), provides useful guidance for future research. Bonnie Kreps, *Guide to the Women's Movement in Canada: A Chatelaine Cope-Kit* (Toronto: Chatelaine, n.d. [1973]), provides a contemporary introduction to mainstream representation of the movement.

A useful collection of primary sources on the impact of feminism on personal politics is Dennis Pilon, "The Personal Dimension," in *Canada since 1960*, ed. Gonick, 524–48.

6. Obsolete Communism and Conflicting Visions? Wafflers, Liberals, and New Leninists, 1968–71

For a nuanced interpretation of world communism after 1968, see Maud Anne Bracke, "1968," in *The Oxford Handbook of the History of Communism*, ed. S.A. Smith (Oxford: Oxford University Press, 2014), 156–70. Norman Penner, *Canadian Communism: The Stalin Years and Beyond* (Toronto: Methuen, 1988), provides a balanced assessment of the CPC. For an innovative discussion of one of its leading intellectual's dealings with the new left, see David Frank, "'A Sense of Direction': l'influence de Stanley B. Ryerson auprès de la nouvelle gauche anglo-canadienne," in *Stanley Bréhaut Ryerson: Un intellectuel de combat*, dirs. Robert Comeau et Robert Tremblay (Hull: Éditions Vents d'ouest, 1996), 339–62.

For general assessments of postwar social democracy, see Sheri Berman, *The Primacy of Politics: Social Democracy and the Making of Europe's Twentieth Century* (Cambridge: Cambridge University Press, 2006); Mark Blyth, *Great Transformations: Economic Ideas and Institutional Change in the Twentieth Century* (Cambridge: Cambridge University Press, 2002); J.F. Conway, "The Crisis of Social

Democracy," *Labour/Le Travail* 17 (Spring 1986): 257–65; Eley, *Forging Democracy*; Bryan Evans and Ingo Schmidt, eds., *Social Democracy after the Cold War* (Edmonton: Athabasca University Press, 2012); Leo Panitch and Colin Leys, *The End of Parliamentary Socialism: From New Left to New Labour*, 2nd ed. (London: Verso, 2001); Thomas Meyer with Lewis Hinchman, *The Theory of Social Democracy* (Cambridge: Polity, 2007); Dennis Pilon, "The Long Lingering Death of Social Democracy." *Labour/Le Travail* 70 (Fall 2012), 245–60; and Adam Przeworski, *Capitalism and Social Democracy* (Cambridge: Cambridge University Press, 1986).

In Canada one of the most important reappraisals of post-1945 social democracy can be found in Christo Aivalis, *The Constant Liberal: Pierre Trudeau, Organized Labour, and the Canadian Social Democratic Left* (Vancouver and Toronto: UBC Press, 2018), which tracks the movement's significant turn to the left after the mid-1960s, in part in response to new leftists; see also Aivalis, "Tommy Douglas, David Lewis, Ed Broadbent, and Democratic Socialism in the New Democratic Party, 1968–1984," in *Party of Conscience: The CCF, the NDP, and Social Democracy in Canada*, ed. Roberta Lexier, Stephanie Bangarth, and Jonathan Weier (Toronto: Between the Lines, 2018).

For the Ontario pattern, see Dan Azoulay, *Keeping the Dream Alive: The Survival of the Ontario CCF/NDP*, 1850–1963 (Montreal and Kingston: McGill-Queen's University Press, 1997), which builds on his "The Cold War Within: The Ginger Group, the Woodsworth Foundation, and the Ontario CCF, 1944–1953," *Ontario History* 84,2 (June 1992), 79–104, and "'This March Forward to a Genuine People's Party'? Rivalry and Deception in the Founding of the Ontario NDP, 1958–61," *Canadian Historical Review* 74,1 (1993), 44–70. For the NDP and labour, see Keith Archer, *Political Choices and Electoral Consequences: A Study of Organized Labour and the New Democratic* Party (Montreal and Kingston: McGill-Queen's University Press, 1990).

Older studies include Gerald Caplan, *The Dilemma of Canadian Socialism: The CCF in Ontario* (Toronto: McClelland and Stewart, 1973); and John Terence Morley, *Secular Socialists: The CCF/NDP in Ontario, A Biography* (Kingston: McGill-Queen's University Press, 1984). See Cameron Smith, *Unfinished Journey: The Lewis Family* (Toronto: Summerhill Press, 1989), for a study of the "first family" of Ontario social democracy.

Charles Taylor, *The Pattern of Politics* (Toronto and Montreal: McClelland and Stewart, 1970), can be read as a defence of social democracy from a prominent new left thinker. For a collection that suggests a certain growth of radicalism within the party by the early 1970s, see Laurier LaPierre et al., eds., *Essays on the Left: In Honour of T.C. Douglas* (Toronto: McClelland and Stewart, 1971).

For period left-wing appraisals of social democracy, see Michael S. Cross, *The Decline and Fall of a Good Idea: CCF-NDP Manifestoes, 1932 to 1969* (Toronto:

New Hogtown Press, 1974); Dick Fidler, *The NDP: The Marxist View* (Toronto: Vanguard Publications, 1973); James Harding, "The NDP, the Regina Manifesto, and the New Left," *Canadian Dimension* 4 (November-December 1966), 18–19; and Gary Teeple, "'Liberals in a Hurry': Socialism and the CCF-NDP," in *Capitalism and the National Question in Canada*, ed. Gary Teeple (Toronto: University of Toronto Press, 1972), 229–50.

The Waffle movement in the NDP has yet to receive the book-length monograph it deserves, but see David Blocker, "Waffling in Winnipeg and London: Canada's New Left and the NDP, 1965–75," in *Party of Conscience*, ed. Lexier, Bangarth, and Weier; Janine Brodie, "From Waffles to Grits: A Decade in the Life of the N.D.P.," in *Party Politics in Canada*, ed. Hugh Thorburn, 5th ed. (Toronto: Prentice-Hall, 1985), 205–17; Robert Hackett, "Pie in the Sky: A History of the Ontario Waffle," *Canadian Dimension* 15 (October-November 1980), which builds on his "The Waffle and the New Democratic Party in Ontario: A Case Study in Canadian Leftist Politics," M.A. thesis, Queen's University, 1976; Roberta Lexier, "Waffling Towards Parity in the New Democratic Party," in *Mind the Gaps: Canadian Perspectives on Gender and Politics*, ed. Roberta Lexier and Tamara A. Small (Halifax: Fernwood Publishing, 2013); and "Two Nations in Canada: The New Democratic Party, the Waffle Movement, and Nationalism in Quebec," *British Journal of Canadian Studies* 30,1 (2017). For an excellent collection of articles about the Waffle experience, see *Studies in Political Economy*, 32 (1990), especially John Smart, "The Waffle's Impact on the New Democratic Party," 177–86; Pat Smart, "The Waffle and Quebec," 195–201; Rianne Mahon, "The Waffle and Canadian Political Economy," 187–94; and Mel Watkins, "The Waffle and the National Question," 173–76.

The Wafflers' own writings are widespread. For James Laxer, see *Centralism, Regionalism, Continentalism: Problems of Canadian Nationhood* (Toronto: Student Union for Peace Action, n.d. [1966?]); "French-Canadian Newspapers and Imperial Defence, 1899–1914," M.A. thesis, Queen's University, 1967; *The Energy Poker Game: The Politics of the Continental Resources Deal* (Toronto: New Press, 1970); and *Canada's Energy Crisis* (Toronto: J. Lewis and Samuel, 1974). For Robert Laxer: *Canada, Ltd.: The Political Economy of Dependency* (Toronto: McClelland and Stewart, 1973). For Krista Maeots: "Some Problems in the Redefinition of Activism: The Rise and Fall of SUPA," in *Social Space: Canadian Perspectives*, ed. D.I. Davies and Kathleen Herman (Toronto: New Press, 1971), 230–33. And for Mel Watkins: *Foreign Ownership and the Structure of Canadian Industry: Report of the Task Force on the Structure of Canadian Industry* (Ottawa; Privy Council Office, 1968); David Godfrey and Melville Watkins, eds., *Gordon to Watkins to You: A Documentary: The Battle for Control of Our Economy* (Toronto: New Press, 1970).

Wafflers were very critical of "international"—that is, American-dominated—trade unions, as were other left nationalists. For one widely read history of trade unions written from this perspective, see Charles Lipton, *The Trade Union Movement of Canada, 1827–1959* (Montreal: Canadian Social Publications, 1967). Jack Scott also produced *Canadian Workers, American Unions: How the American Federation of Labour Took over Canada's Unions* (Vancouver: New Star Books, 1978). Robert Laxer with Paul Craven and Anne Martin, *Canada's Unions* (Toronto: James Lorimer and Company, 1976), presented an equally critical, although more soberly expressed, version of the same critique.

One firm "line of demarcation" found on the English-Canadian left concerned the stance taken with respect to the Trudeau government's repression of Quebec nationalists in October 1970. Fine polemics against the government's position can be found in Denis Smith, *Bleeding Hearts . . . Bleeding Country: Canada and the Quebec Crisis* (Edmonton: M.G. Hurtig, 1971); Abraham Rotstein, ed., *Power Corrupted: The October Crisis and the Repression of Quebec* (Toronto: New Press, 1971); John Saywell, *Quebec 70: A Documentary Narrative* (Toronto: University of Toronto Press, 1971); and R. Haggart and A.E. Golden, *Rumours of War* (Toronto: New Press, 1971), which was also translated and published in Montreal under the title *Octobre 70, un an après. Adaptation français de 'Rumours of War'* (Montreal: H.M.H. Hurtubise, 1971). For a sobering scholarly appraisal, see Dominque Clément, "The October Crisis of 1970: Human Rights Abuses under the War Measures Act," *Journal of Canadian Studies* 42,2 (Spring 2008), 160–86. For an attempt to grasp the October Crisis within the framework of new left humanism, see Charles Taylor, "Behind the Kidnappings: Alienation Too Profound for the System," *Canadian Dimension* 7,5 (December 1970), 26–29.

The disintegration of the SDS and the rise of the Weather Underground have generated an enormous literature, of which Dan Berger, *Outlaws of America: The Weather Underground and the Politics of Solidarity* (Oakland, Cal.: AK Press, 2006), and Jeremy Varon, *Bringing the War Home: The Weather Underground, the Red Army Faction, and Revolutionary Violence in the Sixties and Seventies* (Berkeley and Los Angeles: University of California Press, 2004), stand out analytically; Bill Ayers, *Fugitive Days: Memoirs of an Antiwar Activist* (Boston: Beacon Press, 2008), and Cathy Wilkerson, *Flying Close to the Sun: My Life and Times as a Weatherman* (New York: Seven Stories Press, 2007), are among the more interesting memoirs.

The major book on the emergence of the new communist movements in the United States is Max Elbaum, *Revolution in the Air: Sixties Radicals Turn to Lenin, Mao, and Che* (London: Verso, 2002). A major study of the rise of Maoism in France, with direct implications for Canada, is Richard Wolin, *The Wind from the East: French Intellectuals, the Cultural Revolution, and the Legacy of the 1960s* (Princeton and Oxford: Princeton University Press, 2010); and see also Belden Fields, "French Maoism," in *60s Without Apology*, ed. Sayres et al., 148–77. Michael Staudenmaier, "Unorthodox Leninism: Workplace Organizing and

Anti-Imperialist Solidarity in the Sojourner Truth Organization," in *The Hidden 1970s: Histories of Radicalism*, ed. Dan Berger (New Brunswick, N.J. and London: Rutgers University Press, 2010), 155–74, uncovers a fascinating grassroots experiment in the United States.

In Britain, Smith and Worley, eds., *Against the Grain*, is especially noteworthy. For an empirically rich and comparative analysis, see A. Belden Fields, *Trotskyism and Maoism: Theory and Practice in France and the United States* (Brooklyn, N.Y.: Automedia, 1988).

For global Trotskyism, see Robert J. Alexander, *International Trotskyism, 1929–1985: A Documented Analysis of the Movement* (Durham, N.C.: Duke University Press, 1991); Jan Willem Stutje, "Trotskyism Emerges from Obscurity: New Chapters in Its Historiography," *International Review of Social History* 49,2 (2004), 279–92. Its British career is discussed in John Callaghan, "Engaging with Trotsky: The influence of Trotskyism in Britain," in *Against the Grain*, ed. Smith and Worley, 25–44; and in Phil Burton-Cartledge, "Marching Separately, Seldom Together: The Political History of Two Principal Trends in British Trotskyism, 1945–2009," in *Against the Grain*, ed. Smith and Worley, 80–97. The controversial tactic of entering other parties is examined in Peter Shipley, *Trotskyism: 'Entryism' and Permanent Revolution* (London: Institute for the Study of Conflict, 1977).

In the United States, see especially Donna T. Haverty-Stacke, *Trotskyists on Trial: Free Speech and Political Persecution since the Age of FDR* (New York: New York University Press, 2015); and Bryan D. Palmer, *James P. Cannon and the Origins of the American Revolutionary Left, 1890–1928* (Urbana and Chicago: University of Illinois Press, 2007). Roger O'Toole, *Precipitous Path: Studies in Political Sects* (Toronto: Peter Martin, 1977), attempted to look at Trotskyists and Maoists together; his book builds on "The Sociology of Political Sects: Four Sects in Toronto in 1968–1969," Ph.D. thesis, University of Toronto, 1972.

For the background of Trotskyism in Canada, see the contrasting evaluations of Ian McKay, "Revolution Deferred: Maurice Spector's Political Odyssey, 1928–1941," paper presented to the Canadian Historical Association, Halifax, May 2003, and Bryan D. Palmer, "Maurice Spector, James P. Cannon, and the Origins of Canadian Trotskyism," *Labour/Le Travail* 56 (Fall 2005), 91–148. See also Ernest Tate, *Revolutionary Activism in the 1950s and 60s: A Memoir*, vol. 1, *Canada 1955–1965* (London: Resistance Books, 2014); and Patrick Webber, "Entryism in Theory, in Practice and in Crisis: The Trotskyist Experience in New Brunswick, 1969–1973," *left history* 14,1 (2009), 33–57. A number of Canadian Trotskyist documents are available at the Socialist History Project (socialisthistory.ca).

Period sources for Toronto-based Trotskyists include Ross Dowson, ed., *In the Federal Appeal Court: Between Ross Dowson v. RCMP, A Vivid Episode in the*

Ongoing Struggle for Freedom of Thought and Social Justice in Canada (Toronto: Forward Publications, 1960); and Richard Fidler, *RCMP: The Real Subversives* (Toronto: Vanguard Publications, 1978), both critiques of police surveillance. George Addison, *The Socialist Alternative for Canada* (Toronto: Vanguard Publications, 1974), and John Riddell and Art Young, *Prospects for a Socialist Canada* (Toronto: Vanguard, 1977), present one Trotskyist perspective to the wider public. Judy Rebick provides notable insights into the strengths and limitations of the Trotskyist experience in Judy Rebick, "Interview with Judy Rebick," *Studies in Political Economy* 44 (Summer 1994), 39–71. Heather McLeod, "'Not Another God-Damned Housewife': Ruth Bullock, the 'Woman Question,' and Canadian Trotskyism," M.A. thesis, Simon Fraser University, 1993, brings out the Trotskyists' conflicts on the "Woman Question."

For Hardial Singh Bains, *Necessity for Change* (Ottawa: Communist Party of Canada [Marxist-Leninist], 1976 [first edition 1967]), is of fundamental importance; his later reflections on the period appear in Bains, *Thinking about the Sixties: 1960–1967* (Toronto: The New Magazine Publishing Company, 2006), and *Communism 1989–1991* (Toronto: Ideological Studies Centre, 1991). His reflections on Indian Marxism can be found in Bain, *Crisis of Values: For a Modern Indian Political Theory; Key Problems of Contemporary Marxist-Leninist Thought* (New Delhi: Lok Awaz Publishers and Distributors, 1998). Clarke Mackey's film *The Revolution Begins at Home* (2016) provides an excellent personal account of the early years of CPC-ML. Many documents produced by Canadian Maoists are available at The Encyclopedia of Anti-Revisionism On-Line (marxists.org/history/erol/erol.htm).

7. We Must *All* Be Politicians: Urban Resistance and the Turn to Community, 1971–78

For new leftists, "community" meant something more than a term for people living in the same area or sharing a common characteristic. Rather, it meant shared values and responsibilities that stood apart from, and were largely opposed to, those of capitalism, patriarchy, and possessive individualism. In the 1970s, many new leftists tended increasingly to communitarianism, an outlook emphasizing a self-determining community's irreplaceable role in defining and shaping free individuals. An exemplary case is that of new leftist Charles Taylor of Montreal, whose *Sources of the Self: The Making of Modern Identity* (Cambridge: Harvard University Press, 1992) and *Multiculturalism and the Politics of Recognition* (Princeton: Princeton University Press, 1992) have inspired many left-leaning liberals. The "community" of which new leftists spoke generally had a more anti-capitalist, socialist edge, one that hoped that "grassroots communities" might exemplify participatory democracy, egalitarianism, self-government, human warmth, and gender equality.

The communitarian impulse—the turn to community—took many forms, one of which was the formation of communes. See Bill Metcalf and William James, *Shared Visions, Shared Lives: Communal Living around the Globe* (Scotland: Findhorn Press, 1996); and Barry Shenker, *Intentional Communities: Ideology and Alienation in Communal Societies* (London: Routledge and Kegan Paul, 1986). For explorations of this phenomenon in the United States, see especially Timothy Miller, *The 60s Communes: Hippies and Beyond* (Syracuse: Syracuse University Press, 2015); John Curl, *For All the People: Uncovering the Hidden History of Cooperation, Co-operative Movements, and Communalism in America* (Oakland, Cal.: PM Press, 2009). For assessments from the period, see John Case and Rosemary C.R. Taylor, eds., *Co-ops, Communes, and Collectives: Experiments in Social Change in the 1960s and 1970s* (New York: Pantheon, 1979); Richard Fairfield, *Communes USA: A Personal Tour* (Baltimore: Penguin, 1972); Laurence R. Veysey, *The Communal Experience: Anarchist and Mystical Communities in Twentieth Century America* (New York: Harper and Row, 1973); Laurence Zvesey, *Communal Experience: Anarchist and Mystical Counter-Cultures in America* (New York: Harper and Row, 1973). In Canada, see Andrew Scott, *The Promise of Paradise: Utopian Communities in British Columbia* (Madeira Park, B.C.: Harbour Publishing, 2017).

For innovative studies exploring grassroots community development as a Canadian project with strong transnational connections, see Richard Harris, *Democracy in Kingston: A Social Movement in Urban Politics, 1965–1970* (Kingston and Montreal: McGill-Queen's University Press, 1988); and Langford, "'Helping People Help Themselves.'" For an influential period statement, see Gerry Hunnius, ed., *Participatory Democracy for Canada: Workers' Control and Community Control* (Montreal: Black Rose Books, 1971). A valuable participation-observation study of one of Toronto's largest new left–leaning community organizations is included in Randall White, "Citizen Politics in Riverdale: The Greater Riverdale Organization 1972–1973: An Approach to the Emergence of New Forms of Political Structure in Canadian Society," Ph.D. thesis, University of Toronto, 1976.

For the contradictions and struggles around "urban renewal" in Toronto, see especially Kevin Brushett, "Blots on the Face of the City: The Politics of Slum Housing and Urban Renewal in Toronto, 1940–1970," Ph.D. thesis, Queen's University, 2001; and Sean Purdy, "'Ripped Off' by the System: Housing Policy, Poverty, and Territorial Stigmatization in Regent Park Housing Project, 1951–1991," *Labour/Le Travail* 52 (Fall 2003), 45–108; Purdy, "By the People, for the People: Tenant Organizing in Toronto's Regent Park Housing Project in the 1960s and 1970s," *Journal of Urban History* 30,4 (May 2004), 519–48; Purdy, "Framing Regent Park: The National Film Board of Canada and the Construction of Outcast Spaces in the Inner City, 1953 and 1994," in *Home, Work and Play: Situating Canadian Social History, 1840–1980*, ed. James Opp and John Walsh, 2nd ed. (Toronto: Oxford University Press, 2010), all of which build on Purdy, "From Place of Hope to Outcast Space: Territorial Regulation and Tenant Resistance in Regent Park Housing Project, 1949–2001," Ph.D. thesis, Queen's University, 2003.

For critiques of urban developers from the period, see Graham Fraser, *Fighting Back: Urban Renewal in Trefann Court* (Toronto: Hakkert, 1972); Jack Granatstein, *The Marlborough Marathon: One Street Against a Developer* (Toronto: James Lewis and Samuel, 1971); Wally Seccombe, Jennifer Penny, and Graham Barker, *Highrise and Superprofits: An Analysis of the Development Industry in Canada* (Kitchener: Dumont Press Graphix, 1973); and for an appreciation of working-class community in Toronto, James Lorimer and Myfanwy Phillips, *Working People: Life in a Downtown City Neighbourhood* (Toronto: James Lewis and Samuel, 1971). John Sewell's account of his role in this urban activism appears in Sewell, *How We Changed Toronto: The Inside Story of Twelve Creative Tumultuous Years in Civic Life, 1969–1980* (Toronto: James Lorimer and Company, 2015).

For the anti-poverty movement, see Bryan Palmer and Gaétan Héroux, *Toronto's Poor: A Rebellious History* (Toronto: Between the Lines, 2016); and Paul Weinberg, *When Poverty Was Taken Seriously: The Story of Praxis and the Just Society Movement* (Halifax: Fernwood Publishing, 2019). The limits of state programs are revealed in James Struthers, *The Limits of Affluence: Welfare in Ontario, 1920–1970* (Toronto: University of Toronto Press, 1994). For period sources, see Ian Adams, ed., *The Real Poverty Report* (Edmonton: Hurtig, 1971); Ian Adams, Bill Cameron, Brian Hill, and G. Peter Penz, eds., *The Renegade Report on Poverty* (Montreal: Last Post, 1971); George Ford and Steven Langdon, "Just Society Movement: Toronto's Poor Organize," *Canadian Dimension* 7 (June-July 1970), 19–23; and Howard Buchbinder, "The Just Society Movement," in *Community Work in Canada*, ed. Brian Wharf (Toronto: McClelland and Stewart, 1979), 129–52.

The "rights revolution" manifested in Toronto's legal culture is explored in Dominique Clément, *Canada's Rights Revolution: Social Movements and Social Change, 1937–82* (Vancouver and Toronto: UBC Press, 2008); Jennifer Tunnicliffe, *Resisting Rights: Canada and the International Bill of Rights, 1947–75* (Vancouver and Toronto: UBC Press, 2018); and Ross Lambertson, *Repression and Resistance: Canadian Human Rights Activists, 1930–1960* (Toronto: University of Toronto Press, 2005). From the progressive wing of the medical profession came Martin

Shapiro, *Getting Doctored: Critical Reflections on Becoming a Physician* (Toronto: Between the Lines, 1979).

8. Without Walls—No Ceiling: A Cultural Revolution, 1971–78

The new left conviction that struggles in the cultural sphere were essential was based on the work of prior left-wing formations, particularly that of the Popular Front (1935–39), for which see Michael Denning, *The Cultural Front: The Laboring of American Culture in the Twentieth Century* (London and New York: Verso, 1996; 2000). Important writers for many were the British thinkers historian E.P. Thompson and literary scholar Raymond Williams and the various philosophers associated with the Frankfurt School. See Harvey J. Kaye and Keith McClelland, eds., *E.P. Thompson: Critical Perspectives* (Philadelphia: Temple University Press, 1990); Sean Matthews, *Raymond Williams* (London: Routledge, 2018); W. J. Morgan and Peter Preston, eds., *Raymond Williams: Politics, Education, Letters* (New York: Palgrave Macmillan, 1993); and Martin Jay, *The Dialectical Imagination: A History of the Frankfurt School and the Institute of Social Research, 1923–1950* (Berkeley: University of California Press, 1996).

For U.S. perceptions of cultural change in the 1960s, see Bloom and Breines, eds., *'Takin' It to the Streets'*, ch.5, "'Eight Miles High': The Counterculture," 227–86; Michael Hicks, *Sixties Rock: Garage, Psychedelic, and Other Satisfactions* (Urbana and Chicago: University of Illinois Press, 1999); Scott Saul, *Freedom Is, Freedom Ain't: Jazz and the Making of the Sixties* (Cambridge, Mass.: Harvard University Press, 2003).

For Canada, see Larry Gambone, *No Regrets: Counter-Culture and Anarchism in Vancouver* (Edmonton: Black Cat Press, 2015). For an overview of popular music, see Ryan Edwardson, *Canuck Rock: A History of Canadian Popular Music* (Toronto: University of Toronto Press, 2009). The progressive work of the National Film Board is covered by Thomas Waugh and Michael Brendan, eds., *Challenge for Change: Activist Documentary at the National Film Board of Canada* (Montreal and Kingston: McGill-Queen's University Press, 2010).

An in-depth look at Toronto's arts movement in the late 1970s is provided in Philip Monk, *Is Toronto Burning? Three Years in the Making (and Unmaking) of the Toronto Art Scene* (London: Black Dog Publishing, 2016). Bruce Barber, ed., *Conde and Beveridge: Class Works* (Halifax: The Press of the Nova Scotia College of Art and Design, 2008), discusses the work of two prominent left-wing artists. For more on CEAC and The Funnel, see "The CEAC Was Banned in Canada: Program Notes for a Tragicomic Opera in Three Acts," in Dot Tuer, *Mining the Media*

Archive: Essays on Art, Technology and Cultural Resistance (Toronto: YYZ, 2005); and Michael Hoolboom, *Underground: The Untold Story of the Funnel Film Collective* (Ottawa: Canadian Film Institute, 2016).

No synthesis has yet been attempted on the rise of the academic left in Canada. For leading works of academic Canadian political economy from this period, see Wallace Clement and Glen Williams, eds., *The New Canadian Political Economy* (Kingston and Montreal: McGill-Queen's University Press, 1989); Jorge Niosi, *Canadian Capitalism* (Toronto: James Lorimer, 1981); and Leo Panitch, ed., *The Canadian State* (Toronto: University of Toronto Press, 1977). The Marxist Institute of Toronto has yet to find a historian, but see John Saul and Craig Heron, eds., *Imperialism, Nationalism and Canada: Essays from the Marxist Institute of Toronto* (Toronto and Kitchener: New Hogtown Press and Between the Lines, 1977), its seminal contribution to the discussion of Canada's "national question."

On left publishing in Toronto, see Robert Clarke, *Books Without Bosses: 40 Years of Reading Between the Lines* (Toronto: Between the Lines, 2017); and David McKnight, *New Wave Canada: The Coach House Press and the Small Press Movement in English Canada in the 1960s* (Ottawa: National Library of Canada, 1996). On rebellious music, see Geoff Pevere, *Gods of the Hammer: The Teenage Head Story* (Toronto: Coach House, 2014), a study of a Hamilton band with a considerable Toronto following, which was associated with a near-riot in 1978; Liz Worth, *Treat Me Like Dirt: An Oral History of Punk in Toronto and Beyond, 1977–1981* (Toronto: ECW Press, 2011); and an online history of punk in the city, http://punksandrockers.com/toronto-punk-history/. Progressive theatre can be explored via Neil Carson, *Harlequin in Hogtown: George Luscombe and Toronto Workshop Productions* (Toronto: University of Toronto Press, 1995); Alan Filewod, *Committing Theatre: Theatre Radicalism and Political Intervention in Canada* (Toronto: Between the Lines, 2011); and Denis Johnston, *Up the Mainstream: The Rise of Toronto's Alternative Theatres, 1968–1975* (Toronto: University of Toronto Press, 1991). Progressive art is documented in Fern Bayer, *The Search for the Spirit: General Idea 1968–1975* (Toronto: Art Gallery of Ontario, 1997); and Diana P.C. Nemiroff, "A History of Artist-Run Spaces in Canada, with Particular Reference to Vehicule, A Space and the Western Front," M.A. thesis, Concordia University, 1985. For dance, see Peter Graham, "The New Left Cultural Front: A Lens on Toronto Arts and 15 Dance Lab," in *Renegade Bodies: Canadian Dance in the 1970s*, ed. Allan C. Lingren and Kaija Pepper (Toronto: Dance Collection Danse, 2012), 197–204.

9. Subaltern Identities, Universal Truths, Transnational Complexities: The Rise of Identity-Based Resistance, 1971–78

Although Indigenous struggles in Canada hardly began in 1971—see David T. McNab, *Circles of Time: Aboriginal Land Rights and Resistance in Ontario* (Waterloo, Ont.: Wilfrid Laurier University Press, 1999)—it is striking that it was only in the 1970s that many leftists awoke to the centrality of Indigenous struggles. For overviews, see Peter Kulchyski, "Fifty Years in Indian Country," in *Canada Since 1960*, ed. Gonick, 149–68; and Bryan Palmer, "'Indians of All Tribes': The Birth of Red Power," in *Debating Dissent*, ed. Campbell, Clément, and Kealey, 193–210. For an excellent collection on Indigenous resistance, see Boyce Richardson for the Assembly of First Nations, *Drum Beat: Anger and Renewal in Indian Country* (Toronto: Summerhill Press, 1989).

For pathbreaking scholarly studies, see Howard Ramos, "Divergent Paths: Aboriginal Mobilization in Canada, 1951–2000," Ph.D. thesis, McGill University, 2004; and Scott Rutherford, "Canada's Other Red Scare: The Anicinabe Park Occupation and Indigenous Decolonization," in *The Hidden 1970s: Histories of Radicalism*, ed. Dan Berger (New Brunswick, N.J., and London: Rutgers University Press, 2010), 77–94, which builds on Rutherford, "Canada's Other Red Scare: Rights, Decolonization, and Indigenous Political Protest in the Global Sixties," Ph.D. thesis, Queen's University, 2011.

Waffler Mel Watkins, who served as an intellectual resource for the struggle against the Mackenzie Valley Pipeline, was noteworthy among Toronto leftists who expressed their solidarity with the Indigenous struggle: Mel Watkins, *Dene Nation: The Colony Within* (Toronto: University of Toronto Press, 1977); see also Watkins, "Dene Nationalism," *Canadian Review of Studies in Nationalism* 8,1 (1981), 101–13; and Watkins, "Aboriginal Rights," in Watkins, *Madness and Ruin: Politics and the Economy in the Neoconservative Age* (Toronto: Between the Lines, 1992), 129–52.

For central statements of the Indigenous struggles from the period, see Howard Adams, *Prison of Grass: Canada from a Native Point of View* (Saskatoon: Fifth House, 1989 [1975]); Adams, *A Tortured People: The Politics of Colonization* (Penticton, B.C.: Theytus Books, 1995); Don Barnett and Rick Sterling, eds., *Bobbi Lee: Indian Rebel: Struggles of a Native Canadian Woman* (Richmond, B.C.: Liberation Support Movement Information Center, 1975); George Manuel and Michael Posluns, *The Fourth World: An Indian Reality* (Don Mills, Ont.: Collier-Macmillan Canada, 1974); Vern Harper, *Following the Red Path: The Native Peoples Caravan 1974* (Toronto: NC Press, 1979); and Waubageshig, *The Only Good Indian: Essays by Canadian Indians* (Toronto: New Press, 1970). For an important study of one of the movement's core organic intellectuals, see Peter McFarlane, *Brotherhood to Nationhood: George Manuel and the Making of the Modern Indian Movement* (Toronto: Between the Lines, 1993).

The 1970s witnessed a consolidation of socialist feminism in Canada. The Canadian Women's Educational Press (later the Canadian Women's Press) was founded under collective ownership in 1972. Janice Acton et al., *Women Unite! An Anthology of the Canadian Women's Movement* (Toronto: Women's Educational Press, 1972), was an innovative title that suggested how much socialist feminists pinned their hopes on a working-class feminist movement. For an account of this position, see Meg Luxton, "Feminism as a Class Act: Working-Class Feminism and the Women's Movement in Canada," *Labour/Le Travail* 59 (Spring 2007), 179–97; and Margaret Little, "Militant Mothers Fight Poverty: The Just Society Movement, 1968–1971," *Labour/Le Travail* 49 (Spring 2007), 179–97. From the period, a key text in the wages for housework project was Silvia Federici, *Wages Against Housework* (Bristol: Power of Woman Collective and Falling Wall Press, 1975). Linda Briskin and Lynda Yanz, eds., *Union Sisters: Women in the Labour Movement* (Toronto: Women's Press, 1983) suggests a similar interest in encouraging a working-class feminist movement. Maureen Fitzgerald, Connie Guberman, and Margie Wolfe, eds., *Still Ain't Satisfied: Canadian Feminism Today* (Toronto: Women's Press, 1982), is especially useful for documenting contemporary debates about pornography, heterosexual men, and the emergence of lesbian feminism; it also contains an important collection of articles on women in the workforce and in trade unions.

Other indications of this same hope can be found in the work of Pat Schulz, a crusader for abortion rights, daycare, and forms of vanguardism responsive to the needs of women. An activist in the Trotskyist movement, she wrote an important study of local working-class struggle in the 1930s: *The East York Workers' Association: A Response to the Great Depression* (Toronto: New Hogtown Press, 1975). For a moving portrait of her life and activism, see One Woman Collective with the assistance of Studio D, NFB, *Worth Every Minute,* National Film Board, 1988.

Dorothy Smith, *Feminism and Marxism—A Place to Begin, A Way to Go* (Vancouver: New Star Books, 1977) emphasized the significance of Mao's thought for contemporary feminism; see also Smith, "A Peculiar Eclipsing: Women's Exclusion from Male Culture," *Women's Studies International Quarterly* 1 (1978); Smith, "Where There Is Oppression, There Is Resistance," *Branching Out* 6 (1979), 10–15; and "A Sociology for Women," in *The Prism of Sex*, ed. J. Sherman and E. Beck (Madison: University of Wisconsin Press, 1979). An appreciative assessment of her work, which continued into the next three decades, can be found in Deidre Mary Smyth, "A Few Laced Genes: Sociology, the Women's Movement, and the Work of Dorothy E. Smith," Ph.D. thesis, Ontario Institute for Studies in Education, 1999.

The international emergence of the quite different current of "radical feminism" is tracked by Barbara A. Crow, ed., *Radical Feminism: A Documentary Reader* (New York and London: New York University Press, 2000). Its Canadian impact can be discerned in Geraldine Finn and Angela Miles, *Feminism in Canada: From Pressure to Politics* (Montreal: Black Rose Books, 1982), which contains a forceful intervention by Patricia Hughes on the question of whether men should be allowed to support the cause. For one of its major spokespeople, see Mary O'Brien, *The Politics of Reproduction* (London: Routledge and Kegan Paul, 1981), which is based on her 1976 York Ph.D. dissertation. "Remembering Mary O'Brien," *Canadian Woman Studies/Les cahiers de la femme* 18,4 (Winter 1999), 3–118, is a special issue devoted to her work. Her critique of "Marxist theoreticians" can be found in O'Brien, "Reproducing Marxist Men," in *The Sexism of Social and Political Theory: Women and Reproduction from Plato to Nietzsche*, ed. Lorenne M.G. Clark and Lynda Lange (Toronto: University of Toronto Press, 1979), 99–116, and in O'Brien, "Hegemony and Superstructure: A Feminist Critique of Neo-Marxism," in *The Politics of Diversity: Feminism, Marxism and Nationalism*, ed. Roberta Hamilton and Michèle Barrett (London: Verso, 1986), 256–62. For a critical discussion of her work, see Heather Jon Maroney, "Embracing Motherhood: New Feminist Theory," in *Politics of* Diversity, ed. Hamilton and Barrett, 398–423.

O'Brien was an activist in the short-lived Feminist Party of Canada, for which see Gayle Elizabeth Laws, "The Feminist Party of Canada: An Analysis of Women in Party Politics, M.A. thesis, University of Waterloo, 1989; Dorothy Zaborszky, "Feminist Politics: The Feminist Party of Canada," *Women's Studies International Forum* 10,6 (1987), 613–21; and Trish Wells, *Towards a Canadian Feminist Party* (n.p. [Toronto]: Feminist Party of Canada, 1979), a prospectus for this radical feminist party.

Struggles by gays and lesbians—nowadays commonly referred to as the LGBTQI or queer community—in the 1970s and early 1980s have received much attention. Recent work in the United States has critiqued the "Stonewall Syndrome," which attributed many radical changes in North American gay life to a magic moment in Greenwich Village. See Barry D. Adam, *The Rise of a Gay and Lesbian Movement*, 2nd ed. (New York: Twayne, 1995); Barry D. Adam, Jan Willem Duyvendak, and André Krouwel, *The Global Emergence of Gay and Lesbian Politics: National Imprints of a Worldwide* Movement (Philadelphia: Temple University Press, 1999). The Vancouver story is told in Lawrence Aronsen, "The Sodom of the North: Vancouver's Sexual Revolution 1961–1974," *West Coast Line* 42,4 (Winter, 2009), 4–23.

For a pioneering Canadian thesis that situates Toronto struggles in a transnational context, see Scott de Groot, "Out of the Closet and into Print: Gay Liberation across the Anglo-American World," Ph.D thesis, Queen's University, 2015. Catherine Jean Nash, "Toronto's Gay Ghetto: Politics and the Disciplining of Identity and Space (1969–1982), Ph.D. thesis, Queen's University, 2003, traces the emergence of the gaybourhood. Tim McCaskell, *Queer Progress: From Homophobia to Homonationalism* (Toronto: Between the Lines, 2016) is an outstanding first-person history from a leading gay activist and left intellectual in Toronto; see also McCaskell, "The Bath Raids and Gay Politics," in *Social Movements/Social Change: The Politics and Practice of Organizing*, Socialist Studies 4, ed. Frank Cunningham, Sue Findlay, Marlene Kadar, Allan Lennon, and Ed Silva (Toronto: Between the Lines, 1988), 169–88; and McCaskell, "Pride: A Political History," in *Any Other Way: How Toronto Got Queer*, ed. Stephanie Chambers et al. (Toronto: Coach House Books, 2017), 326–29. Tom Warner, *Never Going Back: A History of Queer Activism in Canada* (Toronto: University of Toronto Press, 2002); and Miriam Smith, *Lesbian and Gay Rights in Canada: Social Movements and Equality-Seeking, 1971–1995* (Toronto: University of Toronto Press, 1999), focus on struggles for equal human rights.

Becki L. Ross, *The House That Jill Built: A Lesbian Nation in Formation* (Toronto: University of Toronto Press, 1995), looks closely at the Toronto lesbian community, and Ross, "Like Apples and Oranges: Lesbian Feminist Responses to the Politics of *The Body Politic*," in *Queerly Canadian: An Introductory Reader in Sexuality Studies*, ed. Maureen FitzGerald and Scott Rayter (Toronto: Canadian Scholars Press, 2012), examines the sometimes fraught relations between gays and lesbians.

Works focusing on the repressive surveillance of queers include Gary Kinsman and Patrizia Gentile, *The Canadian War on Queers: National Security as Sexual Regulation* (Vancouver and Toronto: UBC Press, 2009); and Gary Kinsman, "The Canadian National Security War on Queers and the Left," in *New World Coming*, ed. Dubinsky et al., 77–86.

Research guides include Donald W. McLeod, *Lesbian and Gay Liberation in Canada: A Selected Annotated Chronology, 1964–1975* (Toronto: ECW Press, 1996); and Alan V. Miller, comp., *Our Own Voices: A Directory of Lesbian and Gay Periodicals, 1890–1990, Including the Complete Holdings of the Canadian Gay Archives* (Toronto: Canadian Gay Archives Publication no.12, 1991).

Period sources from this time include W.E. Mann, ed., *The Underside of Toronto* (Toronto: McClelland and Stewart, 1970); and Marion Foster and Kent Murray (pseuds.), *A Not So Gay World: Homosexuality in Canada* (Toronto: McClelland and Stewart, 1972), both of which were pessimistic portraits. Some ten years later, Ed Jackson and Stan Persky, eds., *Flaunting It! A Decade of Gay Journalism from the Body Politic* (Vancouver and Toronto: New Star Books and Pink Triangle Press, 1982), painted a very different picture. Heterosexuality and masculinity are dominant themes in Howard Buchbinder et al., *Who's on Top? The Politics of Heterosexuality* (Toronto: Garamond Press, 1987); and Michael Kaufman, ed., *Beyond Patriarchy: Essays by Men on Pleasure, Power, and Change* (Toronto; New York: Oxford University Press, 1987). Gary Kinsman, *The Regulation of Desire: Homo and Hetero Sexualities* (Montreal: Black Rose Books, 1987), was a pioneering historical study from a long-standing activist on the gay Marxist left.

10. New Leninists and New Constellations: In Quest of the Revolutionary Party, 1971–82

For a number of readings already cited on the vanguard parties, see the section on chapter 6. In addition to those suggestions, for information on the two largest Maoist organizations readers could also consult materials from Quebec, where those groups both had their bases. See Jean-Philippe Warren, *Ils voulaient changer le monde: le militantisme marxiste-léniniste au Québec* (Montréal: vlb éditeur, 2007); and Pierre Milot, *Le paradigme rouge: l'avant-garde politico-littéraire des années 70* (Québec: Editions Balzac, 1992).

En Lutte!/In Struggle! was concerned about grounding its work in the history of the Canadian left, and tasked its militants to identify the key turning points in the history of the CPC. Thus, Fergus McKean's *Communism Versus Opportunism: An Examination of the Revision of Marxism in the Communist Movement of Canada* (Vancouver: The Organizing Committee, 1946), announced his break with the orthodox Communists on the grounds that they had ceased to be revolutionaries; the text was revived, in French, by the Montreal party press in 1980. The group consciously followed the Third Period in much of its thinking: note, for example, *Dump McDermot! Dump the Bourgeois Policy in Trade Unions!* (Montreal: In Struggle! 1979); *For the Political and Organizational Unity of the International Communist Movement: Appeal from the 3rd Congress of IN STRUGGLE! to the Communists (M-L) of the World* (Montreal: Marxist-Leninist Organization of Canada IN STRUGGLE! 1979).

Battles within the vanguard parties over sexuality, and particularly homosexuality, are well documented. Simon Edge, *With Friends Like These . . . Marxism and Gay Politics* (London: Cassell, 1995), assesses the British record, as does Graham Willett, "Something New under the Sun: The Revolutionary Left and Gay Politics," in *Against the Grain*, ed. Smith and Worley, 173–89. Debates within the Toronto revolutionary left on the gay question could be explosive. See Duncan McLean, for the League for Socialist Action, ed., *Gay Liberation in Canada: A Socialist Perspective* (Toronto and New York: Pathfinder Press, 1977), a publication subjected to a pointed critique by the Revolutionary Marxist Group in Toronto: "On 'Gay

Liberation,' A Socialist Perspective, A Critique of the Recent Publication of the League for Socialist Action," *Joint Internal Bulletin*, League for Socialist Action/ Ligue Socialiste Ouvriere and The Revolutionary Marxist Group, 15 (July 1977), 19–23. For a moving text from the struggle against gay repression in the Trotskyist movement, see Gary Kinsman et al., "We May Not Be Witches . . . But We Sure Have Been Burned!" n.d. (1980), an internal mimeographed document from the Revolutionary Workers League.

11. A Long, Ambiguous Goodbye, 1982–85

In the 1980s feminists entered the academy in large numbers and produced a large number of scholarly texts of considerable sophistication. Dorothy Smith, for example, became a renowned feminist sociologist, and her standpoint epistemology was debated in feminist circles around the world. Sandra Harding, in *The Science Question in Feminism* (Ithaca, N.Y. and London: Cornell University Press, 1986) devotes a chapter to Smith. For a direct spinoff from her work, see Marie L. Campbell and Ann Manicom, eds., *Knowledge, Experience and Ruling Relations: Studies in the Social Organization of* Knowledge (Toronto: University of Toronto Press, 1995). For an important text that developed under her intellectual inspiration, see Gillian A. Walker, *Family Violence and the Women's Movement: The Conceptual Politics of Struggle* (Toronto: University of Toronto Press, 1990).

As Smith's case suggests, the 1980s can be seen as the triumph of feminism both within the left and as an active force shaping academic life in Canada and elsewhere. This was the decade in which such figures as Linda Briskin, Marjorie Griffin Cohen, Patricia Connelly, Geraldine Finn, Bonnie Fox, Roberta Hamilton, Patricia Hughes, Diane Lamoureux, Meg Luxton, Chantal Maillé, Heather Jon Maroney, Angela Miles, Roxanna Ng, Mary O'Brien, Marilyn Porter, Wally Seccombe, Jane Ursel, Mariana Valverde, and Jill Vickers—to name but a few—attained prominence in the university system. The age of the polished scholarly article and monograph largely replaced that of the mimeographed manifesto.

Feminist writings suggest three contradictions inherent in this new centrality. There was first a sense that, having entered the state (and such state-funded institutions as universities), feminists had lost something of their radical edge of the 1970s. Sue Findlay, "Facing the State: The Politics of the Women's Movement Reconsidered," in *Feminism and Political Economy*, ed. Heather Jon Maroney and Meg Luxton (Toronto: Methuen, 1987), 31–50, analyzes the Canadian government's formal response to feminist demands, and notes the ways in which "the state demonstrated a commitment to consult with the women of Canada, and in so doing not only validated the faith of liberal feminists in the strategy of reform by the state, but constructed a relationship with them that established liberal feminism as the 'public face' of the women's movement." The state-funded National Action Committee on the Status of Women—for which, see Jill Vickers, Pauline Rankin, and Christine Appelle, *Politics as If Women Mattered: A Political Analysis of the National Action Committee on the Status of Women* (Toronto: University of Toronto Press, 1993)—was the most prominent pan-Canadian women's organization, but it also, as the future would show, was dependent for its functioning on the wider liberal order. A prime example of the transformative power of a liberal order over insurgent feminism can be found in the movement for women's shelters, initially conceived of as integral parts of a movement dedicated to a thoroughgoing revolution in gender politics but then transformed into a provider of social services by the state, which could, with the advent of neo-liberalism, subtly and unsubtly shape their functions and even, through a denial of funds, undermine them altogether. For a discussion, see Margo Goodhand, *Runaway Wives and Rogue Feminists: The Origins of the Women's Shelter Movement in Canada* (Halifax and Winnipeg: Fernwood Publishing, 2017).

Second was the question of race, which cast a shadow over feminism's role as the bearer of universal hopes of liberation. For this debate in the United States, see Wini Breines, *The Trouble Between Us: An Uneasy History of White and Black Women in the Feminist Movement* (New York: Oxford University Press, 2006). Canadian writings on this question include Enakshi Dua and Angela Robertson, *Scratching the Surface: Canadian Anti-Racist Feminist Thought* (Toronto: Women's Press, 1999); Carolyn Egan, Linda Lee Garden, and Judy Vashti Persuad, "The Politics of Transformation: Struggles with Race, Class, and Sexuality in the March 8th Coalition," in *Social Movements/Social Change*, ed. Cunningham et al.; Marlee Kline, "Women's Oppression and Racism: A Critique of the 'Feminist Standpoint,'" in *Race, Class, Gender: Bonds and Barriers*, Socialist Studies/Études socialistes 5, ed. Jesse Vorst et al., revised ed. (Toronto and Winnipeg: Garamond Press and the Society for Socialist Studies, 1991); Sarita Srivastava, "You're Calling Me a Racist? The Moral and Emotional Regulation of Anti-Racism and Feminism," *Signs: Journal of Women and Culture in Society* 31,1 (Fall 2005), 29–62, which draws from her "Facing Race, Saving Face: Anti-Racism, Emotion and Knowledge in Social Movement Organizations," Ph.D. thesis, York University, 2002; and Mariana Valverde, "Racism and Anti-Racism in Feminist Teaching and Research," in *Challenging Times*, ed. Backhouse and Flaherty, 160–64.

Third was the split between socialist and radical feminists, especially with respect to such issues as pornography and censorship, gay/lesbian liberation, and relations with the working class. The rise of radical feminism pushed the pornography debate onto the agenda; many important interventions by radical feminists can be found in the *Canadian Journal of Social and Political Theory* 9,1–2 (1985).

For many, the turning point came with Bonnie Klein's film about pornography, made by Studio D of the National Film Board: *Not a Love Story* (1981), which included commentary from leading North American anti-pornography feminists. The Canadian Advisory Council on the Status of Women was important in influencing the construction of new pornography law, encapsulated in Bill C-54; this law and the judicial rulings flowing from it marked a decisive victory for radical-feminist thought and was directly influenced by such intellectuals as Catherine MacKinnon and Andrea Dworkin. For the other side of the debate, see Varda Burstyn, *Women Against Censorship* (Vancouver: Douglas and McIntyre, 1985); and, more generally, Mariana Valverde, *Sex, Power and Pleasure* (Toronto: Women's Press, 1985).

The transformation of revolutionary gay liberation into a more conservative "homonationalism" is documented in McCaskell, *Queer Progress*, and is unselfconsciously demonstrated in Chambers et al., eds., *Any Other Way*, in which any links to the left are obscured in account after account of struggles over personal and collective identity.

The crisis of Leninist vanguardism is analyzed in Ken Jowitt, "The Leninist Extinction," in *The Crisis of Leninism and the Decline of the Left*, ed. Daniel Chirot (Seattle: University of Washington Press, 1991), and was hastened by the fall of communism after 1989, for which see Ulf Engel, Frank Hadler, and Matthias Middell, eds., *1989 in a Global Perspective* (Leipzig: Leipzig University Press, 2013). The crisis of vanguardism in Canada is studied from within by Charles Gagnon, *Sur la crise du mouvement marxiste-léniniste: notes sur l'évolution récente d'En lutte!* (Montréal: G. Gagnon, n.d. [1981]), translated into English as *On the Crisis in the Marxist-Leninist Movement: Recent Developments in In Struggle! Some Notes* (Montreal: Unity Press, 1981). The anti-poverty movement continued to be a militant force in Toronto—for which see Palmer and Héroux, *Toronto's Poor*—but it has faced similar pressures with respect to keeping hostels and food banks functioning, while gentrification and an implicit policy of "social cleansing" (427) proceed apace. See Jonathan Sydney Greene, "Visibility, Urgency, and Protest: Anti-Poverty Activism in Neo-Liberal Times," Ph.D. thesis, Queen's University, 2006.

Key texts on the 1980s peace movement include Eric Shragge, Ronald Babin, and Jean-Guy Vaillancourt, eds., *Roots of Peace: The Movement Against Militarism in Canada* (Toronto: Between the Lines, 1986); T. James Stark, *Cold War Blues: The Operation Dismantle Story* (Hull: Voyageur Publishing, 1991); Robert A. Hackett, *News and Dissent: The Press and the Politics of Peace in Canada* (Norwood, N.J.: Ablex Pub. Corp., 1991); Rose Fine-Meyer, "'A Good Teacher Is a Revolutionary': Alternative War Perspectives in Toronto Classrooms, 1960s–1990s," in *Worth Fighting For*, ed. Campbell, Dawson, and Gidney.

The coming to power in 1990 of a social-democratic government under Bob Rae, with massive support in Toronto, was equally suggestive of the contradictions of leftists living within an adaptive liberal order. For assessments of the Rae government, see especially, for major critiques from the left, George Ehring and Wayne Roberts, *Giving Away A Miracle: Lost Dreams, Broken Promises and the Ontario NDP* (Oakville, Ont.: Mosaic Press, 1993); other commentaries include Daniel Drache and John O'Grady, eds., *Getting on Track: Social Democratic Strategies for Ontario* (Montreal and Kingston: McGill-Queen's University Press, 1992); Mel Watkins, "Ontario: Discrediting Social Democracy," *Studies in Political Economy* 43 (Spring 1994), 139–48; and Stephen McBride, "The Continuing Crisis of Social Democracy: Ontario's Social Contract in Perspective," *Studies in Political Economy* 50 (Summer 1996), 65–93. Other accounts include Patrick Monahan, *Storming the Pink Palace. The NDP in Power: A Cautionary Tale* (Toronto: Lester Publishing, 1995), Thomas Walkom, *Rae Days: The Rise and Follies of the NDP* (Toronto: Key Porter Books, 1994), and Bob Rae's own account, which can be found in Rae, *From Protest to Power: Personal Reflections on a Life in Politics* (Toronto: Penguin, 1997). Doug Nesbitt and Sean Carleton, *Days of Action: The Character of Class Struggle in 1990s Ontario* (Toronto: Graphic History Collective, 2014) is a graphic novel depicting the difficult task that leftists confronted in fighting the full-bore neo-liberalism of the Mike Harris regime. Many of the strategic discussions and tactical decisions would have been familiar to an earlier cohort of new leftists.

As the "next left" now takes shape, after the full social and economic effects of the global neo-liberal revolution have made themselves evident in environmental crisis and unprecedented social inequality, the lessons to be drawn from the previous left are still being debated. Liberal condescension towards the new left—exemplified by such films as *The Big Chill* (1983) and *The Decline of the American Empire* (1986)—is ceding place to different evaluations: see Jack Whalen, *Beyond the Barricades: The Sixties Generation Grows Up* (Philadelphia: Temple University Press, 1990); Jeremy Varon, "Between Revolution 9 and Thesis 11: Or, Will We Learn (Again) to Start Worrying and Change the World?" in *New Left Revisited*, ed. McMillian and Buhle, 214–40. Many themes familiar to the new left can be found in the anti-racist organizing of Black Lives Matter; for reflections, see Chris Crass, *Towards Collective Liberation: Anti-Racist Organizing, Feminist Praxis, and Movement Building Strategy* (Oakland, Cal.: PM Press, 2013). David Graeber, *The Democracy Project: A History, A Crisis, A Movement* (New York: Spiegel and Grau, 2013), celebrates the anarchism inherent in such movements as Occupy Wall Street; Jonathan Smucker, *Hegemony How-To: A Roadmap for Radicals* (Chico, Cal.: AK Press, 2017), works more impressively to theorize a Gramscian strategy that might overcome the limitations of such anarchism, which seems capable of mounting spectacular protests with intangible and limited long-term consequences. Similar themes are explored in Jane F. McAlevey, *No Shortcuts: Organizing for Power in the New Gilded Age* (New York: Oxford University Press, 2016).

In Canada, Bob Davis, *What Our High Schools Could Be: A Teacher's Reflections from the 60s to the 90s* (Toronto: James Lorimer, 1990), looks back to earlier programs for revolutionizing education; see also Tim McCaskell, *Race to Equity: Disrupting Educational Inequality* (Toronto: Between the Lines, 2005). Some leftists vest considerable hope in the radicalization of struggles for human rights: see Tom Warner, *Losing Control: Canada's Social Conservatives in the Age of Rights* (Toronto: Between the Lines, 2010). For an insightful analyses of the lessons the new left might teach the next left, see Alan Sears, *The Next New Left: A History of the Future* (Halifax and Winnipeg: Fernwood Publishing, 2014); and Christopher Samuel, *Conform, Fail, Repeat: How Power Distorts Collective Action* (Toronto: Between the Lines, 2017).

Index